ACCA

PAPER P6

ADVANCED TAXATION

D1470597

In this new syllabus first edition, approved by ACCA

- We discuss the best strategies for studying for ACCA exams

- We highlight the most important elements in the syllabus and the key skills you will need

- We signpost how each chapter links to the syllabus and the study guide

- We provide lots of exam focus points demonstrating what the examiner will want you to do

- We emphasise key points in regular fast forward summaries

- We test your knowledge of what you've studied in quick quizzes

- We examine your understanding in our exam question bank

- We reference all the important topics in our full index

BPP's **i-Learn** and **i-Pass** products also support this paper.

FOR THE EXAM IN DECEMBER 2007

LEARNING MEDIA

First edition March 2007

ISBN 9780 7517 3305 1

British Library Cataloguing-in-Publication Data
A catalogue record for this book is available from the
British Library

Published by

BPP Learning Media Ltd
BPP House, Aldine Place
London W12 8AA

www.bpp.com/learningmedia

Printed in Great Britain by
WM Print
45-47 Frederick Street
Walsall
West Midlands
WS2 9NE

Your learning materials, published by BPP Learning
Media Ltd, are printed on paper sourced from
sustainable, managed forests.

We are grateful to the Association of Chartered Certified
Accountants for permission to reproduce past
examination questions. The suggested solutions in the
exam answer bank have been prepared by BPP Learning
Media Ltd, except where otherwise stated.

Contents

The BPP Learning Media Effective Study Package

Distance Learning from BPP Professional Education

You can access our exam-focussed interactive e-learning materials over the **Internet**, via BPP Learn Online, hosted by BPP Professional Education.

BPP Learn Online offers **comprehensive tutor support**, **revision guidance** and **exam tips**.

Visit www.bpp.com/acca/learnonline for further details.

Learning to Learn Accountancy

BPP's ground-breaking **Learning to Learn Accountancy** book is designed to be used both at the outset of your ACCA studies and throughout the process of learning accountancy. It challenges you to consider how you study and gives you helpful hints about how to approach the various types of paper which you will encounter. It can help you **focus your studies on the subject and exam**, enabling you to **acquire knowledge**, **practise and revise efficiently and effectively**.

How the BPP ACCA-approved Study Text can help you pass

How the BPP ACCA-approved Study Text can help you pass

Tackling studying

We know that studying for a number of exams can seem daunting, particularly when you have other commitments as well.

- We therefore provide guidance on **what you need to study efficiently and effectively** – to use the limited time you have in the best way possible

- We explain the **purposes** of the **different features** in the BPP Study Text, demonstrating how they help you and improve your chances of passing

Developing exam awareness

We never forget that you're aiming to pass your exams, and our Texts are completely focused on helping you do this.

- In the section **Studying P6** we introduce the key themes of the syllabus, describe the skills you need and summarise how to succeed

- The **Introduction** to each chapter of this Study Text sets the chapter in the context of the syllabus and exam

- We provide specific tips, **Exam focus points**, on what you can expect in the exam and what to do (and not to do!) when answering questions

And our Study Text is **comprehensive**. It covers the syllabus content. No more, no less.

Using the Syllabus and Study Guide

We set out the Syllabus and Study Guide in full.

- Reading the **introduction to the Syllabus** will show you what **capabilities** (skills) you'll have to demonstrate, and how this exam links with other papers.

- The topics listed in the **Syllabus** are the **key topics** in this exam. By quickly looking through the Syllabus, you can see the breadth of the paper. Reading the Syllabus will also highlight topics to look out for when you're reading newspapers or *student accountant* magazine.

- The **Study Guide** provides the **detail**, showing you precisely what you'll be studying. Don't worry if it seems a lot when you look through it; BPP's Study Text will carefully guide you through it all.

- Remember the Study Text shows, at the start of every chapter, which areas of the Syllabus and Study Guide are covered in the chapter.

Testing what you can do

Testing yourself helps you develop the skills you need to pass the exam and also confirms that you can recall what you have learnt.

- We include **Questions** within chapters, and the **Exam Question Bank** provides lots more practice.

- Our **Quick Quizzes** test whether you have enough knowledge of the contents of each chapter.

- Question practice is particularly important if English is not your first written language. ACCA offers an **International Certificate in Financial English** promoting language skills within the international business community.

Example chapter

Topic list

The Topic list gives an overview of the chapter.

Introduction

The Introduction sets the chapter in the context of the whole syllabus.

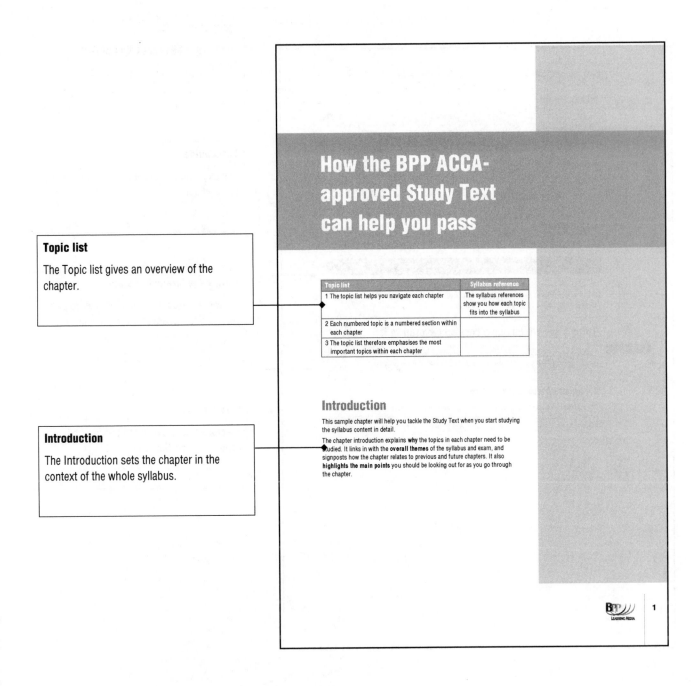

How the BPP ACCA-approved Study Text can help you pass

Topic list	Syllabus reference
1 The topic list helps you navigate each chapter	The syllabus references show you how each topic fits into the syllabus
2 Each numbered topic is a numbered section within each chapter	
3 The topic list therefore emphasises the most important topics within each chapter	

Introduction

This sample chapter will help you tackle the Study Text when you start studying the syllabus content in detail.

The chapter introduction explains **why** the topics in each chapter need to be studied. It links in with the **overall themes** of the syllabus and exam, and signposts how the chapter relates to previous and future chapters. It also **highlights the main points** you should be looking out for as you go through the chapter.

Study guide

	Intellectual level
We list the topics in ACCA's Study guide that are covered in each chapter	The intellectual level indicates the depth in which the topics will be covered

Exam guide

The Exam guide highlights ways in which the main topics covered in each chapter may be examined.

Knowledge brought forward from earlier studies

Knowledge brought forward boxes summarise information and techniques that you are **assumed to know** from your earlier studies. As the exam may test your knowledge of these areas, you should **revise** your previous study material if you are unsure about them.

1 Key topic which has a section devoted to it

FAST FORWARD Fast forwards give you a **summary** of the content of each of the main chapter sections. They are listed together in the roundup at the end of each chapter to allow you to review each chapter quickly.

1.1 Important topic within section

The headings within chapters give you a good idea of the **importance** of the topics covered. The larger the header, the more important the topic is. The headers will help you navigate through the chapter and locate the areas that have been highlighted as important in the front pages or in the chapter introduction.

2 **BPP** LEARNING MEDIA

Study guide

The Study guide links with ACCA's own guidance.

Exam guide

The Exam guide describes the examinability of the chapter.

Knowledge brought forward

Knowledge brought forward shows you what you need to remember from previous exams.

Fast forward

Fast forwards allow you to preview and review each section easily.

BPP LEARNING MEDIA

Example

Examples show you how theory is put into practice.

Key term

Key terms are the core vocabulary.

Exam focus point

Exam focus points provide specific links to the exam.

Formula to learn

You must remember these formulae in the exam.

Question

Questions provide vital practice of what you've learnt.

Case Study

Case Studies link what you've learnt with the business environment.

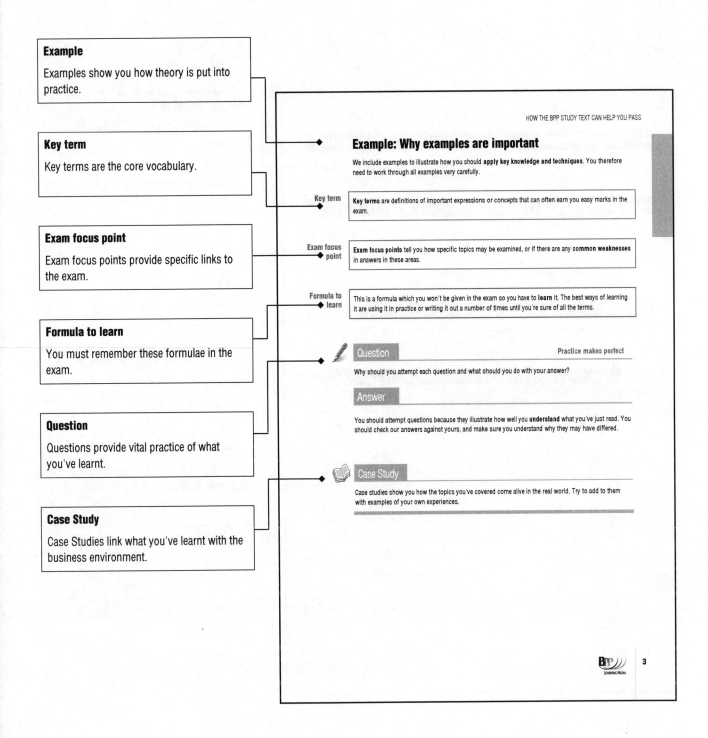

HOW THE BPP STUDY TEXT CAN HELP YOU PASS

Example: Why examples are important

We include examples to illustrate how you should **apply key knowledge and techniques**. You therefore need to work through all examples very carefully.

Key term

Key terms are definitions of important expressions or concepts that can often earn you easy marks in the exam.

Exam focus point

Exam focus points tell you how specific topics may be examined, or if there are any **common weaknesses** in answers in these areas.

Formula to learn

This is a formula which you won't be given in the exam so you have to **learn** it. The best ways of learning it are using it in practice or writing it out a number of times until you're sure of all the terms.

Question — Practice makes perfect

Why should you attempt each question and what should you do with your answer?

Answer

You should attempt questions because they illustrate how well you **understand** what you've just read. You should check our answers against yours, and make sure you understand why they may have differed.

Case Study

Case studies show you how the topics you've covered come alive in the real world. Try to add to them with examples of your own experiences.

BPP LEARNING MEDIA — 3

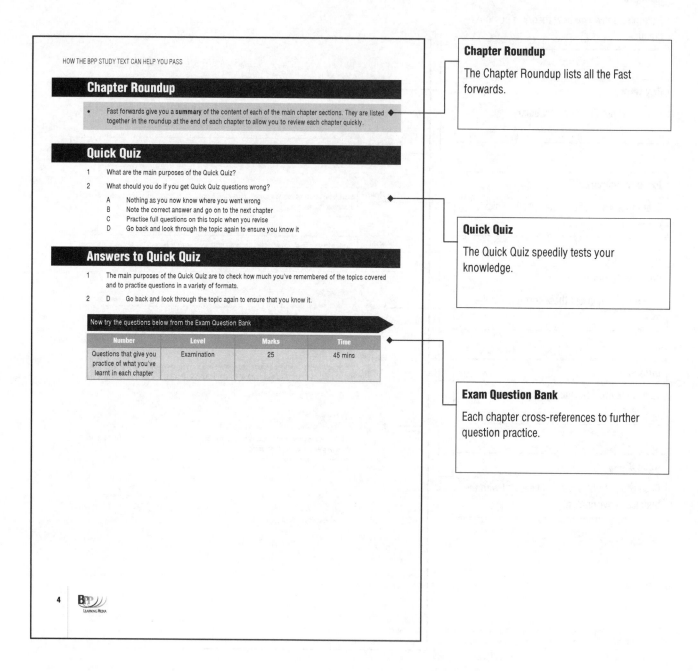

Chapter Roundup

- Fast forwards give you a **summary** of the content of each of the main chapter sections. They are listed together in the roundup at the end of each chapter to allow you to review each chapter quickly.

Quick Quiz

1   What are the main purposes of the Quick Quiz?

2   What should you do if you get Quick Quiz questions wrong?

    A   Nothing as you now know where you went wrong
    B   Note the correct answer and go on to the next chapter
    C   Practise full questions on this topic when you revise
    D   Go back and look through the topic again to ensure you know it

Answers to Quick Quiz

1   The main purposes of the Quick Quiz are to check how much you've remembered of the topics covered and to practise questions in a variety of formats.

2   D   Go back and look through the topic again to ensure that you know it.

Now try the questions below from the Exam Question Bank

Number	Level	Marks	Time
Questions that give you practice of what you've learnt in each chapter	Examination	25	45 mins

Chapter Roundup

The Chapter Roundup lists all the Fast forwards.

Quick Quiz

The Quick Quiz speedily tests your knowledge.

Exam Question Bank

Each chapter cross-references to further question practice.

Learning styles

BPP's guide to studying, *Learning to Learn Accountancy*, provides guidance on identifying how you learn and the variety of intelligences that you have. We shall summarise some of the material in *Learning to Learn Accountancy*, as it will help you understand how to you are likely to approach the Study Text:

If you like	Then you might focus on	How the Study Text helps you
Word games, crosswords, poetry	Going through the detail in the Text	Chapter introductions, Fast forwards and Key terms help you determine the detail that's most significant
Number puzzles, Sudoku, Cluedo	Understanding the Text as a logical sequence of knowledge and ideas	Chapter introductions and headers help you follow the flow of material
Drawing, cartoons, films	Seeing how the ways material is presented show what it means and how important it is	The different features and the emphasis given by headers and emboldening help you see quickly what you have to know
Attending concerts, playing a musical instrument, dancing	Identifying patterns in the Text	The sequence of features within each chapter helps you understand what material is really crucial
Sport, craftwork, hands on experience	Learning practical skills such as preparing a set of accounts	Examples and question practice help you develop the practical skills you need

If you want to learn more about developing some or all of your intelligences, *Learning to Learn Accountancy* shows you plenty of ways in which you can do so.

Studying efficiently and effectively

What you need to study efficiently and effectively

Positive attitude

Yes there is a lot to learn. But look at the most recent ACCA pass list. See how many people have passed. They've made it; you can too. Focus on all the **benefits** that passing the exam will bring you.

Exam focus

Keep the exam firmly in your sights throughout your studies.

- Remember there's lots of **helpful guidance** about P6 in the first part of the Study Text.
- Look out for all the **references to the exam** in the Study Text.

Organisation

Before you start studying you must organise yourself properly.

- We show you how to **timetable** your study so that you can ensure you have enough time to cover all of the syllabus – and revise it.

- Think carefully about the way you take **notes**. You needn't copy out too much, but if you can summarise key areas, that shows you understand them.

- Choose the notes **format** that's most helpful to you; lists, diagrams, mindmaps.

- Consider the **order** in which you tackle each chapter. If you prefer to get to grips with a theory before seeing how it's applied, you should read the explanations first. If you prefer to see how things work in practice, read the examples and questions first.

Active brain

There are various ways in which you can keep your brain active when studying and hence improve your **understanding** and **recall** of material.

- Keep asking yourself how does what I'm studying fit into the **whole picture** of this exam. If you're not sure, look back at the chapter introductions and Study Text front pages.

- Go carefully through every **example** and try every **question** in the Study Text and in the Exam Question Bank. You will be thinking deeply about the syllabus and increasing your understanding.

Review, review, review

Regularly reviewing the topics you've studied will help fix them in your memory. Your BPP Texts help you review in many ways.

- Important points are emphasised **in bold**
- **Chapter roundups** summarise the **Fast forward** key points in each chapter
- **Quick quizzes** test your grasp of the essentials

BPP Passcards present summaries of topics in different visual formats to enhance your chances of remembering them.

Timetabling your studies

As your time is limited, it's vital that you calculate how much time you can allocate to each chapter. Following the approach below will help you do this.

Step 1   Calculate how much time you have

Work out the time you have available per week, given the following.

- The standard you have set yourself

- The time you need to set aside for work on the Practice & Revision Kit, Passcards, i-Learn and i-Pass

- The other exam(s) you are sitting

- Practical matters such as work, travel, exercise, sleep and social life

Hours

Note your time available in box A.   A [   ]

Step 2   Allocate your time

- Take the time you have available per week for this Study Text shown in box A, multiply it by the number of weeks available and insert the result in box B.   B [   ]

- Divide the figure in box B by the number of chapters in this Study Text and insert the result in box C.   C [   ]

Remember that this is only a rough guide. Some of the chapters in this Study Text are longer and more complicated than others, and you will find some subjects easier to understand than others.

Step 3   Implement your plan

Set about studying each chapter in the time shown in box C. You'll find that once you've established a timetable, you're much more likely to study systematically.

BPP
LEARNING MEDIA

Short of time: Skim study technique?

You may find you simply do not have the time available to follow all the key study steps for each chapter, however you adapt them for your particular learning style. If this is the case, follow the **skim study** technique below.

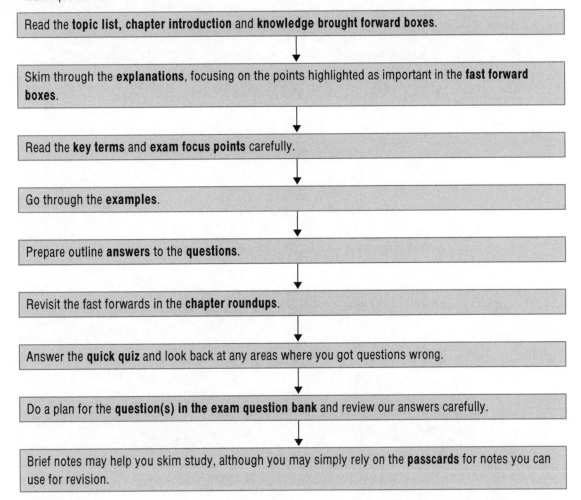

Read the **topic list, chapter introduction** and **knowledge brought forward boxes.**

Skim through the **explanations**, focusing on the points highlighted as important in the **fast forward boxes.**

Read the **key terms** and **exam focus points** carefully.

Go through the **examples.**

Prepare outline **answers** to the **questions.**

Revisit the fast forwards in the **chapter roundups.**

Answer the **quick quiz** and look back at any areas where you got questions wrong.

Do a plan for the **question(s) in the exam question bank** and review our answers carefully.

Brief notes may help you skim study, although you may simply rely on the **passcards** for notes you can use for revision.

Revision

When you are ready to start revising, you should still refer back to this Study Text.

- As a source of **reference** (you should find the index particularly helpful for this)

- As a way to **review** (the Fast forwards, Exam focus points, Chapter roundups and Quick quizzes help you here)

Learning to Learn Accountancy

BPP's guide to studying for accountancy exams, **Learning to Learn Accountancy**, challenges you to think about how you can study effectively and gives you lots and lots of vital tips on studying, revising and taking the exams.

Studying P6

BPP
LEARNING MEDIA

Approaching P6

1   What is P6 about

The impact of major taxes on financial decisions and situations

P6 expands on the knowledge of the range of taxes that you will have encountered before. You must deepen your existing knowledge and study a wider range of taxes as they apply to individuals and businesses. You must be able interpret a given situation, explain the taxes that will be charged and calculate the after tax income or gains. You must also be able to propose alternative strategies and compare and contrast the results. You should always be aware that there may be non-tax matters that should also be taken into account. Being able to communicate your explanations and conclusions effectively is absolutely crucial.

2   What's required

Knowledge and application

You must bring two very different professional attributes to this exam. The first, and easier, is technical knowledge. You will require an easy familiarity with all elements of the basic tax computation for each tax covered by the syllabus.

The second requirement is the ability to apply this knowledge to the different scenarios which you will be presented with in the exam. You must learn to be able to look at a scenario and recognise the underlying issues. Run through all the different taxes, even if only to tick them off as not applicable in this case. If you do not do this it is easy to overlook easy marks.

Calculations

Calculations will only be required in support of explanations or advice and will not be the subject of part of a question in isolation.

Taxation, however, is the imposition of a financial cost on individuals and businesses. To be able to understand the tax charge fully you must be able to calculate it. No recommendation would be complete if you cannot accompany it with a calculation of the expected liability.

Explanation

As well as testing your knowledge and understanding, you will be asked to demonstrate the skill of explaining the tax charges in a particular scenario. Explaining means stating what taxes are applicable and why, usually accompanied by a short calculation.

Analysis

This text sets out the tax rules in a logical order, progressively widening the scope of your studies. Exam questions are not like that; you will be presented with a set of facts and will have to analyse these to ascertain the occasion of charge. You may also have to identify several different options which may be available to the taxpayer.

You must also look out for helpful information that will be given within the question, such as the requirement to obtain loss relief as soon as possible.

Evaluation and recommendation

Once you have explained tax charges and calculated after tax returns, you will often have to evaluate your results and recommend a course of action. You must be able to justify your recommendations, and you may need to set out other factors that a taxpayer should take into account in reaching his decision. You may, for example, be recommending a strategy which involves some investment risk. The client must be made fully aware of this.

You must also be aware of the practical aspects of your recommendations; tax reliefs usually have to be claimed within strict time limits, and these must be drawn to the taxpayer's attention.

3   How to pass

Cover the whole syllabus

Between 50% and 70% of the marks available to you will be for compulsory questions in Section A. Section B will contain three questions for equal marks, of which you must answer two. The questions will be scenario based, will normally cover more than one tax and will involve an element of planning and interaction of taxes. This gives the examiner plenty of opportunity to test a wide range of topics on every paper, but sadly doesn't give you much opportunity to avoid questions you don't like. Do not study the syllabus selectively as the format of the paper enables all topics to be tested in some way in most exams.

Practise

This text gives you ample opportunity to practise by providing questions within chapters, quick quiz questions and questions in the exam question bank at the end.

Examiners routinely identify time management as being a problem. It is particularly important, therefore, that towards the end of your course, you practise examination type questions, only allowing yourself the time you will be given in the exam. You will find plenty of these questions in the BPP practice and revision kit.

Answer selectively

The examiner will expect you to consider carefully what is relevant and significant enough to include in your answers. Exam answers are likely to show various signs that students are not making the necessary judgements:

- Include all the information in the answer that you are asked for; if you are dealing with a loss relief question and are asked to state the loss carried forward don't waste marks by omitting to do so

- Do not include unnecessary information, if you are presented with a scenario do not write all you know if it is outside the scope of the specific scenario

- If you are asked to identify available options make sure that you do, even if only to dismiss one as not beneficial (say why)

- If you are asked to make a recommendation, do so, and say why you have selected it.

Employ good exam technique

The following aspects of exam technique are particularly relevant in this exam

- **Subheadings and leaving spaces between paragraphs** help to demonstrate that your answer is clearly structured and emphasise the points you're making

- **Short paragraphs** (2-3 sentences) help you keep to the point; however avoid 2-3 word bullet points

- **Clear numerical workings** can gain you many marks even if you make a mistake in your calculations

- Time management is likely to be less of a problem if you do the longest question first

- Because you'll often have to give advice, your answer may have to be in the form of a report; using a **proper report style** should gain you easy marks

4   Brought forward knowledge

The P6 syllabus covers almost every topic that was included paper 2.3, with a few minor exceptions. Since tax law changes from time to time, this text covers these topics again. Where a chapter contains a mixture of prior knowledge and new topics a note at the start of the chapter reminds you what you should know already.

Syllabus

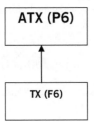

AIM

To apply relevant knowledge and skills and exercise professional judgement in providing relevant information and advice to individuals and businesses on the impact of the major taxes on financial decisions and situations.

MAIN CAPABILITIES

On successful completion of this paper, candidates should be able to:

A Apply further knowledge and understanding of the UK tax system through the study of further capital taxes, together with more advanced topics within the taxes studied previously.

B Evaluate and explain the importance of taxation to personal and corporate financial management.

C Identify and evaluate the impact of relevant taxes on various situations and courses of action, including the interaction of taxes.

D Provide advice on minimising and/or deferring tax liabilities by the use of standard tax planning measures.

E Communicate with clients, HM Revenue and Customs and other professionals in an appropriate manner.

RELATIONAL DIAGRAM OF MAIN CAPABILITIES

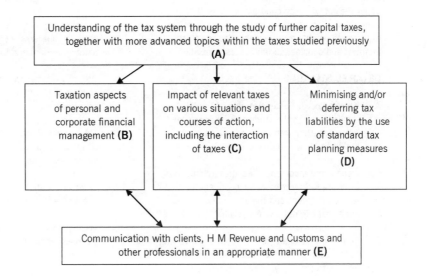

RATIONALE

The Advanced Taxation syllabus further develops the key aspects of taxation introduced in the compulsory Taxation syllabus within the Skills module and extends the candidates' knowledge of the tax system, together with their ability to apply that knowledge to the issues commonly encountered by individuals and businesses, such that successful candidates should have the ability to interpret and analyse the information provided and communicate the outcomes in a manner appropriate to the intended audience.

The syllabus builds on the basic knowledge of core taxes from the earlier taxation paper and introduces candidates to additional capital taxes in the form of inheritance tax, stamp duty and stamp duty land tax. As this is an optional paper, aimed at those requiring/desiring more than basic tax knowledge for their future professional lives, the syllabus also extends the knowledge of income tax, corporation tax and capital gains, to encompass, further overseas aspects of taxation, the taxation of trusts and additional exemptions and reliefs.

Computations will normally only be required in support of explanations or advice and not in isolation.
Candidates are not expected to concentrate on the computational aspects of taxation. Instead this paper seeks to develop candidates' skills of analysis, interpretation and communication. Candidates are expected to be able to use established tax planning methods and consider current issues in taxation.

DETAILED SYLLABUS:

A   Knowledge and understanding of the UK tax system through the study of further capital taxes, together with more advanced topics within the taxes studied previously.

1.   Income and income tax liabilities in situations involving further overseas aspects and in relation to trusts, and the application of additional exemptions and reliefs.

2.   Corporation tax liabilities in situations involving further overseas and group aspects and in relation to special types of company, and the application of additional exemptions and reliefs.

3.   Chargeable gains and capital gains tax liabilities in situations involving further overseas aspects and in relation to closely related persons and trusts, and the application of additional exemptions and reliefs.

4.   Inheritance tax

5.   Stamp duty and stamp duty land tax

6.   National Insurance, value added tax and tax administration

B   The importance of taxation to personal and corporate financial management

1.   The principles underlying personal financial management.

2.   How an individual's personal financial objectives may differ depending on their circumstances and expectations.

3.   The common forms of personal finance and investment products in a given set of circumstances, including ethical considerations.

4.   How a business' financial objectives may differ depending on its circumstances and the business environment.

5.   How taxation can affect the financial decisions made by businesses (corporate and unincorporated) and by individuals.

6.   Other considerations, personal and commercial, which might affect a financial decision.

C   The impact of relevant taxes on various situations and courses of action, including the interaction of taxes

1.   Taxes applicable to a given situation or course of action and their impact.

2.   Alternative ways of achieving personal or business outcomes may lead to different tax consequences.

3.   Tax advantages and/or disadvantages of alternative courses of action.

4. Statutory obligations imposed in a given situation, including any time limits for action and the implications of non-compliance.

D **Minimising and/or deferring tax liabilities by the use of standard tax planning measures**

1. Types of investment and other expenditure that will result in a reduction in tax liabilities for an individual and/or a business.

2. Legitimate tax planning measures, by which the tax liabilities arising from a particular situation or course of action can be mitigated.

3. The appropriateness of such investment, expenditure or measures, given a particular taxpayer's circumstances or stated objectives.

4. The mitigation of tax in the manner recommended, by reference to numerical analysis and/or reasoned argument.

5. Ethical and professional issues arising from the giving of tax planning advice.

6. Current issues in taxation.

E **Communicating with clients, HM Revenue and Customs and other professionals**

1. Communication of advice, recommendations and information in the required format.

2. Presentation of written information, in language appropriate to the purpose of the communication and the intended recipient.

3. Conclusions reached with relevant supporting computations.

4. Assumptions made or limitations in the analysis provided, together with any inadequacies in the information available and/or additional information required to provide a fuller analysis.

5. Other non-tax factors that should be considered.

INTELLECTUAL LEVELS

The syllabus is designed to progressively broaden and deepen the knowledge, skills and professional values demonstrated by the student on their way through the qualification.

The specific capabilities within the detailed syllabuses and study guides are assessed at one of three intellectual or cognitive levels:

Level 1: Knowledge and comprehension
Level 2: Application and analysis
Level 3: Synthesis and evaluation

Very broadly, these intellectual levels relate to the three cognitive levels at which the Knowledge module, the Skills module and the Professional level are assessed.

Each subject area in the detailed study guide is given a 1, 2, or 3 superscript, denoting intellectual level, marked at the end of each relevant line. This gives an indication of the intellectual depth at which an area could be assessed within the examination. However, while level 1 broadly equates with the Knowledge module, level 2 equates to the Skills module and level 3 to the Professional level, some lower level skills can continue to be assessed as the student progresses through each module and level. This reflects that at each stage of study there will be a requirement to broaden, as well as deepen capabilities. It is also possible that occasionally some higher level capabilities may be assessed at lower levels.

Study Guide

A   APPLY FURTHER KNOWLEDGE AND UNDERSTANDING OF THE UK TAX SYSTEM THROUGH THE STUDY OF FURTHER CAPITAL TAXES, TOGETHER WITH MORE ADVANCED TOPICS WITHIN THE TAXES STUDIED PREVIOUSLY.

1. **Income and income tax liabilities in situations involving further overseas aspects and in relation to trusts, and the application of exemptions and reliefs**

a)   The contents of the Paper F6 study guide for income tax, under headings: [2]
*   B1 The scope of income tax
*   B2 Income from employment
*   B3 Income from self employment
*   B4 Property and investment income
*   B5 The comprehensive computation of taxable income and the income tax liability
*   B6 The use of exemptions and reliefs in deferring and minimising income tax liabilities

The following additional material is also examinable:

b)   The scope of income tax: [3]
i)   Explain and apply the concepts of residence, ordinary residence and domicile and advise on the relevance to income tax
ii)   Advise on the tax position of individuals coming to and leaving the UK
iii)   Determine the income tax treatment of overseas income
iv)   Understand the relevance of the OECD model double tax treaty to given situations
vi)   Calculate and advise on the double taxation relief available to individuals

c)   Income from employment: [3]
i)   Advise on the tax treatment of share option and share incentive schemes
ii)   Advise on the tax treatment of lump sum receipts
iii)   Advise on the overseas aspects of income from employment, including travelling and subsistence expenses
iv)   Identify personal service companies and advise on the tax consequences of providing services via a personal service company

d)   Income from self employment:
i)   Recognise the tax treatment of overseas trade travelling expenses [3]
ii)   Evaluate the tax treatment of research and development expenditure [3]
iii)   Establish the relief available on the transfer of a business to a company [3]
iv)   Establish the relief for capital losses on shares in unquoted trading companies [3]
v)   Understand the tax consequences of the disposal of an industrial building after a period of non-industrial use [2]
vi)   Recognise the tax treatment of the investment income and charges of a partnership [2]

e)   Property and investment income: [3]
i)   Assess the tax implications of pre-owned assets
ii)   Recognise income subject to the accrued income scheme
iii)   Advise on the tax implications of jointly held assets
iv)   Income from trusts and settlements: Understand the income tax position of trust beneficiaries

f)   The comprehensive computation of taxable income and the income tax liability: [3]
i) Advise on the income tax position of the income of minor children

g)   The use of exemptions and reliefs in deferring and minimising income tax liabilities:
i)   Understand and apply the rules relating to investments in the enterprise investment scheme [3]
ii)   Understand and apply the rules relating to investments in venture capital trusts [3]
iii)   Explain the conditions that need to be satisfied for pension schemes to be approved by HM Revenue and Customs [2]

Excluded topics

Income from employment:
*   *Explanation of the PAYE system.*
*   *The calculation of a car benefit where emission figures are not available.*

Income from self employment:
- *The 100% first year allowance for information and communication technology equipment.*
- *The 100% first year allowance for expenditure on renovating business premises in disadvantaged areas.*
- *The 100% first year allowance for flats above shops.*
- *The 100% first year allowance for water technologies.*
- *Capital allowances for agricultural buildings, patents, scientific research and know how.*
- *Enterprise zones.*
- *The allocation of notional profits and losses for a partnership.*
- *Farmers averaging of profits.*
- *The averaging of profits for authors and creative artists.*
- *Details of specific anti-avoidance provisions, except as stated in the study guide.*

Income from trusts and settlements:
- *The computation of income tax payable by trustees.*
- *Overseas aspects.*

The comprehensive computation of taxable income and the income tax liability:
- *The blind person's allowance and the married couple's age allowance.*
- *Tax credits*
- *Maintenance payments*
- *Charitable donations.*
- *Social security benefits apart from the State Retirement Pension.*

2. Corporation tax liabilities in situations involving further overseas and group aspects and in relation to special types of company, and the application of additional exemptions and reliefs

a) The contents of the Paper F6 study guide, for corporation tax, under headings:[2]
- C1 The scope of corporation tax
- C2 Profits chargeable to corporation tax
- C3 The comprehensive computation of corporation tax liability

- C4 The effect of a group structure for corporation tax purposes
- C5 The use of exemptions and reliefs in deferring and minimising corporation tax liabilities

The following additional material is also examinable:

b) The scope of corporation tax: [3]
   i) Identify and calculate corporation tax for companies with investment business.
   ii) Close companies:
   - Apply the definition of a close company to given situations
   - Conclude on the tax implications of a company being a close company or a close investment holding company
   iii) Identify and evaluate the significance of accounting periods on administration or winding up
   iv) Conclude on the tax treatment of returns to shareholders after winding up has commenced
   v) Advise on the tax implications of a purchase by a company of its own shares
   vi) Identify personal service companies and advise on the tax consequences of services being provided via a personal service company

c) Profits chargeable to corporation tax: [3]
   i) Identify qualifying research and development expenditure and determine the amount of relief by reference to the size of the individual company/group
   iii) Determine the tax treatment of non trading deficits on loan relationships
   iii) Recognise the alternative tax treatments of intangible assets and conclude on the best treatment for a given company
   iv) Advise on the impact of the transfer pricing and thin capitalisation rules on companies
   v) Advise on the restriction on the use of losses on a change in ownership of a company

d) The comprehensive calculation of corporation tax liability: [3]

i) Advise on the application of the corporate venturing scheme

ii) Assess the impact of the OECD model double tax treaty on corporation tax

iii) Evaluate the meaning and implications of a permanent establishment

iv) Identify and advise on the tax implications of controlled foreign companies

v) Advise on the tax position of overseas companies trading in the UK

e) The effect of a group structure for corporation tax purposes: [3]

i) Advise on the tax consequences of a transfer of intangible assets

ii) Advise on the tax consequences of a transfer of a trade and assets where there is common control

iii) Understand the meaning of consortium owned company and consortium member [2]

iv) Advise on the operation of consortium relief

v) Determine pre-entry gains and losses and understand their tax treatment

vii) Determine the degrouping charge where a company leaves a group within six years of receiving an asset by way of a no gain/no loss transfer

viii) Determine the effects of the anti-avoidance provisions, where arrangements exist for a company to leave a group

ix) Advise on the relief for trading losses incurred by an overseas subsidiary

f) The use of exemptions and reliefs in deferring and minimising corporation tax liabilities:

No additional material at this level.

Excluded topics

The scope of corporation tax:
- *Detailed knowledge of anti-avoidance provisions (except as stated in the Study Guide).*

The comprehensive calculation of the corporation tax liability:
- *Corporation tax rates for companies in the process of winding up.*
- *Relief for overseas tax as an expense.*

- *Detailed knowledge of specific double taxation agreements.*
- *Migration of a UK resident company.*
- *Mixer companies.*
- *Detailed computational questions on the carry back and carry forward of unrelieved foreign tax.*
- *Detailed computational questions on the 'onshore pooling' provisions.*
- *Quarterly accounting for income tax.*

3. **Chargeable gains and capital gains tax liabilities in situations involving further overseas aspects and in relation to closely related persons and trusts together with the application of additional exemptions and reliefs**

a) The contents of the Paper F6 study guide for chargeable gains under headings: [2]
- D1 The scope of the taxation of capital gains
- D2 The basic principles of computing gains and losses
- D3 Gains and losses on the disposal of movable and immovable property
- D4 Gains and losses on the disposal of shares and securities
- D5 The computation of capital gains tax payable by individuals
- D6 The use of exemptions and reliefs in deferring and minimising tax liabilities arising on the disposal of capital assets

The following additional material is also examinable:

b) The scope of the taxation of capital gains: [3]

i) Determine the tax implications of independent taxation and transfers between spouses

ii) Identify the concepts of residence, ordinary residence and domicile and determine their relevance to capital gains tax

iii) Determine the UK taxation of foreign gains, including double taxation relief

iv) Conclude on the capital gains tax position of individuals coming to and leaving the UK

v) Identify the occasions when a capital gain would arise on a partner in a partnership

vi) Capital gains tax and trusts:

Advise on the capital gains tax implications of transfers of property into trust

c) The basic principles of computing gains and losses: [3]

i) Identify connected persons for capital gains tax purposes and advise on the tax implications of transfers between connected persons

ii) Advise on the impact of dates of disposal and conditional contracts

iii) Evaluate the use of capital losses in the year of death

d) Gains and losses on the disposal of movable and immovable property: [3]

i) Advise on the tax implications of a part disposal, including small part disposals of land

ii) Determine the gain on the disposal of leases and wasting assets

iii) Establish the tax effect of appropriations to and from trading stock

iv) Establish the tax effect of capital sums received in respect of the loss, damage or destruction of an asset

v) Advise on the tax effect of making negligible value claims

vi) Determine when capital gains tax can be paid by instalments and evaluate when this would be advantageous to taxpayers

e) Gains and losses on the disposal of shares and securities: [3]

i) Extend the explanation of the treatment of rights issues to include the small part disposal rules applicable to rights issues

ii) Determine the application of the substantial shareholdings exemption

iii) Define a qualifying corporate bond (QCB), and understand what makes a corporate bond non-qualifying. Understand the capital gains tax implications of the disposal of QCBs in exchange for cash or shares

iv) Apply the rules relating to reorganisations, reconstructions and amalgamations and advise on the most tax efficient options available in given circumstances

f) The use of exemptions and reliefs in deferring and minimising tax liabilities arising on the disposal of capital assets: [3]

i) Understand and apply holdover relief on gifts

ii) Understand and apply enterprise investment scheme reinvestment relief

iii) Understand the capital gains tax implications of the variation of wills

Excluded topics

The scope of the taxation of capital gains:
- *Detailed knowledge of the statements of practice on partnership capital gains.*
- *Capital gains tax and trusts:*
- *Overseas aspects of capital gains tax and trusts*

The basic principles of computing gains and losses:
- *Assets held at 31 March 1982.*
- *Relief for losses on loans made to traders.*

Gains and losses on the disposal of movable and immovable property:
- *Chattels where the cost or proceeds are less than £6,000.*
- *Sets of chattels.*
- *The grant of a lease or sub-lease out of either a freehold, long lease or short lease.*

Gains and losses on the disposal of shares and securities:
- *Computation of cost and indexed cost within the s.104 TCGA 1992 share pool*

4. Inheritance tax

a) The scope of inheritance tax: [2]

i) Identify and explain the persons chargeable

ii) Explain the concepts of domicile and deemed domicile and understand the application of these concepts to inheritance tax

b) The basic principles for computing transfers of value: [3]

i) State, explain and apply the meaning of transfers of value, chargeable transfers and potentially exempt transfers

ii) Demonstrate the fall in value principle
iii) Demonstrate the seven year accumulation principle
iv) Identify excluded property [2]
v) Identify and advise on the tax implications of the location of assets
vi) Identify and advise on gifts with reservation of benefit
vii) Identify and advise on the tax implications of associated operations

c) The liabilities arising on chargeable lifetime transfers and death transfers by individuals: [3]
   i) Advise on the tax implications of chargeable lifetime transfers
   ii) Advise on the tax implications of transfers within seven years of death
   iii) Compute the death estate [2]
   iv) Advise on the relief for the fall in value of lifetime gifts
   v) Advise on the operation of quick succession relief
   vi) Advise on the operation of double tax relief for inheritance tax
   vii) Advise on the inheritance tax effects and advantages of the variation of wills

d) Computing transfers of value: [3]
   i) Advise on the principles of valuation
   ii) Advise on the availability of business property relief and agricultural property relief
   iii) Identify exempt transfers [2]

e) The liabilities arising in respect of transfers to and from trusts and on property within trusts: [3]
   i) Define a trust [2]
   ii) Distinguish between an interest in possession trust and a discretionary trust
   iii) Advise on the inheritance tax implications of transfers of property into trust
   iv) Advise on the inheritance tax implications of the termination of the life tenant's interest
   v) Apply the definition of an accumulation and maintenance trust
   vi) Advise on the advantages of using an accumulation and maintenance trust
   vii) Identify the occasions on which inheritance tax is payable by the trustees of a discretionary trust

f) The use of exemptions and reliefs in deferring and minimising inheritance tax liabilities: [3]
   i) Advise on the use of reliefs and exemptions to minimise inheritance tax liabilities, as mentioned in the sections above

g) The system by which inheritance tax is administered, including the instalment option for the payment of tax:
   i) Identify those responsible for the payment of inheritance tax. [2]
   ii) Identify the occasions on which inheritance tax may be paid by instalments. [2]
   iii) Advise on the due dates, interest and penalties for inheritance tax purposes. [3]

Excluded topics

The scope of inheritance tax:
- *Pre 18 March 1986 lifetime transfers*
- *Transfers of value by close companies*

The liabilities arising on chargeable lifetime transfers and on death:
- *Double grossing up on death*
- *Post mortem reliefs*
- *Relief on relevant business property and agricultural property given as exempt legacies*
- *Detailed knowledge of the double charges legislation*

Computing transfers of value:
- *Valuation of an annuity or an interest in possession where the trust interest is subject to an annuity*
- *Woodlands relief*
  Conditional exemption for heritage property

Inheritance tax and trusts:
- *An accumulation and maintenance trust ceasing to qualify*
- *IHT aspects of discretionary trusts prior to 27 March 1974*
- *Computation of ten year charges and exit charges*
- *Overseas aspects of inheritance tax and trusts*

BPP
LEARNING MEDIA

5. **Stamp duties (stamp duty and stamp duty land tax)**

a) The scope of stamp duty and stamp duty land tax: [3]

i) Identify the property in respect of which stamp duty and stamp duty land tax is payable.

b) Identify and advise on the liabilities arising on documented transfers. [3]

i) Advise on the stamp duties payable on transfers of shares and securities

ii) Advise on the stamp duties payable on transfers of land

c) The use of exemptions and reliefs in deferring and minimising stamp duties: [3]

i) Identify transfers involving no consideration

ii) Advise on group transactions

d) Understand and explain the systems by which stamp duties are administered.[2]

Excluded topics

The scope of stamp duty and stamp duty land tax:
- *Leases*

The liabilities arising on documented transfers:
- *The contingency principle*

The systems by which stamp duties are administered:
- *Detailed rules on interest and penalties*

6. **National insurance, value added tax and tax administration:**

a) The contents of the Paper F6 study guide for national insurance under headings:[2]
- E1 The scope of national insurance
- E2 Class 1 and class 1A contributions for employed persons
- E3 Class 2 and class 4 contributions for self-employed persons

No additional material at this level.

b) The contents of the Paper F6 study guide for value added tax (VAT) under headings:

- F1 The scope of value added tax (VAT)
- F2 The VAT registration requirements:
- F3 The computation of VAT liabilities:

The following additional material is also examinable:

i) Advise on the impact of the disaggregation of business activities for VAT purposes [3]

ii) Advise on the impact of group registration and divisional registration [3]

iii) Advise on the VAT implications of the supply of land and buildings in the UK

iv) Advise on the VAT implications of imports and exports

v) Advise on the VAT implications of acquisitions and supplies within the EU

vi) Advise on the VAT implications of partial exemption

vii) Advise on the application of the capital goods scheme

c) The contents of the Paper F6 study guide for the obligations of taxpayers and/or their agents under headings:
- G1 The systems for self assessment and the making of returns
- G2 The time limits for the submission of information, claims and payment of tax, including payments on account
- G3 The procedures relating to enquiries appeals and disputes
- G4 Penalties for non-compliance

No additional material at this level

Excluded topics
Value added tax:
- *The determination of the tax point*
- *The contents of a valid VAT invoice*
- *Do it yourself builders*
- *Second hand goods scheme*
- *Retailers' schemes*
- *Schemes for farmers*

B THE IMPORTANCE OF TAXATION TO PERSONAL AND CORPORATE FINANCIAL MANAGEMENT

1. The principles underlying personal financial management

a) Calculate the receipts from a transaction, net of tax and compare the results of alternative scenarios and advise on the most tax efficient course of action.[3]

2. How an individual's personal financial objectives may differ depending on their circumstances and expectations

a) Understand and apply the effect of age, family commitments, aspirations and the economy on personal financial objectives.[3]

3. The common forms of personal finance and investment products in a given set of circumstances, including ethical considerations

a) Understand and be able to compare and contrast the tax treatment of the sources of finance available to individuals.[3]

b) Understand and be able to compare and contrast the tax treatment of investment products:[3]
   i) Deposit based investments
   ii) Fixed interest securities
   iii) Packaged investments
   iv) Collective investments
   v) Equities
   vi) Enterprise investment scheme
   vii) Venture capital trusts
   viii) Fixed interest securities

4. How a business' financial objectives may differ depending on its circumstances and the business environment.

a) Understand and be able to explain the effect of profitability, future plans, actions of competitors and the economy on a business' financial objectives.[3]

5. How taxation can affect the financial decisions made by businesses (corporate and unincorporated) and by individuals.

a) Understand and explain the tax implications of the effect of the raising of equity and loan finance.[3]

b) Explain the tax differences between decisions to lease, use hire purchase or purchase outright.[3]

c) Understand and explain the impact of taxation on the cash flows of a business.[3]

6. Other considerations, personal and commercial, which might affect a financial decision.[3]

C THE IMPACT OF RELEVANT TAXES ON VARIOUS SITUATIONS AND COURSES OF ACTION, INCLUDING THE INTERACTION OF TAXES

1. Identifying and advising on the taxes applicable to a given course of action and their impact.[3]

2. Identifying and understanding that the alternative ways of achieving personal or business outcomes may lead to different tax consequences.[3]

3. Assessing the tax advantages and disadvantages of alternative courses of action.[3]

4. Understanding the statutory obligations imposed in a given situation, including any time limits for action and advising on the implications of non-compliance.[3]

D MINIMISING AND/OR DEFERRING TAX LIABILITIES BY THE USE OF STANDARD TAX PLANNING MEASURES

1. Identifying and advising on the types of investment and other expenditure that will result in a reduction in tax liabilities for an individual and/or a business.[3]

2. Advising on legitimate tax planning measures, by which the tax liabilities arising from a

particular situation or course of action can be mitigated.[3]

3. Advising on the appropriateness of such investment, expenditure or measures given a particular taxpayer's circumstances or stated objectives.[3]

4. Advise on the mitigation of tax in the manner recommended by reference to numerical analysis and/or reasoned argument.[3]

5. Be aware of the ethical and professional issues arising from the giving of tax planning advice.[3]

6. Be aware of and give advice on current issues in taxation.[3]

E COMMUNICATING WITH CLIENTS, HM REVENUE AND CUSTOMS AND OTHER PROFESSIONALS IN AN APPROPRIATE MANNER

1. Communication of advice, recommendations and information in the required format:[3]

For example the use of:
- Reports
- Letters
- Memoranda
- Meeting notes

2. Presentation of written information, in language appropriate to the purpose of the communication and the intended recipient.[3]

3. Communicating conclusions reached, together, where necessary with relevant supporting computations.[3]

4. Stating and explaining assumptions made or limitations in the analysis provided; together with any inadequacies in the information available and/or additional information required to provide a fuller analysis.[3]

5. Identifying and explaining other, non-tax, factors that should be considered.[3]

The exam paper

The exam is a three-hour paper consisting of two sections.

Section A will contain two compulsory scenario-based questions, usually for the majority of the available marks (between 50 and 70 marks). These questions will normally be broken down into several requirements, allowing students to organise their timing accordingly, and will typically require consideration of the interaction of a number of taxes.

Students will have a choice of two from three Section B questions, which will be shorter in length, but may also cover more than one tax.

Any question may require tax planning considerations.

Computations will normally only be required in support of advice given so no solely numerical questions will be set.

		Number of marks
Section A:	2 compulsory questions	50-70
Section B:	Choice of 2 from 3 questions (equal marks)	30-50
		100

Tax rates, allowances and information on certain reliefs will be given in the exam paper.

Analysis of pilot paper

Section A

1   Trading loss relief for a group of companies; report concerning acquisition of new subsidiary including VAT issues and chargeable gains on sale of factory

2   After tax income comparison for two alternative contracts; employment vs self employment considerations; VAT issues

Section B

3   Incorporation; remuneration package advice
4   Company purchase of own shares; gift of shares
5   Sale of house; IHT gift with reservation rules; shares as part of remuneration package; tax payment due date

Technical articles

You will find technical articles relating to Paper P6 on the ACCA website (ww.accaglobal.com). It is vital that you read the articles written by your examiner, Rory Fish.

Pilot paper

Paper P6

Advanced Taxation

Time allowed

Reading and planning:	15 minutes
Writing:	3 hours

This paper is divided into two sections:

Section A – BOTH questions are compulsory and MUST be attempted

Section B – TWO questions ONLY to be attempted

Do NOT open this paper until instructed by the supervisor.

During reading and planning time only the question paper may be annotated. You must NOT write in your answer booklet until instructed by the supervisor.

This question paper must not be removed from the examination hall.

Warning

The pilot paper cannot cover all of the syllabus nor can it include examples of every type of question that will be included in the actual exam. You may see questions in the exam that you think are more difficult than any you see in the pilot paper.

Section A: BOTH questions are compulsory and MUST be attempted

Question 1

Hutt plc has owned the whole of the ordinary share capital of Rainbow Ltd and Coronet Ltd since 1998. All three companies are resident in the UK. Their results for the year ended 31 March 2007 are as follows:

	Hutt plc £	Rainbow Ltd £	Coronet Ltd £
Taxable trading profit/(loss)	(105,000)	800,000	63,000
Capital gain	144,000	–	–
Rental income	65,000	–	–
UK bank interest receivable	2,000	57,000	18,000

Hutt plc's rental income of £65,000 per annum arises in respect of Hutt Tower, an office building acquired on 1 April 2006.

In the year ended 31 March 2006 Hutt plc had a trading profit of £735,000, UK bank interest receivable of £2,000 and a capital loss of £98,000, which was carried forward as at 31 March 2006.

Hutt plc and Coronet Ltd both carry on trades in the UK. Rainbow Ltd conducts both its manufacturing and trading activities wholly in the country of Prismovia. The system of corporation tax in Prismovia is mainly the same as that in the UK although the rate of corporation tax is 28%. There is no double taxation agreement between the UK and Prismovia.

Hutt plc has agreed that it will purchase the whole of the share capital of Lucia Ltd, a UK resident engineering component manufacturing company, on 1 July 2007 for £130,000.

Hutt plc will need to take out a loan to finance the purchase of Lucia Ltd. The company intends to borrow £190,000 from BHC Bank Ltd on 1 July 2007. BHC Bank Ltd will charge Hutt plc a £1,400 loan arrangement fee and interest at 7.25% per annum. Hutt plc only needs £130,000 of the loan to buy the share capital of Lucia Ltd and intends to use the balance of the loan as follows: £45,000 to carry out repairs to Hutt Tower; and the remainder to help fund the company's ongoing working capital requirements.

Lucia Ltd is a UK resident company. The scale of its activities in the last few years has been very small and it has made tax adjusted trading losses. As at 31 March 2007 Lucia Ltd has trading losses carried forward of £186,000. The company's activities from 1 April 2007 to 30 June 2007 are expected to be negligible and any profit or loss in that period can be ignored. Because of the small scale of its activities Lucia Ltd has not been registered for value added tax (VAT) since March 2006. In arriving at the purchase price for the company, the owners of Lucia Ltd have valued the company's trading losses at £35,340 (£186,000 at 19%), as Lucia Ltd has always been a small company.

On the purchase of Lucia Ltd, Hutt plc has plans to return the company to profitability and the budgeted turnover of Lucia Ltd for the nine months ended 31 March 2008 is as set out below. All amounts relate to the sales of engineering components and are stated exclusive of VAT. It can be assumed that all categories of turnover will accrue evenly over the period.

		£
UK customers:	– VAT registered	85,000
	– non-VAT registered	25,000
European Union customers:	– VAT registered	315,000
	– non-VAT registered	70,000
Other non-UK customers		180,000
		675,000

Lucia Ltd will incur input VAT of £7,800 per month from 1 July 2007 in respect of purchases from UK businesses. It will also purchase raw materials from Dabet Gmbh for £17,000 in November 2007. Dabet Gmbh is resident and registered for VAT in Germany.

Lucia Ltd owns a factory that was built in May 1971 at a cost of £210,000. The factory was acquired by Lucia Ltd on 30 June 2003, for £270,000. It can be assumed that the factory's current value of £80,000 will not change in the foreseeable future. On 1 January 2008, Lucia Ltd will sell this factory and take out a short lease on a new, larger one. The indexation allowance applicable to the period June 2003 to January 2008 can be assumed to be £27,000.

It is proposed that an office building owned by Coronet Ltd be sold to Lucia Ltd in May 2008 at its market value. This building will then be sold on by Lucia Ltd, to Vac Ltd, an unconnected third party in June 2008, giving rise to a capital gain of £92,000. The intention is that this gain will be reduced by the capital loss arising on the sale of the factory.

Required

(a)   Describe and evaluate the options available in respect of the trading losses of Hutt plc for the year ended 31 March 2007. Your answer should include a recommendation on the most tax efficient use of these losses, together with details of and time limits for any elections or claims that would need to be submitted, assuming that the losses are to be used as soon as possible and are not to be carried forward.   **(13 marks)**

(b)   Prepare a report for the management of Hutt plc concerning the acquisition of Lucia Ltd. The report should be in three sections, addressing the three sets of issues set out below, and should, where appropriate, include supporting calculations.

    (i)   The purchase price

        Comment on the valuation placed on Lucia Ltd's trading losses, by the owners of Lucia Ltd.

        Provide an explanation of the tax treatment of the loan arrangement fee and the interest payable on the loan of £190,000, assuming that Hutt plc continues to have bank interest receivable, in the year ended 31 March 2008, of £2,000.   **(9 marks)**

    (ii)   VAT issues

        Provide an explanation of the date by which Lucia Ltd will be required to register for VAT in the UK and any other relevant points in respect of registration.

        Provide a calculation of the VAT payable by, or repayable to, Lucia Ltd in respect of the period from registration to 31 March 2008.

        With reference only to the facts in the question, suggest ONE disadvantage of Lucia Ltd entering into a group VAT registration with Hutt plc.   **(6 marks)**

    (iii)   The office building

        Advise on the tax implications of the proposed sale of the office building by Coronet Ltd to Lucia Ltd in May 2008. Your answer should consider all relevant taxes.

        Evaluate the proposed strategy to reduce the capital gain arising on the sale of the office building by offsetting the capital loss on the sale of the factory, on the assumption that both Lucia Ltd and Coronet Ltd will pay corporation tax at the rate of 30%, for the year ended 31 March 2009.   **(9 marks)**

Appropriateness of the format and presentation of the report and the effectiveness with which its advice is communicated.   **(2 marks)**

You may assume that the tax rates and allowances for the financial year to 31 March 2007 and for the tax year 2006/07 will continue to apply for the foreseeable future.

(Total = 39 marks)

Question 1

You should not be daunted by the apparent length of the question as it subdivides into several distinct areas which you are asked to cover separately in your answer. Note the technique in part (a), describe, evaluate and recommend. This is likely to be a common requirement in future exams. Part (b) requires you to write a report and marks are specifically given for its format, presentation and effective communication. Working through it step by step reduces it to manageable chunks, and you should practise this technique.

Question 2

Your manager has had a meeting with Pilar Mareno, a self-employed consultant, and has sent you a copy of the following memorandum.

To	The files
From	Tax manager
Date	31 May 2007
Subject	Pilar Mareno – Business expansion

Pilar Mareno (PM) has been offered a contract with DWM plc, initially for two years, which will result in fees of £80,000 plus VAT per annum.

In order to service this contract, PM would have to take on additional help in the form of either a part-time employee for two days a week, or the services of a self-employed contractor for 100 days per year. She would also have to acquire a van, which would be used wholly for business purposes. PM has decided that she will only enter into the contract if it generates at least an additional £15,000 per annum, on average, for the family after all costs and taxes.

PM's annual profitability and the profit generated by the contract (before taking into account the costs of the parttime employee/contractor and the van) are summarised below.

	Existing business	New contract
	£	£
Sales	210,000	80,000
Less: Materials, wages and overheads	(120,000)	(35,000)
Profit per accounts and taxable profit	90,000	45,000

Supplies made under the contract will be 65% standard rated and 35% exempt for value added tax (VAT) purposes; this is the same as for PM's existing business. £31,500 of the costs incurred in relation to the contract will be subject to VAT at the standard rate. The equivalent figure for PM's existing business is £100,000.

PM has identified Max Wallen (MW) as a possible self-employed contractor. MW would charge £75 per day plus VAT for a contract of 100 days per year, with a rate of £25 per day plus VAT in respect of any days when he is ill (up to a maximum of 8 days per year). PM has a spare copy of the specialist software that MW would need but MW would use his own laptop computer.

Alternatively, PM could employ her husband, Alec (AM), paying him a gross annual salary of £7,600. AM would have to give up his current full time job, but would expect to do other part-time employed work earning a further £10,000 (gross) per annum.

PM estimates that a second hand van will cost £7,800 plus VAT or alternatively, a van could be leased for £300 plus VAT per month. We can assume that if the van is purchased, it will be sold at the end of the two year contract for £2,500 plus VAT.

Tax manager

An extract from an email from your manager is set out below.

Please prepare a memorandum for me, incorporating the following:

1   Calculations to demonstrate whether or not Pilar's desired annual after tax income from the new contract will be achievable depending on:

- whether she leases or buys the van; and
- whether she employs Alec or uses Max Wallen.

You may find it easier to:

(i)   work out the after tax cost of buying or leasing the van. (When calculating the annual cost of the van, assume that the total cost can be averaged over the two years of the contract.) and then to consider:

(ii)   the after tax income depending on whether Alec is employed or the self-employed contractor, Max, is used.

2   A rationale for the approach you have taken and a summary of your findings.

3   Any other issues we should be considering in respect of Pilar employing Alec, including any alternative to employment.

4   It seems to me that HM Revenue and Customs may be able to successfully contend that Max Wallen would be an employee, rather than a self-employed contractor. Prepare your figures on the basis that he is selfemployed but include a list of factors in your memorandum, based on the information we have, that would indicate either employed or self-employed status.

Take some time to think about your approach to this before you start. Also, as always when working on Pilar's affairs, watch out for the VAT as it can get quite tricky. I suspect the VAT will affect the costs incurred so you'll need to address VAT first. Pilar's estimate of the profit on the contract will have ignored these complications.

Tax manager

You have extracted the following further information from Pilar Mareno's client file.

- None of Pilar's VAT inputs is directly attributable to either standard rated or exempt supplies.
- Alec has worked for a UK bank for many years and is currently paid an annual salary of £17,000.
- The couple have no sources of income other than those set out above.

Required

Prepare the memorandum requested by your manager.

Marks are available for the four components of the memorandum as follows:

1   Relevant calculations.   **(16 marks)**

2   Rationale for the approach taken and summary of findings.   **(2 marks)**

3   Other issues in respect of Pilar employing Alec, together with any suggestions as to an alternative to employment.   **(2 marks)**

4   The employment status of Max Wallen.   **(3 marks)**

Appropriateness of the format and presentation of the memorandum and the effectiveness with which the information is communicated.   **(2 marks)**

You may assume that the rates and allowances for the tax year 2006/07 will continue to apply for the foreseeable future.

(Total = 25 marks)

41

Question 2

This question requires you to calculate the after tax income of a proposed new contract depending on several alternative factors. It helpfully leads you through the route to take in making the comparison, although you will need to work out for yourself the impact that different taxes will have on the options. You are asked to state your findings, and to state any other issues that need to be considered, but you are not required actually to make a recommendation. You just need to be sure that you have provided sufficient information to enable the client to make a considered decision.

You may have spotted that the increase in Alec's income would in fact be at least £554 higher than suggested in the model answer as the earnings threshold of £5,035 for national insurance contributions is available in each of his employments.

Section B: TWO questions ONLY to be attempted

Question 3

Stanley Beech, a self-employed landscape gardener, intends to transfer his business to Landscape Ltd, a company formed for this purpose.

The following information has been extracted from client files and from meetings with Stanley.

Stanley:

- Acquired a storage building for £46,000 on 1 July 1998 and began trading.
- Has no other sources of income.
- Has capital losses brought forward from 2002/03 of £11,400.

The whole of the business is to be transferred to Landscape Ltd on 1 September 2007:

- The market value of the assets to be transferred is £118,000.

- The assets include the storage building and goodwill, valued at £87,000 and £24,000 respectively, and various small pieces of equipment and consumable stores.

- Landscape Ltd will issue 5,000 £1 ordinary shares as consideration for the transfer.

Advice given to Stanley in respect of the sale of the business:

- 'No capital gains tax will arise on the transfer of your business to the company.'

- 'You should take approximately 30% of the payment from Landscape Ltd in shares with the balance left on a loan account payable to you by the company, such that you can receive a cash payment in the future.'

Advice given to Stanley in respect of his annual remuneration from Landscape Ltd:

- 'The payment of a dividend of £21,000 is more tax efficient than paying a salary bonus of £21,000 as you will pay income tax at only 25% on the dividend received, whereas you would pay income tax at 40% on a salary bonus. The dividend also avoids the need to pay national insurance contributions.'

- 'There is no tax in respect of an interest free loan from an employer of less than £5,000.'

- 'The provision of a company car is tax neutral as the cost of providing it is deductible in the corporation tax computation.'

Stanley's proposed remuneration package from Landscape Ltd:

- An annual salary of £40,000 and an annual dividend of approximately £21,000.

- On 1 December 2007 an interest free loan of £3,600, which he intends to repay in two years time.

- A company car with a cost when new of £11,400. The only costs incurred by the company in respect of this car will be lease rentals of £300 per month and business fuel of £100 per month.

- The annual employment income benefit in respect of the car is to be taken as £3,420.

Landscape Ltd:

- Will prepare accounts to 31 March each year.
- Will pay corporation tax at the rate of 19%.

43

Required

(a) (i) Explain why there would be no capital gains tax liability on the transfer of Stanley's business to Landscape Ltd in exchange for shares. Calculate the maximum loan account balance that Stanley could receive without giving rise to a capital gains tax liability and state the resulting capital gains tax base cost of the shares. **(8 marks)**

(ii) Explain the benefit to Stanley of taking part of the payment for the sale of his business in the form of a loan account, which is to be paid out in cash at some time in the future. **(1 mark)**

(b) Comment on the accuracy and completeness of the advice received by Stanley in respect of his remuneration package. Supporting calculations are only required in respect of the company car. **(9 marks)**

Ignore value added tax (VAT) in answering this question.

You may assume that the rates and allowances for the financial year to 31 March 2007 and the tax year 2006/07 will continue to apply for the foreseeable future.

(Total = 18 marks)

Question 3

Part (a) of this question covers a standard topic (incorporation relief) which you should be very familiar with. Part (b) asks you to comment on three pieces of advice which have been given to a client, which is simply another way of asking you to give explanations. The third point asked for calculations and comments on the tax cost of providing a company car. It would be easy to get sidetracked here; the model answer compares the tax cost of providing the benefit with the tax saved on the cost of provision. You may have thought of other points that could conceivably have been required in the answer, such as the tax saved if the employer paid a mileage allowance for use of the employee's own car.

Question 4

Mahia Ltd is an unquoted, UK resident trading company formed in May 2000. One of its shareholders, Claus Rowen, intends to sell his shares back to Mahia Ltd on 31 July 2007. Another shareholder, Maude Brooke, intends to give some of her shares to her daughter, Tessa.

The following information has been extracted from client files and from meetings with the shareholders.

Mahia Ltd

- In May 2000 the company issued 40,000 shares at £3.40 per share as follows:

Claus Rowen	16,000
Charlotte Forde	12,000
Olaf Berne	12,000

- Olaf sold his 12,000 shares to Maude Brooke on 1 October 2005 when they were worth £154,000.

Claus and Charlotte

- Have always lived in the UK.
- Are higher rate taxpayers who use their capital gains tax annual exemption every year.

Maude

- Was born in the UK, but moved to Canada on 1 April 2003 with her daughter, Tessa.

- Has not visited the UK since leaving for Canada, but will return to the UK permanently in December 2012.

- Is employed in Canada with an annual salary equivalent to £70,000.

Sale of shares by Claus

- Charlotte and Maude want to expand the company's activities in the UK but Claus does not. The shareholders have been arguing over this matter for almost a year.

- In order to enable the company to prosper, Claus has agreed to sell his shares to the company on 31 July 2007.

Gift of shares by Maude

- Maude will gift 4,000 shares in Mahia Ltd to her daughter, Tessa, on either 1 August 2007 or 1 June 2008.

- She will delay the gift until 1 June 2008 (Tessa's wedding day) if this reduces the total tax due.

- The tax due in Canada will be the same regardless of the date of the gift.

- She has made no previous transfers of value for UK inheritance tax purposes.

- For the purposes of this gift, you should assume that Maude will die on 31 December 2011.

Market values of shares in Mahia Ltd on all relevant dates are to be taken as:

Size of shareholding %	Market value per share £
< 25	10.20
25 – 35	14.40
> 35	38.60

Market values of the assets of Mahia Ltd on all relevant dates are to be taken as:

	£
Land and buildings used within the trade	1,400,000
Three machines of equal value used within the trade	15,000
Motor cars used by employees	45,000
Quoted shares	42,000
Inventory, trade receivables and cash	145,000

Required

(a) Advise Claus on the tax treatment of the proceeds he will receive in respect of the sale of his shares to Mahia Ltd. Prepare a calculation of the net (after tax) proceeds from the sale based on your conclusions. **(8 marks)**

(b) Advise Maude on the UK tax consequences of gifting the shares to Tessa and prepare computations to determine on which of the two dates the gift should be made, if the total UK tax due on the gift is to be minimised. Your answer should consider all relevant taxes. **(10 marks)**

You may assume that the rates and allowances for the tax year 2006/07 will continue to apply for the foreseeable future.

(Total = 18 marks)

45

Question 4

The first part of this question required you to explain the tax treatment of the purchase by a company of its own shares and calculate the net of proceeds. This simply means that you have to calculate the tax liability and then take the extra step of subtracting it from the proceeds. Part (b) is a straightforward question on the tax consequences of making a gift and the best time to make it. You were told to assume that the table of share values applied at all relevant dates. As there was a repurchase of shares within the period this involved a recalculation of the percentage size of the remaining holdings. Although it may seem unlikely that the values would remain as given you should use the facts as stated in the question. You may have thought of additional points to raise in your answer, such as the fact that if Tessa was likely to sell the shares so that BPR would not be available on Maude's death, the earlier gift would be preferable due to the increased taper of the IHT payable as a result of death within seven years of the gift.

Question 5

Vikram Bridge has been made redundant by Bart Industries Ltd, a company based in Birmingham. He intends to move to Scotland to start a new job with Dreamz Technology Ltd.

The following information has been extracted from client files and from meetings with Vikram.

Vikram Bridge

- Is unmarried, but has been living with Alice Tate since 1996. The couple have four young children.

- Receives dividends of approximately £7,800 each year and makes annual capital gains of approximately £1,200 in respect of shares inherited from his mother.

- The couple have no sources of income other than Vikram's employment income and the £7,800 of dividends.

Made redundant by Bart Industries Ltd on 28 February 2007

- Vikram's employment contract entitled him to two months' notice or two months salary in lieu of notice. On 28 February 2007 the company paid him his salary for the two-month period of £4,700, and asked him to leave immediately.

- On 30 April 2007 the company paid him a further £1,300 in respect of statutory redundancy, together with a non-contractual lump sum of £14,500, as a gesture of goodwill.

Job with Dreamz Technology Ltd

- Starts on 1 October 2007 with an annual salary of £38,500.

- The company will contribute £9,400 in October 2007 towards Vikram's costs of moving to Scotland.

- In November 2008, the company will issue free shares to all of its employees. Vikram will be issued with 200 shares, expected to be worth approximately £2,750.

Moving house

- Vikram's house in Birmingham is fairly small; he intends to buy a much larger one in Glasgow.

- The cost of moving to Glasgow, including the stamp duty land tax in respect of the purchase of his new house, will be approximately £12,500.

- To finance the purchase of the house in Glasgow Vikram will sell a house he owns in Wales, in August 2007.

House in Wales

- Was given to Vikram by his mother on 1 September 1999, when it was worth £145,000.

- Vikram's mother continued to live in the house until her death on 1 May 2007, when she left the whole of her estate to Vikram.

- At the time of her death the house had severe structural problems and was valued at £140,000.

- Vikram has subsequently spent £18,000 improving the property and expects to be able to sell it for £195,000.

- Vikram is keen to reduce the tax payable on the sale of the house and is willing to transfer the house, or part of it, to Alice prior to the sale if that would help.

Required

Prepare explanations, including supporting calculations where appropriate, of the following issues suitable for inclusion in a letter to Vikram.

(a) The capital gains tax payable on the sale of the house in Wales in August 2007, together with the potential effect of transferring the house, or part of it, to Alice prior to the sale, and any other advice you consider helpful. **(7 marks)**

(b) The inheritance tax implications in respect of the house in Wales on the death of Vikram's mother. **(2 marks)**

(c) The income tax treatment of the receipt by Vikram of the shares in Dreamz Technology Ltd. **(3 marks)**

(d) How Vikram's job with Dreamz Technology Ltd will affect the amount and date of payment of the income tax due on his dividend income for 2009/10 and future years. **(6 marks)**

Ignore national insurance contributions in answering this question.

You may assume that the rates and allowances for the tax year 2006/07 will continue to apply for the foreseeable future.

(Total = 18 marks)

Question 5

This question covered a range of topics of taxes. It shows how the use of a scenario based question can test the breadth of your knowledge, and can be regarded as typical of the sort of situation that you are likely to come across in real life.

Part A
Taxation of individuals

Principles of income tax

Topic list	Syllabus reference
1 The aggregation of income	A1(a)B5
2 Various types of income	A1(a)B5
3 Charges on income	A1(a)B5
4 The personal allowance	A1(a)B5
5 The personal tax computation	A1(a)B5
6 Tax reducers	A1(a)B6
7 Families	A1(e)(iii), (f)(i)

Introduction

We start our study of taxation with a look at income tax, which is a tax on what individuals make from their jobs, their businesses and their savings. We see how to collect together all of an individual's income in a personal tax computation, and then work out the tax on that income.

We also look at the family aspects of income tax, how joint income of spouses/civil partners is taxed and the anti-avoidance provisions for minor children.

In later chapters, we look at particular types of income in more detail.

Study Guide

		Intellectual level
1	**Income and income tax liabilities in situations involving further overseas aspects and in relation to trusts, and the application of exemptions and reliefs**	
(a)	The contents of the Paper F6 study guide for income tax, under headings:	2
•	B5 The comprehensive computation of taxable income and the income tax liability	
(e)	Property and investment income:	3
(iii)	Advise on the tax implications of jointly held assets	
(f)	The comprehensive computation of taxable income and the income tax liability:	3
(i)	Advise on the income tax position of the income of minor children	

Exam guide

Although you are unlikely to have to perform a complete income tax computation in the exam, you need to understand how the computation is put together as you may be asked to calculate the after tax income that would be derived from a particular new source. Do not overlook the effect of an increase in income on the age allowance.

The chapter also introduces tax planning concepts. Note the treatment of joint income of spouses/civil partners and the anti-avoidance rules that apply if a parent gives funds to a minor child.

Knowledge brought forward from earlier studies

This chapter revises the basic income tax computation that you will already have met at level 2.3. It also includes material that will be new to you: the age allowance, tax reducers and the taxation of families.

1 The aggregation of income

FAST FORWARD

In a personal income tax computation, bring together income from all sources, splitting the sources into non-savings, savings (excl. dividend) and dividend income.

As a general rule, income tax is charged on receipts which might be expected to recur (such as weekly wages or profits from running a business). **An individual's income from all sources is brought together in a personal tax computation for the tax year**.

Key term

The **tax year**, or **fiscal year**, or **year of assessment** runs from 6 April to 5 April. For example, the tax year 2006/07 runs from 6 April 2006 to 5 April 2007.

Three columns are needed in the computation. Here is an example. All items are explained later in this Text.

RICHARD: INCOME TAX COMPUTATION 2006/07

	Non-savings income £	Savings (excl dividend) Income £	Dividend income £	Total £
Income from employment	41,000			
Building society interest		1,000		
National savings & investments account interest		360		
UK dividends			1,000	
	41,000	1,360	1,000	
Less charges on income	(2,000)			
Statutory total income (STI)	39,000	1,360	1,000	41,360
Less personal allowance	(5,035)			
Taxable income	33,965	1,360	1,000	36,325

	£	£
Income tax on non savings income		
£2,150 × 10%		215
£31,150 × 22%		6,853
£665 × 40%		266
Tax on savings (excl. dividend) income		
£1,360 × 40%		544
Tax on dividend income		
£1,000 × 32.5%		325
		8,203
Less tax reducer		
Investment under the EIS £10,000 × 20%		(2,000)
Add basic rate tax withheld on charges		
paid net £2,000 × 22%		440
Tax liability		6,643
Less tax suffered		
PAYE tax on salary (say)	5,650	
Tax on building society interest	200	
Tax credit on dividend income	100	
		(5,950)
Tax payable		693

Key term

> **Statutory total income** (STI) is all income before deducting the personal allowance or the blind person's allowance. The **tax liability** is the amount which must be accounted for to HMRC. **Tax payable** is the balance of the liability still to be settled in cash.

Income tax is charged on **'taxable income'**. Non-savings income is dealt with first, then savings (excl. dividend) income and then dividend income.

For non-savings income, the first £2,150 (the starting rate band) is taxed at the starting rate (10%), the next £31,150 (the basic rate band) is taxed at the basic rate (22%) and the rest at the higher rate (40%). We will look at the taxation of the other types of income later in this chapter.

The remainder of this chapter gives more details of the income tax computation.

2 Various types of income

FAST FORWARD

Don't forget to gross up dividends by 100/90 and interest by 100/80.

2.1 Classification of income

All income received must be classified according to the nature of the income. This is because different computational rules apply to different types of income. The main types of income are:

- Income from employment, pensions and some social security benefits
- Profits of trades, professions and vocations
- Profits of property businesses
- Savings and investment income, including interest and dividends
- Miscellaneous income.

2.2 Savings income received net of 20% tax

The following savings income is received net of 20% tax. **This is called income taxed at source.**

(a) Bank and building society interest paid to individuals (but not National Savings & Investments account interest)

(b) Interest paid to individuals by unlisted UK companies on debentures and loan stocks

(c) The income portion of a purchased annuity

(d) Savings income (excluding dividends) from non discretionary trusts

The amount received is grossed up by multiplying by 100/80 and is included gross in the income tax computation. The tax deducted at source is deducted in computing tax payable and may be repaid.

Exam focus point

> In examinations you may be given either the net or the gross amount of such income: read the question carefully. If you are given the net amount (the amount received or credited), you should gross up the figure at the rate of 20%. For example, net building society interest of £160 is equivalent to gross income of £160 × 100/80 = £200 on which tax of £40 (20% of £200) has been suffered.

Although bank and building society interest paid to individuals is generally paid net of 20% tax, if a recipient is not liable to tax, he can recover the tax suffered, or he can certify in advance that he is a non-taxpayer and receive the interest gross.

2.3 Dividends on UK shares

FAST FORWARD

Higher rate taxpayers pay an effective rate of 25% on their dividend income.

Dividends on UK shares are received net of a 10% tax credit. This means a dividend of £90 has a £10 tax credit, giving gross income of £100 to include in the income tax computation. The tax credit can be deducted in computing tax payable but it cannot be repaid.

Higher rate taxpayers pay tax at 32½% on their gross dividends and can deduct the 10% tax credit. This is the same as taxing the net dividend at 25%. For example, a higher rate taxpayer receiving a net dividend of £9,000 will pay tax of £2,250, which is £3,250 (£10,000 @ 32½%) less £1,000 (£10,000 @ 10%). This is the same as taking 25% × £9,000.

2.4 Exempt income

Some income is exempt from income tax. Several of these exemptions are mentioned at places in this Text where the types of income are described in detail, but you should note the following types of exempt income now.

- (a) Scholarships (exempt as income of the scholar. If paid by a parent's employer, a scholarship may be taxable income of the parent)

- (b) Betting and gaming winnings, including **premium bond prizes**

- (c) Interest or terminal bonus on **National Savings & Investments Certificates**

- (d) Certain social security benefits

- (e) Gifts

- (f) Damages and payments for personal injury. The exemption applies to lump sum and periodical payments, including payments made via trusts and payments made by buying annuities. Payments under annuities are made gross (unlike most annuities)

- (g) Certain payments under insurance policies to compensate for loss of income on illness or disability (permanent health insurance) or while out of work (eg policies to pay interest on mortgages) (see later in this Text.)

- (h) The amount by which a pension awarded on a retirement due to a disability caused at work, by a work related illness or by war wounds exceeds the pension that would have been payable if the retirement had been on ordinary ill health grounds.

- (i) Interest on amounts repaid to borrowers under the income contingent student loans scheme

- (j) Payments made under the 'new deal 50 plus' scheme and payments made under the employment zones programme.

- (k) Income on investments made through **individual savings accounts (ISAs).**

Exam focus point

Learn the different types of exempt income. They are popular items in the exam. Always state on your exam script that such income is exempt (do not ignore it) to gain an easy half mark.

3 Charges on income

FAST FORWARD

Charges on income are deducted to arrive at Statutory Total Income (STI).

3.1 Types of charges on income

Key term

A **charge on income** is a payment by the taxpayer which income tax law allows as a deduction.

Examples of charges on income are:

- (a) Eligible interest
- (b) Patent royalties
- (c) Copyright royalties

Charges on income broadly fall into two categories: those from which basic rate (22%) income tax is first deducted by the payer (charges paid net) and those which are paid gross (without any tax deduction). Always deduct the gross figure in the payer's tax computation.

Patent royalties are an example of a charge on income which individuals pay net. Eligible interest and copyright royalties are paid gross.

In the personal tax computation of someone who **receives** a charge, you should:

(a) Include the **gross** amount under non-savings income. If the charge is paid gross, the gross amount is the amount received. If it is paid net, the gross amount is the amount received × 100/78.

(b) If the charge was received net, then under the heading 'less tax suffered' (between tax liability and tax payable) include the tax deducted. This is the gross amount × 22%.

3.2 Eligible interest

Interest qualifies for tax relief as a charge if the loan concerned is used for a qualifying purpose:

(a) **The purchase of an interest in a partnership, or contribution to the partnership of capital or a loan**. The borrower must be a partner (other than a limited partner), and relief ceases when he ceases to be one.

(b) **The purchase of ordinary shares in, or the loan of money to, a close trading company.** When the interest is paid the individual must either have (with any associates) a material (more than 5%) interest in the company, or he must hold (ignoring associates) **some** ordinary share capital and work full time as a manager or director of the company. A close company is (broadly) a company controlled by its shareholder-directors or by five or fewer shareholders. Relief for interest paid is not available if relief for the investment is claimed under the enterprise investment scheme (see later in this Text).

(c) **Investment in a co-operative**. This applies to investment in shares/loans to the co-operative. The borrower must work for the greater part of his time in the co-operative.

(d) **The purchase of shares in an employee-controlled company** which must be an unquoted trading company resident in the UK with at least 50% of the voting shares held by employees.

(e) **The payment of inheritance tax by personal representatives** before a grant of representation. Interest is allowed for 12 months only.

(f) **The purchase by a partner of plant or machinery used in the business**. Interest is allowed for three years from the end of the tax year in which the loan was taken out. If the plant is used partly for private purposes, then the allowable interest is apportioned.

(g) **The purchase by an employee of plant or machinery used by him in the performance of his duties**. The interest is allowable for three years from the end of the tax year in which the loan was taken out.

(h) The replacement of other loans qualifying under (a) to (g) above.

Interest on a loan within (a) to (d) above continues to be allowable if a partnership is succeeded by a new partnership or is incorporated into a close company, a co-operative or an employee controlled company, or if shares in a company of one of these kinds are exchanged for shares in a company of another of these kinds, provided that interest on a new loan (to make the loan to or buy the shares in the new entity) would have qualified.

Interest is never allowed if it is payable under a scheme or arrangement of which the expected sole or main benefit was tax relief on the interest. Interest on an overdraft or on a credit card debt does not qualify. Relief under (a) to (d) above is reduced or withdrawn if capital is withdrawn from the business.

3.3 Business interest

A taxpayer paying interest wholly and exclusively for business purposes can deduct such interest in computing his trading profit, rather than as a charge. The interest need not fall into any of the categories outlined above, and it may be on an overdraft or a credit card debt.

If interest is allowable as a trading expense, the amount payable (on an accruals basis) is deducted (see later in this Text).

3.4 Charges in the personal tax computation

The gross amount of any charge is deducted from total income to arrive at STI. Deduct charges from non-savings income, then from savings (excl dividend) income and lastly from dividend income.

If a charge has been paid net, the basic rate income tax deducted (22% of the gross charge) is added to any tax liability. The taxpayer obtained tax relief because the charge reduced his income: he cannot keep the basic rate tax as well, but must pay it to HMRC.

If charges paid net exceed total income (ignoring charges paid net) **minus allowances deductible from STI, the payer of the charge must, under s 350 ICTA 1988, pay HMRC the tax withheld when the excess charge was paid**. In other words, HMRC ensure that you do not get tax relief for charges if you are not a payer of tax.

3.5 Example

Three taxpayers have the following trading income and allowances for 2006/07. Taxpayers A and B pay a patent royalty of £176 (net). Taxpayer C pays a patent royalty of £1,248 (net).

	A £	B £	C £
Trading Income	6,000	4,000	40,795
Less: charge on income (× 100/78)	(226)	(226)	(1,600)
	5,774	3,774	39,195
Less: personal allowance	(5,035)	(5,035)	(5,035)
Taxable income	739	–	34,160
Income tax			
10% on £739/–/£2,150	74	–	215
22% on –/–/£31,150			6,853
40% on –/–/£860			344
	74	–	7,412
Add: 22% tax retained on charge	50	50	352
Tax payable	124	50	7,764

4 The personal allowance

FAST FORWARD

Deduct the personal allowance. There are increased allowances for the over 65s.

Once taxable income from all sources has been aggregated and any charges on income deducted, the remainder is the taxpayer's statutory total income (STI). The personal allowance is deducted from STI. Like charges, it is deducted from non savings income first, then from savings (excl. dividend) income and lastly from dividend income. The amounts given in the following paragraphs are for 2006/07.

All persons (including children) are entitled to the personal allowance of £5,035.

A person aged 65 or over (at any time in the tax year) gets an age allowance of £7,280 instead of the ordinary PA of £5,035.

Where statutory total income exceeds £20,100, cut the age allowance by £1 for every £2 of income over £20,100 until it comes down to £5,035.

Question	Calculation of age allowance

Jonah is 69 and single. In 2006/07 he has pension income totalling £18,000 plus bank interest received of £4,000. What is Jonah's taxable income?

Answer

	Non savings	Savings	Total
2006/07	£	£	£
Pension income	18,000		
Interest 4,000 × 100/80		5,000	
	18,000	5,000	23,000
Less PAA (W1)	(5,830)		
Taxable income	12,170	5,000	17,170

W1

PAA 65+	7,280
Less income restriction (23,000 – 20,100) × ½	(1,450)
	5,830

PAA of £5,830 exceeds basic allowance of £5,035.

Individuals aged 75 or over (at any time in the tax year) get a slightly more generous age allowance of £7,420. In all respects, the higher age allowance works in the same way as the basic age allowance, with the same income limit of £20,100.

Someone who dies in the tax year in which they would have had their 65th or 75th birthday receives the age allowance (for 65 year olds or 75 year olds) for that year.

5 The personal tax computation

FAST FORWARD Work out income tax on the taxable income in three stages then take account of tax retained on charges and tax already suffered.

5.1 Steps in the personal tax computation

Step 1   **The first step in preparing a personal tax computation is to set up three columns.** One column for non-savings income, one for savings (excl. dividend) income and one for dividend income.

Step 2   **Deal with non-savings income first.** Income of up to £2,150 is taxed at 10%. Next any income in the basic rate band is taxed at 22%, and finally income above the basic rate threshold is taxed at 40%.

Step 3   **Now deal with savings (excl dividend) income.** If any of the starting or basic rate bands remain **after taxing non savings income**, they can be used here. Savings (excl) dividend income is taxed at 10% in the starting rate band and in the basic rate band at 20% (not 22%). Once income is above the higher rate threshold, it is taxed at 40%.

Step 4 **Lastly, tax dividend income.** If dividend income falls within the starting or basic rate bands, it is taxed at 10% (never 20% or 22%). If the dividend income exceeds the basic rate threshold of £33,300, it is taxable at 32.5%.

Step 5 Once tax has been computed, deduct any available tax reducers (eg EIS investments).

Step 6 Next, deduct the tax credit on dividends. Although deductible this tax credit cannot be repaid if it exceeds the tax liability calculated so far.

Step 7 Finally deduct the tax deducted at source from savings (excluding dividend) income and any PAYE. These amounts can be repaid to the extent that they exceed the income tax liability.

Question   Calculation of income tax payable

Jules has a business profit of £50,000, net dividends of £6,750 and building society interest of £3,000 net. He pays gross charges of £3,000. How much income tax is payable?

Answer

	Non-savings £	Savings (excl dividend) £	Dividend £	Total £
Business profits	50,000			
Dividends £6,750 × 100/90			7,500	
Building society interest £3,000 × 100/80	–	3,750	–	
	50,000	3,750	7,500	
Less charges	(3,000)			
STI	47,000	3,750	7,500	58,250
Less personal allowance	(5,035)			
Taxable income	41,965	3,750	7,500	53,215

	£
Non savings income	
£2,150 × 10%	215
£31,150 × 22%	6,853
£8,665 × 40%	3,466
	10,534
Savings (excl. dividend) income	
£3,750 × 40%	1,500
Dividend income	
£7,500 × 32.5%	2,438
Less tax credit on dividend income	(750)
Less tax suffered on building society interest	(750)
Tax payable	12,972

Savings (excl. dividend) income and dividend income fall above the basic rate threshold so they are taxed at 40% and 32.5% respectively.

The above question showed a full income tax computation. Often a taxpayer is more interested in looking at the after tax return from a particular investment or transaction. In each of the following examples we will calculate the additional tax due as a result of acquiring a new investment. Note how it is not necessary here to use the full income tax proforma.

5.2 Examples: additional tax due

(a) Kate receives an annual salary of £75,000. Her grandfather dies leaving her shares in Axle plc. She receives dividends of £18,000 during 2006/07. The additional tax due as a result of receiving the dividend income can be calculated as follows:

Income tax on dividends of (£18,000 × 100/90 =) £20,000 is all at the higher rate as there is no basic rate band left:

	£
£20,000 @ 32½%	6,500
Less tax credit @ 10%	(2,000)
Additional tax due	4,500

This is the same as taking 25% of the net dividend taxable at the higher rate ie (£18,000 × 90%) @ 25% = £4,500.

(b) Kate receives an annual salary of £35,000. Her grandfather dies leaving her shares in Axle plc. She receives dividends of £18,000 during 2006/07. The additional tax due as a result of receiving the dividend income can be calculated as follows:

Income tax on dividends of (£18,000 × 100/90 =) £20,000:

Basic rate band remaining:
    £33,300 − (£35,000 − £5,035) = £3,335

	£
£3,335 @ 10%	334
£16,665 @ 32½%	5,416
	5,750
Less tax credit @ 10%	(2,000)
Additional tax due	3,750

Dividend income within the basic rate band is taxed at 10% (*not* 22%).

This is the same as taking 25% of the net dividend taxable at the higher rate ie (£16,665 × 90%) @ 25% = £3,750.

Two types of income (both covered later in this Text) are taxed after dividend income, so that dividend income is not always the top slice of income:

(a) Chargeable gains on life assurance policies.

(b) The taxable portions of partly exempt payments on the termination of employment.

So someone with wages of £15,000, dividend income of £20,000 and a £100,000 termination payment will have dividend income taxed at 10%.

5.3 What is savings income?

'**Savings income**' does not include what you might expect. Here are lists of savings and non-savings income.

5.3.1 Savings income

(a) **Interest** (includes interest from banks, buildings societies, gilts and debentures and under the accrued income scheme)

(b) **Dividends**

(c) **The income part of a purchased life annuity**. This is an annuity which lasts for a period depending on someone's lifespan, and which is bought for a lump sum. Part of each payment is treated as income and is paid net of 20% tax, while the rest is treated as a return of capital and is tax-free (see later in this Text).

(d) Chargeable gains on life assurance policies

5.3.2 Non-savings income

(a)   Income from a job

(b)   Income from running a business (alone or as a partner)

(c)   Rental income

(d)   Charges *received* (other than interest)

(e)   Interest and dividends from abroad are savings income unless the taxpayer is only taxed on money he brings to the UK (the remittance basis). In that case, they are non-savings income (see later in this Text).

5.4 The complete proforma

Here is a complete proforma computation. You can refer back to it as you work through this Text.

	Non-savings £	Savings (excl dividend) £	Dividend £	Total £
Business profits	X			
Less losses set against business profits	(X)			
	X			
Wages less occupational pension contributions	X			
Other non-savings (as many lines as necessary)	X			
Building society interest (gross)		X		
Other savings (excl. dividends) (gross) (as many lines as necessary)		X		
Dividends (gross)			X	
	X	X	X	
Less charges (gross)	(X)	(X)	(X)	
	X	X	X	
Less losses set against general income	(X)	(X)	(X)	
STI	X	X	X	X
Less personal allowance	(X)	(X)	(X)	
Taxable income	X	X	X	X

6 Tax reducers

FAST FORWARD

Tax reducers reduce tax on income at a set rate of relief.

6.1 Introduction

Tax reducers do not affect income; they reduce tax on income. The tax reducers are:

(a)   Investments in venture capital trusts and

(b)   Investments under the enterprise investment scheme.

Investments in the above companies may qualify for a tax reduction of up to the lower of:

(a)   A percentage of the amount subscribed for qualifying investments, and

(b)   The individual's tax liability.

For investments in VCTs, the percentage is 30% for 2006/07 (it was 40% for 2005/06). For investments under the EIS, the percentage is 20%. Further details are given later in this Text.

6.2 Giving tax reductions

Tax reducers are deducted in computing an individual's income tax liability. The full tax reduction can only be given if the individual has enough tax to reduce. If, for example, the tax before the reduction is £50 and the reduction is £200, the tax liability is only reduced to zero. The individual **cannot** claim a repayment of £(50 – 200) = £150.

The tax which can be reduced is the tax on taxable income. It does not include tax retained on charges paid net.

An individual may be entitled to both tax reducers. In such cases the reducer for investments in venture capital trusts is given first, and then the reducer for investments under the enterprise investment scheme, and we must stop when the tax is reduced to zero.

Question

Tax reducers

During 2006/07 Peter, a single man aged 72, makes qualifying investments of £5,000 in a venture capital trusts and of £2,000 a year under the enterprise investment scheme. Show his tax position for 2006/07 if his income consists of:

(a)   trading profits of £40,000;
(b)   trading profits of £8,385.

Answer

	(a): High income Non-savings £	(b): Low income Non-savings £
Trading profits	40,000	8,385
Less personal allowance/age allowance	(5,035)	(7,280)
Taxable income	34,965	1,105
Non savings income		
£2,150/£1,105 × 10%	215	111
£31,150 × 22%	6,853	
£1,665 × 40%	666	
	7,734	111
Tax reducers		
VCT £5,000 × 30%	(1,500)	(111)
	6,234	0
EIS £2,000 × 20%	(400)	–
Tax liability	5,834	0

The tax reducers cannot lead to repayments of tax, so in (b) the EIS relief and some of the VCT relief is wasted.

In (a) Peter is not entitled to the personal age allowance because his STI is too high.

7 Families

FAST FORWARD

Spouses, civil partners and children are all separate taxpayers. There are special rules to prevent parents from exploiting a child's personal allowance.

7.1 Spouses and civil partners

Spouses and civil partners are taxed as two separate people. Each spouse/civil partner is entitled to a personal allowance or an age related personal allowance depending on his or her own age and income.

7.2 Joint property

When spouses/civil partners jointly own income-generating property, it is assumed that they are entitled to equal shares of the income. This does not apply to income from shares held in close companies (see later in this Text for an explanation of close companies).

This rule allows couples to transfer assets between them to use their personal allowances and lower tax rates thereby reducing their overall tax liabilities.

Transfers must be outright gifts and incapable of being revoked, ie with 'no strings attached'.

If the spouses/civil partners are not entitled to equal shares in the income-generating property (other than shares in close companies), **they may make a joint declaration to HMRC, specifying the proportion to which each is entitled.** These proportions are used to tax each of them separately, in respect of income arising on or after the date of the declaration. For capital gains tax purposes it is always this underlying beneficial ownership that is taken into account.

7.3 Example: income tax planning for spouses/civil partners

Mr Buckle is a higher rate taxpayer who owns a rental property producing £20,000 of property income on which he pays tax at 40%, giving him a tax liability of £8,000. His spouse has no income.

If he transfers only 5% of the asset to his wife, they will be treated as jointly owning the property and will each be taxed on 50% of the income. Mr Buckle's tax liability will be reduced to £4,000. His wife's liability is only £834, giving an overall tax saving of £3,166.

7.4 Minor children

There is legislation to prevent the parent of a minor child transferring income to the child in order to use the child's personal allowance and starting and basic rate tax bands. **Income which is directly transferred by the parent, or is derived from capital so transferred, remains income of the parent for tax purposes.** This applies only to parents, however, and tax saving is therefore possible by other relatives. Even where a parent is involved, the child's income is not treated as the parent's if it does not exceed £100 (gross) a year.

This legislation is concerned with gifts from a parent to a child. It may therefore be possible to use the child's personal allowance and starting and basic rate bands if the child is employed in the parent's trade.

The legislation does not apply to income from a Child Trust Fund (CTF). CTFs are dealt with later in this Text.

Chapter roundup

- In a personal income tax computation, bring together income from all sources, splitting the sources into non-savings, savings (excl. dividend) and dividend income.

- Don't forget to gross up dividends by 100/90 and interest by 100/80.

- Higher rate taxpayers pay an effective rate of 25% on their dividend income.

- Charges on income are deducted to arrive at Statutory Total Income (STI).

- Deduct the personal allowance. There are increased allowances for the over 65s.

- Work out income tax on the taxable income in three stages then take account of tax retained on charges and tax already suffered.

- Tax reducers reduce tax on income at a set rate of relief.

- Spouses, civil partners and children are all separate taxpayers. There are special rules to prevent parents from exploiting a child's personal allowance.

Quick quiz

1   At what rates is income tax charged on non-savings income?

2   Is UK rental income savings income?

3   List three types of savings income that is received by individuals net of 20% tax.

4   Which charge on income is paid net?

5   How is dividend income taxed?

6   What is the de minimis threshold below which a child's income deriving from a parental disposition (ie gift) is not taxed as the parents' income?

Answers to quick quiz

1   Income tax on non-savings income is charged at 10% in the starting rate band, at 22% in the basic rate band and at 40% in the higher rate band.

2   No.

3   Interest paid by unquoted UK companies on UK debentures and loan stock, bank and building society interest (but not NS&I account interest), the income portion of a purchased annuity.

4   Patent royalties

5   Dividend income in the starting and basic rate band is taxed at 10%. Dividend income in excess of the higher rate threshold is taxed at 32.5%. A tax credit of 10% is available.

6   £100

Now try the question below from the Exam Question Bank			
Number	**Level**	**Marks**	**Time**
Q1	Introductory	20	36 mins

Pensions and other tax efficient investment products

Topic list	Syllabus reference
1 Types of pension scheme and membership	A1(a)B6
2 Contributing to a pension scheme	A1(a)B6
3 Receiving benefits from pension arrangements	A1(a)B6
4 Registration	A1(g)(iii)
5 The enterprise investment scheme (EIS)	A1(g)(i)
6 Venture capital trusts (VCTs)	A1(g)(ii)

Introduction

In the previous chapter we looked at the basic income tax computation. We now look at some of the tax reliefs given to encourage individuals to invest in certain types of savings.

The most important type of saving is through pensions. Tax relief is given on contributions to pension schemes, and the schemes themselves can grow tax free. There are limits on the amounts that can be invested, and breach of these limits will incur tax charges. Failure to comply with the rules will also result in tax charges.

Investment in smaller companies is encouraged through the enterprise investment scheme and venture capital trusts. We saw how relief is given as a tax reducer in the previous chapter, and here we will examine the conditions which must be satisfied before relief is available.

In the next chapter we will look at income from UK property and other investments.

Study guide

		Intellectual level
1	**Income and income tax liabilities in situations involving further overseas aspects and in relation to trusts, and the application of exemptions and reliefs**	
(a)	The contents of the Paper F6 study guide for income tax, under heading:	2
	B6 The use of exemptions and reliefs in deferring and minimising income tax liabilities	
(g)	The use of exemptions and reliefs in deferring and minimising income tax liabilities:	
(i)	Understand and apply the rules relating to investments in the enterprise investment scheme	3
(ii)	Understand and apply the rules relating to investments in venture capital trusts	3
(iii)	Explain the conditions that need to be satisfied for pension schemes to be approved by HM Revenue and Customs	2

Exam guide

You may well come across pension contributions or investments under the EIS or in VCTs as part of a question. These investments all give tax relief for the amount invested, although the reliefs vary in amount. They are commonly used to mitigate tax liabilities, but you should note that they should be used for in-year tax planning, although there is limited carry back for EIS relief.

> Knowledge brought forward from earlier studies

This chapter builds upon the basic knowledge of tax relief for pension contributions necessary for level 2.3.

1 Types of pension scheme and membership

FAST FORWARD

> An employee may be entitled to join his employer's occupational pension scheme. Both employees and the self employed can take out a 'personal pension' with a financial institution such as a bank or building society. The limits described in this chapter are applied to the total of all the pension arrangements an individual makes, not each of them.

1.1 Types of pension provision

An individual is encouraged by the Government to make financial provision to cover his needs when he reaches a certain age. There are state pension arrangements which provide some financial support, but the Government would like an individual not to rely on state provision but to make his own pension provision.

Therefore tax relief is given for such pension provision. This includes relief for contributions to a pension and an exemption from tax on income and gains arising in a pension fund. There are anti-avoidance provisions preventing the use of pension schemes to gain unauthorised tax-advantages due to the tax-exempt status of pension funds.

1.2 Pension arrangements

An individual may make pension provision in a number of ways. These are called pension arrangements.

If the individual is employed, he may join an **occupational pension scheme run by his employer**.

Any individual (whether employed or not) may join a **personal pension scheme run by a financial institution** such as an insurance company or a bank.

> **Occupational pension schemes** are run by employers for their employees. **Personal pension schemes** are run by financial institutions. Anyone may contribute to a personal pension.

Personal pension schemes and the majority of occupational pension schemes are **money purchase schemes**. These are also known as **defined contributions schemes**. The level of pension that the member can draw from such schemes will depend on the investment performance of the moneys invested.

Some occupational schemes are **final salary schemes**, where the pension depends on the period for which the individual has been a member of the scheme and his salary at the time of retirement. These are also known as **defined benefits schemes**, and are becoming less common due to the high level of contributions required.

An individual may make a number of different pension arrangements depending on his circumstances. For example, he may be a member of an occupational pension scheme and also make pension arrangements independently with a financial provider. If the individual has more than one pension arrangement, the rules we will be looking at in detail later apply to all the pension arrangements he makes. For example, **there is a limit on the amount of contributions that the individual can make in a tax year. This limit applies to all the pension arrangements that he makes, not *each* of them**.

Once we have looked at the tax relief and anti-avoidance provisions we will look in more detail at the different types of pension arrangements available.

1.3 Types of membership

An individual may be a member of a pension scheme in a number of different ways.

An **active member** is an individual for whom there are presently arrangements being made (such as contributions) under the pension scheme for the accrual of benefits to that person or in respect of him (for example, benefits for his dependants).

A **pensioner member** is an individual who is entitled to the present payment of benefits under the pension scheme and is not an active member (so no contributions are being made by or for him).

A **deferred member** is an individual who has accrued rights under a pension scheme and is neither an active member (no contributions are being paid by or for him) nor a pensioner member (so he is not taking benefits from the pension scheme). An example would be a person who has made pension arrangements when he was UK resident but he is no longer UK resident nor of pensionable age. In this case he can no longer make contributions to the scheme nor can he yet receive pension benefits.

2 Contributing to a pension scheme

FAST FORWARD

An individual can make tax deductible contributions to his pension arrangements up to the lower of his earnings and £3,600. Contributions to personal pensions are paid net of basic rate tax. Employers normally operate 'net pay' arrangements in respect of contributions to occupational schemes.

2.1 Contributions by an active scheme member

2.1.1 Eligibility to make contributions attracting tax relief

An individual who is **an active member** of a registered pension scheme and **under the age of 75 is entitled to tax relief on his contributions** to the scheme in a tax year if he is a relevant UK individual.

A **relevant UK individual** is one who:

(a)   has relevant UK earnings chargeable to income tax in the tax year; or

(b)   is resident in the UK at some time in the tax year; or

(c)   was resident in the UK both at some time in the previous five tax years and when he became a member of the pension scheme

Relevant UK earnings are employment income, trading income, patent income in respect of inventions and income from furnished holiday lettings (see later in this Text).

2.1.2 Annual limit for relief

The maximum contributions made by an individual in a tax year attracting tax relief is the higher of:

(a)   **the individual's UK relevant earnings chargeable to income tax in the year; and**

(b)   **the basic amount (set at £3,600 for 2006/07).**

This means that if the individual does not have any UK earnings in a tax year, the maximum contribution he can obtain tax relief on is £3,600.

Where an individual contributes to more than one pension scheme, the aggregate of his contributions will be used to give the total amount of tax relief.

There is an interaction between this provision and the annual allowance, which will be discussed later.

2.1.3 Methods of giving tax relief

2.1.3.1 Relief given at source

This method will be used where an individual makes a contribution to a pension scheme run by a personal pension provider such as an insurance company.

Relief is given at source by the contributions being deemed to be made net of basic rate tax. This applies whether the individual is an employee, self-employed or not employed at all and whether or not he has taxable income. HMRC then pay the basic rate tax to the pension provider.

Further tax relief is given if the individual is a higher rate taxpayer. The relief is given by increasing the basic rate limit for the year by the gross amount of contributions for which he is entitled to relief.

Question   Higher rate relief

Joe has earnings of £50,000 in 2006/07. He pays a personal pension contribution of £7,020 (net). He has no other taxable income.

Show Joe's tax liability for 2006/07.

Answer

	Non savings income £
Earnings/STI	50,000
Less PA	(5,035)
Taxable income	44,965

Tax

	£
£2,150 × 10%	215
£31,150 × 22%	6,853
£9,000 (7,020 × 100/78) × 22%	1,980
£2,665 × 40%	1,066
44,965	10,114

In this example, higher rate relief of 18% relief has been obtained as non savings income ordinarily taxed at 40% has instead been taxed at 22%. Added to the basic rate relief of 22% given at source due to the pension payment being made net, this gives 40% relief.

The effective rate of relief can be higher where dividend income is also received in the year as the higher rate relief on dividends shifted from the higher rate band to the basic rate band is 22½% (32½%-10%).

2.1.3.2 Example: rate of tax relief

Adam has earnings of £40,000 in 2006/07. He also receives net dividends of £9,000. He is thinking of making a contribution of £7,020 (equivalent of £9,000 gross) to his personal pension.

Adam's effective rate of tax saved by making the pension contribution can be found as follows:

	Non savings £	Dividends £
Earnings	40,000	
Dividends × 100/90		10,000
STI	40,000	10,000
Less PA	(5,035)	
Taxable income	34,965	10,000

Tax (before contribution)

	£
£2,150 × 10%	215
£31,150 × 22%	6,853
£1,665 × 40%	666
£10,000 × 32½%	3,250
44,965	10,984

Tax (after contribution)

	£
£2,150 × 10%	215
£31,150 × 22%	6,853
£1,665 × 22%	366
£7,335 × 10%	734
£2,665 × 32½%	866
44,965	9,034

The tax saved by extending the basic rate band is £1,950 (£10,984 – £9,034). If we add to this the basic rate tax saved by making the contribution net (ie £9,000 – £7,020 = £1,980) the total tax saved is £3,930.

The effective rate of tax relief on the pension contribution is $\frac{£3,930}{£9,000} \times 100$, which is 43.7%.

2.1.3.3 Net pay arrangements

An occupational scheme will normally operate net pay arrangements.

In this case, the employer will deduct gross pension contributions from the individual's earnings before operating PAYE. The individual therefore obtains tax relief at his marginal rate of tax without having to make any claim.

Question	Net pay arrangements

Maxine has taxable earnings of £50,000 in 2006/07. Her employer deducts a pension contribution of £9,000 from these earnings before operating PAYE. She has no other taxable income.

Show Maxine's tax liability for 2006/07.

Answer

	£
Earnings	50,000
Less pension contribution	(9,000)
STI	41,000
Less PA	(5,035)
Taxable income	35,965

Tax

	£
£2,150 × 10%	215
£31,150 × 22%	6,853
£2,665 × 40%	1,066
35,965	8,134

This is the same result as Joe in the previous example. Joe had received basic rate tax relief of £(9,000 – 7,020) = 1,980 at source, so his overall tax position was £(10,114 – 1,980) = £8,134.

2.1.4 Contributions by an active scheme member not attracting tax relief

An active scheme member can also make contributions to his pension arrangements which do not attract tax relief, for example out of capital. The member must notify the scheme administrator if he makes contributions in excess of the higher of his UK relevant earnings and the basic amount.

Such contributions do not count towards the annual allowance limit (discussed below) but will affect the value of the pension fund for the lifetime allowance.

2.2 Contributions by people other than the active scheme member

> Employers may make contributions to pension schemes. In certain circumstances employers contributions are spread over a number of years.

Where the active scheme member is an employee, his **employer will often make contributions to his pension scheme**. Such contributions are **exempt benefits** for the employee.

There is **no limit** on the amount of the contributions that may be made by an employer but **they always count towards the annual allowance and will also affect the value of the pension fund for the lifetime allowance** (see further below).

All contributions made by an employer are made gross and the employer will usually obtain tax relief for the contribution by deducting it as an expense in calculating trading profits for the period of account in which the payment is made.

There are two further aspects that need to be considered

First, HMRC may seek to disallow a contribution which it considers is not a revenue expense or is not made wholly and exclusively for the purposes of the trade. Circumstances which might lead to HMRC questioning the contributions include:

(a) where a contribution is made on behalf of a controlling director (or close associate) at a disproportionately high level; or

(b) where contributions are made in connection with the sale or cessation of a trade.

Secondly, there are 'spreading provisions' for large contributions, so that part of the contribution is treated as paid in a later period of account.

These provisions can apply where the pension contributions in the current period exceed 210% of those in the previous period. You then need to calculate the excess of current contributions over 110% of the contribution in the previous period of account. The provisions treat part of the excess contribution to be treated as paid in a later period as follows:

Amount of excess contributions	Fraction and chargeable periods
Less than £500,000	No spreading required
£500,000 or more but less than £1m	$1/2$ treated as paid in current period, $1/2$ treated as paid in the next chargeable period
£1m or more but less than £2m	$1/3$ treated as paid in the current period, $1/3$ treated as paid in each of the next two chargeable periods
£2m or more	$1/4$ treated as paid in the current period, $1/4$ treated as paid in each of the next three chargeable periods.

The amount which is *not* treated as an excess contribution will be given tax relief in the period of account in which it is paid.

2.3 Charge on excess contributions

> The annual allowance is the limit on the amount that can be paid into a pension scheme each year. If this limit is exceeded there is a 40% income tax charge on the excess contributions.

There is an overriding limit on the total pension that can be input into the active member's pension scheme for each tax year. This is called the *annual allowance*.

The amount of the annual allowance is as follows:

Tax year	Annual allowance £
2006/07	215,000
2007/08	225,000
2008/09	235,000
2009/10	245,000
2010/11	255,000

The annual allowance is tested against the *pension input amount* for the *pension input period* which ends in the tax year. The pension input period is basically a period of 12 months chosen by the scheme member or the scheme administrator.

The calculation of the pension input amount depends on the type of pension scheme involved.

Where the pension scheme is a **money purchase arrangement**, the pension input amount is the aggregate of:

(a)   any **tax relievable pension contributions paid by the individual; and**

(b)   **contributions paid in respect of the individual by his employer.**

Only tax relieved contributions made by or behalf of an individual count towards the limit so that contributions on which tax relief is not obtained (eg capital contributions) will not affect the position. On the other hand, all contributions by an employer will count towards the annual allowance.

Where the pension scheme is a **defined benefits arrangement**, the pension input amount is the **increase in value of the individual's rights** under the arrangement during the pension input period, including the effect of any increase in salary. The value of the individual's rights at any time is calculated as 10 × the pension that would be paid if the individual became entitled to payment, plus the lump sum that would also be due.

Exam focus point

> Most pension arrangements are money purchase (or defined contribution) schemes. It is therefore more likely that you will see one of these schemes in the exam.

If the pension input amount exceeds the annual allowance there is an income tax charge on the individual at the rate of 40%.

 Question

Annual allowance charge

Diana is a member of a money purchase personal pension scheme. In the tax year 2006/07, she has UK relevant earnings of £265,000. In the pension input period ending in 2006/07 Diana makes a contribution of £117,000 to the pension scheme and her employer makes a further contribution of £110,000. Diana has no other income in 2006/07.

Show the income tax payable by Diana for 2006/07.

Answer

Diana has made a net contribution of £117,000 to the pension scheme which grosses up to £(117,000 × 100/78) = £150,000. This is all tax-relievable since it is lower than the greater of:

(a)   UK relevant earnings of £265,000; and

(b)   the basic amount of £3,600.

The excess contributions are therefore:

	£
Individual contributions subject to tax relief	150,000
Employer contributions	110,000
Pension input amount	260,000
Less: annual allowance 2006/07	(215,000)
Excess contributions	45,000

Diana's income tax liability is therefore:

	£
Earnings/STI	265,000
Less: PA	(5,035)
Taxable income	259,965

Tax

	£
£2,150 × 10%	215
£31,150 × 22%	6,853
£150,000 × 22% (extended basic rate band)	33,000
£76,665 × 40%	30,666
259,965	
£45,000 × 40%	18,000
Total income tax due	88,734

Note that the employer contributions are not treated as earnings or taxable benefits for NIC purposes. Therefore there is still a slight advantage to the employer making such contributions directly to the pension scheme instead of paying the individual the money for that individual to make contributions, even if the 40% charge applies.

3 Receiving benefits from pension arrangements

FAST FORWARD

The maximum value that can be built up in a pension fund is known as the lifetime allowance.

3.1 The lifetime allowance

An individual is not allowed to build up an indefinitely large pension fund. **There is a maximum value for a pension fund (for money purchase arrangements) or for the value of benefits (for defined benefits arrangements). This is called the *lifetime allowance.***

The amount of the lifetime allowance is as follows:

Tax year	Lifetime Allowance £
2006/07	1,500,000
2007/08	1,600,000
2008/09	1,650,000
2009/10	1,750,000
2010/11	1,800,000

Where the pension scheme is a **money purchase arrangement**, the value of the fund for the lifetime allowance will be the **value of the investments in the fund**. Where the pension scheme is a **defined benefits arrangement**, the **income benefits are usually valued on a 20:1 ratio**, so that, for example, a pension of £10,000 will be valued at £200,000 for this purpose and lump sum benefits are valued at face value (see below for types of pension benefits).

The individual does not have to keep a running total of the value of his pension scheme. Instead, **the lifetime allowance limit is tested only when a *benefit crystallisation event* occurs**. The most common of these are:

(a) when a member becomes **entitled to a scheme pension**

(b) where a scheme pension already being paid is **increased** by more than the greater of 5% or the increase in the RPI

(c) where a member becomes **entitled to a lifetime annuity** under money purchase arrangements

(d) where a member **reaches the age of 75** under a defined benefit arrangement without having vested all or part of his entitlement to a pension and/or lump sum

(e) when a member **becomes entitled to a lump sum**, for example a tax-free lump sum when the entitlement to pension income arises

(f) where a **lump sum is paid on the death of a member**

The consequences of the lifetime allowance being exceeded are discussed below.

3.2 Types of benefits

3.2.1 Benefits taken during lifetime

No pension payment can be made before the member reaches normal minimum pension age (50 for members who reach this age on or before 5 April 2010 and 55 thereafter), unless the member is incapacitated by ill health. **At this age the member may take an income pension and a lump sum from the pension scheme**.

Pension benefits do not all have to be taken or provided for at one time. Between the minimum pension age and 75, an individual may 'vest' the benefits, ie set aside all or part of the pension fund to provide pension benefits. An active member under the age of 75 can make contributions **and** receive pension benefits.

Up to 25% of the pension fund (for money purchase schemes, or 25% of the value of the benefits for defined benefit schemes) **can be taken as a tax free lump sum**, subject to the lifetime allowance limit (see below). There are anti-avoidance rules which prevent a member from 'recycling' the lump sum (ie by immediately reinvesting it in their pension to obtain further tax relief on that contribution).

The remainder must be used to provide a pension income. Pension income is taxable as non savings income.

The pension can be either **secured income** (a guaranteed income), usually provided by the purchase of an annuity, or **unsecured income** (also known as income drawdown), which is only available to members under 75.

3.2.2 Benefits on the death of the member

On the death of a member under 75, the pension scheme may provide for income pensions and/or lump sums to be paid to dependants (including spouse/civil partner, child of the member under 23, or another person who was dependent on the member).

If the member dies having already reached 75, no lump sum can be paid.

3.3 Lifetime allowance charge

3.3.1 Occasions of charge

As we have seen, when a member takes a benefit from a pension scheme, there is usually a benefit crystallisation event so that the value of the pension fund has to be tested against the lifetime allowance for the year in which the event occurs.

In many cases, the lifetime limit will not have been exceeded and there will be no income tax charge. However, the lifetime allowance to be used for further benefit crystallisation events will be reduced by the value of the benefits that have crystallised in the current event. This is discussed further below.

In some cases, the pension fund will exceed the lifetime allowance and this will give rise to an income tax charge on the excess value of the fund which has been vested to provide either a lump sum or a pension income. The rate of the charge depends on the type of benefit that will be taken from the excess funds.

3.3.2 Calculation and payment of the lifetime allowance charge

Where funds are vested to provide a lump sum, there will be a **charge to tax at 55% on the value of the lump sum**.

Where the excess funds are vested to provide a pension income, the rate is 25%. In this case, it is necessary to look at the value of the vested funds to work out the tax charge, not the annual value of the pension income that will be provided.

The different rates apply because the pension income will be taxable in the hands of the individual whereas the lump sum will not.

Where the charge arises in the lifetime of the member, the tax charge primarily falls on him, but the pension scheme administrator has joint liability for the tax charge and will withhold sufficient sums to cover the charge.

Where the charge arises on the payment of a lump sum following the death of a member, the tax charge is payable by the recipient of the lump sum and in this case there will be no withholding tax retained by the scheme administrator.

3.3.3 Example: lifetime allowance exceeded

Amy attained the age of 60 on 1 July 2006 and decided to vest her pension benefits on that date. She has a money purchase fund which was valued at £1,900,000 on 1 July 2006. Amy took the maximum tax-free lump sum of £1,500,000 × 25% = £375,000. The balance of the lifetime allowance is £(1,500,000 − 375,000) = £1,125,000 and this is vested to provide pension income benefits.

Amy also took the excess of the fund over the lifetime allowance as a lump sum ie £(1,900,000 = 1,500,000) = £400,000.

The tax charge is therefore £400,000 × 55% = £220,000.

The scheme administration will therefore pay Amy £(400,000 − 220,000) = £180,000 and withhold £220,000 to pay the tax charge to HMRC.

The pension member may decide to vest benefits over a number of years. In this case, **the lifetime allowance must be adjusted for the value of benefits already vested**. If there has been a change in the value of the lifetime allowance, the benefits vested earlier must be uplifted pro rata to the increase in the lifetime allowance between the two events.

4 Registration

Registration requirements

In order for the tax advantages described above to apply to a pension scheme, the scheme must be registered with HMRC.

Schemes in existence at 6 April 2006 which already has HMRC approval were automatically registered, unless the scheme administrator requested otherwise.

Where a pension scheme commences on or after 6 April 2006, the scheme administrator must make an application to HMRC for registration. A pension scheme may only be registered if it is an occupational pension scheme or if it is established by certain financial institutions such as insurance companies and banks.

HMRC must register the scheme unless it believes that the information in the application is incorrect or that any accompanying declaration is false.

5 The enterprise investment scheme (EIS)

FAST FORWARD

> The enterprise investment scheme and venture capital trusts are designed to help unquoted trading companies raise finance.

Key term

> The **EIS** is a scheme designed to promote enterprise and investment by helping high-risk, unlisted trading companies raise finance by the issue of ordinary shares to individual investors who are unconnected with that company.

5.1 Conditions for relief

Individuals who subscribe for EIS shares are entitled to both income tax and capital gains tax reliefs where certain conditions are satisfied.

5.1.1 The investor

The investor must **subscribe for shares wholly in cash in the company and must not be connected with it**. Connection can broadly occur through employment or owning more than 30% (including holdings of associates ie spouse/civil partner or child, but not a brother or sister) of the issued ordinary share capital, loan capital, issued share capital or voting power of the company or a subsidiary.

The investor must also qualify for the two years prior to and three years after the share issue date or if later, three years from the date trading commences.

5.1.2 The company

The company must be unquoted (which includes AIM for this purpose) and **the funds raised must be used by that company or by a direct 90% subsidiary in carrying out a qualifying trade.** Qualifying trades broadly include all trades except for certain prohibited trades, including dealing in land, financial activities, legal/accountancy services and property backed activities. Research and development prior to starting a trade also qualifies.

At least 80% of the money raised by the EIS share issue must be used for this purpose within twelve months of the issue of the shares (or within twelve months of the commencement of the trade). All of the money must be used for this purpose within a further twelve months (ie within twenty-four months).

The gross assets of the company must not exceed £7m prior to nor £8m after the investment (£15m and £16m respectively for shares subscribed for before 22 March 2006 or issued before 6 April 2006).

5.1.3 The shares

Eligible shares are any new ordinary shares issued for bona fide commercial reasons which, throughout the period of three years beginning with the date on which they are issued, carry no preferential rights to dividends or assets on liquidation of the company. The shares must be fully paid up at the time of issue and they cannot be redeemable.

5.2 Income tax relief

5.2.1 Tax reducer

Individuals can claim a **tax reducer** (see Chapter 1) **of the lower of**:

(a) **20% of the amount subscribed for qualifying investments** (maximum qualifying investment is £400,000 and

(b) **The individual's tax liability for the year** after deducting VCT relief (see below)

| Question | EIS income tax relief |

Mr Matthews has STI of £50,000 (all non-savings income) for 2006/07. He subscribes £75,000 for shares and he claims EIS relief. The shares are issued to him in December 2006. What is his 2006/07 income tax liability?

| Answer |

	£
STI	50,000
Less PA	(5,035)
Taxable income	44,965

	£
£2,150 × 10%	215
£31,150 × 22%	6,853
£11,665 × 40%	4,666
	11,734
Less EIS relief (£75,000 × 20% = £15,000, limited to £11,734)	(11,734)
Income tax liability	Nil

5.2.2 Limits for relief

To be eligible for relief the minimum subscription of shares in any company is £500. The maximum EIS investments qualifying for income tax relief is £400,000 in 2006/07, but individuals can invest in excess of this amount if they wish.

If shares are issued in the first six months of the tax year (ie before 6 October), the investor may claim to have up to half of the shares treated as issued in the previous tax year. This is subject to a maximum carry back of £50,000 if £100,000 or more shares are issued in the first six months.

When carrying back relief, relief given in the previous year must not exceed overall EIS limits for that year. The limit for 2005/06 was £200,000.

5.2.3 Withdrawal of relief

Shares must be held by an investor for at least three years if the income tax relief is not to be withdrawn or reduced if the company was carrying on a qualifying trade at the time of issue. For companies which were preparing to trade at the time of issue, the minimum holding period ends when the company has been carrying on a qualifying trade for three years.

The main reason for the withdrawal of relief will be the sale of the shares by the investor within the three year period mentioned above. The consequences depend on whether the disposal is at arm's length or not:

(a)   If the disposal is not a bargain at arm's length the full amount of relief originally obtained is withdrawn.

(b)   If the disposal is a bargain at arm's length there is a withdrawal of relief on the consideration received. As the relief was originally given as a tax reduction, the withdrawal of relief must be made at the same rate of tax.

Question	Withdrawal of EIS relief

Ted Edwards, a single man, makes a £60,000 EIS investment in 2006/07. His income (all non-savings) for the year is £45,000. In 2007/08, Ted sells the shares (an arm's length bargain) for £50,000. How much EIS relief is withdrawn as a result of the sale of the shares?

Answer

	£
2006/07	
STI	45,000
Less personal allowance	(5,035)
Taxable income	39,965

	£
£2,150 × 10%	215
£31,150 × 22%	6,853
£6,665 × 40%	2,666
	9,734
Less EIS relief: £60,000 × 20% = £12,000, restricted to	(9,734)
Income tax liability	Nil

The effective rate of EIS relief is $\dfrac{9,734}{60,000} \times 100 = 16.2233\%$

2007/08

The sale of the shares for £50,000 as a bargain at arm's length results in the withdrawal of income tax relief in 2007/08 of £8,112 (ie £50,000 × 16.2233%).

Although the company must be unlisted when the EIS shares are issued, there is no withdrawal of relief if the company becomes listed, unless there were arrangements in place for the company to cease to be unlisted at the time of issue.

There are anti-avoidance rules to prevent an individual extracting money from the company without disposing of his shares. However, the rules do not apply where the amount is of an insignificant value (eg any amount of £1,000 or under) or if the receipt is returned without unreasonable delay.

5.3 CGT reliefs

Where shares qualify for income tax relief under the EIS there are also special rules that apply to those shares for capital gains purposes:

(a) Where shares are disposed of after the three year period any gain is exempt from CGT. If the shares are disposed of within three years any gain is computed in the normal way.

(b) If EIS shares are disposed of at a loss at any time, the loss is allowable but the acquisition cost of the shares is reduced by the amount of EIS relief attributable to the shares. The loss is eligible for S574 ICTA 1988 relief (see later in this Text).

Question	Allowable losses

During 2004/05 Martin invested £35,000 in EIS shares and received relief against income tax of £35,000 × 20% = £7,000.

The shares are sold in February 2007 for £15,000. This will lead to a withdrawal of EIS relief of £15,000 × 20% = £3,000. What is the allowable loss for CGT purposes?

Answer

	£	£
Disposal proceeds		15,000
Less: cost	35,000	
EIS relief (7,000 – 3,000)	(4,000)	(31,000)
Allowable loss		(16,000)

If the shares had instead been sold outside the three year relevant period (ie so that there was no withdrawal of income tax relief), the allowable loss would instead be:

	£	£
Disposal proceeds		15,000
Less: cost	35,000	
EIS relief	(7,000)	(28,000)
Allowable loss		(13,000)

EIS reinvestment relief may be available to defer chargeable gains if an individual invests in EIS shares in the period commencing one year before and ending three years after the disposal of the asset (see later in this Text).

5.4 Anti-avoidance

There are a number of provisions designed to prevent abuse of the relief. Relief is usually not given if any of these provisions apply before the investment is made or is withdrawn if the rule is broken. The provisions include:

(a) Shares disposed of in a company and investment made in the same company or member of the same group of companies

(b) There is a pre-arranged exit from the investment

(c) The shares are subject to options to buy or sell

(d) Value is received from the company by the investor or other persons (subject to similar rules as for income tax eg to ignore receipts of insignificant value (see later in this Text))

(e) There is an investment-linked loan

Exam focus point

> Although EIS investments carry attractive tax reliefs remember that they are high risk investments.

6 Venture capital trusts (VCTs)

Key term

> **Venture capital trusts (VCTs)** are listed companies which invest in unquoted trading companies and meet certain conditions.

6.1 Conditions for relief

Individuals who subscribe for VCT shares are entitled to both income tax and capital gains tax reliefs where certain conditions are satisfied.

6.1.1 The investor

The VCT scheme differs from EIS as the individual investor invests directly in a quoted VCT company that itself invests in higher risk unquoted companies. The investor therefore spreads their risk.

6.1.2 The company

A Venture Capital Trust is a company listed on the London Stock Exchange that invests in small unquoted EIS-type companies.

To be HMRC approved, a VCT must satisfy the following conditions:

(a)   Its income comes wholly or mainly from shares or securities

(b)   At least 70% of its investments are in shares in qualifying holdings. Qualifying holdings are broadly holdings in unquoted companies carrying on qualifying trades in the UK.

(c)   At least 30% of its holdings must be in ordinary shares and no one holding can amount to more than 15% of its total investments

(d)   It has not kept more than 15% of its income from shares and securities ie it must distribute 85% of its income from shares and securities

Approval may be withdrawn where a VCT ceases to satisfy the above conditions.

At least 80% of the money invested in a company by the VCT must be used wholly for the purposes of its qualifying trade within 12 months with the balance so used within a further twelve months (ie within twenty-four months).

The gross assets of the company must not exceed £7m prior to nor £8m after the investment (£15m and £16m respectively for funds raised before 6 April 2006).

All income and capital gains received by the VCT are exempt from corporation tax.

6.2 Tax reliefs

An individual investing in a VCT obtains the following tax benefits on a maximum qualifying investment of £200,000 in 2006/07.

- **A tax reduction of 30% of the amount invested** (40% for investments made in 2005/06).

- **Dividends received are tax-free income.**

- **Capital gains on the sale of shares in the VCT are exempt** from CGT (and losses are not allowable).

6.3 Withdrawal of relief

If the shares in the VCT are disposed of within five years of issue (three years for shares issued before 6 April 2006), the following consequences ensue.

- If the shares are not disposed of under a bargain made at arm's length, the tax reduction is withdrawn.

- If the shares are disposed of under a bargain made at arm's length, the tax reduction is withdrawn, up to the disposal proceeds × 30%.

If a VCT's approval is withdrawn within five years of the issue, any tax reduction given is withdrawn.

Note that there is no minimum holding period requirement for the benefits of tax-free dividends and CGT exemption.

Chapter roundup

- An employee may be entitled to join his employer's occupational pension scheme. Both employees and the self employed can take out a 'personal pension' with a financial institution such as a bank or building society. The limits described in this chapter are applied to the total of all the pension arrangements an individual makes, not each of them.

- An individual can make tax deductible contributions to his pension arrangements up to the lower of his earnings and £3,600. Contributions to personal pensions are paid net of basic rate tax. Employers normally operate 'net pay' arrangements in respect of contributions to occupational schemes.

- Employers may make contributions to pension schemes. In certain circumstances employers contributions are spread over a number of years.

- The annual allowance is the limit on the amount that can be paid into a pension scheme each year. If this limit is exceeded there is a 40% income tax charge on the excess contributions.

- The maximum value that can be built up in a pension fund is known as the lifetime allowance.

- The enterprise investment scheme and venture capital trusts are designed to help unquoted trading companies raise finance.

Quick quiz

1   What are the two types of occupational pension scheme?

2   What is the maximum lump sum that can be taken on retirement (lifetime allowance not exceeded)?

3   What is the limit on contributions to an registered pension scheme?

4   What are the consequences of the total of employee and employer contributions exceeding the annual allowance?

5   What are the consequences of exceeding the lifetime allowance?

6   What income tax relief is available in respect of investments under the enterprise investment scheme?

Answers to quick quiz

1   Occupational pension schemes may be final salary schemes or money purchase schemes.

2   25% of the fund.

3   Higher of relevant earnings and the basic amount (£3,600).

4   The excess is subject to the annual allowance charge on the employee at 40%. (Any contributions by the employee which were not eligible for tax relief are ignored).

5   The excess is charged at 55% (if taken as a lump sum) or 25% (if taken as a pension).

6   EIS income tax relief is tax reducer up to 20% of amount subscribed up to £400,000.

Now try the question below from the Exam Question Bank			
Number	**Level**	**Marks**	**Time**
Q2	Introductory	11	20 mins

Property and other investment income

Topic list	Syllabus reference
1 UK property business	A1(a)B4
2 Furnished holiday lettings	A1(a)B4
3 Rent a room relief	A1(a)B4
4 Interest income	A1(a)B4
5 Accrued income scheme	A1(e)(ii)
6 Dividend income	A1(a)B4
7 Miscellaneous income	A1(a)B4
8 Pre-owned assets	A1(e)(i)
9 Trust income	A1(e)(iv)

Introduction

In the previous chapters we have covered the income tax computation, including tax reliefs on certain investments.

This chapter starts with the taxation of income arising from the letting of property in the UK. It looks at the basis of assessment of such income and at the computation of assessable profits and losses, and then covers the special rules for furnished holiday lettings and the rent a room relief.

The chapter then looks at the taxation of income from other investments and from trusts. It also covers the anti-avoidance provisions of the accrued income scheme and for pre-owned assets.

The following chapters will deal with income from employment and self-employment.

Study guide

		Intellectual level
1	**Income and income tax liabilities in situations involving further overseas aspects and in relation to trusts, and the application of exemptions and reliefs**	
(a)	The contents of the Paper F6 study guide for income tax, under headings:	2
•	B4 Property and investment income	
(e)	Property and investment income:	3
(i)	Assess the tax implications of pre-owned assets	
(ii)	Recognise income subject to the accrued income scheme	
(iv)	Income from trusts and settlements: Understand the income tax position of trust beneficiaries	

Exam guide

The computation of income from a UK property business is a generally straight forward matter, but you need to look out for the special areas of lease premiums, furnished holiday lettings and rent a room relief.

You need to watch out for the accrued income scheme if fixed interest securities are bought and sold. You are more likely to have to explain how the scheme works than to calculate the charge or relief.

The rules for pre-owned assets effectively stop inheritance tax mitigation schemes where the donor managed to give away property but still benefit. Although many such gifts are caught by the IHT anti-avoidance provisions the pre-owned assets rule imposes an income tax charge in other cases. You need to remember this when asked to advise on estate planning.

Although you are not required to know how to calculate the income tax liability of trustees, you need to know how the trust income is taxed in the beneficiary's hands. Again this can be a planning point where there are non-tax paying beneficiaries.

Knowledge brought forward from earlier studies

Much of the material in this chapter will be new to you at the P6 level.

1 UK property business

1.1 Profits of a UK property business

FAST FORWARD

Income from a UK property business is computed for tax years on an accruals basis.

Income from land and buildings in the UK, including caravans and houseboats which are not moved, is taxed as non-savings income.

(a) **A taxpayer (or a partnership) with UK rental income is treated as running a business, his 'UK property business'. All the rents and expenses for all properties are pooled, to give a single profit or loss. Profits and losses are computed in the same way as trading profits are computed for tax purposes**, on an accruals basis.

Expenses will often include rent payable where a landlord is himself renting the land which he in turn lets to others. For individuals, interest on loans to buy or improve properties is treated as an expense (on an accruals basis). The rules on post-cessation receipts and expenses apply to UK property businesses in the same way that they apply to trades (see later in this Text).

Relief is available for irrecoverable rent as an impaired debt.

(b) **Capital allowances are given on plant and machinery used in the UK property business and on industrial buildings, in the same way as they are given for a trading business** with an accounting date of 5 April. Capital allowances are not normally available on plant or machinery used in a dwelling. As someone who lets property furnished cannot claim capital allowances on the furniture he can choose instead between the **renewals basis** and the **10% wear and tear allowance**.

(i) Under the **renewals** basis, there is no deduction for the cost of the first furniture provided, but the cost of replacement furniture is treated as a revenue expense. However, the part of the cost attributable to improvement, as opposed to simple replacement, is not deductible.

(ii) Under the **10% wear and tear** basis, the actual cost of furniture is ignored. Instead, an annual deduction is given of 10% of rents. The rents are first reduced by amounts which are paid by the landlord but are normally a tenant's burden. These amounts include any **water rates** and **council tax** paid by the landlord.

If plant and machinery is used partly in a dwelling house and partly for other purposes a just and reasonable apportionment of the expenditure can be made.

(c) **No deduction is usually allowed for capital expenditure**. However, for expenditure incurred before 5 April 2009, there is **an allowable deduction of up to £1,500** for installation of **loft, cavity and solid wall insulation, draught proofing and insulation of hot water systems** in a let dwelling house. This deduction **only applies for income tax purposes**; it does not apply for corporation tax (see later in this Text).

(d) Rent for furniture supplied with premises is taxed as part of the rent for the premises, unless there is a separate trade of renting furniture.

(e) The profits of the UK property business are computed for tax years. Each tax year's profit is taxed in that year.

1.2 Losses of UK property business

A loss on a UK property business is carried forward to set against future profits from the UK property business.

A loss from a UK property business is carried forward to set against the first future profits from the UK property business. It may be carried forward until the UK property business ends, but it must be used as soon as possible.

Certain types of loss from a UK property business may alternatively be set against the taxpayer's total income (after charges but before allowances) for the tax year of loss and/or the next tax year. The loss goes against non-savings income before savings income. The types of loss are:

(a) Losses due to capital allowances up to the lower of:

(i) The excess of capital allowances over balancing charges. Balancing allowances are included in capital allowances.

(ii) The total loss in the UK property business.

(b) Losses due to agricultural expenses up to the lower of:

   (i) The total agricultural expenses. These are expenses on the maintenance, repair, insurance or management of an agricultural estate, excluding any loan interest. Expenses on parts of the land not used for husbandry are excluded.

   (ii) The total loss in the UK property business.

The claim must be for the full amount of the loss, up to the available income, even if this leads to a wasted personal allowance.

Losses from a UK property business brought forward from earlier years are set against the UK property business profit for the year in which relief is claimed before the available income is computed. The taxpayer may claim relief in the year of loss, and then relief for any remaining loss in the next year, or vice-versa, or he may claim for just one year. However, he cannot decide how to split the loss between the two years (for example half for each year). If relief is claimed in a year both for the previous year's loss and for the current year's loss, the previous year's loss must be relieved first.

The time limit for claiming this relief is the 31 January which is nearly two years after the end of the tax year (so 31 January 2009 for relief against 2006/07 income).

Any loss not relieved against total income (because the relief was not claimed or there was less income than loss) is carried forward against future profits from the UK property business.

Question	UK property income

Pete over the last few years has purchased several properties in Manchester as 'buy to let' investments.

5 Whitby Ave is let out furnished at £500 per month. A tenant moved in on 1 March 2005 but left unexpectedly on 1 May 2007 having paid rent only up to 31 December 2006. The tenant left no forwarding address.

17 Bolton Rd has been let furnished to the same tenant for a number of years at £800 per month.

A recent purchase, 27 Turner Close has been let unfurnished since 1 August 2006 at £750 per month having been empty whilst Pete redecorated it after its purchase in March 2006.

Pete's expenses during 2006/07 are:

	No 5	No 17	No 27
	£	£	£
Insurance	250	250	200
Letting agency fees	–	–	100
Repairs	300	40	–
Redecoration	–	–	500

No 27 was in a fit state to let when Pete bought it but he wanted to redecorate the property as he felt this would allow him to achieve a better rental income.

Water rates and council tax are paid by the tenants. Pete made a UK property business loss in 2005/06 of £300.

What is Pete's taxable property income for 2006/07?

Answer

	No 5	No 17	No 27
2006/07	£	£	£
Accrued income			
12 × £500	6,000		
12 × £800		9,600	
8 × £750			6,000
Less:			
Insurance	(250)	(250)	(200)
Letting agency fees			(100)
Impairment (irrecoverable rent)			
3 × £500	(1,500)		
Repairs (note)	(300)	(40)	(500)
Wear and tear allowance			
£(6,000 – 1,500) × 10%	(450)		
£9,600 × 10%		(960)	
Property Income	3,500	8,350	5,200

	£
Total property income	17,050
Less: loss b/fwd	(300)
Taxable property income for 2006/07	16,750

Note. The repairs are allowable as the property was already in a usable state. If the repairs had been needed to put the property into a fit state to be rented, they would not be allowable.

1.3 Premiums on leases

Part of the premium received on the grant of a short lease is taxed as rent. In addition any premiums paid to a tenant to induce him to take out a lease is also taxable as income from a UK property business, or as trading income if the tenant is in business.

When a premium or similar consideration is received on the grant (that is, by a landlord to a tenant) **of a short lease (50 years or less), part of the premium is treated as rent received in the year of grant.** A lease is considered to end on the date when it is most likely to terminate.

The premium taxed as rental income is the whole premium, less 2% of the premium for each complete year of the lease, except the first year using the following formula:

Formula to learn

Premium	P
Less: 2% × (n-1) × P	(a)
Taxable as income	X

This rule does not apply on the **assignment** of a lease (ie one tenant selling his entire interest in the property to another).

1.4 Premiums paid by traders

Where a trader pays a premium for a lease he may deduct an amount from his taxable trading profits in each year of the lease. The amount deductible is the figure treated as rent received by the landlord divided by the number of years of the lease. For example, suppose that B, a trader, pays A a premium of £30,000 for a ten year lease. A is treated as receiving £30,000 – (£30,000 × (10 – 1) × 2%) = £24,600. B can therefore deduct £24,600/10 = £2,460 in each of the ten years. He starts with the accounts year in which the lease starts and apportions the relief to the nearest month.

1.5 Premiums for granting subleases

A tenant may decide to sublet property and to charge a premium on the grant of a lease to the subtenant. This premium is treated as rent received in the normal way (because this is a grant and not an assignment, the original tenant retaining an interest in the property). **Where the tenant originally paid a premium for his own head lease, this deemed rent is reduced by:**

$$\text{Rent part of premium for head lease} \times \frac{\text{duration of sub-lease}}{\text{duration of head lease}}$$

If the relief exceeds the part of the premium for the sub-lease treated as rent (including cases where there is a sub-lease with no premium), the balance of the relief is treated as rent payable by the head tenant, spread evenly over the period of the sub-lease. This rent payable is an expense, reducing the overall profit from the UK property business.

Question	Taxable premium received

C granted a lease to D on 1 March 1996 for a period of 40 years. D paid a premium of £16,000. On 1 June 2006 D granted a sublease to E for a period of ten years. E paid a premium of £30,000. Calculate the amount treated as rent out of the premium received by D.

Answer

	£
Premium received by D	30,000
Less £30,000 × 2% × (10 – 1)	(5,400)
	24,600
Less allowance for premium paid	
(£16,000 – (£16,000 × 39 × 2%)) × 10/40	(880)
Premium treated as rent	23,720

1.6 Reverse premiums

Lump sum payments are sometimes paid by a landlord to induce potential tenants to take out a lease. These payments are often called '**reverse premiums**' and **are taxable on the recipient**.

The timing of the tax charge (to income tax or corporation tax as appropriate) follows accepted accountancy practice and thus will be spread over the period in which the reverse premium is recognised in the accounts.

Where the person receiving the premium is a trader occupying the building for the purposes of his trade then the reverse premium received will be treated as income of the trade. In most other cases, such as a receipt by an intermediate landlord for a lease which will be sublet, the sum received will be taxed as income of the UK property business.

1.7 Real Estate Investment Trusts (REITs)

From January 2007 property companies will be able to operate as **Real Estate Investment Trusts** (REITs).

A REIT will be a listed company (AIM does *not* count for this purpose) owning, managing and earning rental income from commercial or residential property. 75% of its income and asset value must relate to the property letting business and it must distribute 90% of all its profits before its tax return filing date. It must own at least 3 properties but no single property may be more than 40% of the properties' total value.

REITs can elect for their property income (and gains) to be exempt from corporation tax and must withhold basic rate (22%) tax from distributions paid to shareholders (who cannot own more than 10% of a REIT's shares) out of these profits. These distributions are taxed as property income, not as dividends.

Distributions by REITs out of other income (ie not property income or gains) are taxed as dividends in the normal way.

Question   Income and REITs

Sue has a holding of shares in The Property Business which is a REIT. During 2006/07 she received a dividend from her investment of £6,240. She also has a salary of £30,000 and interest income (gross) of £1,000 in the year.

Calculate Sue's tax liability for 2006/07.

Answer

2006/07	Non-savings Income £	Savings Income £	Total £
Salary	30,000		
Dividend from REIT – Property income £6,240 × 100/78	8,000		
Interest		1,000	
STI	38,000	1,000	39,000
PA	(5,035)		
	32,965	1,000	33,965
Non-savings income			
£2,150 @ 10%			215
£30,815 @ 22%			6,779
Savings income			
£335 @ 20%			67
£665 @ 40%			266
Tax liability			7,327

Note. Dividends from REITs are taxed as property income not as company dividends. Basic rate tax (22%) is deducted at source from such distributions.

2 Furnished holiday lettings

There are special rules for furnished holiday accommodation let on a commercial basis with a view to realisation of profit.

There are special rules for furnished holiday lettings. The letting is treated as if it were a trade. This means that, although the income is taxed as income from a UK property business, the provisions which apply to actual trades also apply to furnished holiday lettings, as follows.

(a) Relief for losses is available as if they were trading losses, including the facility to set losses against other income. The usual UK property business loss reliefs do not apply (see later in this Text).

(b) Capital allowances are available on furniture: the renewals basis and the 10% wear and tear basis do not apply if capital allowances are claimed.

(c) The income qualifies as relevant UK earnings for pension relief (see earlier in this Text).

(d) Capital gains tax rollover relief, business asset taper relief and relief for gifts of business assets are available (see later in this Text).

Note, however, that the basis period rules for trades do not apply, and the profits or losses must be computed for tax years.

The letting must be of furnished accommodation made on a **commercial basis with a view to the realisation of profit**. The property must also satisfy the following three conditions.

(a) **The availability condition** – during the **relevant period**, the accommodation is available for **commercial let** as **holiday accommodation** to the **public** generally, for **at least 140 days**.

(b) **The letting condition** – during the **relevant period**, the accommodation is **commercially let** as holiday accommodation to members of the public **for at least 70 days**. If the **landlord has more than one FHL**, at least one of which satisfies the 40 day rule ('qualifying holiday accommodation') and at least one of which does not, ('the underused accommodation') , he may elect to **average the occupation of the qualifying holiday accommodation and any or all of the underused accommodation**. If the average of occupation is at least 70 days, the under-used accommodation will be treated as qualifying holiday accommodation.

(c) **The pattern of occupation condition** – during the **relevant period, not more that 155 days fall during periods of longer term occupation**. Longer term occupation is defined as **a continuous period of more than 31 days during which the accommodation is in the same occupation** unless there are abnormal circumstances.

The relevant period is normally the tax year. Where the FHL starts or ceases in a tax year, the relevant period is the 12 months beginning or ending with the first or last days of letting as appropriate.

If someone has furnished holiday lettings and other lettings, **draw up two profit and loss accounts as if they had two separate UK property businesses**. This is so that the profits and losses treated as trade profits and losses can be identified.

Exam focus point

Always check whether property qualifies as furnished holiday lettings – remember the averaging provisions. It does not have to be a seaside cottage but must be in the UK.

3 Rent a room relief

The first £4,250 of rent received from letting a room or rooms in a main residence is tax free.

If an individual lets a room or rooms, furnished, in his or her main residence as living accommodation, a special exemption may apply.

The limit on the exemption is gross rents (before any expenses or capital allowances) of £4,250 a year. This limit is halved if any other person (including the first person's spouse/civil partner) also received income from renting accommodation in the property while the property was the first person's main residence.

If gross rents (plus balancing charges arising because of capital allowances in earlier years) **are not more than the limit, the rents** (and balancing charges) **are wholly exempt from income tax** and expenses and capital allowances are ignored. However, the taxpayer may claim to ignore the exemption, for example to generate a loss by taking into account both rent and expenses.

If gross rents exceed the limit, the taxpayer will be taxed in the ordinary way, ignoring the rent a room scheme, unless he elects for the 'alternative basis'. If he so elects, he will be taxable on gross receipts plus balancing charges less £4,250 (or £2,125 if the limit is halved), with no deductions for expenses or capital allowances.

An election to ignore the exemption or an election for the alternative basis must be made by the 31 January which is 22 months from the end of the tax year concerned.

An election to ignore the exemption applies only for the tax year for which it is made, but an election for the alternative basis remains in force until it is withdrawn or until a year in which gross rents do not exceed the limit.

Exam focus point

Note the different elections carefully and the relevant time limits.

Question

Rent a Room Relief

Sylvia owns a house near the sea in Norfolk. She has a spare bedroom and during 2006/07 this was let to a chef working at a nearby restaurant for £85 per week which includes the cost of heating, lighting etc.

Sylvia estimates that each year her lodger costs her an extra:

    £50 on gas
    £25 on electricity
    £50 on insurance

How much property income must Sylvia pay tax on?

Answer

Sylvia has a choice:

(1)   Total rental income of £85 × 52 = £4,420 exceeds £4,250 limit so taxable income is £170 (ie £4,420 − 4,250) if rent a room relief claimed.

(2)   Alternatively she can be taxed on her actual profit:

	£
Rental income	4,420
Less expenses (50 + 25 + 50)	(125)
	4,295

Sylvia should be advised to elect for option 1.

4 Interest income

Interest may be received with or without deduction of tax. It is taxed as savings income.

4.1 Interest received without deduction of tax

Interest is taxed as savings income. Some interest, such as bank and building society interest, is taxed at source as we saw earlier in this Text. Other interest is received without deduction of tax at source such as interest on:

- Loans between individuals

- Government stocks (although the individual can opt to have the income paid net of tax if they prefer)

- Debentures and loan stocks of UK companies which are listed on a recognised Stock Exchange

- National Savings & Investments accounts (eg Investment account, Easy Access Savings (EASA) account)

The amount of income taxable for a tax year is the amount arising in that year. Income arises when it is paid or credited: accrued income not yet paid or credited is ignored.

The rules for companies are different. These are covered later in this Text.

4.2 Deeply discounted securities

Some securities are issued at a discount, that is the issue price is less than the redemption price. This is a way of giving investors an extra return in addition to interest. Small discounts are ignored for tax purposes, but if the discount is more than a certain percentage of the redemption price, it is taken into account. This percentage is the lower of 15% and the years from issue to redemption × 0.5%.

When an individual holding such a security sells or redeems it, the profit (selling price – purchase price) is taxed as savings income. We simply tax the profit, and do not give an indexation allowance or taper relief as we would for a capital gain.

These rules do not apply to companies because they take into account all profits and losses on securities, whether they arise from discounts or from some other cause.

5 Accrued income scheme

The accrued income scheme taxes interest that arose up to the date that a security was sold cum interest and gives relief for interest arising between the sale and next interest payment date for sales ex interest.

If the owner of securities sells them before a certain date, he will not be entitled to the next interest payment on them. The new owner will receive it. This is called selling **cum interest.** However, the sale proceeds will include interest accrued to the date of sale.

If securities are sold after a certain date, they are sold **ex interest** and the original owner is entitled to the whole of the next interest payment despite the fact that he has sold the securities to a new owner. This time, the sale proceeds will exclude interest accruing after the date of sale.

Under the **accrued income scheme**, where securities are transferred the accrued interest reflected in the value of securities is taxed separately as savings income. The seller is treated as entitled to the proportion of interest which has accrued since the last interest payment. The buyer is entitled to relief against the interest he receives. This relief is equal to the amount assessable on the seller.

Conversely, where the transfer is ex interest, the seller will receive the whole of the next interest payment. He will be entitled to relief for the amount of interest assessed on the purchaser. The purchaser is treated as entitled to the proportion of the interest accrued between the sale and the next payment date and it is taxed as savings income.

The accrued income scheme does not apply where the seller:

- carries on a trade and the sale is taken into account in computing trading profits

- did not hold securities with a nominal value exceeding £5,000 during the tax year in which the interest period ends

- was neither resident nor ordinarily resident in the UK during any part of the period in question (see later in this Text)

- is taxed on the interest under the manufactured payment rules (not examinable)

Question — Accrued income scheme

Nigel bought £10,000 5% Loan Stock many years ago. Interest is payable on 30 June and 31 December each year. Nigel sells the loan stock to Evie on 30 November 2006 cum interest.

What are the amounts assessable for Nigel and Evie in respect of the loan stock for 2006/07?

Answer

Nigel

	£
Interest paid 30.6.06	
£10,000 × 5% × 6/12	250
Accrued interest deemed received 31.12.06	
£10,000 × 5% × 5/12	208
Total assessable	458

Evie

	£
Interest paid 31.12.06	
£10,000 × 5% × 6/12	250
Less relief for accrued interest	
£10,000 × 5% × 5/12	(208)
Total assessable (ie 1 month's interest)	42

6 Dividend income

Cash dividends and stock dividends are treated as being received net of a 10% tax credit.

6.1 Introduction

We have already seen that **dividends from UK companies are received net of a 10% tax credit and are taxed at special rates**. This also applies to **distributions from authorised unit trusts and open ended investments companies (OEICs)**, other than distributions which are specifically designated as interest distributions.

6.2 Stock dividends

Sometimes a company will offer shares in lieu of a cash dividend. A shareholder who takes the shares receives a stock dividend. The amount of the stock dividend is:

(a)   The cash alternative, if that equals the market value of the shares offered plus or minus 15%.

(b)   The market value of the shares offered, if that differs from the cash alternative by more than 15% or if there is no cash alternative.

The shareholder is treated as receiving a gross dividend of the stock dividend × 100/90, with a tax credit of 10% of the gross dividend.

7 Miscellaneous income

FAST FORWARD

Some income is taxable as miscellaneous income if it does not fall in any other category.

Miscellaneous income includes:

- Income from royalties and other income from intellectual property

- Sales of patents and know how

- Income from settlements which is taxed as the Settlor's income

- Income from estates in administration

- Any other income which is not taxed under any other provision (unless it is specifically exempt), for example casual earnings.

The income arising in a tax year is taxed in that year.

8 Pre-owned assets

FAST FORWARD

There is an income tax charge on the use of pre-owned assets such as land and chattels.

There is an income tax charge on the annual benefit of using or enjoying certain assets that were once owned by the user. The charge does not apply if the asset was sold to an unconnected person, or if it was sold at market value to a connected person either before 7 March 2005 or if the proceeds were not money or readily convertible assets.

There is no charge if the user pays a full market rent for the use of the asset. However, if less than a full rent is paid, any amount paid does not reduce the charge.

The charge applies to:

- **Land:** the taxable amount is **the annual rental value of the land**

- **Chattels**, such as works of art: the taxable amount is **the value of the chattel multiplied by the official rate of interest, and**

- **Intangible property**, such as cash and insurance policies, held in a trust where the settlor can benefit: the taxable amount is **the value of the property multiplied by the official rate of interest, less any income or capital gains tax paid by the settlor in respect of that property**

The property is valued at 6 April 2005, or, if later, the date the asset falls within the scope of the legislation. Land and chattels are valued every 5 years, at the start of the tax year in which the relevant anniversary falls. So if a chattel first comes within the charge on 17 May 2006 it must be valued at that date and then on 6 April 2011.

There is no charge if the taxable amount is £5,000 or less. If this de minimis limit is exceeded the full amount is taxable.

There is no charge if the asset was disposed of before 18 March 1986 or if the disposition falls within the 'gifts with reservation' rules so that the asset is treated as part of the taxpayer's estate for IHT purposes (see later in this Text). **A taxpayer can choose to disapply the income tax charge by electing that the disposition should be treated as a gift with reservation**. The election must be made by 31 January following the first year in which the charge arises, ie by 31 January 2007 for all assets which were caught in 2005/06 (the first year the charge applied), or by 31 January 2008 for assets first caught in 2006/07.

There are various other exemptions including:

(a)   gifts between spouses

(b)   deeds of variation.

9 Trust income

FAST FORWARD

> Income from trusts must be grossed up by either 100/60 (discretionary trusts) or by 100/78, 100/80 or 100/90 (interest in possession trusts).

A trust is a vehicle in which assets are legally owned by the trustees for the benefit of the beneficiaries. There are two types of trust for income tax purposes:

(a)   An interest in possession trust (a 'life interest' trust) where the income must be paid out to the beneficiary (often called the life tenant)

(b)   A discretionary trust where the income (and often capital) is distributed or accumulated at the trustees' discretion.

Income from discretionary trusts is received net of 40% tax. Gross it up in the income tax computation by multiplying by 100/60 and give credit for the tax already suffered when working out the final amount of tax payable. Such income is always treated as non-savings income.

If income from an interest in possession trust is paid out of the trust's non-savings income, it will be received by the beneficiary net of 22% tax and must be grossed up by multiplying by 100/78. If income from an interest in possession trust has been paid out of the trust's savings (excl dividend) income then it is received net of 20% tax and must be grossed up by multiplying by 100/80. If it is paid out of dividend income it must be grossed up by multiplying by 100/90. This tax credit cannot be repaid. Each type of income is then taxed on the beneficiary under the normal rules.

If a **minor beneficiary** receives income from a **trust set up by a parent**, then under the anti-avoidance rules the income is **taxed as the parent's income**. As we saw earlier, there is a £100 de minimis limit.

Question   **Income from trusts**

Victoria, aged 6, received the following income in 2006/07.

	£
Building society interest (received net)	5,000
Dividends	2,250
Income from discretionary trust	6,000
Income from life interest trust	780

The income from the life interest trust was paid out of the trust's rental income. Neither trust was set up by Victoria's parents.

What income tax is payable by/repayable to Victoria?

Answer

	Non savings £	Savings £	Dividends £	£
Building society interest (× 100/80)		6,250		
Dividends (× 100/90)			2,500	
Income from discretionary trust (× 100/60)	10,000			
Income from life interest trust (× 100/78)	1,000			
	11,000	6,250	2,500	19,750
Less: PA	(5,035)			
	5,965	6,250	2,500	14,715

		£
Tax on non savings income	£2,150 × 10%	215
	£3,815 × 22%	839
Tax on savings (excl dividend) income	£6,250 × 20%	1,250
Tax on dividend income	£2,500 × 10%	250
		2,554
Less: Dividend tax credits		(250)
Tax on building society interest		(1,250)
Discretionary trust		(4,000)
Life interest trust		(220)
Income tax repayable		(3,166)

Exam focus point

Although you need to know the rate of tax deducted from income distributions from trusts, you do not need to know how to calculate the trustees' income tax liability.

Chapter roundup

- Income from a UK property business is computed for tax years on an accruals basis.

- A loss on a UK property business is carried forward to set against future profits from the UK property business.

- Part of the premium received on the grant of a short lease is taxed as rent. In addition any premiums paid to a tenant to induce him to take out a lease is also taxable as income from a UK property business, or as trading income if the tenant is in business.

- There are special rules for furnished holiday accommodation let on a commercial basis with a view to realisation of profit.

- The first £4,250 of rent received from letting a room or rooms in a main residence is tax free.

- Interest may be received with or without deduction of tax. It is taxed as savings income.

- The accrued income scheme taxes interest that arose up to the date that a security was sold cum interest and gives relief for interest arising between the sale and next interest payment date for sales ex interest.

- Cash dividends and stock dividends are treated as being received net of a 10% tax credit.

- Some income is taxable as miscellaneous income if it does not fall in any other category.

- There is an income tax charge on the use of pre-owned assets such as land and chattels.

- Income from trusts must be grossed up by either 100/60 (discretionary and accumulating trusts) or by 100/78, 100/80 or 100/90 (interest in possession trusts).

Quick quiz

1   Describe the renewals basis and the 10% wear and tear basis.

2   What are the conditions for a letting to be a furnished holiday letting?

3   What are the tax consequences of selling fixed interest stock cum interest one month after the normal interest payment date?

4   A discretionary beneficiary receives £450 income from a trust. How much does the beneficiary enter as the gross amount in his tax return? Is it savings or non-savings income?

Answers to quick quiz

1   Renewals basis   – no deduction for first furniture costs
                     – replacement furniture is revenue expense

    10% wear and tear – cost of furniture ignored
                     – annual deduction of 10% of rents (less water rates and council tax)

2   FHL is   – available for letting at least 140 days per tax year
             – actually let at least 70 days per tax year
             – not in longer term occupation (more than 31 days) for not more than 155 days

3   The sale price of the stock will reflect the fact that one month's worth of interest is included in the price. This amount is excluded from the proceeds but is taxed as interest (ie savings income).

4   $£450 \times \dfrac{100}{60}$ = £750 gross. Non savings income.

Now try the question below from the Exam Question Bank			
Number	**Level**	**Marks**	**Time**
Q3	Introductory	25	45 mins

Employment income

4

Topic list	Syllabus reference
1 Employment income	A1(a)B2
2 Taxable benefits	A1(a)B2
3 Exempt benefits	A1(a)B2
4 Allowable deductions	A1(a)B2
5 Personal service companies	A1(c)(iv)
6 National insurance	A6(a)E1,E2

Introduction

In the previous chapters we have looked at the basic income tax computation and the taxation of investments.

Most people have jobs, which pay them wages or salaries. They may also get other benefits from their employers and/or they may pay expenses connected with their employment. In this chapter, we see how to work out the basic employment income they must pay tax on.

We also look at the rules for personal service companies, where the taxpayer is deemed to receive employment income even if he has routed his services through a company.

We conclude with a study of the national insurance contributions payable in respect of employees.

In the next chapter we will look at share options and share incentives, and at lump sum receipts.

Study guide

		Intellectual level
1	**Income and income tax liabilities in situations involving further overseas aspects and in relation to trusts, and the application of exemptions and reliefs**	
(a)	The contents of the Paper F6 study guide for income tax, under headings:	2
•	B2 Income from employment	
(c)	Income from employment:	3
(iv)	Identify personal service companies and advise on the tax consequences of providing services via a personal service company	
6	**National insurance, value added tax and tax administration:**	
(a)	The contents of the Paper F6 study guide for national insurance under headings:	2
•	E1 The scope of national insurance	
•	E2 Class 1 and class 1A contributions for employed persons	

Exam guide

In the exam you may get a question which asks you to compare the after tax income from one benefit package with another, or the salary foregone in a salary sacrifice scheme. As well as calculating the marginal tax on the benefit provided or foregone, remember to take into account other costs. For example, an employee who chooses to receive a higher salary and use his own car for business will have to bear the running costs of the car as well as the capital depreciation. Remember to take national insurance into account.

> Knowledge brought forward from earlier studies

With the exception of the rules for personal service companies this chapter is revision of your level 2.3 studies.

1 Employment income

1.1 Outline of the charge

Employment income includes income arising from an employment under a contract of service (see below) and the income of office holders, such as directors. The term 'employee' is used in this text to mean anyone who receives employment income (ie both employees and directors).

There are two types of employment income:

- **General earnings**, and
- **Specific employment income**.

General earnings are an employees' earnings (see key term below) plus the 'cash equivalent' of any taxable non-monetary benefits.

Key term

> **'Earnings'** means any salary, wage or fee, any gratuity or other profit or incidental benefit obtained by the employee if it is money or money's worth (something of direct monetary value or convertible into direct monetary value) or anything else which constitutes an emolument of the employment.

'Specific employment income' includes payments on termination of employment and share related income. This type of income is covered in the next chapter of this Study Text.

The residence and domicile status of an employee determines whether earnings are taxable. If an employee is resident, ordinarily resident and domiciled in the UK, **taxable earnings from an employment in a tax year are the general earnings received in that tax year**. The rules relating to other employees are dealt with later in this Study Text.

1.2 When are earnings received?

FAST FORWARD

> General earnings are taxed in the year of receipt. Money earnings are generally received on the earlier of the time payment is made and the time entitlement to payment arises. Non-money earnings are generally received when provided.

General earnings consisting of money are treated as received at the earlier of:

- **The time when payment is made**
- **The time when a person becomes entitled to payment of the earnings.**

If the employee is a director of a company, earnings from the company are received on the earliest of:

- The earlier of the two alternatives given in the general rule (above)
- The time when the amount is credited in the company's accounting records
- The end of the company's period of account (if the amount was determined by then)
- The time the amount is determined (if after the end of the company's period of account).

Taxable benefits are generally treated as received when they are provided to the employee.

The receipts basis does not apply to pension income or taxable social security benefits. These sources of income are taxed on the amount accruing in the tax year, whether or not it is received in that year.

Question
When are earnings received

John is a director of X Corp Ltd. His earnings for 2006/07 are:

Salary	£60,000
Taxable benefits	£5,000

For the year ended 31 December 2006 the Board of Directors decide to pay John a bonus of £40,000. This is decided on 1 March 2007 at a board meeting and credited in the company accounts 7 days later. However John only received the bonus in his April pay on 30 April 2007.

What is John's taxable income from employment for 2006/07?

Answer

Salary	£60,000
Taxable benefits	5,000
Bonus (1.3.06)	40,000
Taxable employment Income	105,000

The salary and benefits were paid/made available during 2006/07 and hence taxed in 2006/07. The bonus was paid/made available on 30 April 2007 (2007/08) *but* was determined after the company's year end (31.12.06) by the board meeting on 1 March 2007 (2006/07) – hence taxed in 2006/07.

1.3 Net taxable earnings

Total taxable earnings less total allowable deductions (see below) **are net taxable earnings of a tax year. Deductions cannot usually create a loss: they can only reduce the net taxable earnings to nil.**

1.4 Person liable for tax on employment income

The person liable to tax on employment income is generally the **person to whose employment the earnings relate**. However, if the tax relates to general earnings received after the death of the person to whose employment the earnings relate, the person's personal representatives are liable for the tax. The tax is a liability of the estate.

1.5 Employment and self employment

Employment involves a contract of service whereas self employment involves a contract for services.

The distinction between employment (receipts taxable as earnings) and self employment (receipts taxable as trading income) is a fine one. Employment involves a contract of service, whereas self employment involves a contract for services. Taxpayers tend to prefer self employment, because the rules on deductions for expenses are more generous.

Factors which may be of importance include:

- The degree of control exercised over the person doing the work
- Whether he must accept further work
- Whether the other party must provide further work
- Whether he provides his own equipment
- Whether he hires his own helpers
- What degree of financial risk he takes
- What degree of responsibility for investment and management he has
- Whether he can profit from sound management
- Whether he can work when he chooses
- The wording used in any agreement between the parties.

Relevant cases include:

(a)   *Edwards v Clinch 1981*

A civil engineer acted occasionally as an inspector on temporary ad hoc appointments.

Held: there was no ongoing office which could be vacated by one person and held by another so the fees received were from self employment not employment.

(b)   *Hall v Lorimer 1994*

A vision mixer was engaged under a series of short-term contracts.

Held: the vision mixer was self employed, not because of any one detail of the case but because the overall picture was one of self-employment.

(c)   *Carmichael and Anor v National Power plc 1999*

Individuals engaged as visitor guides on a casual 'as required' basis were not employees. An exchange of correspondence between the company and the individuals was not a contract of employment as there was no provision as to the frequency of work and there was flexibility to accept work or turn it down as it arose. Sickness, holiday and pension arrangements did not apply and neither did grievance and disciplinary procedures.

A worker's status also affects national insurance. The self-employed generally pay less than employees.

2 Taxable benefits

2.1 Introduction

Most employees are taxed on benefits under the benefits code. 'Excluded employees' (lower paid/non-directors) are only subject to part of the provisions of the code.

The Income Tax (Earnings and Pensions) Act 2003 (ITEPA 2003) provides comprehensive legislation covering the taxation of benefits. **The legislation generally applies to all employees. However, only certain parts of it apply to 'excluded employees'.**

(a) **An excluded employee is an employee in lower paid employment who is either not a director of a company or is a director but has no material interest in the company** ('material' means control of more than 5% of the ordinary share capital) and either:

    (i) **He is full time working director**, or
    (ii) **The company is non-profit-making or is established for charitable purposes only.**

(b) **The term 'director' refers to any person who acts as a director or any person in accordance with whose instructions the directors are accustomed to act** (other than a professional advisor).

(c) **Lower paid employment is one where earnings for the tax year are less than £8,500.** To decide whether this applies, add together the **total earnings and benefits that would be taxable if the employee were *not* an excluded employee**.

(d) A number of **specific deductions** must be taken into account to determine lower paid employment. These include **contributions to authorised pension schemes and payroll giving**. However, general deductions from employment income (see later in this chapter) are not taken into account.

(e) Where a car is provided but the employee could have chosen a cash alternative, then the higher of the cash alternative and the car benefit should be used in the computation of earnings to determine whether or not the employee is an excluded employee.

Question	Excluded employee?

Tim earns £6,500 per annum working full time as a sales representative at Chap Co Ltd. The company provides the following staff benefits to Tim:

Private health insurance	£300
Company car	£1,500
Expense allowance	£2,000

Tim used £1,900 of the expense allowance on business mileage petrol and on entertaining clients.

Is Tim an excluded employee?

Answer

No. Although Tim's taxable income is less than £8,500 this is only after his expense claim. The figure to consider and compare to £8,500 is the £10,300 as shown below.

	£
Salary	6,500
Benefits: health insurance	300
car	1,500
expense allowance	2,000
Earnings to consider if Tim is lower paid	10,300
Less: claim for expenses paid out	(1,900)
Taxable income	8,400

2.2 General business expenses

If business expenses on such items as travel or hotel stays, are reimbursed by an employer, the reimbursed amount is a taxable benefit for employees other than excluded employees. To avoid being taxed on this amount, **an employee must then make a claim to deduct it as an expense** under the rules set out below. **In practice**, however, **many such expense payments are not reported to HMRC and can be ignored because it is agreed in advance that a claim to deduct them would be possible (a P11D dispensation**).

When an individual has to spend one or more nights away from home, his employer may reimburse expenses on items incidental to his absence (for example meals and private telephone calls). **Such incidental expenses are exempt** if:

(a)   The expenses of travelling to each place where the individual stays overnight, throughout the trip, are incurred necessarily in the performance of the duties of the employment (or would have been, if there had been any expenses).

(b)   The total (for the whole trip) of incidental expenses not deductible under the usual rules is no more than £5 for each night spent wholly in the UK and £10 for each other night. If this limit is exceeded, all of the expenses are taxable, not just the excess. The expenses include any VAT.

This incidental expenses exemption applies to expenses reimbursed, and to benefits obtained using credit tokens and non-cash vouchers.

2.3 Vouchers

If any employee (including an excluded employee):

(a)   receives cash vouchers (vouchers exchangeable for cash)
(b)   uses a credit token (such as a credit card) to obtain money, goods or services, or
(c)   receives exchangeable vouchers (such as book tokens), also called non-cash vouchers

he is taxed on the cost of providing the benefit, less any amount made good.

However, the first 15p per working day of meal vouchers (eg luncheon vouchers) is not taxed. In addition, the first £55 per week of child care vouchers is exempt (see below).

2.4 Accommodation

The benefit in respect of accommodation is its annual value. There is an additional benefit if the property cost the employer over £75,000.

The taxable value of accommodation provided to an employee (including an excluded employee) is the rent that would have been payable if the premises had been let at an amount equal to their annual value (taken to be their **rateable value**). **If the premises are rented** rather than owned by the employer, then **the taxable benefit is the higher of the rent actually paid and the annual value**. If property does not have a rateable value HMRC estimate a value.

If a property cost the employer more than £75,000, an additional amount is chargeable:

Formula to learn

(Cost of providing the accommodation – £75,000) × the official rate of interest at the start of the tax year.

Thus with an official rate of 5%, the total benefit for accommodation costing £90,000 and with an annual value of £2,000 would be £2,000 + £(90,000 – 75,000) × 5% = £2,750.

The 'cost of providing' the living accommodation is the aggregate of the cost of purchase and the cost of any improvements made before the start of the tax year for which the benefit is being computed. It is therefore not possible to avoid the charge by buying an inexpensive property requiring substantial repairs and improving it.

If a property was acquired more than six years before first being provided to the employee, the market value when first provided plus the cost of subsequent improvements is used as the cost of providing the accommodation. However, unless the actual cost plus improvements to the start of the tax year in question exceeds £75,000, the additional charge cannot be imposed, however high the market value. In addition, the additional charge can only be imposed if the employer owns (rather than rents) the property concerned.

Exam focus point

The 'official rate' of interest will be given to you in the exam.

There is no taxable benefit in respect of job related accommodation. Accommodation is job related if:

(a) Residence in the accommodation **is necessary for the proper performance of the employee's duties** (as with a caretaker), or

(b) The accommodation is provided **for the better performance of the employee's duties** and the employment is of a kind in which it is **customary for accommodation to be provided** (as with a policeman), or

(c) The **accommodation is provided as part of arrangements in force because of a special threat to the employee's security**.

Directors can only claim exemptions (a) or (b) if:

(i) They have no **material interest** ('material' means over 5%) in the company, and

(ii) Either they are **full time working directors** or the company is **non-profit making or is a charity**.

Any contribution paid by the employee is deducted from the annual value of the property and then from the additional benefit.

If the employee is given a cash alternative to living accommodation, the benefits code still applies in priority to treating the cash alternative as earnings. If the cash alternative is greater than the taxable benefit, the excess is treated as earnings.

2.5 Expenses connected with living accommodation

In addition to the benefit of living accommodation itself, **employees, other than excluded employees, are taxed on related expenses paid by the employer**, such as:

(a) **Heating, lighting or cleaning the premises**
(b) **Repairing, maintaining or decorating the premises**
(c) **The provision of furniture (the annual value is 20% of the cost)**

Unless the accommodation qualifies as 'job related' (as defined above) **the full cost of ancillary services** (excluding structural repairs) **is taxable. If the accommodation is 'job related'**, however, **taxable ancillary services are restricted to a maximum of 10% of the employee's 'net earnings'**.

For this purpose, net earnings are all earnings from the employment (excluding the ancillary benefits (a)-(c) above) less any allowable expenses, statutory mileage allowances, contributions to registered occupational pension schemes (but not personal pension plans), and capital allowances.

If there are ancillary benefits other than those falling within (a)-(c) above (such as a telephone) they are taxable in full.

Question   Expenses connected with living accommodation

Mr Quinton has a gross salary in 2006/07 of £28,850. He normally lives and works in London, but he is required to live in a company house in Scotland, which cost £70,000 three years ago, so that he can carry out a two year review of his company's operations in Scotland. The annual value of the house is £650. In 2006/07 the company pays an electricity bill of £550, a gas bill of £400, a gardener's bill of £750 and redecoration costs of £1,800. Mr Quinton makes a monthly contribution of £50 for his accommodation. He also pays £1,450 occupational pension contributions.

Calculate Mr Quinton's taxable employment income for 2006/07.

Answer

	£	£
Salary		28,850
Less occupational pension scheme contributions		(1,450)
Net earnings		27,400
Accommodation benefits		
Annual value: exempt (job related)		
Ancillary services		
Electricity	550	
Gas	400	
Gardener	750	
Redecorations	1,800	
	3,500	
Restricted to 10% of £27,400	2,740	
Less employee's contribution	(600)	
		2,140
Employment income		29,540

Council tax and water or sewage charges paid by the employer are taxable in full as a benefit unless the accommodation is 'job-related'.

2.6 Cars

Employees who have a company car are taxed on a % of the car's list price which depends on the level of the car's CO_2 emissions. The same % multiplied by £14,400 determines the benefit where private fuel is also provided. Authorised mileage allowances can be paid tax free to employees who use their own vehicle for business journeys.

A car provided by reason of the employment to an employee or member of his family or household for private use gives rise to a taxable benefit. This does not apply to excluded employees. **'Private use'** **includes home to work travel.**

(a)   A tax charge arises whether the car is provided by the employer or by some other person. The benefit is computed as shown below, even if the car is taken as an alternative to another benefit of a different value.

(b)   The starting point for calculating a car benefit is the list price of the car (plus accessories). **The percentage of the list price that is taxable depends on the car's CO_2 emissions**.

(c)   The price of the car is the sum of the following items.

(i)   The list price of the car for a single retail sale at the time of first registration, including charges for delivery and standard accessories. The manufacturer's, importer's or distributor's list price must be used, even if the retailer offered a discount. A notional list price is estimated if no list price was published.

(ii)   The price (including fitting) of all optional accessories provided when the car was first provided to the employee, excluding mobile telephones and equipment needed by a disabled employee. The extra cost of adapting or manufacturing a car to run on road fuel gases is not included.

(iii)   The price (including fitting) of all optional accessories fitted later and costing at least £100 each, excluding mobile telephones and equipment needed by a disabled employee. Such accessories affect the taxable benefit from and including the tax year in which they are fitted. However, accessories which are merely replacing existing accessories and are not superior to the ones replaced are ignored. Replacement accessories which *are* superior are taken into account, but the cost of the old accessory is then ignored.

(d)   There is a special rule for classic cars. If the car is at least 15 years old (from the time of first registration) at the end of the tax year, and its market value at the end of the year (or, if earlier, when it ceased to be available to the employee) is over £15,000 and greater than the price found under (c), that market value is used instead of the price. The market value takes account of all accessories (except mobile telephones and equipment needed by a disabled employee).

(e)   Capital contributions are payments by the employee in respect of the price of the car or accessories. In any tax year, we take account of capital contributions made in that year and previous years (for the same car). The maximum deductible capital contributions is £5,000; contributions beyond that total are ignored.

(f)   If the price or value found under (c) or (d) exceeds £80,000, then £80,000 is used instead of the price or value. This £80,000 is after capital contributions (see (e) above) have been taken into account.

(g)   For cars that emit **CO_2 of 140g/km (2006/07) or less, the taxable benefit is 15% of the car's list price. This percentage increases by 1% for every 5g/km (rounded down to the nearest multiple of 5) by which CO_2 emissions exceed 140g/km up to a maximum of 35%.**

Exam focus **point**

The CO_2 baseline figure will be given to you in the tax rates and allowances section of the exam paper.

(h) Diesel cars have a supplement of 3% of the car's list price added to the taxable benefit. However, the benefit is discounted for cars that are particularly environmentally friendly. The maximum percentage, however, remains 35% of the list price.

(i) **The benefit is reduced on a time basis where a car is first made available or ceases to be made available during the tax year** or is incapable of being used for a continuous period of not less than 30 days (for example because it is being repaired).

(j) **The benefit is reduced by any payment the user must make for the private use of the car** (as distinct from a capital contribution to the cost of the car). Payments for insuring the car do not count *(IRC v Quigley 1995)*. The benefit cannot become negative to create a deduction from the employee's income.

(k) Pool cars are exempt. A car is a pool car if **all** the following conditions are satisfied.

    (i) It is used by more than one employee and is not ordinarily used by any one of them to the exclusion of the others

    (ii) Any private use is merely incidental to business use

    (iii) It is not normally kept overnight at or near the residence of an employee

There are many ancillary benefits associated with the provision of cars, such as insurance, repairs, vehicle licences and a parking space at or near work. No extra taxable benefit arises as a result of these, with the exception of the cost of providing a driver.

2.7 Fuel for cars

Where fuel is provided there is a further benefit in addition to the car benefit.

No taxable benefit arises where either

(a) **All the fuel provided was made available only for business travel**, or

(b) **The employee is required to make good, and has made good, the whole of the cost of any fuel provided for his private use**.

Unlike most benefits, a reimbursement of only part of the cost of the fuel available for private use does not reduce the benefit.

The taxable benefit is a percentage of a base figure. The base figure for 2006/07 is £14,400. The percentage is the same percentage as is used to calculate the car benefit (see above).

<table>
<tr><td>**Exam focus point**</td><td>The fuel base figure will be given to you in the tax rates and allowances section of the exam paper.</td></tr>
</table>

The fuel benefit is reduced in the same way as the car benefit **if the car is not available for 30 days or more**.

The fuel benefit is also reduced if private fuel is not available for part of a tax year. However, if private fuel later becomes available in the same tax year, the reduction is not made. If, for example, fuel is provided from 6 April 2006 to 30 June 2006, then the fuel benefit for 2006/07 will be restricted to just three months. This is because the provision of fuel has permanently ceased. However, if fuel is provided from 6 April 2006 to 30 June 2006, and then again from 1 September 2006 to 5 April 2007, then the fuel benefit will not be reduced since the cessation was only temporary.

Question — Car and fuel benefit

An employee was provided with a new car (2,500 cc) costing £15,000. The car emits 191g/km of CO_2. During 2006/07 the employer spent £900 on insurance, repairs and a vehicle licence. The firm paid for all petrol, costing £1,500, without reimbursement. The employee paid the firm £270 for the private use of the car. Calculate the taxable benefit.

Answer

Round CO_2 emissions figure down to the nearest 5, ie 190 g/km.

Amount by which CO_2 emissions exceed the baseline:

(190 – 140) = 50 g/km

Divide by 5 = 10

Taxable percentage = 15% + 10% = 25%

	£
Car benefit £15,000 × 25%	3,750
Fuel benefit £14,400 × 25%	3,600
	7,350
Less contribution towards use of car	(270)
	7,080

If the contribution of £270 had been towards the petrol the benefit would have been £7,350.

2.8 Vans and heavier commercial vehicles

If a van (of normal maximum laden weight up to 3,500 kg) **is made available for an employee's private use, there is an annual scale charge of £500, or £350 if the van is at least four years old at the end of the tax year**. The scale charge covers ancillary benefits such as insurance and servicing. Paragraphs 2.6 (i) and (j) above apply to vans as they do to cars.

There is, however, **no taxable benefit where an employee takes a van home** (ie uses the van for home to work travel) but is not allowed any other private use.

From 6 April 2007, the **discount for older vans** will be removed and the **scale charge will rise to £3,000** for unrestricted private use. In addition, if the employer provides **fuel for unrestricted private use**, an additional **fuel charge of £500** will apply.

If a commercial vehicle of normal maximum laden weight over 3,500 kg is made available for an employee's private use, but the employee's use of the vehicle is not wholly or mainly private, no taxable benefit arises except in respect of the provision of a driver.

2.9 Statutory mileage allowances

A single authorised mileage allowance for business journeys in an employee's own vehicle applies to all cars and vans. There is no income tax on payments up to this allowance and employers do not have to report mileage allowances up to this amount. The allowance for 2006/07 is 40p per mile on the first 10,000 miles in the tax year with each additional mile over 10,000 miles at 25p per mile. The authorised mileage allowance for employees using their own motor cycle is 24p per mile. For employees using their own pedal cycle it is 20p per mile.

If employers pay less than the statutory allowance, employees can claim tax relief up to that level.

The statutory allowance does not prevent employers from paying higher rates, but any excess will be subject to income tax. There is a similar (but slightly different) system for NICs, covered below.

Employers can make income tax and NIC free payments of up to 5p per mile for each fellow employee making the same business trip who is carried as a passenger. If the employer does not pay the employee for carrying business passengers, the employee cannot claim any tax relief.

Question   Mileage allowance

Sophie uses her own car for business travel. During 2006/07, Sophie drove 15,400 miles in the performance of her duties. Sophie's employer paid her 35p a mile. How is the mileage allowance received by Sophie treated for tax purposes?

Answer

	£
Mileage allowance received (15,400 × 35p)	5,390
Less tax free [(10,000 × 40p) + (5,400 × 25p)]	(5,350)
Taxable benefit	40

£5,350 is tax free and the excess amount received of £40 is a taxable benefit.

2.10 Beneficial loans

FAST FORWARD

Taxable cheap loans are charged to tax on the difference between the official rate of interest and any interest paid by the employee.

2.10.1 Introduction

Employment related loans to employees (other than excluded employees) and their relatives give rise to a benefit equal to:

(a) **Any amounts written off** (unless the employee has died), and

(b) **The excess of the interest based on an official rate prescribed by the Treasury, over any interest actually charged ('taxable cheap loan').** Interest payable during the tax year but paid after the end of the tax year is taken into account, but if the benefit is determined before such interest is paid a claim must be made to take it into account.

The following loans are normally not treated as taxable cheap loans for calculation of the interest benefits (but not for the purposes of the charge on loans written off).

(a) A loan on normal commercial terms made in the ordinary course of the employer's money-lending business.

(b) A loan made by an individual in the ordinary course of the lender's domestic, family or personal arrangements.

2.10.2 Calculating the interest benefit

There are two alternative methods of calculating the taxable benefit. The simpler **'average' method** automatically applies unless the taxpayer or HMRC elect for the alternative **'strict' method**. (HMRC normally only make the election where it appears that the 'average' method is being deliberately exploited.) In both methods, the benefit is the interest at the official rate minus the interest payable.

The 'average' method averages the balances at the beginning and end of the tax year (or the dates on which the loan was made and discharged if it was not in existence throughout the tax year) and applies the official rate of interest to this average. If the loan was not in existence throughout the tax year only the number of complete tax months (from the 6th of the month) for which it existed are taken into account.

The 'strict' method is to compute interest at the official rate on the actual amount outstanding on a daily basis.

Question | Loan benefit

At 6 April 2006 a taxable cheap loan of £30,000 was outstanding to an employee earning £12,000 a year, who repaid £20,000 on 7 December 2006. The remaining balance of £10,000 was outstanding at 5 April 2007. Interest paid during the year was £250. What was the benefit under both methods for 2006/07, assuming that the official rate of interest was 5%?

Answer

Average method

	£
$5\% \times \dfrac{30{,}000 + 10{,}000}{2}$	1,000
Less interest paid	(250)
Benefit	750

Alternative method (strict method)

	£
$£30{,}000 \times \dfrac{245}{365}$ (6 April - 6 December) $\times 5\%$	1,007
$£10{,}000 \times \dfrac{120}{365}$ (7 December - 5 April) $\times 5\%$	164
	1,171
Less interest paid	(250)
Benefit	921

HMRC might opt for the alternative method.

2.10.3 The de minimis test

The benefit is not taxable if:

(a)   The **total of all taxable cheap loans to the employee did not exceed £5,000** at any time in the tax year, or

(b)   **The loan is not a qualifying loan and the total of all non-qualifying loans to the employee did not exceed £5,000** at any time in the tax year.

A qualifying loan is one on which all or part of any interest paid would qualify as a charge on income.

When the £5,000 threshold is exceeded, a benefit arises on interest on the whole loan, not just on the excess of the loan over £5,000.

When a loan is written off and a benefit arises, there is no £5,000 threshold: writing off a loan of £1 gives rise to a £1 benefit.

2.10.4 Qualifying loans

If the whole of the interest payable on a qualifying loan is eligible for tax relief, then no taxable benefit arises. If the interest is only partly eligible for tax relief, then the employee is treated as receiving earnings because the actual rate of interest is below the official rate. He is also treated as paying interest equal to those earnings. This **deemed interest paid may qualify as a business expense or as a charge in addition to any interest actually paid.**

Question	Beneficial loans

Anna, who is single, has an annual salary of £30,000, and two loans from her employer.

(a)   A season ticket loan of £2,300 at no interest

(b)   A loan, 90% of which was used to buy shares in her employee-controlled company, of £54,000 at 3% interest

The official rate of interest is to be taken as 5%.

What is Anna's tax liability for 2006/07?

Answer

	£
Salary	30,000
Season ticket loan: not over £5,000	0
Loan to buy shares £54,000 × (5 − 3 = 2%)	1,080
Earnings	31,080
Less charge on income (£54,000 × 5% × 90%)	(2,430)
	28,650
Less personal allowance	(5,035)
Taxable income	23,615
Income tax	
£2,150 × 10%	215
£21,465 × 22%	4,722
Tax liability	4,937

2.11 Other assets made available for private use

20% of the value of assets made available for private use is taxable.

When assets are made available to employees or members of their family or household, the taxable benefit is the higher of 20% of the market value when first provided as a benefit to any employee, or on the rent paid by the employer if higher. The 20% charge is time-apportioned when the asset is provided for only part of the year. The charge after any time apportionment is reduced by any contribution made by the employee.

Certain assets, such as bicycles provided for journeys to work, are exempt. These are described later in this chapter.

There is an exemption for computers made available by employers for private use prior to 6 April 2006 for the first £500 worth of benefit.

For example on 6 April 2005 Jane is provided with a new laptop costing £2,800 by her employer. The taxable benefit for 2005/06 was £60 as follows:

£2,800 × 20%	£560
Less exemption	(500)
Taxable benefit	60

The £60 taxable benefit will also be the amount taxed in 2006/07 on Jane. However, if the computer had been provided new on 6 April 2006 Jane's 2006/07 benefit would be £560.

If an asset made available is subsequently acquired by the employee, **the taxable benefit on the acquisition is the *greater* of:**

- The **current market value minus the price paid by the employee**.

- The **market value when first provided minus any amounts already taxed (ignoring contributions by the employee) minus the price paid by the employee**.

This rule prevents tax free benefits arising on rapidly depreciating items through the employee purchasing them at their low second-hand value.

There is an exception to this rule for bicycles which have previously been provided as exempt benefits. The taxable benefit on acquisition is restricted to current market value, minus the price paid by the employee. This also applies to computers which were first provided before 6 April 2006.

2.12 Example: assets made available for private use

A suit costing £400 is purchased by an employer for use by an employee on 6 April 2005. On 6 April 2006 the suit is purchased by the employee for £30, its market value then being £50.

The benefit in 2005/06 is £400 × 20%	£80

The benefit in 2006/07 is £290, being the **greater** of:

		£
(a)	Market value at acquisition by employee	50
	Less price paid	(30)
		20
(b)	Original market value	400
	Less taxed in respect of use	(80)
		320
	Less price paid	(30)
		290

Question	Bicycles

Rupert is provided with a new bicycle by his employer on 6 April 2006. The bicycle is available for private use as well as commuting to work. It cost the employer £1,500 when new. On 6 October 2006 the employer transfers ownership of the bicycle to Rupert when it is worth £800. Rupert does not pay anything for the bicycle.

What is the total taxable benefit on Rupert for 2006/07 in respect of the bicycle?

Answer

	£
Use benefit	*Exempt*
Transfer benefit (use MV at acquisition by employee only)	
MV at transfer	800

LEARNING MEDIA

2.13 Scholarships

If scholarships are given to members an employee's family, the **employee is taxable on the cost** unless the scholarship fund's or scheme's payments by reason of people's employments are not more than 25% of its total payments.

2.14 Residual charge

FAST FORWARD

There is a residual charge for other benefits, usually equal to the cost of the benefits.

We have seen above how certain specific benefits are taxed. **A 'residual charge' is made on the taxable value of other benefits. In general, the taxable value of a benefit is the cost of the benefit less any part of that cost made good by the employee to the persons providing the benefit.**

The residual charge applies to any benefit provided for an employee or a member of his family or household, by reason of the employment. There is an exception where the employer is an individual and the provision of the benefit is made in the normal course of the employer's domestic, family or personal relationships.

This rule does not apply to taxable benefits provided to excluded employees. **These employees are taxed only on the second hand value of any benefit that could be converted into money.**

3 Exempt benefits

FAST FORWARD

Some benefits are exempt from tax such as removal expenses and childcare (subject to certain limits).

Various benefits are exempt from tax. These include:

(a)   **Entertainment provided to employees by genuine third parties** (eg seats at sporting/cultural events), even if it is provided by giving the employee a voucher.

(b)   **Gifts of goods** (or vouchers exchangeable for goods) from third parties (ie not provided by the employer or a person connected to the employer) if the total cost (incl. VAT) of all gifts by the same donor to the same employee in the tax year is £250 or less. If the £250 limit is exceeded, the full amount is taxable, not just the excess.

(c)   **Non-cash awards for long service** if the period of service was at least 20 years, no similar award was made to the employee in the past 10 years and the cost is not more than £50 per year of service.

(d)   **Awards under staff suggestion schemes if**:

   (i)   There is a formal scheme, open to all employees on equal terms.

   (ii)   The suggestion is outside the scope of the employee's normal duties.

   (iii)   Either the award is not more than £25, or the award is only made after a decision is taken to implement the suggestion.

   (iv)   Awards over £25 reflect the financial importance of the suggestion to the business, and either do not exceed 50% of the expected net financial benefit during the first year of implementation or do not exceed 10% of the expected net financial benefit over a period of up to five years.

   (v)   Awards of over £25 are shared on a reasonable basis between two or more employees putting forward the same suggestion.

   If an award exceeds £5,000, the excess is always taxable.

(e)   **The first £8,000 of removal expenses if:**

    (i)   The employee does not already live within a reasonable daily travelling distance of his new place of employment, but will do so after moving.

    (ii)   The expenses are incurred or the benefits provided by the end of the tax year following the tax year of the start of employment at the new location.

(f)   The cost of running a **workplace nursery or play scheme (without limit)**. **Otherwise up to £55 a week of childcare is tax free** if the employer contracts with an approved childcare or provides childcare vouchers to pay an approved childcare. The childcare must be available to all employees and the childcare must either be registered or approved home-childcare.

(g)   **Sporting or recreational facilities available to employees generally and not to the general public**, unless they are provided on domestic premises, or they consist in an interest in or the use of any mechanically propelled vehicle or any overnight accommodation. Vouchers only exchangeable for such facilities are also exempt, but membership fees for sports clubs are taxable.

(h)   **Assets or services used in performing the duties of employment** provided any private use of the item concerned is insignificant. This exempts, for example, the benefit arising on the private use of employer-provided tools.

(i)   **Welfare counselling** and similar minor benefits if the benefit concerned is available to employees generally.

(j)   **Bicycles or cycling safety equipment provided to enable employees to get to and from work or to travel between one workplace and another**. The equipment must be available to the employer's employees generally. Also, it must be used mainly for the aforementioned journeys.

(k)   **Workplace parking**

(l)   **Up to £7,000 a year paid to an employee who is on a full-time course lasting at least a year**, with average full-time attendance of at least 20 weeks a year. If the £7,000 limit is exceeded, the whole amount is taxable.

(m)   **Work related training and related costs. This includes the costs of** training material and assets either made during training or incorporated into something so made.

(n)   **Air miles or car fuel coupons** obtained as a result of business expenditure but used for private purposes.

(o)   **The cost of work buses and minibuses or subsidies to public bus services**.

    A works bus must have a seating capacity of 12 or more and a works minibus a seating capacity of 9 or more but not more than 12 and be available generally to employees of the employer concerned. The bus or minibus must mainly be used by employees for journeys to and from work and for journeys between workplaces.

(p)   Transport/overnight costs where public transport is disrupted by industrial action, late night taxis and travel costs incurred where car sharing arrangements unavoidably breakdown.

(q)   The private use of one **mobile phone**. Top up vouchers for exempt mobile phones are also tax free. If more than one mobile phone is provided to an employee for private use only the second or subsequent phone is a taxable benefit.

(r)   **Employer provided uniforms** which employees must wear as part of their duties.

(s)   The cost of **staff parties** which are open to staff generally provided that the **cost per staff member per year (including VAT) is £150 or less**. The £150 limit may be split between several parties. If exceeded, the full amount is taxable, not just the excess over £150.

(t)   **Private medical insurance premiums paid to cover treatment when the employee is outside the UK in the performance of his duties**. Other medical insurance premiums are taxable as is the cost of medical diagnosis and treatment except for routine check ups. Eye tests and glasses for employees using VDUs are exempt.

(u)   **The first 15p per day of meal vouchers (eg luncheon vouchers).**

(v)   Cheap loans **that do not exceed £5,000** at any time in the tax year (see above).

(w)   **Job related accommodation** (see above).

(x)   **Employer contributions towards additional household costs incurred by an employee who works wholly or partly at home**. Payments up to £2 pw (£104 pa) may be made without supporting evidence. Payments in excess of that amount require supporting evidence that the payment is wholly in respect of additional household expenses.

(y)   **Meals or refreshments for cyclists** provided as part of official 'cycle to work' days.

(z)   Computers provided to employees prior to 6 April 2006 – first £500 of benefit is exempt (see above).

Where a voucher is provided for a benefit which is exempt from income tax the provision of the voucher itself is also exempt.

4 Allowable deductions

FAST FORWARD
To be deductible, expenses must be for qualifying travel or wholly, exclusively and necessarily incurred.

4.1 General principles

Certain expenditure is specifically deductible in computing net taxable earnings:

(a)   **Contributions** (within certain limits) **to registered occupational pension schemes** (see earlier in this Text).

(b)   **Subscriptions to professional bodies** on the list of bodies issued by HMRC (which includes most UK professional bodies), if relevant to the duties of the employment

(c)   Payments for certain **liabilities relating to the employment** and for insurance against them (see below)

(d)   **Payments to charity made under the payroll deduction scheme** operated by an employer

(e)   **Mileage allowance** relief (see above)

Otherwise, **allowable deductions are notoriously hard to obtain. They are limited to**:

- **Qualifying travel expenses** (see below)

- **Other expenses the employee is obliged to incur and pay as holder of the employment which are incurred wholly, exclusively and necessarily in the performance of the duties of the employment**

- **Capital allowances on plant and machinery (other than cars or other vehicles) necessarily provided for use in the performance of those duties.**

4.2 Liabilities and insurance

If a director or employee incurs a liability related to his employment or pays for insurance against such a liability, the cost is a deductible expense. If the employer pays such amounts, there is no taxable benefit.

A liability relating to employment is one which is imposed in respect of the employee's acts or omissions as employee. Thus, for example, liability for negligence would be covered. Related costs, for example the costs of legal proceedings, are included.

For insurance premiums to qualify, the insurance policy must:

(a) Cover only liabilities relating to employment, vicarious liability in respect of liabilities of another person's employment, related costs and payments to the employee's own employees in respect of their employment liabilities relating to employment and related costs, and

(b) It must not last for more than two years (although it may be renewed for up to two years at a time), and the insured person must not be not required to renew it.

4.3 Travel expenses

Tax relief is not available for an employee's normal commuting costs. This means relief is not available for any costs an employee incurs in getting from home to his normal place of work. However **employees are entitled to relief for travel expenses which basically are the full costs that they are obliged to incur and pay as holder of the employment in travelling in the performance of their duties or travelling to or from a place which they have to attend in the performance of their duties (other than a permanent workplace).**

4.4 Example: travel in the performance of duties

Judi is an accountant. She often travels to meetings at the firm's offices in the North of England returning to her office in Leeds after the meetings. Relief is available for the full cost of these journeys as the travel is undertaken in the performance of her duties.

Question
Relief for travelling costs

Zoe lives in Wycombe and normally works in Chiswick. Occasionally she visits a client in Wimbledon and travels direct from home. Distances are shown in the diagram below:

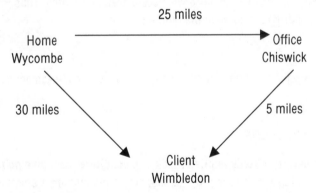

What tax relief is available for Zoe's travel costs?

Answer

Zoe is not entitled to tax relief for the costs incurred in travelling between Wycombe and Chiswick since these are normal commuting costs. However, relief is available for all costs that Zoe incurs when she travels from Wycombe to Wimbledon to visit her client.

To prevent manipulation of the basic rule normal commuting will not become a business journey just because the employee stops en-route to perform a business task (eg make a 'phone call'). Nor will relief be available if the journey is essentially the same as the employee's normal journey to work.

4.5 Example: normal commuting

Judi is based at her office in Leeds City Centre. One day she is required to attend a 9.00 am meeting with a client whose premises are around the corner from her Leeds office. Judi travels from home directly to the meeting. As the journey is substantially the same as her ordinary journey to work relief is not available.

Site based employees (eg construction workers, management consultants etc) who do not have a permanent workplace, are entitled to relief for the costs of all journeys made from home to wherever they are working. This is because these employees do not have an ordinary commuting journey or any normal commuting costs. However there is a caveat that the employee does not spend more than 24 months of continuous work at any one site.

Tax relief is available for travel, accommodation and subsistence expenses incurred by an employee who is working at a temporary workplace on a secondment expected to last up to 24 months. If a secondment is initially expected not to exceed 24 months, but it is extended, relief ceases to be due from the date the employee becomes aware of the change. When looking at how long a secondment is expected to last, HMRC will consider not only the terms of the written contract but also any verbal agreement by the employer and other factors such as whether the employee buys a house etc.

Question

Temporary workplace

Philip works for Vastbank at its Newcastle City Centre branch. Philip is sent to work full-time at another branch in Morpeth for 20 months at the end of which he will return to the Newcastle branch. Morpeth is about 20 miles north of Newcastle.

What travel costs is Philip entitled to claim as a deduction?

Answer

Although Philip is spending all of his time at the Morpeth branch it will not be treated as his normal work place because his period of attendance will be less than 24 months. Thus Philip can claim relief in full for the costs of travel from his home to the Morpeth branch.

There is also tax relief for certain travel expenses relating to overseas employment. These are dealt with later in this text.

4.6 Other expenses

The word 'exclusively' strictly implies that the expenditure must give no private benefit at all. If it does, none of it is deductible. In practice inspectors may ignore a small element of private benefit or make an apportionment between business and private use.

Whether an expense is 'necessary' is not determined by what the employer requires. The test is whether the duties of the employment could not be performed without the outlay.

- *Sanderson v Durbridge 1955*

  The cost of evening meals taken when attending late meetings was not deductible because it was not incurred in the performance of the duties.

- *Blackwell v Mills 1945*

  As a condition of his employment, an employee was required to attend evening classes. The cost of his textbooks and travel was not deductible because it was not incurred in the performance of the duties.

- *Lupton v Potts 1969*

  Examination fees incurred by a solicitor's articled clerk were not deductible because they were incurred neither wholly nor exclusively in the performance of the duties, but in furthering the clerk's ambition to become a solicitor.

- *Brown v Bullock 1961*

  The expense of joining a club that was virtually a requisite of an employment was not deductible because it would have been possible to carry on the employment without the club membership, so the expense was not necessary.

- *Elwood v Utitz 1965*

  A managing director's subscriptions to two residential London clubs were claimed by him as an expense on the grounds that they were cheaper than hotels.

  The expenditure was deductible as it was necessary in that it would be impossible for the employee to carry out his London duties without being provided with first class accommodation. The residential facilities (which were cheaper than hotel accommodation) were given to club members only.

- *Lucas v Cattell 1972*

  The cost of business telephone calls on a private telephone is deductible, but no part of the line or telephone rental charges is deductible.

- *Fitzpatrick v IRC 1994; Smith v Abbott 1994*

  Journalists cannot claim a deduction for the cost of buying newspapers which they read to keep themselves informed, since they are merely preparing themselves to perform their duties.

The cost of clothes for work is not deductible, except that for certain trades requiring protective clothing there are annual deductions on a set scale.

An employee required to work at home may be able to claim a deduction for an appropriate proportion of his or her expenditure on lighting, heating and (if a room is used exclusively for work purposes) **the council tax.** Employers can pay up to £2 per week without the need for supporting evidence of the costs incurred by the employee (see above). Payments above the £2 limit require evidence of the employee's actual costs.

5 Personal service companies

FAST FORWARD

The IR35 provisions prevent avoidance of tax by providing services through a company.

5.1 Application and outline of computation

We looked at the distinction between employment and self employment earlier in this chapter. Taxpayers normally prefer to avoid being classified as employees. Consequently, there are anti-avoidance rules which prevent workers avoiding tax and National Insurance contributions by offering their services through an intermediary, such as a personal service company. **These provisions are commonly known as the IR35 provisions**.

Broadly, the IR35 provisions provide that

(a) if an individual ('the worker') performs, or has an obligation to perform, services for 'a client', and

(b) the performance of those services is referable to arrangements involving a third party (eg the personal service company), rather than referable to a contract between the client and the worker, and

(c) if the services were to be performed by the worker under a contract between himself and the client, he would be regarded as employed by the client

then **a salary payment may be deemed to have been made to the worker at the end of the tax year**. This deemed payment is subject to PAYE and NICs.

The following steps should be followed to compute the amount of the deemed payment.

Step 1 **Take 95% of all payments and benefits received in respect of the relevant engagements by the third party**.

Step 2 **Add amounts received in respect of the relevant engagements by the worker otherwise than from the third party**, if they are not chargeable as employment income, but would have been so chargeable if the worker had been employed by the client.

Step 3 **Deduct expenses met by the third party** if those expenses would have been deductible had they been paid out of the taxable earnings of the employment by the worker. This also includes expenses paid by the worker and reimbursed by the third party. Mileage allowances up to the statutory amounts are also deductible where a vehicle is provided by the third party.

Step 4 **Deduct capital allowances on expenditure incurred by the third party** if the worker would have been able to deduct them had he incurred the expenditure and had he been employed by the client.

Step 5 **Deduct any 'registered' pension contributions and employer's NICs paid by the third party** in respect of the worker.

Step 6 **Deduct amounts received by the worker from the third party** that are chargeable as employment income but were not deducted under Step 3.

Step 7 Find the amount that together with employer's NIC (see below) on it, is equal to the amount resulting from Step 6 above. This means that you should multiply the amount in Step 6 by 12.8/112.8 and deduct this amount from the amount in Step 6.

Step 8 The result is the amount of the deemed employment income.

5.2 Example: personal service company

Alison offers technical writing services through a company. During 2006/07 the company received income of £40,000 in respect of relevant engagements performed by Alison. The company paid Alison a salary of £20,000 plus employer's NIC of £1,916. The company also pays £3,000 into an occupational pension scheme in respect of Alison. Alison incurred travelling expenses of £400 in respect of the relevant engagements.

The deemed employment income taxed on Alison is

	£
Income (£40,000 × 95%)	38,000
Less: travel	(400)
pension	(3,000)
salary	(20,000)
employer's NIC on actual salary	(1,916)
	12,684
Less: employer's NIC on deemed payment	
$\dfrac{12.8}{112.8} \times £12,684$	(1,439)
Deemed employment income	11,245

6 National insurance

6.1 Classes of National Insurance contributions

FAST FORWARD

National Insurance contributions are divided into four classes.

Four classes of national insurance contribution (NIC) exist, as set out below.

(a) **Class 1**. This is divided into:

    (i)   **Primary**, paid by employees

    (ii)   **Secondary**, **Class 1A and Class 1B** paid by employers

(b) **Class 2**. Paid by the self-employed

(c) **Class 3**. Voluntary contributions (paid to maintain rights to certain state benefits)

(d) **Class 4.** Paid by the self-employed

Exam focus point

Class 1B and Class 3 contributions are outside the scope of your syllabus.

In this section we focus on NIC for employees and their employers.

6.2 General principles

FAST FORWARD

Employees pay Class 1 NICs. Employees pay the main primary rate between the earnings threshold and upper earnings limit and the additional rate on earnings above the upper earnings limit. Employers pay Class 1 and Class 1A NICs. For employers, there is no upper earnings limit.

6.2.1 Introduction

The National Insurance Contributions Office (NICO), which is part of HMRC, examines employers' records and procedures to ensure that the correct amounts of NICs are collected.

Both employees and employers pay NICs related to the employee's earnings. NICs are not deductible from an employee's gross salary for income tax purposes. However, employers' contributions are deductible trade expenses.

6.2.2 What is 'earnings'?

'Earnings' broadly comprise gross pay, excluding benefits which cannot be turned into cash by surrender (eg holidays). It also includes mileage payments over the approved amount (see below) and readily convertible assets given to employees. No deduction is made for employee pension contributions.

An employer's contribution to a registered personal pension or a registered occupational pension is not 'earnings'. However, NICs are due on employer contributions to non-registered schemes.

In general income tax and NIC exemptions mirror one another. For example, payment of personal incidental expenses covered by the £5/£10 a night income tax de minimis exemption are excluded from NIC earnings. Relocation expenses of a type exempt from income tax are also excluded from NIC earnings but without the income tax £8,000 upper limit (although expenses exceeding £8,000 are subject to Class 1A NICs as described below). Similarly, the income tax rules for travel expenses are exactly mirrored for NIC treatment.

An expense with a business purpose is not treated as earnings. For example, if an employee is reimbursed for business travel or for staying in a hotel on the employer's business this is not normally 'earnings'. However, if an employee is reimbursed for his own home telephone charges the reimbursed cost of private calls (and all reimbursed rental) is earnings.

Where an employer reimburses an employee using his own car for business mileage, the earnings element is the excess of the mileage rate paid over HMRC's 'up to 10,000 business miles' 'approved mileage allowance payments' (AMAPs). This applies even where business mileage exceeds 10,000 pa.

In general, non cash vouchers are subject to NICs. However, the following are exempt.

- Childcare vouchers up to £55 per week

- Vouchers for the use of sports and recreational facilities (where tax exempt)

- Vouchers for meals on the employer's premises

- Other luncheon vouchers to a maximum of 15p per day

- Transport vouchers where the employee earns less than £8,500 a year

- Top up vouchers for pay as you go mobile phones where the provision of the phone itself is exempt from income tax

- Vouchers for eye tests and glasses for employees using VDUs

- Any other voucher which is exempt from income tax.

6.2.3 Rates

The rates of contribution for 2006/07, and the income bands to which they apply, are set out in the Rates and Allowances Tables in this text.

Non-contracted out **employees pay main primary contributions of 11% of earnings between the earnings threshold of £5,035 and the upper earnings limit of £33,540** or the equivalent monthly or weekly limit (see below). They also pay additional primary contributions of 1% on earnings above the upper earnings limit.

Employers pay secondary contributions of 12.8% on earnings above the earnings threshold of £5,035 or the equivalent monthly or weekly limit. There is no upper limit.

There is a lower earnings limit of £4,368 (or the equivalent monthly or weekly limit). The significance of the lower earnings limit (LEL) is that 'nil rate contributions' will be credited where the employee's earnings are between the LEL and the earnings threshold. These 'nil rate contributions' frank the employee's record and so create an entitlement to certain state benefits.

If an employee is in a contracted out occupational pension scheme, reduced contributions are payable. Employee contributions at the main rate are 9.4% of earnings between the earnings threshold and the upper earnings limit. There is also a rebate of 1.6% on earnings between the lower earnings limit and the earnings threshold. There is an additional rate of 1% on earnings above the upper earnings limit.

Employer rates are also reduced for earnings between the earnings threshold of £5,035 and the upper limit.

If an employee contracts out of the state earnings related pension scheme through a personal pension, full contributions are payable but NICO pays a proportion of these contributions to the insurance company running the personal pension scheme (pensions were covered in detail earlier in this text.)

6.2.4 Earnings period

NICs are based on earnings periods. Directors have an annual earnings period.

NICs are calculated in relation to an earnings period. This is the period to which earnings paid to an employee are deemed to relate. Where earnings are paid at regular intervals, the earnings period will generally be equated with the payment interval, for example a week or a month. An earnings period cannot usually be less than seven days long.

NIC for employees is calculated on a non-cumulative basis, so only the earnings in the earnings period are considered. The monthly limits are the annual limit divided by 12.

Question
Primary and secondary contributions

Sally works for Red plc. She is paid £2,850 per month.

Show Sally's primary contributions for 2006/07, assuming she is not contracted out, and the secondary contributions paid by Red plc.

Answer

Earnings threshold £5,035 ÷ 12 = £420
Upper earnings limit £33,540 ÷ 12 = £2,795

	£
Sally	
Primary contributions	
£(2,795 − 420) = £2,375 × 11% (main) × 12	3,135
£(2,850 − 2,795) = £55 × 1% × 12 (additional)	7
Total primary contributions	3,142
Red plc	
Secondary contributions	£
£(2,850 − 420) = £2,430 × 12.8% × 12	3,733

Special rules apply to company directors, regardless of whether they are paid at regular intervals or not. Where a person is a director at the beginning of the tax year, his earnings period is the tax year, even if he ceases to be director during the year. **The annual limits as shown in the Tax Tables apply.**

Question

Bill and Ben work for Weed Ltd. Bill is a monthly paid employee. Ben who is a director of Weed Ltd, is also paid monthly. Each is paid an annual salary of £33,000 in 2006/07 and received a bonus of £3,000 in December 2006.

Show the primary and secondary contributions due for both Bill and Ben for 2006/07.

Answer

Bill

Earnings threshold £5,035/12 = £420
Upper earnings limit £33,540/12 = £2,795
Regular monthly earnings £33,000/12 = £2,750

Primary contributions

	£
11 months	
£(2,750 − 420) = £2,330 × 11% × 11 (main only)	2,819
1 month (December)	
£(2,795 − 420) = £2,375 × 11% (main)	261
£(5,750 − 2,795) = £2,955 × 1% (additional)	30
Total primary contributions	3,110

Secondary contributions

	£
11 months	
£(2,950 − 420) = £2,330 × 12.8% × 11	3,281
1 month (December)	
£(2,750 + 3,000 − 420) = £5,330 × 12.8%	682
Total secondary contributions	3,963

Ben
Total earnings £(33,000 + 3,000) = £36,000

Primary contributions

	£
Total earnings exceed UEL	
£(33,540 − 5,035) = £28,505 × 11% (main)	3,136
£(36,000 − 33,540) = £2,460 × 1% (additional)	25
Total primary	3,161

Secondary contributions

£(36,000 − 5,035) = £30,965 × 12.8%	3,963

Because Ben is a director an annual earnings period applies. The effect of this is that increased primary contributions are due.

If a director is first appointed as a director during a tax year, the earnings period relating to his directorship is the number of tax weeks from the tax week which includes the date of the appointment to the end of the tax year. The first tax week starts on 6 April. The relevant earnings threshold is then the annual limit divided by 52 times the number of tax weeks in the earnings period, rounded up to the nearest £. The upper earnings limit is the weekly limit times the number of tax weeks in the earnings period.

Question |

Myrtle is appointed as a director of Herbs plc on 29 May 2006 (in tax week 8, ie 7 previous tax weeks in the year). She was not previously employed in the tax year 2006/07. She received a salary of £31,000 between her appointment and 5 April 2007.

What are the total primary and total secondary contributions payable in respect of Myrtle for 2006/07?

Answer

Number of tax weeks in earnings period is 52 − 7 = 45
Earnings threshold is £5,035/52 × 45 = £4,357
Upper earnings limit is £33,540 × 45/52 = £29,025

Primary contributions

	£
Total earnings exceed UEL	
£(29,025 − 4,357) = £24,668 × 11% (main)	2,713
£(31,000 − 29,025) = £1,975 × 1% (additional)	20
Total primary	2,733

Secondary contributions

£(31,000 − 4,357) = £26,643 × 12.8%	£3,410

6.3 Class 1A NIC

Employers must pay Class 1A NIC at 12.8% on most taxable benefits. However, benefits are exempt if they are:

- Within Class 1, or
- Covered by a PAYE dispensation, or
- Provided for employees earning less than £8,500 a year, or
- Included in a PAYE settlement agreement, or
- Otherwise not required to be reported on P11Ds

Childcare provision in an **employer provided nursery or playscheme is wholly exempt** from Class 1A NICs. Provision of **other childcare**, for example where an employer contracts directly for places in a commercial nursery, **is exempt up to £55 per week**.

The provision by an employer of fuel for use in an employee's own car does not lead to a Class 1A charge, instead there is a Class 1 charge (see above.)

6.3.1 Example: Class 1A NICs

An employee is provided with benefits totaling £2,755 during 2006/07. The Class 1A contributions due from the employer are (£2,755 @ 12.8%) = £353.

There is no earnings threshold when calculating Class 1A contributions.

Employee contributions are not charged on benefits.

Class 1A contributions are collected annually in arrears, and are due by 19 July following the tax year.

Chapter roundup

- General earnings are taxed in the year of receipt. Money earnings are generally received on the earlier of the time payment is made and the time entitlement to payment arises. Non-money earnings are generally received when provided.

- Employment involves a contract of service whereas self employment involves a contract for services.

- Most employees are taxed on benefits under the benefits code. 'Excluded employees' (lower paid/non-directors) are only subject to part of the provisions of the code.

- The benefit in respect of accommodation is its annual value. There is an additional benefit if the property cost over £75,000.

- Employees who have a company car are taxed on a % of the car's list price which depends on the level of the car's CO_2 emissions. The same % multiplied by £14,400 determines the benefit where private fuel is also provided. Authorised mileage allowances can be paid tax free to employees who use their own vehicle for business journeys.

- Taxable cheap loans are charged to tax on the difference between the official rate of interest and any interest paid by the employee.

- 20% of the value of assets made available for private use is taxable.

- There is a residual charge for other benefits, usually equal to the cost of the benefits.

- Some benefits are exempt from tax such as removal expenses and childcare (subject to certain limits).

- To be deductible, expenses must be for qualifying travel or wholly, exclusively and necessarily incurred.

- The IR35 provisions prevent avoidance of tax by providing services through a company.

- National Insurance contributions are divided into four classes.

- Employees pay Class 1 NICs. Employees pay the main primary rate between the earnings threshold and upper earnings limit and the additional rate on earnings above the upper earnings limit. Employers pay Class 1 and Class 1A NICs. For employers, there is no upper earnings limit.

- NICs are based on earnings periods. Directors have an annual earnings period.

Quick quiz

1   Ben is paid £14,000 per annum. For the year ended 31 December 2006 he is paid a £5,000 bonus on 1 May 2007. He was paid a similar bonus of £3,000 on 1 May 2006 based on the year ended 31 December 2005 results. How much is Ben's taxable income for 2006/07? Ben is not a director.

2   What accommodation does not give rise to a taxable benefit?

3   Josh was provided with a company car on 1 August 2006. It cost £25,000 and has a CO_2 emission of 160g/km. Josh uses the car 60% for business use as a sales representative. The company pays for Josh's private diesel for use in the car. What is Josh's benefit(s) in respect of the car?

4   When may an employee who is provided with a fuel by his employer avoid a fuel scale charge?

5   To what extent are removal expenses paid for by an employer taxable?

6   When may travel expenses be deducted from the taxable earnings of an employee?

7   Lucy is provided with a mobile phone by her employer costing £350 per annum. What is taxable on Lucy?

8   What are the IR35 provisions designed to prevent?

9   On what and by whom are Class 1A NICs paid?

Answers to quick quiz

1   £17,000 (14,000 + 3,000 bonus paid in 2006/07)

2   Job related accommodation

3   £5,779 (3,667 + 2,112)

Car : $£25,000 \times (\left[\dfrac{160-140}{5}\right] +15\% +3\%)$ (diesel car)

£25,000 × 22%

£5,500 for 12m

£5,500 × 8/12

Car: £3,667

Fuel: £14,400 × 22% × 8/12 = £2,112

4   There is no fuel scale charge if:

(a)   All the fuel provided was made available only for business travel, or

(b)   the full cost of any fuel provided for private use was completely reimbursed by the employee

5   The first £8,000 of removal expenses are exempt. Any excess is taxable.

6   An employee can deduct travel costs incurred in travelling in the performance of his duties or in travelling to a place which he has to attend in the performance of his duties (other than the normal place of work).

7   Nothing. The provision of one mobile phone for private use is an exempt benefit.

8   The provisions are designed to prevent workers avoiding tax and NIC by offering their services through an intermediary, such as a company.

9   Class 1A NICs are paid by employers on taxable benefits.

Now try the question below from the Exam Question Bank

Number	Level	Marks	Time
Q4	Introductory	15	27 mins
Q5	Introductory	15	27 mins

Employment income: additional aspects

Topic list	Syllabus reference
1 Shares and share options	A1(c)(i)
2 Tax efficient share schemes	A1(c)(i)
3 Lump sum payments on the termination of employment	A1(c)(ii)

Introduction

In the last chapter we covered the general rules for employment income, including taxable and exempt benefits.

In this chapter we look at the rules for share incentives and share options. Not only are these tax efficient means by which employees can be remunerated but they also provide a link between remuneration and the company's performance.

Finally we look at the rules for lump sums paid to employees, usually on the termination of the employment.

In the next chapter we will turn our attention to the self-employed.

Study guide

		Intellectual level
1	**Income and income tax liabilities in situations involving further overseas aspects and in relation to trusts, and the application of exemptions and reliefs**	
(c)	Income from employment:	3
(i)	Advise on the tax treatment of share option and share incentive schemes	
(ii)	Advise on the tax treatment of lump sum receipts	

Exam guide

Share incentives and share options may well feature in a question about employees. You may be required to advise the employer as to which incentive scheme would meet his needs. You need to know the different conditions for each scheme – you will not get any marks for recommending an enterprise management incentive scheme to a company whose gross assets exceed £30 million.

Lump sums are commonly paid on the termination of an employment. You may be required to discuss which elements of a termination package are tax free, and the consequences of the ongoing provision of a benefit.

> **Knowledge brought forward from earlier studies**

None of the topics in this chapter were examinable at level 2.3.

1 Shares and share options

FAST FORWARD

> Where shares or share options are provided to an employee outside the approved schemes, a tax charge may arise.

1.1 Introduction

An employer may include shares and share options as part of an incentive package offered to employees. Unless they fall within the special schemes which provide tax reliefs (see below) a tax charge may arise as described below.

1.2 Shares

The ownership of shares in an employing company may lead to a tax charge:

   (a)   **If a director or an employee is given shares, or is sold shares for less than their market value, there is a charge on the difference between the market value and the amount (if any) which the director or employee pays for the shares.**

   (b)   If, while the director or employee still has a beneficial interest in the shares, a 'chargeable event' occurs, there is a charge on the increase in the value of the interest caused by the chargeable event as specific employment income.

A chargeable event is a change of rights or restrictions attaching to either the shares in question or to other shares which leads to the value of the shares in question increasing, and which takes place while the person concerned is a director or employee (of the company or of an associated company) or within seven years of his ceasing to be one. However, where the change applies to all shares of the same class there is not in general a chargeable event.

(c)   If an employee, having obtained shares by reason of his being a director or employee, receives any special benefit because of his owning the shares, he is taxable under on the benefit as specific employment income unless:

(i)   The benefit is available to at least 90% of persons holding shares of the same class, and

(ii)   –   The majority of the shares of the same class are not held by directors or employees, or

–   The company is employee-controlled by virtue of holdings of the same class of shares.

(d)   If an employee or director receives shares which may later be forfeited, there is no income tax charge when the shares are acquired. There is an income tax charge when the risk of forfeiture is lifted or when the shares are sold, if sooner. The amount of specific employment income will be the difference between the market value of the shares less the cost of the shares.

(e)   If shares received as a result of employment are subsequently converted to shares of another class, there is an income tax charge on conversion on the difference between the market value and cost of the shares.

In the above situations when the base cost of the shares is being calculated for capital gains tax purposes (see later in this Text) any amount charged to income tax is added to the acquisition cost of the shares.

1.3 Share options

(a)   **If a director or an employee is granted an option to acquire shares (ie is given the right to buy shares at a future date at a price set now), then, in general, there is no income tax charge on the grant of the option.**

For options granted up to 1 September 2003, if the option could be exercised more than ten years after grant, there was a specific employment income charge at the time of grant. The charge was on the market value of the shares that could be acquired at the time of the grant minus the sum of what the director or employee paid for the option and what he would have to pay for the shares (taking the lowest price at which he could acquire the shares). Any amount taxable under this rule is deducted from the amount taxable on any later specific employment income charge in relation to the same option (see below).

(b)   On the exercise of the option **there is a charge as specific employment income on the market value of the shares after date of exercise minus the sum of what (if anything) was paid for the option and what was paid for the shares**. If he assigns or releases the option for money, or agrees (for money) not to exercise it or to grant someone else a right to acquire the shares, he is likewise taxable on the amount he gets minus the amount he paid for the option.

Question

Mr Wilkes was granted an option to buy 10,000 shares in his employer company in June 1993. The option could be exercised between June 1993 and June 2007. The cost of the option was £1 per share. The value of the shares was £2.50 in June 1993. The price at which the option could be exercised was £1.25.

Mr Wilkes exercised his option in August 2006, when the shares had a market value of £8.

What is the amount of specific employment income taxable in 2006/07?

Answer

Amount taxed on grant of option (could be exercised more than 10 years after grant).

	£
Market value at grant 10,000 × £2.50	25,000
Less cost of option 10,000 × £1	(10,000)
cost of exercise 10,000 × £1.25	(12,500)
Amount charged	2,500

Amount taxed on exercise

	£
Market value at exercise 10,000 × £8	80,000
Less price paid for option	(10,000)
price paid for shares	(12,500)
amount charged on grant	(2,500)
Chargeable on exercise	55,000

The total amount charged £(2,500 + 55,000) is the difference between the market value of shares at exercise and the amount payable by Mr Wilkes for the option and the shares.

If the options had been granted in, say, June 2004, there would have been no tax charge at grant and the amount taxed on exercise would have been £(80,000 − 10,000 − 12,500) = £57,500.

2 Tax efficient share schemes

2.1 Introduction

FAST FORWARD

There are a range of tax efficient HMRC approved share schemes under which an employer may be able to give employees a stake in the business.

Successive governments have recognised the need to encourage schemes that broaden share ownership among employees or reward personnel. A number of tax efficient schemes exist. These are detailed in the following sections.

Exam focus point

If you are asked to recommend an incentive scheme ensure that you select one which fits the employer's requirements.

2.2 SAYE share option schemes

A Save As You Earn (SAYE) share option scheme allows employees to save regular monthly amounts for a fixed period and use the funds to take up options to buy shares free of income tax and NIC. Alternatively they can simply take the cash saved.

An employer can set up a scheme, under which employees can choose to make regular monthly investments in special bank or building society accounts called sharesave accounts.

(a) **Employees can save a fixed monthly amount of between £5 and £250.**

(b) **The investments are made for three or five years, and a tax-free bonus is then added to the account by way of interest.** The employee may either withdraw the money or leave it for another two years. If he leaves it in the account, another tax-free bonus is added.

(c) **At the withdrawal date, the employee may take the money in cash.**

(d) **Alternatively, he may use it to buy ordinary shares in his employer company or its holding company under options granted when the employee started to save in the account.**

(e) **The price of these shares is fixed by the option** and must be at least 80% of the market value at the date the option was granted.

(f) **The only tax charge is to capital gains tax on the gain on the shares when they are finally sold.** The cost in the gain calculation is the price the employee paid for the shares.

(g) A scheme must be open to all employees and full-time directors, and on similar terms. Part-time directors may be included, but can be excluded. However, a minimum qualifying period of employment (of up to five years) may be imposed, and there may be differences based on remuneration or length of service.

(h) Anyone who has within the preceding 12 months held over 25% of the shares of a close company which is the company whose shares may be acquired under the scheme, or which controls that company either alone or as part of a consortium, must be excluded from the scheme.

(i) The costs of setting up the schemes are deductible provided they are paid within nine months of the end of the accounting period.

2.3 Company share option plans (CSOP)

There is no income tax or NIC on the grant of a Company Share Option Plan (CSOP) option. There is also no income tax or NIC on an exercise taking place between three and ten years after the grant. Only CGT will apply to the profit on disposal of the shares.

(a) **An employee can be granted options to buy shares under a CSOP. There is no income tax on the grant of an option, on the profit arising from the exercise of an option between three and ten years after the grant or on the disposal of the shares. Capital gains tax will, however, arise on the gain made when an employee eventually sells his shares. Taper relief will run from the date of exercise (ie purchase.)**

(b) **To obtain HMRC approval schemes must satisfy** the following **conditions**.

(i) The shares must be fully paid ordinary shares.

(ii) The price of the shares must not be less than their market value at the time of the grant of the option.

(iii)   Participation in the scheme must be limited to employees and full-time directors. Options must not be transferable. However, ex-employees and the personal representatives of deceased employees may exercise options; personal representatives must do so within one year after the death. The scheme need not be open to all employees and full-time directors.

(iv)   No options may be granted which take the total market value of shares for which an employee holds options above £30,000. Shares are valued as at the times when the options on them are granted.

(v)   If the issuing company has more than one class of shares, the majority of shares in the class for which the scheme operates must be held other than by:

–   Persons acquiring them through their positions as directors or employees (unless the company is an employee controlled company)

–   A holding company (unless the scheme shares are quoted)

(vi)   Anyone who has within the preceding 12 months held over 25% of the shares of a close company which is the company whose shares may be acquired under the scheme, or which controls that company either alone or as part of a consortium, must be excluded from the scheme.

(c)   The tax exemption is lost in respect of an option if it is exercised earlier than three years or later than ten years after grant. However, this three year waiting period does not need to be observed when personal representatives exercise the options of a deceased employee (but the ten year rule still applies). In addition, if the options are exercised before three years after the grant they will remain tax exempt if the exercise (and exit from the scheme) arises from the injury, disability, redundancy or retirement of the employee.

(d)   Schemes may be altered so that in the event of the company concerned being taken over, employees may exchange their existing options for equivalent options over shares in the acquiring company.

(e)   The costs of setting up the schemes are deductible provided they are paid within nine months of the end of the accounting period.

2.4 Enterprise Management Incentives (EMI)

FAST FORWARD

No income tax or NIC is chargeable on either the grant or exercise of options under the enterprise management incentive (EMI) scheme provided the exercise takes place within 10 years of the grant and the exercise price is the market value of the shares at the date of the grant.

2.4.1 Introduction

This scheme is intended to encourage experienced people to 'take the plunge' and leave established careers in large companies for riskier jobs in smaller, start-up or developing firms.

(a)   **A qualifying company can grant each of its employees options over shares worth up to £100,000 at the time of grant, subject to a maximum of £3m in total.**

(b)   **No income tax or national insurance is chargeable on either the grant or exercise of the options provided the exercise takes place within 10 years of the grant and the exercise price is the market value of the shares at the date of the grant**. If options are granted at a discount, the discount is taxed at the date of exercise.

(c)   An employing company may set a target to be achieved before an option can be exercised. The target must clearly be defined at the time the option is granted.

(d)   **When the shares are sold, the gain is subject to CGT.**

2.4.2 Qualifying company

The company, which can be quoted or unquoted, must meet certain conditions when the options are granted. In particular, **the company's gross assets must not exceed £30m. The company must not be under the control of any other company.**

The company must carry out one of a number of qualifying trades.

2.4.3 Eligible employees

Employees must be employed by the company or group for at least 25 hours a week, or, if less, for at least 75% of their working time (including self-employment). **Employees who own 30% or more of the ordinary shares in the company** (disregarding unexercised options shares) **are excluded**.

2.4.4 Qualifying shares

The share must be **fully paid up irredeemable ordinary shares**. The rules permit restrictions on sale, forfeiture conditions and performance conditions.

2.4.5 Limit

At any one time, an employee may hold EMI options over shares with a value of up to £100,000 at the date of grant. Restrictions and conditions attaching to the shares may not be taken into account when valuing shares. Where options are granted above the £100,000 limit, relief is given on options up to the limit. Once the employee has reached the limit, no more EMI options may be granted for 3 years ie the employee may not immediately top up with new options following the exercise of old options. Any options granted under a **CSOP reduce the £100,000 limit**, but savings related share options can be ignored.

2.4.6 Disqualifying events

There are a number of disqualifying events including an employee ceasing to spend at least 75% of his working time with the company. EMI relief is available up to the date of the event.

2.4.7 Capital gains tax

The shares are a 'business asset' for taper relief purposes. The taper relief period runs from the date the option is granted rather than from exercise like the other option schemes. Where a disqualifying event takes place after the shares have been acquired, business asset taper relief ceases from that time onwards.

2.4.8 Relief for costs

The costs of setting up a scheme and on-going administration are deductible in computing profits.

2.4.9 Approval

It is not necessary to submit schemes to HMRC for approval. Instead, HMRC must be notified of the grant of options within 92 days. HMRC then has 12 months to check whether the grants satisfy the EMI rules.

A company may submit details in writing to the Small Company Enterprise Centre before the options are granted. The Inspector will then confirm in writing whether he is satisfied that the company will be a qualifying company on the basis of information supplied. The details to be submitted include:

(a)   a copy of the latest accounts for the company and its subsidiaries

(b)   a company of the memorandum and articles of association and details of any proposed changes, and

(c)   details of trading and other activities carried on, or to be carried on, by the company or its subsidiaries.

Advance approval is not possible in respect of any other aspect of EMI such as whether an employee is an eligible employee.

2.5 Share Incentive Plans (SIPs)

FAST FORWARD

Employees may be given £3,000 of 'free' shares a year under the share incentive plan (SIP). In addition they can purchase up to £1,500 worth of 'partnership' shares a year and employers can provide up to £3,000 worth of matching shares. Once the shares have been held for five years there is no income tax or NIC.

(a)   **Employers can give up to £3,000 of 'free shares' a year to employees with no tax or NICs**.

(b)   Employees can purchase '**partnership shares**' at any time in the year. These shares are funded through deductions of **up to £1,500 in any tax year**.

(c)   Employers can award 'matching shares' free to employees who purchase partnership shares at a maximum ratio of 2:1.

(d)   Employers offering free shares must offer a minimum amount to each employee on 'similar terms'. Between the minimum and the maximum of £3,000, the employer can offer shares in different amounts and on different bases to different employees. This means that employers can reward either individual or team performance. Employers can set performance targets subject to the overriding requirement that a plan must not contain any features that concentrate rewards on directors and more highly paid employees.

(e)   **Free and matching shares must normally be held in a plan for at least three years. If shares are withdrawn within three years** (because the employee leaves) **there is a charge to income tax (as specific employment income) and NIC on the market value of the shares at the time of withdrawal. If shares are taken out of the plan after three years but before five years, there is charge to income tax and NIC based on the lower of the initial value of the shares** and their value at the date of withdrawal, so any increase in value is free of income tax and NIC. If one of the specified reasons applies, eg redundancy or retirement, there is no tax or NIC charge. **Once the shares have been held for five years there is no income tax or NIC**.

(f)   **Partnership shares can be taken out at any time. If the shares are held for less than three years, there is a charge to income tax and NIC on the market value at the time the shares are removed. If the shares are removed after three years but before five years, the charge to income tax and NIC is based on the lower of salary used to buy the shares and the market value at the date of removal. Once the shares have been held for five years there is no income tax or NICs**.

(g)   **Dividends of up to £1,500 on shares in the plan are tax-free provided the dividends are used to acquire additional shares in the company, which are then held in the plan for three years. These 'dividend' shares do not affect entitlement to partnership or matching shares**.

(h)   A plan may provide for free and matching shares to be forfeited if the employee leaves within three years, unless the employee leaves for specified reasons such as retirement or redundancy. All shares have to come out of a plan if an employee leaves his job.

(i)   Provided they were held in the plan for at least 3 years, there is no charge to CGT on shares taken out of a plan and sold immediately. A charge to CGT will arise on sale to the extent that the shares increase in value after they are withdrawn from the plan.

(j)   The plan must be operated through a UK resident trust. The trustees acquire the shares from the company or – if the plan incorporates partnership shares – from the employees. The existence of arrangements to enable employees to sell shares held in a new plan trust will not of itself make those shares readily convertible into cash and require employers, for example, to operate national insurance.

(k)   Stamp duty is not payable when an employee purchases shares from a SIP trust. The trust must pay stamp duty when it acquires the shares. No taxable benefit arises on an employee as a result of a SIP trust or an employer paying either stamp duty or the incidental costs of operating the plan.

(l)   A deduction in computing profits is given for:

   (i)   The costs of setting up and administering the plan.

   (ii)   The gross salary allocated by employees to buy partnership shares.

   (iii)   The costs of providing shares to the extent that the costs exceed the employees contributions.

   (iv)   The market value of free and matching shares when they are acquired by the trustees.

   (v)   Interest paid by the trustees on borrowing to acquire shares where the company meets the trustees' costs.

(m)   Shares in the plan must be fully paid irredeemable ordinary shares in a company either:

   (i)   Listed on a recognised stock exchange (or in its subsidiary), or
   (ii)   Not controlled by another company.

(n)   A plan established by a company that controls other companies, may be extended to any or all of these other companies. Such a plan is called a group plan.

(o)   A plan need not include all the components – it is possible to have a plan with only free shares.

(p)   Companies must offer all full and part-time employees the opportunity to participate in the plan. A minimum qualifying period of employment of up to 18 months my be specified. Any minimum period specified can be satisfied by working for any company within a group.

(q)   Anyone who has within the preceding 12 months held over 25% of the shares of a close company which is the company whose shares may be acquired under the scheme, or which controls that company either alone or as part of a consortium, must be excluded from the scheme.

2.6 Approved schemes summary

Scheme name	Gift/purchase/option scheme	Tax advantages	Available to?
SIP	Gift from employer and/or purchase by employee	• Favourable income tax charge if shares held ≥ 3yrs • No income tax/NIC if held ≥ 5 yrs	All employees
SAYE	Option scheme	• Tax free savings bonus • No income tax/NIC on exercise • CGT on sale • Taper relief from exercise	All employees
CSOP	Option scheme	• No income tax/NIC on exercise • CGT on sale • Taper relief from exercise	Select employees
EMI	Option scheme	• No income/NIC tax on exercise (unless granted at a discount) • CGT on sale • Taper relief from grant	Key employees

3 Lump sum payments on the termination of employment

Payments made on the termination of employment may be fully taxable, partially exempt or exempt. The first £30,000 of a genuinely *ex gratia* termination payment is normally exempt.

3.1 Payments on the termination of employment

Termination payments may be entirely exempt, partly exempt or entirely chargeable.

3.1.1 Exempt termination payments

The following payments on the termination of employment are exempt.

- Payments on account of injury, disability or accidental death

- Lump sum payments from registered pension schemes

- Legal costs recovered by the employee from the employer following legal action to recover compensation for loss of employment, where the costs are ordered by the court or (for out-of-court settlements) are paid directly to the employee's solicitor as part of the settlement.

3.1.2 Fully taxable termination payments

Payments to which the employee is contractually entitled are, in general, taxable in full as general earnings. Payments for work done (terminal bonuses), for doing extra work during a period of notice, payments in lieu of notice where stated in the original contract, or for extending a period of notice are therefore taxable in full. A payment by one employer to induce an employee to take up employment with another employer is also taxable in full.

An employee may, either on leaving an employment or at some other time, accept a limitation on his future conduct or activities in return for a payment. This is known as a restrictive covenant. **Such payments are taxable as general earnings.** However, a payment accepted in full and final settlement of any claims the employee may have against the employer is not automatically taxable under this rule.

3.1.3 Partly taxable termination payments

Other payments on termination (such as compensation for loss of office and statutory redundancy pay), which are not taxable under the general earnings rules because they are not in return for services, are nevertheless brought in as amounts which count as employment income. These are often called *ex gratia* payments. Such payments **are partly exempt: the first £30,000 is exempt; any excess is taxable as specific employment income**.

3.1.4 Benefits provided on termination

Payments and other benefits provided in connection with termination of employment (or a change in terms of employment) **are taxable in the year in which they are received**. 'Received' in this case means when it is paid or the recipient becomes entitled to it (for cash payments) or when it is used or enjoyed (non-cash benefits).

The provision of **counselling for unemployment** or to help an employee leaving to find new employment or self-employment is **not a taxable benefit**, nor is the reimbursement of the cost of such counselling taxable. Unlike statutory redundancy pay, this does not restrict the £30,000 exemption.

All payments to an employee on termination, both cash and non-cash, should be considered. Non-cash benefits are taxed by reference to their cash equivalent (using the normal benefits rules). Thus if a company car continues to be made available to an ex-employee say for a further year after redundancy he will be taxed on the same benefit value as if he had remained in employment. The normal exemptions apply, so that the continued use of one mobile telephone and work related training would be exempt.

3.1.5 Special situations

HMRC regard payments notionally made as compensation for loss of office but which are made on retirement or death (other than accidental death) as **lump sum payments under non registered pension schemes, and therefore taxable in full**. It may be possible to obtain approval for such a deemed pension scheme so as to make the whole payment tax exempt, provided that the employee is not already a member of a registered pension scheme and the payment is within certain limits. Also, payments in circumstances which amount to unfair dismissal are treated as eligible for the £30,000 exemption.

A payment to an employee as compensation for the loss of rights under a redundancy scheme has been held not to be taxable (*Mairs v Haughey 1993*). A payment to compensate for loss of rights under a share option scheme, following a management buyout of the subsidiary which the employee worked for, has also been held not to be taxable *(Wilcock v Eve 1994)*.

3.1.6 Practical issues

If the termination package is a partially exempt one and exceeds £30,000 then the £30,000 exempt limit is allocated to earlier benefits and payments. In any particular year the exemption is allocated to cash payments before non-cash benefits.

Employers have an obligation to report termination settlements which include benefits to HMRC by 6 July following the tax year end. No report is required if the package consists wholly of cash. Employers must also notify HMRC by this date of settlements which (over their lifetime) may exceed £30,000.

3.2 Example: redundancy package

Jonah is made redundant on 31 December 2006. He receives (not under a contractual obligation) the following redundancy package:

- total cash of £40,000 payable £20,000 in January 2007 and £20,000 in January 2008
- use of company car for period to 5 April 2008 (benefit value per annum £5,000)

In 2006/07 Jonah receives as redundancy:

	£
Cash	20,000
Car (£5,000 × $^3/_{12}$)	1,250
	21,250

Wholly exempt (allocate £21,250 of £30,000 exemption to cash first then benefit).

In 2007/08 Jonah receives:

	£
Cash	20,000
Car	5,000
	25,000
Exemption (remaining)	(8,750)
Taxable	16,250

£11,250 (£20,000 less £8,750) of the cash payment is taxable.

3.3 Other lump sum payments

Where lump sums are received otherwise than in connection with the termination of employment they will be taxable if they derive from the employment. Examples are:

(a) A golden hello, which is a one-off payment made to encourage someone to join a new employer. As it is effectively a reward for future services it is subject to both tax and NIC.

(b) A payment for a change in the terms of employment is also taxable.

Chapter roundup

- Where shares or share options are provided to an employee outside the approved schemes, a tax charge may arise.

- There are a range of tax efficient HMRC approved share schemes under which an employer may be able to give employees a stake in the business.

- A Save As You Earn (SAYE) share option scheme allows employees to save regular monthly amounts for a fixed period and use the funds to take up options to buy shares free of income tax and NIC. Alternatively they can simply take the cash saved.

- There is no income tax or NIC on the grant of a Company Share Option Plan (CSOP) option. There is also no income tax or NIC on an exercise taking place between three and ten years after the grant. Only CGT will apply to the profit on disposal of the shares.

- No income tax or NIC is chargeable on either the grant or exercise of options under the enterprise management incentive (EMI) scheme provided the exercise takes place within 10 years of the grant and the exercise price is the market value of the shares at the date of the grant.

- Employees may be given £3,000 of 'free' shares a year under the share incentive plan (SIP). In addition they can purchase up to £1,500 worth of 'partnership' shares a year and employers can provide up to £3,000 worth of matching shares. Once the shares have been held for five years there is no income tax or NIC.

- Payments made on the termination of employment may be fully taxable, partially exempt or exempt.

- The first £30,000 of a genuinely ex gratia termination payment is normally exempt.

Quick quiz

1   Which approved share option scheme allows employees to take a cash amount instead of exercising their options?

2   What is the maximum amount of enterprise management incentive scheme options that an employee can hold?

3   Matthew is granted EMI options in January 2005. He exercises the options in February 2007. When will taper relief run from?

4   How may 'free shares' can an employee receive under a share incentive plan?

5   How many matching shares can be given in respect of each partnership share purchased?

6   On what value is income tax charged if shares held within a share incentive plan are disposed of within three years?

7   Which termination payments are partly exempt?

8   Thomas was made redundant on 4 January 2007. His severance package was:

Statutory redundancy pay	£12,000
Golden Goodbye	£40,000

The 'Golden Goodbye' was a payment made by the company to 'soften the blow' of redundancy to Thomas. It was not paid as part of his contract of employment.

How much of the above is taxable?

Answers to quick quiz

1   SAYE share option scheme.

2   At any one time an employee may hold options over shares worth up to £100,000 at the date of grant.

3   The date of grant ie January 2005.

4   Up to £3,000 worth of free shares

5   Up to two.

6   Tax is charged on the market value of the shares on the date of withdrawal.

7   The first £30,000 of genuinely *ex gratia* termination payments ie not in return for services.

8   £22,000.

Golden Goodbye	40,000
Partial exemption (30,000 – 12,000)	(18,000)
	22,000

Statutory redundancy of £12,000 is exempt and the £30,000 exemption for *ex gratia* amounts is reduced by this amount.

Now try the question below from the Exam Question Bank

Number	Level	Marks	Time
Q6	Introductory	20	36 mins

Trade profits

Topic list	Syllabus reference
1 The badges of trade	A1(a)B3
2 The computation of trade profits	A1(a)B3, A1(d)(i)
3 Basis periods	A1(a)B3
4 Change of accounting date	A1(a)B3
5 National insurance	A6(a)E3

Introduction

In previous chapters we have looked at the income tax computation, property and investment income and employment income. We are now going to look at the taxation of unincorporated businesses. We work out a business's profit as if it were a separate entity (the separate entity concept familiar to you from basic bookkeeping) but as an unincorporated business has no legal existence apart from its proprietor, we cannot tax it separately. We have to feed its profit into the proprietor's personal tax computation.

In this chapter, we look at the computation and taxation of profits. Standard rules on the computation of profits are used instead of individual traders' accounting policies, so as to ensure fairness. We also need special rules, the basis period rules, to link the profits of periods of account to the personal computations of tax years.

Finally we see how national insurance contributions apply to the self-employed.

In the next chapters we study the allowances available for capital expenditure and then we look at losses and partnerships.

Study guide

		Intellectual level
1	**Income and income tax liabilities in situations involving further overseas aspects and in relation to trusts, and the application of exemptions and reliefs**	
(a)	The contents of the Paper F6 study guide for income tax, under headings:	2
•	B3 Income from self employment	
6	**National insurance, value added tax and tax administration:**	
(a)	The contents of the Paper F6 study guide for national insurance under headings:	2
•	E3 Class 2 and Class 4 contributions	

Exam guide

Rather than being asked to calculate taxable trading profits you are more likely to be asked about the effect on after tax income of taking on an additional contract. This will involve calculating the incremental profits, deducting tax payable, and taking any other costs into account. This will normally include VAT considerations. To be able to do this you need a full understanding of the rules for calculating taxable trade profits and allocating them to tax years.

> Knowledge brought forward from earlier studies

Most of this chapter is revision for students who have studied 2.3.

1 The badges of trade

FAST FORWARD
> The badges of trade can be used to decide whether or not a trade exists.

1.1 Introduction

Before a tax charge can be imposed it is necessary to establish the existence of a trade.

Key term

> A trade is defined in the legislation only in an unhelpful manner as including every trade, manufacture, adventure or concern in the nature of a trade. It has therefore been left to the courts to provide guidance. This guidance is often summarised in a collection of principles known as the **'badges of trade'**. These are set out below. **Profits from professions and vocations are taxed in the same way as profits from a trade.**

1.2 The subject matter

Whether a person is trading or not may sometimes be decided by examining the subject matter of the transaction. Some assets are commonly held as investments for their intrinsic value: an individual buying some shares or a painting may do so in order to enjoy the income from the shares or to enjoy the work of art. A subsequent disposal may produce a gain of a capital nature rather than a trading profit. But **where the subject matter of a transaction is such as would not be held as an investment** (for example 34,000,000 yards of aircraft linen (*Martin v Lowry 1927*) or 1,000,000 rolls of toilet paper (*Rutledge v CIR 1929*)), **it is presumed that any profit on resale is a trading profit.**

1.3 The frequency of transactions

Transactions which may, in isolation, be of a capital nature will be interpreted as trading transactions where their **frequency indicates the carrying on of a trade**. It was decided that whereas normally the purchase of a mill-owning company and the subsequent stripping of its assets might be a capital transaction, where the taxpayer was embarking on the same exercise for the fourth time he must be carrying on a trade *(Pickford v Quirke 1927)*.

1.4 The length of ownership

The courts may infer adventures in the nature of trade where items purchased are sold soon afterwards.

1.5 Supplementary work and marketing

When work is done to make an asset more marketable, or steps are taken to find purchasers, the courts will be more ready to ascribe a trading motive. When a group of accountants bought, blended and recasked a quantity of brandy they were held to be taxable on a trading profit when the brandy was later sold *(Cape Brandy Syndicate v CIR 1921)*.

1.6 A profit motive

The absence of a profit motive will not necessarily preclude a tax charge as trading income, but its presence is a strong indication that a person is trading. The purchase and resale of £20,000 worth of silver bullion by the comedian Norman Wisdom, as a hedge against devaluation, was held to be a trading transaction *(Wisdom v Chamberlain 1969)*.

1.7 The way in which the asset sold was acquired

If goods are acquired deliberately, trading may be indicated. If goods are acquired unintentionally, for example by gift or inheritance, their later sale is unlikely to be trading.

1.8 The taxpayer's intentions

Where a transaction is clearly trading on objective criteria, **the taxpayer's intentions are irrelevant**. If, however, a transaction has (objectively) a dual purpose, the taxpayer's intentions may be taken into account. An example of a transaction with a dual purpose is the acquisition of a site partly as premises from which to conduct another trade, and partly with a view to the possible development and resale of the site.

This test is not one of the traditional badges of trade, but it may be just as important.

Exam focus point

If on applying the badges of trade HMRC do not conclude that income is 'trading income' then they can potentially treat it as other income or a capital gain.

2 The computation of trade profits

FAST FORWARD

The accounts profits need to be adjusted in order to establish the taxable trade profits.

2.1 The adjustment of profits

The net profit before taxation shown in the accounts is the starting point in computing the taxable trade profits. Many adjustments may be required to calculate the taxable amount.

Here is an illustrative adjustment.

	£	£
Net profit per accounts		140,000
Add: expenditure charged in the accounts which is not deductible for tax		
purposes	50,000	
income taxable as trade profits which has not been included in the		
accounts	30,000	
		80,000
		220,000
Less: profits included in the accounts but which are not taxable as trade profits	40,000	
expenditure which is deductible for tax purposes but has not been		
charged in the accounts	20,000	
		(60,000)
Trade profits as adjusted for tax purposes		160,000

You may refer to deductible and non-deductible expenditure as allowable and disallowable expenditure respectively. The two sets of terms are interchangeable.

2.2 Accounting policies

The fundamental concept is that the profits of the business must be calculated in accordance with generally accepted accounting practice (GAAP). These profits are subject to any adjustment specifically required for income tax purposes.

2.3 Capital allowances

Under the Capital Allowances Act 2001 (CAA 2001) **capital allowances are treated as trade expenses and balancing charges are treated as trade receipts** (see later in this Text).

2.4 Non-deductible expenditure

Certain expenses are specifically disallowed by the legislation. These are covered in paragraphs 2.4.1-2.4.11. If however a deduction is specifically permitted this overrides the disallowance.

2.4.1 Capital expenditure

Income tax is a tax solely on income so capital expenditure is not deductible. This denies a deduction for depreciation or amortisation (although there are special rules for companies in relation to intangible assets – see later in this Text). **The most contentious items of expenditure will often be repairs** (revenue expenditure) **and improvements** (capital expenditure).

- The cost of restoration of an asset by, for instance, replacing a subsidiary part of the asset is revenue expenditure. Expenditure on a new factory chimney replacement was allowable since the chimney was a subsidiary part of the factory (*Samuel Jones & Co (Devondale) Ltd v CIR 1951*). However, in another case a football club demolished a spectators' stand and replaced it with a modern equivalent. This was held not to be repair, since repair is the restoration by renewal or replacement of subsidiary parts of a larger entity, and the stand formed a distinct and *separate* part of the club (*Brown v Burnley Football and Athletic Co Ltd 1980*).

- The cost of initial repairs to improve an asset recently acquired to make it fit to earn profits is disallowable capital expenditure. In *Law Shipping Co Ltd v CIR 1923* the taxpayer failed to obtain relief for expenditure on making a newly bought ship seaworthy prior to using it.

- The cost of initial repairs to remedy normal wear and tear of recently acquired assets is allowable. *Odeon Associated Theatres Ltd v Jones 1971* can be contrasted with the *Law Shipping* judgement. Odeon were allowed to charge expenditure incurred on improving the state of recently acquired cinemas.

Other examples to note include:

- A one-off payment made by a hotel owner to terminate an agreement for the management of a hotel was held to be revenue rather than capital expenditure in *Croydon Hotel & Leisure Co v Bowen 1996.* The payment did not affect the whole structure of the taxpayer's business; it merely enabled it to be run more efficiently.

- A one-off payment to remove a threat to the taxpayer's business was also held to be revenue rather than capital expenditure in *Lawson v Johnson Matthey plc 1992.*

- An initial payment for a franchise (as opposed to regular fees) is capital and not deductible.

2.4.2 Expenditure not wholly and exclusively for the purposes of the trade

Expenditure is not deductible if it is not for trade purposes (the remoteness test), or if it reflects more than one purpose (the duality test). The private proportion of payments for motoring expenses, rent, heat and light and telephone expenses of a proprietor is not deductible. If an exact apportionment is possible relief is given on the business element. Where the payments are to or on behalf of employees, the full amounts are deductible but the employees are taxed under the benefits code (see earlier in this Text).

The remoteness test is illustrated by the following cases.

- *Strong & Co of Romsey Ltd v Woodifield 1906*

    A customer injured by a falling chimney when sleeping in an inn owned by a brewery claimed compensation from the company. The compensation was not deductible: 'the loss sustained by the appellant was not really incidental to their trade as innkeepers and fell upon them in their character not of innkeepers but of householders'.

- *Bamford v ATA Advertising Ltd 1972*

    A director misappropriated £15,000. The loss was not allowable: 'the loss is not, as in the case of a dishonest shop assistant, an incident of the company's trading activities. It arises altogether outside such activities'.

- Expenditure which is wholly and exclusively to benefit the trades of several companies (for example in a group) but is not wholly and exclusively to benefit the trade of one specific company is not deductible *(Vodafone Cellular Ltd and others v Shaw 1995).*

- *McKnight (HMIT) v Sheppard (1999)* concerned expenses incurred by a stockbroker in defending allegations of infringements of Stock Exchange regulations. It was found that the expenditure was incurred to prevent the destruction of the taxpayer's business and that as the expenditure was incurred for business purposes it was deductible. It was also found that although the expenditure had the effect of preserving the taxpayer's reputation, that was not its purpose, so there was no duality of purpose.

The **duality test** is illustrated by the following cases.

- *Caillebotte v Quinn 1975*

  A self-employed carpenter spent an average of 40p per day when obliged to buy lunch away from home but just 10p when he lunched at home. He claimed the excess 30p. It was decided that the payment had a dual purpose and was not deductible: a taxpayer 'must eat to live not eat to work'.

- *Mallalieu v Drummond 1983*

  Expenditure by a lady barrister on black clothing to be worn in court (and on its cleaning and repair) was not deductible. The expenditure was for the dual purpose of enabling the barrister to be warmly and properly clad as well as meeting her professional requirements.

- *McLaren v Mumford 1996*

  A publican traded from a public house which had residential accommodation above it. He was obliged to live at the public house but he also had another house which he visited regularly. It was held that the private element of the expenditure incurred at the public house on electricity, rent, gas, etc was not incurred for the purpose of earning profits, but for serving the non-business purpose of satisfying the publican's ordinary human needs. The expenditure, therefore had a dual purpose and was disallowed.

However, the cost of overnight accommodation when on a business trip may be deductible and reasonable expenditure on an evening meal and breakfast in conjunction with such accommodation is then also deductible.

2.4.3 Impaired trade receivables (bad debts)

Under FRS 26 Financial Instruments: *measurement*, a review of all trade receivables should be carried out to assess their fair value at the balance sheet date, and any impairment debts written off. The tax treatment follows the accounting treatment so no adjustment is required for tax purposes.

Loans to employees written off are not deductible unless the business is that of making loans, or it can be shown that the writing-off of the loan was earnings paid out for the benefit of the trade.

Unpaid remuneration

If earnings for employees are charged in the accounts but are not paid within nine months of the end of the period of account, the cost is only deductible for the period of account in which the earnings are paid. When a tax computation is made within the nine month period, it is initially assumed that unpaid earnings will not be paid within that period. The computation is adjusted if they are so paid.

Earnings are treated as paid at the same time as they are treated as received for employment income purposes.

2.4.4 Entertaining and gifts

The general rule is that expenditure on entertaining and gifts is non-deductible. This applies to amounts reimbursed to employees for specific entertaining expenses and gifts, and to round sum allowances which are exclusively for meeting such expenses.

There are specific exceptions to the general rule:

- **Entertaining for and gifts to employees are normally deductible** although where gifts are made, or the entertainment is excessive, a charge to tax may arise on the employee under the benefits legislation.

- **Gifts to customers not costing more than £50 per donee per year are allowed if they carry a conspicuous advertisement for the business and are not food, drink, tobacco or vouchers exchangeable for goods.**

- Gifts to charities may also be allowed although many will fall foul of the 'wholly and exclusively' rule above. If a gift aid declaration is made in respect of a gift, tax relief will be given under the gift aid scheme, not as a trading expense.

2.4.5 Lease charges for expensive cars

Although leasing costs will normally be an allowable expense, there is a restriction for costs relating to expensive cars. **If the retail price of the car when new exceeds £12,000 the deductible part of any leasing charge is reduced by multiplying it by the fraction (£12,000 + RP)/2RP, where RP is the retail price of the car.**

Thus for a car with a retail price of £20,000 and an annual leasing charge of £5,000 the allowable deduction is £5,000 × [(12,000 + 20,000)/2 × 20,000] = £4,000, so £1,000 of the charge is added back.

This restriction does not apply to low emission cars, ie those with carbon dioxide emissions not exceeding 120 g/km and electrically propelled cars.

2.4.6 Patent royalties

Patent royalties are charges and are dealt with in the personal tax computation. They are not also deducted in computing trading profits.

2.4.7 Interest payments

Interest which is allowed as a charge on income (see earlier in this Text) is not also allowed as a trading expense.

2.4.8 National insurance contributions

No deduction is allowed for any national insurance contributions **except for employer's contributions**. For the purpose of your exam, these are Class 1 secondary contributions and Class 1A contributions (Class 1B contributions are not examinable). National insurance contributions for self employed individuals are dealt with later in this chapter.

2.4.9 Penalties and interest on tax

Penalties and interest on late paid tax are not allowed as a trading expense. Tax includes income tax, capital gains tax, VAT and stamp duty land tax.

2.4.10 Crime related payments

A payment is not deductible if making it constitutes an offence by the payer. This covers protection money paid to terrorists, bribes and similar payments made overseas which would be criminal payments if they were made in the UK. Statute also prevents any deduction for payments made in response to blackmail or extortion.

2.5 Deductible expenditure

Most expenses will be deductible under the general rule that expenses incurred wholly and exclusively for the purpose of the trade are not disallowed. Some expenses which might otherwise be disallowed under the 'wholly or exclusively' rule, or under one or other of the specific rules discussed above are, however, specifically allowed by the legislation. These are covered in paragraphs 2.5.1-2.5.12.

2.5.1 Pre-trading expenditure

Expenditure incurred before the commencement of trade is deductible, if it is incurred within seven years of the start of trade and it is of a type that would have been deductible had the trade already started. **It is treated as a trading expense incurred on the first day of trading**.

2.5.2 Incidental costs of obtaining finance

Incidental costs of obtaining loan finance, or of attempting to obtain or redeeming it, are deductible other than a discount on issue or a premium on redemption (which are really alternatives to paying interest). This deduction for incidental costs does not apply to companies because they obtain a deduction for the costs of borrowing in a different way. We will look at companies later in this Text.

2.5.3 Short leases

A trader may deduct an annual sum in respect of the amount liable to income tax on a lease premium which he paid to his landlord (see earlier in this Text). Normally, the amortisation of the lease will have been deducted in the accounts (and must be added back as capital expenditure).

2.5.4 Renewals

Where a tool is replaced or altered then the cost of the renewal or alteration may be deducted as an expense in certain instances. These are that:

- A deduction would only be prohibited because the expenditure is capital expenditure, and

- No deduction can be given under any other provisions, such as under the capital allowances legislation.

2.5.5 Restrictive covenants

When an employee leaves his employment he may accept a limitation on his future activities in return for a payment. **Provided the employee is taxed on the payment as employment income** (see earlier in his Text) **the payment is a deductible trading expense.**

2.5.6 Secondments

The **costs of seconding employees to charities or educational establishments are deductible.**

2.5.7 Contributions to agent's expenses

Many employers run payroll giving schemes for their employees. **Any payments made to the agent who administers the scheme towards running expenses are deductible.**

2.5.8 Counselling and retraining expenses

Expenditure on providing counselling and retraining for leaving employees is allowable.

2.5.9 Redundancy

Redundancy payments made when a trade ends are deductible on the earlier of the day of payment and the last day of trading. If the trade does not end, they can be deducted as soon as they are provided for, so long as the redundancy was decided on within the period of account, the provision is accurately calculated and the payments are made within nine months of the end of the period of account. **The deduction extends to additional payments of up to three times the amount of the redundancy pay on cessation of trade.**

2.5.10 Personal security expenses

If there is a particular security threat to the trader because of the nature of the trade, **expenditure on his personal security is allowable.**

2.5.11 Contributions to local enterprise organisations or urban regeneration companies

This allows a deduction for donations made to a local enterprise agency, a training and enterprise council, a Scottish local enterprise company, a business link organisation or an urban regeneration company. If any benefit is received by the trade from the donation, this must be deducted from the allowable amount.

2.5.12 Patents and trade marks

The costs of **registering patents and trade marks** are deductible for trades only (not professions or vocations).

2.6 Trading income

There are also statutory rules governing whether certain receipts are taxable or not. These are discussed in 2.6.1 to 2.6.6.

2.6.1 Capital receipts

As may be expected, capital receipts are not included in trading income. They may, of course, be taken into account in the capital allowances computation, or as a capital gain.

However, compensation received in one lump sum for the loss of income is likely to be treated as income (*Donald Fisher (Ealing) Ltd v Spencer 1989*).

In some trades, (eg petrol stations and public houses), a wholesaler may pay a lump sum to a retailer in return for the retailer only supplying that wholesaler's products for several years (an **exclusivity agreement**). If the payment must be used for a specific capital purpose, it is a capital receipt. If that is not the case, it is an income receipt. If the sum is repayable to the wholesaler but the requirement to repay is waived in tranches over the term of the agreement, each tranche is a separate income receipt when the requirement is waived.

2.6.2 Debts released

If the trader incurs a deductible expense but does not settle the amount due to the supplier, then if the creditor releases the debt other than under a statutory arrangement, the amount released must be brought into account as trading income.

2.6.3 Takeover of trade

If a trader takes over a trade from a previous owner, then if he receives any amounts from that trade which related to a period before the takeover they must be brought into account unless the previous owner has already done so.

2.6.4 Reverse premiums

If a trader receives a reverse premium in respect of a property used his trade it must be included in trading income (see earlier in this Text).

2.6.5 Insurance receipts

Insurance receipts which are revenue in nature, such as for loss of profits, are trading receipts. Otherwise the receipt must be brought in as trading income if, and to the extent that, any deduction has been claimed for the expense that the receipt is intended to cover.

2.6.6 Gifts of trading stock to educational establishments or schools

When a business makes a gift of equipment manufactured, sold or used in the course of its trade to an educational establishment or for a charitable purpose, nothing need be brought into account as a trading receipt or (if capital allowances had been obtained on the asset) as disposal proceeds, so full relief is obtained for the cost.

2.7 Excluded income

2.7.1 Income taxed in another way

Although the accounts may include other income, such as interest, such income is not trading income. It will instead be taxed under the specific rules for that type of income, such as the rules for savings income.

Certain types of income are specifically exempt from tax, and should be excluded from trade profits.

2.8 Application of general rules

These general rules can be applied to particular types of expenditure and income that you are likely to come across.

2.8.1 Appropriations

Salary or interest on capital paid to a proprietor are not deductible.

2.8.2 Subscriptions and donations

The general 'wholly and exclusively' rule determines the deductibility of expenses. Subscriptions and donations are not deductible unless the expenditure is for the benefit of the trade. The following are the main types of subscriptions and donations you may meet and their correct treatments.

(a)   Trade subscriptions (such as to a professional or trade association) are generally deductible.

(b)   Charitable donations are deductible only if they are small and to local charities. Tax relief may be available for donations under the gift aid scheme. In the latter case they are not a deductible trading expense.

(c)   Political subscriptions and donations are generally not deductible.

(d)   Where a donation represents the most effective commercial way of disposing of stock (for example, where it would not be commercially effective to sell surplus perishable food), the donation can be treated as for the benefit of the trade and the disposal proceeds taken as £Nil. In other cases, the amount credited to the accounts in respect of a donation of stock should be its market value.

2.8.3 Legal and professional charges

Legal and professional charges relating to capital or non-trading items are not deductible. These include charges incurred in acquiring new capital assets or legal rights, issuing shares, drawing up partnership agreements and litigating disputes over the terms of a partnership agreement.

Charges are deductible if they relate directly to trading. Deductible items include:

- Legal and professional charges incurred defending the taxpayer's title to fixed assets
- Charges connected with an action for breach of contract
- Expenses of the **renewal** (not the original grant) of a lease for less than 50 years
- Charges for trade debt collection
- Normal charges for preparing accounts/assisting with the self assessment of tax liabilities

Accountancy expenses arising out of an enquiry into the accounts information in a particular year's return are not allowed where the enquiry reveals discrepancies and additional liabilities for the year of enquiry, or any earlier year, which arise as a result of negligent or fraudulent conduct.

Where, however, the enquiry results in no addition to profits, or an adjustment to the profits for the year of enquiry only and that assessment does not arise as a result of negligent or fraudulent conduct, the additional accountancy expenses are allowable.

2.8.4 Goods for own use

The usual example is when a proprietor takes goods for his own use. In such circumstances the normal selling price of the goods is added to the accounting profit. In other words, the proprietor is treated for tax purposes as having made a sale to himself (*Sharkey v Wernher 1955*). This rule does not apply to supplies of services, which are treated as sold for the amount (if any) actually paid (but the cost of services to the trader or his household is not deductible).

2.8.5 Other items

Here is a list of various other items that you may meet.

Item	Treatment	Comment
Educational courses for staff	Allow	
Educational courses for proprietor	Allow	If to update existing knowledge or skills, not if to acquire new knowledge or skills
Removal expenses (to new business premises)	Allow	Only if not an expansionary move
Travelling expenses to the trader's place of business	Disallow	*Ricketts v Colquhoun 1925*: unless an itinerant trader (*Horton v Young 1971*)
Compensation for loss of office and ex gratia payments	Allow	If for benefit of trade: *Mitchell v B W Noble Ltd 1927*
Pension contributions (to schemes for employees and company directors)	Allow	Special contributions may be spread over the year of payment and future years
Parking fines	Allow	For employees using their employer's cars on business.
	Disallow	For proprietors/directors
Damages paid	Allow	If not too remote from trade: *Strong and Co v Woodifield 1906*
Preparation and restoration of waste disposal sites	Allow	Spread preparation expenditure over period of use of site. Pre-trading expenditure is treated as incurred on the first day of trading. Allow restoration expenditure in period of expenditure
Dividends on trade investments	Deduct	Taxed as savings income
Rental income from letting part of premises	Deduct	Taxed as income of a UK property business unless it is the letting of surplus business accommodation.

Exam focus point

In the exam you could be given a profit and loss account and asked to calculate 'taxable trade profits'. You must look at every expense in the accounts to decide if it is (or isn't) 'tax deductible'. This means that you must become familiar with the many expenses you may see and the correct tax treatment. Look at the above paragraphs again noting what expenses are (and are not) allowable for tax purposes. Similarly you must decide whether income included in the accounts should be included in the taxable trade profits, or whether it should be excluded.

Question
Calculation of taxable trade profits

Here is the profit and loss account of S Pring, a trader.

	£	£
Gross operating profit	30,000	
Taxed interest received	860	
		30,860
Wages and salaries	7,000	
Rent and rates	2,000	
Depreciation	1,500	
Impairment of trade receivables	150	
Entertainment expenses	750	
Patent royalties	1,200	
Bank interest	300	
Legal expenses on acquisition of new factory	250	
		(13,150)
Net profit		17,710

(a)   Salaries include £500 paid to Mrs Pring who works full time in the business.
(b)   No staff were entertained.
(c)   Taxed interest and patent royalties were received and paid net but have been shown gross.

Compute the taxable trade profits.

Answer

	£	£
Profit per accounts		17,710
Add: Depreciation	1,500	
Entertainment expenses	750	
Patent royalties paid (to treat as a charge on income)	1,200	
Legal expenses	250	
		3,700
		21,410
Less interest received (to tax as savings income)		(860)
Taxable trade profits		20,550

2.9 Rounding

Where an individual, a partnership or a single company (not a group of companies) has an annual turnover of at least £5,000,000, and prepares its accounts with figures rounded to at least the nearest £1,000, figures in computations of adjusted profits (including, for companies, non-trading profits but excluding capital gains) may generally be rounded to the nearest £1,000.

2.10 The cessation of trades

2.10.1 Post cessation receipts and expenses

Post-cessation receipts (including any releases of debts incurred by the trader) **are chargeable to income tax as miscellaneous income**.

If they are received in the tax year of cessation or the next six tax years, the trader can elect that they be treated as received on the day of cessation. The time limit for electing is the 31 January which is 22 months after the end of the tax year of receipt.

Certain post cessation expenses paid within seven years of discontinuance may be relieved against other income. The expenses must relate to costs of remedying defective work or goods, or legal expenses of or insurance against defective work claims. Relief is also available for trade receivable that subsequently prove to be impaired.

2.10.2 Valuing trading stock on cessation

When a trade ceases, the closing stock must be valued. The higher the value, the higher the profit for the final period of trading.

If the stock is sold to a UK trader who will deduct its cost in computing his taxable profits, it is valued under the following rules.

    (a)   If the seller and the buyer are unconnected, take the actual price.

    (b)   If the seller and the buyer are connected (see below), take what would have been the price in an arm's length sale.

    (c)   However, if the seller and the buyer are connected, the arm's length price exceeds both the original cost of the stock and the actual transfer price, and both the seller and the buyer make an election, then take the greater of the original cost of the stock and the transfer price. The time limit for election for unincorporated business is the 31 January which is 22 months after the end of the tax year of cessation (for companies, it is two years after the end of the accounting period of cessation).

In all cases covered above, the value used for the seller's computation of profit is also used as the buyer's cost.

Key term

> An individual is **connected** (connected person) with his spouse (or civil partner), with the relatives (brothers, sisters, ancestors and lineal descendants) of himself and his spouse (or civil partner), and with the spouses (or civil partners) of those relatives. In-laws and step family are included; uncles, aunts, nephews, nieces and cousins are not. He is also connected with his business partners (except in relation to bona fide commercial arrangements for the disposal of partnership assets), and with their spouses (or civil partners) and relatives (see diagram below).

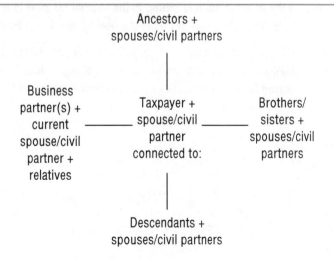

If the stock is not transferred to a UK trader who will be able to deduct its cost in computing his profits, then it is valued at its open market value as at the cessation of trade.

3 Basis periods

Basis periods are used to link periods of account to tax years.

3.1 Introduction

A tax year runs from 6 April to 5 April, but most businesses do not have periods of account ending on 5 April. **Thus there must be a link between a period of account of a business and a tax year.** The procedure is to **find a period to act as the basis period for a tax year. The profits for a basis period are taxed in the corresponding tax year**. If a basis period is not identical to a period of account, the profits of periods of account are time-apportioned as required on the assumption that profits accrue evenly over a period of account. We will apportion to the nearest month for exam purposes.

We will now look at the basis period rules that apply in the opening, continuing and closing years of a business when there is no change of accounting date. Special rules are needed when the trader changes his accounting date. We will look at these rules in the next section.

The first tax year is the year during which the trade commences. For example, if a trade commences on 1 June 2006 the first tax year is 2006/07.

3.2 The first tax year

In opening and closing years, special rules are applied so that a new trader can start to be taxed quickly, and a retiring trader need not be taxed long after his retirement.

The **basis period for the first tax year runs from the date the trade starts to the next 5 April** (or to the date of cessation if the trade does not last until the end of the tax year).

So continuing the above example a trader commencing in business on 1 June 2006 will be taxed on profits arising from 1 June 2006 to 5 April 2007 in 2006/07, their first tax year.

3.3 The second tax year

(a)   **If the accounting date falling in the second tax year is at least 12 months after the start of trading, the basis period is the 12 months to that accounting date**.

(b)   **If the accounting date falling in the second tax year is less than 12 months after the start of trading, the basis period is the first 12 months of trading**.

(c)   **If there is no accounting date falling in the second tax year**, because the first period of account is a very long one which does not end until a date in the third tax year, **the basis period for the second tax year is the year itself (from 6 April to 5 April)**.

The following flowchart may help you determine the basis period for the second tax year.

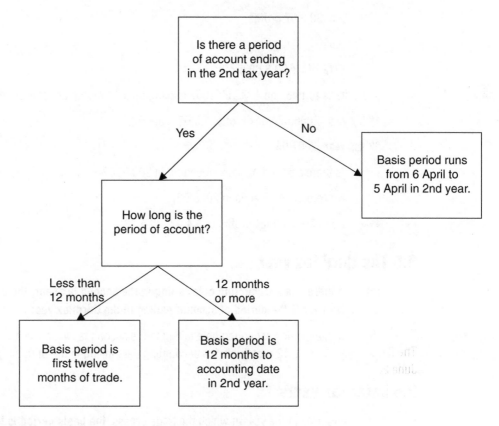

3.4 Examples: the first and second tax year

(a)   John starts to trade on 1 January 2007 making up accounts to 31 December 2007.

1st tax year: 2006/07 – tax profits 1.1.07 – 5.4.07

2nd tax year: 2007/08

- Is there a period of account ending in 2007/08?

    Yes – Y.E. 31.12.07 ends 31.12.07.

- How long is the period of account?

    12 months or more ie 12 months (exactly) to 31.12.07.

- So in 2007/08 tax profits of 12 months to 31.12.07.

(b)   Janet starts to trade on 1 January 2007 making up accounts as follows:

    6 months to 30 June 2007

    12 months to 30 June 2008.

1st tax year: 2006/07 – tax profits 1.1.07 – 5.4.07

2nd tax year: 2007/08.

- Is there a period of account ending in 2007/08?

    Yes – p.e. 30.6.07 ends 30.6.07

- How long is the period of account?

    Less than 12 months ie 6 months long.

- So in 2007/08 tax profits of first 12 months of trade ie 1.1.07 – 31.12.07, ie

  p.e. 30.6.07 profits

  plus

  6/12 of y.e 30.6.08 profits

(c) Jodie starts to trade on 1 March 2007 making up a 14 month set of accounts to 30 April 2008.

1st tax year: 2006/07 – tax profits 1.3.07 – 5.4.07

2nd tax year: 2007/08

- Is there a period of account ending in 2007/08?

  No (p.e. 30.4.08 ends in 2008/09)

- So in 2007/08 tax profits of 6.4.07 – 5.4.08.

3.5 The third tax year

(a) **If there is an accounting date falling in the second tax year, the basis period for the third tax year is the period of account ending in the third tax year.**

(b) If there is no accounting date falling in the second tax year, the basis period for the third tax year is the 12 months to the accounting date falling in the third tax year.

3.6 Later tax years

For later tax years, except the year in which the trade ceases, **the basis period is the period of account ending in the tax year**. This is known as the **current year basis of assessment**.

3.7 The final year

(a) If a trade starts and ceases in the same tax year, the basis period for that year is the whole lifespan of the trade.

(b) If the final year is the second year, the basis period runs from 6 April at the start of the second year to the date of cessation. This rule overrides the rules that normally apply for the second year.

(c) If the final year is the third year or a later year, **the basis period runs from the end of the basis period for the previous year to the date of cessation**. This rule overrides the rules that normally apply in the third and later years.

3.8 Overlap profits

Key term

Profits which have been taxed more than once are called **overlap profits**.

When a business starts, some profits may be taxed twice because the basis period for the second year includes some or all of the period of trading in the first year or because the basis period for the third year overlaps with that for the second year.

Overlap profits may be deducted on a change of accounting date (see below). Any overlap profits unrelieved when the trade ceases are deducted from the final year's taxable profits. Any deduction of overlap profits may create or increase a loss. The usual loss reliefs (covered later in this Text) are then available.

3.9 Example: accounting date in 2nd year at least 12 months

Jenny trades from 1 July 2001 to 31 December 2006, with the following results.

Period	Profit £
1.7.01 – 31.8.02	7,000
1.9.02 – 31.8.03	12,000
1.9.03 – 31.8.04	15,000
1.9.04 – 31.8.05	21,000
1.9.05 – 31.8.06	18,000
1.9.06 – 31.12.06	5,600
	78,600

The profits to be taxed in each tax year from 2001/02 to 2006/07, and the total of these taxable profits are calculated as follows.

Year	Basis period	Working	Taxable profit £
2001/02	1.7.01 – 5.4.02	£7,000 × 9/14	4,500
2002/03	1.9.01 – 31.8.02	£7,000 × 12/14	6,000
2003/04	1.9.02 – 31.8.03		12,000
2004/05	1.9.03 – 31.8.04		15,000
2005/06	1.9.04 – 31.8.05		21,000
2006/07	1.9.05 – 31.12.06	£(18,000 + 5,600 – 3,500)	20,100
			78,600

The overlap profits are those in the period 1 September 2001 to 5 April 2002, a period of seven months. They are £7,000 × 7/14 = £3,500. Overlap profits are either relieved on a change of accounting date (see below) or are deducted from the final year's taxable profit when the business ceases. In this case the overlap profits are deducted when the business ceases. Over the life of the business, the total taxable profits equal the total actual profits.

Question	Calculation of taxable profits

Peter trades from 1 September 2001 to 30 June 2006, with the following results.

Period	Profit £
1.9.01 – 30.4.02	8,000
1.5.02 – 30.4.03	15,000
1.5.03 – 30.4.04	9,000
1.5.04 – 30.4.05	10,500
1.5.05 – 30.4.06	16,000
1.5.06 – 30.6.06	950
	59,450

Show the profits to be taxed in each year from 2001/02 to 2006/07, the total of these taxable profits and the overlap profits.

Answer

Year	Basis period	Working	Taxable profits £
2001/02	1.9.01 – 5.4.02	£8,000 × 7/8	7,000
2002/03	1.9.01 – 31.8.02	£8,000 + (£15,000 × 4/12)	13,000
2003/04	1.5.02 – 30.4.03		15,000
2004/05	1.5.03 – 30.4.04		9,000
2005/06	1.5.04 – 30.4.05		10,500
2006/07	1.5.05 – 30.6.06	£(16,000 + 950 – 12,000)	4,950
			59,450

The overlap profits are the profits from 1 September 2001 to 5 April 2002 (taxed in 2001/02 and in 2002/03) and those from 1 May 2002 to 31 August 2002 (taxed in 2002/03 and 2003/04).

	£
1.9.01 – 5.4.02 £8,000 × 7/8	7,000
1.5.02 – 31.8.02 £15,000 × 4/12	5,000
Total overlap profits	12,000

3.10 Example: no accounting date in the second year

Thelma starts to trade on 1 March 2005. Her first accounts, covering the 16 months to 30 June 2006, show a profit of £36,000. The taxable profits for the first three tax years and the overlap profits are as follows.

Year	Basis period	Working	Taxable profits £
2004/05	1.3.05 – 5.4.05	£36,000 × 1/16	2,250
2005/06	6.4.05 – 5.4.06	£36,000 × 12/16	27,000
2006/07	1.7.05 – 30.6.06	£36,000 × 12/16	27,000

The overlap profits are the profits from 1 July 2005 to 5 April 2006: £36,000 × 9/16 = £20,250.

3.11 The choice of an accounting date

A new trader should consider which accounting date would be best. There are **three factors to consider** from the point of view of taxation.

- **If profits are expected to rise, a date early in the tax year** (such as 30 April) will delay the time when rising accounts profits feed through into rising taxable profits, whereas a date late in the tax year (such as 31 March) will accelerate the taxation of rising profits. This is because with an accounting date of 30 April, the taxable profits for each tax year are mainly the profits earned in the previous tax year. With an accounting date of 31 March the taxable profits are almost entirely profits earned in the current year.

- If the accounting date in the second tax year is less than 12 months after the start of trading, the taxable profits for that year will be the profits earned in the first 12 months. If the accounting date is at least 12 months from the start of trading, they will be the profits earned in the 12 months to that date. **Different profits may thus be taxed twice (the overlap profits),** and if profits are fluctuating this can make a considerable difference to the taxable profits in the first few years. **It may be many years before relief for the overlap profits is obtained.**

- **The choice of an accounting date affects the profits shown in each set of accounts,** and this may affect the taxable profits.

Question | The choice of an accounting date

Christine starts to trade on 1 December 2004. Her monthly profits are £1,000 for the first seven months, and £2,000 thereafter. Show the taxable profits for the first three tax years with each of the following accounting dates (in all cases starting with a period of account of less than 12 months).

(a) 31 March
(b) 30 April
(c) 31 December

Answer

(a) 31 March

Period of account	Working	Profits £
1.12.04 – 31.3.05	£1,000 × 4	4,000
1.4.05 – 31.3.06	£1,000 × 3 + £2,000 × 9	21,000
1.4.06 – 31.3.07	£2,000 × 12	24,000

Year	Basis period	Taxable profits £
2004/05	1.12.04 – 5.4.05	4,000
2005/06	1.4.05 – 31.3.06	21,000
2006/07	1.4.06 – 31.3.07	24,000

(b) 30 April

Period of account	Working	Profits £
1.12.04 – 30.4.05	£1,000 × 5	5,000
1.5.05 – 30.4.06	£1,000 × 2 + £2,000 ×10	22,000

Year	Basis period	Working	Taxable profits £
2004/05	1.12.04 – 5.4.05	£5,000 × 4/5	4,000
2005/06	1.12.04 – 30.11.05	£5,000 + £22,000 × 7/12	17,833
2006/07	1.5.05 – 30.4.06		22,000

(c) 31 December

Period of account	Working	Profits £
1.12.04 – 31.12.04	£1,000 × 1	1,000
1.1.05 – 31.12.05	£1,000 × 6 + £2,000 × 6	18,000
1.1.06 – 31.12.06	£2,000 × 12	24,000

Year	Basis period	Working	Taxable profits £
2004/05	1.12.04 – 5.4.05	£1,000 + £18,000 × 3/12	5,500
2005/06	1.1.05 – 31.12.05		18,000
2006/07	1.1.06 – 31.12.06		24,000

4 Change of accounting date

FAST FORWARD On a change of accounting date, special rules apply for fixing basis periods.

4.1 Introduction

A trader may change the date to which he prepares his annual accounts for a variety of reasons. For example, he may wish to move to a calendar year end or to fit in with seasonal variations of his trade. Special rules normally apply for fixing basis periods when a trader changes his accounting date.

On a change of accounting date there may be

- One set of accounts covering a period of less than twelve months, or
- One set of accounts covering a period of more than twelve months, or
- No accounts, or
- Two sets of accounts

ending in a tax year. In each case, the basis period for the year relates to the new accounting date. We will look at each of the cases in turn.

4.2 One short period of account

When a change of accounting date results in one short period of account ending in a tax year, the basis period for that year is always the 12 months to the new accounting date.

4.3 Example: change of accounting date (1)

Sue prepares accounts to 31 December each year until she changes her accounting date to 30 June by preparing accounts for the six months to 30 June 2006.

There is one short period of account ending during 2006/07. This means the basis period for 2006/07 is the twelve months to 30 June 2006.

Sue's basis period for 2005/06 was the twelve months to 31 December 2005. This means the profits of the six months to 31 December 2005 are overlap profits that have been taxed twice. These overlap profits must be added to any overlap profits that arose when the business began. The total is either relieved when the business ceases or it is relieved on a subsequent change of accounting date.

4.4 One long period of account

When a change of accounting date results in one long period of account ending in a tax year, the basis period for that year ends on the new accounting date. It begins immediately after the basis period for the previous year ends. This means the basis period will exceed 12 months.

No overlap profits arise in this situation. However, more than twelve months worth of profits are taxed in one income tax year and to compensate for this, relief is available for brought forward overlap profits. The overlap relief must reduce the number of months' worth of profits taxed in the year to no more than twelve. So, if you have a fourteen month basis period you can give relief for up to two months worth of overlap profits.

4.5 Example: change of accounting date (2)

Zoe started trading on 1 October 2003 and prepared accounts to 30 September until she changed her accounting date by preparing accounts for the fifteen months to 31 December 2006. Her results were as follows

Year to 30 September 2004	£24,000
Year to 30 September 2005	£48,000
Fifteen months to 31 December 2006	£75,000

Profits for the first three tax years of the business are:

2003/04 (1.10.03 – 5.4.04)	
6/12 × £24,000	£12,000
2004/05 (1.10.03 – 30.9.04)	£24,000
2005/06 (1.10.04 – 30.9.05)	£48,000

Overlap profits are £12,000. These arose in the six months to 5.4.04.

The change in accounting date results in one long period of account ending during 2006/07 which means the basis period for 2006/07 is the fifteen months to 31 December 2006. Three months' worth of the brought forward overlap profits can be relieved.

	£
2006/07 (1.10.05 – 31.12.06)	75,000
Less overlap profits 3/6 × £12,000	(6,000)
	69,000

The unrelieved overlap profits of £6,000 (£12,000 – £6,000) are carried forward for relief either when the business ceases or on a further change of accounting date.

4.6 No accounting date ending in the year

If a change of accounting date results in there being no period of account ending in a tax year there is a potential problem because basis periods usually end on an accounting date. To get round this problem **you must manufacture a basis period by taking the new accounting date and deducting one year. The basis period is then the twelve months to this date**.

4.7 Example: change of accounting date (3)

Anne had always prepared accounts to 31 March. She then changed her accounting date by preparing accounts for the thirteen months to 30 April 2007.

There is no period of account ending during 2006/07 so the basis period for this year is the manufactured basis period of the twelve months to 30 April 2006.

You've probably spotted that this produces an overlap with the previous basis period. The overlap period is the eleven months from 1 May 2005 to 31 March 2006. The overlap profits arising in this period are added to any other unrelieved overlap profits and are carried forward for future relief.

4.8 Two accounting dates ending in the year

When two periods of account end in a tax year, the basis period for the year ends on the new accounting date. It begins immediately following the previous basis period. This means that the basis period will exceed 12 months and overlap relief can be allowed to ensure that only twelve months worth of profits are assessed in the tax year.

4.9 Example: change of accounting date (4)

Elizabeth prepared accounts to 30 September until 2007 when she changed her accounting date by preparing accounts for the six months to 31 March 2007.

The new accounting date is 31 March 2007. This is the end of the basis period for 2006/07. The basis period for 2005/06 ended on 30 September 2005. The 2006/07 basis period is therefore the eighteen month period 1 October 2005 to 31 March 2007. Six months' worth of overlap profits can be relieved in this year.

4.10 Conditions

The above changes in basis period automatically occur if the trader changes his accounting date during the first three tax years of his business.

In other cases **the following conditions must be met before a change in basis periods can occur**:

- The trader must notify HMRC of the change by the 31 January, following the tax year in which the change is made (by 31 January 2008 for a change made during 2006/07.)

- The period of account resulting from the change must not exceed 18 months.

- In general, there must have been no previous change of accounting date in the last 5 tax years. However, a second change can be made within this period if the later change is for genuine commercial reasons. If HMRC do not respond to a notification of a change of accounting date within 60 days of receiving it, the trader can assume that they are satisfied that the reasons for making the change are genuine commercial ones.

If the above conditions are not satisfied because the first period of account ending on the new date exceeds 18 months or the change of accounting date was not notified in time, but the 'five year gap or commercial reasons' condition is satisfied, then the basis period for the year of change is the 12 months to the *old* accounting date in the year of change. The basis period for the next year is then found using rules above as if it were the year of change.

If the 'five year gap or commercial reasons' test is not satisfied, the old accounting date remains in force for tax purposes (with the profits of accounts made up to the new date being time-apportioned as necessary) until there have been five consecutive tax years which were not years of change. The sixth tax year is then treated as the year of change to the new accounting date, and the rules above apply.

5 National insurance

5.1 National insurance contributions (NICs) for the self employed

FAST FORWARD

The self employed pay Class 2 and Class 4 NICs. Class 4 NICs are based on the level of the individual's taxable profits. Class 2 NICs are paid at a weekly flat rate.

The self employed (sole traders and partners) **pay NICs in two ways. Class 2 contributions are payable at a flat rate**. It is possible, however, to be excepted from payment of Class 2 contributions (or to obtain a repayment of contributions already paid) if annual accounts profits are less than £4,465. **The Class 2 rate for 2006/07 is £2.10 a week.**

Self employed people must register with HMRC for Class 2 contributions within three months of the end of the month in which they start self employment. People who fail to register may incur a £100 penalty.

Additionally, **the self employed pay Class 4 NICs, based on the level of the individual's trade profits.**

Main rate Class 4 NICs are calculated by applying a fixed percentage (8% for 2006/07) to the individual's profits between the lower limit (£5,035 for 2006/07) and the upper limit (£33,540 for 2006/07). Additional rate contributions are 1% (for 2006/07) on profits above that limit.

5.2 Example: Class 4 contributions

If a sole trader had profits of £14,080 for 2006/07 his Class 4 NIC liability would be as follows.

	£
Profits	14,080
Less lower limit	(5,035)
	9,045

Class 4 NICs = 8% × £9,045 = £723.60 (main only)

5.3 Example: additional Class 4 contributions

If an individual's profits were £35,000, additional Class 4 NICs are due on the excess over the upper limit. Thus the amount payable in 2006/07 is as follows.

	£
Profits (upper limit)	33,540
Less lower limit	(5,035)
	28,505
Main rate Class 4 NICs 8% × £28,505	2,280
Additional rate class 4 NICs £(35,000 − 33,540) = £1,460 × 1%	15
	2,295

For Class 4 NIC purposes, profits are the trade profits for income tax purposes, less:

(a)   **Trade losses** (see later in this Text)

(b)   **Trade charges on income**

There is no deduction for personal pension premiums.

Class 4 NICs are collected by HMRC. They are paid **at the same time as the associated income tax liability**. Interest is charged on overdue contributions.

5.4 Comparison of NICs for the employees and the self employed

The NIC burden on the self employed tends to be lower than that on employees, although the relative burdens vary with the level of income. The following example shows how a comparison may be made.

5.5 Example: employed and self employed NICs

Two single people, one employed (not in a contracted out pension scheme) and one self employed, each have annual gross income of £18,000. Show their national insurance contributions for 2006/07.

Solution

	Employed £	Self-employed £
NICs		
Class 1: £(18,000 − 5,035) × 11% (main only)	1,426	
Class 2: £2.10 × 52		109
Class 4: £(18,000 − 5,035) × 8%		1,037
	1,426	1,146

The self-employed person is better off by £(1,426 − 1,146) = £280 a year.

Chapter roundup

- The badges of trade can be used to decide whether or not a trade exists.

- The accounts profits need to be adjusted in order to establish the taxable trade profits.

- Basis periods are used to link periods of account to tax years.

- In opening and closing years, special rules are applied so that a new trader can start to be taxed quickly, and a retiring trader need not be taxed long after his retirement.

- On a change of accounting date, special rules apply for fixing basis periods.

- The self employed pay Class 2 and Class 4 NICs. Class 4 NICs are based on the level of the individual's taxable profits. Class 2 NICs are paid at a weekly flat rate.

Quick quiz

1   List the six traditional badges of trade.

2   What are the remoteness test and the duality test?

3   What pre-trading expenditure is deductible?

4   In which period of account are earnings paid 12 months after the end of the period for which they are charged deductible?

5   What is the maximum allowable amount of redundancy pay on the cessation of a trade?

6   What is the basis period for the tax year in which a trade commenced?

7   On what two occasions may overlap profits potentially be relieved?

8   How are Class 4 NICs calculated?

Answers to quick quiz

1   The subject matter
      The frequency of transactions
      The length of ownership
      Supplementary work and marketing
      A profit motive
      The way in which goods were acquired

2   Expenditure is not deductible if it is not for trade purposes (the remoteness test), or if it reflects more than one purpose (the duality test)

3   Pre-trading expenditure is deductible if it is incurred within seven years of the start of the trade and is of a type that would have been deductible if the trade had already started.

4   In the period in which they are paid

5     $3 \times$ statutory amount

6   Date of commencement to 5 April in that year

7   On a change of accounting date where a basis period resulting from the change exceeds 12 months or on the cessation of a business

8   The main rate is a fixed percentage of an individual's profits between the upper limit and lower limit. The additional rate applies above the upper limit.

Now try the question below from the Exam Question Bank

Number	Level	Marks	Time
Q7	Introductory	17	31 mins

Capital allowances

Topic list	Syllabus reference
1 Capital allowances in general	A1(a)B3
2 Plant and machinery – qualifying expenditure	A1(a)B3
3 Allowances on plant and machinery	A1(a)B3
4 Short-term assets	A1(a)B3
5 Long life assets	A1(a)B3
6 Hire purchase and leasing	A1(a)B3
7 Successions	A1(a)B3
8 Industrial buildings – types	A1(a)B3
9 Allowances on industrial buildings	A1(a)B3,(d)(v)

Introduction

In the previous chapter we saw how to adjust the accounting profit to find
taxable trade profits and how to allocate those profits to tax years. The
adjustments included adding back depreciation as a disallowable expenses and
deducting capital allowances instead. In this chapter, we look at capital
allowances, starting with plant and machinery.

Our study of plant and machinery falls into three parts. Firstly, we look at what
qualifies for allowances: many business assets get no allowances at all.
Secondly, we see how to compute the allowances and lastly, we look at special
rules for assets with short and long lives, for assets which the taxpayer does
not buy outright and for transfers of whole businesses.

We then look at industrial buildings. Again, we start off by looking at what
qualifies for the allowances and then how to compute the allowances.

Study guide

		Intellectual level
1	**Income and income tax liabilities in situations involving further overseas aspects and in relation to trusts, and the application of exemptions and reliefs**	
(a)	The contents of the Paper F6 study guide for income tax, under headings:	2
•	B3 Income from self employment	
(d)	Income from self employment:	
(v)	Understand the tax consequences of the disposal of an industrial building after a period of non-industrial use	2

Exam guide

If you are asked to consider the tax costs of business strategies, whether for a sole trader or a company, you should always take capital allowances into account. This could apply when considering a particular contract, or when comparing the costs of different industrial buildings, or it could be in a buy or lease context.

Knowledge brought forward from earlier studies

This chapter is mainly revision for students who studied level 2.3, although the rules for selling an industrial building at less than cost after a period of non-industrial use are new.

1 Capital allowances in general

FAST FORWARD

Capital allowances are available on plant and machinery and industrial buildings.

Capital expenditure cannot be deducted in computing taxable trade profits, but it *may* attract capital allowances. Capital allowances are treated as a trading expense and are deducted in arriving at taxable trade profits. Balancing charges, effectively negative allowances, are added in arriving at those profits.

Capital expenditure on plant and machinery qualifies for capital allowances. Expenditure on industrial buildings may also qualify for allowances.

Both incorporated businesses and companies are entitled to capital allowances. For completeness, in this chapter we will look at the rules for companies alongside those for unincorporated businesses. We will look at companies in more detail later in this Text.

For unincorporated businesses, capital allowances are calculated for periods of account. These are simply the periods for which the trader chooses to make up accounts. For companies, capital allowances are calculated for accounting periods (see later in this Text.)

For capital allowances purposes, expenditure is generally deemed to be incurred when the obligation to pay becomes unconditional. This will often be the date of a contract, but if for example payment is due a month after delivery of a machine, it would be the date of delivery. However, amounts due more than four months after the obligation becomes unconditional are deemed to be incurred when they fall due.

2 Plant and machinery – qualifying expenditure

2.1 Introduction

Capital expenditure on plant and machinery qualifies for capital allowances if the plant or machinery is used for a qualifying activity, such as a trade. 'Plant' is not defined by the legislation, although some specific exclusions and inclusions are given. The word 'machinery' may be taken to have its normal everyday meaning.

2.2 The statutory exclusions

Statutory rules generally exclude specified items from treatment as plant, rather than include specified items as plant.

2.2.1 Buildings

Expenditure on a building and on any asset which is incorporated in a building or is of a kind normally incorporated into buildings does not qualify as expenditure on plant, but see below for exceptions.

In addition to complete buildings, **the following assets count as 'buildings', and are therefore not plant**.

- Walls, floors, ceilings, doors, gates, shutters, windows and stairs
- Mains services, and systems, of water, electricity and gas
- Waste disposal, sewerage and drainage systems
- Shafts or other structures for lifts etc.

2.2.2 Structures

Expenditure on structures and on works involving the alteration of land **does not qualify as expenditure on plant**, but see below for exceptions.

A 'structure' is a fixed structure of any kind, other than a building.

2.2.3 Exceptions

Over the years a large body of case law has been built up under which plant and machinery allowances have been given on certain types of expenditure which might be thought to be expenditure on a building or structure. Statute therefore gives a list of various assets which *may* still be plant. These are:

- Any machinery not within any other item in this list

- Electrical (including lighting), cold water, gas and sewerage systems:

    - Provided mainly to meet the particular requirements of the trade, or

    - Provided mainly to serve particular machinery or plant used for the purposes of the trade

- Space or water heating systems and powered systems of ventilation

- Manufacturing and display equipment

- Cookers, washing machines, refrigeration or cooling equipment, sanitary ware and furniture and furnishings

- Lifts etc

- Sound insulation provided mainly to meet the particular requirements of the trade

- Computer, telecommunication and surveillance systems

- Sprinkler equipment, fire alarm and burglar alarm systems

- Strong rooms in bank or building society premises, safes

- Partition walls, where movable and intended to be moved

- Decorative assets provided for the enjoyment of the public in the hotel, restaurant or similar trades, advertising hoardings

- Glasshouses which have, as an integral part of their structure, devices which control the plant growing environment automatically

- Swimming pools (including diving boards, slides) and structures for rides at amusement parks

- Caravans provided mainly for holiday lettings

- Movable buildings intended to be moved in the course of the trade

- Expenditure on altering land for the purpose only of installing machinery or plant

- Dry docks and jetties

- Pipelines, and also underground ducts or tunnels with a primary purpose of carrying utility conduits

- Silos provided for temporary storage and storage tanks, slurry pits and silage clamps

- Fish tanks, fish ponds and fixed zoo cages

- A railway or tramway

Items falling within the above list of exclusions will only qualify as plant if they fall within the meaning of plant as established by case law. This is discussed below.

2.2.4 Land

Land or an interest in land does not qualify as plant and machinery. For this purpose 'land' excludes buildings, structures and assets which are installed or fixed to land in such a way as to become part of the land for general legal purposes.

2.3 The statutory inclusions

Certain expenditure is specifically deemed to be expenditure on plant and machinery.

The following are deemed to be on plant and machinery.

- Expenditure incurred by a trader in complying with fire regulations for a building which he occupies

- Expenditure by a trader on thermal insulation of an industrial building

- Expenditure by a trader in meeting statutory safety requirements for sports ground

- Expenditure (by an individual or a partnership, not by a company) on *security assets* provided to meet a special threat to an individual's security that arises wholly or mainly due to the particular trade concerned. Cars, ships, aircraft and dwellings are specifically excluded from the definition of a security asset

On disposal, the sale proceeds for the above are deemed to be zero, so no balancing charge (see below) can arise.

Capital expenditure on computer software (both programs and data) **qualifies as expenditure on plant and machinery**:

(a)   Regardless of whether the software is supplied in a tangible form (such as a disk) or transmitted electronically, and

(b)   Regardless of whether the purchaser acquires the software or only a licence to use it.

Disposal proceeds are brought into account in the normal way, except that if the fee for the grant of a licence is taxed as income of the licensor, no disposal proceeds are taken into account in computing the licensee's capital allowances.

Where someone has incurred expenditure qualifying for capital allowances on computer software (or the right to use software), and receives a capital sum in exchange for allowing someone else to use the software, that sum is brought into account as disposal proceeds. However, the cumulative total of disposal proceeds is not allowed to exceed the original cost of the software, and any proceeds above this limit are ignored for capital allowances purposes (although they may lead to chargeable gains).

If software is expected to have a useful economic life of less than two years, its cost may be treated as revenue expenditure.

For companies the rules for computer software are overridden by the rules for intangible fixed assets unless the company elects otherwise.

2.4 Case law

FAST FORWARD

There are several cases on the definition of plant. To help you to absorb them, try to see the function/setting theme running through them.

The original case law **definition of plant** (applied in this case to a horse) is **'whatever apparatus is used by a businessman for carrying on his business: not his stock in trade which he buys or makes for sale; but all goods and chattels, fixed or movable, live or dead, which he keeps for permanent employment in the business'** *(Yarmouth v France 1887)*.

Subsequent cases have refined the original definition and have largely been concerned with the **distinction between plant actively used in the business (qualifying) and the setting in which the business is carried on (non-qualifying). This is the 'functional' test**. Some of the decisions have now been enacted as part of statute law, but they are still relevant as examples of the principles involved.

The whole cost of excavating and installing a swimming pool was allowed to the owners of a caravan park. *CIR v Barclay Curle & Co 1969* was followed: the pool performed **the function** of giving 'buoyancy and enjoyment' to the persons using the pool *(Cooke v Beach Station Caravans Ltd 1974)* (actual item now covered by statute).

A barrister succeeded in his claim for his law library: 'Plant includes a man's tools of his trade. It extends to what he uses day by day in the course of his profession. It is not confined to physical things like the dentist's chair or the architect's table' *(Munby v Furlong 1977)*.

Office partitioning was allowed. Because it was movable it was not regarded as part of the setting in which the business was carried on *(Jarrold v John Good and Sons Ltd 1963)* (actual item now covered by statute).

A ship used as a floating restaurant was regarded as a 'structure in which the business was carried on rather than apparatus employed ... ' (Buckley LJ). No capital allowances could be obtained *(Benson v Yard Arm Club 1978)*. The same decision was made in relation to a football club's spectator stand. The stand performed no function in the actual carrying out of the club's trade *(Brown v Burnley Football and Athletic Co Ltd 1980)*.

At a motorway service station, false ceilings contained conduits, ducts and lighting apparatus. **They did not qualify because they did not perform a function in the business. They were merely part of the setting in which the business was conducted** *(Hampton v Fortes Autogrill Ltd 1979)*.

Light fittings, decor and murals can be plant. A company carried on business as hoteliers and operators of licensed premises. The function of the items was the creation of an atmosphere conducive to the comfort and well being of its customers *(CIR v Scottish and Newcastle Breweries Ltd 1982)* (decorative assets used in hotels etc, now covered by statute).

On the other hand, it has been held that when an attractive floor is provided in a restaurant, the fact that the floor performs the function of making the restaurant attractive to customers is not enough to make it plant. It functions as premises, and the cost therefore does not qualify for capital allowances *(Wimpy International Ltd v Warland 1988)*.

General lighting in a department store is not plant, as it is merely setting. Special display lighting, however, can be plant *(Cole Brothers Ltd v Phillips 1982)*.

Free-standing decorative screens installed in the windows of a branch of a building society qualified as plant. Their function was not to act a part of the setting in which the society's business was carried on; it was to attract local custom, and accordingly the screens formed part of the apparatus with which the society carried on its business *(Leeds Permanent Building Society v Proctor 1982)*.

In *Bradley v London Electricity plc 1996* an electricity substation was held not to be plant because it functioned as premises in which London Electricity carried on a trading activity rather than apparatus with which the activity was carried out.

3 Allowances on plant and machinery

FAST FORWARD

> With capital allowances computations, the main thing is to get the layout right. Having done that, you will find that the figures tend to drop into place.

3.1 Pooling expenditure

Most expenditure on plant and machinery is put into a pool of expenditure on which capital allowances may be claimed. An addition increases the pool whilst a disposal decreases it.

Exceptionally the following items are not pooled.

    (a)   Cars costing more than £12,000
    (b)   Assets with private use by the proprietor
    (c)   Short life assets where an election has been made.

Each of these items is dealt with in further detail below.

3.2 Writing down allowances

FAST FORWARD

> Most expenditure on plant and machinery qualifies for a WDA at 25% every 12 months.

Key term

> A **writing down allowance (WDA)** is given on pooled expenditure **at the rate of 25% a year** (on a reducing balance basis). The WDA is calculated on the written down value (WDV) of pooled plant, after adding the current period's additions and taking out the current period's disposals.

When plant is sold, proceeds (**limited to a maximum of the original cost**) are taken out of the pool. Provided that the trade is still being carried on, the pool balance remaining is written down in the future by WDAs, even if there are no assets left.

3.3 Example: capital allowances

Elizabeth has a balance of unrelieved expenditure on her general pool of plant and machinery of £16,000 on 1.4.06. In the year to 31.3.07 she bought a car for £8,000 and she disposed of plant which originally cost £4,000 for £6,000.

Calculate the capital allowances available for the year.

	£
Pool value b/f	16,000
Addition	8,000
Less: Disposal (limited to cost)	(4,000)
	20,000
WDA @ 25%	(5,000)
TWDV c/f	15,000

WDAs are 25% × months/12:

(a) For unincorporated businesses where the period of account is longer or shorter than 12 months

(b) For companies where the accounting period is shorter than 12 months (a company's accounting period for tax purposes is never longer than 12 months), or where the trade concerned started in the accounting period and was therefore carried on for fewer than 12 months. Remember that we will be studying companies in detail later in this Text.

Expenditure on plant and machinery by a person about to begin a trade is treated as incurred on the first day of trading. Assets previously owned by a trader and then brought into the trade (at the start of trading or later) are treated as bought for their market values at the times when they are brought in.

Allowances are claimed in the tax return.

Exam focus point

Note that from a tax planning point of view any business can claim less than the full allowances. **Adjusting capital allowances may be advantageous, if, for example, a trader wants to avoid making such a large loss claim as to lose the benefit of the personal allowance** (see earlier in this Text). Higher capital allowances will then be available in later years because the WDV carried forward will be higher.

3.4 First year allowances

 FAST FORWARD

First year allowances (FYA) may be available for certain expenditure. FYAs are never pro-rated in short or long periods of account.

3.4.1 Spending by medium sized enterprises

Expenditure incurred on plant and machinery (other than leased assets, cars, sea going ships, railway assets or long life assets) by **medium sized enterprises qualifies for a first year allowance (FYA) of 40%.**

Exam focus point

The rates of FYAs will be given to you in the tax rates and allowances section of the exam paper.

Key term

> A **medium sized enterprise** is an individual, partnership or company that either satisfies at least two of the following conditions in the chargeable period/financial year in which the expenditure is incurred.
>
> (a)   **Turnover not more than £22.8 million**
> (b)   **Assets not more than £11.4 million**
> (c)   **Not more than 250 employees**
>
> or which was medium sized in the previous year. A company must not be a member of a large group when the expenditure is incurred.

3.4.2 Spending by small sized enterprises

Expenditure incurred on plant and machinery by small sized enterprises **qualifies for a FYA** in the same way as for medium sized enterprises, but a higher rate of FYA may be available. The rates are:

Before 6 April 2004 (1 April 2004 for companies)	40%
6 April 2004 to 5 April 2005 (1 April 2004 to 31 March 2005 for companies)	50%
6 April 2005 to 5 April 2006 (1 April 2005 to 31 March 2006 for companies)	40%
6 April 2006 to 5 April 2007 (1 April 2006 to 31 March 2007 for companies)	50%
6 April 2007 (1 April 2007 onwards for companies)	40%

Key term

> A **small enterprise** is an individual, partnership or company, which satisfies at least two of the following conditions in the chargeable period/financial year in which the expenditure is incurred:
>
> (a)   **Turnover not more than £5.6 million**
> (b)   **Assets not more than £2.8 million**
> (c)   **Not more than 50 employees**
>
> or which was small in the previous year. If a company is a member of a group, the group must also be small when the expenditure is incurred.

3.4.3 100% FYAs

A car registered between 17 April 2002 and 31 March 2008 qualifies for 100% FYAs for all businesses if it either:

- **emits not more than 120 gm/km CO_2; or**
- **it is electrically propelled**

In addition, the special rules for expensive cars (see below), which restrict the availability of capital allowances and the deductibility of lease rental payments, do not apply to low emission cars.

A 100% FYA is available to all businesses in respect of expenditure incurred on plant to refuel vehicles with compressed natural gas or hydrogen, between 17 April 2002 and 31 March 2008.

Equipment acquired for leasing does not normally qualify for the 100% FYA. Exceptionally, leased low emission and electric cars and natural gas/hydrogen refuelling equipment do qualify for FYAs.

Exam focus point

> In exam questions you should only treat motor cars as low emission cars if they are specifically described as such. You are not expected to know the 120g/km limit.

3.4.4 Calculation

For FYA purposes, the provisions which treat capital expenditure incurred prior to the commencement of trading as incurred on the first day of trading do not apply except insofar as they require the FYAs to be given in the first period of account (or accounting period for companies).

First year allowances are given in the place of writing down allowances. For subsequent years a WDA is given on the balance of expenditure at the normal rate. You should therefore transfer the balance of the expenditure to the pool at the end of the first period.

FYAs are given for incurring expenditure. It is irrelevant whether the basis period of expenditure is twelve months or not. FYAs are not scaled up or down by reference to the length of the period.

Question	First year allowances

Walton starts a trade on 1 March 2003, and has the following results (before capital allowances).

Period of account	Profits £
1.3.03 – 31.7.04	42,500
1.8.04 – 31.7.05	36,800
1.8.05 – 31.7.06	32,000

Plant (none of which is eligible for 100% FYAs) is bought as follows.

Date	Cost £
1.3.03	13,000
1.6.03	9,603
1.5.05	5,000
1.6.06	1,600

On 1 May 2005, plant which cost £7,000 is sold for £4,000.

Walton's business is a small enterprise for FYA purposes.

Show the taxable trade profits arising in the above periods of account.

Answer

The capital allowances are as follows.

	FYA £	Pool £	Allowances £
FYA			
1.3.03 – 31.7.04			
Additions (1.3.03 and 1.6.03)	22,603		
FYA 40%	(9,041)		9,041
		13,562	
1.8.04 – 31.7.05			
Disposals (1.5.05)		(4,000)	
		9,562	
WDA 25%		(2,391)	2,391
		7,171	
Addition (1.5.05)	5,000		
FYA 40%	(2,000)		2,000
		3,000	4,391
c/f		10,171	

	FYA £	Pool £	Allowances £
b/f		10,171	
1.8.05 – 31.7.06			
WDA 25%		(2,543)	2,543
		7,628	
Addition (1.6.06)	1,600		
FYA 50%	(800)		800
		800	
TWDV c/f		8,428	
			3,343

Note. First year allowances are not pro-rated in a long period of account.

The profits of the first three periods of account are as follows.

Period of account	Working	Profits £
1.3.03 – 31.7.04	£(42,500 – 9,041)	33,459
1.8.04 – 31.7.05	£(36,800 – 4,391)	32,409
1.8.05 – 31.7.06	£(32,000 – 3,343)	28,657

Exam focus point

> Note the tax planning opportunities available. It may be important to buy plant just before an accounting date, so that allowances become available as soon as possible. On the other hand, it may be worthwhile to claim less than the maximum allowances so as to even out the annual assessments and avoid higher rate tax.

3.5 The disposal value of assets

The most common disposal value at which assets are entered in a capital allowances computation is the sale proceeds. But there are a number of less common situations.

Where the asset is sold at below market value (or is given away) the market value is used instead of the actual sale proceeds. This general rule has two exceptions. The actual proceeds of sale are used:

(a)   Where the buyer will be able to claim capital allowances on the expenditure

(b)   Where an employee acquires an asset from his employer at undervalue (or as a gift) and so faces a charge under the employment income benefit rules

If the asset is demolished, destroyed or otherwise lost, the disposal value is taken to be the actual sale proceeds from any resulting scrap, plus any insurance or other compensation monies.

With all these rules, there is an overriding rule that the capital allowances **disposal value cannot exceed the original cost.**

When a building is sold, the vendor and purchaser can make a joint election to determine how the sale proceeds are apportioned between the building and its fixtures. There are anti-avoidance provisions that ensure capital allowances given overall on a fixture do not exceed the original cost of the fixture.

3.6 Balancing charges and allowances

Balancing charges occur when the disposal value deducted exceeds the balance remaining in the pool. The charge equals the excess and is effectively a negative capital allowance, increasing profits. Most commonly this happens when the trade ceases and the remaining assets are sold. It may also occur, however, whilst the trade is still in progress.

Balancing allowances on the capital allowance pool of expenditure arise only when the trade ceases. The balancing allowance is equal to the remaining unrelieved expenditure after deducting the disposal value of all the assets. Balancing allowances also arise on items which are not pooled (see below) whenever those items are disposed of.

3.7 Assets which are not pooled

FAST FORWARD

Private use of assets by sole traders and partners have restricted capital allowances.

A separate record of allowances and WDV must be kept for each asset which is not pooled. When it is sold a balancing allowance or charge arises.

3.7.1 Motor cars

Cars costing more than £12,000 are not pooled. The maximum WDA is £3,000 a year. The limit is £3,000 × months/12:

    (a)   For short or long periods of account of unincorporated businesses

    (b)   For short accounting periods of companies (see later in this Text)

FYAs are not available on cars (except for certain low emission or electric cars – see above).

3.7.2 Private use assets

An asset (eg a car) which is used partly for private purposes by a sole trader or a partner is not pooled. Make all calculations on the full cost but claim only the business use proportion of the allowances. An asset with some private use by an employee (not a proprietor) suffers no such restriction. The employee may be taxed under the benefits code so the business receives capital allowances on the full cost of the asset.

Question   **Capital allowances on a car**

A trader started trading on 1 July 2003, making up accounts to 31 December each year. On 1 August 2003 he bought a car for £15,500. The private use proportion is 10%. The car was sold in July 2006 for £4,000. What are the capital allowances?

Answer

	Car £	Allowances 90% £
1.7.03 – 31.12.03		
Purchase price	15,500	
WDA 25% × 6/12 of £15,500 = £1,938		
Limited to £3,000 × 6/12 = £1,500	(1,500)	1,350
	14,000	
1.1.04 – 31.12.04		
WDA 25% of £14,000 = £3,500, limited to £3,000	(3,000)	2,700
	11,000	
1.1.05 – 31.12.05		
WDA 25% of £11,000	(2,750)	2,475
	8,250	
1.1.06 – 31.12.06		
Proceeds	(4,000)	
Balancing allowance	4,250	3,825

3.7.3 Other assets

Short life assets are not pooled and long life assets are also kept in a separate pool (see below).

3.8 The cessation of a trade

When a business ceases to trade no FYAs or WDAs are given in the final period of account (unincorporated businesses) or accounting period (companies – see later in this Text). Each asset is deemed to be disposed of on the date the trade ceased (usually at the then market value). Additions in the relevant period are brought in and then the disposal proceeds (limited to cost) are deducted from the balance of qualifying expenditure. If the proceeds exceed the balance then a balancing charge arises. If the balance of qualifying expenditure exceeds the proceeds then a balancing allowance is given.

Question	Capital allowances on cessation

Bradley has been trading for many years, preparing accounts to 31 December. He ceases trading on 31 August 2006. The written down value of the general pool at 1 January 2005 was £25,260 and the written down value of the expensive motor car (40% private use by Bradley) was £21,225. Bradley's business is a small sized enterprise for FYA purposes.

Bradley made the following purchases and sales of plant and machinery in the last 20 months to 31 August 2006:

		£
7 June 2005	Bought machinery	2,025
12 May 2006	Bought machinery	1,740
31 August 2006	Sold all pool items (all less than original cost)	24,890
31 August 2006	Sold car	16,500

What is the balancing adjustment required on cessation?

Answer

	FYAs £	General pool £	Car (60%) £	Allowances £
1.1.05 – 31.12.05				
WDV b/f		25,260	21,225	
WDA @ 25%		(6,315)		6,315
WDA @ £3,000 (restricted)			(3,000)	1,800
Addition 7.6.05	2,025			
FYA @ 40%	(810)			810
		1,215		
WDV c/f		20,160	18,225	
Total allowances				8,925
1.1.06 – 31.8.06				
Addition 12.5.06		1,740		
Disposals		(24,890)	(16,500)	
No WDA in year of cessation				
		(2,990)	1,725	
Balancing charge		2,990		(2,990)
Balancing allowance			(1,725)	1,035
Total balancing charge (taxable as profits)				(1,955)

4 Short-life assets

Short life asset elections can bring forward the allowances due on an asset.

A trader can elect that specific items of plant be kept separately from the general pool. The election is irrevocable. For an unincorporated business, the time limit for electing is the 31 January which is 22 months after the end of the tax year in which the period of account of the expenditure ends. (For a company, it is two years after the end of the accounting period of the expenditure.) **Any asset subject to this election is known as a 'short-life asset', and the election is known as a 'de-pooling election'.**

Key term

> Provided that the asset is disposed of within four years of the end of the period of account or accounting period in which it was bought, it is a **short life asset** and a balancing charge or allowance is made on its disposal.

The receipt of a capital sum in return for the right to use computer software does not count as a disposal for this purpose. If the asset is not disposed of in the correct time period, its tax written down value is added to the general pool at the end of that time.

The election should be made for assets likely to be sold within four years for less than their tax written down values. It should not be made for assets likely to be sold within four years for more than their tax written down values. (These are, of course, only general guidelines based on the assumption that a trader will want to obtain allowances as quickly as possible. There may be other considerations, such as a desire to even out annual taxable profits.)

Question
Short life assets

Caithlin bought an asset on 1 May 2002 for £12,000 and elected for de-pooling. Her accounting year end is 30 April. Calculate the capital allowances due if:

(a) The asset is scrapped for £300 in August 2006.
(b) The asset is scrapped for £200 in August 2007.

Answer

(a) Year to 30.4.03	£
Cost	12,000
WDA 25%	(3,000)
	9,000
Year to 30.4.04	
WDA 25%	(2,250)
	6,750
Year to 30.4.05	
WDA 25%	(1,688)
	5,062
Year to 30.4.06	
WDA 25%	(1,266)
	3,796
Year to 30.4.07	
Disposal proceeds	(300)
Balancing allowance	3,496

(b)   If the asset is still in use at 30 April 2007, a WDA of 25% × £3,796 = £949 would be claimable in the year to 30 April 2007. The tax written down value of £3,796 – £949 = £2,847 would be added to the general pool at the beginning of the next period of account. The disposal proceeds of £200 would be deducted from the general pool in that period's capital allowances computation and no balancing allowance would arise.

Short-life asset treatment cannot be claimed for:

- Motor cars
- Plant used partly for non-trade purposes
- Plant brought into use for the trade following non-business use
- Plant received by way of gift
- Plant in respect of which a subsidy is received
- Long life assets

Where a short-life asset is disposed of within the four year period to a connected person.

(a)   The original owner receives a balancing allowance calculated as normal and the new owner receives WDAs on the cost to him, but

(b)   **If both parties so elect, the asset is treated as being sold for its tax written down value at the start of the chargeable period in which the transfer takes place, so there is no balancing charge or allowance for the vendor.**

In both situations, the acquiring party will continue to 'de-pool' the asset up to the same date as the original owner would have done.

5 Long life assets

Key term

Long life assets are assets with an expected working life of 25 years or more.

The writing down allowance available on such assets is 6% per annum on a reducing balance basis. Expenditure on such assets must be kept in a pool that is separate from the general pool.

The following are not **treated as long life assets** (and therefore (with the exception of expensive cars: see above) still qualify for writing down allowances of 25% per annum):

(a)   **Plant and machinery in dwelling houses, retail shops, showrooms, hotels and offices**
(b)   **Motor cars**
(c)   **Ships and railways assets** bought before 1 January 2011
(d)   **Second-hand machinery in respect of which the vendor obtained allowances at 25%**

The **long life asset rules do not apply to companies whose total expenditure on long life assets in a chargeable period is £100,000**, or less. If the expenditure exceeds £100,000, the whole of the expenditure qualifies for allowances at 6% per annum only. For this purpose all expenditure incurred under a contract is treated as incurred in the first chargeable period to which that contract relates.

Individuals and partnerships spending less than £100,000 a year are also excluded from the long life asset rules provided the individual, or at least half the partners, works full time in the business.

The £100,000 limit is reduced or increased proportionately in the case of a chargeable period of less or more than 12 months. In the case of groups of companies, the limit must be divided between the number of associated companies in the group (see later in this Text).

The £100,000 exclusion is not available in respect of leased assets, second-hand assets where the vendor was only able to claim allowances of 6%, or assets in which the trader has only bought a share.

6 Hire purchase and leasing

Capital allowances are available on assets acquired by hire purchase or lease.

6.1 Assets on hire purchase or long term leases

Any asset (including a car) bought on hire purchase (HP) is treated as if purchased outright for the cash price. Therefore:

(a) The buyer normally obtains **capital allowances on the cash price** when the agreement begins.

(b) He may write off the **finance charge as a trade expense** over the term of the HP contract.

Long term leases, (those with a term of 5 or more years), are treated in the same way as HP transactions.

6.2 Assets on long term leases

Under a long term lease, the lessee merely hires the asset over a period. The hire charge can normally be deducted in computing trade profits. If an expensive car (one costing over £12,000) is leased, the maximum allowable deduction from trading profits for lease rentals is limited as described earlier in this Text.

A long term lessor of plant normally obtains the benefit of capital allowances although there are anti-avoidance provisions which deny or restrict capital allowances on certain finance leases. Leasing is thus an activity which attracts tax allowances and which can be used to defer tax liabilities where the capital allowances given exceed the rental income. For individuals, any losses arising from leasing are available for offset against other income only if the individual devotes substantially all of his time to the conduct of a leasing business.

7 Successions

Balancing adjustments are calculated when a business ceases. If the business is transferred to a connected person, the written down value can be transferred instead.

Balancing adjustments arise on the cessation of a business. No writing down allowances are given, but the final proceeds (limited to cost) on sales of plant are compared with the tax WDV to calculate balancing allowances or charges.

Balancing charges may be avoided where the trade passes from one connected person to another. If a succession occurs both parties must elect if the avoidance of the balancing adjustments is required. **An election will result in the plant being transferred at its tax written down value for capital allowances purposes**. The predecessor can write down the plant for the period prior to cessation and the successor can write it down from the date of commencement. The election must be made within two years of the date of the succession.

If no election is made on a transfer of business to a connected person, assets are deemed to be sold at their market values.

As we saw earlier, an individual is connected with his spouse, his, or his spouse's brothers, sisters, ancestors and lineal descendants, with their spouses, with business partners and their spouses and relatives, and with a company he controls. 'Spouses' includes civil partners.

Where a person succeeds to a business under a will or on intestacy, then even if he was not connected with the deceased he may elect to take over the assets at the lower of their market value and their tax written down value.

For both connected persons transfers and transfers on death, where the elections are made, the limit on proceeds to be brought into account on a later sale of an asset is the original cost of the asset, not the deemed transfer price.

8 Industrial buildings – types

Industrial buildings allowances equal to the fall in value of the building whilst it was being used industrially are available to the trader.

8.1 Introduction

A special type of capital allowance (an **industrial buildings allowance** or IBA) is available in respect of **expenditure on industrial buildings**.

The allowance is available to:

- Traders
- Landlords who let qualifying buildings to traders.

Traders can choose whether to segregate expenditure on long life assets in buildings and claim plant and machinery allowances (see above) or whether to claim industrial buildings allowances on the expenditure.

Key term

> **Industrial buildings** include:
>
> (a) All factories and ancillary premises used in:
>
>   (i)   A manufacturing business
>   (ii)   A trade in which goods and materials are subject to any process
>   (iii)   A trade in which goods or raw materials are stored
>
> (b) Staff welfare buildings (such as workplace nurseries and canteens, but not directors' restaurants) where the trade is qualifying
>
> (c) Sports pavilions in any trade
>
> (d) Buildings in use for a transport undertaking, agricultural contracting, mining or fishing
>
> (e) Roads operated under highway concessions. The operation of such roads is treated as a trade for capital allowances purposes. The operator is treated as occupying the roads.

The key term in (a) (ii) above is 'the subjection of goods to any process'.

- The unpacking, repacking and relabelling of goods in a wholesale cash and carry supermarket did not amount to a 'process' but was a mere preliminary to sale (*Bestway Holdings Ltd v Luff 1998*).

- The mechanical processing of cheques and other banking documents was a process but pieces of paper carrying information were not 'goods' and thus the building housing the machinery did not qualify (*Girobank plc v Clarke 1998*).

Estate roads on industrial estates qualify, provided that the estate buildings are used wholly or mainly for a qualifying purpose.

Dwelling houses, retail shops, showrooms and offices are not industrial buildings (although see below for exception.)

Drawing offices (ie those used for technical product and manufacturing planning) which serve an industrial building are regarded as industrial buildings themselves (*CIR v Lambhill Ironworks Ltd 1950*).

Warehouses used for storage often cause problems in practice. A warehouse used for storage which is merely a transitory and necessary incident of the conduct of the business is not an industrial building. Storage is only a qualifying purpose if it is an end in itself.

Any building is an industrial building if it is constructed for the welfare of employees of a trader whose trade is a qualifying one (that is, the premises in which the trade is carried on are industrial buildings). Sports pavilions provided for the welfare of employees qualify as industrial buildings. In this case, it does not matter whether the taxpayer is carrying on a trade in a qualifying building or not. Thus a retailer's sports pavilion would qualify for IBAs.

8.2 Hotels

Allowances on hotels are given as though they were industrial buildings.

Key term

> For a building to qualify as a '**hotel**' for industrial buildings allowance purposes:
>
> (a)   It must have at least ten letting bedrooms
>
> (b)   It must have letting bedrooms as the whole or main part of the sleeping accommodation
>
> (c)   It must offer ancillary services including at least:
>
> > (i)   Breakfast
> > (ii)   Evening meals
> > (iii)   The cleaning of rooms
> > (iv)   The making of beds
>
> (d)   It must be open for at least four months during the April to October season.

8.3 Eligible expenditure

Capital allowances are computed on the amount of eligible expenditure incurred on qualifying buildings. The eligible expenditure is:

- The original cost of a building if built by the trader, or
- The purchase price if the building was acquired from a person trading as a builder.

If the building was acquired other than from a person trading as a builder, the eligible expenditure is the lower of the purchase price and the original cost incurred by the person incurring the construction expenditure.

If a building is sold more than once before being brought into use, the last buyer before the building is brought into use obtains the allowances. If, in such cases, the building was first sold by someone trading as a builder, the eligible expenditure is the lower of the price paid by the first buyer and the price paid by the last buyer.

In all cases where a building is sold before use and artificial arrangements have increased the purchase price, it is reduced to what it would have been without those arrangements.

Where part of a building qualifies as an industrial building and part does not, the whole cost qualifies for IBAs, provided that the cost of the non-qualifying part is not more than 25% of the total expenditure. If the non-qualifying part of the building does cost more than 25% of the total, its cost must be excluded from the capital allowances computation.

Difficulties arise where non-qualifying buildings (particularly offices and administration blocks) are joined to manufacturing areas. In *Abbott Laboratories Ltd v Carmody 1968* a covered walkway linking manufacturing and administrative areas was not regarded as creating a single building. The administrative area was treated as a separate, non-qualifying building.

The cost of land is disallowed but expenditure incurred in preparing land for building does qualify. The cost of items which would not be included in a normal commercial lease (such as rental guarantees) also does not qualify.

Professional fees, for example architects' fees, incurred in connection with the construction of an industrial building qualify. The cost of repairs to industrial buildings also qualifies, provided that the expenditure is not deductible as a trading expense.

9 Allowances on industrial buildings

FAST FORWARD

An allowance, normally at the rate of 4% per annum, is given if a building is in industrial use on the last day of the period of account concerned. If the building is in non industrial use a notional allowance may be given.

9.1 Writing down allowances

A writing down allowance (WDA) is given to the person holding the 'relevant interest'. Broadly, the relevant interest is the interest of the first acquirer of the industrial building and may be a freehold or leasehold interest.

Where a long lease (more than 50 years) has been granted on an industrial building, the grant may be treated as a sale so that allowances may be claimed by the lessee rather than the lessor. A claim must be made by the lessor and lessee jointly, within two years of the start of the lease. The election allows allowances to be claimed on industrial buildings where the lessor is not subject to tax (as with local authorities).

The WDA is given for a period provided that the industrial building was in use as such on the last day of the period concerned.

If the building was not in use as an industrial building at the end of the relevant period it may have been:

- **Unused** for any purpose, or
- **Used for a non-industrial purpose.**

The distinction is important in ascertaining whether WDAs are due to the taxpayer. **If any disuse is temporary and previously the building had been in industrial use, WDAs may be claimed in exactly the same way as if the building were in industrial use.** The legislation does not define 'temporary' but in practice, any subsequent qualifying use of the building will usually enable the period of disuse to be regarded as temporary.

Non-industrial use has different consequences. If this occurs a notional WDA is deducted from the balance of unrelieved expenditure but no WDA may be claimed by the taxpayer.

The WDA is 4% of the eligible expenditure incurred by the taxpayer.

The allowance is calculated on a straight line basis (in contrast to WDAs on plant and machinery which are calculated on the reducing balance), starting when the building is brought into use.

The WDA is 4% × months/12 if the period concerned is not 12 months long.

Buildings always have a **separate computation for each building**. They are never pooled.

9.2 Balancing adjustments on sale

9.2.1 The tax life

The 'tax life' of an industrial building is 25 years after it is first used. Balancing adjustments apply only if a building is sold within its tax life.

On a sale between connected persons, the parties may jointly elect that the transfer price for IBAs purposes should be the lower of the market value and the residue of unallowed expenditure before the sale. This avoids a balancing charge unless there has been non-industrial use.

9.2.2 Sales without non-industrial use

The seller's calculation is quite straightforward providing the building has not been put to non-industrial use at any time during his ownership. It takes the following form.

	£
Cost	X
Less allowances previously given	(X)
Residue (ie WDV) before sale	X
Less proceeds (limited to cost)	(X)
Balancing (charge)/allowance	(X)

The buyer obtains annual straight line WDAs for the remainder of the building's tax life. This life is calculated to the nearest month. The allowances are granted on the residue after sale which is computed thus.

	£
Residue before sale	X
Plus balancing charge or less balancing allowance	X
Residue after sale	X

This means that the second owner will write off the lower of his cost or the original cost.

Question   Calculation of IBAs

Frankie, who started to trade in 2001 preparing accounts to 31 December, bought an industrial building for £100,000 (excluding land) on 1 October 2002. He brought it into use as a factory immediately. On 1 September 2006 he sells it for £120,000 to Holly, whose accounting date is 30 September and who brought the building into industrial use immediately. Show the IBAs available to Frankie and to Holly.

Answer

Frankie	£
Cost 1.10.02	100,000
Y/e 31.12.02 to y/e 31.12.05 WDA 4 × 4%	(16,000)
Residue before sale	84,000
Y/e 31.12.06 Proceeds (limited to cost)	(100,000)
Balancing charge	(16,000)
Holly	
Residue before sale	84,000
Add: balancing charge	16,000
Residue after sale	100,000

The tax life of the building ends on 1.10.02 + 25 years = 30.9.2027

The date of Holly's purchase is 1.9.06. The unexpired life is therefore 21 years 1 month

	£
Y/e 30.9.06 WDA £100,000/21.083333	4,743
Next 20 accounting periods at £4,743 a year	94,860
Y/e 30.9.27 (balance)	397
	100,000

HMRC allow IBAs equal to the fall in value of a building over the trader's use of that building. As a general rule if an industrial building is sold for more than its original cost a balancing charge equal to the allowances given to date will arise. This is because there was no fall in value so no allowances are actually due.

If it is sold for less than original cost we could calculate the fall in value of the building and that would equal the allowances available for this building. If we compare this to the allowances already given, the difference would be the balancing adjustment due on the sale.

In the above question if Frankie sold the building Holly for £90,000:

	£
Fall in value (£100,000 – £90,000) = allowances due	10,000
Less: allowances already given to Frankie	(16,000)
Balancing adjustment = Balancing charge	(6,000)

Over the use of the building by Frankie £16,000 of IBAs were claimed. On the sale of the building the fall in value is calculated as £10,000. Thus Frankie should only have received £10,000 of allowances not £16,000. So £6,000 is paid back as a balancing charge.

Businesses are denied a balancing allowance where disposal proceeds are less than they would have been as a result of a tax avoidance scheme.

9.3 Sales after non-industrial use

If at the end of a period, an industrial building was in non-industrial use, then the owner will not have been able to claim WDAs, but the building will have been written down by notional WDAs.

9.3.1 Sales for more than cost

If, following a period of non-industrial use, an industrial building is sold for more than its original cost, the balancing charge is the actual allowances given. The residue after sale is the original cost minus the notional allowances.

Question	Non-industrial use

The facts are as in the above question except that on 1 October 2003 Frankie ceases manufacturing in the building, letting it out as a theatrical rehearsal studio. On 1 June 2005 he recommences manufacturing in the building and, as before, sells it to Holly for £120,000 on 1 September 2006. Show the IBAs available to Frankie and to Holly.

Answer

	£
Frankie	
Cost 1.10.02	100,000
Y/e 31.12.02 WDA 4%	(4,000)
	96,000
Y/e 31.12.03 and y/e 31.12.04 No WDA since not in industrial use at the ends of the accounting periods, but deduct notional allowances 2 × 4%	(8,000)
	88,000
Y/e 31.12.05 WDA 4%	(4,000)
Residue before sale	84,000
Balancing charge for y/e 31.12.06: real (not notional) allowances £(4,000 + 4,000)	£(8,000)

	£
Holly	
Residue before sale	84,000
Add balancing charge	8,000
Residue after sale	92,000

	£
Y/e 30.9.06 WDA £92,000/21.083333	4,364
Next 20 account periods at £4,364 a year	87,280
Y/e 30.9.27 (balance)	356
	92,000

9.3.2 Sales for less than cost

If, following a period of non-industrial use, an industrial building is sold for less than its original cost, the actual allowances given are compared with the adjusted net cost, and a balancing allowance or charge made for the difference.

Formula to learn

The adjusted net cost is: $\dfrac{\text{(capital expenditure sale proceeds)}}{\text{total period from first use to sale}} \times \text{period of industrial use}$

The residue after sale is the residue before sale plus or minus the balancing charge or allowance, but it cannot exceed the actual sale price.

Question
Non-industrial use

The facts are as in the above question except that on the sale proceeds are £80,000. On 1 October 2003 Frankie ceases manufacturing in the building, letting it out as a theatrical rehearsal studio. On 1 June 2005 he recommences manufacturing in the building and, as before, sells it to Holly on 1 September 2006. Show the IBAs available to Frankie and to Holly.

Answer

	£
Frankie	
Cost 1.10.02	100,000
Sale proceeds	(80,000)
Net cost (ie fall in value)	20,000
Period of industrial use 1.10.02 – 30.9.03 + 1.6.05 – 31.8.06 = 27 months	
Period of ownership 1.10.02 – 31.8.06 = 47 months	
Adjusted net cost £20,000 × 27/47	11,489
Allowances actually given 2 × 4%	(8,000)
Balancing allowance	3,489

	£
Holly	
Residue before sale (as before)	84,000
Less balancing allowance	(3,489)
	80,511
Residue after sale restricted to sale proceeds	80,000

	£
Y/e 30.9.06 WDA £80,000/21.083333	3,794
Next 20 account periods at £3,794 a year	75,880
Y/e 30.9.27 (balance)	326
	80,000

Chapter roundup

- Capital allowances are available on plant and machinery and industrial buildings.

- Statutory rules generally exclude specified items from treatment as plant, rather than include specified items as plant.

- There are several cases on the definition of plant. To help you to absorb them, try to see the function/setting theme running through them.

- With capital allowances computations, the main thing is to get the layout right. Having done that, you will find that the figures tend to drop into place.

- Most expenditure on plant and machinery qualifies for a WDA at 25% every 12 months.

- First year allowances (FYA) may be available for certain expenditure. FYAs are never pro-rated in short or long periods of account.

- Private use of assets by sole traders and partners have restricted capital allowances.

- Short life asset elections can bring forward the allowances due on an asset.

- Capital allowances are available on assets acquired by hire purchase or lease.

- Balancing adjustments are calculated when a business ceases. If the business is transferred to a connected person, the written down value can be transferred instead.

- Industrial buildings allowances equal to the fall in value of the building whilst it was being used industrially are available to the trader.

- An allowance, normally at the rate of 4% per annum, is given if a building is in industrial use on the last day of the period of account concerned. If the building is in non industrial use a notional allowance may be given.

Quick quiz

1   For what periods are capital allowances for unincorporated businesses calculated?

2   Are writing down allowances pro-rated in a six month period of account?

3   Are first year allowances pro-rated in a six month period of account?

4   When may balancing allowances arise?

5   Within what period must an asset be disposed of if it is to be treated as a short life asset?

6   List four types of building which do not usually qualify for industrial buildings allowance.

7   When are drawing offices industrial buildings?

8   What are the conditions for a hotel to qualify for allowances?

9   When must a 'notional allowance' be deducted from the qualifying cost of an industrial building?

10   What is the amount of the balancing charge on a sale above cost where there been non-industrial use?

11   How is balancing charge or allowance calculated on a sale below cost where there been non-industrial use?

Answers to quick quiz

1   Periods of account

2   Yes. In a six month period, writing down allowance are pro-rated by multiplying by 6/12.

3   No. First year allowances are given in full in a short period of account.

4   Balancing allowances may arise in respect of pooled expenditure only when the trade ceases. Balancing allowances may arise on non-pooled items whenever those items are disposed of.

5   Within four years of the end of the period of account (or accounting period) in which it was bought.

6   Dwelling houses, retail shops, showrooms and offices.

7   Drawing offices are industrial buildings if they serve an industrial building.

8   (a)   It must have ten letting bedrooms

    (b)   It must have letting bedrooms as the whole or main part of the sleeping accommodation

    (c)   It must offer ancillary services including at least

        (i)   Breakfast
        (ii)   Evening meals
        (iii)   The cleaning of rooms
        (iv)   The making of beds

    (d)   It must be open for at least four months during the April to October letting season.

9   A notional allowance will be given if a building was in non-industrial use at the end of the period of account (accounting period) concerned.

10   The balancing charge is equal to the industrial buildings allowances actually given.

11   The adjusted net cost, ie cost less proceeds scaled down to reflect period of non-industrial use, is compared with the allowances actually given.

Now try the question below from the Exam Question Bank

Number	Level	Marks	Time
Q8	Introductory	25	45 mins

Trading losses

Topic list	Syllabus reference
1 Losses – an overview	A1(a)B3
2 Carrying forward losses: s 385 ICTA 1988	A1(a)B3
3 Setting trading losses against total income: s 380 ICTA 1988	A1(a)B3
4 Businesses transferred to companies: s 386 ICTA 1988	A1(d)(iii)
5 Trade charges: s 387 ICTA 1988	A1(a)B3
6 Losses in the early years of a trade: s 381 ICTA 1988	A1(a)B3
7 Losses on the cessation of a trade: s 388 ICTA 1988	A1(a)B3
8 Losses on unquoted shares: s 574 ICTA 1988	A1(d)(iv)

Introduction

In earlier chapters we have seen how to compute taxable trading profits, after capital allowances, and allocate them to tax years.

Traders sometimes make losses rather than profits. In this chapter we consider the reliefs available for losses. A loss does not in itself lead to receiving tax back from HMRC. Relief is obtained by setting a loss against trading profits, against other income or against capital gains, so that tax need not be paid on them. An important consideration is the choice between different reliefs. The aim is to use a loss to save as much tax as possible, as quickly as possible.

Finally we consider how a loss on the disposal of shares in an unquoted trading company can be relieved against income in a similar fashion.

In the next chapter we will see how individuals trading in partnership are taxed.

Study guide

		Intellectual level
1	**Income and income tax liabilities in situations involving further overseas aspects and in relation to trusts, and the application of exemptions and reliefs**	
(a)	The contents of the Paper F6 study guide for income tax, under headings:	2
•	B3 Income from self employment	
(d)	Income from self employment:	
(iii)	Establish the relief available on the transfer of a business to a company	3
(iv)	Establish the relief for capital losses on shares in unquoted trading companies	3

Exam focus

There are various ways in which a trader can obtain relief for trading losses. You are likely to have to advise the most beneficial way of obtaining relief. This will involve considering the rate of tax relief, the potential waste of personal allowances, and how soon relief can be obtained. Read the question carefully to establish if the taxpayer has any particular requirements such as to obtain relief as soon as possible.

Knowledge brought forward from earlier studies

Trading losses have been covered at level 2.3. The relief for capital losses on unquoted shares is new.

1 Losses – an overview

FAST FORWARD

Trade losses may be relieved against future profits of the same trade, against total income and against capital gains.

1.1 Trade losses in general

This chapter considers how losses are calculated and how a loss-suffering taxpayer can use a loss to reduce his tax liability. Most of the chapter concerns the trade losses in respect of trades, professions and vocations.

The rules in this chapter apply only to individuals, trading alone or in partnership. Loss reliefs for companies are completely different and are covered later in this Text.

When computing taxable trade profits, profits may turn out to be negative, that is a loss has been made in the basis period. **A loss is computed in exactly the same way as a profit**, making the same adjustments to the accounts profit or loss.

If there is a loss in a basis period, the taxable trade profits for the tax year based on that basis period are nil.

Losses of one spouse/civil partner cannot be relieved against income of the other spouse/civil partner.

1.2 The computation of the loss

The trade loss for a tax year is the trade loss in the basis period for that tax year. However, **if basis periods overlap then a loss in the overlap period is a trade loss for the earlier tax year only**.

1.3 Example: computing the trading loss

Here is an example of a trader who starts to trade on 1 July 2006 and makes losses in opening years.

Period of account			Loss £
1.7.06 – 31.12.06			9,000
1.1.07 – 31.12.07			24,000

Tax year	Basis period	Working	Trade loss for the tax year £
2006/07	1.7.06 – 5.4.07	£9,000 + (£24,000 × 3/12)	15,000
2007/08	1.1.07 – 31.12.07	£24,000 – (£24,000 × 3/12)	18,000

1.4 Example: losses and profits

The same rule against using losses twice applies when losses are netted off against profits in the same basis period. Here is an example, again with a commencement on 1 July 2006 but with a different accounting date.

Period of account		(Loss)/profit £
1.7.06 – 30.4.07		(10,000)
1.5.07 – 30.4.08		24,000

Tax year	Basis period	Working	Trade (Loss)/Profit £
2006/07	1.7.06 – 5.4.07	£(10,000) × 9/10	(9,000)
2007/08	1.7.06 – 30.6.07	£(10,000) × 1/10 + £24,000 × 2/12	3,000

1.5 Other losses

Losses incurred in foreign trades are computed and relieved in a similar manner to those of UK trades and are discussed later in this Text.

Losses from a UK property business have been discussed earlier, and losses on an overseas property business are relieved similarly.

If a loss arises on a transaction which, if profitable, would give rise to taxable miscellaneous income (see earlier in this Text), it can be set against any other similar income in the same year, and any excess carried forward for relief against miscellaneous income in future years.

2 Carrying forward losses: s 385 ICTA 1988

FAST FORWARD

A trade loss carried forward must be set against the first available trade profits of the same trade.

A trade loss not relieved in any other way must be **carried forward to set against the first available trade profits of the same trade**. Losses may be carried forward for any number of years.

2.1 Example: carrying forward losses

B has the following results.

Year ending	£
31 December 2004	(6,000)
31 December 2005	5,000
31 December 2006	11,000

B's taxable profits, assuming that he claims loss relief only under s 385 are:

	2004/05 £		2005/06 £		2006/07 £
Trade profits	0		5,000		11,000
Less s 385 relief	(0)	(i)	(5,000)	(ii)	(1,000)
Profits	0		0		10,000

Loss memorandum		£
Trading loss, y/e 31.12.04		6,000
Less: claim in y/e 31.12.05	(i)	(5,000)
claim in y/e 31.12.06 (balance of loss)	(ii)	(1,000)
		0

3 Setting trading losses against total income: s 380 ICTA 1988

FAST FORWARD

Where a loss relief claim is made, trade losses can be set against STI (ie income after charges) and then gains in the current and/or prior year.

3.1 Introduction

Instead of carrying a trade loss forward against future trade profits, it may be relieved against current income of all types.

3.2 Relieving the loss

Relief under s 380 **is against the income of the tax year in which the loss arose. In addition or instead,** relief may be claimed **against the income of the preceding year**.

If there are losses in two successive years, and relief is claimed against the first year's income both for the first year's loss and for the second year's loss, relief is given for the first year's loss before the second year's loss.

A claim for a loss must be made by the 31 January which is 22 months after the end of the tax year of the loss: so by 31 January 2009 for a loss in 2006/07.

The taxpayer cannot choose the amount of loss to relieve: so the loss may have to be set against income part of which would have been covered by the personal allowance. However, the taxpayer can choose whether to claim full relief in the current year and then relief in the preceding year for any remaining loss, or the other way round.

Set the loss against non-savings income then against savings (excluding dividend) income and finally against dividend income.

Relief is available by carry forward under s 385 for any loss not relieved under s 380.

Question | s 380 relief

Janet has a loss in her period of account ending 31 December 2006 of £25,000. Her other income is £18,000 rental income a year, and she wishes to claim loss relief for the year of loss and then for the preceding year. Show her taxable income for each year, and comment on the effectiveness of the loss relief. Assume that tax rates and allowances for 2006/07 have always applied.

Answer

The loss-making period ends in 2006/07, so the year of the loss is 2006/07.

	2005/06 £	2006/07 £
Income	18,000	18,000
Less s 380 relief	(7,000)	(18,000)
STI	11,000	0
Less personal allowance	(5,035)	(5,035)
Taxable income	5,965	0

In 2006/07, £5,035 of the loss has been wasted because that amount of income would have been covered by the personal allowance. If Janet claims s 380 relief, there is nothing she can do about this waste of loss relief or the personal allowance.

3.3 Capital allowances

The trader may adjust the size of the total s 380 claim by not claiming all the capital allowances he is entitled to: a reduced claim will increase the balance carried forward to the next year's capital allowances computation. This may be a useful **tax planning point where the effective rate of relief for capital allowances in future periods will be greater than the rate of tax relief for the s 380 loss**.

3.4 Trading losses relieved against capital gains

Where relief is claimed against total income of a given year, the taxpayer may include **a further claim to set the loss against his chargeable gains for the year** less any allowable capital losses for the same year or for previous years. This amount of net gains is computed ignoring taper relief and the annual exempt amount (see later in this Text).

The trading loss is first set against total income of the year of the claim, and only any excess of loss is set against capital gains. The taxpayer cannot specify the amount to be set against capital gains, so the annual exempt amount may be wasted. We include an example here for completeness. You will study chargeable gains later in this Text and we suggest that you come back to this example at that point.

Question

Sibyl had the following results for 2006/07.

	£
Loss available for relief under s 380	27,000
Income	19,500
Capital gains less current year capital losses	10,000
Annual exemption for capital gains tax purposes	8,800
Capital losses brought forward	4,000

Assume no taper relief is due.

Show how the loss would be relieved against income and gains.

Answer

	£
Income	19,500
Less loss relief	(19,500)
STI	0
Capital gains	10,000
Less loss relief: lower of £(27,000 – 19,500) = £7,500 (note 1) and	
£(10,000 – 4,000) = £6,000 (note 2)	(6,000)
	4,000
Less annual exemption (restricted)	(4,000)
	0

Note 1 This equals the loss left after the S380 claim
Note 2 This equals the gains left after losses b/fwd but ignoring taper relief and the annual exemption.

A trading loss of £(7,500 – 6,000) = £1,500 is carried forward. Sibyl's personal allowance and £(8,800 – 4,000) = £4,800 of her capital gains tax annual exemption are wasted. Her capital losses brought forward of £4,000 are carried forward to 2007/08. Although we deducted this £4,000 in working out how much trading loss we were allowed to use in the claim, we do not actually use any of the £4,000 unless there are gains remaining in excess of the annual exemption.

3.5 Restrictions on s 380 relief

Relief cannot be claimed under s 380 unless a business is conducted on a commercial basis with a view to the realisation of profits; this condition applies to all types of business.

3.6 The choice between loss reliefs

FAST FORWARD

It is important for a trader to choose the right loss relief, so as to save tax at the highest possible rate and so as to obtain relief reasonably quickly.

When a trader has a choice between loss reliefs, he should aim to obtain relief both quickly and at the highest possible tax rate. However, do consider that losses relieved against income which would otherwise be covered by the personal allowance are wasted.

Another consideration is that a trading loss cannot be set against the capital gains of a year unless relief is first claimed under s 380 against income of the same year. It may be worth making the claim against income and wasting the personal allowance in order to avoid a CGT liability.

Question   The choice between loss reliefs

Felicity's trading results are as follows.

Year ended 30 September	Trading profit/(loss)
	£
2004	1,900
2005	(21,000)
2006	13,000

Her other income (all non-savings income) is as follows.

	£
2004/05	2,200
2005/06	26,500
2006/07	15,000

Show the most efficient use of Felicity's trading loss. Assume that the personal allowance has been £5,035 throughout.

Answer

Relief could be claimed under s 380 for 2004/05 and/or 2005/06, with any unused loss being carried forward under s 385. Relief in 2004/05 would be against total income of £(1,900 + 2,200) = £4,100, all of which would be covered by the personal allowance anyway, so this claim should not be made. A s 380 claim should be made for 2005/06 as this saves tax more quickly than a s 385 claim in 2006/07 would. The final results will be as follows:

	2004/05	2005/06	2006/07
	£	£	£
Trading income	1,900	0	13,000
Less s 385 relief	(0)	(0)	(0)
	1,900	0	13,000
Other income	2,200	26,500	15,000
	4,100	26,500	28,000
Less s 380 relief	(0)	(21,000)	(0)
STI	4,100	5,500	28,000
Less personal allowance	(5,035)	(5,035)	(5,035)
Taxable income	0	465	22,965

Exam focus point

Before recommending s 380 loss relief consider whether it will result in the waste of the personal allowance and any tax reducers. Such waste is to be avoided if at all possible.

4 Businesses transferred to companies: s 386 ICTA 1988

FAST FORWARD ▶▶ If a business is transferred to a company, a loss of the unincorporated business can be set against income received from the company.

Although the set-off under s 385 is restricted to future profits of the same business, this is extended to cover income received from a company to which the business is sold, under s 386.

The amount carried forward is the total unrelieved trading losses of the business. The set-off must be made against the first available income from the company.

The order of set-off is:

(a)   Against **salary** derived from the company by the former proprietor of the business; **then**

(b)   Against **interest and dividends** from the company

The consideration for the sale must be wholly or mainly shares, which must be retained by the vendor throughout any tax year in which the loss is relieved; HMRC treat this condition as being satisfied if 80% or more of the consideration consists of shares.

5 Trade charges: s 387 ICTA 1988

FAST FORWARD

Excess trade charges can be used in the same way as losses under s 385.

5.1 Introduction

Annual charges on income, such as patent royalties, whilst paid out wholly and exclusively for business purposes, are nevertheless not deducted in arriving at the adjusted trade profits or losses.

But it is possible to suffer a 'loss' if STI is reduced to zero by such a charge because HMRC will collect the tax withheld from the charge under s 350 ICTA 1988. **Excess trade charges can be carried forward against future profits from the same trade** in the same way as losses under s 385. Non-trade charges however cannot be relieved in this way.

5.2 Example: excess trade charges

A taxpayer has the following results for 2006/07.

	£
Trading profit	4,000
Other income	1,000
	5,000
Less patent royalty	(7,000)
STI	0

Basic rate tax would be due on the unrelieved £2,000, so that the taxpayer accounted for 22% × £2,000 = £440, but the taxpayer could then carry forward the £2,000 against future profits from the trade.

6 Losses in the early years of a trade: s 381 ICTA 1988

FAST FORWARD

In opening years, a special relief involving the carry back of losses against total income is available. Losses arising in the first four tax years of a trade may be set against total income in the three years preceding the loss making year, taking the earliest year first.

S 381 relief is available for **trading losses incurred in the first four tax years of a trade**.

Relief is obtained by **setting the allowable loss against total income in the three years preceding the year of loss**, applying the loss to the earliest year first. Thus a loss arising in 2006/07 may be set off against income in 2003/04, 2004/05 and 2005/06 in that order.

A claim under s 381 applies to all three years automatically, provided that the loss is large enough. The taxpayer cannot choose to relieve the loss against just one or two of the years, or to relieve only part of the loss. However, the taxpayer could reduce the size of the loss by not claiming the full capital allowances available to him. This will result in higher capital allowances in future years.

Do not double count a loss. If basis periods overlap, a loss in the overlap period is treated as a loss for the earlier tax year only. This is the same rule as applies for s 380 purposes.

Claims for the relief must be made by the 31 January which is 22 months after the end of the tax year in which the loss is incurred.

The 'commercial basis' test is stricter for loss relief under s 381 than under s 380. The trade must be carried on in such a way that profits could reasonably have been expected to be realised in the period of the loss or within a reasonable time thereafter.

Question

s 381 loss relief

Mr A is employed as a dustman until 1 January 2005. On that date he starts up his own business as a scrap metal merchant, making up his accounts to 30 June each year. His earnings as a dustman are:

	£
2001/02	5,000
2002/03	6,000
2003/04	7,000
2004/05 (nine months)	6,000

His trading results as a scrap metal merchant are:

	Profit/(Loss) £
Six months to 30 June 2005	(3,000)
Year to 30 June 2006	(1,500)
Year to 30 June 2007	(1,200)

Assuming that loss relief is claimed as early as possible, show the final taxable income before personal allowances for each of the years 2001/02 to 2007/08 inclusive.

Answer

Since reliefs are to be claimed as early as possible, s 381 ICTA 1988 is applied. The losses available for relief are as follows.

	£	£	Years against which relief is available
2004/05 (basis period 1.1.05 – 5.4.05)			
3 months to 5.4.05 £(3,000) × 3/6		(1,500)	2001/02 to 2003/04
2005/06 (basis period 1.1.05 – 31.12.05)			
6 months to 30.6.05			
(omit 1.1.05 – 5.4.05: overlap) £(3,000) × 3/6	(1,500)		
6 months to 31.12.05 £(1,500) × 6/12	(750)		
		(2,250)	2002/03 to 2004/05
2006/07 (basis period 1.7.05 – 30.6.06)			
12 months to 30.6.06			
(omit 1.7.05 – 31.12.05: overlap) £(1,500) × 6/12		(750)	2003/04 to 2005/06
2007/08 (basis period 1.7.06 – 30.6.07)			
12 months to 30.6.07		(1,200)	2004/05 to 2006/07

The revised taxable income before personal allowances is as follows.

	£	£
2001/02		
Original	5,000	
Less 2004/05 loss	(1,500)	
		3,500
2002/03		
Original	6,000	
Less 2005/06 loss	(2,250)	
		3,750
2003/04		
Original	7,000	
Less 2006/07 loss	(750)	
		6,250
2004/05		
Original	6,000	
Less 2007/08 loss	(1,200)	
		4,800

The taxable trade profits for 2004/05 to 2007/08 are zero. There were losses in the basis periods.

7 Losses on the cessation of a trade: s 388 ICTA 1988

On the cessation of trade, a loss arising in the last 12 months of trading may be set against trade profits of the tax year of cessation and the previous 3 years, taking the last year first.

S 380 relief will often be insufficient on its own to deal with a loss incurred in the last months of trading. For this reason there is a special relief, **terminal loss relief, which allows a loss on cessation to be carried back for relief against taxable trading profits in previous years.**

7.1 Computing the terminal loss

A terminal loss under s 388 is **the loss of the last 12 months of trading**.

It is built up as follows.

		£
(a)	The actual trade loss for the tax year of cessation (calculated from 6 April to the date of cessation)	X
(b)	The actual trade loss for the period from 12 months before cessation until the end of the penultimate tax year	X
(c)	Any excess trade charges for the tax year of cessation	X
(d)	A proportion of any excess trade charges for the penultimate tax year	X
	Total terminal loss	X

If either (a) or (b) above yields a profit rather than a loss, the profit is treated as zero.

Any unrelieved overlap profits are included within (a) above.

If any loss cannot be included in the terminal loss (eg because it is matched with a profit) it can be relieved instead under s.380.

7.2 Relieving the terminal loss

The loss is relieved against trade profits ensuring that no trade charges become unrelieved as a result.

Relief is given in the tax year of cessation and the three preceding years, later years first.

Question	Terminal loss relief

Set out below are the results of a business up to its cessation on 30 September 2006.

	Profit/(loss) £
Year to 31 December 2003	2,000
Year to 31 December 2004	400
Year to 31 December 2005	300
Nine months to 30 September 2006	(1,950)

Overlap profits on commencement were £450. These were all unrelieved on cessation.

Show the available terminal loss relief, and suggest an alternative claim if the trader had had other non-savings income of £10,000 in each of 2005/06 and 2006/07. Assume that 2006/07 tax rates and allowances apply to all years.

Answer

The terminal loss comes in the last 12 months, the period 1 October 2005 to 30 September 2006. This period is split as follows.

2005/06	Six months to 5 April 2006
2006/07	Six months to 30 September 2006

The terminal loss is made up as follows.

Unrelieved trading losses		£	£
2006/07			
6 months to 30.9.06	£(1,950) × 6/9		(1,300)
Overlap relief			(450)
2005/06			
3 months to 31.12.05	£300 × 3/12	75	
3 months to 5.4.06	£(1,950) × 3/9	(650)	
			(575)
			(2,325)

Taxable trade profits will be as follows.

Year	Basis period	Profits £	Terminal loss relief £	Final taxable profits £
2003/04	Y/e 31.12.03	2,000	1,625	375
2004/05	Y/e 31.12.04	400	400	0
2005/06	Y/e 31.12.05	300	300	0
2006/07	1.1.06 – 30.9.06	0	0	0
			2,325	

If the trader had had £10,000 of other income in 2005/06 and 2006/07, we could consider S380 claims for these two years, using the loss of £(1,950 + 450) = £2,400 for 2006/07.

The final results would be as follows (we could alternatively claim loss relief in 2005/06.)

	2003/04	2004/05	2005/06	2006/07
	£	£	£	£
Trade profits	2,000	400	300	0
Other income	0	0	10,000	10,000
	2,000	400	10,300	10,000
Less s 380 claim	0	0	0	(2,400)
STI	2,000	400	10,300	7,600

Another option would be to make a s.380 claim for the balance of the loss not relieved under s.388 £(2,400 − 2,325) = £75 in either 2005/06 or 2006/07.

However, as there is only taxable income in 2005/06 and 2006/07 the full s.380 claim is more tax efficient.

8 Losses on unquoted shares: s 574 ICTA 1988

FAST FORWARD

Capital losses arising on certain unquoted shares can be set against total income of the year of the loss and then against total income of the preceding year.

Relief is available for capital losses on shares in unquoted trading companies (originally **subscribed for**) against total income of the taxpayer for the year **in which the loss arose and/or the preceding year** (ie the operation of the relief mirrors s 380).

In summary, the relief is available only if the shares satisfy the conditions of the Enterprise Investment Scheme (see earlier in this Text). It is not, however, necessary for income tax relief to have been claimed on the shares.

A claim must be made by 31 January 22 months after the end of the year of the loss. Relief is given against income of the year of the loss and if there is an unused balance, against income of the preceding year.

Chapter roundup

- Trade losses may be relieved against future profits of the same trade, against total income and against capital gains.

- A trade loss carried forward must be set against the first available trade profits of the same trade.

- Where a loss relief claim is made, trade losses can be set against STI (ie income after charges) and then gains in the current and/or prior year.

- It is important for a trader to choose the right loss relief, so as to save tax at the highest possible rate and so as to obtain relief reasonably quickly.

- If a business is transferred to a company, a loss of the unincorporated business can be set against income received from the company.

- Excess trade charges can be used in the same way as losses under s 385.

- In opening years, a special relief involving the carry back of losses against total income is available. Losses arising in the first four tax years of a trade may be set against total income in the three years preceding the loss making year, taking the earliest year first.

- On the cessation of trade, a loss arising in the last 12 months of trading may be set against trade profits of the tax year of cessation and the previous 3 years, taking the last year first.

- Capital losses arising on certain unquoted shares can be set against total income of the year of the loss and then against total income of the preceding year.

Quick quiz

1   Against what income trade losses carried forward be set off?

2   When a loss is to be relieved against total income, how are losses linked to particular tax years?

3   Against which years' total income may a loss be relieved under s 380 ICTA 1988?

4   For which losses is s 381 relief available?

5   In which years may relief for a terminal loss be given?

Answers to quick quiz

1   Against trade profits from the same trade.

2   The loss for a tax year is the loss in the basis period for that tax year. However, if basis periods overlap, a loss in the overlap period is a loss of the earlier tax year only.

3   The year in which the loss arose and/or the preceding year.

4   Losses incurred in the first four tax years of a trade.

5   In the year of cessation and then in the three preceding years, later years first.

Now try the question below from the Exam Question Bank

Number	Level	Marks	Time
Q9	Introductory	25	45 mins

Partnerships and limited liability partnerships

Topic list	Syllabus reference
1 Partnerships	A1(a)B3,(d)(vi)
2 Limited liability partnerships	A1(a)(B3)

Introduction

In the previous chapters we have dealt with the income tax rules for sole traders. We now see how those rules are adapted to deal with business partnerships.

On the one hand, a partnership is a single trading entity, making profits as a whole. On the other hand, each partner has a personal tax computation, so the profits must be apportioned to the partners. The general approach is to work out the profits of the partnership, then tax each partner as if he were a sole trader running a business equal to his slice of the partnership (for example 25% of the partnership).

This concludes our study of the different types of UK income to be included in an income tax computation. In the following chapter we will turn our attention to the overseas aspects of income tax.

Study guide

		Intellectual level
1	**Income and income tax liabilities in situations involving further overseas aspects and in relation to trusts, and the application of exemptions and reliefs**	
(a)	The contents of the Paper F6 study guide for income tax, under headings:	2
•	B3 Income from self employment	
(d)	Income from self employment:	
(vi)	Recognise the tax treatment of the investment income and charges of a partnership	2

Exam guide

A question involving any aspect of unincorporated businesses may deal with a partnership rather than a sole trader. The principles are exactly the same, whether you are considering incremental income, possible claims for capital allowances or loss reliefs. Just remember that profits are apportioned to partners in the profit sharing ratio for the period of account after allocating interest on capital and/or salaries.

> Knowledge brought forward from earlier studies

This chapter is mainly revision of the partnership rules covered at level 2.3. Partnership investment income and charges are new areas.

1 Partnerships

FAST FORWARD

> A partnership is simply treated as a source of profits and losses for trades being carried on by the individual partners. Divide profits or losses between the partners according to the profit sharing ratio in the period of account concerned. If any of the partners are entitled to a salary or interest on capital, apportion this first, not forgetting to pro-rate in periods of less than 12 months.

1.1 Introduction

A partnership is treated like a sole trader when computing its profits. Partners' salaries and interest on capital are not deductible expenses and must be added back in computing profits, because they are a form of drawings.

Once the partnership's profits for a period of account have been computed, they are shared between the partners according to the profit sharing arrangements for that period of account.

1.2 The tax positions of individual partners

Each partner is taxed like a sole trader who runs a business which:

- Starts when he joins the partnership

- Finishes when he leaves the partnership

- Has the same periods of account as the partnership (except that a partner who joins or leaves during a period will have a period which starts or ends part way through the partnership's period)

- Makes profits or losses equal to the partner's share of the partnership's profits or losses

1.3 Changes in profit sharing ratios

The profits for a period of account are allocated between the partners according to the profit sharing agreement. If the salaries, interest on capital and profit sharing ratio change during the period of account the profits are time apportioned to the periods before and after the change and allocated accordingly. The constituent elements are then added together to give each partner's share of profits for the period of account.

1.4 Changes in membership

FAST FORWARD
> The commencement and cessation rules apply to partners individually when they join or leave.

When a trade continues but partners join or leave (including cases when a sole trader takes in partners or a partnership breaks up leaving only one partner as a sole trader), **the special rules for basis periods in opening and closing years do not apply to the people who were carrying on the trade both before and after the change. They carry on using the period of account ending in each tax year as the basis period for the tax year ie the current year basis. The commencement rules only affect joiners, and the cessation rules only affect leavers.**

However, when no one same individual carries on the trade both before and after the change, as when a partnership transfers its trade to a completely new owner or set of owners, the cessation rules apply to the old owners and the commencement rules apply to the new owners.

1.5 Loss reliefs

FAST FORWARD
> There are restrictions on loss reliefs for non-active partners in the first four years of trading.

Partners are entitled to the same loss reliefs as sole traders. A partner is entitled to s 381 relief for losses in the four tax years starting with the year in which he is treated as starting to trade and he is entitled to terminal loss relief when he is treated as ceasing to trade. This is so even if the partnership trades for many years before the partner joins or after he leaves. Loss relief under s 380 and s 385 is also available to partners. Different partners may claim loss reliefs in different ways.

There is a restriction for loss relief for a partner who does not spend a significant amount of time (less than 10 hours a week) in running the trade of the partnership. Such a partner can only use loss relief under s 380 and s 381 ICTA 1988 or against capital gains **up to an amount equal to the amount that he contributes to the partnership.** These rules apply in any of the first four years in which the partner carries on a trade.

1.6 Example: loss relief restriction

Laura, Mark and Norman form a partnership and each contribute £10,000. Laura and Mark run the trade full time. Norman is employed elsewhere and plays little part in running the trade. Profits and losses are to be shared 45:35:20 to L:M:N. The partnership makes a loss of £60,000 of which £12,000 is allocated to Norman.

Norman may only use £10,000 of loss under s 380 (plus against capital gains) or s 381. £2,000 is carried forward, for example to be relieved against future profits under s 385.

When a partnership business is transferred to a company, each partner can carry forward his share of any unrelieved losses against income from the company under s 386 ICTA 1988.

1.7 Assets owned individually

Where the partners own assets (such as their cars) individually, a capital allowances computation must be prepared for each partner in respect of the assets he owns (not forgetting any adjustment for private use). **The capital allowances must go into the partnership's tax computation.**

1.8 Example: a partnership

Alice and Bertrand start a partnership on 1 July 2003, making up accounts to 31 December each year. On 1 May 2005, Charles joins the partnership. On 1 November 2006, Charles leaves. On 1 January 2007, Deborah joins. The profit sharing arrangements are as follows.

	Alice	Bertrand	Charles	Deborah
1.7.03 – 31.1.04				
Salaries (per annum)	£3,000	£4,500		
Balance	3/5	2/5		
1.2.04 – 30.4.05				
Salaries (per annum)	£3,000	£6,000		
Balance	4/5	1/5		
1.5.05 – 31.10.06				
Salaries (per annum)	£2,400	£3,600	£1,800	
Balance	2/5	2/5	1/5	
1.11.06 – 31.12.06				
Salaries (per annum)	£1,500	£2,700		
Balance	3/5	2/5		
1.1.07 onwards				
Salaries (per annum)	£1,500	£2,700		£600
Balance	3/5	1/5		1/5

Profits and losses as adjusted for tax purposes are as follows.

Period	Profit(loss)
	£
1.7.03 – 31.12.03	22,000
1.1.04 – 31.12.04	51,000
1.1.05 – 31.12.05	39,000
1.1.06 – 31.12.06	15,000
1.1.07 – 31.12.07	(18,000)

Show the taxable trade profits for each partner for 2003/04 to 2006/07, and outline the loss reliefs available to the partners in respect of the loss in the year ending 31 December 2007. All the partners work full time in the partnership. Assume that the partnership will continue to trade with the same partners until 2018.

Solution

We must first share the trade profits and losses for the periods of account between the partners, remembering to adjust the salaries for periods of less than a year.

	Total £	Alice £	Bertrand £	Charles £	Deborah £
1.7.03 – 31.12.03					
Salaries	3,750	1,500	2,250		
Balance	18,250	10,950	7,300		
Total (P/e 31.12.03)	22,000	12,450	9,550		
1.1.04 – 31.12.04					
January					
Salaries	625	250	375		
Balance	3,625	2,175	1,450		
Total	4,250	2,425	1,825		
February to December					
Salaries	8,250	2,750	5,500		
Balance	38,500	30,800	7,700		
Total	46,750	33,550	13,200		
Total for y/e 31.12.04	51,000	35,975	15,025		
1.1.05 – 31.12.05					
January to April					
Salaries	3,000	1,000	2,000		
Balance	10,000	8,000	2,000		
Total	13,000	9,000	4,000		
May to December					
Salaries	5,200	1,600	2,400	1,200	
Balance	20,800	8,320	8,320	4,160	
Total	26,000	9,920	10,720	5,360	
Total for y/e 31.12.05	39,000	18,920	14,720	5,360	
1.1.06 – 31.12.06					
January to October					
Salaries	6,500	2,000	3,000	1,500	
Balance	6,000	2,400	2,400	1,200	
Total	12,500	4,400	5,400	2,700	
November and December					
Salaries	700	250	450		
Balance	1,800	1,080	720		
Total	2,500	1,330	1,170		
Total for y/e 31.12.06	15,000	5,730	6,570	2,700	
1.1.07 – 31.12.07					
Salaries	4,800	1,500	2,700		600
Balance	(22,800)	(13,680)	(4,560)		(4,560)
Total loss for y/e 31.12.07	(18,000)	(12,180)	(1,860)		(3,960)

The next stage is to work out the basis periods and hence the taxable trade profits for the partners. All of them are treated as making up accounts to 31 December, but Alice and Bertrand are treated as starting to trade on 1 July 2003, Charles as trading only from 1 May 2005 to 31 October 2006 and Deborah as starting to trade on 1 January 2007. Applying the usual rules gives the following basis periods and taxable profits.

Alice

Year	Basis period	Working	Taxable profits £
2003/04	1.7.03 – 5.4.04	£12,450 + (£35,975 × 3/12)	21,444
2004/05	1.1.04 – 31.12.04		35,975
2005/06	1.1.05 – 31.12.05		18,920
2006/07	1.1.06 – 31.12.06		5,730

Note that for 2003/04 we take Alice's total for the year ended 2004 and apportion that, because the partnership's period of account runs from 1 January to 31 December 2004. Alice's profits for 2003/04 are *not* £12,450 + £2,425 + (£33,550 × 2/11) = £20,975.

Alice will have overlap profits for the period 1 January to 5 April 2004 (£35,975 × 3/12 = £8,994) to deduct when she ceases to trade.

Bertrand

Year	Basis period	Working	Taxable profits £
2003/04	1.7.03 – 5.4.04	£9,550 + (£15,025 × 3/12)	13,306
2004/05	1.1.04 – 31.12.04		15,025
2005/06	1.1.05 – 31.12.05		14,720
2006/07	1.1.06 – 31.12.06		6,570

Bertrand's overlap profits are £15,025 × 3/12 = £3,756.

Charles

Year	Basis period	Working	Taxable profits £
2005/06	1.5.05 – 5.4.06	£5,360 + (£2,700 × 3/10)	6,170
2006/07	6.4.06 – 31.10.06	£2,700 × 7/10	1,890

Because Charles ceased to trade in his second tax year of trading, his basis period for the second year starts on 6 April and he has no overlap profits.

Deborah

Year	Basis period	Working	Taxable profits £
2006/07	1.1.07 – 5.4.07	A loss arises	0

Finally, we must look at the loss reliefs available to Alice, Bertrand and Deborah. Charles is not entitled to any loss relief, because he left the firm before any loss arose.

Alice and Bertrand

For 2007/08, Alice has a loss of £12,180 and Bertrand has a loss of £1,860. They may claim relief under s 380 or under s 385.

Deborah

Deborah's losses are as follows, remembering that a loss which falls in the basis periods for two tax years is only taken into account in the earlier year.

Year	Basis period	Working	Loss £
2006/07	1.1.07 – 5.4.07	£3,960 × 3/12	990
2007/08	1.1.07 – 31.12.07	£3,960 – £990 (used in 2006/07)	2,970

Deborah may claim relief for these losses under s 380, s 381 (because she has just started to trade) or s 385.

Exam focus point

Partners are effectively taxed in the same way as sole traders with just one difference. Before you tax the partner you need to take each set of accounts (as adjusted for tax purposes) and divide the trade profit (or loss) between each partner.

Then carry on as normal for a sole trader – each partner is that sole trader in respect of his trade profits for each accounting period.

1.9 Partnership investment income and charges

A partnership may have non-trading income, such as interest on the partnership's bank deposit account or dividends on shares, or non-trading losses. **Such items are kept separate from trading income, but they** (and any associated tax credits) **are shared between the partners in a similar way to trading income.** That is, the following steps are applied.

Step 1   Find out which period of account the income arose in

Step 2   Share the income between the partners using the profit sharing arrangements for that period. If partners have already been given their salaries and interest on capital in sharing out trading income, do not give them those items again in sharing out non-trading income

Step 3   For income not taxed at source attribute each partner's share of the income to tax years using the same basis periods as are used to attribute his share of trading profits to tax years. When working out the basis periods for untaxed income (which excludes income taxed at source and dividends) or for non-trading losses, we always have a commencement when the partner joins the partnership and a cessation when he leaves, even if he carried on the trade as a sole trader before joining or after leaving. If the relief for overlap untaxed income on leaving the firm exceeds the partner's share of untaxed income for the tax year of leaving, the excess is deducted from his total income for that year

Step 4   For income taxed at source assume that income accrued evenly over the accounting period and time apportion on an actual basis into tax years (6 April to 5 April)

Charges are allocated between partners in accordance with the profit sharing ratio for tax years.

2 Limited liability partnerships

FAST FORWARD

Limited liability partnerships are taxed on virtually the same basis as normal partnerships but loss relief is restricted for all partners.

It is possible to form a limited liability partnership. The difference between a limited liability partnership (LLP) and a normal partnership is that **in a LLP the liability of the partners is limited to the capital they contributed.**

The partners of a LLP are taxed on virtually the same basis as the partners of a normal partnership (see above). However, the amount of loss relief that a partner can claim under s 380 and s 381 ICTA 1988 when the claim is against non-partnership income is restricted to the capital he contributed. This rule is not restricted to the first four years of trading and the rules apply to all partners whether or not involved in the running of the trade.

Chapter roundup

- A partnership is simply treated as a source of profits and losses for trades being carried on by the individual partners. Divide profits or losses between the partners according to the profit sharing ratio in the period of account concerned. If any of the partners are entitled to a salary or interest on capital, apportion this first, not forgetting to pro-rate in periods of less than 12 months.

- The commencement and cessation rules apply to partners individually when they join or leave.

- There are restrictions on loss reliefs for non-active partners in the first four years of trading.

- Limited liability partnerships are taxed on virtually the same basis as normal partnerships but loss relief is restricted for all partners.

Quick quiz

1   How are partnership trading profits divided between the individual partners?

2   What loss reliefs are partners entitled to?

3   Janet and John are partners sharing profits 60:40. For the years ended 30 June 2006 and 2007 the partnership made profits of £100,000 and £150,000 respectively. What are John's taxable trading profits in 2006/07?

4   Pete and Doug have been joint partners for many years. On 1 January Dave joins the partnership and it is agreed to share profits 40:40:20. For the year ended 30 June 2006 profits are £100,000.

 What is Doug's share of these profits?

Answers to quick quiz

1   Profits are divided in accordance with the profit sharing ratio that existed during the period of account in which the profits arose.

2   Partners are entitled to the same loss reliefs as sole traders. This means that partners may claim relief for their share or a loss under s 380, s 381, s 385, s 388 or s 386 as appropriate.

3   £40,000.

 2006/07: ye 30 June 2006

 £100,000 × 40% = £40,000.

4   £45,000

	Pete £	Doug £	Dave £
Ye 30 June 2006			
1.7.05 – 31.12.05			
6m × 100,000			
£50,000 50:50	25,000	25,000	
1.1.06 – 30.6.06			
6m × £100,000			
£50,000 40:40:20	20,000	20,000	10,000
	45,000	45,000	10,000

Now try the question below from the Exam Question Bank

Number	Level	Marks	Time
Q10	Introductory	25	45 mins

10

Overseas aspects of income tax

Topic list	Syllabus reference
1 Residence, ordinary residence and domicile	A1(a)B1,(b)(i),(ii)
2 Overseas investment income	A1(b)(iii)
3 Employment abroad and non-residents employed in the UK	A1(c)(iii)
4 Overseas trades	A1(d)(i)
5 Double taxation relief (DTR)	A1(b)(iv),(vi)

Introduction

In the previous chapters we have studied most aspects of income tax. In this chapter we will look at the overseas aspects of income tax.

We start this chapter by looking at where taxpayers live and at how that affects their tax position. We then consider the special rules which apply to people working away from their home countries. We then look at the rules for foreign investment income of people in the UK. Finally, we look at the tax relief which can be available when income is taxed both abroad and in the UK.

In the next chapter will we turn our attention to CGT. We will consider the administration of income tax when we have finished studying CGT as the personal tax return deals with both income and capital gains.

Study guide

		Intellectual level
1	**Income and income tax liabilities in situations involving further overseas aspects and in relation to trusts, and the application of exemptions and reliefs**	
(a)	The contents of the Paper F6 study guide for income tax, under headings:	2
•	B1 The scope of income tax	
(b)	The scope of income tax:	3
(i)	Explain and apply the concepts of residence, ordinary residence and domicile and advise on the relevance to income tax	
(ii)	Advise on the tax position of individuals coming to and leaving the UK	
(iii)	Determine the income tax treatment of overseas income	
(iv)	Understand the relevance of the OECD model double tax treaty to given situations	
(vi)	Calculate and advise on the double taxation relief available to individuals	
(c)	Income from employment	3
(iii)	Advise on the overseas aspects of income from employment, including travelling and subsistence expenses	
(d)	Income from self employment:	
(i)	Recognise the tax treatment of overseas trade travelling expenses	3

Exam guide

In an exam question you may have to advise an individual how he will be taxed on his income from overseas. You may also need to advise an individual who has gone abroad how he will be taxed on his UK income, or how a foreigner is taxed on his foreign income whilst he is resident in the UK. You must be sure that you can correctly determine an individual's residence status.

Knowledge brought forward from earlier studies

This chapter is new.

1 Residence, ordinary residence and domicile

FAST FORWARD

An individual may be any or all of resident, ordinarily resident and domiciled in the UK, and his liability to UK tax will be determined accordingly. Foreign income is only taxable if the individual is UK resident.

1.1 Introduction

A taxpayer's **residence**, **ordinary residence** and **domicile** have important consequences in establishing the treatment of his UK and overseas income.

1.2 Residence and ordinary residence

1.2.1 Residence

An individual is resident in the UK for a tax year if:

(a) **He is present in the UK for 183 days (ie 6 months) or more** (excluding days of arrival and departure)

(b) **He makes substantial annual visits to the UK** averaging 91 days (ie 3 months) or more a year for each of four or more consecutive years, ignoring days spent in the UK due to circumstances beyond the individual's control (eg illness). He will be resident for each of these tax years. For someone leaving the UK, the four years are reduced to three.

1.2.2 Ordinary residence

A person who is resident in the UK will be ordinarily resident where his residence is of a habitual nature. Ordinary residence implies a greater degree of permanence than residence.

The significance of ordinary residence is principally in connection with the basis of assessment for overseas income (see below), and exemption for interest on some government securities and bank deposit interest.

A person who is ordinarily resident in the UK and who goes abroad for a period which does not include a complete tax year, is regarded as remaining resident and ordinarily resident throughout.

1.2.3 Example: non UK individual

Hans has always lived in Austria. He comes to the UK on 1 July 2006 and returns to Austria on 1 March 2007.

Hans is present in the UK for 242 days during 2006/07 (ignoring days of arrival and departure). This is greater than 183 days so he will be treated as UK resident, but not ordinarily resident, for 2006/07.

1.2.4 Splitting the tax year

Strictly, each tax year must be looked at as a whole. A person is resident and/or ordinarily resident either for a whole tax year or not at all. By concession an individual can **split the tax year** if he:

(a) Is **a new permanent resident** or comes to stay in the UK for at least two years, provided he has not been ordinarily resident

(b) Has left the UK for **permanent residence abroad** provided that he becomes not ordinarily resident, or

(c) Is going abroad **to take up employment for at least a whole tax year** (see below).

1.2.5 Coming to the UK

A person who comes to the UK from abroad to take up permanent residence, or intending to stay for at least three years, is regarded as resident and ordinarily resident from the date of his arrival.

A person who comes to the UK to work for a period of at least two years is treated as resident for the whole period from arrival to departure.

A person who comes to the UK who does not originally intend to stay for at least three years is treated as ordinarily resident in the UK from 6 April following the third anniversary of his arrival in the UK. However, once an intention to stay for at least three years is shown (for example by acquiring accommodation with a lease of three years or more), he is treated as ordinarily resident from the start of the tax year in which the intention is shown.

Someone who comes to the UK only for temporary purposes (such as a brief spell of employment) is not UK resident for a tax year unless he spends 183 days or more in the UK in that year. Someone who expects to spend fewer than 91 days a year in the UK for a limited period (for example a five year term of duty) will be treated as in the UK for temporary purposes.

1.2.6 Leaving the UK

A person who has been resident or ordinarily resident here is treated as remaining resident if he goes abroad for short periods which do not span a complete tax year.

If a person claims that he has ceased to be resident and ordinarily resident in the UK and can produce some evidence for this, such as selling his UK home and setting up a permanent home abroad, then his claim is normally provisionally admitted from the day of his departure. If no such evidence can be produced the decision will be postponed for three years and then retrospective adjustments will be made.

If a person goes abroad for full-time service under a contract of employment such that:

(a)   **his absence from the UK is for a period which includes a complete tax year, and**

(b)   **interim visits to the UK do not amount to six months or more in any one tax year or three months or more per tax year on average,**

he is normally regarded as not resident and not ordinarily resident for the whole period of the contract.

If the employee's spouse/civil partner accompanies him, and the spouse/civil partner also satisfies conditions (a) and (b), the spouse/civil partner is also regarded as not resident and not ordinarily resident for the whole period of the contract.

1.2.7 Example: Short periods of absence

Jennifer has always lived in the UK. She goes on a year long trip around the world starting 1 June 2006. She returns to the UK on 31 May 2007.

Even though Jennifer is only in the UK for 56 days during 2006/07, which is less than 183 days, she will be treated as UK resident for the whole period of absence because she is ordinarily resident (habitually lives in the UK) and only left the UK for a short period which did not span an entire tax year.

1.2.8 Example: full time overseas employment contract

Sarah's employer wants to send her abroad for fifteen months to work in an overseas office. Sarah has the option to start the assignment either on 1 March 2006 returning 31 May 2007, or on 1 June 2006, returning 31 August 2007. She has always been UK resident and ordinarily resident. She will return to the UK for two weeks during the period.

Sarah should start the assignment on 1 March 2006 as she will be on a full time contract overseas for a complete tax year. She will be treated as not resident and not ordinarily resident from 1 March 2006 until 31 May 2007. If she starts on 1 June 2006 she will not be overseas for a complete tax year so will remain UK resident and ordinarily resident throughout the contract.

1.2.9 Spouses/civil partners

A spouse/civil partner's residence and ordinary residence is not governed by the other spouse/civil partner's status but is determined independently. If for example, one spouse/civil partner is employed abroad full-time, and the other one also goes abroad but later returns to the UK without having been away for a complete tax year, then the latter is regarded as remaining resident and ordinarily resident in the UK although the former may be not resident and not ordinarily resident.

1.3 Domicile

A person is domiciled in the country in which he has his permanent home. Domicile is distinct from nationality or residence. A person may be resident in more than one country, but he can be domiciled in only one country at a time.

A person acquires a domicile of origin at birth; this is normally the domicile of his father (or that of his mother if his father died before he was born or his parents were unmarried at his birth) and therefore not necessarily the country where he was born.

A person retains this domicile until he acquires a different domicile of dependency (if, while he is under 16, his father's domicile changes) or domicile of choice. A domicile of choice can be acquired only by individuals aged 16 or over.

To acquire a domicile of choice a person must sever his ties with the country of his former domicile and settle in another country with the clear intention of making his permanent home there. Long residence in another country is not in itself enough to prove that a person has acquired a domicile of choice: there has to be evidence that he firmly intends to live there permanently.

1.4 Application of the rules

1.4.1 General principle

Generally, a UK resident is liable to UK income tax on his UK and overseas income whereas a non-resident is liable to UK income tax only on income arising in the UK.

1.4.2 Allowances

In general, non-residents are not entitled to personal allowances. However, the following people are entitled to allowances despite being non-resident:

- Citizens of European Economic Area and Commonwealth countries
- Individuals resident in the Isle of Man and the Channel Islands
- Current or former Crown servants and their bereaved spouses/civil partners
- Former residents who have left the country for health reasons
- Missionaries

There is a special limit on the income tax borne by someone who is, for a complete tax year, not resident in the UK. (The limit does not apply to a year which is split under the concessionary rule described above.) The tax cannot exceed the sum of:

(a) The tax which would be borne if they were taxed on all their income apart from their excluded income, and they had no allowances.

(b) The tax deducted at source from excluded income (including tax credits on dividends).

Excluded income is income which is not from the trade, profession or vocation of a UK branch or agency, nor derived from property or rights used or held by a UK branch or agency, and which falls within one of the following categories.

- UK interest, deeply discounted securities, purchased life annuities

- UK dividends

- Profits on dealing in deposits

- Taxable social security benefits

- Pensions from retirement annuity contracts (old style pensions which are not examinable)

- Other investment income arising from transactions carried out through a broker or investment manager

1.4.3 The remittance basis

A UK resident who is not domiciled in the UK is liable to UK tax on overseas income on a remittance basis only, at the non savings rates (see below), that is only income brought to the UK is taxable. There are special rules for earnings dealt with later in this chapter.

The remittance basis for overseas income also applies to British subjects resident but not ordinarily resident in the UK.

1.4.4 Savings income and charges received

Interest payable on all gilt-edged securities (UK government securities) is exempt from UK income tax if the recipient is not ordinarily resident in the UK.

Income tax must be deducted at source from the following payments to non-UK residents.

- Proceeds of the sale of UK patent rights: tax at 22%
- Copyright royalties and public lending right payments: tax at 22%
- Interest: tax at 20%

However, banks and building societies pay interest gross to persons who have certified that they are not ordinarily resident in the UK.

2 Overseas investment income

Income from overseas sources is taxed on a similar basis to UK income. It is charged on a remittance basis for non-UK domiciled individuals and British subjects not ordinarily resident in the UK.

2.1 Introduction

UK residents are taxable on their overseas investment income. Non-residents are not taxable in the UK on overseas investment income, although they are taxable on their UK investment income.

Foreign income is identified and taxed in broadly the same way as UK income, but the points set out below should be noted.

2.2 Overseas property business

An individual who receives rents and other income from property abroad is treated as carrying on an overseas property business. The income from the overseas property business is liable to income tax in the same way as income from a UK property business, and is calculated in the same way. If an individual has both a UK and an overseas property business, the profits must be calculated separately.

If a loss arises in an overseas property business, it may be carried forward and set against future income from the overseas property business, as soon as it arises.

The special treatment of furnished holiday lettings does not apply to overseas properties.

2.3 Foreign dividends

Foreign dividends are dividends from non-UK companies. The income is taxable in the year it arises, as it is taxed in the same way as UK dividend income, ie at 10% if it falls within the starting and basic rate bands and at 32.5% if it falls within the higher rate band. Foreign dividends do not, however, have the notional 10% tax credit that UK dividends do.

2.4 Other savings income

Other foreign savings income, such as interest, purchased life annuities etc are taxed in the same way as UK savings income, ie at 10% in the starting rate band, 20% in the basic rate band, and at 40% in the higher rate band.

2.5 Remittance basis

A claim for the remittance basis (under which only income brought to the UK is taxed) to apply may be made by:

- **Persons not domiciled in the UK, and**
- **British subjects not ordinarily resident in the UK.**

Where the remittance basis applies, all income from the relevant source counts as non-savings income. It is taxed in the same way as other non-savings income ie at 10% in the starting rate band, 22% in the basic rate band at the higher rate of 40%, even if it is interest or dividends.

2.6 Taxation of investment income – summary

Residence status and domicile	Investment income	
	Arising in the UK	Arising outside the UK
Resident and ordinarily resident, and domiciled	Taxable on receipts basis	Taxable on receipts basis
Resident and either not ordinarily resident or not domiciled	Taxable on receipts basis	Taxable on remittance basis
Not resident	Taxable on receipts basis	Not taxable

3 Employment abroad and non-residents employed in the UK

3.1 Chargeability of employment income

FAST FORWARD

The residence, ordinary residence and domicile status of an employee (and, in some cases, whether he carries out his duties in the UK or outside it) determine the tax treatment of his earnings.

3.1.1 Individual resident and ordinarily resident and domiciled in the UK

A resident, ordinarily resident and domiciled individual is taxed on his general earnings on a receipts basis (see Chapter 4) whether the duties of the employment are carried out in the UK or outside it.

3.1.2 Individual resident and ordinarily resident, but not domiciled in the UK

A resident and ordinarily resident, but not domiciled individual, is usually taxed on all general earnings on the receipts basis, wherever the duties of his employment are carried out. However, only any **'overseas earnings' remitted to the UK are chargeable in the UK**. Overseas earnings arise where the employer is a foreign employer and the duties of the employment are performed *wholly* outside the UK.

3.1.3 Individual resident, but not ordinarily resident in the UK

A resident, but not ordinarily resident, individual is subject to tax on his earnings in two ways. First, he is taxable on his general earnings in respect of duties performed in the UK on the normal receipts basis. Second, he is taxable on his 'foreign earnings' (those relating to non-UK duties) remitted to the UK. In this circumstance, the residence status of the employer is not relevant.

3.1.4 Individual not resident in the UK

A non resident is taxed on his general earnings in respect of UK duties on the receipts basis but there is no UK income tax on foreign earnings (those in respect of non-UK duties).

If the person is absent for a complete tax year as described in Section 1 above then he becomes non-resident for the period of the contract of employment. There will be no UK tax on the foreign earnings.

3.1.5 Taxation of earned income – summary

		Duties performed wholly or partly in the UK		Duties performed wholly outside the UK
		in the UK	outside the UK	
'Overseas earnings' Not UK domiciled Foreign employer	Employee resident and ordinarily resident in the UK	Taxable on receipts basis	Taxable on receipts basis	Taxable on remittance basis
	Resident but not ordinarily resident	Taxable on receipts basis	Taxable on remittance basis	Taxable on remittance basis
	Not resident	Taxable on receipts basis	Not taxable	Not taxable
Other earnings	Resident and ordinarily resident	Taxable on receipts basis	Taxable on receipts basis	Taxable on receipts basis
	Resident but not ordinarily resident	Taxable on receipts basis	Taxable on remittance basis	Taxable on remittance basis
	Not resident	Taxable on receipts basis	Not taxable	Not taxable

3.2 Travel and subsistence expenses for employment abroad

FAST FORWARD

Individuals working abroad may claim certain deductions for travel expenses.

3.2.1 Travel expenses incurred by the employee

Travel expenses relating to employment duties abroad (whether or not reimbursed by the employer) may be deducted from earnings in certain circumstances.

(a) **A deduction is allowed for starting and finishing travel expenses.** Starting travel expenses are those incurred by the employee in travelling from the UK to take up employment abroad and finishing travel expenses are those incurred by the employee in travelling to the UK on the termination of the employment. **Three conditions need to be met:**

(i) **The duties of the employment are performed wholly outside the UK (incidental UK duties are ignored)**

(ii) **The employee is resident and ordinarily resident in the UK**

(iii) **If the employer is a foreign employer, the employee is domiciled in the UK**

If the travel is only partly attributable to the taking up or termination of the employment, the deduction applies only to that part of the expenses.

(b) **There is also a deduction from earnings from an employment for travel expenses where an employee has two or more employments and the duties of at least one of them are performed abroad.** The following conditions must be met:

(i) **The travel is for the purpose of performing duties of the employment at the destination**

(ii) **The employee has performed duties of another employment at the place of departure**

(iii) **The place of departure or the destination or both are outside the UK**

(iv) **The duties of one or both of the employments are performed wholly or partly outside the UK**

(v) **The employee is resident and ordinarily resident in the UK**

(vi) **If the employer is a foreign employer, the employee is domiciled in the UK**

3.2.2 Travel expenses borne by employer

There are a number of deductions which may be made from a person's earnings where an amount has been included in those earnings **in respect of provision of (or reimbursement of expenses relating to) travel abroad. The allowable deduction is generally equal to the amount included in the earnings. Note that these deductions do not apply where the employee incurs such costs but does not receive reimbursement.**

(a) **The first deduction relates to the provision of travel facilities for a journey made by the employee.** This deduction applies in two circumstances:

(i) **The employee is absent from the UK wholly and exclusively for the purpose of performing the duties of one or more employments, the duties can only be performed outside the UK and the journey is from a place outside the UK to the UK or a return journey following such a journey**

(ii) **The duties of the employment are performed partly outside the UK, the journey is between the UK and the place the non-UK duties are performed, the non-UK duties can only be performed there and the journey is made wholly and exclusively for the purpose of performing the duties or returning after performing them**

The deduction only applies from earnings which are chargeable because the individual is UK resident and ordinarily resident but not from 'overseas earnings' (foreign employer/non-domiciled employee/non-UK duties). This is because the overseas earnings are taxed on the remittance basis.

(b) **There is also a deduction for the provision of travel facilities for a journey made by the employee's spouse/civil partner or child** (aged under 18 at the beginning of the outward journey) **or the reimbursement of expenses incurred by the employee on such a journey.** The following conditions need to be met:

     (i)   **The employee is absent from the UK for a continuous period of at least 60 days for the purpose of performing the duties of the employment**

     (ii)   **The journey is between the UK and the place outside the UK that the duties are performed**

     (iii)   **The employee's spouse/civil partner/child is either accompanying the employee at the beginning of the period of absence or visiting the employee during that period or is returning to the UK after accompanying or visiting the employee**

A deduction is not allowed for more than two outward and two return journeys by the same person in a tax year.

Again, the deduction only applies from earnings which are chargeable because the individual is UK resident and ordinarily resident, but not from 'overseas earnings' taxed on the remittance basis.

(c) **There are also rules which apply to non-domiciled employee's travel costs and expenses where duties are performed in the UK. The deduction is only from earnings for duties performed in the UK.**

The first deduction applies to the provision of travel facilities for a journey made by the employee or the reimbursement of expenses incurred by the employee for such a journey. The conditions that must be met are:

     (i)   **The journey ends on or during the period of 5 years beginning with a qualifying arrival date** (see below)

     (ii)   **The journey is made from the country outside the UK where the employee normally lives to the UK in order to perform the duties of the employment or to that country from the UK after performing such duties**

If the journey is only partly for such a purpose, the deduction is equal to so much of the included journey as is properly attributable to that purpose.

A 'qualifying arrival date' is a date on which the person arrives in the UK to perform UK duties where either:

     (i)   The person has not been in the UK for any purpose during the two tax years before the tax year in which the date falls, or

     (ii)   The person was not UK resident in either of the two tax years before the tax year in which the date falls.

Exam focus point

> Note carefully the rules under which relief is given. In particular, the costs must be borne by the employer. Note also the limits on journeys for spouses/civil partners/children.

3.2.3 Foreign accommodation and subsistence costs and expenses

A deduction from earnings from an employment is allowed if:

- **The duties of the employment are performed wholly outside the UK (incidental UK duties ignored)**

- **The employee is resident and ordinarily resident in the UK**

- **If the employer is a foreign employer, the employee is domiciled in the UK**

- **The earnings include an amount in respect of the provision of accommodation or subsistence outside the UK to enable the employee to perform the duties of the employment or the reimbursement of such expenses incurred by the employee.**

The deduction is equal to the amount included in the earnings.

3.3 Foreign pensions

For persons taxed on the arising basis (but not those on the remittance basis), only 90% of the amount of a foreign pension is taxed.

3.4 Tax planning when employed abroad

3.4.1 General considerations

The following points highlight the pitfalls and planning possibilities to be considered when going to work abroad.

(a)   Timing is vital. Leaving just before the end of a tax year may enable the taxpayer to spend a complete year outside the UK so qualifying for non-resident status.

(b)   Insurance policies are available to cover the risk of extra tax liabilities should an early return to the UK be necessary.

(c)   If the employer bears the cost of board and lodging abroad this will represent a tax-free benefit. The employee may visit home as many times as he likes without the costs being taxed as benefits. Likewise, for absences of 60 days or more, travelling expenses for a spouse/civil partner and minor children are also tax-free if paid or reimbursed by the employer. Up to two return visits per person per tax year are allowed.

(d)   Where the remittance basis applies it may be advisable to keep funds abroad separate so that it can be proved that sums remitted to the UK are capital (not subject to income tax) or income from a specific source.

(e)   Having established non-residence in the UK, any UK investments should be reviewed to ensure they are still tax effective. Bank and building society interest, otherwise paid net, may be paid gross where the deposit-taker is given a written declaration that the recipient is not ordinarily resident in the UK.

(f)   Consider carefully the tax system in the foreign country concerned and the terms of any double taxation agreement. The UK has such agreements with most countries: they contain rules on where income and gains are to be taxed, and on other matters (see below).

3.4.2 The OECD model agreement

Most double taxation agreements follow fairly closely the Organisation for Economic Co-operation and Development (OECD) Model Double Taxation Agreement. Under that Model, someone who is resident in country R but is employed in country E will normally be taxed on the earnings in country E. He may only be taxed on the earnings in country R if:

- He is in country E for less than 184 days in total in any 12 month period starting or ending in the year,

- The employer is not resident in country E, and

- The earnings are not borne by a permanent establishment or fixed base which the employer has in country E.

If an individual resident in country R is a director of a company resident in country D, his director's fees may be taxed in country D.

4 Overseas trades

FAST FORWARD

Profits of an overseas trade are computed as for UK trades. However, the remittance basis applies for non-UK domiciled individuals.

4.1 General principles

If a UK resident trader has a business which is conducted wholly or mainly overseas, the trade profits are chargeable to income tax. The trade profits are calculated in the same way as are UK trade profits, and the basis periods are determined in the same way also.

If the trader:

- **is not domiciled in the UK or**
- **is a British subject not ordinarily resident in the UK,**

then the trader may claim that the trade profits should be assessed on the remittance basis.

A person who is not UK resident is only taxable in the UK on UK income. The profits of trades carried on abroad by non-residents are therefore not liable to UK income tax. Where a person who carries on a trade wholly or partly abroad becomes or ceases to be UK resident, the profits of the trade carried on abroad will become or cease to be liable to UK income tax respectively. To ensure that only the foreign profits which arise whilst the trader is UK resident are taxed there is a deemed cessation and recommencement of the trade. This rule also applies to a partner who changes residence if the partnership is carrying on a trade wholly or partly abroad.

This deemed cessation and recommencement does not prevent any losses that were being carried forward from before the change from being set off under s 385 ICTA 1988 against profits arising after the change.

Under the OECD Model Agreement, a resident of country R trading in country T is taxable in country T on his profits only if he has a permanent establishment there (see later in this text). A resident of country R carrying on a profession in country P is taxable in country P on his profits only if he has a fixed base regularly available to him in country P.

The general rule for overseas traders doing business with UK customers is that they are trading in the UK (and therefore liable to UK tax on their profits) if contracts are concluded in the UK.

4.2 Travel expenses

A deduction is available against trade profits income for travel expenses incurred by UK domiciled individuals who carry on a trade wholly outside the UK and who travel to and from the UK. So long as the taxpayer's absence abroad is wholly and exclusively for the purposes of his trade then any travel expenses to and from the UK together with the cost of board and lodging at the overseas location are deductible. If the taxpayer's absence is for a continuous period of 60 days or more, the cost of up to two visits in any tax year by his spouse/civil partner and/or children under 18 is also deductible.

No deduction is however given for these travel expenses where the trade profits are taxed on a remittance basis. Instead the trader should arrange and pay for the travel whilst abroad, thus avoiding the need to remit that amount to the UK.

4.3 Overseas losses

A loss sustained in a trade (or profession or vocation) carried on abroad can be relieved in the same manner as UK trade losses: s 380, s 381, s 385 and s 388 all apply.

However, if relief is sought under ss 380 and 381 for a loss in a trade which is wholly carried on abroad, the income which the loss can be set against is restricted to:

- Overseas trade profits
- Overseas pensions
- Overseas earnings

5 Double taxation relief (DTR)

FAST FORWARD

Double taxation relief may be available to reduce the burden of taxation. It is generally given by reducing the UK tax charged by the foreign tax suffered.

5.1 Introduction

As we have seen, **UK tax applies to the worldwide income of UK residents and the UK income of non-residents.**

When other countries adopt the same approach it is clear that some income may be taxed twice:

- Firstly in the country where it arises
- Secondly in the country where the taxpayer resides

Double taxation relief (DTR) as a result of international agreements may avoid the problem, or at least diminish its impact.

5.2 Double taxation agreements

Typical provisions of double taxation agreements based on the OECD Model are:

(a) Total exemption from tax is given in the country where income arises in the hands of, for example visiting diplomats and teachers on exchange programmes

(b) Preferential rates of withholding tax are applied to, for example, payments of rent, interest and dividends. The usual rate is frequently replaced by 15% or less

(c) DTR is given to taxpayers in their country of residence by way of a credit for tax suffered in the country where income arises. This may be in the form of relief for withholding tax only or, given a holding of specified size in a foreign company, for the underlying tax on the profits out of which dividends are paid

(d)   There are exchange of information clauses so that tax evaders can be chased internationally

(e)   There are rules to determine a person's residence and to prevent dual residence (tie-breaker clauses)

(f)   There are clauses which render certain profits taxable in only one rather than both of the contracting states

(g)   There is a non-discrimination clause so that a country does not tax foreigners more heavily than its own nationals

5.3 Unilateral relief

If no relief is available under a double taxation agreement, UK legislation provides for unilateral relief. However, unilateral relief is not available if relief is specifically excluded under the terms of a double tax agreement.

Foreign income must be included gross (ie including foreign tax) in the UK tax computation. The foreign tax is deducted from the UK tax liability (this is credit relief) but the relief cannot exceed the UK tax on the foreign income so the taxpayer bears the higher of:

- The UK tax
- The foreign tax

The UK tax on the foreign income is the difference between:

(a)   The UK tax before DTR on all income including the foreign income

(b)   The UK tax on all income except the foreign income

In both (a) and (b), we take account of tax reducers.

Question	Double tax relief

A UK resident, ordinarily resident and domiciled individual has the following income for 2006/07.

	£
UK salary	30,212
Interest on foreign debenture (net of foreign tax at 5%)	4,750
Foreign rents (net of foreign tax at 60%)	1,500

Assuming that maximum DTR is claimed, show the UK tax liability.

Answer

	Non-savings £	Savings (excl dividends) £	Total £
Salary	30,212		
Foreign interest £4,750 × 100/95		5,000	
Overseas property business £1,500 × 100/40	3,750		
STI	33,962	5,000	38,962
Less personal allowance	(5,035)		
Taxable income	28,927	5,000	33,927

	£
Non-savings income	
£2,150 × 10%	215
£26,777 × 22%	5,891
Savings (excl dividend) income	
£4,373 × 20%	875
£627 × 40%	251
	7,232

		£
Less double taxation relief		
Interest	250	
Rents (see below)	951	
		(1,201)
UK tax liability		6,031

Since the rents are taxed more highly overseas, these should be regarded as the top slice of UK taxable income. Taxable income excluding the rents is £30,177 and the UK tax on this is:

	£
Non-savings income	
£2,150 × 10%	215
£23,027 × 22%	5,066
Savings (excl. dividend) income	
£5,000 × 20%	1,000
	6,281

The UK tax on the rents is £951 (£7,232 – 6,281). Since foreign tax of £2,250 (60% of £3,750) is greater, the DTR is the smaller figure of £951. Foreign interest was taxed abroad at the rate of 5% (£250). Since the UK rate (20%) is clearly higher, the DTR given is £250.

Where there is no point in claiming this credit relief, perhaps because loss relief has eliminated any liability to UK tax, the taxpayer may elect for expense relief instead. No credit is given for foreign tax suffered, but only the income after foreign taxes is brought into the tax computation.

If foreign taxes are not relieved in the year in which the income is taxable in the UK, no relief can be obtained in any earlier or later year.

Credit relief, whether under a treaty or unilateral, is ignored when working out the tax which remains to be reduced by tax reducers.

Taxpayers who have claimed relief against their UK tax bill for taxes paid abroad must notify HMRC in writing of any changes to the foreign liabilities if these changes result in the DTR claimed becoming excessive. This rule applies to all taxes not just income tax.

Chapter roundup

- An individual may be any or all of resident, ordinarily resident and domiciled in the UK, and his liability to UK tax will be determined accordingly. Foreign income is only taxable if the individual is UK resident.

- Income from overseas sources is taxed on a similar basis to UK income. It is charged on a remittance basis for non-UK domiciled individuals and British subjects not ordinarily resident in the UK.

- The residence, ordinary residence and domicile status of an employee (and, in some cases, whether he carries out his duties in the UK or outside it) determine the tax treatment of his earnings.

- Individuals working abroad may claim certain deductions for travel expenses.

- Profits of an overseas trade are computed as for UK trades. However, the remittance basis applies for non-UK domiciled individuals.

- Double taxation relief may be available to reduce the burden of taxation. It is generally given by reducing the UK tax charged by the foreign tax suffered.

Quick quiz

1 When will an individual be resident in the UK?

2 On what basis is a UK resident who is not domiciled in the UK taxed on overseas income?

3 What earnings are taxed on a remittance basis?

4 How many return journeys by John's family can an employer pay for tax free for John if he is working overseas for 100 days?

5 How will a foreign dividend be taxed on a higher rate taxpayer if he is:

   (a) domiciled in the UK
   (b) not domiciled in the UK?

6 What is the maximum amount of credit relief that can be given for overseas tax on overseas income?

Answers to quick quiz

1   An individual is resident in the UK if he is here for 183 days or more, or he makes visits to the UK averaging 91 days or more a year for each of four consecutive years.

2   On the remittance basis

3   (a)   Individual resident and ordinarily resident in UK, but not UK domiciled, working for a foreign employer, duties performed wholly outside UK ('overseas earnings')

    (b)   Individual resident but not ordinarily resident in UK relating to duties performed outside UK ('foreign earnings')

4   Two

5   (a)   On an arising basis as dividend income liable to tax at 32.5%.

    (b)   On a remittance basis as non-savings income liable to tax at 40%.

6   The lower of:

    (i)   UK tax on the overseas income, and

    (ii)   The overseas tax on the overseas income

Now try the question below from the Exam Question Bank

Number	Level	Marks	Time
Q11	Introductory	20	36 mins

Part B
Capital taxes

Chargeable gains: an outline

Topic list	Syllabus reference
1 Chargeable and exempt persons, disposals and assets	A3(a)D1,D2,(c)(ii), (iii),(d)(iii)
2 CGT payable by individuals	A3(a)D5

Introduction

Now that we have concluded our study of the income tax computation we can consider the capital gains tax computation. The two must be kept separate.

Capital gains arise when taxpayers dispose of assets, such as investments or capital assets used in the business. If, for example, you buy a picture for £10,000, hang it on your wall for 20 years and then sell it for £200,000, you will have a capital gain.

In this chapter we see when a capital gain will be liable to tax and how to work out the tax on an individual's taxable gains.

In the next chapter, we will see how to calculate a chargeable gain.

Study guide

		Intellectual level
3	**Chargeable gains and capital gains tax liabilities in situations involving further overseas aspects and in relation to closely related persons and trusts together with the application of additional exemptions and reliefs**	
(a)	The contents of the Paper F6 study guide for chargeable gains under headings:	2
•	D1 The scope of the taxation of capital gains	
•	D2 The basic principles of computing gains and losses	
•	D5 The computation of capital gains tax payable by individuals	
(c)	The basic principles of computing gains and losses:	3
(ii)	Advise on the impact of dates of disposal and conditional contracts	
(iii)	Evaluate the use of capital losses in the year of death	
(d)	Gains and losses on the disposal of movable and immovable property:	3
(iii)	Establish the tax effect of appropriations to and from trading stock	

Exam guide

Taxpayers normally plan major disposals of capital assets so you may get a question asking when would be the best time to make a disposal. You need to know the rules about the date of disposal, and then you need to be able to quantify any tax savings that might result from delaying or advancing a sale. This is particularly important where business assets have not been held for two years so that a delay may significantly increase the taper relief available.

> Knowledge brought forward from earlier studies

This chapter revises topics covered at level 2.3. The carry back of losses in the year of death is new.

1 Chargeable and exempt persons, disposals and assets

FAST FORWARD
> For CGT to apply, there needs to be a chargeable person, a chargeable disposal and a chargeable asset.

Exam focus point

For a chargeable gain to arise there must be:

- A chargeable person; and
- A chargeable disposal; and
- A chargeable asset

otherwise no charge to tax occurs.

1.1 Chargeable persons

The following are chargeable persons.

- Individuals
- Partnerships
- Companies
- Trustees

We will look at the taxation of chargeable gains on companies later in this Text.

The following are exempt persons.

- Charities using gains for charitable purposes
- Registered pension funds
- Local authorities
- Registered friendly societies
- Approved scientific research associations
- Authorised unit trusts and investment trusts
- Diplomatic representatives
- Persons who are neither resident nor ordinarily resident in the UK

1.2 Chargeable disposals

FAST FORWARD

A chargeable disposal occurs on the date of the contract or when a conditional contract becomes unconditional.

The following are chargeable disposals.

- Sales of assets or parts of assets
- Gifts of assets or parts of assets
- Receipts of capital sums following the surrender of rights to assets
- The loss or destruction of assets
- The appropriation of assets as trading stock

A chargeable disposal occurs on the date of the contract (where there is one, whether written or oral), or the date of a conditional contract becoming unconditional. This may differ from the date of transfer of the asset. However, when a capital sum is received on a surrender of rights or the loss or destruction of an asset, the disposal takes place on the day the sum is received.

The timing of a disposal should be carefully considered bearing in mind these rules. For example, an individual may wish to accelerate a gain into an earlier tax year to obtain earlier loss relief or to delay a gain until a later tax year when a lower rate of tax may be applicable.

Where a disposal involves an acquisition by someone else, their date of acquisition is the same as the date of disposal.

The following are exempt disposals.

- **Transfers of assets on death** (the heirs inherit assets as if they bought them at death for their then market values, but there is no capital gain or allowable loss on death). It is possible to vary or disclaim inherited assets. The CGT effect of such a variation or disclaimer is dealt with later in this Text.

- Transfers of assets as security for a loan or mortgage

Chargeable gains do not arise in respect of betting winnings or cashbacks, for example on new mortgages or cars.

1.3 Transfers to and from trading stock

When a taxpayer acquires an asset other than as trading stock and then uses it as trading stock, **the appropriation to trading stock normally leads to an immediate chargeable gain or allowable loss**, based on the asset's market value at the date of appropriation. The asset's cost for income tax purposes is that market value.

Alternatively, the trader can elect to have no chargeable gain or allowable loss: if he does so, the cost for income tax purposes is reduced by the gain or increased by the loss.

When an asset which is trading stock is appropriated to other purposes, the trade profits are calculated as if the trader had sold it for its market value, and for capital gains tax purposes as if he had bought it at the time of the appropriation for the same value.

1.4 Chargeable assets

All forms of property, wherever in the world they are situated, are chargeable assets unless they are specifically designated as exempt.

The following are exempt assets (so gains are not taxable and losses on their disposal are not in general allowable losses, the few exceptions are explained in this Text).

- Motor vehicles suitable for private use

- National Savings & Investments certificates and premium bonds

- Foreign currency for private use

- Decorations awarded for bravery (unless purchased)

- Damages for personal or professional injury

- Life assurance policies (only exempt in the hands of the original beneficial owner)

- Works of art, scientific collections and so on given for national purposes

- Gilt-edged securities

- Qualifying corporate bonds (QCBs) (although any gain deferred when a security changed status to a QCB remains taxable)

- Certain chattels

- Debts (except debts on a security)

- Pension rights and annuity rights

- Investments held in individual savings accounts

There are also exemptions for enterprise investment scheme (EIS) shares and venture capital trust (VCT) shares (see earlier in this Text).

2 CGT payable by individuals

Individuals pay CGT on their taxable gains. Gains are taxed after income at the rates applicable to savings (excl dividend) income. Individuals are entitled to taper relief and an annual exemption.

2.1 Introduction

Individuals are liable to CGT on the disposal of assets situated anywhere in the world if for any part of the tax year of disposal they are resident or ordinarily resident in the UK. 'Residence' and 'ordinary residence' have the same meaning as for income tax purposes (see earlier in this Text). Trustees also pay CGT on their gains.

An individual pays CGT on any taxable gains arising in the tax year. **Taxable gains are the net chargeable gains (gains minus losses) of the tax year reduced by unrelieved losses brought forward from previous years, taper relief and the annual exemption.**

The annual exemption applies each tax year. For 2006/07 it is £8,800. It is the **last deduction** to be made in the calculation of taxable gains.

2.2 Calculating CGT

Taxable gains are chargeable to CGT, not income tax, and are never included in the income tax computation.

They are taxed *after* income at the rates applicable to savings (excl dividend) income. So, an individual with £2,000 of taxable income and gains of £50,000 in the year would pay CGT at 10% (on £150), 20% (on £31,150) and 40% (on the balance).

Question	Rates of CGT

In 2006/07, Carol, a single woman, has the following income, gains and losses. Find the CGT payable.

	£
Salary	36,050
Chargeable gains (not eligible for taper relief – see later)	26,700
Allowable capital losses	7,700

Answer

(a) Carol's taxable income is as follows.

	£
Salary	36,050
Less personal allowance	(5,035)
Taxable income	31,015

(b) The gains to be taxed are as follows.

	£
Gains	26,700
Less losses	(7,700)
	19,000
Less annual exemption	(8,800)
Taxable gains	10,200

(c)   The tax bands are allocated as follows.

	Total	Income	Gains
Starting rate	2,150	2,150	0
Basic rate	31,150	28,865	2,285
Higher rate	7,915	0	7,915
		31,015	10,200

(d)   The CGT payable is as follows.

	£
£2,285 × 20%	457
£7,915 × 40%	3,166
Total CGT payable	3,623

2.3 Allowable losses

Deduct allowable capital losses from chargeable gains in the tax year in which they arise. Any loss which cannot be set off is carried forward to set against future chargeable gains. Losses must be used as soon as possible (subject to the following paragraph). Losses may not normally be set against income (unless they arise on the disposal of certain unquoted trading company shares – see earlier in this Text.)

Allowable losses brought forward are only set off to reduce current year chargeable gains less current year allowable losses to the annual exempt amount. No set-off is made if net chargeable gains for the current year do not exceed the annual exempt amount.

2.4 Example: the use of losses

(a)   George has chargeable gains for 2006/07 of £10,000 and allowable losses of £6,000. As the losses are **current year losses** they must be fully relieved against the £10,000 of gains to produce net gains of £4,000, despite the fact that net gains are below the annual exemption.

(b)   Bob has gains of £12,700 for 2006/07 and allowable losses brought forward of £6,000. Bob restricts his loss relief to £3,900 so as to leave net gains of £(12,700 – 3,900) = £8,800, which will be exactly covered by his annual exemption for 2006/07. The remaining £2,100 of losses will be carried forward to 2007/08.

(c)   Tom has chargeable gains of £5,000 for 2006/07 and losses brought forward from 2005/06 of £4,000. He will leapfrog 2006/07 and carry forward all of his losses to 2007/08. His gains of £5,000 are covered by his annual exemption for 2006/07.

2.5 Losses in the year of death

One of the only two occasions when capital losses may be carried back arises on the death of an individual. We look at the other occasion (relating to deferred consideration) in the next chapter.

Losses arising in the tax year in which an individual dies can be carried back to the previous three tax years, later years first, and used so as to reduce gains for each of the years to an amount covered by the appropriate annual exemption. Only losses in excess of gains in the year of death can be carried back.

Question Loss in year of death

Joe dies on 1 January 2007. His chargeable gains (no taper relief available – see later) and allowable loss have been as follows.

	Gain/(loss) £	Annual exemption £
2006/07	2,000	8,800
	(12,000)	
2005/06	8,700	8,500
2004/05	4,000	8,200
2003/04	28,000	7,900

How will the loss be set off?

Answer

The £10,000 net loss which arises in 2006/07 will be carried back. We must set off the loss against the 2006/07 gains first even though the gains are covered by the 2006/07 annual exemption.

£200 of the loss will be used in 2005/06. None of the loss will be used in 2004/05 (because the gains for that year are covered by the annual exemption), and so the remaining £9,800 will be used in 2003/04. Repayments of CGT will follow.

2.6 Taper relief

FAST FORWARD

Taper relief is more generous for business assets than non-business assets.

Taper relief may be available to reduce gains realised by individuals after 5 April 1998.

Taper relief reduces the percentage of the gain chargeable according to how many complete years the asset has been held since acquisition or 6 April 1998 if later. Taper relief is more generous for business assets than for non-business assets.

The percentages of gains which remain chargeable after taper relief are set out below.

Number of complete years after 5.4.98 for which asset held	Gain on business assets % of gain chargeable	Gain on non business assets % of gain chargeable
0	100	100
1	50	100
2	25	100
3	25	95
4	25	90
5	25	85
6	25	80
7	25	75
8	25	70
9	25	65
10	25	60

Exam focus point

You will be given the above percentages in the rates and allowances section of the exam paper.

Non-business assets acquired before 17 March 1998 qualify for an additional 1 year (a 'bonus year') to the period for which they are actually held after 5 April 1998.

2.7 Example: taper relief years

Peter buys a non business asset on 1 January 1998 and sells it on 1 July 2006. For the purposes of the taper Peter is treated as if he had held the asset for 9 complete years (eight complete years after 5 April 1998 plus one additional year).

If the asset had been a business asset, Peter holds the asset for eight years only but in any case has maximum taper relief after two years ownership.

2.8 Application of taper relief

FAST FORWARD Losses are set off before taper relief against gains of the same year or of future years.

2.9 Example: use of losses and taper relief

Ruby sold a business asset in July 2006 which she had purchased in January 2005. She realised a chargeable gain (before taper relief) of £18,000. She also sold a painting in 2006/07 realising a capital loss of £6,000. She has a capital loss brought forward from 2005/06 of £10,000.

Losses are dealt with **before** taper relief. However losses brought forward are only deducted from net current gains to the extent that the gains exceed the CGT annual exemption:

	£
Gain	18,000
Loss	(6,000)
Current net gains	12,000
Less brought forward loss	(3,200)
Gains before taper relief	8,800
Gains after taper relief (1 year ownership) £8,800 × 50%	4,400
Less annual exemption	(8,800)
Taxable gains	Nil

Note that the benefit of the taper relief is effectively wasted since the brought forward loss reduces the gain down to the annual exemption amount but the taper is then applied to that amount reducing it further.

The loss carried forward is £6,800 (£10,000 – £3,200).

2.10 Allocation of losses to gains

Where there are several gains eligible for different rates of taper relief allocate losses to gains in the way that produces the lowest tax charge. Losses should therefore be deducted from the gains attracting the lowest rate of taper (ie where the highest percentage of the gain remains chargeable).

The following proforma should be used.

Summary

	Business		Non-business	
	X yrs	X yrs	X yrs	X yrs
	£	£	£	£
Gains	X	X	X	X
Less current year losses (best use)			(X)	(X)
Less loss b/f (best use)		(X)	(X)	(X)
Gains before taper relief	X	X	Nil	Nil
Percentage of gain remaining chargeable	X%	X%	X%	X%
Gains after taper relief	X	X	Nil	Nil

		£
Total gains £(X + X)		X
Less annual exemption		(8,800)
Taxable gains		X

Follow the steps below to ensure you work through the proforma in the correct order.

Step 1   List the gains in order of percentage of gain remaining chargeable

Step 2   Set off current year losses, against gain with highest percentage remaining chargeable first, and then in descending order

Step 3   Set off brought forward losses (or losses carried back from the year of death) in the same order.

Step 4   Remember to restrict set off of brought forward losses (or losses carried back) so that net gains after losses, but before taper relief, is not less than the annual exemption.

Step 5   Apply taper relief

Step 6   Deduct the annual exemption

Step 7   The result is the net taxable gains for the year.

2.11 Example: allocation of losses to gains

Alastair made the following capital losses and gains in 2006/07:

	£
Loss	10,000
Gains (before taper relief)	
Asset A (non-business asset)	25,000
Asset B (business asset)	18,000

Asset A was purchased in December 1997 and sold in January 2007. Taper relief reduces the gain to 65% of the original gain (9 years including additional year; non-business asset). Asset B was purchased on 5 November 2003 and sold on 17 December 2006. Taper relief reduces the gain to 25% of the original gain (3 years; business asset).

The best use of the loss is to offset it against the gain on the non-business asset:

	Business 3 yrs £	Non-business 9 yrs £
Gains	18,000	25,000
Less current year losses (best use)		(10,000)
Gains before taper relief	18,000	15,000
Percentage of gain remaining chargeable	25%	65%
Gains after taper relief	4,500	9,750

	£
Total gains £(4,500 + 9,750)	14,250
Less annual exemption	(8,800)
Taxable gains	5,450

2.12 Other points

There are certain special situations which will affect the operation of taper relief:

    (a)   Where there has been a transfer of assets between spouses/civil partners (a no loss/no gain transfer – see later in this Text) the taper on a subsequent disposal will be based on the combined period of holding by the spouses/civil partners.

    (b)   Where gains have been relieved under a provision which reduces the cost of the asset in the hands of a new owner (such as gift relief – see later in this Text) the taper will operate by reference to the holding period of the new owner.

2.13 Shares and securities

Special rules apply to shares and securities. We cover these later in this Text.

2.14 Business assets

A business asset is:

- An asset **used for the purposes of a trade** carried on by any individual, partnership, trustee or personal representative (whether or not the owner of the asset is involved in carrying on the trade concerned) or by a qualifying company.

- An asset **held for the purposes of any office or employment** held by the individual owner with a person carrying on a trade.

- **Shares in a qualifying company** held by an individual.

A qualifying company is a **trading company** (or holding company of a trading group) where:

    (a)   The company is **not listed** on a recognised stock exchange nor is a 51% subsidiary of a listed company (companies listed on the Alternative Investment Market (AIM) are unlisted for this purpose), or

    (b)   The individual is an **officer or employee** of the company or of a company with a **relevant connection**, or

    (c)   The individual holds at least **5% of the voting rights** in the company.

A company is also a qualifying company if it is a **non-trading company** (or holding company of a non-trading group) where:

    (a)   The individual is an **officer or employee** of the company or a company with a relevant connection, and

    (b)   The individual did not have a **material interest** in the company or in any other company which at that time had control of the company.

A **material interest** is defined as possession or the ability to control more than 10% of the issued shares in the company, or more than 10% of the voting rights in the company, or an entitlement to more than 10% of the income of the company or more than 10% of the assets of the company available for distribution.

For this purpose, an individual is treated as having a material interest if he, together with one or more connected persons (see next chapter) has a material interest. For example, if A holds 5% of the voting rights in the company and his brother B (a connected person) has 15% of the voting rights, A will have a material interest in the company as between them A and B hold more than 10% of the voting rights.

A company has a **relevant connection** with another company if:

(a)   The companies are both members of a 51% group, or

(b)   The companies are under common control and they carry on a complementary business which can reasonably be regarded as one composite undertaking, or

(c)   One company (X Ltd) is a joint enterprise company in which 75% or more of the ordinary shares capital is held by five or fewer persons and the other company (Y Ltd) holds 10% or more of the ordinary share capital in X Ltd.

The rules for business assets apply in a similar way to assets held by trustees.

If an asset qualifies as a business asset for part of the time of ownership, and part not, the business part and the non-business part are treated as separate assets calculated by time apportionment over the period of ownership of the asset (not just complete years). Taper relief applies to each gain separately but the period of ownership for calculating the taper relief percentage is taken to be the **whole** number of years of ownership of the asset.

Question
Mixed use asset

Robert bought a warehouse on 5 August 2000. He used the whole of the building for his trade until 4 April 2004. The building was then let out to a quoted company until it was sold on 4 December 2006. The gain on sale was £140,000.

Show Robert's gain after taper relief.

Answer

	Business use	*Non business use*
Period between 5.8.00 – 4.4.04	44 months	
Period between 5.4.04 – 4.12.06		32 months

Number of complete years ownership is 5.8.00 – 4.8.06 = 6 years

Gain on business asset after taper relief is:

£140,000 × 44/76 × 25% (6 years) = £20,263

Gain on non-business asset after taper relief is:

£140,000 × 32/76 × 80% (6 years) = £47,158

Total gain 20,263 + 47,158 = £67,421

If the asset was acquired before 6 April 1998, only use on or after that date is taken into account. If the asset is owned for more than ten years after 5 April 1998, only the use in the **last ten years** of ownership is taken into account. This rule will clearly only apply from 2008/09.

Chapter roundup

- For CGT to apply, there needs to be a chargeable person, a chargeable disposal and a chargeable asset.

- A chargeable disposal occurs on the date of the contract or when a conditional contract becomes unconditional.

- Individuals pay CGT on their taxable gains. Gains are taxed after income at the rates applicable to savings (excl dividend) income. Individuals are entitled to taper relief and an annual exemption.

- Taper relief is more generous for business assets than non-business assets.

- Losses are set off before taper relief against gains of the same year or of future years.

Quick quiz

1   Give some examples of chargeable disposals.

2   Are the following assets chargeable to CGT or exempt?

    (a)   Shares (not held in ISA)
    (b)   Car
    (c)   Land
    (d)   Victoria Cross awarded to owner
    (e)   National Savings & Investments Certificates

3   At what rate or rates do individuals pay CGT?

4   To what extent must allowable losses be set against chargeable gains?

5   What is a qualifying company for business asset taper relief?

Answers to quick quiz

1   Sales of assets or parts of assets
    Gifts of assets or parts of assets
    Receipts of capital sums following the surrender of rights to assets
    Loss or destruction of assets
    Appropriation of assets as trading stock

2   (a)   Shares – Chargeable
    (b)   Car – Exempt as motor vehicle suitable for private use
    (c)   Land – Chargeable
    (d)   Victoria Cross – Exempt as medal for bravery not acquired by purchase
    (e)   National Savings & Investments Certificates – Exempt

3   10%, 20% and 40%

4   Current year losses must be set off against gains in full, even if this reduces gains below annual exemption. Losses brought forward or carried back from year of death, are set off to bring down untapered gains to level of annual exemption.

5   A trading company (or holding company of trading group) which is unlisted or of which the individual is an officer or employee or of which the individual holds at least 5% voting rights.

    A non-trading company (or holding company of a non-trading group) of which the individual is an officer or employee and in which the individual does not have a material interest.

Now try the question below from the Exam Question Bank

Number	Level	Marks	Time
Q12	Introductory	25	45 mins

Computing gains and losses

12

Topic list	Syllabus reference
1 The basic computation	A3(a)D2
2 The indexation allowance	A3(a)D2
3 Valuing assets	A3(a)D2
4 Connected persons	A3(c)(i)
5 Married couples and civil partners	A3(b)(i)
6 Business partnerships	A3(b)(v)
7 Part disposals	A3(d)(i)

Introduction

In the previous chapter we saw how to work out the CGT payable by an individual on his taxable gains. We now see how to compute a chargeable gain.

The basic computation is to take the proceeds minus the cost. In certain cases we then deduct an allowance for inflation (the indexation allowance). We see how to adapt the computation where only part of an asset is disposed of.

We also look at some special cases where the rules are modified because of the relationship between the disposer and the acquirer of an asset; without such rules, people could do deals with their relatives to avoid tax.

We also look at how chargeable gains on partnership assets are dealt with.

In the following chapters we will look at the special rules for certain types of assets and at what reliefs are available.

Study guide

		Intellectual level
3	**Chargeable gains and capital gains tax liabilities in situations involving further overseas aspects and in relation to closely related persons and trusts together with the application of additional exemptions and reliefs**	
(a)	The contents of the Paper F6 study guide for chargeable gains under headings:	2
•	D2 The basic principles of computing gains and losses	
(b)	The scope of the taxation of capital gains:	3
(i)	Determine the tax implications of independent taxation and transfers between spouses	
(v)	Identify the occasions when a capital gain would arise on a partner in a partnership	
(c)	The basic principles of computing gains and losses:	3
(i)	Identify connected persons for capital gains tax purposes and advise on the tax implications of transfers between connected persons	
(d)	Gains and losses on the disposal of movable and immovable property:	3
(i)	Advise on the tax implications of a part disposal, including small part disposals of land	

Exam guide

To be able to answer a question on any aspect of capital gains tax you must be able to calculate the chargeable gain so you must know the basic computation. You may be asked to give advice about family taxation; you will therefore need to understand how to deal with assets transferred between spouses/civil partners and the special rules for connected persons. Watch out for losses on gifts to connected persons. To deal with partnerships you need to grasp the concept that each partner has a share of each asset, based on the capital profit sharing ratio.

Knowledge brought forward from earlier studies

This chapter revises the computation of chargeable gains from level 2.3 and the rules for spouses/civil partners.

1 The basic computation

FAST FORWARD

A chargeable gain is computed by taking the proceeds and deducting both the costs and the indexation allowance. For individuals indexation is not given after April 1998 but taper relief may be available.

1.1 Introduction

A chargeable gain (or an allowable loss) is generally calculated as follows.

	£
Disposal consideration (usually market value)	45,000
Less incidental costs of disposal	(400)
Net proceeds	44,600
Less allowable costs	(21,000)
Unindexed gain	23,600
Less indexation allowance (if available)	(7,000)
Indexed gain	16,600

For individuals, taper relief may then apply (see the previous chapter).

Incidental costs of disposal may include:

- Valuation fees (but not the cost of an appeal against HMRC's valuation)
- Estate agency fees
- Advertising costs
- Legal costs

These costs should be deducted separately from any other allowable costs (because they do not qualify for any indexation allowance if it was available on that disposal).

Allowable costs include:

- The original cost of acquisition
- Incidental costs of acquisition
- Capital expenditure incurred in enhancing the asset

Incidental costs of acquisition may include the types of cost listed above as incidental costs of disposal, but acquisition costs do qualify for indexation allowance (from the month of acquisition) where it is available on the disposal.

Enhancement expenditure is capital expenditure that enhances the value of the asset and is reflected in the state or nature of the asset at the time of disposal, or expenditure incurred in establishing, preserving or defending title to, or a right over, the asset. Excluded from this category are:

- Costs of repairs and maintenance
- Costs of insurance
- Any expenditure deductible for income tax purposes
- Any expenditure met by public funds (for example council grants)

Enhancement expenditure may qualify for indexation allowance from the month in which it becomes due and payable.

Taper relief applies to the whole gain, regardless of when the enhancement expenditure was incurred.

1.2 The consideration for a disposal

Usually the disposal consideration is the proceeds of sale of the asset, but a disposal is deemed to take place at market value:

(a) Where the disposal is **not a bargain at arm's length**

(b) Where the disposal is made for a **consideration which cannot be valued**

(c) Where the disposal is by way of a **gift**

Sometimes an asset is sold for a fixed sum plus a possible addition depending on some condition. For example, land might be sold without planning permission, with an extra payment to be made to the vendor if planning permission is obtained. In such cases, **the contingent right to additional proceeds must be valued, and that value must be added to the known proceeds.**

If additional proceeds are in fact received, that receipt is treated as proceeds of the disposal of the contingent right. A chargeable gain or allowable loss will then arise: the allowable cost is the value of the right brought into account in the initial computation of the capital gain (*Marren v Ingles 1980*).

Taxpayers (other than companies) can carry back a loss on the disposal of the contingent right to the tax year in which the gain on the main disposal arose. This does not apply where the right to the deferred consideration was acquired second-hand.

1.3 Example: conditional consideration

Deirdre acquired 10,000 shares in Flowers Ltd for £20,000 in May 2001. In November 2006 she agreed to sell her shares for £120,000 cash and 20% of the profits of the company made in the year ended 30 April 2007. The value of the right to receive the additional consideration was agreed by HMRC at the time to be £10,000.

The actual profits of that year were £70,000 and she received the additional consideration in January 2008.

The shares are business assets for taper relief purposes. The right to receive additional consideration is not a business asset for taper relief purposes.

In November 2006 Deirdre's gain is:

	£
Proceeds (£120,000 + £10,000)	130,000
Less cost	(20,000)
Gain before taper relief	110,000
Gain after taper relief (> 2yrs: 25%)	27,500

In January 2008 the receipt of additional consideration is a disposal of the right:

	£
Proceeds (20% × £70,000)	14,000
Less cost	(10,000)
Gain before taper relief	4,000

No taper relief available (non business asset held for < 3 years)

2 The indexation allowance

Indexation allowance removes the inflationary element of a capital gain. It is restricted for individuals.

2.1 Introduction

The purpose of having an indexation allowance is to remove the inflationary element of a gain from taxation.

Individuals are entitled to an indexation allowance from the date of acquisition of an asset until April 1998.

Companies are entitled to an indexation allowance from the date of acquisition until the date of disposal of an asset, even if this is after April 1998. We look at companies in more detail later in this Text.

2.2 Example: indexation allowance

John bought a painting on 2 January 1987 and sold it on 19 November 2006.

Indexation allowance is available from January 1987 until April 1998.

Exam formula

The indexation factor is:

$$\frac{\text{RPI for month of disposal (or April 1998)} - \text{RPI for month of acquisition}}{\text{RPI for month of acquisition}}$$

The calculation is expressed as a decimal and is rounded to three decimal places.

The indexation factor is multiplied by the cost of the asset to calculate the indexation allowance. If the RPI has fallen, the indexation allowance is zero: it is not negative. RPI values are given in questions where required.

Question   The indexation allowance

An asset is acquired by an individual on 15 February 1983 (RPI = 83.0) at a cost of £5,000. Enhancement expenditure of £2,000 is incurred on 10 April 1984 (RPI = 88.6). The asset is sold for £20,500 on 20 December 2006. Incidental costs of sale are £500. Calculate the chargeable gain before taper relief.

Answer

The indexation allowance is available until April 1998 (RPI = 162.6) and is computed as follows.

	£
$\frac{162.6 - 83.0}{83.0} = 0.959 \times £5,000$	4,795
$\frac{162.6 - 88.6}{88.6} = 0.835 \times £2,000$	1,670
	6,465

The computation of the chargeable gain is as follows.

	£
Proceeds	20,500
Less incidental costs of sale	(500)
Net proceeds	20,000
Less allowable costs £(5,000 + 2,000)	(7,000)
Unindexed gain	13,000
Less indexation allowance (see above)	(6,465)
Chargeable gain before taper relief	6,535

2.3 Indexation and losses

The indexation allowance cannot create or increase an allowable loss. If there is a gain before the indexation allowance, the allowance can reduce that gain to zero, but no further. If there is a loss before the indexation allowance, no indexation allowance is available.

3 Valuing assets

FAST FORWARD

Market value must be used in certain capital gains computations. There are special rules for shares and securities.

3.1 General rules

Where market value is used in a chargeable gains computation (see Section 1 above), **the value to be used is the price which the assets in question might reasonably be expected to fetch on a sale in the open market**.

3.2 Shares and securities

Quoted shares and securities are valued using prices in The Stock Exchange Daily Official List, taking the lower of:

(a) Lower quoted price + ¼ × (higher quoted price – lower quoted price) ('quarter up' rule).

(b) The average of the highest and lowest marked bargains (ignoring bargains marked at special prices).

| Question | Calculation of CGT value |

Shares in A plc are quoted at 100-110p. The highest and lowest marked bargains were 99p and 110p. What would be the market value for CGT purposes?

| Answer |

The value will be the lower of:

(a) $100 + \frac{1}{4} \times (110 - 100) = 102.5$

(b) $\frac{110 + 99}{2} = 104.5$

The market value for CGT purposes will therefore be 102.5p per share.

Unquoted shares are harder to value than quoted shares. HMRC have a special office, the Shares Valuation Division, to deal with the valuation of unquoted shares.

4 Connected persons

Disposals between connected persons are always deemed to take place for a consideration equal to market value. Any loss arising on a disposal to a connected person can be set only against a gain arising on a disposal to the same connected person.

4.1 Definition and effect

A transaction between 'connected persons' is treated as one between parties to a transaction otherwise than by way of a bargain made at arm's length. This means that the acquisition and disposal are deemed to take place for a consideration equal to the market value of the asset, rather than the actual price paid. In addition, if a loss results, it can be set only against gains arising in the same or future years from disposals to the same connected person and the loss can only be set off if he or she is still connected with the person sustaining the loss.

Key term

> **Connected person**. An individual is connected with:
>
> * His spouse/civil partner
> * His relatives (brothers, sisters, ancestors and lineal descendants)
> * The relatives of his spouse/civil partner
> * The spouses/civil partners of his and his spouse/civil partner's relatives

4.2 Assets disposed of in a series of transactions

A taxpayer might attempt to avoid tax by disposing of his property piecemeal to persons connected with him. For example, a majority holding of shares might be broken up into several minority holdings, each with a much lower value per share, and each of the shareholder's children could be given a minority holding.

To prevent the avoidance of tax in this way, **where a person disposes of assets to one or more persons, with whom he is connected, in a series of linked transactions, the disposal proceeds for each disposal will be a proportion of the value of the assets taken together**. Thus in the example of the shareholding, the value of the majority holding would be apportioned between the minority holdings. Transactions are linked if they occur within six years of each other.

5 Married couples and civil partners

Spouses/civil partners are treated as separate people. Transfers of assets between spouses/civil partners give rise to neither a gain nor a loss.

Spouses/civil partners are taxed as two separate people. Each has an annual exemption, and losses of one spouse/civil partner cannot be set against gains of the other.

Disposals between spouses/civil partners who are living together give rise to no gain and no loss, whatever actual price (if any) **was charged by the person transferring the asset** to their spouse/civil partner. A couple are treated as living together unless they are separated under a court order or separation deed, or are in fact separated in circumstances which make permanent separation likely.

Special rules apply to the indexation allowance and taper relief on no gain/no loss disposals. To illustrate the rules, we assume that a husband (H) buys an asset and later transfers it to his wife (W). The wife sells the asset to a third party.

H buys an asset and transfers it to W. W is deemed to have bought the asset at the time when H transferred it to her. Her cost is H's cost plus indexation allowance up to the time of the transfer (or 6 April 1998 if earlier). When she sells the asset, she computes indexation allowance from the time of the transfer. If the transfer was after 5 April 1998, no further indexation allowance is given.

For taper relief purposes, the ownership period of W will be treated as the combined ownership period of H and W. For assets other than shares, business use by one spouse is treated as business ownership by the other spouse.

Where an asset is jointly owned, the beneficial interests of the spouses/civil partners will determine the treatment of any gain on disposal. If, for example, there is evidence that the wife's share in an asset was 60%, then 60% of any gain or loss on disposal would be attributed to her. If there is no evidence of the relative interests, HMRC will normally accept that the asset is held in equal shares. Where a declaration of how income from the asset is to be shared for income tax purposes has been made (see earlier in this Text), there is a presumption that the same shares will apply for CGT purposes.

If a spouse/civil partner whose marginal tax rate is 40% wishes to dispose of an asset at a gain and the other spouse/civil partner would only be taxed on the gain at a lower rate, the asset should first be transferred to the spouse/civil partner with the lower tax rate. Similarly, assets or parts of assets should be transferred between spouses/civil partners to use both CGT annual exemptions.

6 Business partnerships

The CGT position of partnerships recognises the fact that individual partners have (potentially variable) stakes in partnership assets.

6.1 Actual disposals

When a business partnership disposes of an asset, any chargeable gain or allowable loss is apportioned to the partners in their capital profit sharing ratio.

6.2 Change in PSR

Partners may decide to change their profit shares in the firm, for example when a new partner joins the firm or a partner retires. Each partner is treated as acquiring or disposing of an appropriate share in the partnership assets. Thus a partner whose share rises from 20% to 50% acquires a 30% share.

On these deemed disposals, the assets of the firm are treated as sold for their current balance sheet values plus the indexation allowance which would apply on an actual disposal. If assets have not been revalued in the balance sheet, the consequence is that the partners reducing their shares have chargeable gains of zero. If assets have been revalued, each such partner will have gains equal to the revaluations × the percentage fall in his share. A corresponding allowable loss arises if assets have been revalued downwards.

When one partner pays another and the payment does not go through the accounts, each partner receiving money has a chargeable gain equal to the amount he receives, in addition to any gain outlined above.

A partner whose share is increased (including a new partner) has a deemed acquisition cost equal to the deemed disposal proceeds of the share he is acquiring from the other partners. If he makes a payment outside the accounts, it is generally treated as being for goodwill.

6.3 Revaluations with no change in PSR

When assets are revalued with no changes in shares in the firm, there is no chargeable gain or allowable loss at that time.

7 Part disposals

FAST FORWARD

On a part disposal, the cost must be apportioned between the part disposed of and the part retained.

7.1 Basic rule

The disposal of part of a chargeable asset is a chargeable event. The chargeable gain (or allowable loss) is computed by deducting from the disposal value a fraction of the original cost of the whole asset.

Formula to learn

The fraction is:

$$\frac{A}{A+B} = \frac{\text{value of the part disposed of}}{\text{value of the part disposed of} + \text{market value of the remainder}}$$

In this fraction, A is the proceeds (for arm's length disposals) *before* deducting incidental costs of disposal.

The part disposal fraction should not be applied indiscriminately. Any expenditure incurred wholly in respect of a particular part of an asset should be treated as an allowable deduction in full for that part and not apportioned. An example of this is incidental selling expenses, which are wholly attributable to the part disposed of.

Question | Part disposals

Mr Heal owns a painting which originally cost him £27,000 in March 1984 (RPI = 87.5). He sold a quarter interest in the painting in July 2006 for £18,000. The market value of the three-quarter share remaining is estimated to be £36,000. What is the chargeable gain after taper relief? RPI April 1998 = 162.6

Answer

The amount of the original cost attributable to the part sold is

$$\frac{18,000}{18,000+36,000} \times £27,000 = £9,000$$

	£
Proceeds	18,000
Less cost (see above)	(9,000)
Unindexed gain	9,000
Less indexation allowance (March 1984 to April 1998)	
$\frac{162.6-87.5}{87.5} = 0.858 \times £9,000$	(7,722)
Gain before taper relief	1,278

Gain after taper relief (6.4.98 – 5.4.06 = 8 years plus additional year = 9 years)

65% × £1,278	£831

7.2 Land: small part disposal proceeds

Where the **consideration** for a part disposal of land **does not exceed 20% of the market value of the entire holding** of land prior to the part disposal, a chargeable disposal does not take place. The taxpayer must make a **claim** by the first anniversary of 31 January following the end of the tax year. The net disposal proceeds are deducted from allowable expenditure when computing a gain on a later disposal of the remaining land.

Question

Small part disposals of land

Bertha buys 10 acres of land in January 2000 for £20,000. She sells 1½ acres for £5,000 in June 2006 and disposal costs amount to £50. Market value of the land immediately prior to the disposal is £30,000.

You are required to show Bertha's CGT position.

Answer

The consideration (£5,000) is less than 20% of market value (20% of £30,000 = £6,000). Bertha may therefore claim for the relief to apply. As a result, no chargeable disposal takes place in June 2006.

Allowable cost of the land retained is:

	£
Cost of 10 acres	20,000
Deduct: net proceeds of part disposal (£5,000 – £50)	(4,950)
Allowable expenditure of land retained	15,050

There are two further conditions to meet before this relief can apply:

- proceeds from the part disposal do not exceed £20,000; and
- aggregate proceeds from the part disposal and any other disposals of land (including buildings) in the same tax year do not exceed £20,000.

7.3 Example: proceeds exceeding £20,000

If, in the previous example, Bertha had made another disposal of land for £15,750 in 2006/07, the relief could not apply since proceeds for the tax year (ie. £15,750 + £5,000 = £20,750) would exceed £20,000. The normal part disposal rules would apply.

Where the capital sum received is not treated as a disposal, but is instead deducted from allowable expenditure as above, any indexation calculation on a later disposal is calculated in two stages:

(a) the indexed rise on the original expenditure is calculated and deducted normally from date of purchase, to date of sale or April 1998 if earlier, then

(b) the indexed rise on a notional item of expenditure equal to the amount of the capital sum received, from date of receipt to date of sale or April 1998 if earlier, is added back. This is effectively 'negative indexation'.

Taper relief applies to the whole gain from the later of the acquisition and 6 April 1998.

Chapter roundup

- A chargeable gain is computed by taking the proceeds and deducting both the costs and the indexation allowance. For individuals indexation is not given after April 1998 but taper relief may be available.

- Indexation allowance removes the inflationary element of a capital gain. It is restricted for individuals.

- Market value must be used in certain capital gains computations. There are special rules for shares and securities.

- Disposals between connected persons are always deemed to take place for a consideration equal to market value. Any loss arising on a disposal to a connected person can be set only against a gain arising on a disposal to the same connected person.

- Spouses/civil partners are treated as separate people. Transfers of assets between spouses/civil partners give rise to neither a gain nor a loss.

- The CGT position of partnerships recognises the fact that individual partners have (potentially variable) stakes in partnership assets.

- On a part disposal, the cost must be apportioned between the part disposed of and the part retained.

Quick quiz

1   Jed buys a house. He repairs the roof, installs central heating and builds an extension. The extension is blown down in a storm and not replaced. Which of these improvements is allowable as enhancement expenditure on a subsequent sale?

2   Shares in A plc are quoted at 410 – 414, with bargains at 408, 410 and 416. What is the value for CGT?

3   With whom is an individual connected?

4   What is the CGT effect of a change in partnership profit sharing ratios without any revaluation of assets or payment between business partners?

5   10 acres of land are sold for £15,000 out of 25 acres. Original cost in 1990 £9,000. Costs of sale £2,000. Rest of land valued at £30,000. What is the allowable expenditure?

Answers to quick quiz

1   Repairs to roof – not allowable as enhancement expenditure because not capital in nature
Central heating – allowable as enhancement expenditure
Extension – not allowable as not reflected in state of asset at time of disposal.

2   Lower of:

$410 + ¼ (414 − 410) = 411$

$\dfrac{416 + 408}{2} = 412$

ie 411

3   An individual is connected with:

- his spouse ('spouse' includes civil partners)
- his relatives (brothers, sisters, ancestors and lineal descendants)
- the relatives of his spouse
- the spouses of his and his spouse's relatives

4   The assets of the firm are treated as sold at current balance sheet values plus indexation. Where there has been no revaluation, the disposing partner will have a nil gain. The acquiring partner will have a base cost equal to the deemed sale proceeds.

5   $\dfrac{15,000}{15,000 + 30,000} \times £9,000 = £3,000 + £2,000$ (costs of disposal) = £5,000

Now try the question below from the Exam Question Bank

Number	Level	Marks	Time
Q13	Introductory	25	45 mins

13

Shares and securities

Topic list	Syllabus reference
1 The matching rules for individuals	A3(a)D4
2 The FA 1985 pool	A3(a)D4
3 Post April 1998 acquisitions and disposals	A3(a)D4
4 Alterations of share capital	A3(e)(i)(iv)
5 Gilts and qualifying corporate bonds	A3(e)(iii)

Introduction

In the previous two chapters we have revised the basic computation of chargeable gains and how to calculate the CGT payable. In this chapter, we look at shares and securities held by individuals.

Shares and securities need special treatment because an investor may hold several shares or securities in the same company, bought at different times for different prices but otherwise identical.

The rules for shares and securities held by companies are different and are dealt with later in this text.

In the next chapter we will consider CGT deferral reliefs and the CGT implications of varying a will.

Study guide

		Intellectual level
3	**Chargeable gains and capital gains tax liabilities in situations involving further overseas aspects and in relation to closely related persons and trusts together with the application of additional exemptions and reliefs**	
(a)	The contents of the Paper F6 study guide for chargeable gains under headings:	2
•	D4 Gains and losses on the disposal of shares and securities	
(e)	Gains and losses on the disposal of shares and securities:	3
(i)	Extend the explanation of the treatment of rights issues to include the small part disposal rules applicable to rights issues	
(iii)	Define a qualifying corporate bond (QCB), and understand what makes a corporate bond non-qualifying. Understand the capital gains tax implications of the disposal of QCBs in exchange for cash or shares	
(iv)	Apply the rules relating to reorganisations, reconstructions and amalgamations and advise on the most tax efficient options available in given circumstances	

Exam guide

Shares and securities are some of the more common assets held by individuals, and knowing how to compute the gain on their disposal is fundamental to an understanding of capital gains. Shares may be held simply as investments, or an entrepreneur may run his business through an unquoted company in which he has a substantial holding. The same identification rules apply to both types of shareholdings.

> **Knowledge brought forward from earlier studies**

This chapter revises the identification rules for individuals and the computation of gains on disposals that were covered at level 2.3. It expands on the rules for rights issues, takeovers and reorganisations. The rules for gilts and qualifying corporate bonds are new.

1 The matching rules for individuals

> **FAST FORWARD**
>
> There are different share matching rules for individuals and companies.

Quoted and unquoted shares and securities and units in a unit trust present special problems when attempting to compute gains or losses on disposal. For instance, suppose that an individual buys some quoted shares in X plc as follows.

Date	Number of shares	Cost £
5 May 1983	100	150
17 January 1999	100	375

On 15 June 2006, he sells 120 of the shares for £1,450. To determine the chargeable gain, we need to be able to work out which shares out of the two original holdings were actually sold.

We therefore need **matching rules**. These **allow us to decide which shares have been sold and so work out what the allowable cost on disposal should be.**

At any one time, we will only be concerned with shares or securities of the same class in the same company. If an individual owns both ordinary shares and preference shares in X plc, we will deal with the two classes of share separately, because they are distinguishable.

In what follows, we will use 'shares' to refer to both shares and securities.

For individuals, share disposals are matched with acquisitions in the following order.

(a) Same day acquisitions.

(b) Acquisitions within the following 30 days (known as the 'bed and breakfast rule').

(c) Previous acquisitions after 5 April 1998 identifying the most recent acquisition first (a LIFO basis).

(d) Any shares in the FA 1985 pool at 5 April 1998 (see below).

The 'bed and breakfast' rule stops shares being sold to crystallise a capital gain or loss and then being repurchased a day or so later. Without the rule a gain or loss would arise on the sale since it would be 'matched' to the original acquisition.

Exam focus point

> Learn the 'matching rules' because a crucial first step to getting a shares question right is to match the shares sold to the original shares purchased correctly.

2 The FA 1985 pool

FAST FORWARD

> When dealing with shares held by individuals we need to construct a FA 1985 pool running (with indexation allowance) to 5 April 1998 and then a list of shares acquired from 6 April 1998 onwards.

2.1 Composition of the FA 1985 pool

We treat shares purchased up until 5 April 1998 as a 'pool' which grew as new shares were acquired and shrunk as they were sold. **The FA 1985 pool** (so called because it was introduced by rules in the Finance Act 1985) **comprises the following shares of the same class in the same company.**

- **Shares held by an individual on 5 April 1985 and acquired by that individual on or after 6 April 1982.**

- **Shares acquired by that individual on or after 6 April 1985, but before 6 April 1998.**

In making computations which use the FA 1985 pool, we must keep track of:

(a) The **number** of shares
(b) The **cost** of the shares ignoring indexation
(c) The **indexed cost** of the shares

The FA 1985 pool may also be called the **s.104 TCGA 1992 pool**.

Exam focus point

> The computation of the cost and indexed cost within the FA 1985 pool is excluded from the syllabus. In an exam you will be told the number of shares within the pool and the balance of cost and indexed cost remaining. This will include indexation up until April 1998 and no further indexation will be due.

In the case of a disposal the cost and the indexed cost attributable to the shares disposed of are deducted from the amounts within the FA 1985 pool. The proportions of the cost and indexed cost to take out of the pool should be computed using the A/(A + B) fraction that is used for any other part disposal. However, we are not usually given the value of the remaining shares (B in the fraction). We then just use numbers of shares.

The indexation allowance is the indexed cost taken out of the pool minus the cost taken out. As usual, the indexation allowance cannot create or increase a loss.

Question

The FA 1985 pool

On 6 April 2006 Oliver held 4,000 shares in Judith plc with a cost of £10,000 and an indexed cost of £17,461. Oliver sold 3,000 shares on 10 July 2006 for £17,000. Compute the gain before taper relief, and the value of the FA 1985 pool following the disposal.

Answer

	No of shares	Cost £	Indexed cost £
Balance at 6.4.98	4,000	10,000	17,461
Disposal	(3,000)		
Cost and indexed cost $\frac{3,000}{4,000}$ × £10,000 and £17,461		(7,500)	(13,096)
	1,000	2,500	4,365

The gain is computed as follows:

	£
Proceeds	17,000
Less cost	(7,500)
	9,500
Less indexation allowance £(13,096 – 7,500)	(5,596)
Chargeable gain before taper relief	3,904

Taper relief will then apply.

3 Post April 1998 acquisitions and disposals

FAST FORWARD

Shares acquired after 6.4.98 are deemed to be disposed of first on a LIFO basis.

3.1 Introduction

There will be no indexation in respect of shares acquired after April 1998. However, taper relief (see earlier in this text) may be available to reduce the amount of the gain arising. We look below at a comprehensive example which includes both acquisitions and the disposal of shares after 6 April 1998.

3.2 Example: Post April 1998 disposals for individuals

At 6 April 2006 Ron held 25,000 shares in First plc acquired as follows:

Date of acquisition	No of shares	Cost
FA 1985 pool balance	15,000	£25,000 (indexed cost £31,269)
4.8.05	5,000	£19,400
15.7.06	5,000	£19,000

He disposed of 20,000 of the shares on 10 July 2006 for £80,000. The shares are not business assets for the purposes of taper relief. We match the shares as follows:

(a)   Acquisition in 30 days after disposal:

	£
Proceeds $\dfrac{5,000}{20,000} \times £80,000$	20,000
Less cost (15.7.06)	(19,000)
Gain	1,000

(b)   Post 5.4.98 acquisitions

	£
Proceeds $\dfrac{5,000}{20,000} \times £80,000$	20,000
Less cost (4.8.05)	(19,400)
Gain	600

Note. No taper relief is due since the period of ownership was only 11 months.

(c)   FA 1985 pool

	Number of shares	Cost £	Indexed cost £
Pool at 6.4.98	15,000	25,000	31,269
7.06 sale (× 10/15)	(10,000)	(16,667)	(20,846)
	5,000	8,333	10,423

Gain

	£
Proceeds $\dfrac{10,000}{20,000} \times £80,000$	40,000
Less cost	(16,667)
	23,333
Less indexation from FA 1985 pool £(20,846 – 16,667)	(4,179)
Gain before taper relief	19,154

Gain after taper relief (6.4.98 – 5.4.06 = 8 years plus additional year = 9 years)

65% × £19,154	£12,450

Total gains £(1,000 + 600 + 12,450)	£14,050

4 Alterations of share capital

FAST FORWARD

On an alteration of share capital, the general principle is only to tax gains immediately if cash is paid to the investors.

4.1 General principle

On a reorganisation we must apportion the original base cost of whatever the shareholder had beforehand between the elements of whatever the shareholder has afterwards.

4.2 Capital distributions

Normally a capital distribution is treated as a part disposal of an asset. If, however, the distribution is small (normally taken to mean not more than the higher of 5% of the value of the shares and £3,000) **then any gain can be deferred by treating the distribution as a deduction from the cost of the shares for the purposes of calculating any gains or losses on future disposals.** Where the shares are held in the FA 1985 pool the distribution must also be deducted from the indexed cost.

If the taxpayer wants a part disposal (for example to use his annual exemption) HMRC will allow this even if the proceeds are small.

Question

Capital distributions

S Barr holds 1,000 shares in Woodleigh plc. These are all held in the FA 1985 pool which had a cost of £3,000 and an indexed cost of £4,849. The company is now in liquidation and in June 2004 the liquidator made a distribution of 35p per share. The market value of the shares after the distribution was £7,000. In November 2006 S Barr received a final distribution of £7,200.

Show any chargeable gains arising, assuming that there is no part disposal in June 2004 and the shares do not meet the definition of 'business asset'.

Answer

No gain arises in June 2004 as the distribution in June 2004 is not more than the higher of £3,000 and 5% of the value of the shares: £(350 + 7,000) × 5% = £368. The November 2006 distribution is treated as follows.

	Cost £
Proceeds	7,200
Less cost less £350	(2,650)
Unindexed gain	4,550
Less indexation (£4,849 – £350) = £4,499 – £2,650	(1,849)
	2,701

The chargeable gain before taper relief on the November 2006 distribution is £2,701.

Gain after taper relief (6 April 1998 – 5 April 2006 = 8 years plus additional year = 9 years)

65% × £2,701	£1,756

4.3 Bonus issues (scrip issues)

When a company issues bonus shares all that happens is that the size of the original holding is increased. Since bonus shares are free shares, issued at no cost, there is no need to adjust the original cost. Instead the numbers purchased at particular times are increased by the bonus. The normal matching rules will then be applied.

4.4 Example: bonus issues

The following transactions in the ordinary shares of X plc would be matched as shown below

6.4.98	Balance on FA 1985 pool 1,000 shares
6.10.03	Bonus issue of one for four
6.5.06	Sale of 750 shares

(a) *The FA 1985 pool*

	No of shares
6.4.98 Balance	1,000
6.10.03 Bonus issue one for four	250
	1,250
6.5.06 Disposal	(750)
Balance carried forward	500

4.5 Rights issues

The difference between a bonus issue and a rights issue is that in a rights issue the new shares are paid for and this results in an adjustment to the original cost.

As with bonus issues, rights shares derived from shares in the FA 1985 pool go into that pool with the cost and indexed cost of the pool being increased by the amount paid for those shares. For individuals, rights shares derived from post 5.4.98 holdings attach to those holdings.

In an **open offer**, shareholders have a right to subscribe for a minimum number of shares based on their existing holdings and may buy additional shares. Subscriptions up to the minimum entitlement are treated as a rights issue. Additional subscriptions are treated as new purchases of shares.

Question   **Rights issues after 5 April 1998**

Simon had the following transactions in S Ltd.

6.4.98	Balance on FA 1985 pool, 10,000 shares, cost £15,000, indexed cost £16,282
11.9.05	Bought 2,000 shares for £5,000
1.2.06	Took up rights issue 1 for 2 at £2.75 per share
14.10.06	Sold 5,000 shares for £15,000

Compute the gain arising in October 2006, after taper relief (if applicable). The shares have always been a business asset for taper relief purposes.

Answer

(a) *Post 5.4.98 holding*

	Number	Cost
		£
Shares acquired 11.9.05	2,000	5,000
Shares acquired 1.2.06 (rights) 1:2 @ £2.75	1,000	2,750
	3,000	7,750

Gain

		£
Proceeds $\frac{3,000}{5,000} \times £15,000$		9,000
Less cost		(7,750)
Gain		1,250

Taper relief (based on ownership of original holding 11.9.05 – 10.9.06)

50% (One year: business asset) × £1,250   £625

(b)   *FA 1985 pool*

	Number	*Cost*	*Indexed cost*
		£	£
Pool at 5.4.98	10,000	15,000	16,282
Rights issue 1.2.06	5,000	13,750	13,750
	15,000	28,750	30,032
14.10.06 Sale	(2,000)	(3,833)	(4,004)
c/F	13,000	24,917	26,028

Gain

	£
Proceeds $\frac{2,000}{5,000} \times £15,000$	6,000
Less cost	(3,833)
Unindexed gain	2,167
Less indexation £(4,004 – 3,833)	(171)
Indexed gain	1,996

Taper relief (based on original holding 6.4.98 – 5.4.06)

25% (Eight years: business asset) × £1,996   £499

(c)   Total gains (after taper relief)

£(625 + 499)   £1,124

4.6 Sales of rights nil paid

Where the shareholder does not take up his rights but sells them to a third party without paying the company for the rights shares, the proceeds are treated as a capital distribution (see above) **and will be dealt with either under the part disposal rules or, if not more than the higher of £3,000 and 5% of the value of the shareholding giving rise to the disposal, as a reduction of original cost** (unless the taxpayer wants a part disposal).

4.7 Stock dividends

A stock dividend is the receipt of a dividend by the issue of additional shares rather than cash. For shareholders which are companies, **a stock dividend is treated as a rights issue taken up** (see later in this text for details of the treatment of shares held by companies). For individuals such shares are treated as free-standing acquisitions and any gain on their disposal is tapered by reference to the period from that acquisition to the disposal of the shares. In both cases, the shares are treated as bought for the value of the (net) stock dividend as calculated for income or corporation tax purposes.

4.8 Reorganisations

A reorganisation takes place where new shares or a mixture of new shares and debentures are issued in exchange for the original shareholdings. The new shares take the place of the old shares. The problem is how to apportion the original cost between the different types of capital issued on the reorganisation.

If the new shares and securities are quoted, then the cost is apportioned by reference to the market values of the new types of capital on the first day of quotation after the reorganisation.

Question   **Reorganisations**

An original quoted shareholding is made up of ordinary shares purchased as follows.

FA 1985 pool   3,000 shares costing £13,250, indexed cost £16,500
2001   2,000 shares costing £9,000

In 2006 there is a reorganisation whereby each ordinary share is exchanged for two 'A' ordinary shares (quoted at £2 each) and one preference share (quoted at £1 each). Show how the original costs will be apportioned.

Answer

Original holdings

	Original	New ords 2:1	MV £2 £	New prefs 1:1	MV £1 £
FA85 Pool	3,000	6,000	12,000	3,000	3,000
2001 holding	2,000	4,000	8,000	2,000	2,000
Total	5,000	10,000	20,000	5,000	5,000

FA1985 holding

	New holding	MV £	Cost £	Indexed cost £
Ords	6,000	12,000	10,600	13,200
Prefs	3,000	3,000	2,650	3,300
Total	9,000	15,000	13,250	16,500

Original cost/ indexed cost is split 12,000:3,000

2001 holding

	New holding	MV £	Cost £
Ords	4,000	8,000	7,200
Prefs	2,000	2,000	1,800
Total	6,000	10,000	9,000

Original cost is split 8,000:2,000

Where a reorganisation takes place and the new shares and securities are unquoted, the cost of the original holding is apportioned using the values of the new shares and securities when they come to be disposed of.

For both quoted and unquoted shares and securities, any incidental costs (such as professional fees) are treated as additional consideration for the new shares and securities.

4.9 Takeovers

The special rules on takeovers only apply if the exchange is for bona fide commercial reasons and not for the avoidance of tax.

A chargeable gain does not arise on a 'paper for paper' takeover. The cost of the original holding is passed on to the new holding which takes the place of the original holding. **If part of the takeover consideration is cash then a gain must be computed**: the normal part disposal rules will apply.

If the cash received is not more than the higher of 5% of the total value on the takeover, **and £3,000, then the small distribution rules apply** and the cash received will be deducted from cost for the purpose of further disposals, unless the taxpayer chooses the part disposal treatment.

The takeover rules apply where the company issuing the new shares ends up with more than 25% of the ordinary share capital of the old company or the majority of the voting power in the old company, or the company issuing the new shares makes a general offer to shareholders in the other company which is initially made subject to a condition which, if satisfied, would give the first company control of the second company.

The exchange must take place for bona fide commercial reasons and must not have as its main purpose, or one of its main purposes, the avoidance of CGT or corporation tax.

Provision is made for the acquiring company to obtain advance clearance from HMRC that the above condition has been met. HMRC must, within 30 days of receiving the application, either ask for further information or give notice of its decision. If further information is given, HMRC must give its decision within 30 days of the receipt of information. There is an appeal against an HMRC decision that the condition has not been satisfied to the Special Commissioners.

Question
Takeovers

Mr Le Bon held 20,000 £1 shares out of a total number of issued shares of one million in Duran plc. The shares were held in the FA 1985 pool, cost £40,000, indexed cost £47,200. In 2006 the board of Duran plc agreed to a takeover bid by Spandau plc under which shareholders in Duran received three Spandau shares plus 90p cash for every four shares held in Duran plc. Immediately following the takeover, the shares in Spandau plc were quoted at £5 each. What gain (before taper relief) has Mr Le Bon made?

Answer

The total value due to Le Bon on the takeover is as follows.

		£
Shares	$20,000 \times 3/4 \times £5$	75,000
Cash	$20,000 \times 1/4 \times 90p$	4,500
		79,500

Since the cash (£4,500) exceeds both £3,000 and 5% of £79,500 it cannot be rolled over by deducting it from the acquisition cost. There is a part disposal.

	£
Disposal proceeds (ie cash received)	4,500

Apportioned cost:

$$\frac{\text{Value of disposal}}{\text{Value of disposal} + \text{value of part retained}} \times \text{cost}$$

$\dfrac{£4,500}{£4,500 + £75,000} \times £40,000$	(2,264)
	2,236

Less indexation allowance

$\dfrac{£4,500}{£4,500 + £75,000} \times £47,200 = £2,672 - £2,264$	(408)
Indexed gain before taper relief	1,828

Part of the takeover consideration may include the right to receive deferred consideration in the form of shares or debentures in the new company. The amount of the deferred consideration may be unascertainable at the date of the takeover, perhaps because it is dependent on the future profits of the company whose shares are acquired. The right is valued and treated as a security. This means the takeover rules apply and there is no need to calculate a gain in respect of the right. The issue of shares or debentures as a result of the right is treated as a conversion of the right and, again, no gain arises.

5 Gilts and qualifying corporate bonds

FAST FORWARD

Gilts and QCBs held by individuals are exempt from CGT.

5.1 Definitions and treatment

Key term

> **Gilts are British Government and Government guaranteed securities** as shown on the Treasury list. Gilt strips (capital or interest entitlements sold separately) are also gilts. You may assume that the list of gilts includes all issues of Treasury Loan, Treasury Stock, Exchequer Loan, Exchequer Stock and War Loan.

Disposals of gilt edged securities (gilts) and qualifying corporate bonds by individuals and trusts are exempt from CGT. The rules for companies are different, and are explained later in this text.

Key term

> A **qualifying corporate bond (QCB)** is a security (whether or not secured on assets) which:
>
> (a) Represents a **'normal commercial loan'**. This excludes any bonds which are convertible into shares (although bonds convertible into other bonds which would be QCBs are not excluded), or which carry the right to excessive interest or interest which depends on the results of the issuer's business
>
> (b) Is **expressed in sterling** and for which no provision is made for conversion into or redemption in another currency
>
> (c) Was **acquired** by the person now disposing of it **after 13 March 1984**, and
>
> (d) Does not have a redemption value which depends on a published index of share prices on a stock exchange.
>
> Permanent interest bearing shares issued by building societies which meet condition (b) above are also QCBs.

5.2 Reorganisations involving QCBs

Special rules apply when a reorganisation involves qualifying corporate bonds, either as the security in issue before the reorganisation (the 'old asset') or as a security issued on the reorganisation (a 'new asset').

Where QCBs are the old asset, the newly issued shares are treated as acquired at the time of the reorganisation, for the then market value of the old asset. This market value is reduced by any money paid to the security-holders, or increased by any money paid by them. If a company holds the QCBs, then the QCBs are treated as sold at the same time for their market value, so as to find the company's profit or loss.

Where QCBs are the new asset, the chargeable gain which would have accrued if the old asset had been sold at its market value at the time of the reorganisation must be computed, and apportioned between the new assets issued. When the QCBs are disposed of, the part of that gain apportioned to them becomes chargeable. However, if that disposal is a no gain/no loss disposal to a spouse/civil partner, the gain does not become chargeable until a disposal outside the marriage. Furthermore, if the reorganisation is followed by the owner's death while he still owns the QCBs, the gain never becomes chargeable.

QCBs are often used in takeover situations instead of cash where for most shareholders the cash would not be a small capital distribution. **This enables the shareholder to defer the gain until the QCBs are disposed of.** This is often done over a period of time so as to use the annual exemption and any other reliefs available.

Chapter roundup

- There are different share matching rules for individuals and companies.

- When dealing with shares held by individuals we need to construct a FA 1985 pool running (with indexation allowance) to 5 April 1998 and then a list of shares acquired from 6 April 1998 onwards.

- Shares acquired after 6.4.98 are deemed to be disposed of first on a LIFO basis.

- On an alteration of share capital, the general principle is only to tax gains immediately if cash is paid to the investors.

- The special rules on takeovers only apply if the exchange is for bona fide commercial reasons and not for the avoidance of tax.

- Gilts and QCBs held by individuals are exempt from CGT.

Quick quiz

1   In what order are acquisitions of shares acquired since 6 April 1982 matched with disposals for individuals?

2   An individual acquired 1,000 shares on each of 15 January 1990, 15 January 2004 and 15 January 2007 in X plc. He sells 2,500 shares on 10 January 2007. How are the shares matched on sale?

3   Sharon acquired 10,000 share in Z plc in 1986. She takes up a 1 for 2 rights offer in 2006. How are the rights issue shares dealt with?

4   What is a qualifying corporate bond?

Answers to quick quiz

1   (a)   Same day acquisitions
    (b)   Acquisitions in following 30 days
    (c)   Previous acquisitions after 5 April 1998 on LIFO basis
    (d)   Shares in FA 1985 pool

2   January 2007 1,000 shares (following 30 days)
    January 2004 1,000 shares (after 5 April 1998)
    January 1990 (FA 1985 pool) 500 shares

3   The rights issue shares are added to the FA 1985 pool holding.

4   A qualifying corporate bond is a security which:

    •   represents a normal commercial loan
    •   is expressed in sterling
    •   was acquired after 13 March 1984
    •   is not redeemable in relation to share prices on a stock exchange

Now try the question below from the Exam Question Bank

Number	Level	Marks	Time
Q14	Introductory	25	45 mins

Chargeable gains: deferral reliefs and variation of a will

14

Topic list	Syllabus reference
1 Gift relief (holdover relief)	A3(f)(i)
2 The replacement of business assets (rollover relief)	A3(a)D6
3 The transfer of a business to a company (incorporation relief)	A3(a)D6
4 EIS deferral relief	A3(f)(ii)
5 Altering dispositions made on death	A3(f)(iii)

Introduction

In the previous chapters we have seen how to calculate chargeable gains. In certain circumstances it may be possible to defer a gain – that is to remove it from an immediate charge to CGT. However, it is important to realise the gain has not been exempted and it may become charged in the future.

Deferral reliefs operate in two ways. First, the gain may be deducted from the base cost of an asset (for example, roll over relief for replacement with non-depreciating business assets, incorporation relief, gift relief). Second, the gain may be 'frozen' until a certain event occurs (deferral relief for replacement with depreciating business assets, EIS deferral relief).

Finally we consider the CGT implications of varying a will,

In the next chapter we will look some further rules for gains and losses.

Study guide

		Intellectual level
3	**Chargeable gains and capital gains tax liabilities in situations involving further overseas aspects and in relation to closely related persons and trusts together with the application of additional exemptions and reliefs**	
(a)	The contents of the Paper F6 study guide for chargeable gains under headings:	2
•	D6 The use of exemptions and reliefs in deferring and minimising tax liabilities arising on the disposal of capital assets	
(f)	The use of exemptions and reliefs in deferring and minimising tax liabilities arising on the disposal of capital assets:	3
(i)	Understand and apply holdover relief on gifts	
(ii)	Understand and apply enterprise investment scheme reinvestment relief	
(iii)	Understand the capital gains tax implications of the variation of wills	

Exam guide

Deferring and minimising tax liabilities is likely to feature at some point in your exam. The methods of deferring capital gains should be very familiar to you. Always look out for the purchase of a new assets where a business asset has been disposed of, but double check that both assets qualify for rollover relief. Holdover relief is usually available for gifts of business assets, but note the effect on taper relief if the donee sells the asset shortly after acquisition. EIS deferral relief is a useful way of deferring gains, but do not overlook the risk of investing in an unquoted company.

> **Knowledge brought forward from earlier studies**

This chapter revises gift relief, rollover relief for the replacement of business assets and incorporation relief which you will have studied at level 2.3. Gift relief for gifts to trusts, EIS deferral relief and the CGT consequences of varying a will are new.

1 Gift relief (holdover relief)

1.1 The relief

FAST FORWARD

Gift relief is available on both outright gifts and sales at an undervalue of business assets. Gift relief is also available on gifts which are immediately chargeable to inheritance tax.

If an individual gives away a qualifying asset, the transferor and the transferee can jointly elect, or where a trust is the transferee, the transferor alone can elect, by the 31 January which is nearly six years after the end of the tax year of the transfer, **that the transferor's gain be reduced, possibly to nil. The transferee is then deemed to acquire the asset for market value at the date of transfer less the transferor's deferred gain** (no taper relief given). The transferee will qualify for further indexation allowance (if available) on that reduced base cost from the date of the transfer. The transferee will start a new period for taper relief from the date of his acquisition or 6 April 1998, if later.

If a disposal involves actual consideration rather than being an outright gift but is still not a bargain made at arm's length, the proceeds are deemed to be the market value of the asset **and any excess of actual consideration over allowable costs** (excluding indexation allowance) **is chargeable immediately and only the balance of the gain is deferred**. The amount chargeable immediately is limited to the full gain (after indexation allowance).

1.2 Qualifying assets

Gift relief can be claimed on gifts or sales at undervalue as follows.

(a) Transfers of **business assets**

(i) Trade assets
(ii) Agricultural property
(iii) Shares and securities (except where the transferee is a company)

(b) Transfers subject to an **immediate inheritance tax (IHT) charge. IHT is covered later in this Text.**

Transfers of business assets are transfers of assets

(a) **Used in a trade, profession or vocation** carried on:

(1) By the donor

(2) If the donor is an individual, by a trading company which is his 'personal company' or a member of a trading group of which the holding company is his 'personal company' (a personal company is one in which the individual can exercise at least 5% of the voting rights).

(3) If the donor is a trustee, by the trustee or by a beneficiary who has an interest in possession in the settled property (see later in this Text).

If the asset was used for the purposes of the trade, profession or vocation for only part of its period of ownership, the gain to be held over is the gain otherwise eligible × period of such use/total period of ownership.

If the asset was a building or structure only partly used for trade, professional or vocational purposes, only the **part of the gain attributable to the part so used is eligible for gift relief**

(b) **Agricultural property** which would attract inheritance tax agricultural property relief (see later in this Text). The restrictions for periods of non-trade use and for partial trade use mentioned above do not apply.

(c) **Shares and securities in trading companies**, or holding companies of trading groups, where:

(1) The shares or securities are **not listed on a recognised stock exchange** (but they may be on the AIM), or

(2) If the donor is an individual, the company concerned is his **personal company** (defined as above), or

(3) If the donor is a trustee, the trustee can exercise 25% or more of the voting rights.

If the company has chargeable non-business assets (ie investments) at the time of the gift, and either (2) or (3) applied at any time in the last 12 months, **the gain to be held over is the gain otherwise chargeable × the value of the chargeable business assets/the value of the chargeable assets.**

If relief is claimed on a transfer of business assets, and that transfer is (or later becomes) chargeable to inheritance tax, then when the transferee disposes of the assets his gain is reduced by the IHT finally payable (but not so as to create a loss).

Transfers subject to an immediate IHT charge include most gifts to trusts. A transfer will be regarded as chargeable to IHT even if it falls within the nil rate band of that tax or is covered by the IHT annual exemption. Gifts to settlor interested trusts, however, do not qualify for gift relief.

If a transfer of business assets could also be subject to an immediate charge to inheritance tax, the rules relating to the latter category apply and the restrictions related to period of use and to chargeable business assets therefore do not apply.

Remember that IHT is covered in detail later in this Text. You should return to this section once you have studied the relevant chapters.

Question	Gift relief

On 6 December 2006 Angelo sold a freehold shop valued at £200,000 to his son Michael for £50,000, and claimed gift relief. Angelo had originally purchased the shop, from which he had run his business, in July 2002 for £30,000. Michael continued to run a business from the shop premises but decided to sell the shop in May 2008 for £195,000. Compute any chargeable gains arising. Assume the rules of CGT in 2006/07 continue to apply in May 2008.

Answer

(a)   *Angelo's CGT position (2006/07)*

	£
Proceeds (market value)	200,000
Less cost	(30,000)
Gain	170,000
Less gain deferred	
£170,000 – £(50,000 – 30,000)	(150,000)
Gain left in charge	20,000
Gain after taper relief (note 1)	£5,000

(b)   *Michael's CGT position (2008/09)*

	£
Proceeds	195,000
Less cost £(200,000 – 150,000)	(50,000)
Gain	145,000
Chargeable gain after taper relief (50%) (note 2)	£72,500

Notes.

1   Taper relief is available for Angelo since the asset disposed of in December 2006 is a 'business asset'. The period of ownership is four complete years. Only 25% of the gain will be taxable.

2   Michael acquired the asset on 6 December 2006 and sold it in May 2008. He therefore owned the asset for one complete year. 50% of the gain is taxable.

1.3 Anti-avoidance rules

Gift relief is not available if the transferee is neither resident nor ordinarily resident in the UK at the time of the gift. If the transferee is an individual who becomes neither resident nor ordinarily resident in the UK in any of the six tax years following the year of the transfer and before disposing of the asset transferred, then the gain held over is chargeable on him as if it arose immediately before he becomes neither resident nor ordinarily resident in the UK.

It is not possible to claim gift relief on transfers to a settlor-interested trust (see later in this Text).

Exam focus point

Gift relief is normally used whenever a business or business asset is gifted, but you should look out for the restriction for a non-resident donee.

Also look out for the effect on taper relief if the donee sells the business or asset shortly afterwards. You should also consider whether retaining the asset until death so as to obtain the tax free uplift to probate value would be advantageous.

2 The replacement of business assets (rollover relief)

2.1 Conditions

FAST FORWARD

When assets falling within certain classes are sold and other such assets are bought, it is possible to defer gains on the assets sold by claiming rollover relief.

A gain may be 'rolled over' (deferred) where it arises on the disposal of a business asset which is replaced. This is **rollover relief**. A claim cannot specify that only part of a gain is to be rolled over.

All the following conditions must be met.

(a) **The old asset sold and the new asset bought are both used only in the trade** or trades carried on **by the person claiming rollover relief**. Where part of a building is in non-trade use for all or a substantial part of the period of ownership, the building (and the land on which it stands) can be treated as two separate assets, the trade part (qualifying) and the non-trade part (non-qualifying). This split cannot be made for other assets.

(b) **The old asset and the new asset both fall within one** (but not necessarily the same one) **of the following classes.**

   (i) Land and buildings (including parts of buildings) occupied, as well as used, only for the purpose of the trade

   (ii) Fixed (that is, immovable) plant and machinery

   (iii) Ships, aircraft and hovercraft

   (iv) Goodwill

   (v) Satellites, space stations and spacecraft

   (vi) Milk quotas, potato quotas and ewe and suckler cow premium quotas

   (vii) Fish quota

(c) **Reinvestment of the proceeds of the old asset takes place in a period beginning one year before and ending three years after the date of the disposal.**

(d) **The new asset is brought into use in the trade on its acquisition** (not necessarily immediately, but not after any significant and unnecessary delay).

Goodwill and the various quotas are not qualifying assets for the purposes of corporation tax (ie for companies). Companies are covered later in this Text.

The new asset can be for use in a different trade from the old asset.

A rollover claim is not allowed when a taxpayer buys premises, sells part of the premises at a profit and then claims to roll over the gain into the part retained. However, a rollover claim is allowed (by concession) when the proceeds of the old asset are spent on improving a qualifying asset which the taxpayer already owns. The improved asset must already be in use for a trade, or be brought into trade use immediately the improvement work is finished.

2.2 Operation of relief

If an amount less than the proceeds of the old asset is invested in the new assets, a gain equal to the difference will be chargeable, if this is less than the actual gain.

Deferral is obtained by deducting the chargeable gain from the cost of the new asset. For full relief, the whole of the consideration for the disposal must be reinvested. Where only part is reinvested, a part of the gain equal to the lower of the full gain and the amount not reinvested will be liable to tax immediately.

The new asset will have a base cost for chargeable gains purposes, of its purchase price less the gain rolled over into its acquisition.

If a trader expects to buy new assets, he can make a provisional rollover claim on the tax return which includes the gain on the old asset. The gain is reduced accordingly. If new assets are not actually acquired, HMRC collect the tax saved by the provisional claim.

Question

Rollover relief

A freehold factory was purchased by Zoë for business use in August 1997. It was sold in December 2006 for £70,000, giving rise to an indexed gain of £17,950. A replacement factory was purchased in June 2007 for £60,000. Compute the base cost of the replacement factory, taking into account any possible rollover of the gain from the disposal in December 2006. Ignore taper relief.

Answer

	£
Total gain	17,950
Less gain rolled over	(7,950)
Chargeable immediately (ie amount not reinvested: £(70,000 – 60,000))	10,000
Cost of new factory	60,000
Less rolled over gain	(7,950)
Base cost of new factory	52,050

Rollover relief applies to the untapered gain. Any gain left in charge will then be eligible for taper relief. So, in the above example, Zoë's gain of £10,000 would be reduced to £2,500 (business asset held for more than 2 years: 25%).

When the replacement asset is sold taper relief on that sale will be given, as usual, by reference to the holding period for that asset (assuming further rollover relief is not claimed on this disposal). **Effectively, taper relief on the rolled over gain, for the period of ownership of the original asset, is lost.**

Question	Rollover relief and taper relief interaction

Karen is a sole trader who bought a business asset for £170,625 on 5 November 1991 (RPI = 135.6) and sold it on 31 December 2006 for £491,400. A replacement business asset was acquired on 1 November 2006 at a cost of £546,000. The new asset was sold on 3 September 2008 for £914,550. Karen made a claim for rollover relief on the first asset sale but not on the second asset sale.

Calculate the taxable gains for each asset disposal. RPI April 1998 = 162.6.

Answer

31 December 2006 disposal

	£
Sale proceeds	491,400
Cost (5.11.91)	(170,625)
	320,775

Less indexation allowance to April 1998

$$\frac{162.6 - 135.6}{135.6} = 0.199 \times £170,625 \qquad (33,954)$$

Chargeable gain before taper relief	286,821

Since the asset was sold for £491,400 and within the required time period a replacement asset was purchased for £546,000 there was a full reinvestment of the sale proceeds. Thus the full gain before taper relief of £286,821 is rolled over against the cost of the new asset.

3 September 2008 disposal

	£	£
Sale proceeds		914,550
Cost (1 November 2006)	546,000	
Less rollover relief	(286,821)	
		(259,179)
Gain		655,371

Ownership period is 1 November 2006 to 3 September 2008
  = 1 complete year of ownership
Gain after taper relief

Taxable gain (50%) for Karen	£327,686

2.3 Non-business use

Where the old asset has not been used in the trade for a fraction of its period of ownership, the amount of the gain that can be rolled over is reduced by the same fraction. If the proceeds are not fully reinvested the restriction on rollover by the amount not reinvested is also calculated by considering only the proportion of proceeds relating to the part of the asset used in the trade or the proportion relating to the period of trade use.

Watch out for the interaction of rollover relief and taper relief when there is some non-business use. Rather unfairly, once the rollover amount has been calculated, the business and non-business elements of the gain remaining chargeable must be added together and then re-split using the same fraction; the appropriate taper relief rates then apply to each element as normal.

Question

John bought a factory for £150,000 on 11 November 2001, for use in his business. From 11 November 2002, he let the factory out to a quoted company, for a period of two years. He then used the factory for his own business again, until he sold it on 10 May 2006 for £225,000. On 13 December 2006, he purchased another factory for use in his business. This second factory cost £100,000.

Calculate the chargeable gain on the sale of the first factory and the base cost of the second factory.

Answer

Gain on first factory – May 2006

	Non business £	Business £
Proceeds of sale (24:30) (W1)	100,000	125,000
Less cost (24:30)	(66,667)	(83,333)
Gain (no indexation allowance)	33,333	41,667
Less rollover relief		(16,667)
Chargeable gain before taper relief (W2)	33,333	25,000
Total gain before taper relief £(33,333 + 25,000)		58,333
Split gain again for taper relief purposes (24:30)	25,956	32,407
Gain after taper relief 90%/25%	23,360	8,102
Total gain after taper relief £(23,360 + 8,102)		31,462

Base cost of second factory

	£
Cost	100,000
Less gain rolled over	(16,667)
Base cost c/f	83,333

Workings

1   *Use of factory*

Total ownership period:

11.11.01 – 10.05.06 = 54 months

Attributable to non business use:

11.11.02 – 10.11.04 = 24 months

Attributable to business use (remainder: 54m – 24m) = 30 months

2   *Proceeds not reinvested*

	£
Proceeds of business element	125,000
Less: cost of new factory	(100,000)
Not reinvested	25,000

2.4 Depreciating assets

Where the replacement asset is a depreciating asset, the gain is not rolled over by reducing the cost of the replacement asset. Rather it is 'frozen', ie deferred, until it crystallises (ie becomes chargeable) on the earliest of:

(a) The disposal of the replacement asset

(b) The date the replacement asset ceases to be used in the trade (but the gain does not crystallise on the taxpayer's death)

(c) Ten years after the acquisition of the replacement asset

Key term

An asset is a **depreciating asset** if it is, or within the next ten years will become, a wasting asset. So, any asset with an expected life of 60 years or less is covered by this definition. Plant and machinery (including ships, aircraft, hovercraft, satellites, space stations and spacecraft) is always treated as depreciating unless it becomes part of a building; in that case, it will only be depreciating if the building is held on a lease with 60 years or less to run.

Taper relief is applied to the original gain **before** it is deferred, in relation to the ownership of the original asset. No further relief is given for the time that the gain is deferred. Taper relief applies on the depreciating asset from the date of purchase in the normal way.

Question
Deferred gain on investment into depreciating asset

Norma bought a freehold shop for use in her business in June 2005 for £125,000. She sold it for £140,000 on 1 August 2006. On 10 July 2006, Norma bought some fixed plant and machinery to use in her business, costing £150,000. She then sells the plant and machinery for £167,000 on 19 November 2008. Show Norma's CGT position.

Answer

Gain deferred

	£
Proceeds of shop	140,000
Less cost	(125,000)
Gain	15,000

Gain after taper relief (1 year)

50% × £15,000 (deferred in relation to the purchase of the plant and machinery)	£7,500

Sale of plant and machinery

	£
Proceeds	167,000
Less cost	(150,000)
Gain	17,000

Gain after taper relief (2 years)

£17,000 × 25%	£4,250

Total gain chargeable on sale (gain on plant and machinery plus crystallised gain)

£(4,250 + 7,500)	£11,750

Where a gain on disposal is deferred on the purchase of a replacement depreciating asset it is possible to transfer the deferred, or 'frozen', gain to a non-depreciating asset provided the non-depreciating asset is bought before the deferred gain has crystallised.

Question	Transfer of frozen gain into non-depreciating asset

In July 1996, Julia sold a warehouse used in her trade, realising a gain of £30,000. Julia invested the whole of the proceeds of sale of £95,000 into fixed plant and machinery in January 1997 and made a claim to defer the gain on the warehouse.

In August 2006, Julia bought a freehold shop for use in her business costing £100,000. Julia has not bought any other assets for use in her business and wishes to minimise chargeable gains arising in 2006/07. What advice would you give Julia? Ignore taper relief.

Answer

Julia should claim to transfer the deferred gain of £30,000 to the purchase of the shop. If she does not do so, the deferred gain will be chargeable in January 2007 at the latest (10 years after the acquisition of the plant and machinery). The effect of the claim will be to reduce the base cost of the shop to £(100,000 – 30,000) = £70,000.

Both types of relief can also be claimed by an individual on assets owned by him but used in the trade of his 'personal company' (defined as for gift relief above).

2.5 The choice of assets for claims

Sometimes more than one eligible asset will be sold, but acquisitions will not allow all the gains to be rolled over or deferred. A choice must then be made, and the choice may affect the total gains rolled over or deferred and thus the total immediately chargeable.

Question	The choice of assets

Asset A was bought for £98 and is sold for £108, giving a gain of £10.

Asset B was bought for £45 and is sold for £50, giving a gain of £5.

Asset C is bought for £100, and gains on assets A and B could be rolled over against this purchase. Compute the gains chargeable immediately under the possible claims.

Answer

If a claim is made for asset A, the gains chargeable immediately will be £8 (proceeds not reinvested) + £5 (asset B) = £13.

If a claim is made for asset B, the gain chargeable immediately will be £10 (asset A). There are no proceeds not reinvested. Note that an additional claim for asset A would have no effect, because the balance of cost of asset C after claiming for asset B would be £(100 – 50) = £50, and the proceeds of asset A not reinvested would be £(108 – 50) = £58, which exceeds the gain on asset A.

If there are plenty of acquisitions, but not enough disposals to make full use of the capacity to rollover or defer gains consider the following points:

(a) Rollover claims against non-depreciating assets allow gains to be deferred indefinitely, whereas gains deferred against depreciating assets will crystallise within ten years (unless rollover claims are substituted).

(b) If two alternative rollover claims or two alternative deferral claims are possible, it is probably better to choose the new assets which are likely to be retained for longer, so as to maximise the period before the gains become chargeable.

(c) If an asset is likely to be retained until the trader's death, it is good tax planning to use it for rollover claims, because the gain on its disposal (as increased by the effect of the rollover claim) may escape tax altogether.

3 The transfer of a business to a company (incorporation relief)

FAST FORWARD

When an individual incorporates his business, the gain arising will be deducted from the cost of the shares received, unless the individual elects otherwise.

If a person transfers his business to a company then he makes a disposal of the business assets for CGT purposes and realises net chargeable gains (chargeable gains less allowable losses) on those assets. (Note that the individual assets are disposed of. Contrast this with a sale of shares, when shares are disposed of but business assets remain the property of the company which issued the shares, and are not disposed of.) It is, however, clearly undesirable to discourage entrepreneurs from incorporating their businesses and so a relief is available.

The relief (incorporation relief) is automatic (so no claim need be made). **All or some of the gains are held over if all the following conditions are met.**

(a) The **business is transferred as a going concern**
(b) **All its assets** (or all its assets other than cash) **are transferred**
(c) **The consideration is wholly or partly in shares**

Formula to learn

The amount deferred is found by applying the fraction:

$$\frac{\text{Value of shares received from the company}}{\text{Total value of consideration from the company}} \times \textbf{gain before taper}$$

This amount is then deducted from the base cost of the shares received. The company is deemed to acquire the assets transferred at their market values.

Question

Incorporation relief

Mr P transferred his business to a company in May 2006, realising a gain before taper relief of £24,000 on its only business asset (a factory). The consideration comprised cash of £15,000 and shares at a market value of £75,000.

(a) What is the gain on the transfer before taper relief?
(b) What is the base cost of the shares for any future disposal?

Answer

(a)

		£
Gain		24,000
Less incorporation relief: $\dfrac{75,000}{15,000+75,000} \times £24,000$		(20,000)
Chargeable gain before taper relief		4,000

(b)

	£
Market value	75,000
Less gain deferred	(20,000)
Base cost of shares	55,000

Although the relief cannot be restricted to utilise losses brought forward, taper relief and the annual exemption, it is possible to manipulate the amount of non-share consideration received (whether in cash or left on loan account) so that the gain remaining chargeable (before taper relief) is equal to losses plus the annual exemption.

Question

Antonio transferred his business (market value £120,000) to a company on 16 August 2006, realising a gain before taper relief of £85,436. He had run the business since September 2000 and had capital losses brought forward of £10,000.

Advise Antonio how much of the consideration he should take as shares and how much he should leave on loan account.

Answer

Antonio should take shares worth £56,514 and leave the balance of £63,486 (£120,000 - £56,514) on loan account. These figures are found as follows:

	£
Gain before taper relief	85,436
Less incorporation relief (W)	(40,236)
Gain before taper relief	45,200
Less losses brought forward	(10,000)
Gain before taper relief	35,200
Gain after taper relief (25%)	8,800
Less annual exemption	(8,800)
Taxable	nil

Working

Work backwards to calculate the incorporation relief required to defer sufficient gains to utilise annual exemption, taper relief and losses:

	£
Annual exemption	8,800
Gross up for taper relief × 100/25	35,200
Add losses	10,000
Gain	45,200
Less total gain	(85,436)
Incorporation relief required	40,236

Once the incorporation relief figure is obtained, we can calculate the share consideration required:

Total consideration $\times \dfrac{\text{Deferred gain}}{\text{Gain before taper}}$

$£120,000 \times \dfrac{40,236}{85,436}$
$\underline{\underline{£56,514}}$

Exam focus point

When advising on the amount of share consideration to take on an incorporation consider losses, taper relief and the annual exemption. You may find it easier to work backwards from the annual exemption.

An individual can elect not to receive incorporation relief. He might do this, for example, to keep his entitlement to, say, maximum taper relief on the gain arising on incorporation where he does not expect to retain the shares for at least two years. The election must usually be made by 31 January, 34 months after the end of the tax year of disposal.

Exam focus point

This long time limit is to allow shareholders to see whether they want to elect to disapply incorporation relief depending on whether they have built up two years (the maximum) taper relief on shares between incorporation and disposal. For example if a business is incorporated on 1 April 2007 (2006/07) the shares will need to be held at least until 1 April 2009 (tax year 2008/09) to obtain full taper relief. In this case an election need not be made until 31 January 2010.

4 EIS deferral relief

FAST FORWARD

Gains can be deferred if an individual invests in shares in a EIS company.

4.1 Introduction

An individual may defer a gain arising on the disposal of any type of asset if he invests in qualifying Enterprise Investment Scheme (EIS) shares (see earlier in this Text). The 'frozen', or deferred, gain will usually become chargeable when the shares are disposed of (subject to a further claim for the relief being made).

It is not necessary for the shares acquired to qualify for the EIS income tax relief.

4.2 Calculation of relief

The amount of the gain (before taper relief) that can be deferred is the **lower of:**

(a) **The amount subscribed by the investor for his shares**, which has not previously been matched under this relief, and

(b) **The amount specified by the investor in the claim. This can take into account the availability of losses, taper relief and the annual exemption.**

Taper relief is then applied to any remaining gain in the usual way.

Question

Robert made a gain of £196,000 (before taper relief) on the disposal of a property in 2006/07. The property qualifies for one year taper relief as a business asset. He subscribed for some shares in a company which qualified under the EIS rules. What will the gain to defer be if:

(a) The shares cost £200,000 and Robert wants to take the maximum deferral relief possible.

(b) The shares cost £170,000 and Robert wants to take the maximum deferral relief possible.

(c) The shares cost £200,000 and Robert, who has no other chargeable assets, wishes to utilise his annual exemption.

Answer

(a) £196,000. The qualifying expenditure on the shares exceeds the gain, so the whole gain can be deferred. (See below for the taper relief position when the gain becomes chargeable eg when the shares are sold.)

(b) £170,000. The gain deferred is restricted to the qualifying expenditure. The remainder of the gain of £26,000 will remain in charge (subject to relief for any further investment). If no further EIS investment is made and there are no losses to take into account, the gain after taper relief will be £26,000 × 50% = £13,000.

(c) A claim can be made to defer £178,400. This is calculated as follows:

	£
Gain before relief	196,000
Less EIS reinvestment relief (balancing figure)	(178,400)
Gain before taper relief	17,600
Gain after taper relief (50%)	8,800
Less annual exemption	(8,800)
Taxable	nil

Exam focus point

When advising on the optimum claim for EIS deferral relief you will find it easier to work backwards from the annual exemption.

4.3 Conditions for the relief

4.3.1 The gain to be deferred

The gain must either arise due to the disposal of an asset or on a gain coming back into charge under this relief.

4.3.2 The investor

The investor must be an individual who is UK resident or ordinarily resident at the time the gain to be deferred was made and at the time the investment was made in the shares.

4.3.3 The company

The company must be a qualifying company under the EIS rules (see earlier in this Text).

4.3.4 The shares

The shares must be qualifying shares under the EIS rules (see earlier in this Text).

4.3.5 Time for investment

The shares must be issued to the investor within the period of one year before and three years after the gain to be deferred accrues (or such longer period as HMRC may allow). If the gain accrues after the issue of the shares, the shares must still be held by the investor at the time that the gain arises.

4.3.6 The claim

The latest date for a claim to be made is 31 January nearly six years after the end of the tax year in which the gain to be deferred arose ie by 31 January 2013 for a disposal in 2006/07.

4.4 Gain coming back into charge

The deferred gain will crystallise, ie come back into charge, on the following events:

(a) **The investor disposing of the shares except by an inter-spouse disposal**.

(b) The spouse/civil partner of an investor disposing of the shares, if the spouse/civil partner acquired the shares from the investor.

(c) **The investor becoming non resident, broadly within three years of the issue of the shares** (except if employed full time abroad for up to three years and retaining the shares until his return to the UK).

(d) The spouse/civil partner of an investor becoming non resident, broadly within three years of the issue of the shares (except if employed full time abroad for up to three years and retaining the shares until his return to the UK), if the spouse/civil partner acquired the shares from the investor.

(e) **The shares ceasing to be eligible shares**, eg the company ceases to be a qualifying company, the money subscribed not being used for a qualifying business activity. However, relief is not withdrawn if the company becomes a quoted company. This is provided that there were no arrangements in existence at the time of the issue of the shares for the company to cease to be unquoted.

Note that the gain becomes chargeable in the year of the event, not the year when the original gain was made (if different). It will be charged on the holder of the shares at the date of the event, eg on the investor if he/she still holds the shares or the spouse/civil partner if the shares have been passed to her/him.

Taper relief will apply to the deferred gain with reference to the original asset which gave rise to the deferred gain. No further taper relief is given to the deferred gain. However, separate taper relief will apply to the holding of the EIS shares.

Question	Gain coming back into charge

In 2006/07, Victor made a gain of £160,000 on the disposal of a business asset, qualifying for one year's taper relief. He invested £180,000 in eligible EIS shares on 13 August 2007 and made a claim for EIS deferral relief. The shares were business assets for the purposes of taper relief. Victor sold the shares on 15 October 2009 for £240,000. Show the gains chargeable as a result of the sale in October 2009.

Answer

	£
Proceeds	240,000
Less cost	(180,000)
Gain	60,000
Gain after taper relief (2 years business) (25%)	15,000
Gain deferred recharged after taper relief (1 year business) (50% × £160,000)	80,000
Total gains arising on sale	95,000

There is special taper relief treatment for investors who defer a gain on the disposal of EIS shares into the purchase of further EIS shares. In this case the taper relief given on the disposal of the second investment of shares is cumulative (ie. includes the ownership of the first *and* second investment of shares on the disposal of the second investment of shares). This rule only applies to the gain on the original EIS shares, not the gain on the asset which was originally deferred into the EIS shares.

4.5 Reorganisations and amalgamations

There are rules relating to reorganisations and amalgamations to enable the identification of the original EIS shares (and any associated relief) with replacement shares and to stop the dilution of the relief into rights issue shares. In certain circumstances a reorganisation or amalgamation may result in a chargeable event, for example, if the replacement shares are not new ordinary shares or on a takeover if the new company does not satisfy the rules for EIS qualifying companies.

4.6 Anti-avoidance

The same provisions that apply for EIS income tax relief apply here (see earlier in this Text).

Exam focus point

Never overlook investment considerations; shares in an unquoted company are a high risk investment.

5 Altering dispositions made on death

FAST FORWARD

A variation or disclaimer can be used to vary a will after death. This can have IHT and CGT consequences.

A variation or disclaimer can be used to secure a fairer distribution of a deceased person's estate. More commonly they are used to allow a tax inefficient will to be amended to a more tax efficient distribution of the assets.

If, within two years of a death the terms of a will are changed, in writing, either by a variation of the terms of the will made by the persons who benefit or would benefit under the dispositions, or by a disclaimer, the change will not be a disposal for CGT purposes. The assets disposed of are taken by the new beneficiaries at their probate value (ie market value at death), rather than at the value at the date of the disclaimer or variation, as if the assets had been left directly to those persons by the deceased.

If the beneficiaries making a variation wish the relevant terms of the will to be treated as replaced by the terms of the variation for CGT purposes, it is necessary to state this in the variation.

Where a disclaimer is made, the relevant terms in the will are *automatically* treated as replaced by the terms of the disclaimer for CGT purposes, regardless of whether this is stated in the disclaimer or not.

Similar provisions apply for IHT purposes (see later in this Text).

Chapter roundup

- Gift relief is available on both outright gifts and sales at an undervalue of business assets. Gift relief is also available on gifts which are immediately chargeable to inheritance tax.

- When assets falling within certain classes are sold and other such assets are bought, it is possible to defer gains on the assets sold by claiming rollover relief.

- If an amount less than the proceeds of the old asset is invested in the new assets, a gain equal to the difference will be chargeable, if this is less than the actual gain.

- When an individual incorporates his business, the gain arising will be deducted from the cost of the shares received, unless the individual elects otherwise.

- Gains can be deferred if an individual invests in shares in a EIS company.

- A variation or disclaimer can be used to vary a will after death. This can have IHT and CGT consequences.

Quick quiz

1   Which disposals of shares qualify for gift relief?

2   What assets are eligible for rollover relief on the replacement of business assets by an individual?

3   What deferral of a gain is available when a business asset is replaced with a depreciating business asset?

4   What are the conditions for deferring gains on the incorporation of a business?

5   When is EIS deferral relief available?

6   When will a gain deferred using EIS deferral relief come back into charge?

Answers to quick quiz

1   Shares which qualify for gift relief are those in trading companies which

- are not listed on a recognised stock exchange, or

- where the donor is an individual, which are in that individual's personal company, or

- where the donor is a trustee, where the trustee can exercise 25% or more of the voting rights in the company

2   Assets eligible for rollover relief by an individual are:

- land and buildings
- fixed plant and machinery
- ships, aircraft and hovercraft
- goodwill
- satellites, space stations and spacecraft
- milk quota, potato quota, ewe and suckler cow premium quota
- fish quota

3   Where a depreciating asset is acquired, the gain is 'frozen', or deferred until it crystallises on the earliest of the replacement of the replacement asset, the date the replacement asset ceases to be used in the trade and ten years after the acquisition of the replacement asset.

4   The conditions for incorporation relief are:

- the business is transferred as a going concern,
- all of its assets (or all assets other than cash) are transferred,
- the consideration is wholly or partly in shares

5   EIS deferral relief is available where an individual makes a gain (on any type of asset) and invests in EIS shares within a certain time period.

6   A deferred gain will come back into charge where:

- investor disposes of the shares (except inter-spouse/civil partner)

- investor's civil partner/spouse disposes of shares (if acquired from investor)

- investor (or investor's spouse/civil partner who acquires shares from investor) becomes non-resident within 3 years of issue of shares, unless employed full-time abroad for up to 3 years

- shares cease to be eligible shares (does not generally include becoming quoted)

Now try the question below from the Exam Question Bank

Number	Level	Marks	Time
Q15	Examination	25	45 mins

15

Chargeable gains: additional aspects

Topic list	Syllabus reference
1 Chattels and wasting assets	A3(a)D3,(d)(ii)
2 Wasting assets	A3(d)(ii)
3 Leases	A3(d)(ii)
4 Private residences	A3(a)D6
5 Loss, damage or destruction of an asset	A3(d)(iv),(v)
6 CGT and trusts	A3(b)(vi)
7 Overseas aspects of CGT	A3(b)(ii)-(iv)

Introduction

In the previous chapters we have learnt how to calculate capital gains and we have looked at some of the reliefs available. We now look at some more of the rules for particular assets and particular situations.

First we look at wasting assets. Unless capital allowances have been claimed there are special rules to ensure that the cost of the asset is restricted to reflect the fall in value of the asset over time.

Leases of land also fall in value over their lives: a lease with ten years left to run is worth less than one with thirty years left to run. The rules for wasting assets are modified to reflect the fact that the value of a lease falls more steeply the shorter it becomes.

We then look at the gains people make on their homes which are usually exempt. This means there is no capital gains tax charge when people move home, but also means that there is no relief if their house is sold at a loss.

We next look at the rules which apply when an asset is damaged or destroyed and the reliefs available where insurance proceeds are applied to restore or replace the asset.

Next we consider how CGT applies when assets are transferred into trusts and finally we look at the overseas aspects of capital gains tax.

In the next chapter we will study the administration of income tax and capital gains tax.

Study guide

		Intellectual level
3	**Chargeable gains and capital gains tax liabilities in situations involving further overseas aspects and in relation to closely related persons and trusts together with the application of additional exemptions and reliefs**	
(a)	The contents of the Paper F6 study guide for chargeable gains under headings:	2
•	D1 The scope of the taxation of capital gains	
•	D3 Gains and losses on the disposal of movable and immovable property	
(b)	The scope of the taxation of capital gains:	3
(ii)	Identify the concepts of residence, ordinary residence and domicile and determine their relevance to capital gains tax	
(iii)	Determine the UK taxation of foreign gains, including double taxation relief	
(iv)	Conclude on the capital gains tax position of individuals coming to and leaving the UK	
(vi)	Capital gains tax and trusts:	
	Advise on the capital gains tax implications of transfers of property into trust	
(d)	Gains and losses on the disposal of movable and immovable property:	3
(ii)	Determine the gain on the disposal of leases and wasting assets	
(iv)	Establish the tax effect of capital sums received in respect of the loss, damage or destruction of an asset	
(v)	Advise on the tax effect of making negligible value claims	

Exam guide

You may come across the disposal of wasting assets as part as a question on the disposal of a business, so you must understand the interaction of capital allowances and capital gains. The rules for the damage or destruction of an asset are further rollover reliefs which can be used to defer capital gains. A negligible value claim can be used to crystallise a loss, and you must consider the time of the claim carefully to ensure the best possible use of the loss.

The exemption for the principal private residence and the rules for transfers into trust may be examined in a question about families; watch out for where the PPR relief is restricted or where holdover relief is not available on a gift into a trust.

Do not be caught out by the overseas aspects. For CGT purposes the most useful exclusion is the fact that individuals who are not resident *and* not ordinarily resident in the UK are not taxable on their UK gains. Note, however, how these rules are applied to temporary non-residents so that gains made whilst abroad are taxed on the individual's return.

Knowledge brought forward from earlier studies

This chapter is new.

1 Chattels and wasting assets

Gains on most wasting chattels are exempt, and losses on them are not allowable. The CGT rules are modified for assets eligible for capital allowances.

1.1 Introduction

Key term

> A **chattel** is tangible movable property.
>
> A **wasting asset** is an asset with an estimated remaining useful life of 50 years or less.

Special rules apply for wasting assets to prevent taxpayers from realising a capital loss simply due to the fall in value of a wasting asset over time. The rules are modified where capital allowances are available.

1.2 Chattels

Plant and machinery, whose predictable useful life is always deemed to be less than 50 years, is an example of a wasting chattel (unless it is immovable, in which case it will be wasting but not a chattel). Machinery includes, in addition to its ordinary meaning, motor vehicles (unless exempt as cars), railway and traction engines, engine-powered boats and clocks.

Wasting chattels are exempt (so that there are no chargeable gains and no allowable losses). There is one **exception** to this: assets used for the purpose of a trade, profession or vocation in respect of which **capital allowances** have been or could have been claimed. This means that items of plant and machinery used in a trade are not exempt merely on the ground that they are wasting. However, cars are always exempt.

Exam focus point

> The special rules for non-wasting chattels where the cost and/or sale proceeds are less than £6,000 are excluded from the syllabus. Any disposal of a non-wasting chattel in the exam will therefore give rise to a gain or loss calculated under the normal rules

1.3 Chargeable gains and capital allowances

The wasting chattels exemption does not apply to chattels on which capital allowances have been claimed or could have been claimed.

Where capital allowances have been obtained on any asset, and a loss would arise before indexation allowance, the allowable cost for chargeable gains purposes must be reduced by the lower of the unindexed loss and the net amount of allowances (taking into account any balancing allowances or charges, but not any notional allowances during periods of non-industrial use of buildings). For plant and machinery, and for industrial buildings which have always been in industrial use, the result is no gain and no loss.

Question

CGT and capital allowances

David buys a machine for £100,000 in June 2000 and sells it for £70,000 in June 2006. Show the capital gains consequences.

Answer

The capital allowances after any balancing adjustment, are £(100,000 – 70,000) = £30,000.

	£
Proceeds	70,000
Less reduced cost £(100,000 – 30,000)	(70,000)
No gain and no loss	0

If there is a gain before indexation allowance, the cost is not adjusted for capital allowances. As usual, the indexation allowance may only reduce the gain to zero.

2 Wasting assets

FAST FORWARD
> Other wasting assets generally have their cost written down over time.

2.1 Introduction

A wasting asset is one which has an estimated remaining useful life of 50 years or less and whose original value will depreciate over time. **Freehold land is never a wasting asset**, and there are special rules for leases of land (see below).

Wasting chattels are exempt except for those on which capital allowances have been (or could have been) **claimed**.

2.2 Options

An option (for example an option to buy shares) is a right to buy or sell something at a specified price within a specified time. **An option is usually a wasting asset** because after a certain time it can no longer be exercised.

2.2.1 The grant of an option

The grant of an option is the disposal of an asset, namely the option itself, rather than a part disposal of the asset over which the option has been granted. The only allowable expenditure will be the incidental costs of the grant, such as legal fees. If the option is exercised the CGT treatment changes.

2.2.2 The exercise of an option

Where an option is exercised, the granting of the option and the subsequent disposal of the asset under the option are treated as a single transaction taking place when the option is exercised. Proceeds from the grant of the option plus the disposal of the asset are combined and become the disposal proceeds of the grantor and the allowable base cost of the grantee.

Where tax was paid on the original grant of the option it will usually be treated as a payment on account of the tax on the exercise.

For taper relief purposes, the exercise of the option determines the end of the qualifying taper period for the grantor now disposing of the asset and the start of the qualifying period for the grantee now acquiring the asset. Business status of the asset is determined by reference to the option to which the option related and not to the option itself.

There is one exception. If an individual exercises a share option granted under the Enterprise Management Incentive Scheme (see earlier in this Text), the shares are treated for taper relief purposes as if they had been acquired at the date the option was granted.

2.2.3 Example: exercise of an option

Tom owns a plot of investment land which he bought for £10,000 in May 1999. He grants an option to Penelope for £1,000 in July 2001 whereby he will sell the land for £25,000 at any time nominated by Penelope before 30 June 2008. Penelope exercises her option in July 2006.

Tom's gain in 2006/07 will be:

	£
Proceeds (£1,000 + £25,000)	26,000
Less cost	(10,000)
Gain before taper relief	16,000
Gain after taper relief (5.99 – 7.06 = 7 years)	
£16,000 × 75%	12,000
Penelope's base cost will be: £1,000 + £25,000 =	26,000

The date of disposal is July 2006 (ie when the option is exercised).

2.2.4 Abandoned options

Where an option is abandoned, the position of the grantor and grantee are different. The grantor makes a chargeable disposal at the time when the option is granted. The grantee acquires a chargeable asset at the same time, but the abandonment of the option amounts to a disposal only where the option is:

(a) a quoted option to subscribe for shares in a company
(b) a traded option or financial option
(c) an option to acquire assets for the purposes of a trade

2.2.5 Example: abandoned option

Fred grants an option to sell a plot of land to Barney for £25,000 for which Barney pays £2,500. Barney decides not to proceed with the purchase.

Fred has a chargeable gain equal to the forfeited deposit (ie the proceeds from the option) ie £2,500.

Barney does not have a chargeable disposal because the asset (land) does not fall within the three types of option listed above. No allowable loss arises. The position would be different if, for example, Barney was a trader acquiring the land in order to build a factory on it in which case the normal CGT computation rules would apply.

2.2.6 Disposal of an option

The disposal (eg by sale to a third party) of an option (other than a quoted, traded or financial option) to buy or sell quoted shares or securities gives rise to a chargeable gain or allowable loss computed in accordance with the normal rules for wasting assets (see below). These options are assets which waste on a straight line basis.

2.3 Other wasting assets

The cost is written down on a straight line basis before calculating the indexation allowance. So, if a taxpayer acquires such an asset with a remaining life of 40 years and disposes of it after 15 years (with 25 years remaining) only 25/40 of the cost is deducted from the disposal consideration. Indexation allowance is computed on the written down cost rather than the full original cost.

Examples of such assets are **copyrights** (with 50 years or less to run) and **registered designs**.

Where the asset has an estimated residual value at the end of its predictable life, it is the cost less residual value which is written off on a straight line basis over the asset's life. Where additional expenditure is incurred on a wasting asset the additional cost is written off over the life remaining when it was incurred.

Assets eligible for capital allowances and used throughout the period of ownership in a trade, profession or vocation do not have their allowable expenditure written down.

3 Leases

FAST FORWARD

An ordinary disposal computation is made on the disposal of a lease with 50 years or more to run. For leases of land with less than 50 years to run, a special table of percentages is used.

3.1 Types of disposal

The gain that arises on the disposal of a lease will be chargeable according to the terms of the lease disposed of. We must consider:

(a) The assignment of a lease or sub-lease with 50 years or more to run.
(b) The assignment of a lease or sub-lease with less than 50 years to run.

There is an assignment when a lessee sells the whole of his interest. There is a grant when a new lease or sub-lease is created out of a freehold or existing leasehold, the grantor retaining an interest.

Exam focus point

The CGT rules for the **grant** of leases will not be examined.

The duration of the lease will normally be determined by the contract terms. The expiry date, however, will be taken as the first date on which the landlord has an option to terminate the lease or the date beyond which the lease is unlikely to continue because of, for example, the likelihood that the rent will be substantially increased at that date.

3.2 The assignment of a lease with 50 years or more to run

An **ordinary disposal computation** is made and the whole of any gain on disposal will be chargeable to CGT (subject to any private residence exemption, see below).

3.3 The assignment of a lease with less than 50 years less to run

In calculating the gain on the disposal of a lease with less than 50 years to run only a certain proportion of the original expenditure counts as an allowable deduction. This is because a lease is losing value anyway as its life runs out: only the cost related to the tail end of the lease being sold is deductible. The proportion is determined by a table of percentages.

Exam focus point

The appropriate lease percentages will be given by the examiner.

Formula to learn

The allowable cost is given by:

$$\text{Original cost} \times \frac{X}{Y}$$

where X is the percentage for the number of years left for the lease to run at the date of the assignment, and Y is the percentage for the number of years the lease had to run when first acquired by the seller.

The table only provides percentages for exact numbers of years. Where the duration is not an exact number of years the relevant percentage should be found by adding 1/12 of the difference between the two years on either side of the actual duration for each extra month. Fourteen or more odd days count as a month.

Question

The assignment of a short lease

Mr A acquired a 20 year lease on a block of flats on 1 August 2000 for £15,000. He assigned it on 2 August 2006 for £19,000. Compute the chargeable gain arising.

The percentage form the lease percentage table for 20 years is 72.770, for 14 years is 58.971 and for 6 years is 39.195.

Answer

	£
Proceeds	19,000
Less cost £15,000 × $\dfrac{\%14 \text{ years} : 58.971}{\%20 \text{ years} : 72.770}$	(12,156)
Gain	6,844
Gain after taper relief (6 years) 80% × £6,844	£5,475

4 Private residences

4.1 General principles

There is an exemption for gains on principal private residences, but the exemption may be restricted because of periods of non-occupation or because of business use.

A gain arising on the sale of an individual's only or main private residence (his principal private residence or PPR) is exempt from CGT. The exemption also covers grounds of up to half a hectare. The grounds can exceed half a hectare if the house is large enough to warrant it, but if not, only the gain on the excess grounds is taxable. If the grounds do not adjoin the house (for example when a road separates the two), they **may** still qualify but they may not; each case must be argued on its merits.

For the exemption to be available the taxpayer must have occupied the property as a residence rather than just as temporary accommodation. In the case of *Goodwin v Curtis 1998* the Court held that a considerable degree of permanence and continuity is required in order to turn a simple occupation into a residence. This meant the taxpayer was not entitled to the exemption in respect of one of three properties which he had consecutively acquired and disposed of between April and December 1985 because he had only occupied the property concerned for a short time during which the property was up for sale.

Case law has introduced a restriction of the exemption. In *Varty v Lynes 1976*, the dwelling house and part of the garden were sold, leaving the rest of the garden to be sold separately (for development purposes) at a later date. When this later sale took place, the PPR exemption was not available since the garden was no longer part of the individual's PPR, the house having been sold some time previously.

In *Batey v Wakefield 1981*, the taxpayer had built a bungalow for the use of a caretaker who occupied it rent-free. Since the bungalow was within the grounds of the main dwelling house it formed part of the taxpayer's principal private residence.

However, a gardener's cottage 175m from the main house was held not to be part of the same residence in *Lewis v Rook 1992*. Several flats close together in different buildings in a single London square and used by members of one family for various domestic purposes, have been held not to constitute a single private residence: *Honour v Norris 1992*. In *Green v CIR 1982* it was held that the unoccupied wings of a mansion house partly occupied by the taxpayer were not necessarily a part of his main residence. A caravan connected to mains water and electricity has been held to be a qualifying dwelling for the purposes of principal private residence relief: *Makins v Elson 1977*.

4.2 The exemption

The gain is wholly exempt where the owner has occupied the whole of the residence throughout his period of ownership. Where occupation has been for only part of the period, a proportion of the gain is exempted.

Formula to learn

> The exempt proportion is:
>
> $$\text{Gain before taper relief} \times \frac{\text{Period of occupation}}{\text{Total period of ownership}}$$

A further proportionate restriction is made where only part of the property has been occupied as the owner's residence.

Where a loss arises but all or a proportion of any gain would have been exempt, all or the same proportion of the loss is not allowable.

The **last 36 months of ownership are always** treated as **a period of occupation**, if at some time the residence has been the taxpayer's main residence, even if within those last 36 months the taxpayer also has another house which is his principal private residence.

The **period of occupation is also deemed to include certain periods of absence, provided the individual had no other exempt residence at the time and the period of absence was at some time both preceded by and followed by a period of actual occupation.** Deemed but non-actual occupation during the last 36 months of ownership does not count for this purpose.

These periods of **deemed occupation** are:

(a) Any period (or periods taken together) of absence, for any reason, **up to three years,** and

(b) **Any periods** during which the owner was **required by his employment (ie employed taxpayer) to live abroad**, and

(c) Any period (or periods taken together) **up to four years** during which the owner was **required to live elsewhere due to his work** (ie both employed and self employed taxpayer) so that he could not occupy his private residence.

It does not matter if the residence is let during the absence.

Exempt periods of absence must normally be preceded and followed by periods of **actual occupation**. An extra-statutory concession relaxes this where an individual who has been required to work abroad or elsewhere (ie the latter two categories mentioned above) is unable to resume residence in his home because the terms of his employment require him to work elsewhere.

Where a taxpayer buys land and builds a house on it, or buys a house but delays moving in because he has work done on it or he is still disposing of his old house, the period from purchase to actual moving in counts as a period of residence if it is immediately followed by actual residence, and does not exceed one year. The one year period may be increased by up to a further year if there are good reasons.

Principal private residence relief

Mr A purchased a house on 31 March 1983 for £50,000. He lived in the house until 30 June 1983. He then worked abroad for two years before returning to the UK to live in the house again on 1 July 1985. He stayed in the house until 31 December 1999 before retiring and moving out to live with friends in Spain until the house was sold on 28 December 2006 for £150,000.

Calculate any chargeable gain arising. Assume an indexation factor March 1983 to April 1998 = 0.956

Answer

(a)   *Exempt and chargeable periods*

		Exempt months	*Chargeable months*
Period			
(ii)	April 1983 – June 1983 (occupied)	3	0
(iii)	July 1983 – June 1985 (working abroad)	24	0
(iv)	July 1985 – December 1999 (occupied)	174	0
(v)	January 2000 – December 2003 (see below)	0	48
(vi)	January 2004 – December 2006 (last 36 months)	36	0
		237	48

No part of the period from January 2000 to December 2003 can be covered by the exemption for three years of absence for any reason because it is not followed at any time by actual occupation.

(b)   *The chargeable gain*

	£
Proceeds	150,000
Less cost	(50,000)
Unindexed gain	100,000
Less indexation allowance (March 1983 to April 1998)	
0.956 × £50,000	(47,800)
Gain before taper relief	52,200
Less exempt under PPR provisions:	
$\dfrac{237}{285} \times £52,200$	(43,408)
Chargeable gain	8,792
Gain after taper relief (9 years including additional year) 65% × £8,792	£5,715

Exam focus point

To help you to answer questions such as that above it is useful to draw up a table showing period of ownership, exempt months (real/deemed occupation) and chargeable months (non-occupation). You should also provide an explanation for any periods of deemed occupation.

4.3 Relocations

When an employee is required to move by his employer, and sells his house to the employer or to a relocation company for a guaranteed value plus a share in any profit made by the employer or relocation company when it sells the house, the profit share is exempt to the same extent as the initial gain on selling the house. Thus if only 60% of that gain was exempt, 60% of the profit share will also be exempt. This is an extra-statutory concession.

4.4 More than one residence

4.4.1 The election for a residence to be treated as the main residence

Where a person has more than one residence (owned or rented), he may elect for one to be regarded as his main residence by notice to HMRC within two years of commencing occupation of the second residence. An election can have effect for any period beginning not more than two years prior to the date of election until it is varied by giving further notice. (The further notice may itself be backdated by up to two years.)

In order for the election to be made, the individual must actually reside in both residences.

Any period of ownership of a residence not nominated as the main residence will be a chargeable period for that residence.

Where there are two residences and the second one is being treated as a residence under the 'delay in moving in' rule (see above), the election is not needed and both may count as principal private residences simultaneously.

4.4.2 Job-related accommodation

The rule limiting people to only one main residence is relaxed for individuals living in job-related accommodation.

Such individuals will be treated as occupying any second dwelling house which they own if they intend in due course to occupy the dwelling house as their only or main residence. Thus it is not necessary to establish any actual residence in such cases. This rule extends to self-employed persons required to live in job-related accommodation (for example tenants of public houses).

Key term

A person lives in **job-related accommodation** where:

(a)   It is necessary for the **proper performance of his duties**, or

(b)   It is provided for the **better performance of his duties** and his is one of the kinds of employment in which it is **customary** for employers to provide accommodation, or

(c)   There is a **special threat to the employee's security** and use of the accommodation is part of security arrangements.

4.5 Spouses/civil partners

Where a married couple/civil partners live together only one residence may qualify as the main residence for relief. If each owned one property before marriage/registration of the civil partnership, a new two year period for electing for which is to be treated as the main residence starts on marriage/registration.

Where a marriage/civil partnership has broken down and one spouse/civil partner owning or having an interest in the matrimonial home has ceased to occupy the house, by concession the departing spouse/civil partner will continue to be treated as resident for capital gains tax purposes provided that the other has continued to reside in the home and the departing spouse/civil partner has not elected that some other house should be treated as his or her main residence for this period. This only applies where one spouse disposes of his interest to the other spouse.

Where a house passes from one spouse/civil partner to the other (for example on death), the new owner also inherits the old owner's periods of ownership and occupation for PPR relief purposes.

4.6 Letting relief

FAST FORWARD

> There is also a relief for letting out a principal private residence if the gain arising during the letting would not be covered by the main relief.

The principal private residence exemption is extended to any gain accruing while the property is let, up to a certain limit. The two main circumstances in which the letting exemption applies are:

(a) When the owner is absent and lets the property, where the absence is not a deemed period of occupation.

(b) When the owner lets part of the property while still occupying the rest of it. The absence from the let part cannot be a deemed period of occupation, because the owner has another residence (the rest of the property). However, the let part will qualify for the last 36 months exemption **if** the let part has **at some time** been part of the only or main residence.

In both cases the letting must be for residential use. **The extra exemption is restricted to the lowest of:**

(a) The amount of the total **gain** which is already **exempt under the PPR provisions** (including the last 36 months exemption)

(b) The gain accruing during the letting period (the **letting part of the gain**)

(c) **£40,000**

The letting exemption cannot convert a gain into an allowable loss.

If a lodger lives as a member of the owner's family, sharing their living accommodation and eating with them, the whole property is regarded as the owner's main residence.

Question	Letting relief

Miss Coe purchased a house on 31 March 1993 for £90,000. She sold it on 31 August 2006 for £340,000. In 1995 the house was redecorated and Miss Coe began to live on the top floor renting out the balance of the house (constituting 60% of the total house) to tenants between 1 January 1996 and 31 December 2005. On 2 January 2006 Miss Coe put the whole house on the market but continued to live only on the top floor until the house was sold. What was the chargeable gain? Assume an indexation factor March 1993 to April 1998 = 0.167.

Answer

	£
Proceeds	340,000
Less: cost	(90,000)
Unindexed gain	250,000
Less indexation allowance (March 1993 to April 1998)	
0.167 × £90,000	(15,030)
Indexed gain	234,970
Less PPR exemption	
$£234,970 \times \dfrac{105.8}{161}$	(154,409)
	80,561

Less letting exemption
Lowest of:

(a) gain exempt under PPR rules: £154,409

(b) gain attributable to letting $£234,970 \times \dfrac{55.2}{161}$: £80,561

(c) £40,000	(40,000)
Gain left in charge	40,561

Gain after taper relief (9 years including additional year): 65% × £40,561	£26,365

Working

Period	Exempt months	Chargeable months
1.4.93 – 31.12.95 (occupied)	33	
1.1.96 – 31.8.03 (40% occupied: 60% let)	36.8	55.2
1.9.03 – 31.8.06 (last 36 months – treated as 100% occupied)	36	
Total	105.8	55.2

Note. The gain on the 40% of the house always occupied by Miss Coe is fully covered by PPR relief. The other 60% of the house has not always been occupied by Miss Coe and thus any gain on this part of the house is taxable where it relates to periods of time when Miss Coe was not actually (or deemed to be) living in it.

As a further point if Miss Coe had reoccupied the lower floors (60% part) of the house prior to the sale then 3 years' worth of the non-occupation period between 1.1.96 and 31.8.03 could have been treated as deemed occupation under the special 3 years absence for any reason rule.

4.7 Business use

Where part of a residence is used exclusively for business purposes throughout the period of ownership, the gain attributable to use of that part is taxable.

The 'last 36 months always exempt' rule does not apply to that part.

Question — Business use of PPR

Mr Smail purchased a property for £35,000 on 31 May 2001 and began operating a dental practice from that date in one quarter of the house. On 31 December 2004 he purchased a second house and submitted an election to treat this second house as his main residence from the date of purchase. He closed the dental practice on 31 December 2006, selling the old house on that date for £130,000.

Compute the chargeable gain, if any, arising before taper relief.

Answer

	£
Proceeds	130,000
Less: cost	(35,000)
Gain	95,000
Less PPR exemption 0.75 × £95,000	(71,250)
Chargeable gain before taper relief	23,750

Exemption is lost on one quarter throughout the period of ownership (including the last 36 months) because of the use of that fraction for business purposes. The last 36 months are exempt (for the non-business part), despite the acquisition of a second house which is treated as the PPR.

If part of a house was used for business purposes for part of the period of ownership, the gain is apportioned between chargeable and exempt parts in a just and reasonable manner. If the business part was **at some time** used as part of the only or main residence, the gain apportioned to that part **will** qualify for the last 36 months exemption.

4.8 Tax planning points

Where a second residence is acquired, careful consideration should be given as to which residence is to be treated as the main residence. One should generally choose the residence on which the greatest gain is likely to arise.

When considering what proportion of relief can be claimed for household expenses where part of the residence is used for business, a taxpayer should take care not to jeopardise any PPR exemption.

There are no exemptions on properties acquired wholly or partly to make a gain. HMRC normally only apply this rule when a residence appears to have been bought with the primary purpose of an early disposal. More commonly, gains attributed to the extra expenditure incurred wholly or partly to make a gain are denied the exemption. An example is the conversion of a house into flats.

5 Loss, damage or destruction of an asset

The gain which would otherwise arise on the receipt of insurance proceeds may, subject to certain conditions, be deferred.

5.1 Destroyed assets

If an asset is destroyed (compared to merely being damaged – see below) any compensation or insurance monies received will normally be brought into an ordinary CGT disposal computation as proceeds. The date of disposal is the date the insurance proceeds are received and not the date the asset is destroyed. If all the insurance proceeds from a non-wasting asset are applied for the replacement of the asset within 12 months, any gain can be deducted from the cost of the replacement asset. If only part of the proceeds are used, the gain immediately chargeable can be limited to the amount not used. The rest of the gain is then deducted from the cost of the replacement. This is similar to rollover relief for replacement of business assets (see earlier in this Text.)

Question

Destroyed assets

Fiona bought a non-business asset for £25,000 in June 2003. It was destroyed in March 2006. Insurance proceeds of £34,000 were received in September 2006, and Fiona spent £35,500 on a replacement asset. Compute the chargeable gain and the base cost of the new asset.

Answer

2006/07	£
Proceeds	34,000
Less cost	(25,000)
Gain (can be fully deferred as all insurance monies are spent on replacement)	9,000

The base cost of the new asset is £(35,500 – 9,000) = £26,500.

5.2 Damaged assets

If an asset is damaged and compensation or insurance money is received as a result, then **this will normally be treated as a part disposal.**

By election, however, the taxpayer can avoid a part disposal computation. **A capital sum received can be deducted from the cost of the asset rather than being treated as a part disposal if:**

    (a)   **Any amount not spent in restoring the asset is small**, or

    (b)   **The capital sum is small.**

HMRC accept a sum as 'small' if it is either less than 5% of the value of the asset or is less than £3,000. There are special restrictions if the asset is wasting (that is, it has a remaining useful life of 50 years or less).

    (a)   The **whole** capital sum must be spent on restoration.

    (b)   The capital sum can only be deducted from what would have been the allowable expenditure on a sale immediately after its application. If the asset is a wasting asset this will be less than the full cost of the asset, because the cost of a wasting asset is written down over its life.

If the amount not used in restoring the asset is not small, then the taxpayer can elect for the amount used in restoration to be deducted from the cost; the balance will continue to be treated as a part disposal.

Question | Damaged asset

Mr J bought an office block for renting out which cost £18,000 on 15 August 1983. On 10 September 2006 it was damaged in a fire and, as a result, £27,000 insurance proceeds were received in December 2006. £20,000 was spent to restore the building in October 2006; the market value of the building immediately after restoration was £62,000. What gain arose and what will be the base cost of the building in future computations? Assume that Mr J elects for the amount used in restoration to be deducted from the base cost of the building. Assume an indexation factor of August 1993 to April 1998 = 0.897.

Answer

The part disposal in December 2006

	£	£
Capital sum not used for restoration		
£(27,000 - 20,000)		7,000
Less: part of original cost (incurred August 1983)		
£18,000 × $\dfrac{7,000}{7,000+62,000}$	1,826	
part of restoration cost (incurred October 2006)		
£20,000 × $\dfrac{7,000}{7,000+62,000}$	2,029	
		(3,855)
Unindexed gain		3,145
Less indexation allowance (August 1983 to April 1998)		
0.897 × £1,826		(1,638)
Indexed gain		1,507
Gain after taper relief £1,507 × 65%		980

The base cost of the restored building

	£	£
Original cost		18,000
Restoration expenditure		20,000
		38,000
Less: costs used in part disposal	3,855	
restoration expenditure rolled over	20,000	
		(23,855)
Base cost		14,145

The date of the part disposal is the date of receipt of the insurance monies (December 2006). Mr J purchased the asset in August 1983 and also spent £20,000 in restoring the building in October 2006. There is an indexation allowance from August 1983 to April 1998 on the part of the original cost but there is no indexation allowance on the part of the restoration cost since this was incurred post April 1998 (the date on which indexation allowance was abolished). Taper relief is due for 9 years as the asset is not a business asset. There are 8 years ownership post 6 April 1998 plus the additional year.

5.3 Negligible value claims

If a chargeable asset's value becomes negligible a claim may be made to treat the asset as though it were sold, and then immediately reacquired at its current market value. This will usually give rise to an allowable loss.

The sale and reacquisition are treated as taking place when the claim is made, or at a specified earlier time. The earlier time can be any time up to two years before the start of the tax year in which the claim is made. (For companies, it can be as far back as the start of the earliest accounting period which ends within two years of the date of claim.) The asset must have been of negligible value at the specified earlier time.

On a subsequent actual disposal, any gain is computed using the negligible value as the acquisition cost.

<table>
<tr><td>**Exam focus point**</td><td>Since a negligible value claim can be backdated it can be used to generate an allowable loss to set against a gain that has already been realised.</td></tr>
</table>

6 CGT and trusts

FAST FORWARD

CGT may arise when assets are transferred into trust.

6.1 Assets being put into trusts

If a settlor puts an asset into any type of trust during his lifetime, he makes a disposal for CGT purposes. It will be deemed to take place at market value and gift relief will be available (unless the trust is a settlor-interested trust – see below). This is because there is also an inheritance tax charge (see later in this Text) when the assets enter the trust.

As there is no CGT on death, where a trust is created on death there is no deemed disposal. The trustees of a trust created under a will or on intestacy acquire the trust assets at their market value at death (ie probate value).

<table>
<tr><td>**Exam focus point**</td><td>Inheritance tax for trusts is covered later in this Text. You should return to this section once you have completed your study of the relevant chapters.</td></tr>
</table>

6.2 Settlor-interested trusts

It is not possible to claim gift relief on transfers to a settlor-interested trust. This is a trust from which the settlor, or his spouse/civil partner or minor child (who is neither married nor in a civil partnership) can benefit.

Gift relief may have been claimed on a transfer to a trust which becomes settlor interested. If the **trust becomes settlor interested within six tax years of the end of the tax year in which the transfer was made there is a claw back of the gift relief.**

The gain that was deferred using gift relief will be treated as becoming taxable on the settlor when the trust becomes settlor interested. The trustees' allowable cost will be increased by the amount of the gain taxable on the settlor. If the trustees have already disposed of the gifted asset before the gain is clawed back, the trustees' gain or loss will be recomputed as if the gift relief had never been claimed and the tax payable or repayable is adjusted accordingly.

7 Overseas aspects of CGT

CGT applies primarily to persons resident or ordinarily resident in the UK and persons only temporarily abroad.

7.1 General principles

An individual's liability to capital gains tax is affected by his residence, ordinarily residence and domicile. The meaning of these terms has been discussed earlier in this Text .

Individuals are liable to CGT on the disposal of assets situated anywhere in the world if for any part of the tax year in which the disposal occurs they are resident or ordinarily resident in the UK. By concession, when a person first becomes resident in the UK, he is normally charged to CGT only on those gains which arise after his arrival provided he has not been resident or ordinarily resident in the UK for four out of the last seven years.

If a person is not domiciled in the UK but is resident or ordinarily resident in the UK, gains on the disposal of assets situated overseas are taxable only to the extent that the proceeds of the sale are remitted to the UK. No account is given for overseas capital losses for this person even if all of the proceeds are remitted.

Some of the rules about where assets are situated are contained in legislation. Some of them are a matter of general law. Most of the rules are obvious, for example, land is situated where it actually is, chattels are situated where they are physically present. There are special rules relating to intangible assets, the most important of which are shares and securities in a company. **All shares and securities of a UK incorporated company are treated as situated in the UK, regardless of where the share certificate is kept**.

If a gain made on the disposal of an overseas asset suffers overseas taxation, relief will be available in the UK against any CGT on the same disposal.

If an asset is bought and/or sold for amounts in a foreign currency, each such amount is first translated into sterling (using the rate at the time of purchase or sale), and the gain or loss is computed using these sterling amounts.

Tax on gains accruing on assets situated outside the UK may be deferred if:

- The taxpayer makes a claim
- The gain could not be remitted to the UK because of the laws of the country where it arose, because of executive action of its government or because it was impossible to obtain foreign currency, and
- This was not because of any lack of reasonable endeavours on the taxpayer's part.

The time limit for this claim, for individuals, is the 31 January which is nearly 6 years after the end of the tax year of disposal. For companies, it is six years after the end of the accounting period of disposal.

However, the gain deferred is taxable if it becomes remittable, as if it were a gain accruing in the year in which it ceases to be non-remittable.

7.2 Non-UK residents

Normally a disposal of assets situated in the UK is not a chargeable event if the vendor is neither resident nor ordinarily resident in the UK at the time of disposal. However, a liability to CGT may arise if the person is carrying on a trade, profession or vocation in the UK through a branch or agency and an asset which has been used for the purpose of the branch or agency is either disposed of or removed from the UK.

A charge will also arise if the UK trade, profession or vocation ceases. In this case, and in the case of removal of assets from the UK, there is a deemed disposal of assets at their market value.

7.3 Temporary non-residence

Temporary non residents may be taxable on gains realised whilst they are abroad if:

(a)   They are outside the UK for less than five years between the years of departure and return.

(b)   They were UK resident or ordinarily resident for the four out of the seven years immediately preceding the year of departure.

Net gains realised in the year of departure are taxed in that year (this applies whether the absence is temporary or permanent, under general principles). Subsequent gains/ losses are chargeable/allowable in the year of return as if they were gains/losses of that year. Taper relief applies until the date of actual disposal as usual, not until the time the gain becomes chargeable.

Gains on assets acquired in the non-resident period are not included in the above charge nor are gains which are already chargeable because they arise on branch or agency assets (see above).

Question	Temporary non residence

Sue was resident in the UK until January 2006. She then left the UK and was not resident or ordinarily resident in the UK until she returned in December 2010. In July 2006 Sue sold a business asset for £150,000 that she had acquired in May 2005 for £87,000. In June 2008 she sold an investment asset for £80,000 that she had bought in May 2004 for £100,000. Sue makes no other disposals. Show the amount of Sue's net taxable gains in 2010/11. Assume 2006/07 tax rates and allowances continue to apply.

Answer

As Sue has been outside of the UK for less than five years, the gains/ losses arising whilst she was abroad on assets she owned before leaving the UK will be taxable/ allowable in the year of return.

2006 disposal

	£
Proceeds	150,000
Less cost	(87,000)
Gain	63,000

This business asset was held for 1 year: 50%

2008 disposal

	£
Proceeds	80,000
Cost	(100,000)
Loss	(20,000)

Net gain chargeable 2010/11

	£
Gain	63,000
Loss	(20,000)
	43,000
Gain after taper relief (50%)	21,500
Less annual exemption	(8,800)
	12,700

Exam focus point	Note carefully the rules for temporary non-residence, in particular that taper relief is given for the ownership period to the date of sale even though the gain accrues in a later year. Also note the exclusion for assets purchased whilst abroad.

7.4 The OECD model agreement

Where a double tax agreement follows the OECD model, a person resident in country R disposing of an asset in country A may be taxed in country A on any gain only if the asset is:

- Immovable property in country A, or

- A permanent establishment (see later in this Text) used for a business carried on in country A, a fixed base used for carrying on a profession in country A or movable property pertaining to such an establishment or base.

Otherwise, a gain may be taxed only in country R.

Chapter roundup

- Gains on most wasting chattels are exempt, and losses on them are not allowable. The CGT rules are modified for assets eligible for capital allowances.

- Other wasting assets generally have their cost written down over time.

- An ordinary disposal computation is made on the disposal of a lease with 50 years or more to run. For leases of land with less than 50 years to run, a special table of percentages is used.

- There is an exemption for gains on principal private residences, but the exemption may be restricted because of periods of non-occupation or because of business use.

- There is also a relief for letting out a principal private residence if the gain arising during the letting would not be covered by the main relief.

- The gain which would otherwise arise on the receipt of insurance proceeds may, subject to certain conditions, be deferred.

- CGT may arise when assets are transferred into trust.

- CGT applies primarily to persons resident or ordinarily resident in the UK and persons only temporarily abroad.

Quick quiz

1. What is the general treatment of intangible wasting assets (eg a copyright)?
2. When a lease with less than 50 years to run is assigned, what proportion of the cost is allowable?
3. For what periods may an individual be deemed to occupy his principal private residence?
4. What is the maximum letting exemption?
5. Emma drops and destroys a vase. She receives compensation of £2,000 from her insurance company. How can she avoid a charge to CGT arising?

Answers to quick quiz

1 The cost is written down on a straight line basis

2 Allowable cost is original cost × X/Y where X is the % for the years left of the lease to run at assignment and Y is the % for the years the lease had to run when first acquired by the seller.

3 Periods of deemed occupation are:

- last 36 months of ownership, and

- any period of absence up to three years, and

- any period during which the owner was required by his employment to work abroad, and

- any period up to four years during which the owner was required to live elsewhere due to his work (employed or self-employed) so that he could not occupy his private residence.

4 £40,000

5 Emma can avoid a charge to CGT on receipt of the compensation by investing at least £2,000 in a replacement asset within 12 months.

Now try the questions below from the Exam Question Bank

Number	Level	Marks	Time
Q16	Introductory	25	45 mins

Self assessment for individuals and partnerships

16

Topic list	Syllabus reference
1 The administration of taxation	A6(c)
2 Notification of liability of income tax and CGT	A6(c)
3 Tax returns and keeping records	A6(c)
4 Self-assessment and claims	A6(c)
5 Payment of income tax and capital gains tax	A3(d)(vi),A6(c)
6 Enquiries, determinations and discovery assessments	A6(c)

Introduction

In the previous chapters we have studied the comprehensive computation of income tax and capital gains tax liabilities.

In this chapter we look at the overall system for the administration of tax. We then see how individuals and partnerships must 'self assess' their liability to income tax and capital gains tax. We deal with self assessment for companies later in this Text.

In the next chapter we will commence our study of inheritance tax.

Study guide

		Intellectual level
3	**Chargeable gains and capital gains tax liabilities in situations involving further overseas aspects and in relation to closely related persons and trusts together with the application of additional exemptions and reliefs**	
(d)	Gains and losses on the disposal of movable and immovable property:	3
(vi)	Determine when capital gains tax can be paid by instalments and evaluate when this would be advantageous to taxpayers	
6	**National insurance, value added tax and tax administration:**	
(c)	The contents of the Paper F6 study guide for the obligations of taxpayers and/or their agents under headings:	2
•	G1 The systems for self assessment and the making of returns	
•	G2 The time limits for the submission of information, claims and payment of tax, including payments on account	
•	G3 The procedures relating to enquiries appeals and disputes	
•	G4 Penalties for non-compliance	

Exam guide

In any tax advice question you must consider the administrative requirements and time limits. You must know the taxpayer's responsibilities for making returns and paying tax, and the rules that HMRC can use to enforce compliance.

> **Knowledge brought forward from earlier studies**

This chapter is a revision of material studied at level 2.3.

1 The administration of taxation

FAST FORWARD

> Direct taxes are administered by Her Majesty's Revenue and Customs.

The **Treasury** formally imposes and collects taxation. The management of the Treasury is the responsibility of the Chancellor of the Exchequer. **The administrative function for the collection of tax is undertaken by Her Majesty's Revenue and Customs (HMRC).** Previously there were two separate bodies called the Inland Revenue (responsible for direct taxes such as income tax and corporation tax) and HM Customs and Excise (responsible for indirect taxes such as VAT). Rules on these administrative matters are contained in the **Taxes Management Act 1970 (TMA 1970)**.

HMRC consists of the commissioners for Her Majesty's Revenue and Customs and staff known **as Officers of Revenue and Customs.**

The UK has historically been divided into **tax districts**. These are being merged into larger **areas**, with the separate offices in each area being responsible for different aspects of HMRC's work. For example, one office may be designated to deal with taxpayer's queries, another to deal with the PAYE procedures for joiners and leavers, whilst end of year PAYE returns may be dealt with by a third office. Some offices also act as **enquiry offices**, where taxpayers can visit the office and see a member of HMRC staff in person without an appointment.

Each area is headed by an area director. HMRC staff were historically described as **'Inspectors'** and **'Collectors'**. The legislation now refers to an **'Officer of the Revenue and Customs'** when setting out HMRC's powers. They are responsible for supervising the self-assessment system and agreeing tax liabilities. Collectors (or **receivable management officers**) are local officers who are responsible for following up amounts of unpaid tax referred to them by the **HMRC Accounts Office.**

The structure of offices is also being changed. **Taxpayer service offices** are being set up to do routine checking, computation *and* collection work, while **Taxpayer district offices** investigate selected accounts, deal with corporation tax and enforce the payment of tax when it is not paid willingly. **Taxpayer assistance offices** handle enquiries and arrange specialist help for taxpayers.

The **General Commissioners** (not to be confused with the Commissioners for HMRC) are (currently) appointed by the Lord Chancellor to hear **appeals** against HMRC decisions. They are part-time and unpaid. They are appointed for a local area (a **division**). They appoint a clerk who is often a lawyer or accountant and who is paid for his services.

The **Special Commissioners** are also appointed by the Lord Chancellor. They are full-time paid professionals. They generally hear the more complex appeals.

Many taxpayers arrange for their accountants to prepare and submit their tax returns. The taxpayer remains responsible for submitting the return and for paying the tax; the accountant acts as the taxpayer's agent.

2 Notification of liability to income tax and CGT

FAST FORWARD

Individuals who do not receive a tax return or who have a new source of income or gains must notify their chargeability to income tax or CGT.

Individuals who have not received a notice to file a return, or who have a new source of income or gains in the tax year, are required to give notice of chargeability to HMRC within six months from the end of the year ie by 5 October 2007 for 2006/07.

A person who has no chargeable gains and who is not liable to higher rate tax does not have to give notice of chargeability if all his income:

  (a)   Is taken into account under PAYE
  (b)   Is from a source of income not subject to tax under a self-assessment
  (c)   Has had (or is treated as having had) income tax deducted at source, or
  (d)   Is a UK dividend.

The maximum mitigable penalty where notice of chargeability is not given is 100% of the tax assessed which is not paid on or before 31 January following the tax year.

3 Tax returns and keeping records

FAST FORWARD

Tax returns must be filed within certain time limits. There are penalties for late submission.

3.1 Tax returns

The tax return comprises a Tax Form, together with supplementary pages for particular sources of income. Taxpayers are sent a Tax Form and a number of supplementary pages depending on their known sources of income, together with a Tax Return Guide and various notes relating to the supplementary pages. Taxpayers with new sources of income may have to ask the order line for further supplementary pages.

If a return for the previous year was filed electronically, or a computer generated substitute form used, the taxpayer may be sent a notice to file a return, rather than the official HMRC form.

Taxpayers with simple tax affairs may be asked to complete a Short four page Tax Return. Short Tax Returns may be sent to employees (not directors) with taxable benefits, sole traders with three line accounts and pensioners who have pensions and simple investment income. HMRC process these returns using an automated data capture facility. Taxpayers can also choose to file the return online.

Partnerships must file a separate return which includes 'a partnership statement' showing the firm's profits, losses, proceeds from the sale of assets, tax suffered, tax credits, charges on income and the division of all these amounts between partners. The partnership return must normally be made by the senior partner (or whomever else may be nominated by the partnership), but HMRC have power to require any, all, or some of the partners (or their nominated successors) to submit the return.

A partnership return must include a declaration of the name, residence and tax reference of each partner, as well as the usual declaration that the return is correct and complete to the best of the signatory's knowledge. **Each partner must then include his share of partnership profits on his personal tax return.**

3.2 Time limit for submission of tax returns

FAST FORWARD

Taxpayers normally self assess their income tax, Class 4 NIC and CGT liabilities but HMRC will calculate the tax on their behalf if they file their tax return by 30 September following the end of the tax year.

Key term

The **filing due date for filing a tax return is the later of:**

*   **31 January following the end of the tax year which the return covers.**
*   **Three months after the notice to file the return was issued.**

If an individual or trustees wish HMRC to prepare the self-assessment (see below) on their behalf, earlier deadlines apply. The filing date is then the later of:

*   **30 September following the tax year eg for 2006/07, by 30 September 2007.**
*   **Two months after notice to file the return was issued.**

Since a partnership return does not include a self-assessment these revised deadlines do not apply to partnership returns. This may, of course, create problems if one of the partners wishes HMRC to complete his personal self-assessment.

The filing due dates are to be advanced for 2007/08 onwards as part of the move towards online filing. The deadline for paper returns will be 31 October following the tax year, although the deadline for online returns will remain at 31 January following the tax year.

3.3 Penalties for late filing

3.3.1 Individual returns

The maximum penalties for delivering a tax return after the filing due date are:

(a)	**Return up to 6 months late:**	£100
(b)	**Return more than 6 months but not more than 12 months late:**	£200
(c)	**Return more than 12 months late:**	£200 + 100% of the tax liability

In addition, the General or Special Commissioners can direct that a maximum penalty of £60 per day be imposed where failure to deliver a tax return continues after notice of the direction has been given to the taxpayer. In this case the additional £100 penalty, imposed under (b) if the return is more than six months late, is not charged.

The fixed penalties of £100/£200 can be set aside by the Commissioners if they are satisfied that the taxpayer had a reasonable excuse for not delivering the return. If the tax liability shown on the return is less than the fixed penalties, the fixed penalty is reduced to the amount of the tax liability. The tax geared penalty is mitigable by HMRC or the Commissioners.

3.3.2 Partnership returns

The maximum penalties for late delivery of a partnership tax return are as shown above, save that there is no tax-geared penalty if the return is more than 12 months late. The penalties apply separately to each partner.

3.3.3 Reasonable excuse

A taxpayer only has a reasonable excuse for a late filing if a default occurred because of a factor outside his control. This might be non-receipt of the return by the taxpayer, an industrial dispute in the post office after the return was posted, serious illness of the taxpayer or a close relative, or destruction of records through fire and flood. Illness etc is only accepted as a reasonable excuse if the taxpayer was taking timeous steps to complete the return, and if the return is filed as soon as possible after the illness etc.

3.3.4 Returns rejected as incomplete

If a return, filed before the filing date, is rejected by HMRC as incomplete later than 14 days before the filing deadline of 31 January, a late filing penalty will not be charged if the return is completed and returned within 14 days of the rejection. This only applies if the omission from the return was a genuine error. It does not apply if a return was deliberately filed as incomplete in the hope of extending the time limit.

3.4 Electronic lodgement of tax returns

The electronic lodgement of tax returns and other documents is possible if:

(a) The information is transferred by persons approved by HMRC.

(b) The information is transmitted using approved hardware and software.

(c) A hard copy of the information (signed by the taxpayer etc) was made before the information is transmitted electronically and the fact that this has been done is signified as part of the transmission.

(d) The information is accepted by HMRC's computer.

Where a return is filed electronically, supporting documents may be sent separately (eg. by post). Provided they are submitted within one month of the return and have been referred to in the return HMRC accept that they 'accompany' the return.

3.5 Standard accounting information

'Three line' accounts (ie income less expenses equals profit) only need be included on the tax return of businesses with a turnover (or gross rents from property) of less than £15,000 pa. This is not as helpful as it might appear, as underlying records must still be kept for tax purposes (disallowable items etc) when producing three line accounts.

Large businesses with a turnover of at least £5 million which have used figures rounded to the nearest £1,000 in producing their published accounts can compute their profits to the nearest £1,000 for tax purposes.

The tax return requires trading results to be presented in a standard format. Although there is no requirement to submit accounts with the return, accounts may be filed. If accounts accompany the return, HMRC's power to raise a discovery assessment (see below) is restricted.

3.6 Keeping of records

All taxpayers must keep and retain all records required to enable them to make and deliver a correct tax return.

Records must be retained until the later of:

(a) (i) **5 years after the 31 January following the tax year where the taxpayer is in business** (as a sole trader or partner or letting property), or

(ii) **1 year after the 31 January following the tax year, or**

(b) Provided notice to deliver a return is given before the date in (a):

(i) **The time after which enquiries by HMRC into the return can no longer be commenced**, or

(ii) **The date any such enquiries have been completed.**

Where a person receives a notice to deliver a tax return after the normal record keeping period has expired, he must keep all records in his possession at that time until no enquiries can be raised in respect of the return or until such enquiries have been completed.

The maximum (mitigable) penalty for each failure to keep and retain records is £3,000 per tax year/accounting period.

The duty to preserve records can generally be satisfied by retaining copies of original documents except that the originals of documents which show domestic or foreign tax deducted or creditable (eg dividend certificates) must be kept.

Record keeping failures are taken into account in considering the mitigation of other penalties. Where the record keeping failure is taken into account in this way, a penalty will normally only be sought in serious and exceptional cases where, for example, records have been destroyed deliberately to obstruct an enquiry or there has been a history of serious record keeping failures.

4 Self-assessment and claims

4.1 Self assessment

Every full personal and trust tax return must be accompanied by a self-assessment.

Key term

> **A self-assessment** is a calculation of the amount of taxable income and gains after deducting reliefs and allowances, and a calculation of the income tax, Class 4 NIC and CGT payable after taking into account tax deducted at source and tax credits.

Although Tax Calculation Working Sheets are provided with the tax return there is no requirement for the taxpayer to use these in computing his self-assessment. It is sufficient to enter the appropriate figures on the tax return.

The self-assessment calculation may either be made by the taxpayer or HMRC. If a return is filed within certain time limits (normally, 30 September following the tax year to which it relates, see above) an Officer of Revenue and Customs must make a self-assessment on the taxpayer's behalf on the basis of the information contained in the return. He must send a copy of the assessment to the taxpayer. These assessments, even though raised by HMRC, are treated as self-assessments.

If the taxpayer files a return after the above deadline but without completing the self-assessment, HMRC will not normally reject the return as incomplete. However HMRC are not then bound to complete the self-assessment in time to notify the taxpayer of the tax falling due on the normal due date (generally the following 31 January), and it is the taxpayer's responsibility to estimate and pay his tax on time.

Within nine months of receiving a tax return, HMRC can amend a taxpayer's self-assessment to correct any obvious errors or mistakes; whether errors of principle, arithmetical mistakes or otherwise. The taxpayer does have the right to reject any corrections of obvious errors made by HMRC.

Within 12 months of the due filing date (*not* the actual filing date), the taxpayer can give notice to an officer to amend his tax return and self-assessment. Such amendments by taxpayers are not confined to the correction of obvious errors. An amendment may be made whilst HMRC are making enquiries into the return, but will not take effect until the end of the enquiry.

The same rules apply to corrections and amendments of partnership statements and stand alone claims (see below).

The Short Tax Return form does not have the facility for the taxpayer to complete a self-assessment although if needed there is a two-page simple calculation to give people a rough idea of their tax liability. HMRC calculate the tax for such returns. Therefore HMRC encourage taxpayers to file the return by 30 September following the tax year. However, the latest date for filing is 31 January.

4.2 Claims

4.2.1 Introduction

All claims and elections which can be made in a tax return must be made in this manner if a return has been issued. A claim for any relief, allowance or repayment of tax must be quantified at the time it is made. These rules do not apply to claims involving two or more years.

Certain claims have a time limit that is longer than the time limit for filing or amending a tax return. A claim may therefore be made after the time limit for amending the tax return has expired. Claims not made on the tax return are referred to as **'stand alone' claims**.

Claims made on a tax return are subject to the administrative rules governing returns, for the making of corrections, enquiries etc.

4.2.2 Stand alone claims

Claims and elections not made in a tax return are governed by provisions which are similar to the rules governing the treatment of tax returns. The rules cover:

(a)   Keeping supporting records. Records must be kept until enquiries may no longer be made into the claim, or until any enquiries which are made have been completed

(b)   Amending the claim. HMRC's nine month time limit is unchanged, but the taxpayer has twelve months from the date the claim was made (see below)

(c)   Giving effect to the claim (ie repaying the tax)

(d)   Enquiring into the claim and making any necessary amendments (see below)

4.2.3 Claims involving more than one year

Self-assessment is intended to avoid the need to reopen earlier years, so relief should be given for the year of the claim. This rule can best be explained by considering a claim to carry back a trade loss to an earlier year of assessment:

(a) The claim for relief is treated as made in relation to the year in which the loss was actually incurred

(b) The amount of any tax repayment due is calculated in terms of tax of the earlier year to which the loss is being carried back, and

(c) Any tax repayment etc is treated as relating to the later year in which the loss was actually incurred. A repayment supplement may accrue from the later year.

These rules apply not only to trading losses, but also to the carry back of post cessation receipts.

4.2.4 Time limits

The time limit for making a claim is 5 years from 31 January following the tax year, unless a different limit is specifically set for the claim. Many reliefs have a shorter time limit specifically set – of one year from the 31 January following the end of the tax year. These time limits are mentioned, where relevant, throughout this Text.

Since a taxpayer needs to be able to calculate his tax liability under self-assessment a certain amount of formality in the claims procedure is needed. For example, capital losses are only allowable if notified to an officer of the Board and such notification is treated as a claim for relief for the year in which the loss accrues. Therefore, notification of such losses has to be made within 5 years from 31 January following the tax year in which they accrue.

A taxpayer may normally make a claim if the conditions for relief are fulfilled. A claim for enterprise investment scheme deferral relief, however, may not be made until the relevant certificates have been received from the EIS company. It may be necessary to submit the tax return before the certificate is available, and to claim the relief subsequently.

4.2.5 Error or mistake claims

An error or mistake claim may be made for errors in a return or partnership statement where tax would otherwise be overcharged. The claim may not be made where the tax liability was computed in accordance with practice prevailing at the time the return or statement was made.

An error or mistake claim may not be made in respect of a claim. If a taxpayer makes an error or mistake in a claim, he may make a supplementary claim within the time limits allowed for the original claim.

The taxpayer may appeal to the Special Commissioners against any refusal of an error or mistake claim.

5 Payment of income tax and capital gains tax

Two payments on account and a final balancing payment of income tax and Class 4 NICs are due. All capital gains tax is due on 31 January following the end of the tax year.

5.1 Payment dates

The self-assessment system may result in the taxpayer making three payments of income tax and Class 4 NICs.

Date	Payment
31 January in the tax year	1st payment on account
31 July after the tax year	2nd payment on account
31 January after the tax	Final payment to settle the remaining liability

HMRC issue payslips/demand notes in a credit card type 'Statement of Account' format, but there is no statutory obligation for it to do so and **the onus is on the taxpayer to pay the correct amount of tax on the due date.**

Key term

Payments on account are usually required where the income tax and Class 4 NICs due in the previous year exceeded the amount of income tax deducted at source; this excess is known as **'the relevant amount'**. Income tax deducted at source includes tax suffered, PAYE deductions and tax credits on dividends.

The payments on account are each equal to 50% of the relevant amount for the previous year.

Question

Payments on account

Sue is a self employed writer who paid tax for 2006/07 as follows:

		£
Total amount of income tax charged		9,200
This included:	Tax deducted on savings income	3,200
She also paid:	Class 4 NIC	1,900
	Class 2 NIC	109
	Capital gains tax	4,800

How much are the payments on account for 2007/08?

Answer

	£
Income tax:	
Total income tax charged for 2006/07	9,200
Less: tax deducted for 2006/07	(3,200)
	6,000
Class 4 NIC	1,900
'Relevant amount'	7,900
Payments on account for 2007/08:	
31 January 2008 £7,900 × ½	3,950
31 July 2008 As before	3,950

There is no requirement to make payments on account of capital gains tax nor Class 2 NIC.

Payments on account are not required if the relevant amount falls below a de minimis limit of £500. Also, payments on account are not required from taxpayers who paid 80% or more of their tax liability for the previous year through PAYE or other deduction at source arrangements.

If the previous year's liability increases following an amendment to a self-assessment, or the raising of a discovery assessment, an adjustment is made to the payments on account due.

Payments on account are normally fixed by reference to the previous year's tax liability but if a taxpayer expects his liability to be lower than this **he may claim to reduce his payments on account to:**

(a)   **A stated amount**, or

(b)   **Nil**.

The claim must state the reason why he believes his tax liability will be lower, or nil.

If the taxpayer's eventual liability is higher than he estimated he will have reduced the payments on account too far. Although the payments on account will not be adjusted, the taxpayer will suffer an interest charge on late payment.

A penalty of the difference between the reduced payment on account and the correct payment on account may be levied if the reduction was claimed fraudulently or negligently.

The balance of any income tax and Class 4 NICs together with all CGT due for a year, is normally payable on or before the 31 January following the year.

Exam focus point

CGT is never included in payments on account.

Question

Payments of tax

Giles made payments on account for 2006/07 of £6,500 each on 31 January 2007 and 31 July 2007, based on his 2005/06 liability. He then calculates his total income tax and Class 4 NIC liability for 2006/07 at £18,000 of which £2,750 was deducted at source. In addition he calculated that his CGT liability for disposals in 2006/07 is £5,120.

What is the final payment due for 2006/07?

Answer

Income tax and Class 4 NIC: £18,000 – £2,750 – £6,500 – £6,500 = £2,250. CGT = £5,120.

Final payment due on 31 January 2008 for 2006/2007 £2,250 + £5,120 = £7,370

In one case the due date for the final payment is later than 31 January following the end of the year. **If a taxpayer has notified chargeability by 5 October but the notice to file a tax return is not issued before 31 October, then the due date for the payment is three months after the issue of the notice.**

Tax charged in an amended self-assessment is usually payable on the later of:

(a)   The normal due date, generally 31 January following the end of the tax year, and

(b)   The day following 30 days after the making of the revised self-assessment.

Tax charged on a discovery assessment (see below) is due thirty days after the issue of the assessment.

5.2 Surcharges

Self assessment is enforced through a system of automatic surcharges, penalties and interest.

Key term

Surcharges are normally imposed in respect of amounts paid late:

	Paid	Surcharge
(a)	Within 28 days of due date:	none
(b)	More than 28 days but not more than six months after the due date:	5%
(c)	More than six months after the due date:	10%

Surcharges apply to:

    (a)   Balancing payments of income tax and Class 4 NICs and any CGT under self-assessment or a determination

    (b)   Tax due on the amendment of a self-assessment

    (c)   Tax due on a discovery assessment

The surcharge rules do not apply to late payments on account.

No surcharge will be applied where the late paid tax liability has attracted a tax-geared penalty on the failure to notify chargeability to tax, or the failure to submit a return, or on the making of an incorrect return (including a partnership return).

5.3 Interest

Interest is chargeable on late payment of both payments on account and balancing payments. In both cases interest runs from the due date until the day before the actual date of payment.

Interest is charged from 31 January following the tax year (or the normal due date for the balancing payment, in the rare event that this is later), even if this is before the due date for payment on:

    (a)   Tax payable following an amendment to a self-assessment
    (b)   Tax payable in a discovery assessment, and
    (c)   Tax postponed under an appeal which becomes payable.

Since a determination (see below) is treated as if it were a self-assessment, interest runs from 31 January following the tax year.

If a taxpayer claims to reduce his payments on account and there is still a final payment to be made, interest is normally charged on the payments on account as if each of those payments had been the lower of:

    (a)   the reduced amount, plus 50% of the final income tax liability; and
    (b)   the amount which would have been payable had no claim for reduction been made.

Question   Interest

Herbert's payments on account for 2006/07 based on his income tax liability for 2005/06 were £4,500 each. However when he submitted his 2005/06 income tax return in January 2006 he made a claim to reduce the payments on account for 2006/07 to £3,500 each. The first payment on account was made on 29 January 2007, and the second on 12 August 2007.

Herbert filed his 2006/07 tax return in December 2007. The return showed that his tax liabilities for 2006/07 (before deducting payments on account) were income tax and Class 4 NIC: £10,000, capital gains tax: £2,500. Herbert paid the balance of tax due of £5,500 on 19 February 2008.

For what periods and in respect of what amounts will Herbert be charged interest?

Answer

Herbert made an excessive claim to reduce his payments on account, and will therefore be charged interest on the reduction. The payments on account should have been £4,500 each based on the 2005/06 liability (not £5,000 each based on the 2006/07 liability). Interest will be charged as follows:

(a) First payment on account

     (i)   On £3,500 – nil – paid on time

     (ii)   On £1,000 from due date of 31 January 2007 to day before payment, 18 February 2008

(b) Second payment on account

     (i)   On £3,500 from due date of 31 July 2007 to day before payment, 11 August 2007

     (ii)   On £1,000 from due date of 31 July 2007 to day before payment, 18 February 2008

(c) Balancing payment

     On £3,500 from due date of 31 January 2008 to day before payment, 18 February 2008

Where interest has been charged on late payments on account but the final balancing settlement for the year produces a repayment, all or part of the original interest is repaid.

If a taxpayer provided HMRC in good time with the information needed to calculate the payment on account due on 31 January but did not receive a Statement of Account in time to make the correct payment by 31 January, it is HMRC practice to treat the due date for interest purposes as 30 days after the issue of the Statement.

5.4 Repayment of tax and repayment supplement

Tax is repaid when claimed unless a greater payment of tax is due in the following 30 days, in which case it is set-off against that payment.

Interest is paid on overpayments of:

     (a)   Payments on account

     (b)   Final payments of income tax and Class 4 NICs and CGT, including tax deducted at source or tax credits on dividends, and

     (c)   Penalties and surcharges.

Repayment supplement runs from the original date of payment (even if this was prior to the due date), until the day before the date the repayment is made. Income tax deducted at source and tax credits are treated as if they were paid on the 31 January following the tax year concerned.

Tax repaid is identified with tax payments in the following order:

     (a)   Final balancing payment

     (b)   Equally to the payments on account

     (c)   Income tax deducted at source/tax credits

     (d)   If it is attributable to tax paid in instalments (see below), to a later instalment before an earlier one.

5.5 Payment of CGT by instalments

5.5.1 Transfers not eligible for gift relief

CGT can be paid by instalments on transfer of certain assets where gift relief is not available.

Any **CGT payable** on transfers of certain assets **where no gift relief is available** (and any CGT payable because part of a gain cannot be deferred) **can be paid by annual instalments over ten years**. These assets are:

(a) Land

(b) A controlling holding of shares or securities in a company

(c) Minority holdings of shares or securities in a company which is not listed on a stock exchange (but it may be on the AIM)

Note that gift relief must be **unavailable**, not merely not elected for, for example where there is a gift of shares and the company owns chargeable non business assets.

Interest is chargeable on the outstanding balance from the normal due date.

The first instalment is due on the normal due date. If, for example, land is given away on 30 June 2006 and the instalment option is claimed, the first instalment will be due for payment on 31 January 2008.

If the transfer is to a connected person and the asset is subsequently sold within the ten year instalment period, any outstanding tax and accrued interest will become payable immediately.

If the taxpayer wishes, the balance with interest to date may be paid at any time.

5.5.2 Sales where consideration received in instalments

Where the consideration for a disposal of an asset is receivable in instalments over a period exceeding 18 months, the taxpayer has the option to pay the CGT arising in instalments. HMRC then allow payment of CGT to be spread over the shorter of:

(a) The instalment period, and
(b) Eight years.

6 Enquiries, determinations and discovery assessments

Strict procedural rules govern HMRC enquiries into tax returns.

6.1 Enquiries into returns

An officer of the Revenue and Customs has a limited period within which to commence enquiries into a return or amendment. The officer must give written notice of his intention by:

(a) The **first anniversary of the due filing date (not the actual filing date)**, or

(b) **If the return is filed after the due filing date, the quarter day following the first anniversary of the actual filing date. The quarter days are 31 January, 30 April, 31 July and 31 October.**

If the taxpayer amended the return after the due filing date, the enquiry 'window' extends to the quarter day following the first anniversary of the date the amendment was filed. Where the enquiry was not raised within the limit which would have applied had no amendment been filed, the enquiry is restricted to matters contained in the amendment.

Enquiries may be made into partnership returns (or amendments) upon which a partnership statement is based within the same time limits. A notice to enquire into a partnership return is deemed to incorporate a notice, to enquire into each individual partner's return.

Enquiries may also be made into stand alone claims, provided notice is given by the Officer of Revenue and Customs by the later of:

(a)   The quarter day following the first anniversary of the making or amending of the claim

(b)   31 January next but one following the tax year, if the claim relates to a tax year, or

(c)   The first anniversary of the end of the period to which a claim relates if it relates to a period other than a tax year.

The procedures for enquiries into claims mirror those for enquiries into returns.

The officer does not have to have, or give, any reason for raising an enquiry. In particular the taxpayer will not be advised whether he has been selected at random for an audit. Enquiries may be full enquiries, or may be limited to 'aspect' enquiries.

In the course of his enquiries **the officer may require the taxpayer to produce documents, accounts or any other information required. The taxpayer can appeal to the Commissioners.**

During the course of his enquiries an officer may amend a self-assessment if it appears that insufficient tax has been charged and an immediate amendment is necessary to prevent a loss to the Crown. This might apply if, for example, there is a possibility that the taxpayer will emigrate.

If a return is under enquiry HMRC may postpone any repayment due as shown in the return until the enquiry is complete. HMRC have discretion to make a provisional repayment but there is no facility to appeal if the repayment is withheld.

At any time during the course of an enquiry, the taxpayer may apply to the Commissioners to require the officer to notify the taxpayer within a specified period that the enquiries are complete, unless the officer can demonstrate that he has reasonable grounds for continuing the enquiry.

If both sides agree, disputes concerning a point of law can be resolved through litigation without having to wait until the whole enquiry is complete.

An officer must issue a notice that the enquiries are complete, state his conclusions and make any necessary amendments to the tax return, or the amounts which should be contained in the partnership statement, or the amount of the claim.

If the taxpayer is not satisfied with the officer's amendment he may, within 30 days, appeal to the Commissioners.

Once an enquiry is complete the officer cannot make further enquiries. HMRC may, in limited circumstances, raise a discovery assessment if they believe that there has been a loss of tax (see below).

6.2 Determinations

HMRC may only raise enquiries if a return has been submitted.

If notice has been served on a taxpayer to submit a return but the return is not submitted by the due filing date, an officer of Revenue and Customs may make a determination of the amounts liable to income tax and CGT and of the tax due. Such a determination must be made to the best of the officer's information and belief, and is then treated as if it were a self-assessment. This enables the officer to seek payment of tax, including payments on account for the following year and to charge interest.

The determination must be made within the period ending 5 years after 31 January following the tax year. It may be superseded by a self-assessment made within the same period or, if later, within 12 months of the date of the determination.

6.3 Discovery assessments

If an officer of Revenue and Customs discovers that profits have been omitted from assessment, that any assessment has become insufficient, or that any relief given is, or has become excessive, an assessment may be raised to recover the tax lost.

If the tax lost results from an error in the taxpayer's return but the return was made in accordance with prevailing practice at the time, no discovery assessment may be made.

A discovery assessment may only be raised where a return has been made if:

(a) There has been fraudulent or negligent conduct by the taxpayer or his agent, or

(b) At the time that enquiries into the return were completed, or could no longer be made, the officer did not have information to make him aware of the loss of tax.

Information is treated as available to an officer if:

(a) It is contained in the taxpayer's return for the period (or for either of the two preceding periods) or in any accompanying documents.

(b) It is contained in a claim made in respect of that period or in any accompanying documents;

(c) It is contained in any documents, produced in connection with an enquiry into a return (or claim) for the period or either of the two preceding periods;

(d) It is information, the existence and relevance of which, could reasonably be expected to be inferred by an officer from the information described above, or which was notified in writing by or on behalf of the taxpayer to an officer. The information supplied must be sufficiently detailed to draw HMRC's attention to contentious matters, such as the use of a valuation or estimate.

These rules do not prevent HMRC from raising assessments in cases of genuine discoveries, but prevent assessments from being raised due to HMRC's failure to make timely use of information or to a change of opinion on information made available.

6.4 Appeals and postponement of payment of tax

A taxpayer may appeal against an amendment to a self-assessment or partnership statement, or an amendment to or disallowance of a claim, following an enquiry, or against an assessment which is not a self-assessment, such as a discovery assessment.

The appeal must normally be made within 30 days of the amendment or self-assessment.

The notice of appeal must state the *grounds* of appeal. These may be stated in general terms. At the hearing the Commissioners may allow the appellant to put forward grounds not stated in his notice if they are satisfied that his omission was not wilful or unreasonable.

In some cases it may be possible to agree the point at issue by negotiation with HMRC, in which case the appeal may be settled by agreement. If the appeal cannot be agreed, it will be heard by the General or Special Commissioners.

An appeal does not relieve the taxpayer of liability to pay tax on the normal due date unless he obtains a 'determination' from the Commissioners or agreement of the Inspector that payment of all or some of the tax may be postponed pending determination of the appeal. The amount not postponed is due 30 days after the determination or agreement is issued, if that is later than the normal due date.

If any part of the postponed tax becomes due a notice of the amount payable is issued and the amount is payable 30 days after the issue of the notice. Interest, however, is still payable from the normal due date.

6.5 Income tax fraud

There is a statutory offence of evading income tax. The penalty may be up to seven years in prison or an unlimited fine, or both.

Chapter roundup

- Direct taxes are administered by Her Majesty's Revenue and Customs.

- Individuals who do not receive a tax return or who have a new source of income or gains must notify their chargeability to income tax or CGT.

- Tax returns must be filed within certain time limits. There are penalties for late submission.

- Taxpayers normally self assess their income tax, Class 4 NIC and CGT liabilities but HMRC will calculate the tax on their behalf if they file their tax return by 30 September following the end of the tax year.

- Two payments on account and a final balancing payment of income tax and Class 4 NICs are due. All capital gains tax is due on 31 January following the end of the tax year.

- Self assessment is enforced through a system of automatic surcharges, penalties and interest.

- CGT can be paid by instalments on transfer of certain assets where gift relief is not available.

- Strict procedural rules govern HMRC enquiries into tax returns.

Quick quiz

1   By when must a taxpayer who has a new source of income give notice of his chargeability to capital gains tax due in 2006/07?

2   By when must a taxpayer, who intends to calculate his own tax, file a tax return for 2006/07?

3   What are the normal payment dates for income tax?

4   What surcharges are due in respect of income tax payments on account that are paid two months late?

5   When may CGT be paid by ten annual instalments?

Answers to quick quiz

1   Within six months of the end of the year, ie by 5 October 2007.

2   By 31 January 2008 or, if later, 3 months after a notice to file the return was issued.

3   Two payments on account of income tax are due on 31 January in the tax year and on the 31 July following. A final balancing payment is due on 31 January following the tax year.

4   None. Surcharges do not apply to late payment of payment on account.

5   Provided a transfer is not eligible for gift relief, the ten annual instalment option is available on transfers of:

- land, or
- controlling holdings of share or securities in a company, or
- minority holdings of shares or securities in an unlisted company

Now try the question below from the Exam Question Bank

Number	Level	Marks	Time
Q17	Introductory	17	31 mins

17

An introduction to inheritance tax

Topic list	Syllabus reference
1 Basic principles	A4(a)(i)
2 Computing transfers of value	A4(b)(i)-(iv)
3 Exemptions	A4(d)(iii)
4 Excluded property	A4(b)(iv)
5 Calculation of tax on lifetime transfers	A4(c)(i), (ii), (iv)
6 Relief for the fall in value of lifetime gifts	A4(c)(iv), (f)(i)

Introduction

In this chapter we introduce a new tax, inheritance tax (IHT). IHT is primarily a tax on wealth left on death. It also applies to gifts within seven years of death and to certain lifetime transfers of wealth.

The tax is different from income tax and CGT, where the basic question is: how much has the taxpayer made? With IHT, the basic question is, how much has he given away? We tax the amount which the taxpayer has transferred - the amount by which he is worse off. If the taxpayer pays IHT on a lifetime gift, he is worse off by the amount of the gift plus the tax due, and we have to take that into account. Some transfers are, however, exempt from IHT.

We will see that the first £285,000 of transfers is taxed at 0% (the 'nil rate band'), and is therefore effectively tax-free. To stop people from avoiding IHT by, for example, giving away £1,425,000 in five lots of £285,000, we need to look back seven years every time a transfer is made to decide how much of the nil rate band is available to set against the current transfer.

In the next chapter we will look at transfers on death.

Study guide

		Intellectual level
4	**Inheritance tax**	
(a)	The scope of inheritance tax:	2
(i)	Identify and explain the persons chargeable	
(b)	The basic principles for computing transfers of value:	3
(i)	State, explain and apply the meaning of transfers of value, chargeable transfers and potentially exempt transfers	
(ii)	Demonstrate the fall in value principle	
(iii)	Demonstrate the seven year accumulation principle	
(iv)	Identify excluded property	2
(c)	The liabilities arising on chargeable lifetime transfers and death transfers by individuals:	3
(i)	Advise on the tax implications of chargeable lifetime transfers	
(ii)	Advise on the tax implications of transfers within seven years of death	
(iv)	Advise on the relief for the fall in value of lifetime gifts	
(d)	Computing transfers of value:	3
(iii)	Identify exempt transfers	2
(f)	The use of exemptions and reliefs in deferring and minimising inheritance tax liabilities:	3
(i)	Advise on the use of reliefs and exemptions to minimise inheritance tax liabilities, as mentioned in the sections above	

Exam guide

As you have not studied Inheritance tax (IHT) before, it is likely to examined in most, if not all, sittings at P6. The concepts of potentially exempt transfers (PETs), chargeable lifetime transfers (CLTs) and the seven year cumulation principle are all fundamental to an understanding of IHT and you must learn how to calculate lifetime tax and any additional tax arising on death. Making full use of any available exemptions is a straightforward but very important part of any IHT planning exercise.

1 Basic principles

IHT is a tax on gifts or '**transfers of value**' made by **chargeable persons**. This generally involves a transaction as a result of which wealth is transferred by one person to another, either directly or via a trust.

1.1 Chargeable persons

Chargeable persons for IHT purposes are:

    (a)   **Individuals**, and
    (b)   **Trustees of settled property.**

Companies are not chargeable persons although if companies are used to transfer wealth an IHT liability can be charged on the shareholders (the details are outside the scope of your syllabus).

Spouses and civil partners are taxed separately although there is an exemption for transfers between the couple. There are also special valuation rules which are dealt with later.

1.2 The scope of the charge

All transfers of assets (worldwide) made by persons domiciled in the UK (see later in this Text) **whether during lifetime or on death are within the charge to IHT.**

For individuals not domiciled in the UK, only transfers of UK assets are within the charge to IHT.

2 Computing transfers of value

2.1 Introduction

There are two main chargeable occasions for individuals:

    (a)   gifts made in the lifetime of the donor (**lifetime transfers**), and

    (b)   gifts made on death, for example when property is left in a will (**death estate**).

We will look in detail at lifetime transfers later in this chapter and at the death estate in the next chapter.

First, however, we start our study of IHT by looking at some general principles which apply to both chargeable occasions.

2.2 Transfers of value and chargeable transfers

FAST FORWARD

IHT applies to transfers to trusts, transfers on death and to transfers within the seven years before death.

IHT cannot arise unless there is a transfer of value. This is any gratuitous disposition (eg gift) made by a person which results in his being worse off, that is, he suffers a diminution (ie reduction) in the value of his estate.

The measure of a gift is always the loss to the transferor (the diminution in value of his estate), not the amount gained by the transferee.

2.3 Chargeable transfers

Inheritance tax arises on any **chargeable transfer. This is any transfer of value not covered by an exemption.**

Transfers made during the individual's lifetime are called **chargeable lifetime transfers (CLTs).**

On death, an individual is treated as if he had made a transfer of value of the property comprised in his estate. This, then, will be a chargeable transfer to the extent that it is not exempt.

2.4 Potentially exempt transfers

Key term

A **PET** is a **lifetime transfer made by an individual to another individual**. Any other lifetime transfer by an individual (eg gift to a trust) not covered by an exemption is a CLT.

Prior to 22 March 2006 certain other gifts by an individual were also treated as PETs. These are not examinable in Paper P6.

A PET is exempt from IHT when made, and will remain so if the transferor survives for at least seven years from making the gift. If the transferor dies within seven years of making the gift, it will become chargeable to IHT.

2.5 Diminution in value

In many cases the diminution in value of the transferor's estate will be the same as the increase in the value of the transferee's estate. However, sometimes the two will not be the same.

2.6 Example: diminution in value

A holds 5,100 of the shares in an unquoted company which has an issued share capital of 10,000 shares. Currently A's majority holding is valued at £15 per share.

A wishes to give 200 shares to his son, B. However, to B the shares are worth only £2.50 each, since B will have only a small minority holding in the company. After the gift A will hold 4,900 shares and these will be worth £10 each. The value per share to A will fall from £15 to £10 per share since he will lose control of the company.

The diminution in value of A's estate is £27,500, as follows.

	£
Before the gift: 5,100 shares × £15	76,500
After the gift: 4,900 shares × £10	(49,000)
Diminution in value	27,500

B has only been given shares with a market value of 200 × £2.50 = £500. Remember, a gift is also a deemed disposal at market value for CGT purposes, and it is this value that will be used in any CGT computation. IHT, however, uses the principle of diminution in value which can, as in this case, give a much greater value than the value of the asset transferred.

2.7 Exceptions to the IHT charge

The following are not chargeable to IHT:

(a) **Transfers where there is no gratuitous intent**: for example selling a painting for £1,000 which later turns out to be worth £100,000. The transaction must have been made at arm's length between unconnected persons

(b) **Transfers made in the course of a trade**: for example Christmas gifts to employees

(c) **Expenditure on family maintenance**: for example school fees paid for a child

(d) Waivers of remuneration

(e) Waivers of dividends provided the waiver is made within the 12 months before the dividend is declared

(f) Any transfer covered by a specific exemption (see further below)

(g) **Transfers of excluded property** (see below)

3 Exemptions

Exemptions may apply to make transfers or parts of transfers non chargeable. Some exemptions only apply on lifetime transfers (annual, normal expenditure out of income, marriage/civil partnership), whilst some apply on both life and death transfers (eg spouses, charities, political parties).

3.1 Introduction

There are various exemptions available to eliminate or reduce the chargeable amount of a lifetime transfer or property passing on an individual's death. Some exemptions apply to both lifetime transfers and property passing on death, whilst others apply only to lifetime transfers.

The lifetime exemptions apply to PETs as well as to CLTs. Only the balance of such gifts after the lifetime exemptions have been taken into account is then potentially exempt.

Exam focus point

Where CLTs and PETS made in the same year the CLTs should be made first to use any available exemptions. If used up against the PETs an exemption will be wasted if the PET never becomes chargeable.

3.2 Exemptions applying to lifetime transfers (including PETs) only

3.2.1 The small gifts exemptions

Outright gifts to individuals totalling £250 or less per donee in any one tax year are exempt. If gifts total more than £250 the whole amount is chargeable. A donor can give up to £250 each year to each of as many donees as he wishes. The small gifts exemption cannot apply to gifts into trusts.

3.2.2 The annual exemption (AE)

The first £3,000 of value transferred in a tax year is exempt from IHT. The annual exemption is used only after all other exemptions (such as for transfers to spouses/civil partners or charities (see below)). If several gifts are made in a year, the £3,000 exemption is applied to earlier gifts before later gifts. The annual exemption is used up by PETs as well as CLTs, even though the PETs might never become chargeable.

Any unused portion of the annual exemption is carried forward for one year only. Only use it the following year *after* that year's own annual exemption has been used.

Question   Annual exemptions

F has no unused annual exemption brought forward at 6 April 2005.

On 1 August 2005 he makes a transfer of £600 to P.
On 1 September 2005 he makes a transfer of £2,000 to Q.
On 1 July 2006 he makes a transfer of £3,300 to a trust for his grandchildren.
On 1 June 2007 he makes a transfer of £5,000 to R.

Show the application of the annual exemptions.

Answer

2005/06		£
1.8.05 Gift to P		600
Less AE 2005/06		(600)
		0

		£
1.9.05 Gift to Q		2,000
Less AE 2005/06		(2,000)
		0

The unused annual exemption carried forward is £3,000 – £600 – £2,000 = £400.

2006/07	£	£
1.7.06 Gift to trust		3,300
Less: AE 2006/07	3,000	
AE 2005/06 b/f	300	
		(3,300)
		0

The unused annual exemption carried forward is zero because the 2006/07 exemption must be used before the 2005/06 exemption brought forward. The balance of £100 of the 2005/06 exemption is lost, because it cannot be carried forward for more than one year.

2007/08		£
1.6.07 Gift to R		5,000
Less AE 2007/08		(3,000)
		2,000

3.2.3 Normal expenditure out of income

Inheritance tax is a tax on transfers of capital, not income. A transfer of value is exempt if:

(a)   It is made as part of the normal expenditure of the transferor

(b)   Taking one year with another, it was made out of income, and

(c)   It leaves the transferor with sufficient income to maintain his usual standard of living.

As well as covering such things as regular presents **this exemption can cover regular payments out of income such as a grandchild's school fees or the payment of life assurance premiums on a policy for someone else.** In general there should be evidence of a prior commitment or a settled pattern of expenditure: *Bennett v IRC 1995.*

3.2.4 Gifts in consideration of marriage/civil partnership

Gifts in consideration of marriage/civil partnership are exempt up to:

(a)   **£5,000 if from a parent of a party to the marriage/civil partnership**

(b)   **£2,500 if from a remoter ancestor or from one of the parties to the marriage/civil partnership**

(c)   **£1,000 if from any other person.**

The limits apply to gifts from any one donor for any one marriage/civil partnership.

The exemption is available only if the marriage/civil partnership actually takes place.

3.3 Exemptions applying to both lifetime transfers and transfers on death

3.3.1 Gifts between spouses/civil partners

Any transfers of value between spouses/civil partners are exempt provided the transferee is domiciled (see later in this Text) in the UK at the time of transfer. The exemption covers lifetime gifts between them and property passing under a will or on intestacy.

If the transferor spouse/civil partner is domiciled in the UK but the transferee spouse/civil partner is not domiciled in the UK the exemption is limited to a cumulative total of £55,000, but any gift in excess of the £55,000 cumulative total will be a PET. If neither spouse/civil partner is domiciled in the UK there is no limit on the exemption.

Two simple planning points follow from this exemption:

(a)   A couple may avoid IHT, at least in the short term, if each makes a will leaving most of his property to the other

(b)   A couple should consider making lifetime transfers between themselves so as to achieve, as far as possible, estates of equal value. If they should die together the combined estate will then enjoy the full benefit of two nil rate bands.

Question	Exemptions

D made a gift of £141,000 to her son on 17 October 2002 on the son's marriage. D gave £100,000 to her spouse on 1 January 2006. D gave £70,000 to her daughter on 11 May 2006. The only other gifts D made were birthday and Christmas presents of £100 each to her grandchildren.

Show what exemptions are available assuming:

(a)   D's spouse is domiciled in the UK
(b)   D's spouse is not domiciled in the UK

Answer

(a)   *17 October 2002*

	£
Gift to D's son	141,000
Less: ME	(5,000)
AE 2002/03	(3,000)
AE 2001/02 b/f	(3,000)
	130,000

1 January 2006

	£
Gift to D's spouse	100,000
Less spouse exemption	(100,000)
	0

11 May 2006

	£
Gift to D's daughter	70,000
Less: AE 2006/07	(3,000)
AE 2005/06 b/f	(3,000)
	64,000

The gifts to the grandchildren are covered by the small gifts exemption.

(b)   *17 October 2002*

As in part (a)

1 January 2006

	£
Gift to D's spouse	100,000
Less spouse exemption (restricted)	(55,000)
Less: AE 2005/06	(3,000)
AE 2004/05 b/f	(3,000)
	39,000

Note that the annual exemption is available to set against the gift remaining after deducting the spouse exemption.

11 May 2006

	£
Gift to D's daughter	70,000
Less AE 2006/07	(3,000)
	67,000

3.3.2 Other exempt transfers

Transfers (whether outright or by settlement) **to UK charities are exempt** from inheritance tax.

Gifts to a qualifying political party are exempt. A political party qualifies if, at the general election preceding the transfer of value, either:

(a)   At least two members were elected to the House of Commons, or

(b)   One member was elected and the party polled at least 150,000 votes.

Gifts for national purposes are exempt. Eligible recipients include:

(a)   Museums

(b)   Art galleries

(c)   The National Trust

(d)   Universities

(e)   Local authorities

(f)   Government departments

Maintenance settlements can be made free of inheritance tax if they are for the upkeep of historic property.

Gifts of land to housing associations are exempt.

Where there is a transfer of shares to an employee trust (eg one set up by a company to operate a share option scheme) this is usually an exempt transfer.

4 Excluded property

If excluded property is given away, there are no IHT consequences.

4.1 Types of excluded property

The following are examples of excluded property.

(a) A reversionary interest in settled property. A reversionary interest is a future interest in trust property. An example is when an income beneficiary (with the present interest) dies and the capital passes to the remainderman. A reversionary interest will not, however, be treated as excluded property if:

    (i) it has been acquired at any time for consideration in money or money's worth, or

    (ii) either the settlor or his spouse is or has been beneficially entitled to the interest at any time

(b) Foreign assets owned by non-UK domiciled individuals (see later in this Text).

5 Calculation of tax on lifetime transfers

5.1 Basic principles

Transfers are cumulated for seven years so that the nil rate band is not available in full on each of a series of transfers in rapid succession.

There are two aspects of the calculation of tax on lifetime transfers:

(a) **lifetime tax on CLTs,** and

(b) **additional death tax on CLTs and on PETs where the transferor dies within seven years of making the transfer.**

Exam focus point

You should always calculate the lifetime tax on any CLTs first, then move on to calculate the death tax on all CLTs and PETs made within seven years of death.

5.2 Lifetime tax

IHT is charged on what a donor loses. If the donor pays the IHT on a lifetime gift he loses both the asset given away and the money with which he paid the tax due on it. Grossing up is required.

5.2.1 Transferee pays tax

When a CLT is made and the transferee (ie the trustees) pays the lifetime tax, follow these steps to work out the lifetime IHT on it:

Step 1 Look back seven years from the date of the transfer to see if any other CLTs have been made. If so, these transfers use up the nil rate band available for the current transfer. Work out the value of any nil rate band still available.

Step 2 Compute the gross value of the CLT. You may be given this in the question or you may have to work out the diminution of value, deduct reliefs (such as business property relief as described later in the Text) or exemptions (such as the annual exemption described earlier in this chapter).

Step 3 Any part of the CLT covered by the nil rate band is taxed at 0%. Any part of the CLT not covered by the nil rate band is charged at 20%.

> The nil band will be given in the rates and allowances section of the exam paper.

Question
Transferee pays the lifetime tax

Eric makes a chargeable lifetime transfer of £296,000 to a trust on 10 July 2006. The trustees agree to pay the tax due.

Calculate the lifetime tax payable by the trustees if Eric has made:

(a) a lifetime chargeable transfer of value of £100,000 in August 1998
(b) a lifetime chargeable transfer of value of £100,000 in August 1999
(c) a lifetime chargeable transfer of value of £300,000 in August 1999.

Answer

(a) **Step 1** No lifetime transfers in seven years before 10 July 2006. Nil rate band of £285,000 available.

Step 2

	£
Gift	296,000
Less: AE 2006/07	(3,000)
AE 2005/06 b/f	(3,000)
	290,000

Step 3

	IHT £
£285,000 × 0%	0
£5,000 × 20%	1,000
£290,000	1,000

(b) **Step 1** Lifetime transfer of value of £100,000 in seven years before 10 July 2006 (transfers after 10 July 1999). Nil rate band of £(285,000 − 100,000) = £185,000 available.

Step 2 Value of CLT is £290,000 (as before).

Step 3

	IHT £
£185,000 × 0%	0
£105,000 × 20%	21,000
£290,000	21,000

(c) **Step 1** Lifetime transfer of value of £300,000 in seven years before 10 July 2006 (transfers after 10 July 1999). No nil rate band available as all covered by previous transfer.

Step 2 Value of CLT is £290,000 (as before)

Step 3

	IHT £
£290,000 @ 20%	58,000

5.2.2 Transferor pays tax

Where IHT is payable on a CLT, the **primary liability to pay tax is on the transferor,** although the transferor may agree with the transferee (as in the above example) that the transferee is to pay the tax instead.

If the transferor pays the lifetime IHT due on a CLT, the total reduction in value of his estate is the transfer of value plus the IHT due on it. The transfer is therefore a net transfer and must be grossed up in order to find the gross value of the transfer. **We do this by working out the tax as follows.**

Formula to learn

$$\text{Chargeable amount (ie not covered by nil band)} \times \frac{20\,(\text{rate of tax})}{80\,(100 \text{ minus the rate of tax})}$$

When a CLT is made and the transferor pays the lifetime tax, follow these steps to work out the lifetime IHT on it:

Step 1 Look back seven years from the date of the transfer to see if any other CLTs have been made. If so, these transfers use up the nil rate band available for the current transfer. Work out the value of any nil rate band still available.

Step 2 Compute the net value of the CLT. You may be given this in the question or may have to work out the diminution of value, deduct reliefs (such as business property relief as described later in the Text) or exemptions (such as the annual exemption discussed earlier in this chapter).

Step 3 Any part of the CLT covered by the nil rate band is taxed at 0%. Any part of the CLT not covered by the nil rate band is taxed at 20/80.

Step 4 Work out the gross transfer by adding the net transfer and the tax together. You can check your figure by working out the tax on the gross transfer.

Question   Transferor pays the lifetime tax

James makes a chargeable lifetime transfer of £296,000 to a trust on 10 July 2006. James will pay the tax due.

Calculate the lifetime tax payable, if James has made:

(a)   a lifetime chargeable transfer of value of £100,000 in August 1998
(b)   a lifetime chargeable transfer of value of £100,000 in August 1999
(c)   a lifetime chargeable transfer of value of £300,000 in August 1999.

Answer

(a)   **Step 1**   No lifetime transfers in seven years before 10 July 2006. Nil rate band of £285,000 available.

Step 2

	£
Gift	296,000
Less: AE 2006/07	(3,000)
AE 2005/06 b/f	(3,000)
Net CLT	290,000

Step 3

	IHT
	£
£285,000 × 0%	0
£5,000 × 20/80	1,250
£290,000	1,250

Step 4 Gross transfer is £(290,000 + 1,250) = £291,250. *Check:* Tax on the gross transfer would be:

	IHT
	£
£285,000 × 0%	0
£6,250 × 20%	1,250
£291,250	1,250

(b) **Step 1** Lifetime transfer of value of £100,000 in seven years before 10 July 2006 (transfers after 10 July 1999). Nil rate band of £(285,000 – 100,000) = £185,000 available.

Step 2 Net value of CLT is £290,000 (as before).

Step 3

	IHT
	£
£185,000 × 0%	0
£105,000 × 20/80	26,250
£290,000	26,250

Step 4 Gross transfer is £(290,000 + 26,250) = £316,250. *Check:* Tax on the gross transfer would be:

	IHT
	£
£185,000 × 0%	0
£131,250 × 20%	26,250
£316,250	26,250

(c) **Step 1** Lifetime transfer of value of £300,000 in seven years before 10 July 2006 (transfers after 10 July 1999). No nil rate band available as all covered by previous transfer.

Step 2 Net value of CLT is £290,000 (as before).

Step 3

	IHT
	£
£290,000 × 20/80	72,500

Step 4 Gross transfer is £(290,000 + 72,500) = £362,500. Tax on the gross transfer would be:

	IHT
	£
£362,500 × 20%	72,500

5.3 Death tax

The longer the transferor survives after making a gift, the lower the death tax. This is because taper relief applies to lower the amount of death tax payable as follows:

Years between transfer and death	% reduction in death tax
3 years or less	0
More than 3 but less than 4	20
More than 4 but less than 5	40
More than 5 but less than 6	60
More than 6 but less than 7	80

Death tax on a lifetime transfer is **always** payable by the transferee, so grossing up is not relevant.

Follow these steps to work out the death tax on a CLT:

Step 1   Look back seven years from the **date of the transfer** to see if any other chargeable transfers were made. If so, these transfers use up the nil rate band available for the current transfer. Work out the value of any nil rate band remaining.

Step 2   Compute the value of the CLT. This is the gross value of the transfer that you worked out for computing lifetime tax.

Step 3   Any part of the CLT covered by the nil rate band is taxed at 0%. Any part of the CLT not covered by the nil rate band is charged at 40%.

Step 4   Reduce the death tax by taper relief (if applicable).

Step 5   Deduct any lifetime tax paid. The death tax may be reduced to nil, but there is no repayment of lifetime tax.

Exam focus point

> The death rate of 40% will be given in the rates and allowances section of the exam paper.
>
> Watch IHT taper relief which is deducted from the IHT due; do not confuse it with CGT taper, which instead reduces a chargeble gain.

Question — Lifetime tax and death tax on CLTs

Trevor makes a gross chargeable transfer of value of £181,000 in December 1999. He then makes a gift to a trust of £198,000 on 15 November 2006 and the trustees pay the lifetime tax due.

Trevor dies in February 2010.

Compute:

(a)   the lifetime tax payable by the trustees on the lifetime transfer in November 2006, and

(b)   the death tax payable on the lifetime transfer in November 2006 assuming the nil rate band in February 2010 remains £285,000.

Answer

Lifetime tax

Step 1   Lifetime transfer of value of £181,000 in seven years before 15 November 2006 (transfers after 15 November 1999). Nil rate band of £(285,000 − 181,000) = £104,000 available.

Step 2

		£
Gift		198,000
Less	AE 2006/07	(3,000)
	AE 2005/06 b/f	(3,000)
		192,000

Step 3

	IHT £
£104,000 × 0%	0
£ 88,000 × 20%	17,600
£192,000	17,600

Death tax

Step 1   Lifetime transfer of value of £181,000 **in seven years before 15 November 2006** (transfers after 15 November 1999). Nil rate band of £(285,000 − 181,000) = £104,000 available.

Step 2   Value of CLT is £192,000 as before

Step 3

		IHT
		£
£ 104,000 × 0%		0
£ 88,000 × 40%		35,200
£192,000		35,200

Step 4   Death more than 3 years but less than 4 years after transfer

	£
Death tax	35,200
Less: taper relief @ 20%	(7,040)
Death tax left in charge (80%)	28,160

Step 5   Tax due £(28,160 – 17,600)   10,560

5.4 Death tax on potentially exempt transfers

If the transferor dies within seven years of making a PET it will become chargeable to death tax in the same way as a CLT. There will be no lifetime tax paid, so Step 5 above will not apply.

Remember that the exemptions which apply to lifetime transfers only, such as the annual exemption and the marriage/civil partner exemption, are available to set against PETs. **You must apply them in chronological order**, so that if a PET is made before a CLT in the same tax year, the exemption is set against the PET. This may waste the exemption (unless the donor dies within seven years), and is disadvantageous in cash flow terms since lifetime tax is paid on CLTs but not on PETs.

We will now work through an example where there is both a PET and a CLT.

Exam focus point

Calculate lifetime tax on CLTs first. Then move on to death tax, working through all CLTs and PETs in chronological order. Remember: on death PETs become chargeable so must be taken into account when calculating the death tax on later CLTs.

 Question   Lifetime tax and death tax on CLTs and PETs

Louise gave £299,000 to her son on 1 February 2003. This was the first transfer she had made for IHT.

On 10 October 2006, Louise gave £344,000 to a trust. The trustees paid the lifetime IHT due. On 11 January 2007, Louise died.

Compute:

(a)   the lifetime tax payable by the trustees on the lifetime transfer made in 2006,
(b)   the death tax payable on the lifetime transfer made in 2003, and
(c)   the death tax payable on the lifetime transfer made in 2006.

Answer

(a) *Lifetime tax – 2006 CLT*

Step 1 There are no chargeable lifetime transfers in the seven years before 10 October 2006 because the 2003 transfer is a PET and therefore exempt during Louise's lifetime. Nil rate band of £285,000 available.

Step 2

		£
Gift		344,000
Less	AE 2006/07	(3,000)
	AE 2005/06 b/f	(3,000)
CLT		338,000

Step 3

	IHT £
£285,000 × 0%	0
£ 53,000 × 20%	10,600
£338,000	10,600

(b) *Death tax – 2003 PET becomes chargeable*

Step 1 No lifetime transfers of value in seven years before 1 February 2003 (transfers after 1 February 1996). Nil rate band of £285,000 available.

Step 2

		£
Gift		299,000
Less	AE 2002/03	(3,000)
	AE 2001/02 b/f	(3,000)
CLT		293,000

Step 3

	IHT £
£285,000 × 0%	0
£ 8,000 × 40%	3,200
£293,000	3,200

Step 4 Death more than 3 years but less than 4 years after transfer

	£
Death tax	3,200
Taper relief @ 20%	(640)
Death tax due (ie 80%)	2,560

(c) *Death tax – 2006 CLT additional tax*

Step 1 Lifetime transfer of value of £293,000 in seven years before 10 October 2006 (transfers after 10 October 1999). Note that as the PET becomes chargeable on death, its value is now included in calculating the death tax on the CLT. No nil rate band available.

Step 2 Value of CLT is £338,000 as before

Step 3

	IHT £
£338,000 @ 40%	135,200

Step 4 Death within 3 years of transfer so no taper relief.

Step 5 Tax due £(135,200 – 10,600) 124,600

6 Relief for the fall in value of lifetime gifts

> If an asset falls in value between a lifetime gift and death, fall in value relief reduces the death tax payable. The relief affects the tax on the transfer concerned. It does not reduce the value of the gross chargeable transfer for the purpose of computing later IHT.

Where a PET or CLT becomes chargeable to IHT on death and the value of the gift has fallen between the date of the gift and the death of the transferor (or the sale of the property if this precedes death) **fall in value relief may be claimed. Relief is available only if the transferee** (or his spouse/civil partner) **still holds the property at the date of death, or it has been sold in an arm's length transaction** to an unconnected person.

Only the tax on the transfer is reduced by the relief. It does not affect the value of the gross chargeable transfer when considering how much of the nil band is used by the gift.

Question

The fall in value of lifetime gifts

H transferred a house worth £307,000 to his son on 1 June 2003. H then gave £205,000 cash to his daughter on 20 August 2005. Shortly before H's death his son sold the house on the open market for £242,000. H died on 14 July 2006. Calculate the IHT liabilities arising.

Answer

1 June 2003

There is no IHT liability when the gift is made because it is a PET.

	£
Gift	307,000
Less AE 2003/04	(3,000)
Less AE 2002/03 b/f	(3,000)
PET	301,000

The PET becomes chargeable as a result of death within seven years. The value of the chargeable transfer is reduced by the fall in value of the house:

Death tax	*Chargeable Transfer*
	£
PET	301,000
Less relief for fall in value (307,000 – 242,000)	(65,000)
	236,000

This is within the nil band so the IHT payable by the son is £Nil.

20 August 2005

There is no IHT liability when the gift is made because it is a PET.

	£
Gift	205,000
Less AE 2005/06	(3,000)
Less AE 2004/05 b/f	(3,000)
PET	199,000

Gross chargeable transfers in the seven years prior to the gift total £301,000 (not *£236,000*), so none of the nil band remains available to use when calculating IHT on the PET to the daughter. The IHT payable by her is, therefore, £199,000 × 40% = £79,600. No taper relief applies as gift was within three years of death.

Chapter roundup

- IHT applies to transfers to trusts, transfers on death and to transfers within the seven years before death.

- Exemptions may apply to make transfers or parts of transfers non chargeable. Some exemptions only apply on lifetime transfers (annual, normal expenditure out of income, marriage/civil partnership), whilst some apply on both life and death transfers (eg spouses, charities, political parties).

- If excluded property is given away, there are no IHT consequences.

- Transfers are cumulated for seven years so that the nil rate band is not available in full on each of a series of transfers in rapid succession.

- IHT is charged on what a donor loses. If the donor pays the IHT on a lifetime gift he loses both the asset given away and the money with which he paid the tax due on it. Grossing up is required

- If an asset falls in value between a lifetime gift and death, fall in value relief reduces the death tax payable. The relief affects the tax on the transfer concerned. It does not reduce the value of the gross chargeable transfer for the purpose of computing later IHT.

Quick quiz

1 What is a transfer of value?

2 Who is chargeable to inheritance tax?

3 What is the effect of property being excluded property?

4 What types of transfer during 2006/07 by an individual are potentially exempt transfers?

5 To what extent may unused annual exemption be carried forward?

6 Don gives some money to his daughter on her marriage. What marriage exemption is applicable?

7 Which lifetime transfers may lead to tax being charged on death of the transferor?

8 Why must some lifetime transfers be grossed up?

9 What is taper relief?

Answers to quick quiz

1   A transfer of value is any gratuitous disposition by a person resulting in a diminution of the value of his estate.

2   Individuals and trustees.

3   Excluded property is ignored for IHT purposes.

4   A potentially exempt transfer is a lifetime transfer made by an individual to another individual.

5   An unused annual exemption can be carried forward one tax year.

6   The marriage exemption for a gift to the transferor's child is £5,000.

7   An IHT charge on death arises on PETs and CLTs made within seven years of the transferor's death

8   Where the donor pays the lifetime tax due it must be grossed up to calculate the total reduction in value of the estate.

9   Taper relief reduces death tax where a transfer is made between three and seven years before death.

Now try the question below from the Exam Question Bank

Number	Level	Marks	Time
Q18	Introductory	16	29 mins

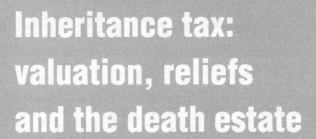

Inheritance tax: valuation, reliefs and the death estate

Topic list	Syllabus reference
1 The valuation of assets for IHT purposes	A4(d)(i)
2 Business property relief (BPR)	A4(d)(ii), (f)(i)
3 Agricultural property relief (APR)	A4(d)(ii), (f)(i)
4 The death estate	A4(c)(iii)
5 Quick succession relief (QSR)	A4(c)(v), (f)(i)
6 Grossing up gifts on death	A4(c)(iii)

Introduction

We started our study of IHT in the previous chapter with a look at which transfers are exempt from IHT and the charge to IHT on lifetime transfers which are, or become, chargeable.

This chapter opens with a section on how assets are valued. Pay particular attention to the related property rules, which prevent one way of avoiding IHT.

Two of the reliefs described in this chapter, business property relief and agricultural property relief, are very generous. If the conditions are satisfied, assets can be exempted from IHT without any limit on the value of the assets. These reliefs are meant to ensure that a family business or farm does not have to be sold when an owner dies, but they also extend to non-family businesses and farms.

Finally, we will see how to bring together all of a deceased person's assets at death, and compute the tax on the estate.

In the next chapter we turn our attention to some additional aspects of IHT including the overseas aspects and administration rules.

Study guide

		Intellectual level
4	**Inheritance tax**	
(c)	The liabilities arising on chargeable lifetime transfers and death transfers by individuals:	3
(iii)	Compute the death estate	2
(v)	Advise on the operation of quick succession relief	
(d)	Computing transfers of value	3
(i)	Advise on the principles of valuation	
(ii)	Advise on the availability of business property relief and agricultural property relief	
(f)	The use of exemptions and reliefs in deferring and minimising inheritance tax liabilities:	3
(i)	Advise on the use of reliefs and exemptions to minimise inheritance tax liabilities, as mentioned in the sections above	

Exam guide

Business and agricultural property reliefs are extremely valuable reliefs as they enable assets to be passed on tax free, and they are therefore likely to feature in IHT planning. You should note the withdrawal of the relief on lifetime transfers if the donee sells the property or ceases to use if for business or agricultural purposes. There is no such limitation for gifts on death.

1 The valuation of assets for IHT purposes

FAST FORWARD

There are special rules for valuing particular kinds of assets, such as quoted shares and securities. The related property rules prevent artificial reductions in value.

1.1 The general principle

The value of any property for the purposes of IHT is the price which the property might reasonably be expected to fetch if sold in the open market at the time of the transfer.

Two or more assets can be valued jointly if disposal as one unit is the course that a prudent hypothetical vendor would have adopted in order to obtain the most favourable price: *Gray v IRC 1994*.

1.2 Quoted shares and securities

The valuation of quoted shares and securities is easy: the Stock Exchange daily official list gives the closing bid and offer prices of all quoted securities. **Inheritance tax valuations are done on the same basis as for CGT ie taking the lower of:**

(a) **The value on the quarter up basis.**

(b) **The average of the highest and lowest marked bargains** for the day, ignoring those marked at special prices.

The transfer may take place on a day on which the Stock Exchange is closed, in which case the valuation is done on the basis of the prices or bargains marked on the last previous day of business or the first following day of business. The lowest of, in this case, the four alternatives will be taken.

Valuations for transfers on death must be cum dividend or cum interest, including the value of the right to the next dividend or interest payment. However, if the question gives an **ex dividend** or an ex interest price and the transfer is on death then the valuation is done on the basis of **adding the whole of the impending net dividend**, or the whole of the impending interest payment net of 20% tax.

> If a question just gives a closing price you may assume that it is the cum dividend or cum interest price.

For lifetime transfers, the Stock Exchange list prices are used without adjustment, whether they are cum or ex dividend or interest.

1.3 Example: securities quoted ex interest

If someone owned £10,000 12% Government stock (interest payable half yearly) quoted at 94-95 ex interest, the valuation on death would be as follows.

	£	£
£10,000 at 94.25 (quarter up rule)		9,425
Add ½ × 12% × £10,000	600	
Less income tax at 20%	(120)	
		480
		9,905

1.4 Unquoted shares and securities

There is no easily identifiable open market value for shares in an unquoted company. The Shares Valuation Division of HMRC is the body with which the taxpayer must negotiate. If agreement cannot be reached, appeal lies to the Special Commissioners and then to the courts.

1.5 Unit trusts

Units in authorised unit trusts are valued at the managers' bid price (**the lower of the two published prices**).

1.6 Life assurance policies

Where a person's estate includes a life policy which matures on his death, the proceeds payable to his personal representatives must be included in his estate for IHT purposes. But where a person's estate includes a life policy which matures on the death of someone else, the open market value must be included in his estate.

If an individual writes a policy in trust, or assigns a policy, or makes a subsequent declaration of trust, the policy proceeds will not be paid to his estate but to the assignee or to the trustees for the trust beneficiaries. The proceeds will, therefore, not be included as part of his free estate at death. It is common to write policies in trust for the benefit of dependants to avoid IHT. In many cases these transfers will be exempted as normal expenditure out of income.

1.7 Overseas property

The basis of valuation is the same as for UK property. The value is converted into sterling at the exchange rate (the 'buy' or 'sell' rate) which will give the lower sterling equivalent. Overseas debts are deductible.

If the property passes on death, the costs of administering and realising overseas property are deductible up to a maximum of 5% of the gross value of the property, so far as those expenses are attributable to the property's location overseas. **Capital taxes paid overseas which are the foreign equivalent of IHT may give rise to double taxation relief** (see later in this Text). Such taxes are given as a credit against the IHT payable; they do not reduce the value of the asset.

1.8 Related property

FAST FORWARD

Related property must be valued as a proportion of the value of the whole of the related property if this produces a higher value than the stand alone value.

Key term

Property is related to that in a person's estate (**related property**) if:

(a)   It is included in the estate of his spouse/civil partner, or

(b)   It has been given to a charity, political party, national public body or housing association as an exempt transfer by either spouse or civil partner and still is, or within the preceding five years has been, the property of the body it was given to.

To reduce the value transferred individuals might fragment an asset into several parts which are collectively worth less than the whole. This way of reducing the value of an asset or set of assets is normally prevented using the diminution in value principle. However, this application of the principle could be thwarted by use of exempt inter-spouse/civil partner transfers. To deter this method of avoiding IHT, there are provisions under which related property is taken into account.

Property which is related to other property must be valued as a proportion of the value of the whole of the related property but only if, by so doing, a higher value is produced. For example, where a husband and wife each hold 40% of the issued shares of a company, the husband's holding will normally be valued as a proportion (one half) of the price which an 80% shareholding would fetch, as an 80% interest would normally be more valuable than two 40% interests.

1.9 Example: related property

Lofty has a leasehold interest in a property. The value of his interest is £25,000. His wife Michelle holds the freehold reversion of the property, which has a market value of £40,000. The value of the freehold not subject to the lease (that is the value of the freehold reversion plus the lease) is £80,000. If Lofty wishes to transfer his interest to their daughter Vicky the value transferred will be the greater of:

(a)   The value of the interest by itself, £25,000, and

(b)   The value of his part of the total related property, which is

$$\frac{\text{The value of the property transferred at its } \textit{unrelated} \text{ value}}{\text{The value of the property transferred at its } \textit{unrelated} \text{ value} + \text{The value of any related property at its } \textit{unrelated} \text{ value}} \times \text{The value of the whole property}$$

$$\frac{25,000}{25,000 + 40,000} \times £80,000 = £30,769.$$

The higher value is £30,769. This is therefore the value transferred by Lofty.

Exam focus point

If the property in question is shares, then in arriving at the fraction set out above, the numbers of shares held are used instead of unrelated values.

Question
Valuation of shares

Shares in an unquoted company are held as follows.

	Number of shares
Husband (H)	4,000
Wife (W)	2,000
Son (S)	750
Shares given by H to a charity by an exempt transfer eight years ago (and still owned by the charity)	3,250
	10,000

Estimated values for different sizes of shareholding are as follows.

Number of shares	Pence per share	£
750	60	450
2,000	90	1,800
4,000	130	5,200
7,250	200	14,500
9,250	250	23,125

What is the value of H's holding, taking into account related property?

Answer

There are three related holdings.

	Shares
H	4,000
W	2,000
Charity	3,250
	9,250

The value of H's 4,000 shares is $\dfrac{4,000}{9,250} \times £23,125 = £10,000$ (ie 250 pence × 4,000 shares).

If in the above exercise H gives away half of his holding to his son, the transfer of value is as follows.

	£
Holding before transfer (as above)	10,000
Less holding after transfer	
$\dfrac{2,000}{7,250} \times £14,500$	(4,000)
Transfer of value	6,000

If H transferred all his shares the value transferred would be £10,000 (no holding after, so no value in the calculation performed above).

2 Business property relief (BPR)

FAST FORWARD
BPR can reduce the values of assets by 100% or 50%. However, there are strict conditions, which are largely intended to prevent people near death from obtaining the reliefs by investing substantial sums in businesses.

2.1 Business property

BPR is applied to the value of relevant business property transferred, to prevent large tax liabilities arising on transfers of businesses.

Relevant business property is:

(a)   Property consisting of a **business or an interest** (such as a partnership share) **in a business**

(b)   **Securities of a company which are unquoted and which** (alone or with other securities or unquoted shares) **gave the transferor control of the company** immediately before the transfer **(control may be achieved by taking into account related property)**

(c)   **Any unquoted shares** (not securities) **in a company**

(d)   **Shares in or securities of a company which are quoted and which** (alone or with other such shares or securities) **gave the transferor control of the company** immediately before the transfer (control may be achieved by taking into account related property)

(e)   **Any land or building, machinery or plant which**, immediately before the transfer, **was used wholly or mainly for the purposes of a business carried on by a company of which the transferor then had control, or by a partnership of which he was then a partner**

Shares or securities on the AIM count as unquoted.

The reliefs available are percentage reductions in the value transferred: 100% for assets within Paragraph (a), (b) or (c) above, and 50% for assets within Paragraph (d) or (e) above.

2.2 Conditions for BPR

BPR is only available if the relevant business property:

(a)   was owned by the transferor for at least the two years preceding the transfer, or

(b)   replaced other relevant business property (which includes agricultural property used in a farming business) where the combined period of ownership of both sets of property was at least two out of the last five years. In this situation relief is given on the lower of the values of the two sets of property.

If the property was inherited, it is deemed to have been owned from the date of the death unless it was inherited from the transferor's spouse or civil partner, in which case the transferor is deemed to have owned it for the period the spouse or civil partner owned it.

BPR is still available even if the transferor cannot fulfil either of the two year ownership criteria if when he acquired the property it was eligible for BPR and either the previous or this current transfer was made on death.

2.3 Additional conditions for BPR on lifetime transfers

If, as a result of the donor's death within seven years of a gift, a PET becomes chargeable or additional tax is due on a CLT, two further conditions must be fulfilled for BPR to be available.

(a) The donee must still own the original property at the date of the donor's death, or the donee's death if earlier.

(b) The original property must still qualify as relevant business property at the date of the donor's death, or the donee's death if earlier.

These conditions are fulfilled if the donee disposed of the original property but reinvested **all** of the disposal proceeds in replacement property within three years of the disposal.

2.4 Non-qualifying businesses

BPR is not available if the business consists wholly or mainly of:

(a) Dealing in securities, stocks and shares (except for discount houses and market makers on the Stock Exchange or on LIFFE)

(b) Dealing in land or buildings

(c) Making or holding investments (including land which is let)

Shares in holding companies, where the subsidiaries have activities which would qualify shares in them for BPR, are eligible for relief.

2.5 Excepted assets

Relevant business property excludes assets which were neither used wholly or mainly for the purposes of the business in the two years preceding the transfer nor required at the time of the transfer for future use in the business.

Formula to learn

> **For shares or securities in a company, the value which we compute BPR on (at 100% or 50%) is:**
>
> $$\text{Total value} \times \frac{\text{the company's relevant business property}}{\text{the company's total assets before deducting liabilities}}$$

2.6 Contracts for sale

BPR is not available if at the date of transfer there is a binding contract for the sale of a business or an interest in a business, unless the sale is to a company which will continue the business and the consideration is wholly or mainly shares or securities in the company.

BPR is not available if at the date of the transfer there is a binding contract for the sale of shares or securities of a company unless the sale is for the purpose of reconstruction or amalgamation.

If any other relevant business property is subject to a binding contract for sale, BPR is not available on it at all.

Partnership agreements often contain a buy/sell clause under which surviving partners must buy a deceased partner's share in the partnership. HMRC regard such a clause as a binding contract for sale which disentitles the deceased partner to BPR. However, neither an accruer clause whereby the deceased partner's share accrues to the surviving partners, nor an option for the surviving partners to buy the deceased partner's share is regarded as binding contract for sale. This means that from a tax planning point of view the later types of arrangement should be used.

Question

BPR

On 31 July 2006 relevant business property valued at £16,800 is transferred to a trust. Assuming that the 2005/06 and 2006/07 annual exemptions have not been used what will the chargeable transfer be if:

(a) The property consists of unquoted shares?
(b) The property consists of land used by a company in which the transferor has a controlling interest?
(c) The property consists of quoted shares which formed part of a 20% interest before the transfer?

Answer

	(a) £	(b) £	(c) £
Value transferred	16,800	16,800	16,800
Less BPR	(16,800)	(8,400)	0
	0	8,400	16,800
Less: AE 2006/07		(3,000)	(3,000)
2005/06 b/f		(3,000)	(3,000)
Chargeable transfer	0	2,400	10,800

Question

BPR and related property

J had shares in a quoted trading company, J plc. The shares in the company were held as follows.

	%
J	40
J's wife	30
Other unconnected persons	30
	100

The shareholdings have been unchanged since 1987. On 1 May 2006 J gave a 30% holding to his son. The values of the shares in May 2006 were agreed as follows.

	£
70% holding	1,600,000
40% holding	900,000
30% holding	840,000
10% holding	200,000

J, who had made a previous chargeable lifetime transfer of £300,000 in 2000, died in January 2007.

Calculate the IHT arising on the gift of the shares, if

(a) J's son still holds the shares in January 2007
(b) J's son sells the shares in June 2006 and retains the cash proceeds.

Answer

No IHT arises when the gift was made, because it was a PET. It becomes chargeable as a result of J's death within seven years as follows.

PET – May 2006

(a)   If J's son still holds the shares, BPR at 50% is available to reduce the chargeable transfer:

	£
Before: $\dfrac{40\%}{40\%+30\%} \times £1,600,000$	914,286
After: $\dfrac{10\%}{10\%+30\%} \times £900,000$	(225,000)
	689,286
Less BPR at 50% (control (with related property) of quoted company)	(344,643)
	344,643
Less: AE 2006/07	(3,000)
AE 2005/06 b/f	(3,000)
Chargeable transfer	338,643

Gross chargeable transfers in the seven years before May 2006 amount to £300,000. This means none of the nil band remains and IHT payable on death amounts to:

IHT at 40% = £135,457

(b)   If J's son does not hold the shares on J's death, BPR is not available to reduce the value of the chargeable transfer:

	£
Transfer (see above)	689,286
Less: AE (2006/07)	(3,000)
AE (2005/06)	(3,000)
Chargeable transfer	683,286

IHT @ 40% = £273,314

3 Agricultural property relief (APR)

FAST FORWARD

APR usually reduces a transfer of agricultural property by 100% of agricultural value.

3.1 Agricultural property

APR is available on the agricultural value of agricultural property.

Agricultural property is agricultural land or pasture (including short rotation coppice) situated in the UK, the Channel Islands or the Isle of Man and includes woodland and any building used in connection with the intensive rearing of livestock or fish where the occupation of the woodland or building is ancillary to that of the land or pasture. It also includes cottages, farm buildings and farm houses of a character appropriate to the property.

Exam focus point

The agricultural value will be given to you in the exam.

APR works like BPR in reducing the value being transferred by a certain percentage before any exemptions. APR is given before BPR and double relief cannot be obtained on the agricultural value. The non-agricultural part of the value of the property meets the relevant business property conditions, however, BPR will be available on that value.

The percentage reduction in agricultural value is, in general, 100% (it is 50% on some land held under pre-September 1995 tenancies.)

3.2 Conditions for relief

For relief to apply the transferor must either:

    (a)   **Own the property and have occupied it themselves for the purpose of agriculture for the two years before the transfer (ie they farm the land themselves)**, or

    (b)   **Own the property for at least the seven years before the transfer, during which it must have been occupied for the purposes of agriculture by either the transferor or a tenant (ie the property is or has been let out).**

If a company controlled by the transferor occupies the property the transferor is treated as occupying it. A farmhouse which is being redecorated, renovated or altered is not treated as though it is occupied for agricultural purposes.

If the property transferred replaces other agricultural property, the condition will be satisfied provided that:

    (a)   The transferor has occupied the properties for the purposes of agriculture for at least two out of the last five years, or

    (b)   The transferor has owned the properties (and somebody has occupied them for agricultural purposes) for at least seven out of the last ten years.

If agricultural properties have been replaced the APR will apply only to the lowest of the values of the various properties considered.

If the property transferred was acquired on the death of the transferor's spouse or civil partner then the period of ownership or occupation of the first spouse or civil partner can count towards the seven years or the two years required. If the property transferred was acquired on the death of somebody else the transferor will be deemed to own it from the date of death and if he subsequently occupies it, to have occupied it from the date of death.

3.3 Additional conditions for lifetime transfers

If, as a result of the donor's death within seven years of a gift, a PET becomes chargeable or additional tax is due on a CLT, two further conditions must be fulfilled for APR to be available.

    (a)   The donee must still own the original property at the date of the donor's death, or the donee's death if earlier.

    (b)   The original property must still qualify as agricultural property immediately prior to the date of the donor's death, or the donee's death if earlier, and must have been occupied as such since the original transfer.

These conditions are fulfilled if the donee disposed of the original property but reinvested **all** of the disposal proceeds in replacement property within three years of the disposal.

3.4 Shares in companies owning agricultural property

If a company owns agricultural property and satisfies the occupation or ownership conditions above then APR is available in respect of the agricultural value that can be attributed to shares or securities transferred by an individual who controls the company. The shares or securities must have been held by the transferor for the relevant period (two years or seven years).

Question   **Farming companies**

On 13 June 2006 K gives his shares in Farm Ltd to his son. K owns 65% of the shares in issue, with an agreed value of £400,000. K has owned the shares for nine years. The company has owned and occupied farmland (for agricultural purposes) for the last eight years. The agricultural value of this land represents 20% of the total value of the company's net assets.

Calculate the chargeable transfer assuming that K dies on 14 July 2007 and the son still holds the shares at the date of his father's death.

Answer

	£
Unquoted trading company shares	
Value of holding	400,000
Less: APR 100% × 20% × £400,000 (on agricultural value)	(80,000)
BPR 100% × 80% × £400,000 (on balance)	(320,000)
Chargeable transfer	0

3.5 Contracts for sale

No APR is available if, at the time of the transfer, a binding contract for sale of the agricultural property exists unless the sale is to a company (the consideration being wholly or mainly shares or securities which will give the transferor control), or is to enable a reorganisation or reconstruction of a farming company.

4 The death estate

FAST FORWARD   When someone dies, we must bring together all their assets to find the value of their death estate.

4.1 Composition of death estate

An individual's death estate consists of all the property he owned immediately before death, with the exception of excluded property. The estate also includes anything acquired as a result of death, for example the proceeds of a life assurance policy.

The estate at death may include:

(a) **Free estate** (everything not within (b) or (c) below).

(b) **Property given subject to a reservation**. This is property given away before death, but with strings attached (see next chapter). For example, someone might give away a house but continue to live in it.

The primary responsibility for payment of tax depends on the type of property:

(a) **Tax on the free estate is payable by the personal representatives (PRs)** (executors or administrators).

(b) **Tax on property given subject to a reservation is payable by the person in possession of the property.**

The whole of the death estate will be chargeable to tax, subject to reliefs (such as BPR and APR) and any exemptions which may be available on death. In particular, if property passes to the deceased person's spouse this will be an exempt transfer. A transfer to any other person eg. children, will be chargeable to IHT, whether this is made outright or to any type of trust.

In order to calculate the tax on the death estate, use the following steps:

Step 1   Look back seven years from the date of death to see if any CLTs or PETs which have become chargeable have been made. If so, these transfers use up the nil rate band available for the death estate. Work out the value of any nil rate band still available.

Step 2   Compute the gross value of the death estate (see further below).

Step 3   Any part of the death estate covered by the nil rate band is taxed at 0%. Any part of the death estate not covered by the nil rate band is charged at 40%. Deduct relevant reliefs from the death tax (eg quick succession relief – see below)

Step 4   Where relevant divide the tax due between PRs and the person in possession of a gift subject to a reservation.

Usually, it will not be necessary to consider grossing up. The situation where it will be needed is dealt with below.

Question

Tax on death estate

Laura dies on 1 August 2006, leaving a free estate valued at £400,000 to a discretionary trust for her children.

Laura had made a transfer of value of £123,000 to her sister on 11 September 2005. The amount stated is after all exemptions and reliefs.

Compute the tax payable by Laura's personal representatives.

Answer

Death tax

Note. There is no death tax on the September 2005 PET which becomes chargeable as a result of Laura's death, as it is within the nil rate band at her death. However, it will use up part of the nil rate band, as shown below.

Step 1   Lifetime transfer of value of £123,000 in seven years before 1 August 2006 (transfers after 1 August 1999). Nil rate band of £(285,000 – 123,000) = £162,000 available.

Step 2   Value of death estate is £400,000.

Step 3

	IHT £
£162,000 × 0%	0
£238,000 × 40%	95,200
£400,000	95,200

Step 4   Tax payable by personal representatives   £95,200

The computation of an individual's chargeable estate at death should be set out as follows.

Death estate	£	£
Personalty		
Stocks and shares		X
Insurance policy proceeds		X
Personal chattels		X
Cash		X
		X
Less debts due by deceased	X	
funeral expenses	X	
		(X)
		X
Realty		
Freehold property (keep UK and foreign property separate)	X	
Less mortgages	(X)	
		X
		X
Net estate		X
Gifts with reservation		X
Chargeable estate		X

4.2 Debts and funeral expenses

The rules on debts are as follows.

(a) Only debts incurred by the deceased *bona fide* and for full consideration may be deducted.

(b) The debts must be such as an executor could pay without making himself personally liable for a misuse of the assets of the estate. So gaming debts are not deductible but statute barred debts are, provided the executor pays them.

(c) **Debts incurred by the deceased but payable after the death may be deducted** but the amount should be discounted because of the future date of payment.

(d) Rent and similar amounts which accrue day by day should be accrued up to the date of death.

(e) **Taxes to the date of death may be deducted** as they are a liability imposed by law.

(f) **Debts incurred by the executor are not allowed.**

(g) **If a debt is charged on a specific property it is deductible primarily from that property**; a mortgage on freehold property is therefore deductible from that freehold.

(h) Debts contracted abroad must first be deducted from non-UK property (whether or not the value of that property is chargeable to inheritance tax). If the foreign debts exceed the value of the foreign property the excess is allowed as a deduction from UK property provided it represents debts recoverable in the UK.

Reasonable funeral expenses may be deducted.

(a) What is reasonable depends on the deceased's condition in life.

(b) Reasonable costs of mourning for the family (and servants) are allowed.

(c) **The cost of a tombstone is deductible.**

Question

Z died on 19 June 2006. His estate consisted of the following.

10,000 shares in A plc, quoted at 84p – 89p with bargains marked at 85p, 87p and 90p

8,000 shares in B plc, quoted ex div at 111p – 115p. A net dividend of 4p per share was paid on 21 July 2005

Freehold property valued at £150,000 subject to a mortgage of £45,040

Liabilities and funeral expenses amounted to £2,450.

Z had made a chargeable lifetime transfer of £295,000 in July 2001. Calculate the IHT liability on the death estate.

Answer

Free estate

	£	£
Personalty		
A plc shares		
10,000 at lower of 85.25p and 87.5p		
10,000 × 85.25p		8,525
B plc		
8,000 × 112p	8,960	
Net dividend 8,000 × 4p	320	
		9,280
		17,805
Less debts and funeral expenses		(2,450)
		15,355
Realty		
Freehold property	150,000	
Less mortgage	(45,040)	
		104,960
Chargeable estate		120,315

Chargeable transfers in the seven years prior to death exceeded the nil band, so IHT on the death estate is £120,315 at 40% = £48,126.

5 Quick succession relief (QSR)

FAST FORWARD

Quick succession relief applies where there are two charges to IHT within five years.

If a person dies shortly after receiving property by way of a chargeable transfer the same property will be taxed twice within a short space of time: it will be taxed as the original chargeable transfer and it will be taxed again as part of the estate of the deceased transferee. QSR reduces the tax on the estate.

The tax on the estate is calculated normally. A credit is then given as follows.

Formula to learn

$$\text{Tax paid on first transfer} \times \frac{\text{net transfer}}{\text{gross transfer}} \times \text{percentage}$$

The percentage to use is as follows.

Period between the transfer and the death of the transferee	Relief
	%
1 year or less	100
1-2 years	80
2-3 years	60
3-4 years	40
4-5 years	20
Over 5 years	0

If the period is precisely two years, 80% relief is given, and so on.

The relief applies even where the asset has been disposed of before death.

Question

QSR

Oscar died on 29 September 2006 leaving an estate valued at £347,000 to his son. Oscar had received £28,000 gross in July 2002 from his uncle's estate. IHT of £4,200 had been payable by Oscar on this legacy.

Calculate the IHT payable on Oscar's estate, assuming he has made no lifetime transfers.

Answer

	£
IHT on £347,000 (£285,000 @ 0% + £62,000 @ 40%)	24,800
Less QSR: £4,200 × (23,800/28,000) × 20% (4-5 years)	(714)
IHT payable on Oscar's estate	24,086

6 Grossing up gifts on death

FAST FORWARD

Gross up specific gifts on death if the residue of the estate is left to an exempt recipient.

We saw that grossing up applies to CLTs when the donor pays the IHT. **We must also gross up on a death when there is a specific legacy (ie gift on death) of UK property, and the residue of the estate (ie what's left of the estate after specific gifts have been paid out) is exempt. This can happen when the residue is left to a spouse/ civil partner or charity.**

The reason for this is that the recipients of specific gifts of UK property do not pay the tax on the gift. Instead this must be borne by the residue of the estate – which is exempt. Specific gifts of foreign property, on the other hand, do bear their own tax (ie the recipient must pay any IHT) and do not need to be grossed up.

Do not gross up specific gifts if the whole estate is chargeable. In such cases, work out IHT as normal.

Specific gifts of UK property are given to the heirs in full (unless there is not enough residue to pay the IHT), and the IHT on those gifts comes out of the residue. In this case, the formula used to calculate the tax is as follows.

Formula to learn

Chargeable amount (in excess of the nil band) $\times \dfrac{40}{60}$ ie $\dfrac{\text{rate of tax}}{100 \text{ minus the rate of tax}}$

Question

R dies on 29 May 2006 leaving an estate valued at £451,000. Included in this is UK property valued at £359,000 which he leaves to his son. He leaves the residue of the estate to his wife.

Calculate the IHT liability arising on death assuming R has made no lifetime transfers.

Answer

There is an exempt residue and a specific gift of a UK asset. Therefore the specific gift must be grossed up:

	IHT
	£
£285,000 @ 0%	0
£74,000 @ 40/60	49,333
£359,000	49,333

The gross transfer is £(359,000 + 49,333) = £408,333.

Check tax £(408,333 − 285,000) = £123,333 @ 40% = £49,333.

The son receives £359,000, HMRC receives £49,333.

The residue available to the wife is £451,000 − £408,333 = £42,667.

This calculation would not have applied if:

(a)   The residue of the estate had been chargeable rather than exempt, in which case IHT would have been calculated on a gross chargeable estate of £451,000 in the normal way, or

(b)   The will had left a specific gift of £92,000 to the wife and the residue to the son. In that case, the son would have received £359,000 less tax of £(359,000 − 285,000) × 40% = £29,600, giving the son a net amount of £329,400, and the wife would have received £92,000.

Chapter roundup

- There are special rules for valuing particular kinds of assets, such as quoted shares and securities. The related property rules prevent artificial reductions in value.

- Related property must be valued as a proportion of the value of the whole of the related property if this produces a higher value than the stand alone value

- BPR and APR can reduce the values of assets by 100% or 50%. However, there are strict conditions, which are largely intended to prevent people near death from obtaining the reliefs by investing substantial sums in businesses and in farms.

- APR usually reduces a transfer of agricultural property by 100% of agricultural value.

- When someone dies, we must bring together all their assets to find the value of their death estate.

- Quick succession relief applies where there are two charges to IHT within five years.

- Gross up specific gifts on death if the residue of the estate is left to an exempt recipient.

Quick quiz

1   How are quoted securities valued?

2   What is related property?

3   What rate of BPR is given on a controlling shareholding in

    (a)   a quoted trading company, and
    (b)   an unquoted trading company?

4   What periods of ownership or occupation are required to obtain agricultural property relief?

5   How is quick succession relief calculated?

6   Sonia dies leaving the following debts:

    (a)   Grocery bill
    (b)   HM Revenue and Customs – income tax to death
    (c)   Mortgage on house
    (d)   Gambling debt

    Which are deductible against her death estate and why?

Answers to quick quiz

1   The value is the lower of:

-   the value on the quarter up basis (bid price plus 1/4 of the difference between the bid and offer prices).

-   the average of highest and lowest marked bargains for the day (ignoring special price bargains).

2   Related property is property:

-   comprised in the estate of the transferor's spouse, or

-   which has been given to a charity, political party, national public body or housing association as an exempt transfer by either spouse and still is, or has been within the past five years, been the property of the body it was given to.

3   (a)   50%
    (b)   100%

4   For APR the transferor must have either:

-   owned and farmed the land themselves for two years before the transfer, or

-   owned the property for at least seven years before the transfer during which time it was farmed either by the transferor or a tenant.

5   QSR is calculated as:

$$\text{Tax paid on first transfer} \times \frac{\text{net transfer}}{\text{gross transfer}} \times \%$$

6   (a)   grocery bill – deductible as incurred for full consideration
    (b)   income tax to death – deductible as imposed by law
    (c)   mortgage – deductible, will be set against value of house primarily
    (d)   gambling debt – not allowable as executor be liable for misuse of estate assets if paid

Now try the question below from the Exam Question Bank

Number	Level	Marks	Time
Q19	Introductory	25	45 mins

Inheritance tax: additional aspects

19

Topic list	Syllabus reference
1 Overseas aspects	A4(a)(ii), (b)(v), (c)(vi)
2 Gifts with reservation	A4(b)(vi)
3 Associated operations	A4(b)(vii)
4 Altering dispositions made on death	A4(c)(vii)
5 The administration of IHT	A4(g)(iii)
6 The payment of IHT	A4(g)(i), (ii)

Introduction

In the previous two chapters we have studied the charge to IHT both on lifetime transfers and on death, and have looked at some exemptions and reliefs.

In this chapter, we look at overseas aspects, including relief where property is subject both to IHT and to a similar tax abroad.

We also look at two important sets of anti-avoidance provisions. The rules on gifts with reservation prevent people from avoiding IHT by claiming to give property away before death while in fact retaining rights over it. The rules on associated operations allow HMRC to defeat tax avoidance schemes which rely on breaking down one transaction into several artificial steps to avoid IHT.

We also consider how a will can be altered and, finally, we look at the administration and payment of IHT.

In the next chapter we conclude our study of capital taxes by looking at trusts and stamp duties.

Study guide

		Intellectual level
4	**Inheritance tax**	
(a)	The scope of inheritance tax:	2
(ii)	Explain the concepts of domicile and deemed domicile and understand the application of these concepts to inheritance tax	
(b)	The basic principles for computing transfers of value:	3
(v)	Identify and advise on the tax implications of the location of assets	
(vi)	Identify and advise on gifts with reservation of benefit	
(vii)	Identify and advise on the tax implications of associated operations	
(c)	The liabilities arising on chargeable lifetime transfers and death transfers by individuals:	3
(vi)	Advise on the operation of double tax relief for inheritance tax	
(vii)	Advise on the inheritance tax effects and advantages of the variation of wills	
(g)	The system by which inheritance tax is administered, including the instalment option for the payment of tax:	
(i)	Identify those responsible for the payment of inheritance tax.	2
(ii)	Identify the occasions on which inheritance tax may be paid by instalments.	2
(iii)	Advise on the due dates, interest and penalties for inheritance tax purposes.	2

Exam guide

The topics covered in this chapter are important for tax planning questions. The anti-avoidance rules for gifts with reservation and associated operations are designed to ensure that individuals are taxed on what they have effectively given away entirely. The rules for foreign assets are beneficial to non-domiciliaries. Note, however, that you have to take positive action to change your domicile, and that the deemed domicile rules mean that it takes at least three years to escape the UK IHT net.

1 Overseas aspects

1.1 Domicile

Domicile for IHT has the same meaning as in general law, namely **the country of one's permanent home**.

Also, a person is **deemed to be domiciled in the UK for IHT purposes**:

(a)   If he has been **resident in the UK for at least 17 out of the 20 tax years** ending with the year in which any chargeable transfer is made. The term 'residence' has the same meaning as for income tax (see earlier in this Text).

(b)   **For 36 months after ceasing to be domiciled in the UK** under general law.

1.1.1 UK domicile

If an individual is **UK domiciled**, or deemed UK domiciled, **transfers of all assets, wherever situated, are subject to IHT**.

1.1.2 Foreign domicile

FAST FORWARD

> Non-UK assets of individuals not domiciled in the UK are not subject to IHT. Because of the value of this exemption some individuals not UK domiciled are treated as UK domiciled under general law for IHT purposes.

For individuals **not domiciled in the UK, only transfers of UK assets are within the charge to IHT**, and even some assets within the UK are excluded property.

1.2 The location of assets

For someone not domiciled in the UK, the location of assets is clearly important:

(a) **Land and buildings**, freehold or leasehold, are in the country in which they are **physically situated**.

(b) **A debt** is in the **country of residence of the debtor** unless it is a debt evidenced by a deed, when the debt is where the deed is. Judgement debts are situated wherever the judgement is recorded.

(c) **Life policies** are in the **country where the proceeds are payable**.

(d) **Registered shares and securities** are in the **country where they are registered**, or where they would normally be dealt with in the ordinary course of business.

(e) **Bearer securities** are **where the certificate of title is located** at the time of transfer.

(f) **Bank accounts** are at the **branch** where the account is kept.

(g) **An interest in a partnership** is where the partnership **business is carried on**.

(h) **Goodwill** is where the **business** to which it is attached is **carried on**.

(i) **Tangible property** is at its **physical location**.

(j) Property held in trust follows the above rules regardless of the rules of the trust or residence of the trustees.

1.3 Excluded property

As we saw earlier, foreign property of a non-UK domiciled individual is excluded property so is ignored for IHT purposes. The following are also excluded property.

(a) Foreign assets in a trust established when the settlor was non-UK domiciled for IHT purposes. No IHT is due on the trust assets even if the settlor later becomes UK domiciled at a later date.

(b) Certain British Government securities whose terms of issue provide that they shall be exempt from taxation so long as they are owned by non-UK domiciled or not ordinarily resident individuals (the extended IHT definition of deemed domicile above does not apply).

(c) The following savings if held by persons domiciled in the Channel Islands or the Isle of Man (the extended IHT definition of deemed domicile above does not apply):

    (i) War savings certificates

    (ii) National Savings & Investments certificates

    (iii) Premium savings bonds

    (iv) Deposits in National Savings & Investments accounts or with a trustee savings bank

    (v) SAYE savings schemes (see earlier in this Text)

(e) Unit trust units or shares in open ended investment companies (OEICs) held by non-UK domiciliaries.

In addition, if someone dies when neither domiciled, resident nor ordinarily resident in the UK, a foreign currency account held at a UK bank is ignored in computing his death estate.

1.4 Double taxation relief (DTR)

Double taxation relief may reduce the IHT on assets also taxed overseas.

DTR applies to transfers (during lifetime and on death) of assets situated overseas which suffer tax overseas as well as IHT in the UK. Relief may be given under a treaty, but if not then the following rules apply.

DTR is given as a tax credit against the IHT payable on the overseas asset. The amount available as a tax credit is the lower of the foreign tax liability and the IHT (at the average rate) on the asset.

Question   DTR

P died on 15 October 2006 leaving a chargeable estate of £282,000. Included in this total is a foreign asset valued at £80,000 in respect of which foreign taxes of £20,000 were paid.

Calculate the IHT payable on the estate assuming that P made a gross chargeable lifetime transfer of £147,000 one year before his death.

Answer

	£
IHT on chargeable estate of £282,000	
(available nil rate band £(285,000 − 147,000) = £138,000 @ 0%, £144,000 @ 40%	57,600
(Average rate: 57,600/282,000 = 20.42553%)	
Less DTR: lower of:	
(a) £20,000	
(b) £80,000 × 20.42553% = £16,340	(16,340)
IHT payable on the estate	41,260

2 Gifts with reservation

The rules on gifts with reservation ensure that gifts which are effectively made on death or within the seven years before death, even though apparently made earlier, are taxed.

2.1 Introduction

There are rules to prevent the avoidance of IHT by the making of gifts while reserving some benefit. Without these rules, incomplete lifetime gifts would escape IHT by being PETs but would also reduce the individual's estate at death. The value of the assets could thus escape tax entirely, despite the original owner deriving some benefit from them up to his death.

The obvious example is a gift of a home to the donor's children but with the donor continuing to live in it rent free. Another example is a gift of income-producing assets, for example shares, but with the income continuing to be received by the donor.

Key term

> Property given subject to a reservation (**gifts with reservation**) is property where:
>
> (a)   Such property is not enjoyed virtually to the entire exclusion of the donor (in the case of land only, also the donor's spouse or civil partner), or
>
> (b)   Possession and enjoyment of the property transferred is not *bona fide* assumed by the donee.

'Virtually to the entire exclusion' would, for example, allow a donor occasional brief stays in a house he had given away without creating a reservation, but spending most weekends in the house would create a reservation.

2.2 IHT consequences

Where a gift with reservation is made, it is treated in the same way as any other gift at the time it is made (as a PET or a CLT, as appropriate). **However, special rules apply on the death of the donor.**

(a)   **If the reservation still exists at the date of the donor's death, the asset is included in the donor's estate at its value at that time** (not its value at the date the gift was made).

(b)   **If the reservation ceases within the seven years before death, then the gift is treated as a PET made at the time the reservation ceased.** The charge is based on its value at that time. The annual exemption cannot be used against such a PET.

If the gift could be taxed as a PET or CLT when made, as well as taxed under (a) or (b) above, it will be taxed either under (a) or (b), or as a PET or CLT when made (but not both), whichever gives the higher total tax.

2.3 Exceptions

There are **exceptions to the gifts with reservation rules** as follows.

(a)   A gift will not be treated as being with reservation if **full consideration is given** for any right of occupation or enjoyment retained or assumed by the donor (or his spouse or civil partner, in the case of land), and the property is land or chattels. For example, an individual might give away his house and continue to live in it, but pay a full market rent for doing so.

(b)   A gift will not be treated as being with reservation if the circumstances of the donor change in a way that was unforeseen at the time of the original gift and the benefit provided by the donee to the donor only represents reasonable provision for the **care and maintenance of the donor, being an elderly or infirm relative**. This exception only applies to interests in land.

2.4 Pre owned assets

If the gift with reservation rules do not apply **an income tax charge may apply if individuals have entered into tax planning to reduce their inheritance tax liability** without completely divesting themselves of the asset. **This was covered in Chapter 3.** The transferor may, however, elect that the asset should be treated as remaining within their estate under the gift with reservation rules so that an income tax charge does not arise.

3 Associated operations

Associated operations (ie transactions affecting the same property) are treated as dispositions for IHT.

Key term

> **Associated operations** are:
>
> (a)   Two or more operations which affect the same property or one of which affects the property whilst other operations affect other property directly or indirectly representing the property, or
>
> (b)   Any two operations, one of which is effected with reference to the other, or with a view to enabling the other to be effected.

All associated operations are considered as one disposition. If a transfer of value has been made it is treated as made at the time of the last operation in the chain of associated operations. For this purpose, if the earlier operations themselves constituted transfers of value then the value transferred by these is deducted from the value transferred by all associated operations taken together.

The associated operations rule is a powerful weapon against schemes to avoid inheritance tax by using several transactions instead of one.

For example, trustees might own some valuable paintings. They could give D, an individual, custody of the paintings for several years, on normal commercial terms (so that there would be no gratuitous intent). The trustees' interest in the paintings would be reduced in value, because someone else had custody of them. The trustees could then give an interest in the paintings to D's son. The value of what was given to D's son would be lower than it would otherwise have been, saving tax. HMRC would, however, retrieve the tax by treating the arrangement with D and the gift to his son as associated operations *(Macpherson and another v CIR 1988).*

4 Altering dispositions made on death

A variation or disclaimer can be used to vary a will after death. This can have IHT and CGT consequences.

4.1 Introduction

There are **two main ways in which dispositions on death may be altered: by application to the courts, and by means of a voluntary variation or a disclaimer** of a legacy. Application to the courts may be made if the family and dependants of the deceased feel that the will has not made adequate provision for them. Any changes to the will made in this way will be treated for IHT purposes as if made by the deceased when writing his will.

4.2 IHT and CGT consequences

Within two years of a death the terms of a will can be changed in writing, either by a variation of the terms of the will made by the persons who benefit or would benefit under the dispositions, or by a disclaimer, with the change being effective for IHT purposes. The variation or disclaimer will not be treated as a transfer of value. Inheritance tax will be calculated as if the terms contained in the variation replaced those in the will. If a legacy is disclaimed, it will pass under the terms of the will (or possibly under the intestacy rules) to some other person, usually the residuary legatee, and tax will apply as if the will originally directed the legacy to that new recipient.

There is a similar provision for CGT. **This was covered in Chapter 14.**

If the beneficiaries making the variation wish the relevant terms of the will to be treated as replaced by the terms of the variation, it is necessary to state this in the variation. The statement can apply for inheritance tax or capital gains tax or both. Where a disclaimer is made, the relevant terms in the will *must* be treated as replaced by the terms of the disclaimer for both IHT and CGT purposes (subject to exceptions listed below), regardless of whether this is stated in the disclaimer or not.

A variation or disclaimer may be of benefit in reducing tax or in securing a fairer distribution of the deceased's estate or both.

4.3 Miscellaneous points

These provisions do not apply where the variation or disclaimer is made for consideration.

Property which is deemed to be included in an estate at the date of death because the deceased made a previous gift with reservation cannot be redirected by a deed of variation in a way which is effective for IHT purposes.

Variations or disclaimers can be made in respect of property passing under the intestacy rules in the same way as for property passing under a will, and with the same IHT and CGT consequences.

Exam focus point

A variation is a planning tool to allow a tax inefficient will to be amended to a more tax efficient distribution of the assets. For example instead of leaving say £285,000 of assets to a spouse to pass onto the children when the spouse dies, leave the assets directly to the children.

Although the first will arranges for an exempt transfer to the spouse, the nil band is wasted. The assets will thus be added to the surviving spouse's own assets on their death. The varied will utilises the nil band passing those assets to the children IHT free.

5 The administration of IHT

FAST FORWARD

IHT is administered by HMRC (Capital Taxes). The due date for payment depends on the type of event giving rise to the charge to tax.

5.1 Accounts

IHT is administrated by HMRC (Capital Taxes), part of HMRC's capital and savings section.

There is no system of regular returns as for income tax, corporation tax and capital gains tax. **Instead, any person who is liable for IHT on a transfer is required to deliver an account giving details of the relevant assets and their value. An account delivered by the personal representatives (PRs) of a deceased person has to provide full details of the assets in the death estate. The PRs also have to include in their account details of any chargeable transfers made by the deceased person in the seven years before his death.**

PRs must deliver an account within 12 months following the end of the month in which death occurred or, if later, three months following the date when they become PRs. **Where no tax is due, and certain other conditions are satisfied, it is not necessary to submit an account. Estates where no account needs to be submitted are called excepted estates.**

A person responsible for the delivery of an account in relation to a PET that has become chargeable by reason of death, must do so within 12 months following the end of the month in which death occurred unless already reported by the PRs.

Any other account (such as for a chargeable lifetime transfer) must be delivered within 12 months of the end of the month in which the transfer was made or, if later, within three months from the date liability to tax arose.

5.2 Corrective accounts

If a person has delivered an account and then discovers a material defect in it, he must deliver a corrective account within six months.

5.3 Power to call for documents

HMRC may require any person to provide any information, documents, etc needed for the purposes of IHT. There is a right of appeal against such an information notice.

5.4 Determinations and appeals

HMRC issue a written notice of determination where for example they do not agree a value of transfer or where payment of tax has not been made. It may be made on the basis of a submitted account or to the best of the inspector's judgement.

An appeal against a notice of determination may be made to the Special Commissioners within 30 days of its being served, and an appeal may be made against their decision to the courts (but only on a question of law, not on a question of fact). If the issues are substantially confined to questions of law, an appeal may be made directly to the High Court instead of to the Special Commissioners. Questions of land valuation are dealt with by the Lands Tribunal.

HMRC cannot take legal proceedings to recover tax charged by a notice of determination while an appeal is pending.

6 The payment of IHT

6.1 Liability

FAST FORWARD The liability to pay IHT depends on the type of transfer and whether it was made on death.

On death, liability for payment is as follows.

(a)   **Tax on the free estate is paid by the PRs** out of estate assets, with the burden generally falling on the residuary legatee (ie the recipient of the assets in the residue).

(b)   **Tax on property** not in the possession of the personal representatives, having been transferred by the donor **subject to a reservation, is payable by the person in possession of the property.**

(c)   **Tax on PETs that have become chargeable is paid and borne by donees**.

(d)   **Additional liabilities on CLTs must be paid and borne by the donees**.

HMRC can look beyond the person primarily responsible. Most significantly a PR may become liable where the tax remains unpaid. This overall liability is limited to the value of estate assets in his possession. HMRC will not pursue the PR for tax if lifetime transfers are later discovered and the PR has made the fullest reasonably practicable enquiries to discover lifetime transfers and has obtained a certificate of discharge before distributing the estate.

If the PRs do not pay IHT due on an estate, HMRC may collect the tax from beneficiaries under the will to the extent they receive assets under the will.

The donor is primarily liable for the tax due on chargeable lifetime transfers.

6.2 Due dates

(a) **For chargeable lifetime transfers the due date is the later of:**

(i) **30 April just after the end of the tax year of the transfer.**

(ii) **Six months after the end of the month of the transfer.**

Interest (not tax deductible) is payable from the due date to the day before the day on which payment is made (inclusive).

(b) **Tax arising on the free estate at death (and on gifts with reservation if the reservation still existed at death) is payable by the PRs on delivery of their account.** The time limit for this is 12 months from the end of the month in which the death occurred or, if earlier, when probate is obtained. Interest, however, runs from six months after the end of the month when death occurred.

(c) **Tax arising on death in respect of PETs and CLTs with additional tax is payable within six months from the end of the month of death, and interest runs from this due date.**

Interest (not taxable) may be obtained on repayments of tax or of interest on tax, from the date of payment to the date of repayment.

Question   Interest on IHT

Peter died on 10 March 2006. IHT of £375,000 on his estate was paid on 10 November 2006, and IHT of £27,300 was repaid on 18 January 2007. Calculate the interest payments to and by HMRC, assuming an interest rate of 5% for both overpayments and underpayments of IHT.

Answer

Interest payment to HMRC

Interest runs from 30 September to 9 November inclusive.

Interest = £375,000 × 5% × 41/365 = £2,106.16

Interest payment by HMRC

The interest paid to HMRC on £27,300 was £27,300 × 5% × 41/365 = £153.33.

The interest payment by HMRC runs from 10 November to 17 January inclusive. It is £(27,300.00 + 153.33) × 5% × 69/365 = £259.49.

6.3 The instalment option

IHT on certain property can be paid by ten equal annual instalments on CLTs where tax is borne by the donee, or on the transfer of a person's death estate.

The instalment option may also be used for IHT payable due to the death of the donor within seven years of making a PET. In this case, the donee must have kept the property (or replacement property qualifying for business or agricultural property relief) until the donor's death (or his own, if earlier), and if the property qualifies under (c) or (d) below the shares must remain unquoted until the earlier of the two deaths.

The first instalment is due for payment:

(a)   On transfers on death and liabilities arising as a result of death, six months after the end of the month of death.

(b)   On chargeable lifetime transfers, on the normal due date.

The instalment option applies to:

(a)   **Land and buildings**

(b)   **Shares or securities in a company controlled by the transferor** immediately before the transfer

(c)   **Other holdings in unquoted companies** where the tax on them together with that on other instalment property represents **at least 20% of the total liability** on the estate on a death, **or where the tax cannot all be paid at once without undue hardship**

(d)   **Shares in an unquoted company (including an AIM listed company) representing at least 10%** of the nominal value of the issued share capital and **valued for IHT purposes at not less than £20,000**

(e)   **A business or an interest in a business**

No interest is charged on the instalments if paid on the due dates, unless the property is land not attracting agricultural property relief, or is shares or securities of an investment company or a company whose business is wholly or mainly dealing in securities, stocks or shares or land or buildings. For such property, interest is charged on the balance outstanding, from the normal due date for paying tax in one amount.

If the property is sold, all outstanding tax must then be paid.

6.4 Transfers reported late

Where a transfer is reported late and that transfer was made within the seven years preceding a later transfer, then the tax charge on the earlier transfer (the one reported late) is the liability that would have arisen if the transfer had been reported on time together with the additional IHT that would have been payable on the later transfer if the earlier transfer had been properly taken into account.

Chapter roundup

- Non-UK assets of individuals not domiciled in the UK are not subject to IHT. Because of the value of this exemption some individuals not UK domiciled are treated as UK domiciled under general law for IHT purposes.

- Double taxation relief may reduce the IHT on assets also taxed overseas.

- The rules on gifts with reservation ensure that gifts which are effectively made on death or within the seven years before death, even though apparently made earlier, are taxed.

- Associated operations (ie transactions affecting the same property) are treated as dispositions for IHT.

- A variation or disclaimer can be used to vary a will after death. This can have IHT and CGT consequences.

- IHT is administered by HMRC (Capital Taxes). The due date for payment depends on the type of event giving rise to the charge to tax.

- The liability to pay IHT depends on the type of transfer and whether it was made on death.

Quick quiz

1   How is domicile defined for IHT purposes?

2   How is double taxation relief given?

3   Within what time limit must a variation of a will be made?

4   When is lifetime inheritance tax on a chargeable lifetime transfer due for payment?

Answers to quick quiz

1 Domicile for IHT is:

- domicile under the general law (permanent home) and
- deemed domicile in the UK if resident for at least 17 out of 20 tax years, and
- deemed domicile in the UK if ceased to be domiciled under general law in last 36 months

2 DTR is given as a tax credit against IHT payable on the overseas asset to the extent of the lower of foreign tax and the IHT (at average rate) on it.

3 A variation of a will must be made within two years of death.

4 The due date for lifetime tax on a chargeable lifetime transfer is the later of:

(a) 30 April just after the end of the tax year of the transfer, and
(b) 6 months after the end of the month of transfer

Now try the question below from the Exam Question Bank

Number	Level	Marks	Time
Q38	Examination	25	45 mins

This question has been analysed to show you how to approach paper P6 exams.

Trusts and stamp duties

Topic list	Syllabus reference
1 Trusts	A4(e)(i)
2 IHT for discretionary trusts	A4(e)(iii), (vii)
3 Tax planning using trusts	A4(f)(i)
4 Scope of stamp duties	A5(a)(i)
5 Stamp duties on shares and securities	A5(b)(i)
6 Stamp duty land tax (SDLT)	A5(b)(ii)
7 Exemptions and reliefs	A5(c)(i), (ii)
8 Administration of stamp duties	A5(d)

Introduction

In the last three chapters we have studied the impact of IHT on transfers by individuals, whether during lifetime or on death.

This chapter reviews the IHT charge on gifts into discretionary trusts and the subsequent impact of IHT on those trusts. Trusts have historically been used in estate planning as they allow the settlor to direct how the assets should be dealt with even after they have been given away. Even though there are periodic and exit charges, discretionary trusts can still be used for tax mitigation. This concludes our study of IHT and trusts.

In the remainder of this chapter we look at stamp duties. Stamp duty and stamp duty reserve taxes impose a charge on transfers of shares and securities of 0.5% of the consideration for the sale. Stamp duty land tax is charged on transfers of land. The rate of charge can be as high as 4%.

In the next chapter we will turn our attention to corporation tax.

Study guide

		Intellectual level
4	**Inheritance tax**	
(e)	The liabilities arising in respect of transfers to and from trusts and on property within trusts:	3
(i)	Define a trust	2
(iii)	Advise on the inheritance tax implications of transfers of property into trust	
(vii)	Identify the occasions on which inheritance tax is payable by the trustees of a discretionary trust	
(f)	The use of exemptions and reliefs in deferring and minimising inheritance tax liabilities	3
(i)	Advise on exemptions and reliefs to minimise inheritance tax liabilities as mentioned in the sections above.	
5	**Stamp duties (stamp duty and stamp duty land tax)**	
(a)	The scope of stamp duty and stamp duty land tax:	3
(i)	Identify the property in respect of which stamp duty and stamp duty land tax is payable.	
(b)	Identify and advise on the liabilities arising on documented transfers.	3
(i)	Advise on the stamp duties payable on transfers of shares and securities	
(ii)	Advise on the stamp duties payable on transfers of land	
(c)	The use of exemptions and reliefs in deferring and minimising stamp duties:	3
(i)	Identify transfers involving no consideration	
(ii)	Advise on group transactions	
(d)	Understand and explain the systems by which stamp duties are administered.	2

Exam guide

Trusts are useful in tax planning. The trustees retain control over assets until they deem a beneficiary to be sufficiently capable of looking after them. Be aware of the IHT implications for discretionary trusts.

Stamp duties are unlikely to form a major part of a question, but must not be overlooked as they can be a significant cost in many transactions.

1 Trusts

1.1 What is a trust?

A trust is an arrangement under which a person, the **settlor**, transfers property to another person, the **trustee** or trustees, who is required to deal with the **trust property** on behalf of certain specified persons, the **beneficiaries**.

A trust may be created during the **lifetime of the settlor**, in which case the terms of the trust will be contained in the trust deed. Alternatively a trust may arise on the **death of the settlor**, in which case the terms of the trust will be laid down in the will, or by the statutory provisions which apply on an intestacy.

The first trustee will normally be specified in the trust deed or will. Trustees may retire and new trustees may be appointed, but for tax purposes they are regarded as a single continuing body of persons.

The beneficiaries will also be specified in the trust deed or will. They may be separately named, 'my daughter Ann', or may be members of a particular class of persons, 'my children'.

The trust property will comprise the original property settled (or property replacing it), plus any property added to the trust, plus income accumulated as an addition to capital, less any amounts advanced to beneficiaries.

1.2 Example of a discretionary trust

A discretionary trust for a family may have the following provisions:

(a)   Settlor: James Brown

(b)   Trustees, John Brown (son) and Jean White (daughter)

(c)   Beneficiaries: the children and remoter issue of the settlor, and their spouses/civil partners

(d)   Trust property: £100,000 originally settled and any property deriving therefrom

(e)   Income may be accumulated for up to 21 years from the date of the settlement; subject to which it is to be distributed to the beneficiaries at the trustees' discretion.

(f)   Capital may be advanced to beneficiaries at the trustees' discretion. Any capital remaining undistributed on the 80th anniversary of the date of settlement is to be distributed to the settlor's grandchildren then living, failing which to Oxfam.

This gives the trustees complete discretion over income and capital.

2 IHT for discretionary trusts

FAST FORWARD

There is a CLT when a discretionary trust is set up. The trust suffers the IHT principal charge once every ten years and the exit charge when property leaves the trust.

2.1 IHT on creation

As we saw earlier in this Text, **when an individual makes a gift to a discretionary trust it is a CLT for IHT purposes**. If the gift is made on death, IHT is charged on the death estate in the normal way before the assets enter the trust.

2.2 IHT charges on the trust

The property in the trust is known as 'relevant property'. So long as it remains relevant property it is subject to the **principal charge** on every tenth anniversary from the start of the trust.

If property leaves the trust (and so ceases to be relevant property) an **exit charge** arises.

Exam focus point

> All trusts set up during the settlor's lifetime, whether they are interest in possession or discretionary trusts, are 'relevant property trusts' for IHT purposes, and the rules below apply. However, the examiner has stated that he will only refer to discretionary trusts in the exam.

Exit charge before first principal charge

The amount subject to the exit charge is the amount distributed from the trust. The rate of IHT is 30% of the (lifetime) rate that would apply to a notional (ie pretend) transfer of the initial value of the trust, assuming cumulative transfers by the trust equal to those made by the settlor in the seven years prior to the setting up of the trust. Once the rate of IHT has been established, it is then further reduced by multiplying by x/40 where x is the number of complete successive quarters that have elapsed since the trust commenced.

The principal charge

IHT is charged on the value of the property in the trust at each tenth anniversary of the trust. The rate is 30% of the (lifetime) rate that would apply to a transfer of the property in the trust at the tenth anniversary, assuming cumulative transfers equal to the gross amount of any capital paid out of the trust in the previous ten years **plus** the settlor's transfers in the seven years prior to the creation of the trust.

Exit charge after a principal charge

Use the rate that applied at the last tenth anniversary, reduced by multiplying by a fraction that reflects the time elapsed since the tenth anniversary. The fraction is x/40, where x is the number of complete quarters since the last tenth anniversary. If there has been a change in the nil band, the rate applied at the last tenth anniversary is recomputed using the new nil band.

Exam focus point

Although you must have an awareness of these exit and principal charges, you will not be expected to perform a computation in the exam.

3 Tax planning using trusts

FAST FORWARD

Trusts help preserve family wealth while maintaining flexibility over who should benefit. Use of a nil rate band discretionary will trust should be considered where there is a surviving spouse/civil partner.

3.1 Inheritance tax planning

Trusts are useful vehicles for non-tax reasons such as to preserve family wealth, to provide for those who are deemed to be incapable (minors, and the disabled) or unsuitable (due to youth or poor business sense) to hold assets directly.

3.2 Will trusts

A discretionary trust may be set up by will. The rate of inheritance tax on principal charges and exit charges within the trust will then depend on the settlor's cumulative transfers in the seven years before his death and the value of the trust property.

'Nil rate band' discretionary trust are commonly used in tax planning where there is a surviving spouse/civil partner. By including the spouse/civil partner as a beneficiary of the discretionary trust the deceased can ensure that the survivor is provided for financially without wasting the nil rate band. The amount passing into the trust is limited to any unused part of the nil rate band so that there is no IHT on death, the balance of the estate passing to the surviving spouse/civil partner. There will therefore be no IHT on any amounts advanced before the first ten year anniversary. IHT will only arise on the ten year anniversary and on later advances if the value of the trust property has increased by more than the nil rate band.

3.3 Lifetime trusts

Although gifts to trusts during lifetime can lead to an IHT charge (a CLT), there can be tax benefits from setting up trusts during the settlor's lifetime. As long as the cumulative total of CLTs in any seven year period does not exceed the nil rate band there will be no lifetime IHT to pay on creation of the trust. The trust will be subject to IHT at nil% on the ten year anniversary and later advances, unless the value of the trust property grows faster than the nil rate band.

The settlor can preserve the maximum flexibility in the class of beneficiaries and how income and capital should be dealt with.

If the settlor is included as a beneficiary of a discretionary trust the gift will be treated as a gift with reservation.

4 Scope of stamp duties

There are three distinct taxes which come under the description of stamp duties.

The oldest is stamp duty, which is a tax on written documents ('instruments'). Stamp duty now generally only applies to transactions in shares and securities which are effected by an instrument.

Stamp duty reserve tax is a special tax for transactions involving shares and securities where there is no written document. This prevents the avoidance of tax on paperless transfers.

Stamp duty land tax applies to land transactions. It replaced the stamp duty charge, and applies to all land transactions whether or not there is a written document.

5 Stamp duties on shares and securities

5.1 Stamp duty

FAST FORWARD

Stamp duty applies to share transactions.

Stamp duty applies to transfers of shares and securities transferred by a stock transfer form. It is payable by the purchaser.

Transfers of shares are charged to stamp duty at 0.5% of the consideration unless they fall within one of the specific exemptions. The duty is rounded up to the nearest £5.

The exemptions are primarily for transfers where is no consideration, such as:

- Gifts
- Changes in trustees
- Divorce arrangements
- Variation of wills

To qualify for the exemption the transfer document must state which exemption is being claimed. The categories of exemption are printed on the back of the stock transfer form.

5.2 Stamp duty reserve tax (SDRT)

FAST FORWARD

Stamp Duty Reserve Tax (SDRT) applies to paperless share transactions instead of Stamp Duty.

SDRT is not a stamp duty, but a separate tax with its own rules. It applies to agreements to transfer **chargeable securities for consideration in money or money's worth**.

SDRT is charged at **0.5% of the amount or value of the consideration for the sale**.

SDRT applies to the **agreement to transfer (whether oral or written)** and does not depend on the execution of the written instrument of transfer for a charge to arise. Thus, it applies to paperless Stock Exchange transactions and is collected automatically on such dealings.

The **tax charge arises on the date the agreement is made or becomes unconditional**.

6 Stamp duty land tax (SDLT)

6.1 Land transactions

Stamp Duty Land Tax (SDLT) applies to the sale of land, or of rights over land.

Stamp duty land tax applies to land transactions. A land transaction is a transfer of land or an interest in, or right over, land. **SDLT is generally payable as a percentage of the consideration paid for the land. It is payable by the purchaser.**

The following land transactions are exempt:

- A transfer for no chargeable consideration (except a gift to a connected company)
- A transfer on divorce, annulment of marriage or judicial separation
- Variations of a will or intestacy made within 2 years of death for no consideration
- Transfers to charities if the land is to be used for charitable purposes

If land is transferred to a company, for example on incorporation, SDLT is payable on the market value of land.

Exam focus point

The charge to stamp duty land tax on leases is outside the scope of your syllabus.

6.2 Rate of charge

The amount of the charge to SDLT depends on whether the land is residential or non-residential and whether or not it is in a designated disadvantaged area. The following rates apply:

Rate (%)	Non-disadvantaged area		Disadvantaged area
	Residential	Non-residential	Residential and non-residential
0	Up to £125,000	Up to £150,000	Up to £150,000
1	£125,001 – £250,000	£150,001 – £250,000	£150,001 – £250,000
3	£250,001 – £500,000	£250,001 – £500,000	£250,001 – £500,000
4	£500,001 +	£500,001+	£500,001+

Once the relevant rate of SDLT has been ascertained, it applies to the whole of the consideration, not just that above the band threshold.

6.3 Example

Beryl buys a house in a non-disadvantaged area for £300,000. Her stamp duty land tax is £300,000 × 3% = £9,000.

7 Exemptions and reliefs

7.1 Transfers with no consideration

Stamp duties are charged on the consideration passing under the document or transaction. If there is no chargeable consideration, there is no charge to tax.

If the consideration is not in money, the market value is used.

7.2 Company transactions

Relief from stamp duty and SDLT is given for transfers of assets between associated companies.

There are two conditions which must be met to attract the relief, namely that:

- the effect must be to transfer the **beneficial interest** in property from one body corporate to another, and

- those bodies corporate must be **associated** at the time of transfer, ie one must be the parent of the other or they must have a common parent.

(The term 'body corporate' includes foreign companies.)

For the 'associated companies' test, one company is regarded as the parent of another if it has:

- beneficial ownership of at least **75% of the ordinary share capital**, ie if all the issued share capital of a company, other than fixed rate preference shares, *and*

- a 75% interest in dividends and assets in a winding up, *and*

- there must not be 'arrangements' for a non-associated person to acquire control of the transferee.

It is necessary for there to be a **parent company**, ie two companies owned by the same *individual* are not 'associated' for stamp duty or SDLT purposes (even though they would be associated for corporation tax purposes). For indirect holdings, it is necessary to reduce the degree of ownership at each level to the appropriate fraction in determining whether the 75% test is met (as for group relief).

Question

Stamp duty relief

Allegri Ltd owns 90% of the ordinary share capital of Byrd Ltd, which in turn owns 85% of the ordinary share capital of Corelli Ltd.

Shares are transferred from Corelli Ltd to Allegri Ltd under an instrument executed on 1 June 2006.

Is stamp duty relief available?

Answer

Relief is available, since Allegri Ltd owns indirectly 76½ % (ie. 90% x 85%) of the ordinary share capital of Corelli Ltd.

SDLT relief is withdrawn where land has been transferred from one associated company to another and within three years of the transfer the purchaser company leaves the group whilst still owning the land. Note that the *vendor* company leaving the group does not cause the SDLT relief to be withdrawn as the land is still held within the group.

8 Administration of stamp duties

8.1 Stamp duty

Documents which are chargeable to stamp duty must be sent to HMRC (Stamp Taxes) with the duty payable. The document is then impressed with a duty stamp, usually in red, showing the duty paid and the date of payment.

To be certain that the correct amount of duty has been paid the taxpayer may request that the document be adjudicated, in which case HMRC will examine the underlying facts and determine the duty payable. This is most commonly used where the value of the consideration needs to be ascertained, and must be used in certain cases, such as for intra-group transfers

Documents must be presented for stamping within 30 days of execution. Interest runs from this date until the document is stamped, and a late filing penalty may be charged.

Unstamped documents are not admissible as evidence.

8.2 Stamp duty land tax

FAST FORWARD ⟩⟩ Stamp Duty Land Tax is collected under a self assessment system.

If a land transaction takes place which is not exempt a land transaction return must be filed within 30 days of the transaction. There are late filing penalties of £100 if the return is less than 3 months late, or £200 otherwise. HMRC can apply to the Commissioners for a daily penalty, and the penalty is tax geared if the return is over 12 months late.

Interest is charged on late paid tax.

The taxpayer may amend the return within 12 months of the filing date, and HMRC may amend the return to correct obvious errors within 9 months of the actual filing date.

HMRC may raise enquiries into the return within 9 months of the later of the due and actual filing dates. On completion of the enquiry they must issue a closure notice stating their conclusions and making any necessary amendments to the return.

If no return is filed HMRC may issue a determination of the tax due, and they have the power to raise a discovery assessment.

Land transactions cannot be registered with the Land Registry unless accompanied by a certificate from HMRC that duty has been paid or by a self-certificate from the taxpayer that no duty is due.

Chapter roundup

- A trust is an arrangement under which a person, the settlor, transfers property to another person, the trustee or trustees, who is required to deal with the trust property on behalf of certain specified persons, the beneficiaries.

- There is a CLT when a discretionary trust is set up. The trust suffers the IHT principal charge once every ten years and the exit charge when property leaves the trust.

- Trusts help preserve family wealth while maintaining flexibility over who should benefit. Use of a nil rate band discretionary will trust should be considered where there is a surviving spouse/civil partner.

- Stamp duty applies to share transactions.

- Stamp Duty Reserve Tax (SDRT) applies to paperless share transactions instead of Stamp Duty.

- Stamp Duty Land Tax (SDLT) applies to the sale of land, or of rights over land.

- Stamp Duty Land Tax is collected under a self assessment system.

Quick quiz

1   What is the IHT principal charge?

2   What are the IHT consequences of advancing capital from a discretionary trust to a beneficiary 20 months after the tenth anniversary?

3   When would you advise the use of a nil rate band discretionary trust on death?

4   At what rate is SDLT charged on the sale of land worth £600,000?

5   On what is stamp duty reserve tax charged?

6   What is the stamp duty on a share transfer form if the consideration for sale was £50,000?

Answers to quick quiz

1.   The principal charge is a charge on relevant property held in trust at each ten year anniversary of the trust.

2.   If capital is advanced from a discretionary trust there is an exit charge. This is calculated using the rate of tax that applied on the ten year anniversary × 6/40 as between 6 and 7 quarters have elapsed since then.

3.   A nil rate band discretionary trust may be used on the death of the first spouse/civil partner to ensure the deceased's nil rate band is not wasted. The remaining assets pass to the surviving spouse/civil partner.

4.   4%

5.   On agreements to transfer chargeable securities for consideration in money or money's worth.

6.   £50,000 × 0.5% = £250

Now try the question below from the Exam Question Bank

Number	Level	Marks	Time
Q20	Introductory	11	20 mins

Part C
Taxation of companies

Computing profits chargeable to corporation tax

Topic list	Syllabus reference
1 The scope of corporation tax	A2(a)C1
2 Profits chargeable to corporation tax	A2(a)C2,C5
3 Chargeable gains	A3(e)(ii)
4 Loan relationships	A2(c)(ii)
5 Intellectual property (intangible fixed assets)	A2(c)(iii)
6 Transfer pricing	A2(c)(iv)
7 Research and development	A2(c)(i),(f)
8 Personal service companies	A2(b)(vi)

Introduction

At this point in our studies we turn to corporation tax, covering the basic corporation tax rules in this chapter.

We start by looking at accounting periods, which are the periods for which companies pay corporation tax. We then see how to bring together all of a company's profits in a corporation tax computation and discuss the special rules for certain types of income and gains that apply to companies.

In the next chapter we will see how to work out the corporation tax payable.

Study guide

		Intellectual level
2	**Corporation tax liabilities in situations involving further overseas and group aspects and in relation to special types of company, and the application of additional exemptions and reliefs**	
(a)	The contents of the Paper F6 study guide, for corporation tax, under headings:	2
•	C1 The scope of corporation tax	
•	C2 Profits chargeable to corporation tax	
•	C5 The use of exemptions and reliefs in deferring and minimising corporation tax liabilities	
(b)	The scope of corporation tax:	3
(vi)	Identify personal service companies and advise on the tax consequences of services being provided via a personal service company	
(c)	Profits chargeable to corporation tax:	3
(i)	Identify qualifying research and development expenditure and determine the amount of relief by reference to the size of the individual company/group	
(iii)	Recognise the alternative tax treatments of intangible assets and conclude on the best treatment for a given company	
(iv)	Advise on the impact of the transfer pricing and thin capitalisation rules on companies	
(f)	The use of exemptions and reliefs in deferring and minimising corporation tax liabilities	
3	**Chargeable gains and capital gains tax liabilities in situations involving further overseas aspects and in relation to closely related persons and trusts together with the application of additional exemptions and reliefs**	
(e)	Gains and losses on the disposal of shares and securities:	3
(ii)	Determine the application of the substantial shareholdings exemption	

Exam guide

Although you are unlikely to get a question requiring a detailed computation of PCTCT you may be asked to comment on how certain types of income would be included in the computation where there are special rules, such as for loan relationships, intangible fixed assets and research and development expenditure. You may also be asked to discuss how the transfer pricing rules work. It is less likely that you will be examined in detail on the more straightforward adjustments to profits or the rules for capital allowances.

Knowledge brought forward from earlier studies

This chapter revises the scope of corporation tax and the basic computation of profits chargeable to corporation tax. It also expands on the treatment of loan relationships and transfer pricing and introduces three new topics: substantial shareholdings, intangible fixed assets and research and development.

1 The scope of corporation tax

1.1 Introduction

Companies pay corporation tax on their profits chargeable to corporation tax of each accounting period. The profits chargeable to corporation tax are income plus gains minus charges.

Corporation tax is paid by companies. It is charged on the profits (including chargeable gains) of each accounting period. Corporation tax is not charged on dividends received from UK resident companies (see below for exception).

A 'company' is any corporate body (limited or unlimited) or unincorporated association eg sports clubs.

1.2 The residence of companies

A company incorporated in the UK is resident in the UK. A company incorporated abroad is resident in the UK if its central management and control are exercised here.

1.3 Accounting periods

An accounting period cannot exceed twelve months in length. A long period of account must be split into two accounting periods, the first of which is twelve months long.

Corporation tax is chargeable in respect of accounting periods. It is important to understand the difference between an accounting period and a period of account. A period of account is any period for which a company prepares accounts; usually this will be 12 months in length but it may be longer or shorter than this. An accounting period starts when a company starts to trade, or otherwise becomes liable to corporation tax, or immediately after the previous accounting period finishes. An accounting period finishes on the earliest of:

- 12 months after its start
- The end of the company's period of account
- The commencement of the company's winding up or administration (see later in this Text)
- The company ceasing to be resident in the UK
- The company ceasing to be liable to corporation tax

In many cases the company will have a period of account of 12 months and an accounting period of 12 months. We will deal with long periods of account (exceeding 12 months) later in this chapter.

Companies' taxable profits are always computed for accounting periods, not tax years. There are no basis period rules, there is no personal allowance and there is no taper relief or annual exemption for capital gains.

2 Profits chargeable to corporation tax

The profits chargeable to corporate tax (PCTCT) are the total profits less charges on income.

2.1 The schedular system

The corporation tax computation draws together all of the company's income and gains from various sources. The income from each different type of source must be computed separately because different computational rules apply.

The corporation tax rules (with the exception of capital allowances) have not yet been rewritten under the Tax Law Rewrite project which has rewritten much of the income tax legislation. The various sources of income are technically still described using the old system of Schedules and Cases. Each type of income is defined in accordance with a Schedule. There are only two kinds of Schedule now relevant to corporation tax: Schedule D and Schedule A. Schedule D is subdivided into Cases.

Although this Text will use the more general descriptive terminology as used for income tax, a list of the relevant cases and schedules is given below for completeness.

- **Schedule D Case I**, equivalent to trading income under the income tax rules.

- **Schedule D Case III**, equivalent to interest income under the income tax rules.

- **Schedule D Case V**, equivalent to foreign income under the income tax rules.

- **Schedule D Case VI**, equivalent to miscellaneous income under the income tax rules, including any annual profits not falling under any other Schedule or Case, such as income from intangible fixed assets which are held as investments.

- **Schedule A**, equivalent to property income under the income tax rules.

The profits chargeable to corporation tax for an accounting period are derived as follows.

	£
Trading income	X
Interest income	X
Foreign income	X
Miscellaneous income	X
Property income	X
Chargeable gains	X
Total profits	X
Less charges on income (gross)	(X)
Profits chargeable to corporation tax (PCTCT) for an accounting period	X

Each of the above items is dealt with in further detail later in this Text.

Exam focus point

> It would be of great help if you could learn the above proforma. The calculation of profits chargeable to corporation tax may be required in an exam, so you must understand how different types of income and gains are dealt with. You will then be able to advise on the marginal tax effects of suggested courses of action.

2.2 Trading income

The trading income of companies is derived from the net profit figure in the accounts. The adjustments that need to be made to the accounts are broadly the same for companies as they are for income tax purposes even though the legislation has not been rewritten (see Chapter 6). Companies may also claim relief for the expenses of managing their investments (see Chapter 25). Where shares in UK companies are held as trading assets, and not as investments, any dividends on those shares will be treated for tax purposes as trading profits.

Charges are added back in the calculation of adjusted profit. They are treated instead as a deduction from total profits. **The only charge on income examinable is a charitable gift aid donation**.

Patent and copyright royalties are not charges on income for corporation tax. Royalties paid for trade purposes are deducted in computing trading profits on the same basis as they have been deducted in accounts.

Interest received on a trading loan relationship (see later in this chapter) is included within trading profits on an accruals basis. Similarly, interest paid on a trading loan relationship is deducted at arriving at trading profits.

Exam focus point

When adjusting profits as supplied in a profit and loss account confusion can arise as regards to whether the figures are net or gross. Properly drawn up company accounts should normally include all income gross. Charges should also be shown gross. However, some examination questions include items 'net'. Read the question carefully.

The calculation of capital allowances follows income tax principles. However, for companies, there is never any restriction of allowances to take account of any private use of an asset. The director or employee suffers a taxable benefit instead.

2.3 Property income

The taxation of UK property income follows similar rules to those for income tax (see earlier in this Text). In summary:

(a) All UK rental activities are treated as a single source of income calculated in the same way as trading profits.

(b) Capital allowances on plant and machinery (but not furniture) are taken into account when computing property income or losses.

However **there are certain differences for companies**:

(a) **Property income losses are first set off against other income and gains of the company for the current period and any excess is:**

(i) **Carried forward** as a property income loss of the following accounting period provided (except for investment companies) that the property letting business has not ceased, or

(ii) **Available for surrender as group relief** (see later in this Text).

(b) **Interest paid by a company on a loan to buy or improve property is not a property income expense. The loan relationship rules apply instead** (see later in this chapter).

(c) **There is no landlords energy saving allowance** for insulation and draught proofing.

2.4 Income received net of tax

Examples of income received net of tax are:

(a) Patent royalties where the payer is not a UK company: tax at 22%
(b) Annuities and annual payments are paid net of tax where the payer is not a UK company.

Patent royalties and annuities which relate to the trade are included in trading profits normally on an accruals basis. Patent royalties and annuities which do not relate to the trade are taxed as miscellaneous income.

Income which suffers a deduction of tax at source is included within the profits chargeable to corporation tax at its gross equivalent. For example £4,875 of patent royalties relating to the trade received net of tax would need to be grossed up by multiplying by 100/78 to include £6,250 within trading income. If tax suffered on income received net exceeds tax deducted from amounts paid net, the difference is subtracted in calculating the mainstream corporation tax due.

2.5 Interest income

UK companies normally receive interest gross. Interest relating to non-trading loan relationships is taxed separately as interest income on an accruals basis (see later in this chapter for the loan relationship rules).

2.6 Chargeable gains

Companies do not pay capital gains tax. Instead their chargeable gains are included in the profits chargeable to corporation tax. We look at the computations of a company's chargeable gains later in this chapter.

2.7 Unit trusts

If a company holds units in a unit trust, then in general it is in the same position as if it held shares in a company. Dividends from the trust are, like dividends on shares, not taxable income for a company. There are the following exceptions to this rule.

(a)   If more than 60% (by market value) of the unit trust's investments are interest-bearing investments, then the units are treated as a creditor loan relationship (see below) for the company. The amortised cost basis of accounting cannot be used; the fair value basis must be used instead and distributions out of the unit trust's interest income are treated as interest received.

(b)   In other cases, a proportion of a dividend paid by the unit trust is treated as interest. This is called the unfranked part of the distribution; it corresponds to the proportion of the unit trust's income which is not dividend income.

2.8 Charges on income

Having arrived at a company's total profits, charges on income are deducted to arrive at the profits chargeable to corporation tax (PCTCT). The only charge on income examinable is a **payment under the gift aid scheme.**

Almost all donations of money to charity qualify as charges on income under the gift aid scheme whether they are one off donations or are regular donations. **Gift aid donations are paid gross.**

A donation will not be a qualifying donation under the gift aid scheme if:

(a)   The company, persons connected with it, or persons connected with those connected persons, receive benefits from the charity, as a result of the donation worth more than:

Donation	Maximum benefit
< £100	25% of the total donations made in that accounting period
> £100 < £1,000	£25
> £1,000 < £10,000	2.5% of the total donations made in that accounting period
> £10,000	£250

(b)   The gift is subject to any condition of repayment.

Donations to charities which are incurred wholly and exclusively for the purposes of the trade are trading deductions instead of charges on income.

Corporation tax relief is also given for gifts of quoted shares or land or buildings made to a charity and for donations to non-UK charities of medical supplies and equipment for humanitarian purposes.

Question

The calculation of PCTCT

The following is a summary of the profit and loss account of A Ltd for the year to 31 March 2007.

	£	£
Gross profit on trading		180,000
Treasury stock interest (non-trading investment)		700
Dividends from UK companies (net)		3,600
Loan interest from UK company (non-trading investment)		4,000
Building society interest received (non-trading investment)		292
Less: trade expenses (all allowable)	62,000	
gift aid donation paid	1,100	
		(63,100)
		125,492

The capital allowances for the period total £5,500. There was also a capital gain of £13,867.

Compute the profits chargeable to corporation tax.

Answer

	£	£
Net profit per accounts		125,492
Less: Treasury stock interest	700	
dividends received	3,600	
building society interest	292	
loan interest received	4,000	
		(8,592)
		116,900
Add gift aid donation		1,100
		118,000
Less capital allowances		(5,500)
Trading income		112,500
Interest income £(700 + 292 + 4,000)		4,992
Chargeable gain		13,867
		131,359
Less charges: gift aid donation		(1,100)
Profits chargeable to corporation tax (PCTCT)		130,259

2.9 Long periods of account

If a company has a long period of account, exceeding 12 months, it is split into two accounting periods: the first 12 months and the remainder.

Where the period of account differs from the corporation tax accounting periods, profits are **allocated to the relevant periods** as follows:

- **Trading income** before capital allowances is apportioned on a **time basis**.
- **Capital allowances** and balancing charges are **calculated for each accounting period.**
- **Other income is allocated to the period to which it relates** (eg rents to the period when accrued). Miscellaneous income, however, is apportioned on a time basis.
- **Chargeable gains and losses** are allocated to the **period in which they are realised.**
- **Charges on income** are deducted in the accounting **period in which they are paid.**

Question

Xenon Ltd makes up an 18 month set of accounts to 30 June 2007 with the following results.

	£
Trading profits	180,000
Property income	
18 months @ £500 accruing per month	9,000
Capital gain (1 May 2007 disposal)	250,000
Less gift aid donation (paid 31.12.06)	(50,000)
	389,000

What are the profits chargeable to corporation tax for each of the accounting periods based on the above accounts?

Answer

The 18 month period of account is divided into:

Year ending 31 December 2006
6 months to 30 June 2007

Results are allocated:

	Y/e 31.12.06 £	6m to 30.6.07 £
Trading profits 12:6	120,000	60,000
Property Income		
12 × £500	6,000	
6 × £500		3,000
Capital gain (1.5.07)		250,000
Less charge on income (31.12.06)	(50,000)	
PCTCT (profits chargeable to corporation tax)	76,000	313,000

3 Chargeable gains

FAST FORWARD

Companies pay corporation tax on their capital gains. Indexation allowance is available until disposal. Chargeable gains arising on the disposal of substantial shareholdings are exempt.

3.1 Introduction

Companies do not pay capital gains tax. Instead their chargeable gains are included in the profits chargeable to corporation tax. A company's capital gains or allowable losses are computed in a similar way to individuals (see earlier in this Text) but with a few major differences:

(a) Indexation allowance calculations can include periods of ownership after 6 April 1998. **Indexation is calculated to the month of disposal of an asset.**

(b) **The FA 1985 pool for shares does not close at 5 April 1998; it runs to the month of disposal of the shares.** This means that different matching rules are needed (see below)

(c) **Taper relief does not apply**

(d) **No annual exemption is available**

Key term

All companies under common control are **connected persons** for chargeable gains purposes.

3.2 Shares and securities

For companies the matching of shares sold is in the following order.

1st   Shares acquired on the **same day**
2nd   Shares acquired in the **previous nine days**, taking earlier acquisitions first
3rd   Shares from the **FA 1985 pool**

Where shares are disposed of within nine days of acquisition, no indexation allowance is available even if the acquisition and disposal fall within different months. Acquisitions matched with disposals under the nine day rule never enter the FA 1985 pool.

Exam focus point

> The computation of the cost and indexed cost within the FA 1985 share pool are excluded from the syllabus. You must, however, understand that shares which are acquired by a company enter the FA 1985 pool unless they have been matched with shares disposed of on the same day or within the following 9 days.

The rules on alterations of share capital are similar to those for individuals. Bonus or rights issue shares will be added to the underlying holding from which the entitlement to the additional shares arose. In effect this means that the shares are included within the FA 1985 share pool, unless they have been matched with shares disposed of on the same day or within the following 9 days.

This rule about rights issue shares also applies to the shares acquired by way of scrip dividend (contrast the treatment of individuals where the scrip dividend shares are treated as a completely new acquisition).

The profit or loss on disposal of debentures and gilts are dealt with under the loan relationship rules and not as a chargeable gain or allowable capital loss (see below).

3.3 Disposal of substantial shareholdings

There is an exemption from corporation tax for any gain arising when a **trading company (or member of a trading group) disposes of the whole or any part of a substantial shareholding in another trading company** (or in the holding company of a trading group or sub-group).

Key term

> A **substantial shareholding** is one where the investing company holds 10% of ordinary share capital and is beneficially entitled to at least 10% of the
>
> (a)   profits available for distribution to equity holders, and
> (b)   assets of the company available for distribution to equity holders on a winding up.

To meet the 10% test shares owned by members of a chargeable gains group (see later in this Text) may be amalgamated. **The 10% test must have been met for a continuous twelve month period during the two years preceding the disposal.**

The exemption is given automatically and cannot be disclaimed. This means that as well as exempting gains, it denies relief for losses.

The exemption applies to the disposal of part of a substantial holding. This means that if A Ltd owns 10% of the ordinary share capital in B Ltd, and disposes of 1% of that share capital, any gain will be exempt. In addition, the disposal of the remaining 9% may result in an exempt gain.

3.4 Example: disposal of substantial shareholding

On 1.12.01 SD Ltd bought 20% of the shares in AM Ltd. The shareholding qualifies for the substantial shareholding exemption. During its accounting period to 31 March 2007, SD Ltd made the following disposals:

(a)   On 30 June 2006 it disposed of a 15% holding in AM Ltd.

(b)   On 30 December 2006 it disposed of the remaining 5% holding in AM Ltd.

Both of these shareholdings qualify for the substantial shareholdings exemption. Clearly the first disposal is of at least a 10% holding which was held for twelve months prior to disposal. The second disposal also qualifies despite being only a 5% holding, because SD Ltd owned a 10% holding throughout a twelve month period beginning in the two years prior to this second disposal.

Where there has been a qualifying share-for-share exchange, the holding period of the original shares is amalgamated with the holding period of the replacement shares in determining whether the '12 month' rule has been satisfied.

The company making the disposal must have been a trading company (or member of a qualifying group, which is essentially a group of trading companies) throughout the period:

(a)   beginning with the start of the latest 12 month period in relation to which the company disposing of the shares met the substantial shareholding requirement, and

(b)   ending with the time of disposal.

It must also be a trading company or member of a qualifying group immediately after the disposal.

4 Loan relationships

> **FAST FORWARD**
>
> A loan relationship arises when a company lends or borrows money. Trading loan relationships are dealt with as trading income. Non-trading loan relationships are dealt with as interest income.

4.1 Introduction

If a company borrows or lends money, including issuing or investing in debentures or buying gilts, it has a loan relationship. This can be a creditor relationship (where the company lends or invests money) or a debtor relationship (where the company borrows money or issues securities). The loan relationship rules apply to both revenue and capital items.

4.2 Trading loan relationships

If the company is a party to a **loan relationship for trade purposes, any debits, ie interest payable or other debt costs, charged through its accounts are allowed as a trading expense** and are therefore deductible in computing trading profits. For example, a company paying interest on a loan taken out to purchase plant and machinery, or a factory or office premises for use in the trade will be able to deduct the interest payable for tax purposes.

Similarly **if any credits, ie interest income or other debt returns, arise on a trading loan these are treated as a trading receipt and are taxable as part of trading profit**. This is not likely to arise unless the trade is one of money lending so will usually fall within the rules for non-trading loan relationships (below).

4.3 Non-trading loan relationships

If the company is a party to a **loan relationship for non-trade purposes, any debits and credits must be pooled.** For example, a company paying interest on a loan taken out to purchase an investment property will not be able to deduct the interest from trading profits for tax purposes. Instead this 'non-trade debit' must be netted off against 'non trade credits' such as bank interest.

A net credit (ie income) on the pool is chargeable as interest income. Relief is available if there is a net 'deficit' (ie loss) (see later in this Text).

4.4 Example: loan relationships

During its year ended 31 December 2006 Jello Ltd received bank interest of £13,500 and debenture interest from Wobble Ltd of £45,400. It also paid debenture interest of £40,000 to Shaker Ltd on a loan of £1,000,000. The debentures were issued to Shaker Ltd in May 2005 to raise £700,000 for the purchase of a factory to use in the trade and £250,000 for the purchase of an investment property. The balance was used as working capital. All figures are stated gross and are the amounts shown in the accounts.

The debenture interest payable to Shaker Ltd was used partly for trade purposes, and partly for non trade purposes and must be apportioned:

	£
Non-trade purposes 250,000 × £40,000/1,000,000	10,000
Trade purposes (700,000 + 50,000 (bal)) = 750,000 × 40,000/1,000,000	30,000
Non-trading loan relationship credit	40,000

The £30,000 of interest paid for trade purposes is deducted in the computation of trading profits.

The £10,000 of interest paid for non-trade purposes is deducted from non-trading interest received. The amount taxable as a non-trading loan relationship credit is:

	£
Bank interest (received gross)	13,500
Debenture interest receivable from Wobble Ltd	45,400
	58,900
Non-trade debenture interest paid to Shaker Ltd	(10,000)
Non-trading loan relationship credit	48,900

4.5 Accounting methods

Debits and credits must be brought into account using UK generally accepted accounting practice (UK GAAP) or International Accounting Standards (IAS). Under UK GAAP this will generally be either:

    (a)   The amortised cost basis of accounting, or

    (b)   The fair value basis.

Under the amortised cost basis the cost of the asset or liability must be included in the accounts at cost less cumulative amortisation. The debit or credit brought into account will be the amortisation for the period, together with any interest for the period. This method is effectively the accruals basis, and is used in this Text.

Under the fair value basis the cost of the asset or liability must be included in the accounts at its fair value. The debit or credit brought into account will be the change in value for the period, together with any interest for the period. This method is commonly only used by companies in the financial sector, such as banks.

If the company changes its basis of accounting, any change in value of the loan relationship from the end of the previous period to the start of the current period must be brought into account. This applies especially if there is a change in accounting basis on moving from UK GAAP to IAS or vice versa.

If neither UK GAAP nor IAS are used, the debits and credits must be recalculated using a 'correct' method.

4.6 Incidental costs of loan finance

Under the loan relationship rules expenses ('debits') are allowed if incurred directly:

    (a)   Bringing a loan relationship into existence

    (b)   Entering into or giving effect to any related transactions

    (c)   Making payment under a loan relationship or related transactions, or

    (d)   Taking steps to ensure the receipt of payments under the loan relationship or related transaction.

A related transaction means 'any disposal or acquisition (in whole or in part) of rights or liabilities under the relationship, including any arising from a security issue in relation to the money debt in question'.

The above categories of incidental costs are also allowable even if the company does not enter into the loan relationship (ie abortive costs). Cost directly incurred in varying the terms of a loan relationship are also allowed.

4.7 Other matters

It is not only the interest costs of borrowing that are allowable or taxable. The capital costs are treated similarly. Thus if a company issues a loan at a discount and repays it eventually at par, the capital cost is allowed over the life of the loan.

Relief for pre-trading expenditure extends to expenses incurred on trading loan relationships in accounting periods ending within seven years of the company starting to trade. An expense that would have been a trading debit if it was incurred after the trade had commenced, is treated as a trading debit of the first trading period. An election has to be made within two years of the end of the first trading period.

Payments of interest between UK companies are paid gross. Short interest or interest to a UK bank is payable gross while 'yearly' interest is payable net of 20% tax if not paid to a corporate recipient.

Interest charged on underpaid tax is deductible and interest received on overpaid tax is assessable under the loan relationship rules as interest income.

5 Intellectual property (intangible fixed assets)

FAST FORWARD

> Gains/losses arising on intangible assets are recognised for tax purposes on the same basis as they are recognised in the accounts. Intangible assets that are not amortised in the accounts, or are amortised very slowly, may be written off for tax purposes at the rate of 4% per annum.

5.1 Definition and treatment

Any income or expenditure (including depreciation or amortisation) associated with:

    (a)   intellectual property (including patents and copyrights)
    (b)   goodwill
    (c)   other intangible assets (including agricultural quotas and brands)

is, in general, taxable/deductible as trading income. Provided the accounts have been prepared using generally accepted accounting practice, no adjustment will be needed to net profits for tax purposes.

Exam focus point

Exam questions in this area will normally cover goodwill and/or patents.

All debits/credits relating to intellectual property are brought in/deducted either as:

(a)   trading income, if the asset is used for trade purposes, or

(b)   as income from property if the asset is used for a property letting business, or

(c)   as miscellaneous income.

As for loan relationships, the rules apply to capital debits and credits as well as revenue items. Thus amounts relating to disposals are also dealt with in the profit and loss account. **An election may be made to disallow amortisation and instead write off the cost of a capitalised intangible asset for tax purposes at the rate of 4% per annum** (pro-rated for short accounting periods). The election is irrevocable and must be made within two years of the end of the accounting period of acquisition. The 4% relief is available for expenditure on the creation or enhancement of capital assets as well as on the cost of acquisition. The election may be beneficial if an asset is not amortised in the accounts (or only over a very long time).

5.2 Example: intangible fixed assets

During its six month accounting period to 31 March 2007, Dex Ltd purchased goodwill for £400,000. The goodwill is capitalised in the balance sheet and not amortised.

In the six month period to 31.3.07

$6/12 \times 4\% \times £400,000 = £8,000$

may be deducted from trading profits for tax purposes provided an election to do so is made by 31.3.09.

When the asset is disposed of sale proceeds are compared with the tax written down value (this will be cost less amounts amortised or the 4% straight line write off claimed) and the gain/loss is included within trading profits. For example, if the goodwill in the above example was sold in the year to 31.3.08 for £420,000, the amount taxable as part of trading profits would be

£420,000 − (£400,000 − £8,000) = £28,000.

5.3 Rollover relief

The capital gains tax rollover relief rules do not apply to goodwill and other intangible fixed assets for companies. However, if an intangible asset is sold for more than its original cost and other intangible assets are acquired in the period commencing one year before and ending three years after the sale, a form of rollover relief can be claimed.

Where full reinvestment takes place the relief is the excess of proceeds over original cost. Where the amount reinvested is less than the proceeds received the relief is restricted to the amount by which the reinvestment exceeds the cost of the asset.

A claim for relief must specify the 'old' asset, the amount of relief claimed and the amount of expenditure on the new asset.

5.4 Example: rollover relief for fixed intangible assets

On 1.1.07 Gateway Ltd sold goodwill which originally cost £400,000, for £500,000. The tax and accounting written down value of the goodwill was £360,000. New goodwill was purchased for £550,000 on 31.3.07.

The gain in the P&L account is £(500,000 − 360,000) = £140,000.

£100,000 (£500,000 − £400,000) of the gain on the sale of the 'old' goodwill can be deducted from trading profits. The remaining £40,000 will remain within the trading profits. £450,000 (£550,000 − £100,000) is the cost of the new goodwill for the purpose of computing any future tax deductions.

If only £450,000 had been reinvested the relief would be restricted to £50,000.

5.5 Accounting methods

Debits and credits for intangible fixed assets must be calculated using generally accepted accounting practice, and if the accounts do not comply the debits and credits must be recalculated using the correct basis. Most accounts will be prepared using the accruals basis, and this has been followed in this Text. The accounts may be prepared using either UK generally accepted accounting practice (UK GAAP) or International Accounting Standards (IAS).

If the company changes its basis of accounting, any change in value of intangible fixed assets from the end of the previous period to the start of the current period must be brought into account. This applies especially if there is a change in accounting basis on moving from UK GAAP to IAS or vice versa.

6 Transfer pricing

> The transfer pricing legislation prevents manipulation of profits between members of a group which can occur when a company chooses to buy and sell goods at a price which is not a market price.

6.1 General rules

Companies under common control can structure their transactions in such a way that they can shift profit (or losses) from one company to another. For example consider a company which wishes to sell goods valued at £20,000 to an independent third party.

| Selling company | ——— Goods invoice value: £20,000 ———→ | Buying company |

In this case all the profit on the sale arises to the selling company. Alternatively the sale could be rearranged:

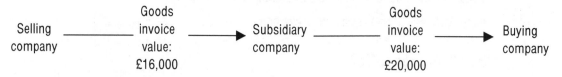

In this case £4,000 of the profit has been diverted to the subsidiary.

This technique could be used to direct profits to a company with a lower tax rate, or where they can be sheltered by losses brought forward, or even to an overseas company paying tax at a lower rate. This is a 'tax advantage' and there is **anti avoidance legislation** which **requires the profit to be computed as if the transactions had been carried out at arm's length and not at the prices actually used.**

The transfer pricing rules apply to transactions between two persons if either:

(a)   one person directly or indirectly participates in the management, control or capital of the other, or

(b)   a third party directly or indirectly participates in the management, control or capital of both.

6.2 Exemption for small and medium sized enterprises

Small and medium-sized enterprises (SMEs) are normally exempt from the transfer pricing requirements.

The definition of SMEs for the purposes of the transfer pricing rules are that the number of staff must be less than, and either the turnover or the balance sheet total not more than, the limits in the table below:

	Staff	Turnover	Balance Sheet
Small	50	€10M (£7m)	€43M (£30m)
Medium	250	€50M (£35m)	€10M (£7m)

The exemption does not apply to transactions with parties which are resident in a non-qualifying territory. This includes most foreign countries which do not have a double tax treaty with the UK, and certain other designated countries.

HMRC may direct that a medium sized enterprise should be brought within the scope of the legislation.

6.3 Transactions affected

The rules apply to all types of transactions. This includes not only the simple cases of sales of goods or provision of services, but also **loans**. A transfer pricing adjustment may be required if the loan would not have been made between the companies had there not been a relationship between them, or if a different amount would have been lent, or if the interest rate would have been different. Thus an adjustment to the interest charged in the accounts would be needed if the loan was sufficiently large that in an arm's length situation the lending company would have required equity, ie shares, instead of the loan. This situation is referred to as '**thin capitalisation**'.

6.4 Tax implications

Companies must self-assess their liability to tax under the transfer pricing rules and pay any corporation tax due. A statutory procedure exists for advance pricing arrangements (APAs) whereby a company can agree in advance that its transfer pricing policy is acceptable to HMRC ie not requiring a self-assessment adjustment. The APA facility is voluntary but companies may feel the need to use the facility as it provides necessary advance confirmation that their approach to transfer pricing in their self-assessment is acceptable.

7 Research and development

FAST FORWARD

> SMEs can obtain 150% relief for qualifying research and development expenditure and large companies may obtain 125% relief.

7.1 General rules

The general rule is that **research and development may be deducted as allowable expenditure if it is related to the trade.** 'Research and development' covers any activities that would be described as such under generally accepted accounting practice.

Research and development is related to the trade if it will lead to an extension of the trade, or is directed towards the medical welfare of workers employed in the trade. It does not cover expenditure incurred on acquiring rights arising from research and development, and only covers expenses of a revenue nature.

7.2 R&D relief: SMEs

A **small or medium sized enterprise** which incurs research and development expenditure of a specific nature may claim R&D tax relief.

The definition of an SME for R&D purposes is the same as for the transfer pricing rules (see above). It must not be owned as to 25% or more by a non-SME.

The company must spend **at least £10,000** on qualifying research and development expenditure related to its own trade in the accounting period. The limit is scaled down for short accounting periods. Research and development expenditure which **qualifies for the relief** is revenue expenditure on:

(a)   **staff costs**, ie salaries but not benefits, pension contributions and employer's Class 1 NICs

(b)   **software and consumable items**, including fuel, power and water

(c)   subcontracted expenditure of the same nature, and

(d)   expenditure on externally related workers. Unless the workers are provided by a connected company this is limited to 65% of the amounts paid in respect of these workers.

R&D relief for SMEs is given by allowing the company to claim 150% of the expenditure as a deduction instead of the actual cost.

7.3 R&D tax credits

If a company that qualifies for 150% R&D relief makes a trading loss it may claim a tax credit which will entitle it to an immediate repayment. The credit is 16% of the lower of the trading loss or 150% of qualifying R&D expenditure. The trading loss eligible for relief under the normal rules (see later in this Text) is reduced accordingly. The credit is also restricted to the amount of PAYE and NICs payable by the company for the accounting period.

7.4 R&D relief: large companies

A large company, ie one which is not an SME, that incurs research and development expenditure of a specific nature may claim a less generous R&D tax relief.

The company must spend **at least £10,000** on qualifying research and development expenditure related to its own trade in the accounting period. The limit is scaled down for short accounting periods. Research and development expenditure which **qualifies for the relief** is revenue expenditure on:

(a)   **staff costs, software and consumable items, and** expenditure on externally related workers in connection with its own research or with research subcontracted to the company by a large company or non-trading organisation

(b)   expenditure of the same nature **subcontracted** by the company to a research organisation, an individual or a partnership of individuals.

R&D relief for large companies is given by allowing the company to claim 125% of the expenditure as a deduction instead of the actual cost.

SMEs may claim this 125% relief on expenditure contracted to it by a large company.

8 Personal service companies

If a worker provides his services through a company special rules apply to deem a salary payment to have been made to the worker at the end of the tax year, resulting in an employment income charge. This was fully discussed earlier in this Text.

The income received by the company from contracts caught by these rules is taxable in the usual way, with a deduction being allowed as normal for expenses. **A deduction is also allowed for the amount of any deemed salary payment (and related employer's Class 1 NICs).** The deduction is given **in the accounting period in which the date of the deemed payment (normally 5 April) occurs**. For this reason an accounting date shortly after the end of the tax year should be chosen; if a 31 March year end is used relief for any deemed salary payment for the year to 31 March will not be given until the following year.

Where the actual expenses of the company exceed the automatic 5% deduction allowed (since only 95% of the income is chargeable), the deduction of the deemed salary payment may generate a trading loss. Although this can be relieved under the normal rules (see later in this Text), this situation may continue year after year, effectively denying any tax relief for the loss.

Chapter roundup

- Companies pay corporation tax on their profits chargeable to corporation tax of each accounting period. The profits chargeable to corporation tax are income plus gains minus charges.

- An accounting period cannot exceed twelve months in length. A long period of account must be split into two accounting periods, the first of which is twelve months long

- The profits chargeable to corporate tax (PCTCT) are the total profits less charges on income

- Companies pay corporation tax on their capital gains. Indexation allowance is available until disposal. Chargeable gains arising on the disposal of substantial shareholdings are exempt.

- A loan relationship arises when a company lends or borrows money. Trading loan relationships are dealt with as trading income. Non-trading loan relationships are dealt with as interest income.

- Gains/losses arising on intangible assets are recognised for tax purposes on the same basis as they are recognised in the accounts. Intangible assets that are not amortised in the accounts, or are amortised very slowly, may be written off for tax purposes at the rate of 4% per annum.

- The transfer pricing legislation prevents manipulation of profits between members of a group which can occur when a company chooses to buy and sell goods at a price which is not a market price.

- SMEs can obtain 150% relief for qualifying research and development expenditure and large companies may obtain 125% relief.

Quick quiz

1   When does an accounting period end?

2   How are trading profits (before capital allowances) of a long period of account divided between accounting periods?

3   Does a company pay debenture interest to another UK company gross or net of tax?

4   Any gain arising on the disposal of a 'substantial shareholding' is exempt from corporation tax. Define a substantial shareholding for these purposes.

5   Co Ltd has a long standing 15% holding in Jo Ltd, an investment company. If Co Ltd sells its holding will this disposal fall into the 'substantial shareholding' provisions?

6   How is interest arising on a non-trading loan relationship taxed?

7   What steps can be taken against the use of artificial transfer prices?

Answers to quick quiz

1   An accounting period ends on the earliest of:

    (a)   12 months after its start

    (b)   the end of the company's period of account

    (c)   the commencement of the company's winding up

    (d)   the company ceasing to be resident in the UK

    (e)   the company ceasing to be liable to corporation tax

2   Trading income (before capital allowances) is apportioned on a time basis.

3   Gross.

4   Broadly, a substantial shareholding is one where the investing company holds 10% of the ordinary share capital concerned.

5   No, although a 15% holding is a 10% or more holding Jo Ltd is not a trading company.

6   Interest on a non-trading loan relationship is aggregated with all other income and gains from non-trading loans. From this is deducted interest paid on and losses on non-trading loans. The resulting net amount is taxed as interest income.

7   Although a company may buy and sell goods at any price it wishes, the transfer pricing anti-avoidance legislation requires profit to be computed as if the transactions had been carried out at arm's length, in certain circumstances

Now try the question below from the Exam Question Bank

Number	Level	Marks	Time
Q21	Introductory	15	27 mins

Computing corporation tax payable

Topic list	Syllabus reference
1 Charge to corporation tax	A2(a)C3
2 The corporate venturing scheme	A2(d)(i)
3 Returns, records, enquiries, assessments and claims	A6(c)
4 Payment of corporation tax and interest	A6(c)

Introduction

In the last chapter we saw how to compute profits chargeable to corporation tax.

In this chapter we look at how to calculate the corporation tax payable on the profits chargeable to corporation tax. We look at the effect of short accounting periods and associated companies on the rate of corporation tax payable. We also consider the relief available for investments under the corporate venturing scheme.

Finally we look at the administration of corporation tax.

In the next chapter we will consider the rules for winding up companies and for companies purchasing their own shares.

Study guide

		Intellectual level
2	**Corporation tax liabilities in situations involving further overseas and group aspects and in relation to special types of company, and the application of additional exemptions and reliefs**	
(a)	The contents of the Paper F6 study guide, for corporation tax, under headings:	2
•	C3 The comprehensive computation of corporation tax liability	
(d)	The comprehensive calculation of corporation tax liability:	3
(i)	Advise on the application of the corporate venturing scheme	
6	**National insurance, value added tax and tax administration:**	
(c)	The contents of the Paper F6 study guide for the obligations of taxpayers and/or their agents under headings:	
•	G1 The systems for self assessment and the making of returns	
•	G2 The time limits for the submission of information, claims and payment of tax, including payments on account	
•	G3 The procedures relating to enquiries appeals and disputes	
•	G4 Penalties for non-compliance	

Exam guide

Although you are unlikely simply to be asked to calculate the corporation tax payable for an accounting period you are very likely to have to be able to work out marginal tax rates when giving advice about using losses, new projects, etc. It is therefore very important to know the rules for small companies' rate and marginal relief, and how the limits are affected by the length of the accounting period and the number of associated companies. The corporate venturing scheme is a useful relief for investing companies. You must know the rules regarding administration as the company's obligations could form a part of any question.

Knowledge brought forward from earlier studies

This chapter revises the computation of corporation tax payable that you will have studied previously. The rules for administration are also revision. The corporate venturing scheme is new.

1 Charge to corporation tax

FAST FORWARD

A company pays corporation tax on its profits chargeable to corporation tax (PCTCT).

1.1 'Profits'

FAST FORWARD

'Profits' is PCTCT plus franked investment income (FII).

Although we tax PCTCT another figure needs to be calculated ('profits') to determine the rate of corporation tax to use to tax PCTCT.

'Profits' means profits chargeable to corporation tax plus the grossed-up amount of dividends received from UK companies other than those in the same group. The grossed-up amount of UK dividends is the dividend received multiplied by 100/90. This is because dividends are treated as paid net of a 10% tax credit (see earlier in this Text). You may see the grossed up amount of dividend received referred to as **franked investment income (FII)**.

Do not include overseas dividends in the computation of FII. These will have been included as foreign income when calculating PCTCT (see later in this Text).

Exam focus point

Be careful to charge corporation tax on PCTCT, not on profits.

1.2 Financial years

FAST FORWARD

Tax rates are set for financial years.

The rates of corporation tax are fixed for financial years.

A financial year runs from 1 April to the following 31 March and is identified by the calendar year in which it begins. For example, the year ended 31 March 2007 is the Financial Year 2006 (FY 2006). This should not be confused with a tax year, which runs from 6 April to the following 5 April.

1.3 The full rate

FAST FORWARD

Companies are taxed at either the starting rate, the small companies' rate or receive marginal relief, depending on their 'profits'.

The full rate of corporation tax is 30% for FY 2006, and applies to companies with 'profits' of £1,500,000 or more, having remained unchanged since FY 1999. A company with PCTCT of, say, £2 million, will pay £600,000 corporation tax.

1.4 The small companies' rate (SCR)

The SCR of corporation tax of 19% for FY 2006 (unchanged since FY 2002) applies to the profits chargeable to corporation tax of UK resident companies whose 'profits' are not more than £300,000. In FY 2005 and prior years the SCR applied where 'profits' were more than £50,000 but not more than £300,000.

Question
The small companies' rate

B Ltd had the following results for the year ended 31 March 2007.

	£
Trading profits	42,000
Dividend received 1 May 2006	9,000

Compute the corporation tax payable.

Answer

	£
Trading profits	42,000
Dividend plus tax credit £9,000 × 100/90	10,000
'Profits' (between £50,000 and £300,000 limit)	52,000
Corporation tax payable	
£42,000 × 19%	£7,980

1.5 Marginal relief

Small companies' marginal relief applies where the 'profits' of an accounting period of a UK resident company are over £300,000 but under £1,500,000. We first calculate the corporation tax at the full rate and then deduct:

(M – P) × I/P × marginal relief fraction

where M = upper limit (currently £1,500,000)
P = 'profits' (see above Paragraph)
I = PCTCT

The marginal relief fraction is 11/400 for FY 2006 (unchanged since FY 2002).

You will be given this formula in the rates and allowances section of the exam paper.

Question	Small companies' marginal relief

Lenox Ltd has the following results for the year ended 31 March 2007.

	£
PCTCT	296,000
Dividend received 1 December 2006	12,600

Calculate the corporation tax liability.

Answer

	£
PCTCT	296,000
Dividend plus tax credit £12,600 × 100/90	14,000
'Profits'	310,000

'Profits' are above £300,000 but below £1,500,000, so marginal relief applies.

	£
Corporation tax on PCTCT £296,000 × 30%	88,800
Less small companies' marginal relief	
£(1,500,000 – 310,000) × 296,000/310,000 × 11/400	(31,247)
	57,553

FAST FORWARD

The marginal rate of corporation tax between the small companies' limits is 32.75%. The marginal tax rate is an effective rate; it is never actually used in working out corporation tax.

In exam questions you often need to be aware that there is a **marginal rate of 32.75 %** which applies to any PCTCT that lies in between the small companies' limits.

This is calculated as follows:

	£				£
Upper limit	1,500,000	@	30%		450,000
Lower limit	(300,000)	@	19%		(57,000)
Difference	1,200,000				393,000

$$\frac{393,000}{1,200,000} = 32.75\%$$

Effectively the band of profits (here £1,200,000) falling between the upper and lower limits are taxed at a rate of 32.75%

1.6 Example: effective marginal rate of tax

A Ltd has PCTCT of £350,000 for the year ended 31 March 2007. Its corporation tax liability is

	£
£350,000 × 30%	105,000
Less small companies' marginal relief	
11/400 (1,500,000 – 350,000)	(31,625)
	73,375

This is the same as calculating tax at 19% × £300,000 + 32.75% × £50,000 = £57,000 + £16,375 = £73,375.

Consequently tax is charged at an effective rate of 32.75% on PCTCT that exceeds the small companies' lower limit.

Note that although there is an effective corporation tax charge of 32.75%, this rate of tax is never used in actually calculating corporation tax. The rate is just an effective marginal rate that you must be aware of. It is particularly important when considering loss relief and group relief (see later in this Text).

1.7 The starting rate (FY 2005 and earlier)

FAST FORWARD

A starting rate of corporation tax applied from FY02 to FY05. A starting rate marginal rate of 23.75% also applied.

A starting rate of corporation tax of 0% applied to companies with 'profits' of up to £10,000 for FY 2002 to FY 2005.

Companies with 'profits' in the starting rate band could be subject to extra tax if they made distributions to non corporate shareholders.

Exam focus point

You will not be examined on the effect on a company's corporation tax liability of dividends paid to non-corporate shareholders.

Question

The starting rate of corporation tax

Dexter Limited had the following income for the year ended 31 March 2006.

(a)   Trading profits of £9,500, and
(b)   Franked investment income of £300.

Calculate the corporation tax liability for the year. Assume all profits are retained in the company.

Answer

	£
Trading profits	9,500
Franked investment income	300
'Profits'	9,800
Corporation tax on PCTCT £9,500 × 0%	£nil

For companies with 'profits' between £10,001 and £50,000, the small companies' rate less a starting rate marginal relief applied. The formula for calculating this marginal relief is the same as that given above except that 'M' is the upper limit for starting rate purposes, (£50,000). **However the fraction used here is 19/400.** The small companies' rate only applied in full when 'profits' exceeded £50,000.

Starting rate marginal relief

Armstrong Ltd had the following income for its year ended 31 March 2006:

		£
(a)	Trading profits	29,500
(b)	Franked investment income	3,000

Calculate the corporation tax liability, if all profits are retained in the company for future use in the business.

Answer

	£
Trading profits	29,500
Franked investment income	3,000
Profits	32,500

	£
Corporation tax at small companies' rate:	
£29,500 × 19%	5,605
Less starting rate marginal relief	
19/400 × ((£50,000 – £32,500) × £29,500/£32,500)	(755)
Corporation tax payable	4,850

The effective marginal rate of tax when PCTCT fell between the starting rate limits was 23.75%. Again, this is an effective marginal rate of tax that you need to be aware of but it is a rate that is never actually used in working out the CT charge. It was calculated as:

	£				£
Upper limit	50,000	@	19%		9,500
Lower limit	(10,000)	@	0%		Nil
Difference	40,000				9,500

$$\frac{9,500}{40,000} = 23.75\ \%$$

PCTCT falling into the band (here £40,000) suffered tax at an effective rate of 23.75%.

1.8 Changes in the rate – accounting periods straddling 31 March

If there is a change in the corporation tax rate, and a company's accounting period does not fall entirely within one financial year, the profits of the accounting period are apportioned to the two financial years on a time basis. Note that the profits as a whole are apportioned. We do not look at components of the profit individually, unlike apportionment of profits of a long period of account to two accounting periods.

The 'profits' falling into each financial year determines the rate of corporation tax that applies to the PCTCT of that year. This could be the full rate, the small companies' rate or, before FY 2006, the starting rate.

Frances Ltd makes up accounts to 31 December each year. For the year ended 31 December 2006 its profit and loss account was as follows.

	£
PCTCT	40,000
Dividends plus tax credits	2,500
'Profits'	42,500

Calculate the corporation tax liability for the year.

Answer

	FY 2005 3 months to 31 March 2006 £	FY 2006 9 months to 31 December 2006 £
PCTCT (divided 3:9)	10,000	30,000
'Profits' (divided 3:9)	10,625	31,875
FY 2005 (W): £10,000 × 19%	1,900	
Less starting rate marginal relief		
19/400 × £(12,500 − 10,625) × 10,000/10,625	(84)	
	1,816	
FY 2006: £30,000 × 19%		5,700
Corporation tax payable (£1,816 + £5,700)		7,516
Working		
Corporation tax limits		
Lower limit for starting rate		
FY 2005 £10,000 × $^{3}/_{12}$	2,500	
FY 2006 N/A		
Upper limit for starting rate		
FY 2005 £50,000 × $^{3}/_{12}$	12,500	
FY 2006 N/A		
Lower limit for small companies' rate		
FY 2005 N/A		
FY 2006 £300,000 × $^{3}/_{12}$		225,000

1.9 Associated companies and short accounting periods

The upper and lower limits which are used to be determine tax rates are divided by the number of associated companies and may also need to be pro-rated on a time basis if an accounting period lasts for less than 12 months.

Key term

The expression **'associated companies'** in tax has no connection with financial accounting. For tax purposes a company is associated with another company if either controls the other or if both are under the control of the same person or persons (individuals, partnerships or companies). Whether such a company is UK resident or not is irrelevant (even though non-UK resident companies cannot benefit from the starting rate, small companies' rate or from marginal relief). Control is given by holding over 50% of the share capital or the voting power or being entitled to over 50% of the distributable income or of the net assets in a winding up.

If a company has one or more 'associated companies', then the profit limits for starting rate and small companies' rate purposes are divided by the number of associated companies + 1 (for the company itself).

Companies which have only been associated for part of an accounting period are deemed to have been associated for the whole period for the purpose of determining the profit limits.

An associated company is ignored for these purposes if it is dormant ie has not carried on any trade or business at any time in the accounting period (or the part of the period during which it was associated). A holding company counts as not carrying on any trade or business so long as:

- Its only assets are shares in subsidiaries

- It is not entitled to deduct any outgoings as charges or management expenses, and

- Its only profits are dividends from subsidiaries, which are distributed in full to its shareholders.

The profit limits are reduced proportionately if an accounting period lasts for less than 12 months.

Question   Associated companies and short accounting periods

For the nine months to 31 January 2007 a company with two other associated companies had PCTCT of £78,000 and no dividends paid for or received. Compute the corporation tax payable.

Answer

(a) Reduction in the upper limit for SCR

Multiply by 1/(number of associated companies + 1) = $^1/_3$

Then multiply by number of months in AP/12 = $^9/_{12}$

£1,500,000 × $^1/_3$ × $^9/_{12}$ = £375,000

(b) Reduction in the lower limit for SCR

£300,000 × $^1/_3$ × $^9/_{12}$ = £75,000

(c) 'Profits' = £78,000

As 'profits' fall between the lower and upper limits for SCR purposes, the full rate less small companies' marginal relief applies:

(d) Corporation tax

	£
£78,000 × 30%	23,400
Less small companies' marginal relief £(375,000 − 78,000) × 11/400	(8,168)
Corporation tax	15,232

2 The corporate venturing scheme

FAST FORWARD

Companies can obtain tax relief on certain investments they make under the Corporate Venturing Scheme (CVS).

2.1 Introduction

The corporate venturing scheme (CVS) allows an investing company to obtain corporation tax relief at 20% on amounts invested in ordinary shares held for at least 3 years.

The investment must be in new ordinary shares of an unquoted 'small high risk trading company'. As long as the small company is unquoted at the time the shares are issued and there are no arrangements in place (or planned) at that time for seeking a listing, relief will not be withdrawn if the company subsequently becomes quoted during the three year period for which the shares must be held.

The investing company can defer any chargeable gains made on corporate venturing investments that it reinvests in another shareholding under the scheme.

Any capital loss (net of corporation tax relief) arising on a disposal of the shares can be set against the company's income.

Tax relief is withdrawn if the shares are not held for three years.

A corporate venturer cannot obtain tax relief under the scheme if it controls the small company in which it has invested.

2.2 The investing company

The investing company must either be:

    (a)   A trading company which is neither engaged in a financial trade nor a member of a group whose business consists of financial trades or non-trading activities, or

    (b)   An investment company which is a member of a non-financial trading group.

The investing company must not hold more than 30% of the:

    (a)   Ordinary share capital, or
    (b)   The combined share and loan capital which can be converted into ordinary share capital

of the company in which the investment is made (the issuing company).

2.3 The issuing company

The issuing company must not have gross assets of more than £7 million before the investment and not more than £8 million immediately after it.

For a period of three years from the later of the issue of shares and the start of trading:

    (a)   The issuing company must carry on a qualifying trade or be a parent company whose business does not consist to a substantial extent of excluded activities and which has at least one group member carrying on a qualifying trade. If the issuing company is a parent company, each of the other group members (other than property companies) must be at least 51% owned by the company or another of its subsidiaries. If the subsidiary holds and manages property, it must be at least 90% owned by the company or another of it's subsidiaries.

    (b)   The issuing company must not be under the control of any other company.

415

(c) The issuing company must not be involved in a partnership or joint venture with another company which is owned by the same person as owns the issuing company.

(d) At least 20% of the issuing company's ordinary share capital must be owned by individuals who are not employees or directors of the investing company.

2.4 Qualifying trade

A trade must be carried on on a commercial basis and must not consist to a substantial extent of certain excluded activities.

Research and development which is intended to lead to or benefit a qualifying trade is treated as a qualifying trade.

2.5 Anti-avoidance rules

There are extensive anti-avoidance rules designed to ensure that money invested is genuinely put at risk.

2.6 Clearance

The issuing company can apply for advance clearance from HMRC that an issue will meet the qualifying conditions.

3 Returns, records, enquiries, assessments and claims

3.1 Notification to HMRC

FAST FORWARD

A company must notify HMRC within 3 months of starting to trade.

A company must notify HMRC of the beginning of its first accounting period (ie usually when it starts to trade) and the beginning of any subsequent period that does not immediately follow the end of a previous accounting period. The notice must be in the prescribed form and submitted within three months of the relevant date.

3.2 Returns

FAST FORWARD

CT 600 returns must usually be filed within twelve months of the end of an accounting period.

A company's tax return (CT 600) must include a self assessment of any tax payable.

An obligation to file a return arises only when the company receives a notice requiring a return. A return is required for each accounting period ending during or at the end of the period specified in the notice requiring a return. A company also has to file a return for certain other periods which are not accounting periods (eg for a period when the company is dormant).

A company that does not receive a notice requiring a return must, if it is chargeable to tax, **notify HMRC within twelve months of the end of the accounting period**. Failure to do so results in a maximum penalty equal to the tax unpaid twelve months after the end of the accounting period. Tax for this purpose includes corporation tax and notional tax on loans to participators of close companies (see later in this Text).

A notice to file a return may also require other information, accounts and reports. For a UK resident company the requirement to deliver accounts normally extends only to the accounts required under the Companies Act.

A return is due on or before the filing date. This is the later of:

(a) **12 months after the end of the period to which the return relates**

(b) **if the relevant period of account is not more than 18 months long, 12 months from the end of the period of account**

(c) **if relevant the period of account is more than 18 months long, 30 months from the start of the period of account**, and

(d) **three months from the date on which the notice requiring the return was made**.

The relevant period of account is that in which the accounting period to which the return relates ends.

Question
Filing date

A Ltd prepares accounts for the eighteen months to 30 June 2006. A notice requiring a return for the period ended 30 June 2006 was issued to A Ltd on 1 September 2006. State the periods for which A Ltd must file a tax return and the filing dates.

Answer

The company must file a return for the two accounting periods ending in the period specified in the notice requiring a return. The first accounting period is the twelve months to 31 December 2005 and the second is the six months to 30 June 2006. The filing date is twelve months after the end of the relevant period of account, 30 June 2007.

There is a £100 penalty for a failure to submit a return on time, rising to £200 if the delay exceeds three months. These penalties become £500 and £1,000 respectively when a return was late (or never submitted) for each of the preceding two accounting periods.

An additional tax geared penalty is applied if a return is more than six months late. The penalty is 10% of the tax unpaid six months after the return was due if the total delay is up to 12 months, and 20% of that tax if the return is over 12 months late.

There is a tax geared penalty for a fraudulent or negligent return and for failing to correct an innocent error without unreasonable delay. The maximum penalty is equal to the tax that would have been lost had the return been accepted as correct. HMRC can mitigate this penalty. If a company is liable to more than one tax geared penalty, the total penalty is limited to the maximum single penalty that could be charged.

A company may amend a return within twelve months of the filing date. HMRC may amend a return to correct obvious errors within nine months of the day the return was filed, or if the correction is to an amended return, within nine months of the filing of an amendment. The company may amend its return so as to reject the correction. If the time limit for amendments has expired, the company may reject the correction by giving notice within three months.

3.3 Records

Companies must keep records until the latest of:

(a) six years from the end of the accounting period
(b) the date any enquiries are completed
(c) the date after which enquiries may not be commenced.

All business records and accounts, including contracts and receipts, must be kept.

If a return is demanded more than six years after the end of the accounting period, any records which the company still has must be kept until the later of the end of any enquiry and the expiry of the right to start an enquiry.

Failure to keep records can lead to a penalty of up to £3,000 for each accounting period affected. However, this penalty does not apply when the only records which have not been kept are ones which could only have been needed for the purposes of claims, elections or notices not included in the return.

HMRC do not generally insist on original records being kept but original records of the following must be preserved:

(a) Qualifying distributions (eg dividends) and tax credits

(b) Gross and net payments and tax deducted for payments made net of tax

(c) Certificates of payments made to sub-contractors net of tax

(d) Details of foreign tax paid, although HMRC will accept photocopies of foreign tax assessments when calculating underlying tax (see later in this Text) on dividends from abroad

3.4 Enquiries

FAST FORWARD

HMRC can enquire into returns.

A return or an amendment need not be accepted at face value by HMRC. **They may enquire into it, provided that they first give written notice that they are going to enquire.** The notice must be given by a year after the later of:

(a) The filing date

(b) The 31 January, 30 April, 31 July or 31 October next following the actual date of delivery of the return or amendment.

Only one enquiry may be made in respect of any one return or amendment.

If a notice of an enquiry has been given, HMRC may demand that the company produce documents for inspection and copying. However, documents relating to an appeal need not be produced and the company may appeal against a notice requiring documents to be produced.

If HMRC demand documents, but the company does not produce them, there is a penalty of £50. There is also a daily penalty, which applies for each day from the day after the imposition of the £50 penalty until the documents are produced. The daily penalty may be imposed by HMRC, in which case it is £30. If, however, HMRC ask the Commissioners to impose the penalty, it is £150.

HMRC may amend a self assessment at any time during an enquiry if they believe there might otherwise be a loss of tax. The company may appeal against such an amendment within 30 days. The company may itself make amendments during an enquiry under the normal rules for amendments. No effect will be given to such amendments during the enquiry but they may be taken into account in the enquiry.

An enquiry ends when HMRC give notice that it has been completed and notify what they believe to be the correct amount of tax payable. Before that time, the company may ask the Commissioners to order HMRC to notify the completion of its enquiry by a specified date. Such a direction will be given unless HMRC can demonstrate that they have reasonable grounds for continuing the enquiry.

The company has 30 days from the end of an enquiry to amend its self assessment in accordance with HMRC's conclusions. If HMRC are not satisfied with the company's amendments, they have a further 30 days to amend the self assessment. The company then has another 30 days in which it may appeal against HMRC's amendments.

3.5 Determinations and discovery assessments

If a return is not delivered by the filing date, HMRC may **issue a determination of the tax payable** within the five years from the filing date. This is **treated as a self assessment** and there is no appeal against it. However, it is automatically replaced by any self assessment made by the company by the later of five years from the filing date and 12 months from the determination.

If HMRC believe that not enough tax has been assessed for an accounting period they can make a discovery assessment to collect the extra tax. However, when a tax return has been delivered this power is limited as outlined below.

No discovery assessment can be made on account of an error or mistake as to the basis on which the tax liability ought to be computed, if the basis generally prevailing at the time when the return was made was applied.

A discovery assessment can only be made if either:

(a)   the loss of tax is due to fraudulent or negligent conduct by the company or by someone acting on its behalf or

(b)   HMRC could not reasonably be expected to have been aware of the loss of tax, given the information so far supplied to them, when their right to start an enquiry expired or when they notified the company that an enquiry had finished. The information supplied must be sufficiently detailed to draw HMRC's attention to contentious matters such as the use of a valuation or estimate.

The time limit for raising a discovery assessment is six years from the end of the accounting period but this is extended to 21 years if there has been fraudulent or negligent conduct. The company may appeal against a discovery assessment within 30 days of issue.

3.6 Claims

Wherever possible claims must be made on a tax return or on an amendment to it and must be quantified at the time the return is made.

If a company believes that it has paid excessive tax because of an error in a return, an error or mistake claim may be made within six years from the end of the accounting period. An appeal against a decision on such a claim must be made within 30 days. An error or mistake claim may not be made if the return was made in accordance with a generally accepted practice which prevailed at the time.

Other claims must be made by six years after the end of the accounting period, unless a different time limit is specified. These time limits are mentioned, where relevant, throughout this Text.

If an error or mistake is made in a claim, a supplementary claim may be made within the time limit for the original claim.

If HMRC amend a self assessment or issue a discovery assessment then the company has a further period to make, vary or withdraw a claim (unless the claim is irrevocable) even if this is outside the normal time limit. The period is one year from the end of the accounting period in which the amendment or assessment was made, or one year from the end of the accounting period in which the enquiry was closed if the amendment is the result of an enquiry. The relief is limited where there has been fraudulent or negligent conduct by the company or its agent.

4 Payment of corporation tax and interest

Large companies pay their corporation tax in four quarterly instalments. Other companies pay their tax nine months after the end of an accounting period.

4.1 Due dates

Corporation tax is due for payment by small and medium sized companies **nine months after the end of the accounting period**.

Large companies, however, must pay their corporation tax in instalments. **Broadly, a large company is any company that pays corporation tax at the full rate** (profits exceed £1,500,000 in a 12 month period where there are no associated companies).

Instalments are due on the 14th day of the month, starting in the seventh month. Provided that the accounting period is twelve months long subsequent instalments are due in the tenth month during the accounting period and in the first and fourth months after the end of the accounting period.

If an accounting period is less than twelve months long subsequent instalments are due at three monthly intervals but with the final payment being due in the fourth month of the next accounting period.

4.2 Example: quarterly instalments

X Ltd is a large company with a 31 December accounting year end. Instalments of corporation tax will be due to be paid by X Ltd on:

- 14 July and 14 October in the accounting period
- 14 January and 14 April after the accounting period ends

So for the year ended 31 December 2006 instalment payments are due on 14 July 2006, 14 October 2006, 14 January 2007 and 14 April 2007.

Instalments are based on the estimated corporation tax liability for the current period (not the previous period). It will be extremely important for companies to forecast their tax liabilities accurately. Large companies whose directors are poor at estimating may find their company's incurring significant interest charges. The amount of each instalment is computed by:

(a) working out 3 × CT/n where CT is the amount of the estimated corporation tax liability payable in instalments for the period and n is the number of months in the period

(b) allocating the smaller of that amount and the total estimated corporation tax liability to the first instalment

(c) repeating the process for later instalments until the amount allocated is equal to the corporation tax liability. This gives four equal instalments for 12 month accounting periods and also caters for periods which end earlier than expected.

The company is therefore required to estimate its corporation tax liability before the end of the accounting period, and must revise its estimate each quarter.

 Question   **Short accounting period**

A large company has a CT liability of £880,000 for the eight month period to 30 September 2006. Accounts had previously always been prepared to 31 January. Show when the CT liability is due for payment.

Answer

£880,000 must be paid in instalments.

The amount of each instalment is $3 \times \dfrac{£880,000}{8} = £330,000$

The due dates are:

	£
14 August 2006	330,000
14 November 2006	330,000
14 January 2007	220,000 (balance)

A company is not required to pay instalments in the first year that it is 'large', unless its profits exceed £10 million. The £10 million limit is reduced proportionately if there are associated companies. For this purpose only, a company will be regarded as an associated company where it was an associated company at the **start** of an accounting period. (This differs from the normal approach where being an associated company for any part of the AP affects the CT thresholds of both companies for the whole of the AP).

Any company whose liability does not exceed £10,000 need not pay by instalments.

Interest runs from the due date on over/underpaid instalments. The position is looked at cumulatively after the due date for each instalment. HMRC calculate the interest position after the company submits its corporation tax return.

4.3 Example: interest on quarterly instalments

X plc prepared accounts to 31 December 2006. The company has always prepared accounts to 31 December each year. It paid CT instalments of:

Date	Amount
	£m
14.7.06	3.5
14.10.06	8.5
14.01.07	4.5
14.4.07	4.5
	21.0

X plc's CT return showed a CT liability of £22m. The £1m balance was paid on 1.10.07. £22m should have been paid in instalments.

The under(over) payments were:

Date	Paid	Correct	Under(over) paid
	£m	£m	£m
14.7.06	3.5	5.5	2
14.10.06	8.5	5.5	
	12.0	11.0	(1)
14.1.07	4.5	5.5	
	16.5	16.5	–
14.4.07	4.5	5.5	
	21.0	22.0	1

Interest would be charged (received) as follows.

14.7.06 – 13.10.06   Interest charged on £2m
14.10.06 – 13.1.07   Interest received on £1m
14.1.07 – 13.4.07   No interest
14.4.07 – 30.9.07   Interest charged on £1m

Interest paid/received on late payments or over payments of corporation tax is dealt with as interest paid/received on a non trading loan relationship (see earlier in this Text).

There are penalties if a company deliberately and flagrantly fails to pay instalments of sufficient size. After a company has filed its return or HMRC has determined its liability, HMRC may wish to establish the reason for inadequate instalment payments. It can do this by asking the company to produce relevant information or records (presumably to decide if a penalty applies). The failure to supply these will lead to an initial fixed penalty which may also be followed by a daily penalty which may continue until the information/records are produced.

Companies can have instalments repaid if they later conclude they ought not to have been paid.

4.4 Group payment arrangements

Where more than one company in a group is liable to pay their tax by instalments, arrangements may be made for the instalments to be paid by one company (the nominated company), and allocated amongst the group. These provisions were introduced because groups often have uncertainties over the tax liabilities of individual group members until all relevant group reliefs and claims are decided upon following the end of the accounting period.

Chapter roundup

- A company pays corporation tax on its profits chargeable to corporation tax (PCTCT).

- 'Profits' is PCTCT plus franked investment income (FII)

- Tax rates are set for financial years.

- Companies are taxed at either the starting rate, the small companies' rate or receive marginal relief, depending on their 'profits'

- The marginal rate of corporation tax between the small companies' limits is 32.75%. The marginal tax rate is an effective rate; it is never actually used in working out corporation tax

- A starting rate of corporation tax applied from FY02 to FY05. A starting rate marginal rate of 23.75% also applied

- The upper and lower limits which are used to be determine tax rates are divided by the number of associated companies and may also need to be pro-rated on a time basis if an accounting period lasts for less than 12 months

- Companies can obtain tax relief on certain investments they make under the Corporate Venturing Scheme (CVS).

- A company must notify HMRC within 3 months of starting to trade.

- CT 600 returns must usually be filed within twelve months of the end of an accounting period.

- HMRC can enquire into returns.

- Large companies pay their corporation tax in four quarterly instalments. Other companies pay their tax nine months after the end of an accounting period.

Quick quiz

1   Which companies are entitled to the small companies' rate of corporation tax in FY 2006?

2   What is the marginal relief formula?

3   What is an associated company?

4   What tax relief is available under the corporate venturing scheme?

5   Youngs Ltd makes up a 12 m set of accounts to 31 December 2006. When must the company file its CT return based on these accounts?

6   What are the fixed penalties for failure to deliver a corporation tax return on time?

7   When must HMRC give notice that they are going to start an enquiry if a return was filed on time?

8   Which companies must pay quarterly instalments of their corporation tax liability?

9   State the due dates for the payment of quarterly instalments of corporation tax for a 12 month accounting period.

10   Freeman Ltd changes its accounting date and makes up accounts for the 8 months to 31 December 2006. The company is large and is due to pay tax by instalments. Outline when the tax is due.

11   In question 10 if the CT liability is £1,000,000 for the 8 month period what amount is due at each date?

Answers to quick quiz

1   Companies with profits of up to £300,000

2   (M – P) × I/P × marginal relief fraction

where:

M = upper limit
P = 'profits'
I = PCTCT

3   A company is associated with another company if either controls the other or if both are under the control of the same person or persons (Individual, partnership or companies).

4   The corporate venturing scheme allows an investing company to obtain corporation tax relief at 20% on amounts invested in ordinary shares held for at least three years.

5   By 31 December 2007.

6   There is a £100 penalty for failure to submit a return on time rising to £200 if the delay exceeds three months. These penalties increased to £500 and £1,000 respectively when a return was late for each of the preceding two accounting periods.

7   Notice must be given by one year after the filing date.

8   'Large' companies ie: companies that pay corporation tax at the full rate.

9   14th day of:

(a)   7th month in AP
(b)   10th month in AP
(c)   1st month after AP ends
(d)   4th month after AP ends

10   Due dates are:

14 November 2006
14 February 2007
14 April 2007.

11   £375,000, £375, 000 and finally £250,000.

Now try the question below from the Exam Question Bank			
Number	**Level**	**Marks**	**Time**
Q22	Introductory	20	36 mins
Q23	Introductory	13	23 mins
Q24	Introductory	10	18 mins

Administration, winding up, purchase of own shares

Topic list	Syllabus reference
1 Winding up	A2(b)(iii),(iv)
2 The purchase by a company of its own shares	A2(b)(v)

Introduction

In the last two chapters we have studied the computation of profits chargeable to corporation tax and the corporation tax payable.

In this chapter we look at some of the consequences of placing a company into administration or liquidation.

We also consider the tax consequences which accrue when a company purchases its own shares.

In the next chapters we will consider further aspects of corporation tax, starting with losses.

Study guide

		Intellectual level
2	**Corporation tax liabilities in situations involving further overseas and group aspects and in relation to special types of company, and the application of additional exemptions and reliefs**	
(b)	The scope of corporation tax:	3
(iii)	Identify and evaluate the significance of accounting periods on administration or winding up	
(iv)	Conclude on the tax treatment of returns to shareholders after winding up has commenced	
(v)	Advise on the tax implications of a purchase by a company of its own shares	

Exam guide

If the exam includes a question which includes the purchase by a company of its own shares you must be careful to consider whether the capital gains treatment will apply, and if so, whether it is beneficial. You must be prepared to advise whether any variation to a suggested purchase would be beneficial.

1 Winding up

FAST FORWARD

A new accounting period (AP) begins when a winding up commences. Thereafter APs are for 12 months until the winding up is complete. Distributions made during a winding up are capital. There are special rules in respect of accounting periods when companies go into administration.

1.1 Liquidation

A company **in liquidation is chargeable to corporation tax on the profits arising during the winding up.**

An accounting period ends and a new one beings when a winding up commences. Thereafter, accounting periods end *only* on each anniversary of the commencement of winding up, until the final period which ends when the winding up is completed. A cessation of trade after a winding up has commenced will not bring an accounting period to an end.

1.2 Example: accounting periods on a winding up

Totterdown Ltd, a company with a 31 December year end, ceased trading on 10 June 2005. The members passed a resolution to wind up the company on 12 September 2005 and the winding up was completed on 15 January 2007. From 1 January 2005 the accounting periods will be:

1.1.05 – 10.6.05	To the date trade ceased.
11.6.05 – 11.9.05	The commencement of a winding up brings an AP to an end.
12.9.05 – 11.9.06	Anniversary of commencement of winding up.
12.9.06 – 15.1.07	Final AP ends when winding up complete.

1.3 Administration

The Enterprise Act 2002 provides for companies to go from liquidation to administration and for assets to be distributed without a formal liquidation. In such cases, the following rules apply relating to when an accounting period will be deemed to end.

A new accounting period begins when a company goes into administration. An accounting period ends when a company ceases to be in administration and a new accounting period begins when a company moves out of liquidation into administration.

In contrast to the position in liquidation, where the corporation tax accounting periods are then annual from the date of appointment of the liquidator, there is no requirement to change the accounting reference date of the company. Therefore, future accounting periods in administration follow the original accounting dates.

1.4 Example: accounting periods in administration

Company A has a normal accounting date of 31 December annually. An administrator is appointed on 17 August 2006. As a result, for corporation tax purposes the company's accounting periods will be 1 January to 16 August 2006 before administration and 17 August to 31 December 2006 after the appointment of the administrator. Accounting periods will then be 31 December annually while the company remains in administration.

When an administration ceases, a new accounting period must start for tax purposes, whether the company comes out of administration and recommences to trade normally or goes from administration into winding up.

1.5 Example: administration to liquidation

Company A remains in administration for 16 months and a liquidator is appointed on 10 October 2007.

The accounting period in administration will therefore be 1 January 2007 to 9 October 2007. The next accounting period will be the first liquidation accounting period, 10 October 2007 to 9 October 2008. Accounting periods will then be annually to 9 October until the company ceases to be in liquidation (either by striking off or returning to administration).

When a company comes out of liquidation into administration, a new accounting period must start. Again, this permits proper computation of the tax due as an expense of liquidation or administration.

1.6 Example: liquidation to administration

Following the above example, company A remains in liquidation for only three months, and a court order appointing a new administrator is granted on 14 January 2008.

The accounting periods are therefore 10 October 2007 to 13 January 2008 in liquidation, then 14 January to (presumably) 31 December 2008 in administration.

If the company had been in liquidation for some time, so that liquidation accounts had been prepared to 9 October for a number of years, the post-liquidation accounting periods would end on 9 October annually unless the administrator changed the accounting reference date.

1.7 Significance of accounting periods

The date on which an accounting period ends will affect the accounting periods into which income and capital profits and losses fall. This may prevent relief being obtained in the most beneficial way. For example trading losses of the current year or carried back can be set against other income or gains, whilst trading losses carried forward can only be set against trading profits. Capital gains may therefore be taxable if made after trade ceases even though there may be unrelieved trading losses.

1.8 Distributions

Distributions made after the liquidation has started are capital and treated as a part disposal of shares in the hands of the shareholder. This is the position even if the distributions include accumulated net profits of the company out of which dividends could be paid.

Where a company has distributable profits, it may be preferable to pay these out as a dividend before the liquidation starts. Any such distribution will be chargeable to income tax on a shareholder who is an individual.

Assets distributed in specie (ie in their existing form rather than sold and distributed as cash) by the liquidator are deemed to be disposed of at market value. Where the assets are chargeable assets, any chargeable gain arising is charged to corporation tax in accordance with the normal rules. Consequently there is double taxation on assets distributed to shareholders in the liquidation since the asset distribution will also be treated as a capital distribution in the hands of the shareholders.

Ordinarily, assets distributed outside a formal winding up represent an income distribution.

It may, however, be possible by concession (ESC C16) to treat certain distributions as capital providing certain assurances are given beforehand as follows:

- (a)   that the company has **ceased trading**

- (b)   that the company will **collect its debts, pay off its creditors** and **distribute its remaining assets** to its shareholders

- (c)   that it will **thereafter seek to be struck off the Companies Register and be dissolved** and

- (d)   that the **shareholders agree to pay any tax liabilities arising on the concessionary basis**.

Once they have received these assurances HMRC is prepared to regard the distribution as having been made **under a formal winding up**. The value of the distribution is then treated as capital receipts of the shareholders for the purpose of calculating any chargeable gains arising to them on the disposal of their shares. This may or may not be advantageous to the shareholders.

1.9 Other points

The appointment of a receiver, a manager or administrator has no tax consequences, apart from determining accounting periods as discussed above.

When a company is put into liquidation, it loses beneficial ownership of its assets. If the company to be liquidated is a parent company, it will therefore lose its group relationship with its former subsidiaries. No group relief (see later in this text) will be available to any of the companies in the former group.

By contrast, a group continues to exist for chargeable gains purposes (see later in this text), notwithstanding the commencement of liquidation.

2 The purchase by a company of its own shares

FAST FORWARD

A purchase of a company's own shares may be treated as a capital distribution or as an income distribution.

If a company buys its own shares for more than the amount originally subscribed, general tax rules state that there is a distribution of the excess.

Recipients of such distributions are treated in the same way as recipients of ordinary dividends which means that starting and basic rate taxpayers have no further tax to pay and higher rate taxpayers must pay additional tax. The company cannot obtain a tax deduction for those distributions.

However, a capital gains tax disposal automatically occurs rather than an income distribution, when an unquoted trading company (or the unquoted parent of a trading group) buys back its own shares in order to benefit its trade and certain other conditions are satisfied. The trade must not consist of dealing in shares, securities, land or futures. The company may be on the AIM. The capital gains treatment is not given if a main objective is tax avoidance.

The 'benefit to the trade' test will be satisfied where:

- a dissident and disruptive shareholder is bought out
- the proprietor wishes to retire to make way for new management
- an outside investor who provided equity wishes to withdraw his investment
- a shareholder dies and his personal representatives do not wish to retain his shares.

The conditions to be satisfied by the vendor shareholder are as follows.

(a)   He must be resident and ordinarily resident in the UK when the purchase is made

(b)   **The shares must have been owned by the vendor or his spouse throughout the five years preceding the purchase**. This is reduced to three years if the vendor is the personal representative or the heir of a deceased member, and previous ownership by the deceased will count towards the qualifying period

(c)   **The vendor and his associates must as a result of the purchase have their interest in the company's share capital reduced to 75% or less of their interest before the disposal**. Associates include spouses, minor children, controlled companies, trustees and beneficiaries. Where a company is a member of a group the whole group is effectively considered as one for this test

(d)   **The vendor must not be connected with the company or any company in the same 51% group after the transaction**. A person is connected with a company if he can control more than 30% of the ordinary share capital, the issued share capital and loan capital or the voting rights in the company.

Any shares repurchased by the company must usually be cancelled and cannot be re-issued.

Question		The reduction of a shareholding

Henry holds 300 of H Ltd's 1,000 issued ordinary shares. Will there be a capital distribution if the company buys 80 shares back from him?

Answer		

	Total shares	Held by Henry
Initially	1,000	300
Less repurchased (and cancelled)	(80)	(80)
	920	220

Henry originally had a 30% interest. This is reduced to 220/920 = 23.9%, a reduction to 23.9/30 = 79.7% of his original interest. For a capital distribution he must sell at least 97 shares back to H Ltd, thus reducing his percentage holding below 30% × 75% = 22.5%.

The relief is also available where a company purchases shares to enable the vendor to pay any inheritance tax arising on a death (the 'benefit to the trade' test and the above conditions do not then apply).

Companies considering the purchase of their own shares may seek HMRC clearance to ensure that relief is available.

Exam focus point

The relief applies automatically if the conditions are satisfied. It may be necessary to vary the terms of the purchase to ensure that the relief will not apply where that is preferable.

Chapter roundup

- A new accounting period (AP) begins when a winding up commences. Thereafter APs are for 12 months until the winding up is complete. Distributions made during a winding up are capital. There are special rules in respect of accounting periods when companies go into administration.

- A purchase of a company's own shares may be treated as a capital distribution or as an income distribution.

Quick quiz

1   Inca Ltd makes up accounts to 31 March. The company goes into liquidation on 1 November 2006 and cease to trade on 31 December 2006. The company is finally wound up on 31 July 2007. What are the accounting periods from 1 April 2005?

2   Does the appointment of an administrator affect a company's accounting periods?

3   What is the impact (if any) on a company accounting period when a company moves out of liquidation into administration?

4   Are distributions made during a liquidation treated as capital or income distributions?

5   When a company buys its own shares, what potential tax consequences may occur?

Answers to quick quiz

1   1 April 2005 – 31 March 2006
    1 April 2006 – 31 October 2006
    1 November 2006 – 31 July 2007

2   Yes. A new accounting period begins when a company goes into administration. An accounting period ends when a company ceases to be in administration.

3   A new accounting period begins when a company moves status from liquidation into administration.

4   Distributions are capital distributions and are treated as a part disposal of the shares in the hands of the shareholder.

5   If a company buys its own shares from a shareholder and pays more than the amount originally subscribed the general tax rules treat the excess amount paid as a distribution (dividend) made by the company to the shareholder. Thus there is no tax relief for the company and income tax applies to the shareholder recipient of the dividend.

    If certain conditions are met, however, the full amount paid by the company for a purchase of own shares will be treated as capital. Hence the full amount becomes sale proceeds in a CGT computation for the selling shareholder.

Now try the question below from the Exam Question Bank

Number	Level	Marks	Time
Q25	Introductory	10	18 mins

Losses and deficits on non-trading loan relationships

Topic list	Syllabus reference
1 Reliefs for losses – overview	A2(a)C5
2 Trading losses	A2(a)C5
3 Reliefs for deficits on non-trading loan relationships	A2(c)(ii)
4 Restrictions on loss relief	A2(c)(v)
5 Choosing loss reliefs and other planning points	A2(a)C5

Introduction

We have studied the computation of profits chargeable to corporation tax and the corporation tax payable.

We now see how a company may obtain relief for trading losses and also for deficits on non trading loan relationships. We look at the factors to take into account when deciding which loss relief to choose.

In the next chapter we will look at close companies and investment companies, and then we will turn to groups and consortia.

Study guide

		Intellectual level
2	**Corporation tax liabilities in situations involving further overseas and group aspects and in relation to special types of company, and the application of additional exemptions and reliefs**	
(c)	Profits chargeable to corporation tax:	3
(ii)	Determine the tax treatment of non trading deficits on loan relationships	
(v)	Advise on the restriction on the use of losses on a change in ownership of a company	

Exam guide

You are likely to come across company losses at some point in the exam, although the question may include group relief. Always look to see if any requirements are specified in the question, such as to claim relief as early as possible, and then consider how to optimise the relief.

Knowledge brought forward from earlier studies

This chapter revises the treatment of trading losses. The relief for deficits on non-trading loan relationships and the restriction on the use of losses are new to you.

1 Reliefs for losses – overview

1.1 Trading losses

FAST FORWARD

Trading losses may be relieved against current total profits, against total profits of earlier periods or against future trading income.

In summary, the following reliefs are available for trading losses incurred by a company.

- (a) **Claim to set-off against current profits**
- (b) **Claim to carry back against earlier profits**
- (c) **Make no claim and automatically carry forward against future trading profits**

These reliefs may be used in combination. The options open to the company are:

- (a) Do nothing, so that the loss is automatically carried forward against future trading profits

- (b) Claim to set-off against current profits, and carry any remaining unrelieved loss forward

- (c) Claim to set-off against current profits, then claim to carry any unused loss back against earlier profits, and then carry any remaining unrelieved loss forward.

The reliefs are explained in further detail below.

1.2 Non-trading deficits

Non-trading deficits on loan relationships can be relieved in the same ways as trading losses, but against different profits (see below).

1.3 Capital losses

Capital losses can only be set against capital gains in the same or future accounting periods, never against income (except losses suffered by an investment company on shares in a qualifying trading company). Capital losses must be set against the first available gains.

1.4 Foreign income losses

In the case of a trade which is controlled outside the UK **any loss made in an accounting period can only be set against trading income from the same trade in later accounting periods.** The same rule applies to losses on overseas property businesses.

1.5 Miscellaneous income losses

Where in an accounting period a company makes a loss in a transaction where income would be taxable as miscellaneous income (such as one involving intangible fixed assets used for non trade purposes), **the company can set the loss against any income from other transactions taxable as miscellaneous income in the same or later accounting periods.** The loss must be set against the earliest income available.

1.6 Property income losses

Property income losses are first set off against other income and gains of the company for the current period. Any excess is then:

(a) Carried forward as if a property income loss arising in the later accounting period for offset against future income (of all descriptions), or

(b) Available for surrender as group relief (in a similar fashion to management expenses: see later in this Text).

2 Trading losses

2.1 Loss relief against future trading income: s 393(1) ICTA 1988

FAST FORWARD

Trading losses carried forward can only be set against future trading profits of the same trade.

If a company makes no claim for relief for its trading losses they will be automatically carried forward against income from the same trade in future accounting periods. Relief is against the first available trading profits.

Question | Carrying forward losses

A Ltd has the following results for the three years to 31 March 2007.

	Year ended		
	31.3.05	31.3.06	31.3.07
	£	£	£
Trading profit/(loss)	(8,550)	3,000	6,000
Property income	0	1,000	1,000
Gift aid donation	300	1,400	1,700

Calculate the profits chargeable to corporation tax for all three years showing any losses available to carry forward at 1 April 2007.

Answer

	Year ended		
	31.3.05	31.3.06	31.3.07
	£	£	£
Trading income	0	3,000	6,000
Less s 393(1) carry forward relief		(3,000)	(5,550)
	0	0	450
Property income	0	1,000	1,000
Less gift aid donation	0	(1,000)	(1,450)
PCTCT	0	0	0
Unrelieved gift aid donation	300	400	250

Note that the trading loss carried forward is set only against the trading profit in future years. It cannot be set against the property income.

The non-trade charges that become unrelieved are wasted as they cannot be carried forward.

Loss memorandum

	£
Loss for y/e 31.3.05	8,550
Less s 393(1) relief y/e 31.3.06	(3,000)
Loss carried forward at 1.4.06	5,550
Less s 393(1) relief y/e 31.3.07	(5,550)
Loss carried forward at 1.4.07	0

2.2 Loss relief against total profits: s 393A(1) ICTA 1988

FAST FORWARD

S393A relief is given against total profits before charges. Gift Aid donations remain unrelieved. S393A relief may be given against current period profits and against profits of the previous 12 months (or previous 36 months if the trade is ceasing). A claim for current period S393A relief can be made without a claim for carryback. However, if a loss is to be carried back a claim for current period relief must have been made first.

2.2.1 Current year claim

A company may claim under s 393A(1) to set a trading loss (arising in a UK trade) **incurred in an accounting period against total profits of the same accounting period** *before* **deducting charges (ie gift aid donations).**

Any loss remaining unrelieved is automatically carried forward under s 393(1) to set against future profits of the same trade unless a carry back claim is made.

2.2.2 Carry back claim

Any loss remaining after a current year claim may then be carried back and set against total profits of the previous 12 months (before gift aid donations).

A claim for the current period *must* be made before any excess loss can be carried back to a previous period.

If there is more than one accounting period in the 12 month period, the loss relief available is equal to the proportion of each period that falls within the 12 months. Any carry-back is to later periods before earlier periods. Relief for earlier years' losses is given before relief for later years' losses.

Any loss remaining unrelieved is automatically carried forward under s 393(1) to set against future profits of the same trade.

2.2.3 The claim

A claim for relief against current or prior period profits must be made within two years of the end of the accounting period in which the loss arose.

Any claim must be for the *whole* loss (to the extent that profits are available to relieve it). The loss can however be reduced by not claiming full capital allowances, so that higher capital allowances are given (on higher tax written down values) in future years.

Question	S 393A loss relief

Helix Ltd has the following results.

	Year ended		
	30.9.05	30.9.06	30.9.07
	£	£	£
Trading profit/(loss)	90,500	80,000	(105,000)
Bank interest	500	500	500
Chargeable gains	0	0	4,000
Charges on income:			
Gift Aid donation	250	250	250

Show the PCTCT for all the years affected assuming that s 393A(1) loss relief is claimed. Assume the provisions of FA 2006 continue to apply.

Answer	

The loss of the year to 30.9.07 is relieved under s 393A ICTA 1988 against current year profits and against profits of the previous twelve months.

	Year ended		
	30.9.05	30.9.06	30.9.07
	£	£	£
Trading income	90,500	80,000	0
Interest income	500	500	500
Chargeable gains	0	0	4,000
	91,000	80,500	4,500
Less s 393A current period relief	0	0	(4,500)
	91,000	80,500	0
Less s 393A carryback relief	0	(80,500)	0
	91,000	0	0
Less gift aid donation	(250)	0	0
PCTCT	90,750	0	0
Unrelieved gift aid donation		250	250

S 393A (1) loss memorandum	£
Loss incurred in y/e 30.9.07	105,000
Less s 393A (1): y/e 30.9.07	(4,500)
y/e 30.9.06	(80,500)
Loss available to carry forward under s 393(1)	20,000

The 12 month carry back period is extended to 36 months where the trading loss arose in the 12 months immediately before the company ceased to trade.

Loser Ltd had always made up accounts to 31 December, but ceased to trade on 31 December 2006. Results had been as follows.

	Year ended			
	31.12.03	*31.12.04*	*31.12.05*	*31.12.06*
	£	£	£	£
Trading profit/(loss)	36,000	26,000	23,000	(61,200)
Interest income	2,000	2,000	2,000	0
Gift Aid donation	170	170	170	80

Show the profits chargeable to corporation tax for all years after relief for the loss.

Answer

	Year ended			
	31.12.03	*31.12.04*	*31.12.05*	*31.12.06*
	£	£	£	£
Trading income	36,000	26,000	23,000	0
Interest income	2,000	2,000	2,000	0
	38,000	28,000	25,000	0
Less s 393A carryback	(8,200)	(28,000)	(25,000)	0
	29,800	0	0	0
Less gift aid donations	(170)	0	0	0
	29,630	0	0	0
Unrelieved gift aid donations		170	170	80

S 393A (1) loss memorandum	£
Loss incurred in y/e 31.12.06	61,200
Less s 393A (1): y/e 31.12.05	(25,000)
y/e 31.12.04	(28,000)
y/e 31.12.03	(8,200)
Loss available to carry forward under s 393(1)	Nil

3 Reliefs for deficits on non-trading loan relationships

FAST FORWARD

Deficits on non-trading loan relationships can be used in a similar way to trading losses.

A deficit on a non-trading loan relationship may be set, in whole or part, against any profit of the same accounting period. Relief is given after relief for any trading loss brought forward but before relief is given for a trading loss of the same or future period.

Relief for deficit on non-trading loan relationship

Witherspoon Ltd has the following results for the two years ended 31 December 2006:

	2005	2006
	£	£
Trading profit/(loss)	70,000	(42,000)
Trading losses brought forward	(20,000)	–
Bank interest receivable	2,000	
Interest payable on a loan for non-trading purposes	(11,000)	

Show how relief may be given for the deficit on the non-trading loan relationship in the year ended 31.12.05.

Answer

Y/e 31.12.05	£
Trading income	70,000
s 393(1) losses brought forward	(20,000)
	50,000
Less: non-trading deficit £(11,000 – 2,000)	(9,000)
	41,000
Losses carried back s 393A	(41,000)
Chargeable profits	Nil

Trading loss memorandum	£
Loss incurred in y/e 31.12.06	42,000
Less s 393A (1): y/e 31.12.05	(41,000)
Loss available to carry forward under s 393(1)	1,000

A deficit is eligible for group relief (see later in this Text).

A deficit may be set against non-trading income arising from loan relationships in the previous twelve months provided the income has not been reduced by:

    (a)   Loss relief in respect of a period prior to the deficit period

    (b)   Management expenses of an investment company (see later in this Text)

A claim under the above must be made within two years of the deficit period.

Any deficits unrelieved after claiming the above reliefs are automatically carried forward and set against non trading profits of the company for succeeding accounting periods. If the company does not want this automatic set-off to apply **it has two years from the end of the accounting period to apply for exemption for all or part of the deficit carried forward.**

A company can choose how much deficit to relieve in the current period, how much to carry back and how much to carry forward; unlike s 393A relief, these are not all or nothing claims, and the company can choose to carry back a deficit even if it does not claim current period relief.

4 Restrictions on loss relief

FAST FORWARD

> If there is a change in ownership of a company, the carry forward of losses is restricted if there is also a major change in the nature of the trade within three years of the change in ownership.

4.1 The continuity of trades

Relief under s 393(1) is only available against future profits arising from the same trade as that in which the loss arose.

The continuity of trade for this purpose was considered in a case involving a company trading as brewers: *Gordon & Blair Ltd v CIR 1962*. It ceased brewing but continued to bottle and sell beer. The company claimed that it carried on the same trade throughout so that its losses from brewing could be set off against profits from the bottling trade. The company lost their case and were prevented from obtaining any further relief for losses in the brewing trade under s 393(1).

4.2 The disallowance of loss relief following a change in ownership

Trading losses may be restricted where there is a change in ownership of a company and there is either:

(1)   **A major change in the nature or conduct of the trade within three years before or three years after the change in ownership, or**

(2)   **After the change in ownership there is a considerable revival of the company's trading activities which at the time of the change had become small or negligible.**

If the restriction applies:

- **Any losses incurred before the change in ownership cannot be carried forward against post-acquisition profits under s 393(1)**

- **Any losses incurred after the change in ownership cannot be carried back against profits arising before the date of the change of ownership under s 393A(1)**

For example, if a company changes its ownership on 1 July 2006 and there is a major change in the nature or conduct of its trade between 1 July 2003 and 30 June 2009 the carry back and carry forward of losses is restricted.

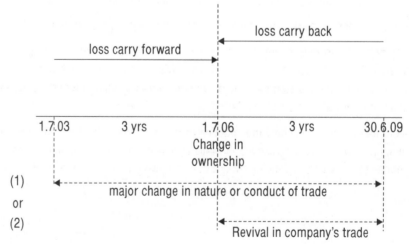

BPP
LEARNING MEDIA

Examples of a major change in the nature or conduct of a trade include changes in:

- The type of property dealt in (for example a company operating a dealership in saloon cars switching to a dealership in tractors)

- The services or facilities provided (for example a company operating a public house changing to operating a discotheque)

- Customers

- Outlets or markets

However, changes to keep up to date with technology or to rationalise existing ranges of products are unlikely to be regarded as major. HMRC consider both qualitative and quantitative issues in deciding if a change is major.

If the change in ownership occurs in (rather than at the end of) an accounting period, the period is divided into two, one up to and one after the change, for the purposes of this rule, with profits and losses being time-apportioned.

A change in ownership is disregarded for this purpose if both immediately before and immediately after the change the company is a 75% subsidiary of the same company.

4.3 Uncommercial trades

A loss made in a trade which is not conducted on a commercial basis and with a view to the realisation of gain cannot be set off against the company's profits in the same or previous accounting periods under s 393A(1). Such losses are only available to carry forward under s 393(1) against future profits of the same trade.

4.4 Farming and market gardening

A company carrying on the trade of farming or market gardening is treated in the same way as one that trades on an uncommercial basis in any accounting period if, in the five successive years immediately before that accounting period, the trade made a loss (before capital allowances).

5 Choosing loss reliefs and other planning points

FAST FORWARD

When selecting a loss relief, firstly consider the rate at which relief is obtained and, secondly, the timing of the relief.

Several alternative loss reliefs may be available. In making a choice consider:

- **The rate at which relief will be obtained:**
  - 30% at the full rate (FY 2006)
  - 19% at the small companies' rate (FY 2006)
  - 32.75% if the small companies' marginal relief applies (FY 2006)

  Where the loss is carried back relief may also be obtained at the starting rate of 0% (FY 2005), or at 23.75% if the starting rate marginal relief applies (FY 2005).

  We previously outlined how the 23.75% and 32.75% marginal rates are calculated. Remember these are just marginal rates of tax; they are never actually used in computing a company's corporation tax.

- **How quickly relief will be obtained**: s 393A(1) relief is quicker than s 393(1) relief.

- **The extent to which relief for gift aid donations might be lost.**

Exam focus point

When choosing between loss relief claims **always** consider the rate of tax 'saved' by the loss first.

If in the current period the loss 'saves' 19% tax but if carried forward saves 30% tax then a carry forward is the better choice (even though the timing of loss relief is later).

If the tax saved now is 30% and in the future is the same (30%) **then** consider timing (in this example a current claim is better timing wise).

So, first – rate of tax saved, second – timing.

Question

The choice between loss reliefs

M Ltd has had the following results.

	Year ended 31 March				
	2003	*2004*	*2005*	*2006*	*2007*
	£	£	£	£	£
Trading profit/(loss)	5,000,000	2,000	(1,000,000)	200,000	138,000
Chargeable gains	0	35,000	750,000	0	0
Gift aid donations paid	20,000	30,000	20,000	20,000	20,000

Recommend appropriate loss relief claims, and compute the mainstream corporation tax for all years based on your recommendations. Assume that future years' profits will be similar to those of the year ended 31 March 2007 and that any profits made by the company are retained for future use in the business.

Answer

A s 393A(1) claim for the year ended 31 March 2005 will save tax partly in the small companies' marginal relief band, partly at the small companies rate and partly in the starting rate marginal relief band. It will waste the gift aid donation of £20,000.

PCTCT in the previous year is £7,000 (£35,000 + £2,000 – £30,000) and falls into the starting rate band lower limit. Corporation tax at 0% would have been due in this year (FY 2003).

If no current period s 393A(1) claim is made, £200,000 of the loss will save tax at the small companies rate and in the starting rate marginal relief band in the year ended 31 March 2006, with £20,000 of gift aid donations being wasted. The remaining £800,000 of the loss, would be carried forward to the year ended 31 March 2007 and later years to save tax at the small companies rate.

To conclude a s 393A(1) claim should be made for the year of the loss but not in the previous year. £20,000 of gift aid donations would be wasted in the current year, but much of the loss would save tax at the small companies' marginal corporation tax rate and relief would be obtained quickly.

The final computations are as follows.

	2003 £	2004 £	2005 £	2006 £	2007 £
			Year ended 31 March		
Trading income	5,000,000	2,000	0	200,000	138,000
Less s 393(1) relief	0	0	0	(200,000)	(50,000)
	5,000,000	2,000	0	0	88,000
Chargeable gains	0	35,000	750,000	0	0
	5,000,000	37,000	750,000	0	88,000
Less s 393A current relief		0	(750,000)	0	0
	5,000,000	37,000	0	0	88,000
Less: gift aid donations	(20,000)	(30,000)	0	0	(20,000)
Profits chargeable to corporation tax	4,980,000	7,000	0	0	68,000
MCT at 30%/0%/0%/19%	1,494,000	0	0	0	12,920
Unrelieved gift aid donations	0	0	20,000	20,000	0

Loss memorandum	£
Loss incurred in y/e 31.3.05	1,000,000
Less s 393A (1): y/e 31.3.05	(750,000)
Less s 393 (1): y/e 31.3.06	(200,000)
y/e 31.3.07	(50,000)
Loss available to carry forward under s 393(1)	Nil

5.1 Other tax planning points

A company must normally claim capital allowances on its tax return. A company with losses could consider claiming less than the maximum amount of capital allowances available. This will result in a higher tax written down value to carry forward and therefore higher capital allowances in future years.

Reducing capital allowances in the current period reduces the loss available for relief under s 393A. As S 393A relief, if claimed, must be claimed for all of a loss available, a reduced capital allowance claim could be advantageous where all of a loss would be relieved at a lower tax rate in the current (or previous) period than the effective rate of relief for capital allowances will be in future periods.

Chapter roundup

- Trading losses may be relieved against current total profits, against total profits of earlier periods or against future trading income.

- Trading losses carried forward can only be set against future profits of the same trade.

- S393A relief is given against total profits before charges. Gift Aid donations remain unrelieved. S393A relief may be given against current period profits and against profits of the previous 12 months (or previous 36 months if the trade is ceasing). A claim for current period S393A relief can be made without a claim for carryback. However, if a loss is to be carried back a claim for current period relief must have been made first.

- Deficits on non-trading loan relationships can be used in a similar way to trading losses.

- If there is a change in ownership of a company, the carry forward of losses is restricted if there is also a major change in the nature of the trade within three years of the change in ownership.

- When selecting a loss relief, firstly consider the rate at which relief is obtained and, secondly, the timing of the relief.

Quick quiz

1   Against what profits may trading losses carried forward be set?

2   To what extent may losses in a continuing trade be carried back?

3   What relief is available in the current AP for a non-trading deficit?

4   Why might a company make a reduced capital allowances claim?

Answers to quick quiz

1   Profits from the same trade.

2   A loss may be carried back and set against total profits (before deducting gift aid donations) of the prior 12 months. The loss carried back is the trading loss left unrelieved after a claim against total profits (before deducting gift aid donations) of the loss making AP has been made.

3   A deficit on a non-trading loan relationship may be set against profits of the same AP. Relief is given after relief for any trading loss brought forward but before relief is given for a current or future trading loss.

   The deficit is also eligible for group relief.

4   Reducing capital allowances in the current AP reduces the loss available for relief under s 393A. Section 393A demands that all of the available loss is utilised. Reducing capital allowances reduces the size of the available loss.

Now try the question below from the Exam Question Bank

Number	Level	Marks	Time
Q26	Introductory	15	27 mins

Close companies and investment companies

Topic list	Syllabus reference
1 Companies with investment business	A2(b)(i)
2 Close companies	A2(b)(ii)

Introduction

Having looked at the general rules for companies we now look at the specific rules for investment companies and close companies.

Companies with investment business are any companies that make investments, for example in shares, and collect the income from them. Expenses of managing those investments are generally deductible for corporation tax purposes.

A close company may have any type of business, but it needs special tax treatment because it is under the control of a few people who might try to take profits out of it in non-taxable forms.

In the next chapter we will go on to look at groups and consortia.

Study guide

		Intellectual level
2	**Corporation tax liabilities in situations involving further overseas and group aspects and in relation to special types of company, and the application of additional exemptions and reliefs**	
(b)	The scope of corporation tax:	3
(i)	Identify and calculate corporation tax for companies with investment business.	
(ii)	Close companies:	
•	Apply the definition of a close company to given situations	
•	Conclude on the tax implications of a company being a close company or a close investment holding company	

Exam guide

Questions involving planning for families may include a consideration of close companies. The rules for treating benefits as distributions are fairly straightforward, but you must be careful not to overlook the disallowance of the expenses in the corporation tax computation. The tax charge for loans to participators is a significant cost of making any such loan, even though it is recovered when the loan is repaid or written off.

1 Companies with investment business

 FAST FORWARD

A company that generates income from investments can usually deduct the expenses of managing their investments for corporation tax purposes.

1.1 Companies with investment business

A company with investment business is any company whose **business consists wholly or partly in making investments.**

The principal overhead of the investment business will be the costs of running the business which are called management expenses. These are generally deductible in computing taxable profits. An unrelieved excess of such expenses in one accounting period may be carried forward as management expenses of the following accounting period and, if still unrelieved, to future accounting periods.

Excessive directors' remuneration is not deductible for tax purposes, whilst earnings of a controlling director of an investment company are not relevant UK earnings for the director's pension contribution purposes although they may contribute up to the threshold of £3,600 each year (see earlier in this Text).

Capital expenditure is excluded from deduction as a management expense and HMRC may also refuse a reduction for any amounts which are not in fact expenses of management.

Capital allowances on plant and machinery used for the investment business are allowed as a management expense if they cannot be relieved in any other way.

Non-trading loan relationships expenses and losses are dealt with under the loan relationship rules, not as a management expense.

An company with investment business may or may not also fall within the definition of a close investment-holding company (see below).

1.2 Corporation tax

Corporation tax is applied to companies with investment business in the normal way (there is an exception for *close* investment holding companies outlined below). Thus companies with investment business can benefit from the small companies' rate or marginal relief.

Question	Investment companies

TC Ltd, a non-close company with wholly investment business, has the following results for the year ended 31 March 2007.

	£
Rental income	150,000
Building society interest	8,000
Chargeable gains	100,000
Management expenses	
Property management	40,000
General	50,000
Capital allowances	
On property	800
General	1,000
Gift aid donations	47,000

Unrelieved management expenses carried forward at 1 April 2006 amounted to £60,500.

Compute the mainstream corporation tax payable.

Answer

	£	£
Rents		150,000
Less: capital allowances	800	
property management expenses	40,000	
		(40,800)
Property income		109,200
Interest income		8,000
Chargeable gains		100,000
		217,200
Less: general management expenses	50,000	
general capital allowances	1,000	
management expenses brought forward	60,500	
		(111,500)
		105,700
Less charges on income (gift aid donations)		(47,000)
PCTCT		58,700
Corporation tax payable £58,700 × 19%		£11,153

2 Close companies

Owner-managed and family-owned companies could easily be used for tax avoidance. **Special rules apply to these 'close' companies** to counteract this. Broadly, a close company is one that is under the control of either five or fewer shareholders or any number of its shareholding directors. Shareholders and shareholding directors are known as 'participators'.

Direct relatives, business partners and certain trusts set up by the participator (or their direct relatives or business partners) are known as 'associates'. The rights and powers of associates are attributed to participators when determining control.

Thus if the five largest shareholders of X Ltd own 9% of the shares each, and they have no associates, the company will not be close. If, however, the wife and son of Mr A, one of the five largest shareholders, each hold 3% the company will be close as Mr A is deemed to hold (9 + 3 + 3) = 15%, so that the holdings of the five largest shareholders is (4 × 9 + 15) = 51%.

2.1 Loans to participators

FAST FORWARD

The rules on loans and benefits from close companies are intended to deter shareholders from using the obvious ways of extracting value from their company without paying tax.

When a close company makes a loan to one of its participators or an associate it must make a tax payment to HMRC equal to 25% of the loan. If the loan is repaid, HMRC will repay this tax charge.

For small and medium sized companies, the tax charge is due for payment nine months after the end of the accounting period. If the loan is repaid before the tax charge is due to be paid then the requirement to pay the penalty tax charge is cancelled. Interest runs from the due date until the earlier of payment of the tax and repayment of the loan. The loan must be notified on the company's tax return. The tax charge is subject to the quarterly payments on account regime if the company is large.

A loan for these purposes includes:

- A debt owed to the company
- A debt incurred by a participator or his associate and assigned to the company
- An advance of money
- A director's overdrawn current account

Certain loans are excluded from these provisions. These are:

- Money owed for goods or services supplied in the ordinary course of the company's trade unless the credit period exceeds:

  - Six months, or, if less
  - The normal credit period given to the company's other customers.

- Loans to directors and employees providing they do not exceed £15,000 in total per borrower and:

  - The borrower works full-time for the close company, and

  - He does not have a material interest (entitlement to over 5% of the assets available for distribution on a winding up) in the close company.

If at the time a loan was made the borrower did not have a material interest but he later acquires one, the company is regarded as making a loan to him at that date.

When all or part of the loan is repaid by the participator to the company, or the company writes off all or part of the loan, then the company can reclaim all or a corresponding part of the tax charge paid over to HMRC. If the loan is repaid or written of after the due date for paying the tax charge, the tax is not repayable until nine months after the end of the accounting period of repayment or write off of the loan.

HMRC pay interest up to the time they repay the tax. If the loan is repaid/written off before nine months from the end of the accounting period in which the loan is made, interest runs from the end of those nine months. Otherwise, it runs from the date when the tax is repayable.

Exam focus point

If a loan made during an accounting period is to be repaid during the next accounting period repayment before the due date for payment of the corporation tax will avoid the need for the penalty tax charge to be paid. Later repayment will defer the refund date for a year.

Although tax is charged on the company when a loan is made to a participator, the loan is not at that stage treated as the participator's income. If the loan is later written off:

(a)   **The amount written off is treated as the participator's income** and is included within his total income grossed up accordingly. It is taxed **as if it were a dividend** received by him (the net dividend equalling the loan written off), so a starting or basic rate taxpayer has no more tax to pay, but a higher rate taxpayer must pay more tax

(b)   If the participator is a director or employee, there is no taxable benefit because the above tax charge applies instead

(c)   The amount included within the participator's income cannot be used to cover charges paid for the purposes of avoiding a liability for tax retained on charges not paid out of taxable income.

Question

Close company loan

C Ltd, a close company which prepares accounts to 31 July each year, lends £50,000 to a shareholder in July 2005. C Ltd is required to account for a tax charge of £12,500 to HMRC. In July 2006 the shareholder repays £20,000. In January 2007 C Ltd writes off the remaining £30,000. Compute the amount of penalty tax recovered by C Ltd following the repayment in July 2006 and the write off in January 2007.

Answer

(a)   The penalty tax recovered after the repayment is $\dfrac{20,000}{50,000} \times £12,500 = £5,000$.

(b)   The penalty tax recovered after the write off is £7,500.

2.2 Benefits treated as distributions

Benefits given by a close company to participators and their associates and which are not taxable earnings, for example where the participator does not work for the company, **are treated as distributions**. The amount of the deemed distribution is the amount that would otherwise be taxed as earnings. The actual cost is a disallowable expense for corporation tax purposes.

Question

Benefits

A close company provides a new car for a participator who is not a director or employee in May 2006. The taxable benefit in 2006/07 under the income tax legislation would be valued at £3,500. No fuel is provided. What are the tax consequences?

Answer

The participator is taxed as if he had received a net dividend of £3,500 in 2006/07. The company cannot deduct capital allowances on the car or any running costs in computing its taxable profits.

2.3 Close investment-holding companies

FAST FORWARD

Close investment-holding companies are singled out for special treatment so as to deter people with substantial investments from putting their investments into a company and using the company status to reduce or defer tax liabilities.

Key term

A **close investment-holding company** (CIC) is a close company which:

- Is not a trading company, and
- Is not a member of a trading group.

A company is a trading company for an accounting period if it exists wholly or mainly for the purpose of trading. A company will not necessarily have to trade in an accounting period in order to satisfy this test but the trade must, when it is carried on, be carried on a commercial basis.

A member of a trading group is a company which co-ordinates the administration of trading companies which it controls.

Companies which deal in land, shares or securities are treated as trading companies for this purpose. Similarly, a company which invests in property let or to be let on a commercial basis will not be treated as a CIC.

A CIC always pays corporation tax at the full rate of 30% whatever its level of profits. However, a CIC associated with another company still counts as an associated company for the purposes of reducing the limits for the small companies rate and marginal relief.

2.4 Taper relief on the sale of shares in a close company

Where shares in a close company are disposed of, any part of a period of ownership during which the company is not active does not count for taper relief purposes (see earlier in this Text).

A company is active if it is preparing to carry on, or actually carrying on, a business of any description or if such a business is being wound up. The business does not have to be carried on with a view to profit nor conducted on a commercial basis. 'Carrying on a business' can include holding assets and managing them.

Chapter roundup

- A company that generates income from investments can usually deduct the expenses of managing their investments for corporation tax purposes.

- The rules on loans and benefits from close companies are intended to deter shareholders from using the obvious ways of extracting value from their company without paying tax.

- Close investment-holding companies are singled out for special treatment so as to deter people with substantial investments from putting their investments into a company and using the company status to defer tax liabilities.

Quick quiz

1   How may an investment company obtain relief for management expenses?

2   What is a close company?

3   What are the immediate consequences of a loan by a close company to a participator?

4   What items are treated as distributions by close companies?

5   What rate(s) of CT may apply to close investment-holding companies?

Answers to quick quiz

1   Management expenses are deductible when computing taxable profits Any unrelieved management expenses may be carried forward to be relieved in a similar fashion in the following accounting period.

2   A close company is one that is under the control of either five or fewer shareholders or any number of shareholding directors.

3   When a close company makes a loan to one of its participators it must make a payment to HMRC equal to 25% of the loan.

4   Benefits given to participators or their associates which are not taxed under the benefits legislation.

5   CICs always pay the full rate of corporation tax (30%) irrespective of the level of their profits.

Now try the question below from the Exam Question Bank

Number	Level	Marks	Time
Q27	Introductory	15	27 mins
Q37	Examination	25	45 mins

Q37 has been analysed to show you how to approach paper P6 exams.

Groups and consortia

Topic list	Syllabus reference
1 Types of group	A2(a)C4
2 Group relief	A2(e)(iii),(iv),(viii), (ix)
3 Capital gains group	A2(e)(i),(v),(vii)
4 Succession to trade	A2(e)(ii)

Introduction

So far we have studied the corporation tax rules for single companies. In this chapter we consider the extent to which tax law recognises group relationships between companies.

Companies in a group are still separate entities with their own tax liabilities but tax law recognises the close relationship between group companies. They can, if they meet certain conditions, share their losses and pass assets between each other without chargeable gains.

Consortium companies are companies which are controlled by several companies. They can also share their losses, but the rules are restricted to recognise the ownership shares of the controlling companies.

In the next chapter we will complete our study of corporation tax by looking at overseas aspects.

Study guide

		Intellectual level
2	**Corporation tax liabilities in situations involving further overseas and group aspects and in relation to special types of company, and the application of additional exemptions and reliefs**	
(a)	The contents of the Paper F6 study guide, for corporation tax, under headings:	2
•	C4 The effect of a group structure for corporation tax purposes	
(e)	The effect of a group structure for corporation tax purposes:	3
(i)	Advise on the tax consequences of a transfer of intangible assets	
(ii)	Advise on the tax consequences of a transfer of a trade and assets where there is common control	
(iii)	Understand the meaning of consortium owned company and consortium member	2
(iv)	Advise on the operation of consortium relief	
(v)	Determine pre-entry gains and losses and understand their tax treatment	
(vii)	Determine the degrouping charge where a company leaves a group within six years of receiving an asset by way of a no gain/no loss transfer	
(viii)	Determine the effects of the anti-avoidance provisions, where arrangements exist for a company to leave a group	
(ix)	Advise on the relief for trading losses incurred by an overseas subsidiary	

Exam guide

Groups and consortia are likely to be examined at most sittings. You must understand the difference between the definitions between a 75% group for group relief and a capital gains group, and understand the definition of a consortium. The question is likely to require a consideration of the various reliefs specifically available in group situations, with a view to minimising the group's tax liability.

Knowledge brought forward from earlier studies

This chapter revises the rules for group relief and for the transfer of capital assets between group companies and extends these to cover intangible fixed assets. It introduces consortium relief, and examines the anti-avoidance rules specifically applicable to groups.

1 Types of group

1.1 Groups

A group exists for taxation purposes where one company is a subsidiary of another. The percentage shareholding involved determines the taxation consequences of the fact that there is a group.

The four types of relationship for tax purposes are:

- **Associated companies**
- **75% subsidiaries**
- **Consortia**
- **Groups for chargeable gains purposes (capital gains groups)**

1.2 Associated companies

Two companies are associated with each other for taxation purposes if one is under the control of the other, or both are under the control of a third party. Control for these purposes means entitlement to more than 50% of any one of:

- The share capital
- The votes
- The income
- The net assets on a winding up

The number of associated companies determines the limits for the small companies' rate of corporation tax and marginal relief.

2 Group relief

2.1 Definitions

FAST FORWARD

Group relief is available where the existence of a group or consortium is established through companies resident anywhere in the world.

The group relief provisions enable companies within a 75% group to transfer trading losses to other profit making companies within the group, in order to reduce the group's overall corporation tax liability.

Key term

For one company to be a **75% subsidiary** of another, the holding company must have:

- At least 75% of the ordinary share capital of the subsidiary
- A right to at least 75% of the distributable income of the subsidiary, and
- A right to at least 75% of the net assets of the subsidiary were it to be wound up.

Two companies are members of a group for group relief purposes where one is a 75% subsidiary of the other, or both are 75% subsidiaries of a third company. Ordinary share capital is any share capital other than fixed dividend preference shares.

Two companies are in a group only if there is a 75% effective interest. Thus an 80% subsidiary (T) of an 80% subsidiary (S) is not in a group with the holding company (H), because the effective interest is only 80% × 80% = 64%. However, S and T are in a group and can claim group relief from each other. S **cannot** claim group relief from T and pass it on to H; it can only claim group relief for its own use.

A group relief group may include non-UK resident companies. **However, losses may generally only be surrendered between UK resident companies although in certain circumstances group relief is available to UK branches of overseas companies and even in specific circumstances for overseas losses.**

Illustration of a group relief group:

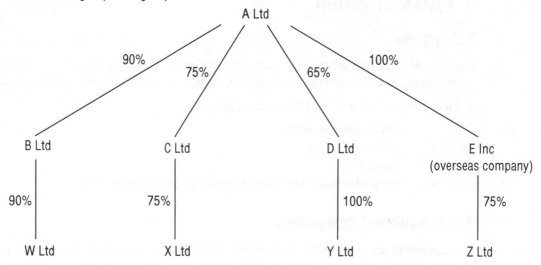

The companies in the group for group relief purposes are:

A Ltd
B Ltd
W Ltd (81% effective holding by A)
C Ltd
E Inc
Z Ltd (75% effective holding by A)

In addition C Ltd and X Ltd and also D Ltd and Y Ltd form their own separate mini-groups.

2.2 The relief

FAST FORWARD

> Within a 75% group trading losses can be surrendered between UK companies.

A **claimant company** is assumed to use its own current year losses or losses brought forward in working out the profits against which it may claim group relief, even if it does not in fact claim s 393A relief for current losses. Furthermore, **group relief is against profits after all other reliefs for the current period or brought forward from earlier periods**, including non-trading deficits on loan relationships and charges. Group relief is given before relief for any amounts brought back from later periods.

A **surrendering company may group relieve a loss before setting it against its own profits for the period of the loss, and may specify any amount to be surrendered.** This is **important for tax planning as it enables the surrendering company to leave profits in its own computation to be charged to corporation tax at the small companies' rate, while surrendering its losses to other companies to cover profits which would otherwise fall into the marginal relief band or be taxed at the full rate.** Note that profits in the small companies' marginal relief band are taxed at the marginal rate of 32.75%. (In FY 2005 profits in the starting rate marginal relief band were taxed at the marginal rate of 23.75%.)

Question

In a group of four companies, the results for the year ended 31 March 2007 are as follows.

	Profit/(loss) £
A Ltd	52,000
B Ltd	212,500
C Ltd	1,000,000
D Ltd	(400,000)

How should the loss be allocated to save as much tax as possible? How much tax is saved?

Answer

The upper and lower limits for small companies' marginal relief are £1,500,000/4 = £375,000 and £300,000/4 = £75,000 respectively.

	A Ltd £	B Ltd £	C Ltd £
Profits before group relief	52,000	212,500	1,000,000
Less group relief (note)	0	(137,500)	(262,500)
PCTCT	52,000	75,000	737,500
Tax saved			
£137,500 × 32.75%		45,031	
£262,500 × 30%			78,750

Total £(45,031 + 78,750) = £123,781

Note. We wish to save the most tax possible for the group.

Since A Ltd is in the small companies' band any loss given to it will save tax at the small companies' rate of 19%.

B Ltd is in the marginal relief for small companies' rate band. Therefore, any loss given to B saves the effective marginal rate of 32.75% until the profits fall to £75,000 (the small companies' lower limit). After this only 19% is saved.

C Ltd is in the full rate band of 30% until profits fall to £375,000 (the small companies' upper limit).

So to conclude it is best to give B Ltd £137,500 of loss and save 32.75% tax on the profits in the marginal relief band. The balance of the loss is then given to C Ltd to save 30% tax.

A company may surrender trading losses, excess property income losses, non-trading deficits on loan relationships and excess charges on income to other group companies. Charges can only be group-relieved to the extent that they exceed profits before taking account of any losses of the current period or brought forward or back from other accounting periods. **Excess management expenses of companies with investment business may also be surrendered.** If there are excess charges, property income losses and management expenses available for surrender then they are surrendered in that order.

Capital losses cannot be group relieved. However, see below for details of how a group may net off its gains and losses.

Only current period losses are available for group relief. Furthermore, they must be set against profits of a corresponding accounting period. If the accounting periods of a surrendering company and a claimant company are not the same this means that both the profits and losses must be apportioned so that only the results of the period of overlap may be set off. Apportionment is on a time basis.

However, in the period when a company joins or leaves a group, an alternative method may be used if the result given by time-apportionment would be unjust or unreasonable.

An overseas subsidiary may only surrender losses to other companies if they would have been within the charge to UK corporation tax had they been profits, and if no relief for those losses is available against foreign tax. This applies to trading losses incurred in the UK. Relief from UK corporation tax cannot be obtained for overseas trading losses, although relief from tax in the country in which the subsidiary is resident may be available, depending on the tax rules for that country.

Question	Corresponding accounting periods
	£
S Ltd incurs a trading loss for the year to 30 September 2006	(150,000)
H Ltd makes taxable profits:	
for the year to 31 December 2005	200,000
for the year to 31 December 2006	100,000

What group relief can H Ltd claim from S Ltd?

Answer

H Ltd can claim group relief as follows.

	£
For the year ended 31 December 2005 profits of the corresponding accounting period (1.10.05 – 31.12.05) are £200,000 × 3/12	50,000
Losses of the corresponding accounting period are £150,000 × 3/12	37,500
A claim for £37,500 of group relief may be made against H Ltd's profits	
For the year ended 31 December 2006 profits of the corresponding accounting period (1.1.06 – 30.9.06) are £100,000 × 9/12	75,000
Losses of the corresponding accounting period are £150,000 × 9/12	112,500
A claim for £75,000 of group relief may be made against H Ltd's profits	

If a claimant company claims relief for losses surrendered by more than one company, the total relief that may be claimed for a period of overlap is limited to the proportion of the claimant's profits attributable to that period. Similarly, if a company surrenders losses to more than one claimant, the total losses that may be surrendered in a period of overlap is limited to the proportion of the surrendering company's losses attributable to that period.

A claim for group relief is normally made on the claimant company's tax return. It is ineffective unless a notice of consent is also given by the surrendering company. Where the surrendering company is also claiming loss relief against its own profits the group relief surrender must be made first.

A claimant company may not amend a group relief claim but it may withdraw it and replace it with a new claim. The **time limit** for making or withdrawing a claim is the latest of:

(a)   **The first anniversary of the filing date for the CT return**

(b)   30 days after the completion of an enquiry into a return

(c)   30 days after the amendment of a self assessment by HMRC following the completion of an enquiry

(d)   30 days after the settlement of an appeal against an amendment to the self assessment made by HMRC following an enquiry.

HMRC has discretion to accept a late claim/withdrawal.

Group wide claims/surrenders can be made as one person can act for two or more companies at once.

Any payment by the claimant company for group relief, up to the amount of the loss surrendered, is ignored for all corporation tax purposes.

Question
Group relief

C Ltd has one wholly owned subsidiary, D Ltd. The results of both companies for the four years ended 31 March 2007 are shown below.

	12 months to 31 March			
	2004	2005	2006	2007
	£'000	£'000	£'000	£'000
C Ltd				
Trading profit (loss)	200	(1,700)	100	(2,000)
Property income	800	800	800	800
Gift aid donation paid	(40)		0	(60)
D Ltd				
Trading profit (loss)	(2,300)	3,260	(870)	2,400
Interest on gilts (non-trading investment) (gross)	1,800	0	1,200	1,300
Gift aid donation paid	0	(400)	(300)	(500)

Show the profits chargeable to corporation tax for both companies for all years shown, assuming that the most beneficial claims for loss relief and group relief are made, and no dividends are paid or received by the companies.

Answer

C Ltd

	Accounting periods to 31 March			
	2004	2005	2006	2007
	£'000	£'000	£'000	£'000
Trading profit	200	0	100	0
Property income	800	800	800	800
	1,000	800	900	800
Less s 393A(1) – current period relief		(650)	0	(800)
		150	900	0
Less s 393A – carry back	0	0	(630)	0
	1,000	150	270	0
Less charges paid	(40)	0	0	0
	960	150	270	0
Less group relief claim	(650)	0	(120)	0
PCTCT	310	150	150	0

Loss memorandum				
Loss		(1,700)		(2,000)
Group relief surrender		1,050		570
		(650)		(1,430)
S 393A(1) claim: current year		650		800
		0		(630)
S 393A(1) claim: carry back				630
		0		0

	Accounting periods to 31 March			
	2004	*2005*	*2006*	*2007*
	£'000	£'000	£'000	£'000
D Ltd				
Trading income	0	3,260	0	2,400
Interest income	1,800	0	1,200	1,300
	1,800	3,260	1,200	3,700
Less s 393A(1) – current period relief	(1,650)		(750)	
	150		450	
Less charges paid	0	(400)	(300)	(500)
	150	2,860	150	3,200
Less group relief claim		(1,050)		(570)
PCTCT	150	1,810	150	2,630
Loss memorandum	£		£	
Loss	(2,300)		(870)	
Group relief surrender	650		120	
	(1,650)		(750)	
S 393A(1) claim	1,650		750	
	0		0	

Note. The excess charges of £60,000 arising in C Ltd for the year to 31.3.07 are wasted.

(1) The most beneficial claims for relief will relieve losses at the small companies' marginal rate, then at the full rate and, where the rate of relief is the same, in the earlier year

(2) C Ltd should claim group relief of £650,000 in the year to 31.3.04 leaving D Ltd sufficient loss to reduce its profits to the small companies' limit of £150,000 (two companies in group)

(3) Similarly in the year to 31.3.05 D Ltd should claim group relief of £1,050,000, leaving sufficient loss to reduce C Ltd's profit to £150,000

(4) In the year to 31.3.06 C Ltd needs to claim group relief of £120,000, leaving D Ltd's profits, after S393A(1) relief, at £150,000

(5) S393A carry back relief is advantageous for C Ltd's loss of the year to 31.3.06, but again group claim by D Ltd should be set so as to leave C Ltd's PCTCT for the year to 31.3.06 at £150,000. Note that the current year claim cannot be restricted

2.3 Arrangements to leave a group

Group relief is not available for any period during which there are arrangements in force for either the surrendering company or the claimant company to leave the group. If necessary, profits and losses are apportioned on a time basis.

The term 'arrangements' is not defined, but HMRC normally accept that negotiations to sell a company are not arrangements until an offer is accepted, even if it is then subject to contract or is conditional. If shareholder approval is required for the sale, arrangements do not exist until approval has been given.

2.4 Consortium relief

FAST FORWARD

Within a consortium there is some scope for loss relief.

The definition of a consortium is given below.

Key term

> A **company is owned by a consortium** (and is known as a consortium-owned company) if:
>
> - 75% or more of its ordinary share capital is owned by companies (the members of the consortium), none of which has a holding of less than 5%, and
>
> - Each member of the consortium is entitled to at least 5% of any profits available for distribution to equity holders of the company and at least 5% of any assets so available on a winding up.

Illustration of a consortium

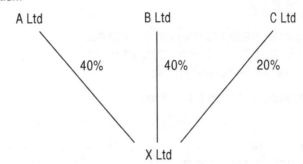

X Ltd is the consortium-owned company A Ltd, B Ltd and C Ltd are the consortium members.

Consortium relief is a loss relief which is available:

(a) Where the surrendering company is a trading company owned by a consortium and is not a 75% subsidiary of any one company and the claimant company belongs to the consortium

(b) Where the surrendering company is a trading company which is a 90% subsidiary of a holding company which is owned by a consortium and is not a 75% subsidiary of any one company and the claimant company is a member of the consortium

(c) Where the surrendering company is a holding company owned by a consortium and is not a 75% subsidiary of any one company and the claimant company is a member of the consortium.

A **trading company** is one whose business consists wholly or mainly in carrying on a trade. A holding company is one whose business consists wholly or mainly in holding shares in companies which are trading companies.

A consortium-owned company can surrender losses in proportion to the stakes of the members of the consortium. Thus if a member holds 20% of the shares in the company, up to 20% of the company's losses can be surrendered to that member.

Consortium relief can also flow downwards. **A consortium member may surrender its losses to set against its share of the consortium-owned company's profits.** So, a member with a 25% stake in the consortium-owned company can surrender losses to cover up to 25% of the company's profits.

Whereas normally a surrendering company can surrender group relief without having to consider any possible s 393A(1) claim, **a loss made by a consortium-owned company must be reduced by any potential s 393A(1) claims against current period profits** (not profits of previous periods) **before it may be surrendered as consortium relief**.

Although a consortium can be established with non-UK resident companies, losses cannot, in general, be surrendered to/from a non-UK resident.

Question

C Ltd is owned 60% by A Ltd, 30% by B Ltd and 10% by an overseas company X Inc. Results for the year ended 31 March 2007 are as follows.

	A Ltd £	B Ltd £	C Ltd £
Trading profit/(loss)	200,000	75,000	(50,000)
Property income	0	0	12,000

No dividends are paid or received by C Ltd.

Compute the corporation tax liabilities of all three companies, assuming that all possible consortium relief claims are made but that C Ltd does not claim s 393A(1) relief.

Answer

A Ltd may claim £(50,000 – 12,000) × 60% = £22,800.
B Ltd may claim £(50,000 – 12,000) × 30% = £11,400.
A Ltd has one associated company (C Ltd).

A Ltd's corporation tax liability is as follows.

	£
Profits	200,000
Less consortium relief	(22,800)
Profits chargeable to corporation tax	177,200

Corporation tax	£
£177,200 × 30%	53,160
Less small companies' rate marginal relief £(750,000 – 177, 200) × 11/400	(15,752)
	37,408

B Ltd's corporation tax liability is £(75,000 – 11,400) × 19% = £63,600 × 19% = £12,084.

C Ltd's corporation tax liability is:

	£
£12,000 × 19%	2,280

Note. The limits for small companies' rate marginal relief are divided by 2 since there are two associated companies (A Ltd and C Ltd).

C Ltd has a loss to carry forward under s 393(1) ICTA 1988 of £(50,000 – 22,800 – 11,400) = £15,800.

2.5 Tax planning for group relief

This section outlines some tax planning points to bear in mind when dealing with a group.

Group relief should first be given in this order:

1st   To companies in the small companies' marginal relief band paying 32.75% tax (but only sufficient loss to bring profits down to the SCR limit)

2nd   To companies paying the full rate of tax at 30%

3rd   To companies paying SCR at 19%

Similarly, a company should make a s 393A(1) claim to use a loss itself rather than surrender the loss to other group companies if the s 393A(1) claim would lead to a tax saving at a higher rate. Remember that where a loss is carried back relief may be at the starting rate (nil%) or the starting rate marginal rate (23.75%)

Companies with profits may benefit by reducing their claims for capital allowances in a particular year. This may leave sufficient profits to take advantage of group relief which may only be available for the current year. The amount on which writing-down allowances can be claimed in later years is increased accordingly.

3 Capital gains group

3.1 Definition

Companies are in a capital gains group if:

(a)   At each level, there is a 75% holding, and

(b)   The top company has an effective interest of over 50% in the group companies.

If A holds 75% of B, B holds 75% of C and C holds 75% of D, then A, B and C are in such a group, but D is outside the group because A's interest in D is only 75% × 75% × 75% = 42.1875%. Furthermore, D is not in a group with C, because the group must include the top company (A). This is illustrated in the diagram below.

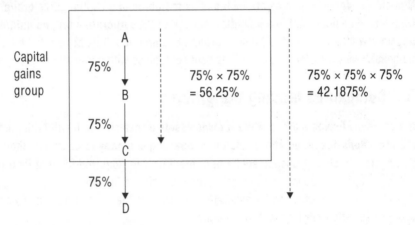

Illustration of a chargeable gains group:

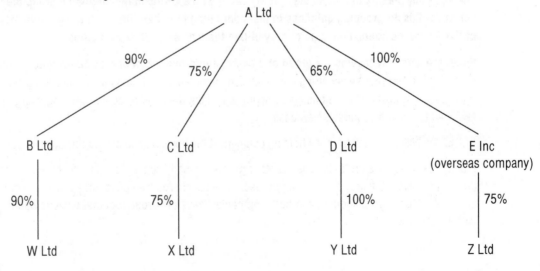

The companies in a group for chargeable gains purposes are:

> A Ltd
> B Ltd
> W Ltd
> C Ltd
> X Ltd (75% subsidiary of 75% subsidiary, effective interest over 50%)
> E Inc
> Z Ltd

There is a separate capital gains group of D Ltd and Y Ltd.

3.2 Intra-group transfers

Within a capital gains group, assets are automatically transferred at no gain/no loss. An election may be made for this tax treatment to apply where an asset is sold outside the group to match group gains and losses.

Companies in a capital gains group make intra-group transfers of chargeable assets without a chargeable gain or an allowable loss arising. No election is needed, as this relief is compulsory. The assets are deemed to be transferred at such a price as will give the transferor no gain and no loss. Similarly, intangible assets can be transferred between members of a capital gains group without a Trading profit or loss arising (see earlier in this Text).

Non-UK resident companies are included as members of a capital gains group. Provided the assets transferred do not result in a potential leakage of UK corporation tax, no gain/no loss transfers are possible within a worldwide (global) group of companies. This means that it may be possible to make no gain/no loss transfers to non-UK resident companies with a branch or agency in the UK.

3.3 Companies leaving the group

If a company leaves a group while it owns assets transferred to it within the previous six years under the provisions described above, then the departing company is treated as though it had, at the time of its acquisition of such assets, sold and immediately re-acquired them at their then market values. However, the consequent gain or loss (computed using indexation allowance up to the time when the departing company acquired the assets) is brought into the departing company's tax computation for the accounting period in which it leaves the group.

The company leaving the group may jointly claim with a UK resident continuing group member to surrender this de-grouping gain/loss to that continuing member. The continuing group member may utilise its losses against the gain or may utilise the loss against its own gains.

Either the company leaving the group or a continuing group member may claim rollover relief for the de-grouping charge. The departing company can claim relief if it retains the de-grouping charge and acquires a new asset. The continuing company can claim the relief if the de-grouping charge has been switched to it and it acquires a new asset.

HMRC can collect the tax from the holding company if the tax is unpaid six months after its due date.

If a company leaves a group because another group company ceases to exist, the first company is not deemed to have left a group for these purposes. The tax charge also does not apply if one company acquired an asset from another, and both companies leave the group together while remaining in a group with each other.

Question

In March 2007, Top Ltd sold the whole of the share capital of Bottom Ltd, a 100% subsidiary, to Take plc. Included in Bottom Ltd's assets is a warehouse acquired by Top Ltd in January 1987 for £96,000. This was transferred to Bottom Ltd in August 2001 for £100,000. Its market value at the date of transfer was £310,000. The indexation allowance on a sale in August 2001 would have been £74,000.

What is the effect of Bottom Ltd leaving the group? Compute Bottom Ltd's mainstream corporation tax for the year ended 31 March 2007 if it has trading income of £2,000,000.

Answer

Bottom Ltd leaves the group within six years of acquiring the warehouse from Top Ltd. Bottom Ltd will be treated as if it had sold the warehouse at its market value in August 2001 and then immediately reacquired it.

	£	£
Proceeds (ie MV in August 2001)		310,000
Less cost: cost to Top Ltd	96,000	
indexation allowance to August 2001	74,000	
		(170,000)
Chargeable gain of Bottom Ltd, in the accounting period which includes March 2007		140,000

Top Ltd will not have a chargeable gain on the sale of its shares in Bottom Ltd, due to the substantial shareholdings relief applying to the sale of the subsidiary.

If no claims are made, Bottom Ltd's MCT for the year to 31.3.07 is as follows.

	£
Trading profits	2,000,000
Chargeable gain	140,000
	2,140,000
Corporation tax £2,140,000 × 30%	£642,000

Alternatively, a claim could be made to surrender the gain of £140,000 to Top Ltd or to rollover the gain against any qualifying asset purchased. In this case the amount to be 'reinvested' to obtain full relief is £310,000 (the market value of the warehouse when the deemed disposal took place).

3.4 Matching group gains and losses

Capital losses cannot be included in a group relief claim. However, **two members of a capital gains group can elect that an asset that has been disposed of outside the group is treated as if it had been transferred between them immediately before disposal**. The deemed transferee company is then treated as having made the disposal. This election may be made within two years of the end of the accounting period in which the disposal took place.

From a tax planning point of view, elections(s) should be made to ensure that net taxable gains arise in the company subject to the lowest rate of corporation tax.

3.5 Rollover relief

Rollover relief is available in a capital gains group.

If a member of a capital gains group disposes of an asset eligible for capital gains rollover relief it may treat all of the group companies as a single unit for the purpose of claiming such relief. Acquisitions by other group members within the qualifying period of one year before the disposal to three years afterwards may be matched with the disposal. However, both the disposing company and the acquiring company must make the claim. If an asset is transferred at no gain and no loss between group members, that transfer does not count as the acquisition of an asset for rollover relief purpose.

Claims may also be made by non-trading group members which hold assets used for other group members' trades.

Exam focus point

Try to remember the following summary – it will be of great help in the exam.

Parent Co controls > 50% of subsidiary

- Associated companies for upper and lower limits

Parent Co owns ≥ 75% of subsidiary and has indirect holding of ≥ 75% of sub-subsidiaries

- Surrender trading losses, excess property income losses, excess charges, loan deficits, excess management expenses to companies with some PCTCT for same time period

Parent Co owns ≥ 75% of subsidiary and has indirect holding of > 50% of sub-subsidiaries (but must be ≥ 75% at each level)

- Transfer assets between companies automatically at no gain/no loss
- Capital gains and losses can be matched between group member companies
- All companies treated as one for rollover relief purposes.

3.6 Intangible fixed assets

Similar rules apply to intangible fixed assets held within a capital gains group. The rules are:

(a) **Rollover relief** can be claimed where an intangible fixed asset used for trade purposes is sold where the reinvestment is made by another member of the capital gains group, and also where the reinvestment is in the shares of another company which becomes a member as a result

(b) **Transfers of intangible assets between members of a capital gains group are on a 'no gain/loss basis'**

(c) Where a company leaves a capital gains group holding an intangible asset transferred to it in the previous six years the gain or loss that would have arisen on the date of the transfer is realised and included in trading profits (if the asset is used for the trade), the profits of a UK property letting business (if the asset is used for letting), or miscellaneous income (if the asset is an investment)

(d) The degrouping charge may be transferred from the company leaving the group to another group company

(e) Either the company leaving the capital gains group or a continuing member can claim to rollover any profit arising. The departing company can claim relief if it retains the profit and acquires a new asset. The continuing company can claim relief if the profit has been switched to it and it acquires a new intangible asset.

3.7 Pre-entry capital losses

Restrictions apply to the use of pre-entry losses and gains within capital gains groups.

A group might acquire a company that has capital losses brought forward, or assets which could be sold to generate capital losses. The use of such 'pre-entry' losses is restricted.

If a company (X) joins a group (G), we must identify X's pre-entry (capital) losses. These are:

- **Losses on disposals before X joined G**

- **The pre-entry proportions of losses on disposals after X joined G of pre-entry assets** (assets X already owned but not yet sold when it joined G).

When a pre-entry asset is sold at a loss after X joins G, the pre-entry proportion of the loss is found by working out the proportion for each item of allowable expenditure (cost or enhancement expenditure) and adding up the results.

The proportion for each item of allowable expenditure is $A \times (B/C) \times (D/E)$, where:

A   is the total allowable loss
B   is the item of allowable expenditure
C   is the sum of all the items of allowable expenditure
D   is the time from when the expenditure was incurred to when X joined G.
E   is the time from when the expenditure was incurred to the disposal

The original cost of the asset is treated as incurred when the asset was acquired.

If X sells a pre-entry asset at a loss and makes an election within two years of the end of the accounting period of the disposal, the above computation is disregarded and instead the pre-entry proportion of the loss is the smaller of:

(a)   The loss which would have arisen on a sale at market value when X joined G (treating a gain as a loss of £0).

(b)   The loss on the actual sale.

X's pre-entry losses may (subject to the usual rule against carrying back capital losses) **be set against gains on assets which:**

- **X disposed of before joining G**

- **X already owned when it joined G, or**

- **X acquired after joining G from someone outside G** and which have, since acquisition, not been used except for the purposes of a trade which X was carrying on immediately before joining G and continued to carry on until the disposals giving rise to the gains.

In any one accounting period, pre-entry losses (whether of the current period or brought forward) are used (so far as possible) before other losses.

Question   Pre-entry losses

X joined the G group on 1 January 1998. X had acquired some land on 1 August 1992 for £700,000, and had incurred enhancement expenditure of £300,000 on 1 April 1995. The land was worth £600,000 on 1 January 1998. On 1 July 2006, X sold the land for £450,000. What is the pre-entry proportion of the loss?

Answer

The total allowable loss is as follows.

	£	£
Proceeds		450,000
Less: cost	700,000	
enhancement expenditure	300,000	
		(1,000,000)
Allowable loss		(550,000)

The pre-entry proportion without an election is as follows.

	£
$£550,000 \times \dfrac{700,000}{1,000,000} \times \dfrac{1.8.92 - 1.1.98 = (65\,\text{months})}{1.8.92 - 1.7.06 = (167\,\text{months})}$	149,850
$£550,000 \times \dfrac{300,000}{1,000,000} \times \dfrac{1.4.95 - 1.1.98 = (33\,\text{months})}{1.4.95 - 1.7.06 = (135\,\text{months})}$	40,333
	190,183

If the land had been sold when X joined the group on 1 January 1998, the loss would have been as follows.

	£	£
Proceeds		600,000
Less: cost	700,000	
enhancement expenditure	300,000	
		(1,000,000)
Allowable loss		(400,000)

The pre-entry proportion with an election would be the lower of £550,000 and £400,000, that is, £400,000.

The company wants the **lowest** possible pre-entry proportion, because that proportion's use is restricted. The company should therefore not make an election, and will then have a pre-entry proportion of £190,183. The balance of the loss, £(550,000 – 190,183) = £359,817, can be set against all gains made by X Ltd in the same or later accounting periods without restriction.

There are anti avoidance rules which further restricts the set off losses if the transaction is part of a tax avoidance scheme.

3.8 Capital gains buying (pre-entry capital gains)

Pre-entry gains are gains realised on pre-change assets, ie assets held by a company at or before the time that it joins a group.

If one of the purposes of the company joining the group was to enable a loss to be set against a pre-entry gain, relief is restricted. In this case the only losses available to set against pre-entry gains **realised before a company joins a group** are:

- Losses that arise in that company before the company joins the new group, and
- Losses that arise after that time on assets that the company held when it joined the group.

4 Succession to trade

FAST FORWARD

A succession occurs when a trade carried on by one company is transferred to another company in substantially the same ownership. In this case losses may be carried forward and balancing adjustments do not arise for capital allowances purposes.

Generally, if a trade is transferred from one company to another, that is treated as a cessation of the trade by the transferor and a commencement of the trade by the transferee. Any trading losses brought forward by the transferor under s 393(1) are extinguished and cannot be utilised by the transferee. In addition, balancing adjustments may arise on assets qualifying for capital allowances. If however the transfer of the trade amounts to a 'succession', it is treated as continuing for certain specific purposes.

Key term

A '**succession to trade**' occurs if a trade carried on by one company (the 'predecessor') is transferred to another company (the 'successor') in **substantially the same ownership**.

The above test is met if the same persons hold an interest of at least 75% in the trade **both**:

(a)   at some time during the 12 months prior to transfer, and

(b)   at some time during the 24 months following the transfer

and throughout those periods the trade is carried on by a company chargeable to tax in respect of it.

The transfer of a trade from a company to its 75% subsidiary will generally qualify as a succession. Such a transfer is often referred to as a 'hive down'.

Other circumstances where a succession takes place include a transfer from a 75% subsidiary to its parent and a transfer of trade between two companies with a common 75% parent (or indeed owned to the extent of at least 75% by the same individual). There is no stipulation that the companies have to be UK resident, so the provisions can apply to UK branches of non-resident companies.

When a trade is transferred in this way:

(a)   an **accounting period ends** on the date of transfer

(b)   the predecessor may claim **capital allowances** in the final accounting period as if no transfer had taken place. The successor takes over the unrelieved expenditure and is entitled to capital allowances thereon in the period in which the transfer takes place

(c)   the successor is entitled to relief under **s 393(1) for trading losses** not utilised by the predecessor, against future profits from the trade in which the losses were incurred.

The following are **not** transferred:

(a)   capital losses

(b)   deficits on non-trading loan relationships.

These remain with the transferor company.

These provisions do **not** enable a trading loss incurred by the successor company to be carried back under s 393A(1)(b) against profits realised by the predecessor. Also, the predecessor's cessation of trade does not qualify it for a three year carry back of losses.

Chapter roundup

- Group relief is available where the existence of a group or consortium is established through companies resident anywhere in the world.

- Within a 75% group trading losses can be surrendered between UK companies.

- Within a consortium there is some scope for loss relief.

- Within a capital gains group, assets are automatically transferred at no gain/no loss. An election may be made for this tax treatment to apply where an asset is sold outside the group to match group gains and losses.

- Rollover relief is available in a capital gains group.

- Restrictions apply to the use of pre-entry losses and gains within capital gains groups.

- A succession occurs when a trade carried on by one company is transferred to another company in substantially the same ownership. In this case losses may be carried forward and balancing adjustments do not arise for capital allowances purposes.

Quick quiz

1   List the losses which may be group relieved.

2   What is the definition of a consortium?

3   When may assets be transferred intra-group at no gain and no loss?

4   How can capital gains and losses within a group be matched with each other?

Answers to quick quiz

1   Trading losses, excess UK property business losses, non-trading deficits on loan relationships, excess charges on income and excess management expenses of investment companies.

2   A company is owned by a consortium if 75% or more of its ordinary share capital is owned by companies none of which have a holding of less than 5%.

     Each consortium member (ie company shareholders) must have at least a 5% stake in profits and assets on a winding up in the consortium company.

3   No gain no loss asset transfers are automatic between companies in a capital gains group.

4   Two member of an 'assets group' can elect that an asset which has been disposed of to a third party is treated as transferred between them prior to disposal. This election effectively allow the group to match its gains and losses in one company.

Now try the question below from the Exam Question Bank			
Number	**Level**	**Marks**	**Time**
Q28	Introductory	25	45 mins

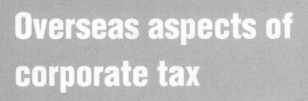

Overseas aspects of corporate tax

Topic list	Syllabus reference
1 Company residence	A2(d)
2 Double taxation relief (DTR)	A2(d)(ii)
3 Groups of companies	A2(e)(ix)
4 Controlled foreign companies	A2(d)(iv)
5 Permanent establishment (PE) or subsidiary abroad	A2(d)(iii)
6 Non-UK resident companies	A2(d)(v)

Introduction

We have nearly completed our study of corporation tax, except for the consideration of overseas aspects.

This chapter starts by considering which country a company 'lives' in. We then see how relief may be given for overseas taxes suffered, how overseas companies may impact a group and how UK companies are taxed on the profits of certain overseas subsidiaries.

Finally, we look at UK companies trading abroad, and some miscellaneous points on overseas companies trading in the UK.

In the next chapter we will turn our attention to VAT.

Study guide

		Intellectual level
2	**Corporation tax liabilities in situations involving further overseas and group aspects and in relation to special types of company, and the application of additional exemptions and reliefs**	
(d)	The comprehensive calculation of corporation tax liability:	3
(ii)	Assess the impact of the OECD model double tax treaty on corporation tax	
(iii)	Evaluate the meaning and implications of a permanent establishment	
(iv)	Identify and advise on the tax implications of controlled foreign companies	
(v)	Advise on the tax position of overseas companies trading in the UK	
(e)	The effect of a group structure for corporation tax purposes:	3
(ix)	Advise on the relief for trading losses incurred by an overseas subsidiary	

Exam guide

A question on the overseas aspects of corporation tax could require you to advise on the tax consequences of relationships with overseas companies. This could involve a discussion of the merits of trading through a permanent establishment (eg a branch) or subsidiary, and could extend to the anti-avoidance controlled foreign company rules where the subsidiary is resident in a low tax country. Double tax relief is an important consideration; the relief is the lower of the UK corporation tax and the foreign tax paid.

> Knowledge brought forward from earlier studies

This chapter revises your basic knowledge of double tax relief and the advantages of trading through a branch or subsidiary. Controlled foreign companies are new.

1 Company residence

FAST FORWARD

Company residence is important in determining whether its profits are subject to UK tax.

1.1 Introduction

A company is resident in the UK if it is incorporated in the UK or if its central management and control are exercised in the UK. Central management and control are usually treated as exercised where the board of directors meets.

A UK resident company is subject to corporation tax on its worldwide profits. It is taxable at the starting rate of corporation tax (FY02 to FY05) or the small companies' rate and can obtain marginal relief.

1.2 Non-UK resident companies trading in the UK

A non-UK resident company will be chargeable to corporation tax if it carries on a trade in the UK through a permanent establishment (PE). The profits of such a company which are chargeable to corporation tax, whether or not they arise in the UK, are:

- any trading income arising directly or indirectly from the PE

- any income from property or rights used by, or held by or for, the PE (other than dividends from UK companies)

- any chargeable gains arising from the disposal of assets situated in the UK.

Key term

> A **permanent establishment** is a fixed place of business through which the business of the enterprise is wholly or partly carried on. It includes a branch, office, factory, workshop, mine, oil or gas well, quarry and construction project lasting more than twelve months. It does not include use of storage facilities, maintenance of a stock of goods and delivery of them or a fixed place of business used solely for purchasing goods or any ancillary activity.

The profits of the permanent establishment are taxable at the full rate of corporation tax only. The small companies' rate and starting rate (FY02 to FY05) do not apply.

1.3 UK resident companies with foreign income

If a UK resident company makes investments abroad it will be liable to corporation tax on the profits made, the taxable amount being before the deduction of any foreign taxes. The profits may be any of the following.

(a) Trading income: profits of an overseas branch or agency controlled from the UK

(b) Interest income: income from foreign securities, for example debentures in overseas companies

(c) Foreign income: income from other overseas possessions including:

  (i) dividends from overseas subsidiaries
  (ii) profits of an overseas branch or agency controlled abroad

(d) Capital gains on disposals of foreign assets

Overseas dividends and interest received by a company are taxed at normal corporation tax rates.

A company may be subject to foreign tax as well as to UK corporation tax on the same profits usually if it has a PE in that foreign country. Double taxation relief (see below) is available in respect of the foreign tax suffered.

2 Double taxation relief (DTR)

FAST FORWARD

A company may obtain DTR for overseas withholding tax, and also (if its investment is large enough) for underlying tax. The allocation of charges and losses can affect the relief.

2.1 General principles

In the UK relief for foreign tax suffered by a company may be currently available in one of three ways.

(a) **Treaty relief**

Under a treaty entered into between the UK and the overseas country, a treaty may exempt certain profits from taxation in one of the countries involved, thus completely avoiding double taxation. More usually treaties provide for credit to be given for tax suffered in one of the countries against the tax liability in the other.

(b) **Unilateral credit relief**

Where no treaty relief is available, unilateral relief may be available in the UK giving credit for the foreign tax against the UK tax.

(c) **Unilateral expense relief** (This is not examinable)

Where neither treaty relief nor unilateral credit relief is available, or unilateral credit relief is not wanted by the taxpayer (because of a lack of UK tax liability against which to obtain credit), relief for overseas tax is given by deducting the overseas tax from the overseas profits prior to including them in the profits chargeable to corporation tax.

2.2 Treaty relief

A tax treaty based on the OECD model treaty may use either the exemption method or the credit method to give relief for tax suffered on income from a business in country B by a resident of country R.

(a) Under the **exemption method**, the income is not taxed at all in country R, or if it is dividends or interest (which the treaty allows to be taxed in country R) credit is given for any country B tax against the country R tax

(b) Under the **credit method**, the income is taxed in country R, but credit is given for any country B tax against the country R tax.

Under either method, any credit given is limited to the country B tax attributable to the income.

2.3 Unilateral credit relief

Relief is available for overseas tax suffered on PE profits, dividends, interest and royalties, up to the amount of the UK corporation tax (at the company's average rate) attributable to that income. The tax that is deducted overseas is usually called withholding tax. The gross income including the withholding tax is included within the profits chargeable to corporation tax.

Question | Unilateral credit relief

On 1 May 2006, AS plc receives a dividend from Bola of £80,000. This has been paid subject to 20% withholding tax. AS plc has UK trading income of £2,000,000 for the year to 31.3.07. Show that the foreign income is £100,000 and compute the corporation tax payable.

Answer

	Total £	UK £	Overseas £
Trading income	2,000,000	2,000,000	
Foreign income (W)	100,000		100,000
PCTCT	2,100,000	2,000,000	100,000

	Total £	UK £	Overseas £
Corporation tax at 30%	630,000	600,000	30,000
Less DTR: lower of:			
(a) overseas tax: £20,000, or			
(b) UK tax on overseas income: £30,000	(20,000)		(20,000)
CT due	610,000	600,000	10,000

Working: Foreign income

£80,000 × 100/(100 − 20) = £100,000.

If the overseas tax rate exceeds the UK tax rate there will be excess foreign tax. This may be eligible for relief against the UK tax on other foreign dividends through 'onshore pooling' where low taxed foreign dividends are pooled and the excess tax can be set against the UK tax due on the pooled dividends.

The excess foreign tax can be relieved as follows.

- (a)   Set off in the current accounting period
- (b)   Carry back for three years on a LIFO basis
- (c)   Carry forward indefinitely
- (d)   Surrender to another group company

Companies must take all reasonable steps to minimise their foreign tax if they are to obtain full relief against UK tax. A failure to claim all overseas tax reliefs, deductions, allowances etc will result in the UK authorities restricting the amount of DTR available.

Exam focus point

No detailed computational questions will be set on the carry back and carry forward of excess foreign tax or 'onshore pooling'. Only an awareness of the general provisions is required.

2.4 Underlying tax relief

In addition to the relief available for withholding tax shown above, relief is available for underlying tax relating to a dividend received from a foreign company in which the UK company owns at least 10% of the voting power, either directly or indirectly. The underlying tax is the tax attributable to the relevant profits out of which the dividend was paid.

Formula to learn

Underlying tax is calculated as:

$$\text{Gross dividend income} \times \frac{\text{foreign tax paid}}{\text{after-tax accounting profits}}$$

Relief for underlying tax is not available to individuals.

We may need to decide which accounting profits have been used to pay a dividend. If the dividend is declared for a particular year, the set of accounts for that year are used. If this information is not given, the relevant profits are those of the period of account immediately before that in which the dividend was payable.

There is an anti-avoidance provision which restricts relief for underlying tax in certain circumstances where there is a scheme the purpose, or one of the main purposes, of which is to obtain relief for underlying tax.

Question   Underlying tax relief

A Ltd, a UK company with no associated companies, holds 30,000 out of 90,000 voting ordinary shares in B Inc (resident in Lintonia).

The profit and loss account of B Inc for the year to 31 March 2007 is as follows (converted into sterling).

		£	£
Trading profit			1,000,000
Less taxation:	provided on profits	300,000	
	transfer to deferred tax account	100,000	
			(400,000)
Profits after tax			600,000
Less dividends:	net	240,000	
	withholding tax (20%)	60,000	
			(300,000)
Retained profits			300,000

The actual tax paid on the profits for the year to 31 March 2007 was £270,000.

Apart from the net dividend of £80,000 received out of the above profits from B Inc on 31 May 2006 the only other taxable profit of A Ltd for its year to 31 March 2007 was £610,000 UK trading profit. A Ltd paid no dividends during the year and received no UK dividends.

Calculate A Ltd's UK corporation tax liability after double taxation relief.

Answer

A LTD: UK CORPORATION TAX LIABILITY

	£	£
Trading income		610,000
Foreign income		
Net dividend	80,000	
Withholding tax at 20%		
£80,000 × 20/80	20,000	
Gross dividend	100,000	
Underlying tax		
£100,000 × $\dfrac{270,000}{600,000}$	45,000	
Gross income		145,000
PCTCT		755,000

	Total £	UK £	Overseas £
Trading income	610,000	610,000	
Foreign income	145,000		145,000
PCTCT	755,000	610,000	145,000
Corporation tax £755,000 × 30%			226,500
Less small companies' marginal relief £(1,500,000 – 755,000) × 11/400			(20,488)
			206,012

The average rate of corporation tax is £206,012/£755,000 = 27.28635%.

	Total	UK	Overseas
Corporation tax at the average rate	206,012	166,447	39,565
Less DTR: lower of:			
(a) overseas tax £(20,000 + 45,000) = £65,000			
(b) UK tax on overseas income £39,565	(39,565)		(39,565)
	166,447	166,447	0

Corporation tax of £166,447 is payable. £(65,000 – 39,565) = £25,435 of overseas tax is unrelieved (ie excess). It is possible to carry the unrelieved tax back or forward.

A company may allocate its non-trading deficits on loan relationships, charges and losses relieved under s 393A(1) in whatever manner it likes for the purpose of computing double taxation relief. (Deficits brought back can as usual only go against interest income, and deficits brought forward can only go against non-trading profits, but the company can choose which interest income or non-trading profits.) **It should set the maximum amount against any UK profits, thereby maximising the corporation tax attributable to the foreign profits and hence maximising the double taxation relief available.**

If a company has several sources of overseas profits, then deficits, charges and losses should be allocated first to UK profits, and then to overseas sources which have suffered the **lowest** rates of overseas taxation.

Losses relieved under s 393(1) must in any case be set against the first available profits of the trade which gave rise to the loss.

A company with a choice of loss reliefs should consider the effect of its choice on double taxation relief. For example, a s 393A(1) claim might lead to there being no UK tax liability, or a very small liability, so that foreign tax would go unrelieved. S 393(1) relief might avoid this problem and still leave very little UK tax to pay for the period of the loss.

Companies that have claimed DTR must notify HMRC if the amount of foreign tax they have paid is adjusted and this has resulted in the DTR claim becoming excessive. The notification must be in writing.

Exam focus point

If there are several sources of overseas income it is important to keep them separate and to calculate double tax relief on each source of income separately. Get into the habit of setting out a working with a separate column for UK income and for each source of overseas income. You should then find arriving at the right answer straightforward.

3 Groups of companies

FAST FORWARD

> The group relief rules allow groups and consortia to be established through companies resident anywhere in the world.

3.1 Introduction

Groups and consortia can be established through companies resident anywhere in the world. However, group relief is normally only available to, and may only be claimed from, UK resident companies.

There is a very limited exception for group companies resident in another country in the European Economic Area. Such companies may, from 1 April 2006, surrender losses to UK group members, but only if they are unable to obtain relief for the loss in any other country.

3.2 Example

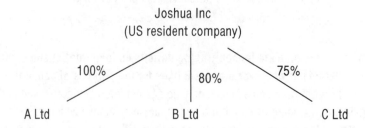

Joshua Inc
(US resident company)

100%   80%   75%

A Ltd   B Ltd   C Ltd

A Ltd, B Ltd and C Ltd are all UK resident companies. As the three UK companies share a common parent they will be treated as part of a group relief group despite the fact that the parent company is not UK resident. The UK companies may surrender losses to each other (but not normally to or from the overseas parent company).

Similarly, a consortium may exist for relief purposes where one or more of the members is not resident in the UK but relief cannot be passed to or from a non UK resident company.

3.3 Permanent establishments (PEs) of companies

Group relief is available to UK PEs of overseas companies. PEs can claim relief from UK resident group members. Alternatively, they can surrender losses, which cannot be relieved against profits in the overseas country, to such group members.

Losses incurred by overseas PEs of UK companies can be surrendered as group relief only if they cannot be relieved against profits in the overseas country.

3.4 The global group concept

The 'global group concept' means that instead of looking at the residence of a company one needs to look at whether the company is subject to UK corporation tax on any of its chargeable gains. Provided the assets transferred do not result in a potential leakage of UK corporation tax, no gain/no loss transfers will be possible within a worldwide (global) group of companies.

The global group concept applies to the transfer of the whole or part of a trade and extends to certain intra-group transfers of assets and to transfers of assets where one company disposes of the whole or part of its business to another company as part of a scheme of reconstruction or amalgamation.

4 Controlled foreign companies

FAST FORWARD

Profits of a CFC are apportioned to UK resident companies entitled to at least 25% of those profits.

4.1 Definition and treatment

Setting up a company in an overseas low tax jurisdiction and keeping it outside of the UK charge to corporation tax is the most popular method of corporate anti-avoidance. Special rules have been introduced to bring the profits of 'controlled foreign companies' (CFCs) into the UK tax net.

A controlled foreign company (CFC) is a company which:

- (a)   **is resident outside the UK**, and
- (b)   **is controlled by persons resident in the UK,** and
- (c)   **is subject to a 'lower level of taxation' in the country in which it is resident.**

A lower level of tax means less than three quarters of the amount which would have been payable had the company been resident in the UK.

Question	Controlled foreign company

Bohemia Limited is resident for tax purposes in the Cayman Islands but also trades through a branch based in Switzerland. It is owned as follows:

	%
Maurice Feischner (Swiss resident Managing Director)	25
Ace Ltd ⎫	25
Beta Ltd ⎬ UK resident companies	10
Cahill Ltd ⎭	10
Michael Brown (UK resident)	30
	100

Bohemia Ltd has chargeable profits of £875,000 in the year to 31 December 2006. The tax rate in the Cayman Islands on these profits is 24%. The UK tax rate would have been 30%. The Swiss tax paid was £90,000 on the profits.

Is Bohemia Limited a controlled foreign company?

Answer

(a) Non UK-resident? – Yes

(b) Is it controlled by UK resident persons? Yes. UK residents own 75% of the company.

(c) Subject to lower tax rate?

	Cayman Islands £	UK equivalent £
Tax payable		
£875,000 × 24%/30%	210,000	262,500
Relief for foreign tax suffered	(90,000)	(90,000)
	120,000	172,500

Tax rates: 24/30 = 80% not lower

Total tax: £210,000/£262,500 = 80% not lower

Local tax/UK tax: £120,000/£172,500 = 69.6% – lower than three quarters limit

Consequently Bohemia Limited is a CFC unless one of the exceptions apply (see below).

4.2 Apportionment of profits

Income profits (not gains) of a CFC are apportioned to UK resident companies (not individuals) entitled to at least 25% of those profits. The apportionment should be made on a 'just and reasonable' basis.

UK companies must self-assess their proportion of the profits. These apportioned profits are brought into the UK company's corporation tax computation as an amount of tax. **The tax rate is always the full rate of corporation tax** irrespective of the rate the UK company pays tax on its other profits.

Question

In the above question how much profits would Ace Ltd be taxed on if Bohemia Ltd is held to be a CFC?

Answer

Ace Ltd would have to apportion 25% of the profit of Bohemia Ltd when calculating CT for self assessment purposes.

Ace Ltd

£875,000 × 25%   £218,750

Where CFC profits are apportioned they are reduced by 'creditable tax' which is the aggregate of:

(a)   any double tax relief (see above) available in the UK in respect of foreign tax due against the chargeable profits

(b)   any income tax deducted at source on income received by the CFC

(c)   corporation tax payable in the UK on any CFC income taxable in this country.

Question

R Inc is a controlled foreign company owned 75% by J Ltd and 25% by Mr J. Its results for the year ended 31 December 2006 were:

	£
Tax adjusted trading profits	
– under UK legislation	650,000
– under foreign legislation (foreign tax rate 8%)	500,000

Show how the profits of R Inc will be apportioned to and taxed on J Ltd. J Ltd has other profits of £2 million.

Answer

	£
UK tax adjusted profit	650,000
Apportioned to J Ltd (75%)	487,500

J Ltd's CT computation

	£	£
Tax on UK profits (£2m × 30%)		600,000
Tax on CFC		
£487,500 × 30%	146,250	
Less foreign tax (8% × £500,000) × 75%	(30,000)	
		116,250
		716,250

4.3 Exceptions

A CFC profits do not need to be apportioned if it falls into one of the six situations outlined below.

(a) **Its chargeable profits for the accounting period do not exceed £50,000 (reduced proportionately for short accounting periods)**

(b) **It is situated in a territory which does not have a lower level of taxation**

(c) **It follows an acceptable distribution policy** ie it distributes by way of a dividend, during or within 18 months of the period for which it is due, at least 90% of its net chargeable profits (as computed for UK corporation tax purposes less chargeable gains and foreign tax)

(d) **It is engaged in exempt activities and satisfies the following four conditions:**

   (i) it has a **real presence** in its territory of residence

   (ii) its main activity does not consist of leasing, dealing in securities or the receipt of income such as dividends, interest or royalties and is not such that the company may be used as an invoicing route

   (iii) its business is not primarily with associates in those trades which frequently involve cross-frontier transactions

   (iv) it does not receive a significant amount of dividends from CFCs except where the exemption for holding companies applies

   A holding company with subsidiaries outside the territory in which it is itself resident meets the exempt activities test only if 90% or more of its income is in the form of non-tax deductible dividends from subsidiaries that are themselves exempt from the CFC rules

(e) **It fulfils the public quotation conditions** ie it is quoted on a recognised stock exchange, and dealing must have taken place within twelve months of the end of the accounting period

(f) It satisfies the **motive test** ie the reduction in UK tax is no more than minimal, or the main purpose of these transactions was not to achieve a reduction, and the reduction in UK tax by the diversion of profit from the UK was not a main reason for the company's existence during that accounting period

There is an **advance clearance procedure** in respect of the **'exempt activities' test**, the **'motive'**; test and the **'acceptable distribution policy'**.

5 Permanent establishment (PE) or subsidiary abroad

FAST FORWARD

A UK resident company intending to do business abroad must choose between a permanent establishment and a subsidiary. If a subsidiary is chosen, the rules on controlled foreign companies and on trading at artificial prices may apply.

5.1 General principles

Where a foreign country has a lower rate of company taxation than the UK, it can be beneficial for the UK company to conduct its foreign activities through a **non-UK resident subsidiary** if profits are anticipated (assuming that the CFC rules (see above) do not apply), and through a **PE if losses are likely to arise**.

The **profits of a foreign PE** are treated as part of the profits of the UK company and are normally included in its computation of trading profits. If, however, the operations of the overseas PE amount to a separate trade which is wholly carried on overseas, the profits are assessed as foreign income.

The losses of a foreign PE are normally netted off against the UK company's trading income and the usual loss reliefs are available. Losses can be surrendered as group relief to the extent they cannot be relieved against profits in the overseas country. Alternatively a foreign income trading loss can be carried forward to set against future profits of the same trade.

The profits of a non-resident **foreign subsidiary** are only liable to UK tax when remitted to the UK, for example in the form of dividends (foreign income). However, no relief can be obtained against the UK parent's profits for any overseas losses of a non-resident subsidiary except in very limited circumstances.

5.2 Incorporating a foreign PE

Where a foreign operation is likely to show a loss in the early years followed by a profit it may be worthwhile to trade through a foreign PE whilst losses arise (these are usually then automatically netted off against the company's UK profits) and then later to convert the PE into a non-UK resident subsidiary company (so that profits can be accumulated at potentially lower rates of foreign tax).

This conversion of a foreign PE into a non-UK resident subsidiary has some important tax implications both in the UK and the overseas country.

5.2.1 Treasury consent

As it is illegal for a UK resident company to cause or permit a non-UK resident company over which it has control to create or issue any shares or debentures it is usually necessary to secure the consent of the Treasury for the transaction. It is also illegal for a UK resident company to transfer to any person, or cause or permit to be transferred to any person, any shares or debentures of a non-UK resident company over which it has control.

The Treasury have published General Consents which permit certain intra-group transactions and third party transactions provided full consideration is given. Additionally certain movements of capital between EEA states are allowed automatically. Thus in practice specific Treasury consent may not always be required.

5.2.2 Postponement of gains

The conversion will constitute a disposal of the assets of the PE giving rise to a chargeable gain or loss in the hands of the UK company. A chargeable gain can be postponed where:

(a)   the trade of the foreign PE is transferred to the non-UK resident company with all the assets used for that trade except cash, and

(b)   the consideration for the transfer is wholly or partly securities (shares or shares and loan stock), and

(c)   the transferring company owns at least 25% of the ordinary share capital of the non-resident company, and

(d)   a claim for relief is made.

There is full postponement of the net gains arising on the transfer where the consideration is wholly securities. Where part of the consideration is in a form other than securities, eg cash, that proportion of the net gains is chargeable immediately.

The postponement is indefinite. The gain becomes chargeable only when:

(a)   the transferor company at any time disposes of any of the securities received on the transfer, or

(b)   the non-UK resident company within six years of the transfer disposes of any of the assets on which a gain arose at the time of the transfer.

The 'global group' concept applies to certain intra-group transfers of assets and also where one company disposes of the whole of part of its business to another company as part of a reconstruction or amalgamation scheme. Such asset transfers are on a no gain/no loss basis provided the assets transferred do not result in a potential leakage of UK corporation tax.

5.3 European Community companies

If all or part of a trade carried on in the UK by a company resident in one EC state is transferred to a company resident in another EC state, then the transfer is deemed to be at a price giving no gain and no loss, if all the following conditions are fulfilled.

(a) The transfer is wholly in exchange for shares or securities

(b) The company receiving the trade would be subject to UK corporation tax on any gains arising on later disposals of the assets transferred

(c) Both parties claim this special treatment

(d) The transfer is for bona fide commercial reasons. Advance clearance that this condition is satisfied may be obtained.

6 Non-UK resident companies

FAST FORWARD

A non resident company is liable to UK corporation tax if it carries on trade in the UK through a permanent establishment.

6.1 Corporation tax charge

A non resident company is liable to tax in the UK if it carries on a trade in the UK through a permanent establishment (defined as above).

The PE has **the profits it would have made if it were a distinct and separate establishment engaged in the same or similar activities in the same or similar conditions, dealing wholly independently with the non resident company attributed to it.** Deductions are available for allowable expenses incurred for the purposes of the PE including executive and general administrative expenses whether in the UK or elsewhere. The term 'allowable expenses' has the same meaning as for a UK resident company. Relief is available for the expenses of managing investments for all companies whether or not they qualify as 'investment companies'.

Transactions between the PE and the non resident company are treated as taking place at **arm's length prices.**

For the purposes of collection of tax a PE will be treated as the UK representative through which the non resident company carries on a trade in the UK.

These rules align with the normal provision in tax treaties (based on the OECD model treaty) **that a foreign trader is taxable on his trading profits in the UK if he has a permanent establishment in the UK.**

6.2 Tax charge on income

Income charged to corporation tax comprises:

(a) Trading income arising directly or indirectly through or from the permanent establishment, and

(b) Any income, wherever arising, from property or rights used by, held by or held for the permanent establishment.

Dividends and other distributions from companies resident in the UK are not charged to corporation tax; nor are they normally charged to income tax. A repayment may arise under the terms of a double taxation agreement.

Annual interest and other annual payments are received under deduction of income tax. Provided that the income is charged to corporation tax, the company can offset the income tax suffered against its corporation tax liability and, in appropriate circumstances, obtain repayment in the same manner as a resident company.

Income from sources within the UK which is not subject to corporation tax is subject to income tax. This could arise, for example, if a non-resident company carries on a trade in the UK without having a permanent establishment, or receives letting income from a UK property.

6.3 Tax charge on capital gains

Capital gains are charged to corporation tax where the company carries on a trade in the UK through a permanent establishment if they arise on:

(a) **Assets situated in the UK used in or for the purposes of the trade at or before the time when the gain accrued**

(b) **Assets situated in the UK held or used for the purposes of the permanent establishment at or before the time when the gain accrued.**

As it would be possible to avoid gains being chargeable by, for example, ceasing to trade in the UK through a permanent establishment prior to selling the asset or exporting the asset, there are two further charging provisions:

(a) Where a non-UK resident company ceases to trade through a permanent establishment in the UK, a charge will arise. Any chargeable asset which would otherwise become non-chargeable shall be deemed to be disposed of and reacquired at market value immediately before it ceases to trade.

(b) Where a non-UK resident company trading through a UK permanent establishment exports a chargeable asset, so that it becomes non-chargeable, the gain will crystallise immediately before it is exported.

6.4 Tax planning

A foreign resident company may have to decide **whether to trade in the UK through a PE or via a UK subsidiary**. The advantage of a subsidiary if profits are low is that it will be able to take advantage of the small companies' rate of tax. However, if the subsidiary makes losses the overseas company may be restricted in the relief it can claim. The overseas company would also need to consider the repatriation of profits and the provision of finance.

Chapter roundup

- Company residence is important in determining whether its profits are subject to UK tax.

- A company may obtain DTR for overseas withholding tax, and also (if its investment is large enough) for underlying tax. The allocation of charges and losses can affect the relief.

- The group relief rules allow groups and consortia to be established through companies resident anywhere in the world.

- Profits of a CFC are apportioned to UK resident companies entitled to at least 25% of those profits.

- A UK resident company intending to do business abroad must choose between a permanent establishment and a subsidiary. If a subsidiary is chosen, the rules on controlled foreign companies and on trading at artificial prices may apply.

- A non resident company is liable to UK corporation tax if it carries on trade in the UK through a permanent establishment.

Quick quiz

1   When is a company UK resident?

2   How is underlying tax calculated?

3   How best should charges be allocated in computing credit relief for foreign tax?

4   What is the definition of a CFC?

5   A UK company is planning to set up a new operation in Australia that will initially be loss making. Should it set up as a permanent establishment or a subsidiary of the UK company?

Answers to quick quiz

1   A company is resident in the UK if it is incorporated in the UK or if its central management and control are exercised in the UK.

2   Underlying tax is calculated as: dividend plus withholding tax $\times \dfrac{\text{foreign tax paid}}{\text{after-tax accounting profits}}$

3   Charges should be set-off firstly from any UK profits, then from overseas income sources suffering the lowest rates of overseas taxation before those suffering at the higher rates.

4   A CFC is a company which

   (a)   is resident outside the UK
   (b)   is controlled by persons resident in the UK
   (c)   is subject to a lower level of taxation in the country in which it is resident.

5   If losses are expected then a PE is best since losses of a foreign PE can be surrendered as group relief.

Now try the question below from the Exam Question Bank

Number	Level	Marks	Time
Q29	Introductory	15	27 mins

Part D

Value added tax

Value added tax 1

28

Topic list	Syllabus reference
1 Basic principles	A6(b)F1
2 The scope of VAT	A6(b)F1
3 Registration	A6(b)F2, (i),(ii)
4 Accounting for VAT	A6(b)F3
5 The valuation of supplies	A6(b)F3
6 Administration	A6(b)F3
7 Penalties	A6(b)F3

Introduction

In this and the next chapter, we study value added tax (VAT). VAT is a tax on turnover rather than on profits.

As the name of the tax suggests, it is charged (usually at 17.5%) on the value added. If someone in a chain of manufacture or distribution buys goods for £1,000 and sells them for £1,200 he has increased their value by £200. (He may have painted them, packed them or distributed them to shops to justify his mark-up, or he may simply be good at making deals to buy cheaply and sell dearly.) Because he has added value of £200, he collects VAT of £200 × 17.5% = £35 and pays this over to the government. The VAT is collected bit by bit along the chain and finally hits the consumer who does not add value, but uses up the goods.

VAT is a tax with simple computations but many detailed rules to ensure its enforcement. You may find it easier to absorb the detail if you ask yourself, in relation to each rule, exactly how it helps to enforce the tax.

In the next chapter we will look at the rules for zero-rated and exempt supplies, the rules for imports and exports and some of the special schemes.

Study guide

		Intellectual level
6	**National insurance, value added tax and tax administration:**	
(b)	The contents of the Paper F6 study guide for value added tax (VAT) under headings:	2
•	F1 The scope of value added tax (VAT)	
•	F2 The VAT registration requirements:	
•	F3 The computation of VAT liabilities:	
	The following additional material is also examinable:	
(i)	Advise on the impact of the disaggregation of business activities for VAT purposes	3
(ii)	Advise on the impact of group registration and divisional registration	3

Exam guide

VAT is a very important tax for businesses as there are very few small enough to avoid it. You may be required to advise on almost any aspect, such as registration, including group and divisional registration.

Knowledge brought forward from earlier studies

This chapter revises your knowledge of the scope of VAT, the requirement to register and the computation of the VAT liability in straightforward cases.

Disaggregation and group and divisional registration are new.

1 Basic principles

FAST FORWARD

VAT is charged on turnover at each stage in a production process, but in such a way that the burden is borne by the final consumer.

1.1 Introduction

The legal basis of value added tax (VAT) is to be found in the Value Added Tax Act 1994 (VATA 1994), supplemented by regulations made by statutory instrument and amended by subsequent Finance Acts. VAT is administered by HM Revenue and Customs (HMRC).

VAT is a tax on turnover, not on profits. The basic principle is that the VAT should be borne by the final consumer. Registered traders may deduct the tax which they suffer on supplies to them (input tax) from the tax which they charge to their customers (output tax) at the time this is paid to HMRC. So, at each stage of the manufacturing or service process, the net VAT paid is on the value added at that stage.

1.2 Example: the VAT charge

A forester sells wood to a furniture maker for £100 plus VAT. The furniture maker uses this wood to make a table and sells the table to a shop for £150 plus VAT. The shop then sells the table to the final consumer for £300 plus VAT. VAT will be accounted for to HMRC as follows.

	Cost £	Input tax 17.5% £	Net sale price £	Output tax 17.5% £	Payable to HMRC £
Forester	0	0	100	17.50	17.50
Furniture maker	100	17.50	150	26.25	8.75
Shop	150	26.25	300	52.50	26.25
					52.50

Because the traders involved account to HMRC for VAT charged less VAT suffered, their profits for income tax or corporation tax purposes are based on sales and purchases net of VAT.

2 The scope of VAT

FAST FORWARD

> VAT is charged on taxable supplies of goods and services made by a taxable person in his business.

2.1 General principles

VAT is charged on taxable supplies of goods and services made in the UK by a taxable person in the course or furtherance of any business carried on by him. It is also chargeable on the import of goods into the UK (whether they are imported for business purposes or not, and whether the importer is a taxable person or not), and on certain services received from abroad if a taxable person receives them for business purposes.

Special rules for trade with the European Union (the EU) are covered later.

Key term

> A **taxable supply** is a supply of goods or services made in the UK, other than an exempt supply.

A taxable supply is either standard-rated or zero-rated. The standard rate is 17.5% (although on certain supplies, for example the supply of domestic fuel and power, a lower rate is charged of 5%) and zero-rated supplies are taxed at 0%. An exempt supply is not chargeable to VAT. The categories of zero-rated and exempt supplies are listed in the next chapter.

2.2 Supplies of goods

Goods are supplied if exclusive ownership of the goods passes to another person.

The following are treated as supplies of goods.

- The supply of any form of power, heat, refrigeration or ventilation, or of water

- The grant, assignment or surrender of a major interest (the freehold or a lease for over 21 years) in land

- Taking goods permanently out of the business for the non-business use of a taxable person or for other private purposes including the supply of goods by an employer to an employee for his private use

- Transfers under an agreement contemplating a transfer of ownership, such as a hire purchase agreement

Gifts of goods are normally treated as sales at cost (so VAT is due). **However, business gifts are not supplies of goods if:**

(a)   **The total cost of gifts made to the same person does not exceed £50 in any 12 month period**. If the £50 limit is exceeded, output tax will be due in full on the total of gifts made. Once the limit has been exceeded a new £50 limit and new 12 month period begins

(b)   **The gift is a sample**. However, if two or more identical samples are given to the same person, all but one of them are treated as supplies.

2.3 Supplies of services

Apart from a few specific exceptions, **any supply which is not a supply of goods and which is done for a consideration is a supply of services**. Consideration is any form of payment in money or in kind, including anything which is itself a supply.

A supply of services also takes place if:

- Goods are lent to someone for use outside the business
- Goods are hired to someone
- Services bought for business purposes are used for private purposes

The European Court of Justice has ruled that restaurants supply services rather than goods.

2.4 Taxable persons

The term 'person' includes individuals, partnerships (which are treated as single entities, ignoring the individual partners), **companies, clubs, associations and charities. If a person is in business making taxable supplies, then the value of these supplies is called the taxable turnover. If a person's taxable turnover exceeds certain limits then he is a taxable person and should be registered for VAT.**

3 Registration

FAST FORWARD

A trader becomes liable to register for VAT if the value of taxable supplies in any period up to 12 months exceeds £61,000 or if there are reasonable grounds for believing that the value of the taxable supplies will exceed £61,000 in the next 30 days. A trader may also register voluntarily.

3.1 Compulsory registration

At the end of every month a trader must calculate his cumulative turnover of taxable supplies to date. However this cumulative period does not extend beyond the previous 12 months. **The trader becomes liable to register for VAT if the value of his cumulative taxable supplies** (excluding VAT) **exceeds £61,000** (from 1 April 2006 onwards). The person is required to notify HMRC within 30 days of the end of the month in which the £61,000 limit is exceeded. HMRC will then register the person with effect from the end of the month following the month in which the £61,000 was exceeded, or from an earlier date if they and the trader agree.

Registration under this rule is not required if HMRC are satisfied that the value of the trader's taxable supplies (excluding VAT) in the year then starting will not exceed £59,000 (from 1 April 2006 onwards).

A person is also liable to register at any time if there are reasonable grounds for believing that his taxable supplies (excluding VAT) in the following 30 days will exceed £61,000. Only taxable turnover of that 30 day period is considered **not** cumulative turnover. HMRC must be notified by the end of the 30 day period and registration will be with effect from the beginning of that period.

When determining the value of a person's taxable supplies for the purposes of registration, supplies of goods and services that are *capital assets* of the business are to be disregarded, except for non zero-rated taxable supplies of interests in land.

Question	VAT registration

Fred started to trade in cutlery on 1 January 2006. Sales (excluding VAT) were £5,325 a month for the first nine months and £7,700 a month thereafter. From what date should Fred be registered for VAT?

Answer

	£
Sales to 31 October 2006	55,625
Sales to 30 November 2006	63,325 (exceeds £61,000)

Fred must notify his liability to register by 30 December 2006 (not 31 December) and will be registered from 1 January 2007 or from an agreed earlier date.

When a person is liable to register in respect of a past period, it is his responsibility to pay VAT. If he is unable to collect it from those to whom he made taxable supplies, the VAT burden will fall on him. A person must start keeping VAT records and charging VAT to customers as soon as it is known that he is required to register. However, VAT should not be shown separately on any invoices until the registration number is known. The invoice should show the VAT inclusive price and customers should be informed that VAT invoices will be forwarded once the registration number is known. Formal VAT invoices should then be sent to such customers within 30 days of receiving the registration number.

Notification of liability to register must be made on form VAT 1. Simply writing to, or telephoning, a local VAT office is not enough. On registration the VAT office will send the trader a certificate of registration. This shows the VAT registration number, the date of registration, the end of the first VAT period and the length of later VAT periods.

If a trader makes a supply before becoming liable to register, but gets paid after registration, VAT is not due on that supply.

3.2 Voluntary registration

A person may decide to become registered even though his taxable turnover falls below the registration limit. Unless a person is registered he cannot recover the input tax he pays on purchases.

Voluntary registration is advantageous where a person wishes to recover input tax on purchases. For example, consider a trader who has one input during the year which cost £1,000 plus £175 VAT; he works on the input which becomes his sole output for the year and he decides to make a profit of £1,000.

(a) If he is not registered he will charge £2,175 and his customer will obtain no relief for any VAT.

(b) If he is registered he will charge £2,000 plus VAT of £350. His customer will have input tax of £350 which he will be able to recover if he, too, is registered.

If the customer is a non-taxable person he will prefer (a) as the cost to him is £2,175. If he is taxable he will prefer (b) as the net cost is £2,000. Thus, a decision whether or not to register voluntarily may depend upon the status of customers. It may also depend on the status of the outputs and the image of his business the trader wishes to project (registration may give the impression of a substantial business). The administrative burden of registration should also be considered.

3.3 Intending trader registration

Providing that a trader satisfies HMRC that he is carrying on a business, and intends to make taxable supplies, he is entitled to be registered if he chooses. But, once registered, he is obliged to notify HMRC within 30 days if he no longer intends to make taxable supplies.

3.4 Exemption from registration

If a person makes only zero-rated supplies, he may request exemption from registration. The trader is obliged to notify HMRC of any material change in the nature of his supplies.

HMRC may also allow exemption from registration if only a small proportion of supplies are standard-rated, provided that the trader would normally receive repayments of VAT if registered.

3.5 Group registration

Companies under common control may apply for group registration. The effects and advantages of group registration are as follows.

- Each VAT group must appoint a representative member which must **account for the group's output tax and input tax, thus simplifying VAT accounting** and allowing payments and repayments of VAT to be netted off. However, all members of the group are jointly and severally liable for any VAT due from the representative member

- **Any supply of goods or services by a member of the group to another member of the group is, in general, disregarded for VAT purposes,** reducing the VAT accounting required

- Any other supply of goods or services by or to a group member is in general treated as a supply by or to the representative member

- Any VAT payable on the import of goods by a group member is payable by the representative member.

Two or more companies are eligible to be treated as members of a group provided each of them is either established in the UK or has a fixed establishment in the UK, and:

- **One of them controls each of the others, or**
- **One person** (which could be an individual or a holding company) **controls all of them**, or
- **Two or more persons carrying on a business in partnership control all of them.**

Anti-avoidance rules prevent a company from belonging to a VAT group where it would otherwise be eligible but it is in fact run for the benefit of an external third party.

An application to create, terminate, add to or delete a company from a VAT group may be made at any time. Applications may be refused when it appears to HMRC to be necessary to do so for the protection of the revenue. However, if a company is no longer eligible to belong to a VAT group because the common control test is failed, the company must leave the VAT group even if revenue might not be lost.

A group registration, or any change therein, will take effect from the date the application is received by HMRC although applications may have an earlier or later effect. Therefore it is possible to apply in advance for group changes and it is also possible to apply for changes having a retrospective effect. However, HMRC have 90 days to refuse an application.

HMRC can cancel a grouping if a company ceases to meet the eligibility requirements or a risk to revenue arises. A risk arises where avoidance is suspected, there is a risk that tax due may not be collectable or the revenue loss goes beyond that arising as a natural consequence of grouping.

Certain 'tax planning' schemes use groups to reduce the Government's overall VAT revenue. (Normal transactions within a VAT group do not do this, because eventually supplies will be made outside the group.) HMRC can deal with such schemes by directing that:

- A supply made within a group is treated as made outside the group, or
- A company within a group is treated as being outside the group for a specified period
- A company eligible to be in a group is treated as being in the group for a specified period.

A company can appeal against a direction on the grounds that a transaction, or a change in group membership, had a genuine commercial purpose as its main purpose.

Individual companies which are within a group for company law purposes may still register separately and stay outside the VAT group. This may be done to ensure that a company making exempt supplies does not restrict the input tax recovery of the group as a whole (see the partial exemption rules in the next chapter).

It is possible for a company to be in two VAT groups at the same time.

3.6 Divisional registration

A company which is divided into several units which each prepare accounts can apply for divisional registration. The only advantage of divisional registration is administrative convenience; the separate divisions do not become separate taxable persons and the company is itself still liable for the VAT. However, if divisions account for VAT separately it may make it more likely that VAT returns will be made on time, because data for the divisions do not have to be consolidated before returns are completed.

Broadly, the conditions for divisional registration are as follows.

(a)   HMRC must be satisfied that there would be real difficulties in submitting a single VAT return by the due date

(b)   Each division must be registered even where that division's turnover is beneath the registration limits

(c)   The divisions must be independent, self-accounting units, carrying on different activities or operating in separate locations

(d)   Input tax attributable or apportioned to exempt supplies (see the partial exemption rules in the next chapter) for the company as a whole must be so low that it can all be recovered (apart from VAT which can never be recovered because of the type of expenditure)

(e)   Each division must make VAT returns for the same tax periods

(f)   Tax invoices must not be issued for supplies between the divisions of the same company as they are not supplies for VAT purposes.

3.7 Deregistration

3.7.1 Voluntary deregistration

A person is eligible for voluntary deregistration if HMRC are satisfied that the value of his taxable supplies (net of VAT and excluding supplies of capital assets) **in the following one year period will not exceed £59,000 (from 1 April 2006)**. However, voluntary deregistration will not be allowed if the reason for the expected fall in value of taxable supplies is the cessation of taxable supplies or the suspension of taxable supplies for a period of 30 days or more in that following year.

HMRC will cancel a person's registration from the date the request is made or from an agreed later date.

3.7.2 Compulsory deregistration

Traders may be compulsorily deregistered. Failure to notify a requirement to deregister within 30 days may lead to a penalty. Compulsory deregistration may also lead to HMRC reclaiming input tax which has been wrongly recovered by the trader since the date on which he should have deregistered.

Other points to note are:

- If HMRC are misled into granting registration then the registration is treated as void from the start.

- A person may be compulsorily deregistered if HMRC are satisfied that he is no longer making nor intending to make taxable supplies.

- Changes in legal status also require cancellation of registration. For example:
    - A sole trader becoming a partnership
    - A partnership reverting to a sole trader
    - A business being incorporated
    - A company being replaced by an unincorporated business

3.7.3 The consequences of deregistration

On deregistration, VAT is chargeable on all stocks and capital assets in a business on which input tax was claimed, since the registered trader is in effect making a taxable supply to himself as a newly unregistered trader. If the VAT chargeable does not exceed £1,000, it need not be paid.

This special VAT charge does not apply if the business (or a separately viable part of it) **is sold as a going concern to another taxable person** (or a person who immediately becomes a taxable person as a result of the transfer). **Such transfers are outside the scope of VAT** (except for certain buildings being transferred which are 'new' or opted buildings and the transferee does not make an election to waive exemption – refer to the section on land in the next chapter).

If the original owner ceases to be taxable, the new owner of the business may also take over the existing VAT number. If he does so, he takes over the rights and liabilities of the transferor as at the date of transfer.

3.8 Pre-registration input tax

VAT incurred before registration can be treated as input tax and recovered from HMRC subject to certain conditions.

If the claim is for input tax suffered on goods purchased prior to registration then the following conditions must be satisfied.

(a)   The goods were acquired for the purpose of the business which either was carried on or was to be carried on by him at the time of supply

(b)   The goods have not been supplied onwards or consumed before the date of registration (although they may have been used to make other goods which are still held)

(c)   The VAT must have been incurred in the three years prior to the effective date of registration.

If the claim is for input tax suffered on the supply of services prior to registration then the following conditions must be satisfied.

(a)   The services were supplied for the purposes of a business which either was carried on or was to be carried on by him at the time of supply

(b)   The services were supplied within the six months prior to the date of registration.

Input tax attributable to supplies made before registration is not deductible even if the input tax concerned is treated as having been incurred after registration.

3.9 Disaggregation

A person's registration covers all his business activities together. **The turnover of all business activities carried on by a 'person' must be aggregated to find taxable turnover.** However, if the same individual both carries on trade A alone and is a member of a partnership carrying on trade B, the turnover of the two trades will not normally be aggregated: the individual will have his taxable turnover in respect of trade A only, and the partnership will have its taxable turnover in respect of trade B only.

For example, a brother and sister might operate a pub with catering and bed and breakfast facilities. The catering could be operated by the brother, the pub could be operated by a partnership of the two people and the bed and breakfast business could be operated by the sister. This could avoid the need to register and account for output tax, if the turnover of each business was below the threshold for registration.

There are anti-avoidance provisions to prevent VAT benefits from the operation of one business through two or more entities. These provisions enable HMRC to direct that any connected businesses which have avoided VAT by artificially separating should be treated as one, whatever the reason for the separation. When deciding whether businesses are artificially separated, HMRC consider the extent to which those persons are bound by financial, economic or organisational links.

4 Accounting for VAT

4.1 VAT periods

VAT is accounted for on regular returns. Extensive records must be kept.

The VAT period (also known as the tax period) is the period covered by a VAT return. It is usually three calendar months. The return shows the total input and output tax for the tax period and must be submitted (along with any VAT due) within one month of the end of the period. (Businesses which pay VAT electronically automatically receive a seven day extension to this time limit.)

HMRC allocate VAT periods according to the class of trade carried on (ending in June, September, December and March; July, October, January and April; or August, November, February and May), to spread the flow of VAT returns evenly over the year. When applying for registration a trader can ask for VAT periods which fit in with his own accounting year. It is also possible to have VAT periods to cover accounting systems not based on calendar months.

A registered person whose input tax will regularly exceed his output tax can elect for a one month VAT period, but will have to balance the inconvenience of making 12 returns a year against the advantage of obtaining more rapid repayments of VAT.

Certain small businesses may submit an annual VAT return (see later in this Text).

4.2 The VAT return

The regular VAT return to HMRC is made on form VAT 100. The boxes on a VAT return which a trader must fill in are as follows.

    (a)   Box 1: the VAT due on sales and other outputs

    (b)   Box 2: the VAT due on acquisitions from other EU member states

    (c)   Box 3: the total of boxes 1 and 2

    (d)   Box 4: the VAT reclaimed on purchases and other inputs

    (e)   Box 5: the net VAT to be paid or reclaimed: the difference between boxes 3 and 4

(f)   Box 6: the total value (before cash discounts) of sales and all other outputs, excluding VAT but including the total in box 8

(g)   Box 7: the total value (before cash discounts) of purchases and all other inputs, excluding VAT but including the total in box 9

(h)   Box 8: the total value of all sales and related services to other EU member states

(i)   Box 9: the total value of all purchases and related services from other EU member states

Input and output tax figures must be supported by the original or copy tax invoices, and records must be maintained for six years.

4.3 Internet filing of VAT returns

It is possible to file VAT returns electronically. The trader must enrol with HMRC before using the service.

4.4 Substantial traders

If the total VAT liability over 12 months to the end of a VAT period exceeds £2,000,000, the trader must make payments on account of each quarter's VAT liability during the quarter. Payments are due at the end of the second and third month of the quarter, with the final payment due at the usual time, a month after the end of the quarter. Electronic payment must be used, with no 7 day grace period available.

The amount of each payment on account is 1/24 of the total annual VAT liability. The obligation to pay on account starts with the first VAT period starting *after* 31 March.

The default surcharge (see below) applies to late payments.

A trader may elect to pay their actual VAT liability monthly. For example, the actual liability for January would be due at the end of February. The trader can continue to submit quarterly returns so long as HMRC is satisfied the trader is paying sufficient monthly amounts.

Question	Payments on account

Large Ltd is liable to make payments on account calculated at £250,000 each for the quarter ended 31 December 2006.

What payments/repayment are due if Large Ltd's VAT liability for the quarter is calculated as:

(a)   £680,000
(b)   £480,000?

Answer

(a)   30 November 2006   – payment of £250,000
       31 December 2006   – payment of £250,000
       31 January 2007   – payment of £180,000 with submission of VAT return for quarter

(b)   30 November 2006   – payment of £250,000
       31 December 2006   – payment of £250,000
       31 January 2007   – on submission of return HMRC will repay £20,000.

If a trader's total annual liability increases to 120% or more of the amount used to calculate the payments on account, then the new higher annual liability is used to calculate new payments on account. The increase applies from the end of the 12 months with the new higher annual liability.

Once a trader is in the scheme, the payments on account are also recomputed annually.

For the purposes of calculating the payments on account (but not for the purposes of the £2,000,000 limit for entry into the scheme), a trader's VAT due on imports from outside the EU is ignored.

4.5 Refunds of VAT

There is a three year time limit on the right to reclaim overpaid VAT. This time limit does not apply to input tax which a business could not have reclaimed earlier because the supplier only recently invoiced the VAT, even though it related to a purchase made some time ago. Nor does it apply to overpaid VAT penalties.

If a taxpayer has overpaid VAT and has overclaimed input tax by reason of the same mistake, HMRC can set off any tax, penalty, interest or surcharge due to them against any repayment due to the taxpayer and repay only the net amount. In such cases the normal three year time limit for recovering VAT, penalties, interest, etc by assessment does not apply.

HMRC can refuse to make any repayment which would unjustly enrich the claimant. They can also refuse a repayment of VAT where all or part of the tax has, for practical purposes, been borne by a person other than the taxpayer (eg by a customer of the taxpayer) except to the extent that the taxpayer can show loss or damage to any of his businesses as a result of mistaken assumptions about VAT.

4.6 Records

Every VAT registered trader must keep records for six years, although HMRC may sometimes grant permission for their earlier destruction. They may be kept on paper, on microfilm or microfiche or on computer. However, there must be adequate facilities for HMRC to inspect records.

All records must be kept up to date and in a way which allows:

- The calculation of VAT due
- Officers of HMRC to check the figures on VAT returns

The following records are needed.

- Copies of VAT invoices, credit notes and debit notes issued

- A summary of supplies made

- VAT invoices, credit notes and debit notes received

- A summary of supplies received

- Records of goods received from and sent to other EU member states

- Documents relating to imports from and exports to countries outside the EU

- A VAT account

- Order and delivery notes, correspondence, appointment books, job books, purchases and sales books, cash books, account books, records of takings (such as till rolls), bank paying-in slips, bank statements and annual accounts

- Records of zero-rated and exempt supplies, gifts or loans of goods, taxable self-supplies and any goods taken for non-business use

5 The valuation of supplies

VAT is charged on the VAT-exclusive price. Where a discount is offered for prompt payment, VAT is chargeable on the net amount even if the discount is not taken up.

5.1 General principles

The value of a supply is the VAT-exclusive price on which VAT is charged. The consideration for a supply is the amount paid in money or money's worth. Thus with a standard rate of 17.5%:

Value + VAT = consideration
£100 + £17.50 = £117.50

The VAT proportion of the consideration is known as the 'VAT fraction'. It is

$$\frac{\text{rate of tax}}{100 + \text{rate of tax}} = \frac{17.5}{100 + 17.5} = \frac{7}{47}$$

Provided the consideration for a bargain made at arm's length is paid in money, the value for VAT purposes is the VAT exclusive price charged by the trader. If it is paid in something other than money, as in a barter of some goods or services for others, it must be valued and VAT will be due on the value.

If the price of goods is effectively reduced with money off coupons, the value of the supply is the amount actually received by the taxpayer.

5.2 Mixed supplies and composite supplies

Different goods and services are sometimes invoiced together at an inclusive price (a *mixed supply*). Some items may be chargeable at the standard rate and some at the zero-rate. **The supplier must account for VAT separately on the standard rated and zero rated elements by splitting the total amount payable in a fair proportion between the different elements and charging VAT on each at the appropriate rate.** There is no single way of doing this: one method is to split the amount according to the cost to the supplier of each element, and another is to use the open market value of each element. Mixed supplies are also known as 'multiple supplies'.

If a supply cannot be split into components, there is a *composite supply*, to which one VAT rate must be applied. The rate depends on the nature of the supply as a whole. Composite supplies are also known as 'compound supplies'.

A supply of air transport including an in-flight meal has been held to be a single, composite supply of transport (zero-rated) rather than a supply of transport (zero-rated) and a supply of a meal (standard-rated). Contrast this with catering included in the price of leisure travel – there are two separate supplies: standard-rated catering and zero-rated passenger transport.

Broadly, a composite supply occurs when one element of the supply is merely incidental to the main element. A mixed supply occurs where different elements of the supply are the subject of separate negotiation and customer choice giving rise to identifiable obligations on the supplier.

5.3 Discounts

Where a discount is offered for prompt payment, VAT is chargeable on the net amount, regardless of whether the discount is taken up (except that for imports from outside the EU, the discount is ignored unless it is taken up). Supplies of retailer vouchers made on contingent discount terms (for example depending on the level of purchases) must be invoiced with VAT based on the full amount, an adjustment being made when the discount is earned. When goods are sold to staff at a discount, VAT is only due on the discounted price.

Generally, the sale of a voucher is VAT free. However, intermediate suppliers of retailer vouchers (ie vouchers for which the seller provides the redemption goods or services), must account for VAT on the purchase and sale of vouchers. Input tax is recoverable by the purchaser. There are additional rules affecting vouchers sold as part of a package of goods for which the price would not be reduced if the vouchers were excluded. These rules aim to prevent the deferral of VAT on sales of vouchers until they are redeemed.

5.4 Miscellaneous

For goods supplied under a hire purchase agreement VAT is chargeable on the cash selling price at the start of the contract.

If a trader charges different prices to customers paying with credit cards and those paying by other means, the VAT due in respect of each standard-rated sale is the full amount paid by the customer × the VAT fraction.

When goods are permanently taken from a business for non-business purposes VAT must be accounted for on their market value. Where business goods are put to a private or non-business use, the value of the resulting supply of services is the cost to the taxable person of providing the services. If services bought for business purposes are used for non-business purposes (without charge), then VAT must be accounted for on their cost, but the VAT to be accounted for is not allowed to exceed the input tax deductible on the purchase of the services.

6 Administration

FAST FORWARD ⟩⟩   VAT is administered by HMRC, and the VAT Tribunal hears appeals.

6.1 Introduction

The administration of VAT is dealt with by HM Revenue and Customs (HMRC).

6.2 Local offices

Local offices are responsible for the local administration of VAT and for providing advice to registered persons whose principal place of business is in their area. They are controlled by regional collectors.

Completed VAT returns should be sent to the VAT Central Unit at Southend, not to a local office.

From time to time a registered person will be visited by staff from a local office (a control visit) to ensure that the law is understood and is being applied properly. If a trader disagrees with any decision as to the application of VAT given by HMRC he can ask his local office to reconsider the decision. It is not necessary to appeal formally while a case is being reviewed in this way. Where an appeal can be settled by agreement, a written settlement has the same force as a decision decided through the normal appeals process (see below). A trader can ask for a reconsideration even if he has already appealed to a VAT Tribunal.

HMRC may issue assessments of VAT due to the best of their judgement if they believe that a trader has failed to make returns or if they believe those returns to be incorrect or incomplete. The time limit for making assessments is normally three years after the end of a VAT period, but this is extended to 20 years in the case of fraud, dishonest conduct, certain registration irregularities and the unauthorised issue of VAT invoices.

HMRC sometimes write to traders, setting out their calculations, before issuing assessments. The traders can then query the calculations.

6.3 Appeals

A trader may appeal to a VAT Tribunal. VAT Tribunals are administered by the Tribunals Service, part of the Department of Constitutional Affairs and are completely independent of HMRC. Provided that VAT returns and payments have been made, appeals can be heard.

The VAT Tribunal can waive the requirement to pay all VAT shown on returns before an appeal is heard in cases of hardship. It cannot allow an appeal against a purely administrative matter such as HMRC's refusal to apply an extra statutory concession.

There may be a dispute over the deductibility of input tax which hinges on the purposes for which goods or services were used, or on whether they were used to make taxable supplies. The trader must show that HMRC acted unreasonably in refusing a deduction, if the goods or services are luxuries, amusements or entertainment.

6.4 Time limits

An appeal must be lodged with the VAT Tribunal (not the local office) within 30 days of the date of any decision by HMRC. If, instead, the trader would like the local office to reconsider the decision he should apply within 30 days of the decision to the relevant office. The local VAT office may either:

*   Confirm the original decision, in which case the taxpayer has a further 21 days from the date of that confirmation in which to lodge an appeal with the Tribunal, or

*   Send a revised decision, in which case the taxpayer will have a further 30 days from the date of the revised decision in which to lodge an appeal with the Tribunal.

If one of the parties is dissatisfied with a decision on a point of law he may appeal to the courts. The Tribunal may award costs.

6.5 The Adjudicator

The Adjudicator for the HMRC is independent of these bodies. The Adjudicator considers complaints about the way in which taxpayers' affairs are handled, for example complaints about delays or the exercise of officials' discretion. The Adjudicator does not consider complaints where there are alternative channels of appeal, such as exist for appeals against assessments.

6.6 Tax avoidance and evasion

Significant resources are deployed to tackle fraud, tax evasion and avoidance.

Avoidance is also countered by the requirement for traders to disclose to HMRC any use of a notifiable VAT avoidance scheme (see later in this text).

7 Penalties

FAST FORWARD

A default occurs when a trader either submits his VAT return late, or submits the return on time but pays the VAT late. A default surcharge is applied if there is a default during a default surcharge period.

7.1 The default surcharge

A default occurs when a trader either submits his VAT return late, or submits the return on time but pays the VAT late. It also occurs when a payment on account from a substantial trader is late. **If a trader defaults, HMRC will serve a surcharge liability notice on the trader. The notice specifies a surcharge period running from the date of the notice to the anniversary of the end of the period for which the trader is in default.**

If a further default occurs in respect of a return period ending during the specified surcharge period, the original surcharge period will be extended to the anniversary of the end of the period to which the new default relates. In addition, if the default involves the late payment of VAT (as opposed to simply a late return) **a surcharge is levied.**

The surcharge depends on the number of defaults involving late payment of VAT which have occurred in respect of periods ending in the surcharge period, as follows.

Default involving late payment of VAT in the surcharge period	Surcharge as a percentage of the VAT outstanding at the due date
First	2%
Second	5%
Third	10%
Fourth or more	15%

Surcharges at the 2% and 5% rates are not normally demanded unless the amount due would be at least £400 but for surcharges calculated using the 10% or 15% rates there is a minimum amount of £30 payable.

If a substantial trader is late with more than one payment (on account or final) for a return period, this only counts as one default. The total VAT paid late is the total of late payments on account plus the late final payment.

Question
Default surcharge

Peter Popper has an annual turnover of around £300,000. His VAT return for the quarter to 31.12.06 is late. He then submits returns for the quarters to 30.9.07 and 31.3.08 late as well as making late payment of the tax due of £12,000 and £500 respectively.

Peter's VAT return to 31.3.09 is also late and the VAT due of £1,100 is also paid late. All other VAT returns and VAT payments are made on time. Outline Peter Popper's exposure to default surcharge.

Answer

A surcharge liability notice will be issued after the late filing on the 31.12.06 return outlining a surcharge period extending to 31.12.07.

The late 30.9.07 return is in the surcharge period so the period is extended to 30.9.08. The late VAT payment triggers a 2% penalty. 2% × £12,000 = £240. Since £240 is less than the £400 de minimis limit it is not collected by HMRC.

The late 31.3.08 return is in the surcharge period so the period is now extended to 31.3.09. The late payment triggers a 5% penalty. 5% × £500 = £25. Since £25 is less than the £400 de minimis limit it is not collected by HMRC.

The late 31.03.09 return is in the surcharge period. The period is extended to 31.03.10. The late payment triggers a 10% penalty. 10% × £1,100 = £110. This is collected by HMRC since the £400 de minimis does not apply to penalties calculated at the 10% (and 15%) rate.

Peter will have to submit all four quarterly VAT returns to 31.3.10 on time and pay the VAT on time to 'escape' the default surcharge regime.

A trader must submit one year's returns on time and pay the VAT shown on them on time in order to break out of the surcharge liability period and the escalation of surcharge percentages.

A default will be ignored for all default surcharge purposes if the trader can show that the return or payment was sent at such a time, and in such a manner, that it was reasonable to expect that HMRC would receive it by the due date. Posting the return and payment first class the day before the due date is generally accepted as meeting this requirement. A default will also be ignored if the trader can demonstrate a reasonable excuse for the late submission or payment.

The application of the default surcharge regime to small businesses is modified. **A small business is one with a turnover below £150,000.** When a small business is late submitting a VAT return or paying VAT it will receive a letter from HMRC offering help. No penalty will be charged. Four such letters will be issued without penalty. However, on the issue of a fifth letter a 10% penalty will apply which increases to 15% on the issue of a sixth or subsequent letter.

7.2 The misdeclaration penalty: very large errors

The making of a return which understates a person's true liability or overstates the repayment due to him incurs a penalty of 15% of the VAT which would have been lost if the return had been accepted as correct. The same penalty applies when HMRC issue an assessment which is too low and the trader fails to notify the error within 30 days from the issue of the assessment.

These penalties apply only where the VAT which would have been lost equals or exceeds the lower of

(a)   **£1,000,000 or**

(b)   **30% of the sum of the true input tax and the true output tax.** This sum is known as the gross amount of tax (GAT). In the case of an incorrect assessment 30% of the true amount of tax (TAT), the VAT actually due from the trader, is used instead of 30% of the GAT.

The penalty may be mitigated.

Question   Misdeclaration penalty - GAT

A trader declares output tax of £100,000 and claims input tax of £30,000 on the VAT return for the quarter ended 31 March 2007. It is subsequently discovered that output tax is understated by £28,000.

Does a misdeclaration penalty arise?

Answer

The test for misdeclaration penalty is the lower of:

*   30% of GAT (gross amount of tax)
    30% × £(100,000 + 28,000 + 30,000) = £47,400

*   £1,000,000

ie £47,400

Since the error of £28,000 is less than £47,400 the error is not 'large' and hence no penalty arises.

Question

A trader fails to submit a VAT return for the quarter to 30 June 2006. On 31 August 2006 HMRC issue an assessment showing VAT due of £200,000.

The true VAT liability for the quarter is:

	£
Output tax	370,000
Input tax	(80,000)
Net VAT due	290,000

The trader pays the £200,000 of VAT assessed but does not bring the correct position to HMRC's attention.

The true position is discovered during a control visit in December 2007.

Will a misdeclaration penalty apply?

Answer

The under-assessment of £90,000 will attract a penalty if it exceeds the lower of:

- 30% of TAT (True Amount of Tax)
  30% × £290,000 = £87,000

- £1,000,000

ie £87,000.

The £90,000 under-assessment exceeds £87,000, thus a misdeclaration penalty will be charged at £90,000 × 15% = £13,500.

The trader will have to pay the additional £90,000 due as well as the £13,500 penalty.

Errors on a VAT return of up to £2,000 (net: underdeclaration minus overdeclaration) may be corrected on the next return without giving rise to a misdeclaration penalty or interest (see below). Errors over £2,000 cannot be corrected in this way and should be notified to HMRC on form VAT652 or by letter. The misdeclaration penalty may apply.

This penalty does not apply if the trader can show reasonable excuse for his conduct, or if he made a full disclosure when he had no reason to suppose that HMRC were enquiring into his affairs.

If his conduct leads to a conviction for fraud, or to a penalty for conduct involving dishonesty, it cannot also lead to a misdeclaration penalty.

7.3 Interest on unpaid VAT

Interest (not deductible in computing taxable profits) **is charged on VAT which is the subject of an assessment** (where returns were not made or were incorrect), **or which could have been the subject of an assessment but was paid before the assessment was raised. It runs from the reckonable date until the date of payment.** This interest is sometimes called 'default interest'.

The reckonable date is when the VAT should have been paid (one month from the end of the return period), or in the case of VAT repayments, seven days from the issue of the repayment order. However, where VAT is charged by an assessment, interest does not run from more than three years before the date of the assessment. Where the VAT was paid before an assessment was raised, interest does not run for more than three years before the date of payment.

In practice, interest is only charged when there would otherwise be a loss to the Exchequer. It is not, for example, charged when a company failed to charge VAT but if it had done so another company would have been able to recover the VAT.

7.4 Reasonable excuse

A penalty may not be due if the trader can show that there is reasonable excuse for the failure, or the penalty may be mitigated by HMRC or by the VAT Tribunal. There is no definition of 'reasonable excuse'. However the legislation states that the following are not reasonable excuses:

- An insufficiency of funds to pay any VAT due
- Reliance upon a third party (such as an accountant) to perform the task in question

Many cases have considered **what constitutes a reasonable excuse** but decisions often conflict with one another. Each case depends on its own facts. Here are some examples:

(a)   Whilst **'ignorance of basic VAT law'** is not an excuse, ignorance of more complex matters can constitute a reasonable excuse

(b)   There have been a number of cases where it has been accepted that **misunderstandings as to the facts** give rise to a reasonable excuse

(c)   Although the law expressly excludes an insufficiency of funds from providing a reasonable excuse, the Tribunal will, in exceptional circumstances, look behind the shortage of funds itself and examine the case of it – this is generally restricted to cases where an unexpected event (eg bank error) has led to the shortage of funds.

Exam focus point

You are not required to know any of the other VAT penalties for your exam.

BPP LEARNING MEDIA

Chapter roundup

- VAT is charged on turnover at each stage in a production process, but in such a way that the burden is borne by the final consumer.

- VAT is charged on taxable supplies of goods and services made by a taxable person in his business.

- A trader becomes liable to register for VAT if the value of taxable supplies in any period up to 12 months exceeds £61,000 or if there are reasonable grounds for believing that the value of the taxable supplies will exceed £61,000 in the next 30 days. A trader may also register voluntarily.

- VAT is accounted for on regular returns. Extensive records must be kept.

- VAT is charged on the VAT-exclusive price. Where a discount is offered for prompt payment, VAT is chargeable on the net amount even if the discount is not taken up

- VAT is administered by HMRC and the VAT Tribunal hears appeals.

- A default occurs when a trader either submits his VAT return late, or submits the return on time but pays the VAT late. A default surcharge is applied if there is a default during a default surcharge period.

Quick quiz

1   On what transactions will VAT be charged?

2   What is a taxable person?

3   When may a taxable person be exempt from registration?

4   How are transfers between group companies treated under a VAT registration?

5   When may a person choose to be deregistered?

6   What is the time limit in respect of claiming pre-registration input tax on goods?

7   Within what time limit must an appeal to a tribunal be lodged?

8   What is a default?

Answers to quick quiz

1   VAT is charged on taxable supplies of goods and services made in the UK by a taxable person in the course or furtherance of any business carried on by him.

2   Any 'person' whose taxable turnover exceeds the registration limit. The term 'person' includes individuals, partnerships, companies, clubs, associations and charities.

3   If a taxable person makes only zero-rated supplies he may request exemption from registration.

4   Any supplies between VAT group members are ignored for VAT purposes.

5   A person is eligible for voluntary deregistration if HMRC are satisfied that the value of his taxable supplies in the following year will not exceed £59,000.

6   The VAT must have been incurred in the three years prior to the effective date of registration.

7   Within 30 days of the date of the decision by HMRC.

8   A default occurs when a trader either submits his VAT return late or submits the return on time but pays the VAT late.

Now try the question below from the Exam Question Bank

Number	Level	Marks	Time
Q30	Introductory	10	18 mins
Q31	Introductory	10	18 mins

Value added tax 2

Topic list	Syllabus reference
1 Zero-rated and exempt supplies	A6(b)F1
2 Land and buildings	A6(b)(iii)
3 The deduction of input tax	A6(b)F3
4 Partial exemption	A6(b)(vi)
5 Capital goods scheme	A6(b)(vii)
6 Imports, exports, acquisitions and dispatches	A6(b)(iv),(v)
7 Special schemes	A6(b)F4

Introduction

In this chapter we continue our VAT studies by looking at zero-rated and exempt supplies and we see how making exempt supplies can affect the deduction of input tax.

VAT needs to be applied to imports, so that people do not have a tax incentive to buy abroad, and VAT is taken off many exports in order to encourage sales abroad. We see how this is achieved for transactions both within and outside the European Community.

Finally, we look at special VAT schemes designed for particular types of smaller trader.

In the next chapter we will draw together all of our studies by looking at tax planning.

Study guide

		Intellectual level
6	**National insurance, value added tax and tax administration:**	
(b)	The contents of the Paper F6 study guide for value added tax (VAT) under headings:	
•	F1 The scope of value added tax (VAT)	
•	F3 The computation of VAT liabilities	
	The following additional material is also examinable:	
(iii)	Advise on the VAT implications of the supply of land and buildings in the UK	
(iv)	Advise on the VAT implications of imports and exports	
(v)	Advise on the VAT implications of acquisitions and supplies within the EU	
(vi)	Advise on the VAT implications of partial exemption	
(vii)	Advise on the application of the capital goods scheme	

Exam guide

In the exam you may be required to advise on almost any aspect of VAT, such as imports and exports or the special schemes. A question may require you to consider the effect of following a particular course of action, for example commencing to make exempt supplies may lead to a greater than expected VAT cost as the partial exemption rules result in the disallowance of a proportion of input tax.

Knowledge brought forward from earlier studies

This chapter continues to revise your knowledge of the basic principles of VAT, including zero rated and exempt supplies, the deduction of input tax and the special schemes for smaller traders. Imports and exports, partial exemption and the capital goods scheme are all new material.

1 Zero-rated and exempt supplies

FAST FORWARD

Some supplies are taxable (either standard-rated, reduced-rated or zero-rated). Others are exempt.

1.1 Types of supply

Zero-rated supplies are taxable at 0%. A taxable supplier whose outputs are zero-rated but whose inputs are standard-rated will obtain repayments of the VAT paid on purchases.

A **person making exempt supplies is unable to recover VAT on inputs** (in exactly the same way as for a non-registered person). An exempt supplier has to shoulder the burden of VAT. He may increase his prices to pass on the charge, but he cannot issue a VAT invoice which would enable a taxable customer to obtain a credit for VAT, since no VAT is chargeable on his supplies.

1.2 Example: standard-rated, zero-rated and exempt supplies

Here are figures for three traders, the first with standard-rated outputs, the second with zero-rated outputs and the third with exempt outputs. All their inputs are standard-rated.

	Standard-rated £	Zero-rated £	Exempt £
Inputs	20,000	20,000	20,000
VAT	3,500	3,500	3,500
	23,500	23,500	23,500
Outputs	30,000	30,000	30,000
VAT	5,250	0	0
	35,250	30,000	30,000
Pay/(reclaim)	1,750	(3,500)	0
Net profit	10,000	10,000	6,500

VAT legislation lists zero-rated, lower rate and exempt supplies. There is no list of standard-rated supplies.

If a trader makes a supply you need to categorise that supply for VAT as follows:

Step 1   Consider if it is a zero-rated supply. If not:

Step 2   Consider if it is exempt. If not:

Step 3   The supply is standard-rated.

1.3 Zero-rated supplies

The following are some common items on the **zero-rated list**.

(a)   Human and animal food

(b)   Printed matter used for reading (eg books, newspapers)

(c)   Construction work on new homes or the sale of the freehold of (or a lease over 21 years (at least 20 years in Scotland) of) new homes by builders

(d)   Exports of goods to outside the EU

(e)   Clothing and footwear for young children and certain protective clothing eg motor cyclists' crash helmets

1.4 Exempt supplies

The following are some common items on the **exempt** list.

(a)   Sales of freeholds of buildings (other than commercial buildings within three years from completion) and leaseholds of land and buildings of any age including a surrender of a lease

(b)   Financial services

(c)   Insurance

1.5 Lower rate of VAT

Certain supplies are charged at **5%. The supplies are still taxable supplies**.

The main supplies are:

(a)   supplies of fuel for domestic use, and

(b)   supplies of the services of installing energy saving materials to homes

1.6 Exceptions to the general rule

There are many exceptions to the general rule.

For example the zero-rated list states human food is zero-rated. However, the legislation then states that food supplied in the course of catering (eg restaurant meals, hot takeaways) is not zero-rated. Luxury items of food (eg crisps, peanuts, chocolate covered biscuits) are also not zero-rated.

In the exempt list we are told that financial services are exempt. However the legislation then goes on to state that credit management and processing services are not exempt. Investment advice is also not exempt.

Great care must be taken when categorising goods or services as zero-rated, exempt or standard-rated. It is not as straightforward as it may first appear.

1.7 Standard-rated supplies

There is no list of standard-rated supplies. If a supply is not zero-rated and is not exempt then it is treated as standard-rated. The standard rate of VAT is 17.5%.

2 Land and buildings

 FAST FORWARD

Transactions in land may be zero rated, standard rated or exempt.

Transactions in land may be zero rated, standard rated or exempt.

(a) **The construction of new dwellings or buildings to be used for residential or charitable purposes is zero-rated**.

(b) **The sale of the freehold of a 'new' commercial building is standard-rated. The definition of 'new' is less than three years old**. The construction of commercial buildings is also standard-rated.

(c) Other sales and most leases of land and buildings are exempt.

2.1 Option to tax

Owners may elect to treat sales and leases of land and *commercial* buildings as taxable instead of exempt. This is known as 'waiving the exemption' or the option to tax.

The owner must become registered for VAT (if he is not already so registered) in order to make the election. The election replaces an exempt supply with a standard rated one, usually to enable the recovery of input VAT.

The election may be revoked after 20 years with the written consent of HMRC.

3 The deduction of input tax

 FAST FORWARD

Not all input VAT is deductible, eg VAT on most motor cars.

3.1 Introduction

Input tax is deductible for supplies to a taxable person in the course of his business.

3.2 Capital items

There is no distinction between capital and revenue expenditure for VAT. So a manufacturer paying VAT on the purchase of plant to make taxable supplies will be able to obtain a credit for all the VAT immediately (see below for the capital goods scheme).

3.3 Non-deductible input tax

The following input tax is not deductible.

(a) **VAT on motor cars** not used wholly for business purposes. VAT on cars is never reclaimable unless the car is acquired new for resale or is acquired for use in or leasing to a taxi business, a self-drive car hire business or a driving school (see below for treatment of motor expenses).

(b) **VAT on business entertaining** where the cost of the entertaining is not a tax deductible trading expense.

(c) **VAT on expenses incurred on domestic accommodation for directors or proprietors of a business**.

(d) **VAT on non-business items passed through the business accounts.** If goods are bought partly for business use the purchaser may:

(i) Deduct all the input tax, and account for output tax in respect of the private use, or
(ii) Deduct only the business proportion of the input tax.

3.4 Irrecoverable VAT

Where input tax on a purchase is not deductible that input **VAT is included in the cost for income tax, corporation tax, capital allowance or capital gains purposes.**

Deductible VAT is omitted from costs, so that only net amounts are included in accounts. Similarly, sales (and proceeds in chargeable gains computations) **are shown net of VAT**, because the VAT is paid over to HMRC.

3.5 Motoring expenses

3.5.1 Accessories and maintenance costs

Input VAT can be reclaimed if accessories for business use are fitted after the original purchase of a car and a separate invoice is raised. If a car is used for business purposes then any VAT charged on repair and maintenance costs can be treated as input tax.

3.5.2 Fuel

If fuel is supplied for private purposes all input VAT incurred on the fuel is allowed but the business must account for output VAT using a set of scale charges.

The input VAT incurred on fuel is fully deductible even when it is supplied for an individual's private use. However in this case the business must account for output tax using set scale charges per VAT return period, based on the cylinder capacity of the car's engine.

The VAT inclusive scale charges are reproduced below; the relevant figures will be given to you in the exam. However, take care to note whether the examiner has given you the VAT inclusive or the VAT exclusive scale figure.

£

VAT on private petrol – VAT inclusive quarterly scale charge
CC of car: 1400cc or less

	£
CC of car: 1400cc or less	273
Over 1400cc up to 2000cc	346
Over 2000cc	508

The output tax is the VAT inclusive scale charge × 7/47 or the VAT exclusive scale charge × 17.5%.

Question

VAT and private use fuel

Iain is an employee of ABC Ltd. He has the use of a 1000 cc car for one month and an 1800 cc car for two months during the quarter ended 31 March 2007.

ABC Ltd pay all the petrol costs in respect of both cars without requiring Iain to make any reimbursement in respect of private fuel. Total petrol costs for the quarter amount to £300 (including VAT).

What is the VAT effect of the above on ABC Ltd?

VAT Scale rates (VAT inclusive)

	Quarterly	
	Diesel	*Petrol*
	£	£
Up to 1400cc	260	273
1401 to 2000cc	260	346
Over 2000cc	331	508

Answer

Value for the quarter:

	£
Car 1	
Up to 1400 cc £273 × 1/3 =	91.00
Car 2	
1401-2000 cc £346 × 2/3 =	230.67
	321.67
Output tax:	
7/47 × £321.67	£47.91
Input tax	
7/47 × £300	£44.68

3.6 Relief for impairment losses (bad debts)

 FAST FORWARD

Relief for VAT on impairment losses (bad debts) is available if the VAT has been accounted for, the debt is over six months old (measured from when the payment is due) and has been written off in the trader's accounts.

A trader may claim a refund of VAT on amounts unpaid by debtors if:

(a) he has accounted for VAT, and
(b) the debt is over six months old, and
(c) has been written off in the creditor's accounts.

If the debtor later pays all (or part) of the amount owed the corresponding amount of VAT repaid must be paid back to HMRC.

Claims for relief must be made within three years of the time the debt became eligible for relief.

4 Partial exemption

A trader making both taxable and exempt supplies may be unable to recover all of his input tax.

4.1 Introduction

A trader may only recover the VAT on supplies made to him if it is attributable to his taxable supplies. **Where a person makes a mixture of taxable and exempt supplies, he is partially exempt, and not all his input tax is recoverable because some of it is attributable to his exempt supplies.**

4.2 The standard method of attributing input tax

For a trader who is partially exempt, input tax must be apportioned between that relating to **taxable supplies** (and recoverable) **and** that relating to **exempt supplies** (exempt input tax). The standard method of attributing input tax is to:

Step 1   **Calculate how much of the input tax relates to making taxable supplies**: this input tax is deductible in full.

Step 2   **Calculate how much of the input tax relates to making exempt supplies**: this is exempt input tax.

Step 3   **Calculate how much of any residual (ie remaining) input tax is deductible using the percentage:**

Formula to learn

$$\frac{\text{Taxable turnover excluding VAT}}{\text{Total turnover excluding VAT}} \times 100\%, \text{rounded up to the nearest whole percentage}$$

An alternative method of attributing input tax ('special' method) may be agreed in writing with HMRC.

Question   Calculation of recoverable input tax (part 1)

In the three month VAT period to 30 June 2006, Mr A makes £105,000 of exempt supplies and £300,000 of taxable supplies. Most of the goods purchased are used for both types of supply which means that much of the input tax cannot be directly attributed to either type of supply. After directly attributing as much input tax as possible the following position arises.

	£
Attributed to taxable supplies	1,200
Attributed to exempt supplies	600
Unattributed VAT	8,200
	10,000

How much input tax can Mr A recover?

Answer

The amount of unattributed VAT which is apportioned to the making of taxable supplies is

$\dfrac{300,000}{405,000}$ = 74.07% rounded up to 75% × £8,200 = £6,150

Note. The percentage is rounded up since residual (unattributed) input tax does not exceed £400,000 per month.

Mr A can therefore recover £1,200 + £6,150 = £7,350 of his input tax.

The balance of input tax of £2,650 (£600 + £(8,200 − 6,150)) is exempt input tax.

Where the input VAT wholly attributable to exempt supplies plus the residual VAT attributed to exempt supplies (ie the total of exempt input tax) does not exceed:

    (a)   **£625 a month on average and**
    (b)   **50% of all input tax,**

all the input VAT is recoverable.

Question   De minimis limit

Sue makes the following supplies in the quarter ended 31 October 2006.

	£
Taxable supplies (excl. VAT)	28,000
Exempt supplies	6,000
	34,000

Sue analyses her input tax for the period as follows.

	£
Wholly attributable to: taxable supplies	1,500
exempt supplies	900
Non-attributable (overheads)	1,200
	3,600

How much input tax is available for credit on Sue's VAT return?

Answer

	£
Wholly attributable to taxable supplies	1,500
Partly attributable to taxable supplies	
$\dfrac{28,000}{28,000+6,000}$	
ie 82.35% rounded up to 83% × £1,200	996
	2,496
£(900 + (1,200 − 996)) = 1,104	
Exempt input tax is de minimis (W)	1,104
Input tax recoverable	3,600
ie all input tax is recoverable	

Working

De minimis test

- Monthly average $\dfrac{1,104}{3}$ = £368 ie not more than £625.

- Proportion of total $\dfrac{1,104}{3,600}$ = 30.7% ie not more than 50%.

Both tests passed. Thus exempt input tax is de minimis.

4.3 Annual adjustment

An annual adjustment is made with the '£625 a month on average and 50%' test applied to the year as a whole. The result for the year is compared with the total of results for the individual VAT periods and any difference is added to or deducted from the input tax on the return for the *next* period after the end of the tax year.

Question	Calculation of recoverable input tax (part 2)

Following on from the above example Mr A has the following results in the remaining VAT quarters of his VAT year ended 31 March 2007.

		Input tax attributed to	
	Taxable	Exempt	
Quarter to	*supplies*	*supplies*	*Unattributed*
	£	£	£
30.9.06	1,500	1,000	5,000
31.12.06	2,000	500	1,800
31.3.07	1,900	850	7,000
	5,400	2,350	13,800

	Turnover	
Quarter to	*Taxable*	*Exempt*
	£	£
30.9.06	400,000	100,000
31.12.06	500,000	150,000
31.3.07	450,000	120,000
	1,350,000	370,000

Calculate the annual adjustment required and state which return it will be made on.

Answer

First we calculate the recoverable input tax in each VAT return.

		£	*Recovered* £
Return to 30.6.06			
See above	Taxable	7,350	7,350
	Exempt	2,650	
		10,000	

Return to 30.9.06

$\dfrac{400,000}{500,000}$ = 80% × £5,000 = Non-attributable

	£	*Recovered* £
	4,000	
Wholly taxable	1,500	
Taxable total	5,500	5,500
Exempt £(1,000 + 1,000)	2,000	
	7,500	

Return to 31.12.06

$\dfrac{500,000}{650,000}$ = 76.92% rounded up to 77% × £1,800

	£	*Recovered* £
	1,386	
Non-attributable		
Wholly taxable	2,000	
Taxable total	3,386	
Exempt £(500 + 414)	914	
	4,300	4,300

The exempt input tax at £914 is less than £1,875 (£625 × 3 months) and 50% of total input tax (50% × £4,300 = £2,150) so is de minimis and recoverable.

Return to 31.3.07

$\dfrac{450,000}{570,000}$ = 78.94% rounded up to 79% × £7,000

	£	*Recovered* £
	5,530	
Non-attributable		
Wholly taxable	1,900	
Taxable total	7,430	7,430
Exempt £(850 + 1,470)	2,320	
	9,750	
Recovered over the VAT year		24,580

Now we do the same calculation again but using the results for the whole VAT year to 31.3.07.

Annual adjustment

$\dfrac{1,350,000 + 300,000}{1,720,000 + 405,000}$ = 77.64% rounded up to 78% × £(13,800 + 8,200) (note)

	£	*Recovered* £
	17,160	
Wholly taxable £(5,400 + 1,200)	6,600	
Taxable total	23,760	23,760
Exempt £(31,550 − 23,760)	7,790	
	31,550	

VAT to repay to HMRC on VAT return to 30 June 2007 as annual adjustment.   820

Note. We must include the quarter to June 2006's results.

5 Capital goods scheme

> The capital goods scheme (CGS) allows HMRC to ensure the VAT claimed on the purchase of certain capital items accurately reflects the taxable use to which they are put over a period of time.

The scheme mainly affects partially exempt businesses and enables the amount of VAT recovered to be adjusted for each year's use.

The CGS applies to:

(a)   Computers costing £50,000 or more, which are dealt with over 5 VAT years, and

(b)   Land and building costing £250,000 or more, which are dealt with over 10 VAT years.

In the VAT year the asset is acquired the input recovery is initially based on use for the quarter of purchase, and is then subject to the annual adjustment as described above.

For each subsequent VAT year over the recovery period of 5 or 10 years an adjustment is made to the VAT recovery.

Formula to learn

> The adjustment is equal to the difference in percentage use between the first VAT year and the VAT year under review × 1/5 (for computers) or 1/10 (for land and buildings) × the cost

The adjustment is made in the second VAT return following the end of the VAT year.

If the asset is sold before the end of the recovery period, two adjustments are needed:

(a)   the normal adjustment for the VAT year of sale as if the proportion of use for the period from the start of the year until the date of sale had applied for the whole VAT year, and

(b)   an additional adjustment for each remaining VAT year of recovery calculated assuming 100% use for taxable supplies. This additional adjustment cannot exceed the VAT charged on the sale of the item.

Question
Capital goods scheme

Z Ltd purchased a computer for £100,000 + 17.5% VAT on 1 December 2006. It used it 58% for taxable use in the quarter of purchase and 60% for taxable purposes in the year to 31 March 2007.

The taxable use in the year to 31 March 2008 was 50%. The computer was sold for £6,000 + VAT on 10 August 2008. The taxable use in the period 1 April 2008 to 10 August 2008 was 50%.

Calculate the initial input recovery and adjustments required for all other years.

Answer

For the first VAT year to 31 March 2007 the recovery (after the annual partial exemption adjustment) is £100,000 × 17.5% = £17,500 × 60% = £10,500.

For the second VAT year to 31 March 2008 the adjustment is £17,500 × 10% (ie 60%-50%) × 1/5 = £350, payable to HMRC.

For the third VAT year to 31 March 2009 there are two adjustments:

(a)   £17,500 × 10% × 1/5 = £350, payable to HMRC.

(b)   £17,500 × 40% (ie 100%-60%) × 2/5 = £2,800, restricted to the VAT charged on the sale of the computer ie £6,000 × 17.5% = £1,050, recoverable from HMRC.

The net adjustment for the third VAT year to 31 March 2009 is (£(350) + £1,050) = £700 recoverable from HMRC.

6 Imports, exports, acquisitions and dispatches

FAST FORWARD

> Imports from outside the EU are subject to VAT and exports to outside the EU are zero-rated. Taxable acquisitions from other EU states are also subject to VAT and sales to registered traders in other EU states are zero-rated.

6.1 Introduction

The terms **import and export** refer to purchases and sales of goods with countries **outside the EU.**

The terms **acquisition and dispatch** refer to purchases and sales of goods with countries **in the EU.**

The EU comprises Austria, Belgium, Bulgaria, the Czech Republic, Cyprus, Denmark, Estonia, Finland, France, Germany, Greece, Hungary, the Republic of Ireland, Italy, Latvia, Lithuania, Luxembourg, Malta, the Netherlands, Poland, Portugal, Romania, Slovakia, Slovenia, Spain, Sweden and the UK.

Exam focus point

> There are different rules for transactions between EU member states and for transactions with non-EU countries.

6.2 Trade in goods outside the European Union

6.2.1 Imports

An importer of goods from outside the EU must:

   (a)   **account for the output VAT at the point of entry into the UK, and**
   (b)   **can claim the input VAT payable on his next VAT return.**

6.2.2 Exports

The export of goods outside the EU is zero rated.

The trader must provide evidence of the export such as copy invoices and consignment notes.

6.3 Trade in goods within the European Union

6.3.1 Purchases (acquisitions)

Goods acquired by a VAT registered person in the UK from another EU member state are liable to VAT in this country. Consequently, output tax has to be accounted for on the relevant VAT return. **The 'tax point' for such acquisitions is the earlier of:**

   •   **The fifteenth day of the month following the month of acquisition, and**
   •   **The date of issue of an invoice.**

The transaction is entered on the relevant VAT return as an output *and* an input so, subject to the partial exemption provisions, the effect is neutral. Thus the trader is in the same position as he would have been if he had acquired the goods from a UK supplier.

If the goods acquired are zero-rated or exempt under UK VAT legislation there is no requirement to account for VAT at the standard rate.

6.3.2 Sales (dispatches)

Where goods are sold to another EU member state, the supply is zero-rated if:

- **The supply is made to a registered trader**, and
- **The supplier quotes his customer's VAT number on the invoice**, and
- **The supplier holds evidence that the goods were delivered to another member state.**

7 Special schemes

FAST FORWARD

Special schemes include the cash accounting scheme, the annual accounting scheme and the optional flat rate scheme. These schemes make VAT accounting easier for certain types of trader usually with relatively low turnover.

7.1 The cash accounting scheme

The cash accounting scheme enables businesses to account for VAT on the basis of cash paid and received. The date of payment or receipt determines the return in which the transaction is dealt with.

The scheme can only be used by a trader whose annual taxable turnover (exclusive of VAT) does not exceed £660,000 and whose returns and VAT payments are up to date.

If the value of taxable supplies exceeds £825,000 in the 12 months to the end of a VAT period a trader must leave the cash accounting scheme immediately.

Advantages of the scheme are:

- **automatic relief for bad debts**
- **cash flow**

7.2 The annual accounting scheme

The annual accounting scheme is only available to traders who regularly pay VAT to HMRC, not to traders who normally receive repayments.

It is available for traders **whose VAT exclusive taxable turnover is not expected to exceed £1,350,000 over the following 12 months (from 1 April 2006. Prior to this date £660,000).**

Traders file annual VAT returns and must make nine monthly payments on account equal to 90% of their previous year's VAT liability, with the first payment due at the end of the fourth month of the year. An annual VAT return must be submitted to HMRC along with any balancing payment due within two months of the end of the year. There is an option to pay three larger interim instalments.

Late payment of instalments is not a default for the purposes of the surcharge liability notice system.

To use the scheme all returns must have been made up to date. Annual accounting is not available where VAT registration is in the name of a VAT group or a division.

If the expected value of a trader's taxable supplies exceeds £1,600,000 notice must be given to HMRC within 30 days and he may then be required to leave the scheme. If the £1,600,000 limit is actually exceeded, the trader must leave the scheme.

Advantages of annual accounting:

- Only one VAT return each year so fewer occasions to trigger a default surcharge
- Ability to manage cash flow more accurately
- Avoids need for quarterly calculations for partial exemption purposes and input tax recovery

Disadvantages of annual accounting:

- Need to monitor future taxable supplies to ensure turnover limit not exceeded
- Timing of payments have less correlation to turnover (and hence cash received) by business
- Payments based on previous year's turnover may not reflect current year turnover which may be a problem if the scale of activities has reduced

7.3 Flat rate scheme

The flat rate scheme enables businesses to calculate VAT due to HMRC by simply applying a flat rate percentage to their VAT inclusive turnover, including all zero-rated and exempt income. The percentage depends upon the trade sector into which a business falls.

Exam focus point

> The flat rate percentage will be given to you in your examination.

A 1% reduction off the flat rate % can be made by businesses in their first year of VAT registration.

Businesses using the scheme must issue VAT invoices to their VAT registered customers but they do not have to record all the details of the invoices issued or purchase invoices received to calculate the VAT due. Invoices issued will show VAT at the normal rate rather than the flat rate.

To join the flat rate scheme businesses must have:

- **a tax exclusive annual taxable turnover of up to £150,000**, and
- **a tax exclusive annual total turnover, including the value of exempt and/or other non-taxable income, of up to £187,500.**

7.4 Example: flat rate scheme

An accountant undertakes work for individuals and for business clients. In a VAT year, the business client work amounts to £35,000 and the accountant will issue VAT invoices totalling £41,125 (£35,000 plus VAT at 17.5%). Turnover from work for individuals totals £18,000, including VAT. Total gross sales are therefore £59,125. The flat rate percentage for an accountancy businesses is 13%.

VAT due to HMRC will be 13% × £59,125 = £7,686.25

Under the normal VAT rules the output tax due would be:

	£
£35,000 × 17.5%	6,125.00
£18,000 × 7/47	2,680.85
	8,805.85

Whether the accountant is better off under the scheme depends on the amount of input tax incurred as this would be offset, under normal rules, from output tax due.

Chapter roundup

- Some supplies are taxable (either standard-rated, reduced-rated or zero-rated). Others are exempt.

- Transactions in land may be zero rated, standard rated or exempt.

- Not all input VAT is deductible, eg VAT on most motor cars

- If fuel is supplied for private purposes all input VAT incurred on the fuel is allowed but the business must account for output VAT using a set of scale charges

- Relief for VAT on impairment losses (bad debts) is available if the VAT has been accounted for, the debt is over six months old (measured from when the payment is due) and has been written off in the trader's accounts.

- A trader making both taxable and exempt supplies may be unable to recover all of his input tax.

- The capital goods scheme (CGS) allows HMRC to ensure the VAT claimed on the purchase of certain capital items accurately reflects the taxable use to which they are put over a period of time.

- Imports from outside the EU are subject to VAT and exports to outside the EU are zero-rated. Taxable acquisitions from other EU states are also subject to VAT and sales to registered traders in other EU states are zero-rated.

- Special schemes include the cash accounting scheme, the annual accounting scheme and the optional flat rate scheme. These schemes make VAT accounting easier for certain types of trader usually with relatively low turnover.

Quick quiz

1 What input tax is never deductible?

2 What relief is available for bad debts?

3 What is partial exemption?

4 Are goods exported from the EU standard-rated or zero-rated?

5 What are the turnover limits for the annual accounting scheme?

6 What is the optional flat rate scheme?

Answers to quick quiz

1. VAT on:

    - motor cars (where there is an element of private use)
    - business entertaining
    - expenses incurred on domestic accommodation for directors
    - non-business items passed through the accounts

2. Where a supplier has accounted for VAT on a supply and the customer fails to pay, then the supplier may, after 6 months, write it off in the accounts and claim a refund of the VAT.

3. Where a 'person' makes a mixture of taxable and exempt supplies he is partially exempt and cannot recover input tax incurred by the business in full.

4. In general, exports from the EU are zero-rated.

5. Turnover not exceeding £1,350,000 to join the scheme. Once turnover exceeds £1,600,000 must leave the scheme.

6. The optional flat rate scheme enables businesses to calculate VAT simply by applying a percentage to their tax-inclusive turnover ie the total turnover generated, including all zero-rated and exempt income. The percentage depends upon the trade sector into which a business falls.

Now try the question below from the Exam Question Bank

Number	Level	Marks	Time
Q32	Introductory	10	18 mins

Part E

Tax planning and ethics

30

Tax planning and ethics

Topic list	Syllabus reference
1 Introduction	C,D,E
2 Ethics	D5
3 Employment and self-employment	C1-4,D2-6
4 Remuneration packages	C1-4,D1-6
5 The choice of a business medium	C1-4,D1-6
6 The incorporation of a business	C1-4,D1-6
7 Tax efficient profit extraction	C1-4,D1-6
8 Tax efficient exit routes	C1-4,D1-6
9 Planning for corporate growth	C1-4,D1-6
10 Group tax minimisation strategies	C1-4,D1-6
11 Divisionalised v group company structure	C1-4,D1-6
12 Disclosure of tax avoidance schemes	D5-6

Introduction

You have now completed your studies of the individual taxes covered in the syllabus so we will turn our attention to how to use your knowledge. First we consider how to approach and answer the question. Next we consider the ethical rules which should be applied to every situation that you are required to consider. Up to five marks on every paper will be given for your comments on ethical matters. It is therefore important that you identify ethical issues and comment as appropriate.

We then turn to tax planning, which is an integral part of any tax advice you give. Note that tax avoidance is the exploitation of the law to reduce tax liabilities. It is not illegal to attempt tax avoidance and this is what you are doing when you give tax planning advice. Tax avoidance should be distinguished from tax evasion which involves not giving all relevant facts to HMRC. Tax evasion is always illegal and you should never become involved in it. There may be a duty to disclose details of tax avoidance schemes to the relevant HMRC authorities.

We have dealt with various tax planning aspects as they have arisen earlier in this Text. In this chapter, we bring together topics by considering some additional typical tax planning points.

Study guide

		Intellectual level
C	**THE IMPACT OF RELEVANT TAXES ON VARIOUS SITUATIONS AND COURSES OF ACTION, INCLUDING THE INTERACTION OF TAXES**	
1	Identifying and advising on the taxes applicable to a given course of action and their impact.	3
2	Identifying and understanding that the alternative ways of achieving personal or business outcomes may lead to different tax consequences.	3
3	Assessing the tax advantages and disadvantages of alternative courses of action.	3
4	Understanding the statutory obligations imposed in a given situation, including any time limits for action and advising on the implications of non-compliance.	3
D	**MINIMISING AND/OR DEFERRING TAX LIABILITIES BY THE USE OF STANDARD TAX PLANNING MEASURES**	
1	Identifying and advising on the types of investment and other expenditure that will result in a reduction in tax liabilities for an individual and/or a business.	3
2	Advising on legitimate tax planning measures, by which the tax liabilities arising from a particular situation or course of action can be mitigated.	3
3	Advising on the appropriateness of such investment, expenditure or measures given a particular taxpayer's circumstances or stated objectives.	3
4	Advise on the mitigation of tax in the manner recommended by reference to numerical analysis and/or reasoned argument.	3
5	Be aware of the ethical and professional issues arising from the giving of tax planning advice.	3
6	Be aware of and give advice on current issues in taxation.	3
E	**COMMUNICATING WITH CLIENTS, HM REVENUE AND CUSTOMS AND OTHER PROFESSIONALS IN AN APPROPRIATE MANNER**	
1	Communication of advice, recommendations and information in the required format:	3
	For example the use of Reports, Letters, Memoranda and Meeting notes	
2	Presentation of written information, in language appropriate to the purpose of the communication and the intended recipient.	3
3	Communicating conclusions reached together, where necessary with relevant supporting computations.	3
4	Stating and explaining assumptions made or limitations in the analysis provided; together with any inadequacies in the information available and/or additional information required to provide a fuller analysis.	3
5	Identifying and explaining other, non-tax, factors that should be considered.	3

Exam Guide

A significant number of marks in the exam will be available for evaluation and advice. Before you start to write your answer assess what is required. You may simply be asked to advise on the tax consequences of one course of action, or you may have to compare the tax consequences of two or more options. The options may be specified in the question, or you may be required to identify possible options. You may have to cover all taxes, or to restrict your answer to a single tax. Present your answer in the required format; if you are asked for notes do not write an essay; if you are asked to write a letter do so.

In every paper there will be five marks awarded for your comments on ethical matters. You need to know the fundamental principles of the ACCA's code of conduct, and when presented with a scenario you should quickly review these to make sure that they are not compromised. If there is a threat then consider how serious it is and how you should respond.

1 Introduction

1.1 Approach to the question

It would be impossible to write a definitive chapter on tax planning and mitigation, as no two scenarios are ever the same. This chapter covers several typical cases, highlighting the points which need to be considered. You may well think of other situations where taxpayers may seek advice.

You should be methodical in your approach. Unless you are asked to consider only one or more specific taxes, you should get into the habit of running through all the taxes, even if to eliminate them from consideration. This Text covers:

(a) income tax
(b) capital gains tax
(c) inheritance tax
(d) national insurance
(e) stamp duties
(f) corporation tax, and
(g) VAT.

If you are asked to compare the tax consequences of two or more options, you must consider the impact of each tax on each option in order to produce a complete picture.

In some cases you may be asked how to **mitigate a tax liability arising from a particular transaction**. There are several standard options. You will normally be looking for a way to reduce income or gains, for example for an individual by paying a pension contribution, or you may be seeking to reduce a liability by a tax reducer, such as by investing in a VCT, or to defer a gain, using one of the holdover reliefs. Look carefully at the dates, there is less you can do to mitigate a liability for an earlier year than for the current year.

Make sure that you consider the future consequences of your proposals. In particular remember that deferred gains crystallise on certain events; it may not be a good idea to claim gift relief if the donee is likely to sell the asset gifted shortly after receipt because of a loss of capital gains tax taper relief. You should also have spotted in this case that this would lead to a withdrawal of IHT business property relief if the donor died within seven years.

1.2 Approach to the answer

Read the question carefully to ascertain the type of answer that may be required. You may have to prepare a formal report, letter or memorandum, or you may have to write notes for a colleague. In other cases you may just be required to prepare explanations or calculations.

Where the answer is formal, **marks will be specifically awarded for the presentation of the material and the effectiveness with which the information is presented**. You should get used to setting out the points in your answer in a logical order, giving full explanations and yet still being concise. It is often better to present any calculations as an appendix, unless they are extremely short. Look back to the question; if you are asked to draw conclusions or make recommendations have you done so? You may find using headings will help you.

It is important to know who the report, letter etc. is being prepared for. If you are writing to a client they are unlikely to understand technical terms, and certainly will not know, for example, what 's381 relief' is. If, on the other hand, you are writing a memorandum to a partner you can assume a certain degree of familiarity with the underlying concepts.

Sometimes the information not given in the question is as important as the information which is. **You may have to make assumptions** about what the taxpayers has done, or intends to do, or about his personal circumstances. If so, state them in your answer, so that if your assumptions are wrong the reader's attention will be drawn to them. Otherwise the course of action that you are recommending may be totally unsuitable. You may be able to give some indication of how your answer would differ, but do not go wildly off on a tangent.

Remember also that **tax should never be the only factor** in a decision. For example, if you are advising someone to invest under the enterprise investment scheme to obtain a tax reducer and also to defer the gain, stop and think about the nature of the investment. Small unquoted companies often fail, and your client may prefer to pay the tax rather than lose his investment. There may be hints and clues in the question; a 74 year old is not likely to want to invest in a personal pension.

2 Ethics

2.1 Introduction

In common with most professional organisations, the ACCA require members and students to observe the highest professional standards in all aspects of their work. This section discusses how these standards can be maintained, with particular reference to taxation work. The requirements apply equally to members and students, and in this section the term 'members' should be taken to include students.

In addition to the ACCA's own requirements, there are many instances where **members are required to comply with statutory and regulatory requirements imposed by the Government**. If a member is in doubt as to the course of action he should take, he should approach the ACCA for guidance. **Failure to observe the ACCA's standards may result in disciplinary action**.

The ACCA publish a **Code of Ethics and Conduct** covering the standards and ethical requirements which they expect. It details the **fundamental principles and sets out a framework for applying those principles**. Members must apply this framework to particular situations to identify instances where compliance with the ethical standards may be compromised so that safeguards may be put in place to avoid threats, or to reduce them to below the minimum level that can be regarded as acceptable.

Normally a member's responsibility will be to a client, or to an employer, but there may be instances where a member may need to act in the public interest.

2.2 The fundamental principles

The fundamental principles of ethics should underlie all of a member's professional behaviour.

The fundamental principles are:

(a) **Integrity**: Requires all members to be straightforward and honest in professional and business relationships.

A member should not be associated with information if he believes that the information contains a materially false or misleading statement, statements or information furnished recklessly, or omits or obscures information required to be included where such omission or obscurity would be misleading.

(b) **Objectivity**: Imposes an obligation on members not to compromise their professional or business judgement because of bias, conflict of interest or the undue influence of others.

Relationships that bias or unduly influence the professional judgement of the member should be avoided.

(c) **Professional competence and due care**: Requires members to:

(i) Maintain professional knowledge and skill at the level required to ensure that clients or employers receive competent professional service based on current developments in practice, legislation and techniques; and

(ii) Act diligently in accordance with applicable technical and professional standards when providing professional services.

Any limitations relating to the service being provided must be made clear to clients and other users to ensure that misinterpretation of facts or opinions does not take place.

(d) **Confidentiality**: Imposes an obligation on members to refrain from:

(i) Disclosing outside the firm confidential information acquired as a result of professional and business relationships without proper and specific authority or unless there is a legal or professional right or duty to disclose; and

(ii) Using confidential information acquired as a result of professional and business relationships to their personal advantage or the advantage of third parties.

A member should consider the need to maintain confidentiality of information within the firm. A member should also maintain confidentiality of information disclosed by a prospective client or employer.

The need to maintain confidentiality continues even after the end of relationships between a member and a client or employer. When a member changes employment or acquires a new client, the member is entitled to use prior experience, but not confidential information obtained from the previous relationship.

(e) **Professional behaviour**. Imposes an obligation on a member to comply with relevant laws and regulations and avoid any action that may bring discredit to the profession.

This includes actions which a reasonable and informed third party, having knowledge of all relevant information, would conclude negatively affects the good reputation of the profession.

Members should be honest and truthful and should not:

(i) Make exaggerated claims for the services they are able to offer, the qualifications they possess, or experience they have gained

(ii) Make disparaging references or unsubstantiated comparisons to the work of others

2.3 The conceptual framework

2.3.1 Introduction

A member may find himself in a situation where there is a **specific threat to compliance with the fundamental principles**. There are many possible scenarios, and rather than trying to specify how each situation should be dealt with, the ACCA provide a conceptual framework that requires members to identify, evaluate and address such threats. Unless an identified threat is clearly insignificant, members should apply safeguards to eliminate the threat or reduce it to an acceptable level so that compliance with the fundamental principles is not compromised.

2.3.2 Threats

The member is obliged to evaluate any threat as soon as he knows, or should be expected to know, of its existence. Both qualitative and quantitative factors should be taken into account.

Most threats to compliance with the fundamental principles fall into the following categories:

(a) **Self-interest threat**, which may occur as a result of the financial or other interests of a member or of an immediate or close family member

(b) **Self-review threat**, which may occur when a previous judgment needs to be re-evaluated by the member responsible for that judgment

(c) **Advocacy threat**, which may occur when a member promotes a position or opinion to the point that subsequent objectivity may be compromised

(d) **Familiarity threats**, which may occur when, because of a close relationship, a member becomes too sympathetic to the interests of others

(e) **Intimidation threats**, which may occur when a member may be deterred from acting objectively by threats, actual or perceived

2.3.3 Safeguards to offset the threats

If a member cannot implement appropriate safeguards, he should decline or discontinue the specific professional service involved, or where necessary resign from the client.

Safeguards that may eliminate or reduce threats to an acceptable level fall into two broad categories:

(a) **Safeguards created by the profession, legislation or regulation**, such as education and training, continuing professional development, professional or regulatory monitoring and disciplinary procedures

(b) **Safeguards in the work environment**, such as effective, well publicised complaints systems operated by the employing organisation

The nature of the safeguards to be applied will vary depending on the circumstances. In exercising professional judgment, a member should consider what a reasonable and informed third party, having knowledge of all relevant information, including the significance of the threat and the safeguards applied, would conclude to be unacceptable.

2.4 Ethical conflict resolution

There may be instances where a particular situation leads to a **conflict in the application of the fundamental principles**.

When initiating either a formal or informal conflict resolution process, a member should consider five factors:

(a) **Relevant facts**
(b) **Ethical issues**
(c) **Fundamental principles related to the matter**
(d) **Established internal procedures**
(e) **Alternative courses of action**

Having considered these issues, the appropriate course of action can be determined which resolves the conflict with all or some of the five fundamental principles. If the matter remains unresolved, the member should consult with other appropriate persons within the firm for help in obtaining resolution.

Where a matter involves a conflict with, or within, an organisation, a member should also consider consulting with those charged with governance of the organisation.

It is advisable for the member to **document the issue and details of any discussions held or decisions taken, concerning that issue**.

If a significant conflict cannot be resolved, a member may wish to obtain **professional advice from the ACCA or legal advisors**, to obtain guidance on ethical and legal issues without breaching confidentiality.

If, after exhausting all relevant possibilities, **the ethical conflict remains unresolved, a member should, where possible, refuse to remain associated with the matter creating the conflict**.

The member may determine that, in the circumstances, it is appropriate to withdraw from the engagement team or specific assignment, or to resign altogether from the engagement or the firm.

2.5 Disclosure of information

2.5.1 When to disclose

A member may disclose confidential information if:

(a) **Disclosure is permitted by law and is authorised** by the client or the employer

(b) **Disclosure is required by law**, such as under anti-money laundering legislation

(c) **There is a professional duty or right to disclose**, when not prohibited by law, such as under a quality review

2.5.2 Factors to consider regarding disclosure

In deciding whether to disclose confidential information, members should consider:

(a) Whether the interests of all parties, including third parties, could be harmed if the client or employer consents to the disclosure of information

(b) Whether all the relevant information is known and substantiated, to the extent it is practicable to do so. When the situation involves unsubstantiated facts, incomplete information or unsubstantiated conclusions, professional judgment should be used in determining the type of disclosure to be made, if any

(c) The type of communication that is expected and to whom it is addressed; in particular, members should be satisfied that the parties to whom the communication is addressed are appropriate recipients

2.6 Conflicts of interest

> **FAST FORWARD**
>
> A conflict of interest is a commonly met threat to compliance with the fundamental principles.

2.6.1 The threat of a conflict of interest

A member should take reasonable steps to identify circumstances that could pose a conflict of interest. These may give rise to threats to compliance with the fundamental principles.

A conflict may arise between the firm and the client or between two conflicting clients being managed by the same firm. For example where a firm acts for both a husband and wife in a divorce settlement or acts for a company and for its directors in their personal capacity.

Evaluation of threats includes consideration as to whether the member has any business interests or relationships with the client or a third party that could give rise to threats. Safeguards should be considered and applied as necessary.

2.6.2 Safeguards

Depending upon the circumstances giving rise to the conflict, safeguards should ordinarily include the member in public practice:

(a)   **Notifying the client** of the firm's business interest or activities that may represent a conflict of interest

(b)   **Notifying all known relevant parties** that the member is acting for two or more parties in respect of a matter where their respective interests are in conflict

(c)   **Notifying the client that the member does not act exclusively for any one client** in the provision of proposed services (for example, in a particular market sector or with respect to a specific service)

In each case the member should obtain the consent of the relevant parties to act.

Where a member has requested consent from a client to act for another party (which may or may not be an existing client) and that consent has been refused, then he must not continue to act for one of the parties in the matter giving rise to the conflict of interest.

The following additional safeguards should also be considered:

(a)   The use of separate engagement teams

(b)   Procedures to prevent access to information (eg strict physical separation of such teams, confidential and secure data filing)

(c)   Clear guidelines for members of the engagement team on issues of security and confidentiality

(d)   The use of confidentiality agreements signed by employees and partners of the firm

(e)   Regular review of the application of safeguards by a senior individual not involved with relevant client engagements

Where a conflict of interest poses a threat to one or more of the fundamental principles that cannot be eliminated or reduced to an acceptable level through the application of safeguards, the member should conclude that it is not appropriate to accept a specific engagement or that resignation from one or more conflicting engagements is required.

2.6.3 Example

You have acted for Robenick Ltd for several years, and also for the three director shareholders, Rob, Ben and Nick. During 2007 Rob has a disagreement with Ben and Nick over the direction of the company. What should you do?

When you commenced acting for both the company and Rob, Ben and Nick you should have advised each that you were acting for the others, and asked their permission to act. Providing there were no areas where the interests of the clients conflicted, there is no reason why you should not have acted for all the clients, although it may be advisable to have ensured that, for example, a different tax manager was responsible for each client.

However, now that there has been a disagreement between Rob and the other clients the situation has changed and there is a conflict of interest. It is most likely that it would be inappropriate to continue to act for all the clients, and you will need to cease to act, either for Rob, or for Ben, Nick and the company.

2.7 Prospective clients

Members invited to act as tax advisers by clients must **contact the existing tax advisers** to ascertain if there are any matters they should be aware of when deciding whether to accept the appointment.

2.7.1 Acceptance

Before accepting a new client, members should consider whether acceptance of the client or the particular engagement would create any threats to compliance with the fundamental principles.

Potential threats to integrity or professional behaviour may be created from, for example, questionable issues associated with the client, or a threat to professional competence and due care may be created if the engagement team does not possess the necessary skills to carry out the engagement.

Where it is not possible to implement safeguards to reduce the threats to an acceptable level, members should decline to enter into the relationship.

2.7.2 Changes in professional appointment

Members who are asked to replace another accountant should ascertain whether there are any professional or other reasons for not accepting the engagement. This may require direct communication with the existing accountant to establish the facts and circumstances behind the proposed change so that members can decide whether it is appropriate to accept the engagement.

Communication with the existing accountant is not just a matter of professional courtesy. Its main purpose is to enable members to ensure that there has been no action by the client which would on ethical grounds, preclude members from accepting the appointment and that, after considering all the facts, the client is someone for whom members would wish to act. Thus, members must always communicate with the existing accountant on being asked to accept appointment for any recurring work.

The existing accountant is bound by confidentiality. This means the extent to which a client's affairs may be discussed with a prospective accountant will depend on the nature of the engagement and on whether the client's permission has been obtained. **If the client refuses permission, the existing accountant should inform the prospective accountant, who should then inform the client that he is unable to accept the appointment.**

If the existing accountant fails to communicate with the prospective accountant despite the client's permission, the prospective accountant will need to make other enquiries to ensure there are no reasons not to accept the appointment. This could be through communications with third parties, such as banks.

Where the member is the existing accountant then, subject to obtaining the client's permission, he should disclose all information requested without delay.

2.7.3 Example

You have acted for Mr X. but have discovered a serious tax irregularity which Mr X has refused to correct and you have advised Mr X that you can no longer act for him. You receive a letter from another ACCA member advising you that he has been asked to act for Mr X. Mr X has forbidden you to divulge any information to him. What should you do?

You should advise the new accountant that Mr X has not given you permission to divulge any information. The new accountant should then refuse to act for Mr X.

2.7.4 Acting as agent or principal

Where you are performing tax compliance work eg preparing and submitting tax returns, you will be acting as agent to the client. This means that the client remains responsible for all of the information provided in the return.

When you are **providing tax planning advice, however, you will be acting as 'principal'** which means that you are fully responsible for the advice you give.

2.7.5 Tax planning concerns

At the very least **anything you recommend must be legal.** Most people understand the basic distinction between tax avoidance (tax mitigation through legal means) and tax evasion (illegal, such as fraud). Apart from the specific rules regarding disclosure of avoidance schemes (see below), you must understand that the taxpayer has the responsibility of preparing a tax return that is complete and correct (see above), and this will include an accurate disclosure of the facts.

That is not to say that you may not suggest a course of action where HMRC might disagree with your conclusion as to the tax consequences. You need to explain to the client that full details must be given to enable HMRC to consider the matter, and you should warn him that any negotiations with HMRC will take time and incur expense.

Make sure that you **know the time limits for any claims** that need to be made. If you miss the limit, the relief will be denied. Late returns incur penalties, and late payment of tax leads to an interest charge.

2.8 Tax irregularities

FAST FORWARD

If a member discovers that a client has misled him in order to obtain a tax advantage, the member has to consider his position in relation to both the client and the tax authorities.

2.8.1 Discovery of errors

A member may discover that a client has committed a taxation offence. Tax legislation prescribes monetary penalties for a number of offences. There is also the possibility of criminal proceedings being brought against the client.

The evasion or attempted evasion of tax may be the subject of criminal charges under both tax law and money laundering legislation. This applies not only to direct taxes such as income tax or corporation tax, but also to indirect taxes such as VAT.

The member has the following responsibilities:

(a)   If the information obtained concerns computations or returns that the member is currently preparing, the member must ensure that the information is accurately reflected therein. **If the client fails to provide any information requested by the member, or objects to way in which the member has presented the information, the member needs to consider whether he can continue to act for that client.**

(b)   If the information obtained concerns computations or returns that the member has already prepared and submitted to HMRC, the member cannot allow HMRC to continue to rely on them. **He should advise his client to make full disclosure to HMRC, or to authorise him to do so, without delay. If the client refuses, then the member can no longer act for the client.** The client should be advised of this, and also that the member must inform HMRC that they have ceased to act for the client. If the documents submitted to HMRC contain any accountant's report, the member must also advise HMRC that the report should no longer be relied on. The member should not, however, advise HMRC in what way the accounts are defective unless the client has consented to such disclosure.

(c)   If the information relates to a new client and concerns computations or returns that have been prepared by the client or a third party and submitted to HMRC, the member should advise the client to make full and prompt disclosure. If the error affects the current computations or returns then the member must inform the client that an appropriate adjustment must be made in the current accounts, and **if the client refuses the member should consider whether he should act for that client**. Indeed, even if the error does not affect current returns and computations the member should consider whether he should act for the client if the client refuses to disclose the error to HMRC.

Whether or not the member feels able to act for a client, he is still under a **professional duty to ensure that the client understands the seriousness of offences against HMRC**. He should also warn the client that notification that he is no longer acting for a client may alert HMRC, and urge the desirability of making a full disclosure, subject to any legal advice obtained. Any accounts, returns, computations or reports submitted on behalf of taxpayers are deemed to be submitted by the taxpayer and/or with their consent unless they prove otherwise.

This emphasises the need for members to ensure that clients have approved computations and returns, and signified their approval by signing them. There should always be a letter of engagement in place setting out the precise responsibilities of both the member and the client.

2.8.2 Example

You are preparing the tax return for Mrs Y and amongst her papers you find a bank statement for a new account which was opened with the transfer of a significant amount from her own account. Mrs Y says that this new account belongs to her young son, and that the interest should not be put on her tax return. What should you do?

First you should explain that income from funds provided by a parent are taxed as the parent's income, unless the income is less that £100, so that the interest must be shown. If Mrs Y still refuses to enter the interest on her return you should advise her that you can no longer act for her, and you must also advise HMRC that you no longer act. You are not obliged to disclose the reason to HMRC.

At this stage you have a suspicion that a tax offence may be committed, and you should discuss with your firm's money laundering officer.

2.8.3 HMRC powers

HMRC have certain statutory powers to compel disclosure in particular instances. Where information is sought under such powers, members must check that the statutory power being invoked actually covers the information sought and, if in any doubt, should take legal advice.

In some cases HMRC will ask for information to be provided voluntarily, rather than resorting to the use of their statutory powers. In this case the member must consider carefully whether it is in the client's interest to make voluntary disclosure, rather than await a statutory demand, and again may wish to take legal advice.

2.8.4 Errors by HMRC in the taxpayers' favour

Problems may arise if HMRC erroneously makes an excessive repayment of tax to taxpayers, even though they have received full disclosure of the facts.

If the repayment is made directly to the client, the member should urge them to refund the excess sum to HMRC as soon as possible. Failure to correct the error may be a civil and/or criminal offence by the client. **If the client refuses the member must consider whether he should continue to act for the client.** If he ceases to act, he must notify HMRC that he no longer acts for the client, but is under no duty to give HMRC any further details, although it may be necessary to consider whether a report should be made under the money laundering rules.

If the repayment is made to the member on the client's behalf, the member must notify the tax authorities. Failure to do so could involve both the member and client in a civil and/or criminal offence.

It should be noted that if HMRC make the repayment because they have adopted a different treatment of a transaction to that taken by the member and client, this is not an excessive repayment, it merely arises from a different interpretation of the legislation. This is subject to the proviso that full details of the transaction has been returned, so that HMRC have reached their decision on an informed basis.

2.9 Money laundering

Money laundering is the process by which criminals attempt to conceal the true origin and ownership of the proceeds of their criminal activity, often with the unwitting assistance of professionals such as accountants and lawyers.

Members are bound by legislation to implement preventative measures and to report suspicions to the appropriate authority. Failure to follow these legislative requirements will often be a criminal offence, leading to a fine and/or imprisonment. The legal position and its application to any given set of facts may not be straightforward and members are advised to take legal advice whenever they are uncertain as to their conduct.

Members should have appropriate procedures to ensure that client identification procedures are carried out correctly and that knowledge and suspicions of money laundering are reported to the firm's money laundering officer.

2.9.1 Client identification procedures

Where a new client is taken on a member should verify his identity by reliable and independent means. This could comprise the following:

(a)   where the client is an individual: by obtaining independent evidence, such as a passport, driving licence, HMRC document such as a notice of coding, and proof of address;

(b)   where the client is a company: by obtaining proof of incorporation; by establishing the primary business address; by identifying the members and directors of the company; and by establishing the identities of those persons instructing the member on behalf of the company and verifying that those persons are authorised to do so;

If members satisfactory evidence cannot be obtained, no work should be undertaken.

Members should **retain all client identification records for at least five years after the end of the client relationship**, together with records of all work carried out for the client.

2.9.2 Suspicions of money laundering

During the course of the engagement, members should regularly review the client's actions to satisfy themselves that they are consistent with the client's usual activities. Anything which appears to be out of the ordinary should be closely examined and a written record made of the member's conclusions. **If members' suspicions are aroused, a money laundering report should be made**.

Suspicion is more than mere speculation, but which falls short of proof based on firm evidence. What is suspicious in relation to one client may not be suspicious in relation to another client. Therefore, the key to recognising a suspicious transaction or situation is for members to have a full understanding of the client and his activities.

Transactions which appear to have no apparent economic or visible lawful purpose should be looked at carefully to establish their purpose and any findings recorded in writing. If no purpose for the transaction can be established, this may be a ground for suspicion.

Where members know or suspect that funds are directly or indirectly the proceeds of crime, they should report their suspicions promptly to the Serious Organised Crime Agency. Where tax evasion is involved members will also need to examine their responsibilities to the tax authorities.

Where the work done by members for their clients is covered by legal professional privilege, members are not required to report their suspicions. Whether or not legal professional privilege applies to members and in what circumstances will depend on local law and members are strongly advised to seek legal advice as and when the issue arises.

2.9.3 Tipping off

Members should not 'tip off' a client that a report has been made. This may cause a member difficulties if a client refuses to disclose tax irregularities to HMRC as ceasing to act for the client might tip off the client that a report has been made. Any attempts to persuade a client not to proceed with an intended crime will not constitute tipping off.

Members faced with money laundering issues may call upon the Advisory Services Section of the ACCA for confidential advice.

3 Employment and self-employment

FAST FORWARD

As a general rule, self-employment leads to lower overall tax and NIC burdens than employment.

A taxpayer who has a choice between being employed and being self-employed, on similar gross incomes, should consider the following points.

(a) An employee must pay **income tax and NICs as salary is received, under the PAYE system** and on a current year basis. A self-employed person pays **Class 2 NICs during the year, but income tax and Class 4 NICs are at least partly payable after all of the profits concerned have been earned**. There is thus a cash flow advantage in self-employment.

(b) **An employee is likely to suffer significantly higher NICs in total than a self employed person**, although the employee's entitlement to state benefits will also be higher. In particular, note that the self-employed earn no entitlement to the State Second Pension.

(c) An **employee may receive benefits as well as salary**. Taxable values of benefits may be less than their actual value to the employee and benefits do not attract employee NICs (this is however only relevant if salary does not exceed the upper NIC limit). Most benefits attract employer's Class 1A NIC.

(d) The **rules on the deductibility of expenses are much stricter for employees** (incurred wholly, exclusively and necessarily in the performance of duties) than for the self-employed (normally incurred wholly and exclusively for the purposes of the trade).

4 Remuneration packages

FAST FORWARD

If someone is to be an employee, the tax effects of the remuneration package should be taken into account.

4.1 Income tax planning for employment situations

An employee will usually be rewarded largely by salary, but several other elements can be included in a remuneration package. Some of them bring tax benefits to the employee only, and some will also benefit the employer.

Bonuses are treated like salary, except that if a bonus is accrued in the employer's accounts but is paid more than nine months after the end of the period of account, its deductibility for tax purposes will be delayed.

The general position for **benefits** is that they are subject to **income tax and employer Class 1A NICs**. The cost of providing benefits is generally deductible in computing trading profit for the employer (but if a car costing over £12,000 is provided, the employer's capital allowances (or deductions for lease payments) are restricted).

However, there are a large number of **tax and NI free benefits** and there is a great deal of planning that can be done to ensure a tax and NIC efficient benefits package for directors and employees. The optimum is to ensure that the company receives a tax deduction for the expenditure whilst creating tax and NI free remuneration for employees. The main tax free benefits are:

(a)	Growth in value and exercise in shares in approved share option schemes
(b)	Free car parking at/near place of work
(c)	Contributions to registered occupational or personal pension scheme
(d)	Mileage paid at statutory rates
(e)	Training courses provided (day release, block release, sandwich courses etc)
(f)	Air miles obtained through business travel
(g)	Beneficial loans under £5,000
(h)	Long service awards (20 years, max £50 pa)
(i)	Staff suggestion schemes
(j)	Free or subsidised canteens available to all staff
(k)	Sports facilities provided on the employer's premises
(l)	Workplace nursery or childcare provision
(m)	Staff uniforms
(n)	Provision of goods or services at marginal cost only
(o)	Gifts from third parties up to £250 per source
(p)	Removal expenses up to £8,000
(q)	Health checks, screening and eye tests
(r)	Mobile phones (one only)
(s)	The first £30,000 of an ex gratia termination payment

For further details of taxable and exempt benefits see earlier in this Text.

Comparison of two remuneration packages

Employee A receives a salary of £20,000.

Employee B receives a salary of £15,000, the use of a new video camera which cost £800 on 6.4.06 and the use of a car which cost £17,732 on 1.1.06. The taxable benefit for this car is £4,433. No fuel is supplied.

Employee B is also in a pension scheme (not contracted out) to which he contributes 5% of his gross salary (excluding benefits) and his employer company contributes 10% of his gross salary (excluding benefits).

A and B are both single and have no other income.

Show the tax and the NIC effects of the two remuneration packages on both the employees and their employers. Assume the employer company does not meet the definition of 'small' or 'medium' sized. Use 2006/07 tax rates and allowances and assume that the employer prepares accounts to 31 March each year.

Answer

A's income tax and NIC computations are as follows.

	£
Earnings	20,000
Less personal allowance	(5,035)
Taxable income	14,965

Income tax
£2,150 × 10%	215
£12,815 × 22%	2,819
	3,034

NICs
£(20,000 − 5,035) × 11%	£1,646

A's employer must pay NICs of £20,000 − £5,035 × 12.8% = £1,916, and can deduct £(20,000 + 1,916) = £21,916 in computing trading profits.

B's income tax and NIC computations are as follows.

	£
Salary	15,000
Use of video camera £800 × 20%	160
Car	4,433
	19,593
Less pension contribution £15,000 × 5%	(750)
Earnings	18,843
Less personal allowance	(5,035)
Taxable income	13,808

Income tax
	£
£2,150 × 10%	215
£11,658 × 22%	2,565
	2,780

NICs
£(15,000 − 5,035) × 11%	1,096

B's employer must pay NICs as follows.

Class 1 NICs
£(15,000 − £5,035) × 12.8%   1,276

Class 1A NICs
£(4,433 + 160) × 12.8%   588
                                                                                                                            1,864

B's employer will have the following deductions in computing profits.

	£	£
Salary		15,000
Pension contribution £15,000 × 10%		1,500
NICs		1,864
Capital allowances		
Car (WDV maximum)	3,000	
Video camera £800 × 25%	200	
		3,200
		21,564

4.2 NIC planning for employment situations

NIC is payable on 'earnings' which is defined as 'any remuneration or profit derived from employment'. Remuneration packages structured to include the following items which are not 'earnings' would reduce the NIC burden.

(a) **Dividends** – director/shareholders could take remuneration in the form of dividends. Dividend waivers and adjustments to bonuses would probably be required. There are CT implications as salary and NIC costs are allowable business expenses whereas dividends are not.

Dividends are an efficient way of avoiding NIC. However dividend income is not earnings for pension purposes. There is also a cash flow impact since PAYE does not apply to dividends.

(b) **Rents** – a director owning a property used by a company could be paid rent instead of remuneration. This will not impact business asset taper relief (if available) on the subsequent sale of the property. The rental expense is a deductible business expense for the company but the income is not earnings for pension contribution purposes for the individual.

5 The choice of a business medium

An entrepreneur must choose between trading as a sole trader and trading through a company. That choice, and if a company is chosen, the choice between dividends and remuneration, can significantly affect the overall tax and NIC burden. Cashflow is also an important consideration.

5.1 General considerations

When starting in business the first decision must be whether to trade as a company (with the entrepreneur as a director taxable on earnings) or as an unincorporated business, either as a sole trader or a partnership. Certain professions may not be practised through a limited company (although unlimited companies and limited liability partnerships may be allowed).

The attraction of incorporation lies in the fact that a sole trader or a partner is liable for business debts to the full extent of his personal assets. A limited company's shareholder's liability is limited to the amount, if any, unpaid on his shares. However, limited liability is often reduced by the demands of bankers or landlords for personal guarantees from company directors. In addition, compliance with the statutory obligations (eg annual returns, audits etc) that apply to a company can be costly.

A company often finds raising finance easier than an unincorporated business. This is partly because of the misguided view that a company has greater reliability and permanence. A company can obtain equity finance through venture capital institutions and can borrow by giving a floating charge over its assets as security whereas a sole trader or partnership cannot do this.

A business may be seen as **more reputable or creditworthy if conducted through the medium of a company.** Companies, however, have to comply with disclosure requirements and this may be unattractive to proprietors who wish to keep information from employees, potential competitors etc. This could be avoided by using an unlimited company but in that case any advantage of limited status is lost. The disclosure requirements could be reduced by filing abbreviated accounts.

5.2 The effect of marginal tax rates and national insurance

A trader's profits whether retained or withdrawn are taxed at a marginal rate of 40% on taxable income in excess of £33,300. In addition Class 2 and Class 4 national insurance contributions are payable.

A controlling director/shareholder can decide whether profits are to be paid out as remuneration or dividends, or retained in the company.

If profits are retained, the consequent growth in asset values will increase the potential capital gain when shares are sold (although taper relief may reduce the amount of the taxable gain). Where remuneration is paid the total national insurance liability is greater than for the proprietor of an unincorporated business.

Where a spouse is employed his or her salary must be justifiable as 'wholly and exclusively for the purposes of the trade'; HMRC may seek to disallow excessive salary cost. On the other hand, a spouse as active partner can take any share in profits, provided that he or she is personally active in the business and there is evidence of a bona fide partnership. Thus the spouse's personal allowance and starting and basic rate bands can be used.

In choosing a business medium, we should also remember that a sole trader will be denied the enhanced state benefits that are available to an employee who pays Class 1 national insurance contributions. In particular, note that the self-employed do not build an entitlement to the State Second Pension.

Question	Net income from a business

Alan, who is single, expects to make annual profits of £30,000 before tax and national insurance. Consider the fiscal effects of his choosing to trade as a sole trader or, alternatively, through a company, paying him a salary of £15,000 and then the largest possible dividend not giving rise to a loss of capital. Assume that accounting profits equal taxable trade profits. Use 2006/07 tax rates.

Answer

As a sole trader

	£
Profits	30,000
Less personal allowance	(5,035)
Taxable income	24,965
Tax thereon at 10%/22%	5,234
National Insurance Classes 2 (52 × £2.10) and 4 (£(30,000 − 5,035) × 8%)	2,106
	7,340
Net income £(30,000 − 7,340)	22,660

Through a company

	£
Profits	30,000
Less: salary	(15,000)
employer's NI 12.8% (£15,000 − £5,035)	(1,276)
Taxable profits	13,724
Less: corporation tax 19% × £13,724	(2,608)
Net profits	11,116

A dividend of £11,116 can be paid without loss of capital.

	Non-savings £	Dividends £	Total £
Earnings	15,000		
Dividends £11,116 × 100/90		12,351	
STI	15,000	12,351	27,351
Less personal allowance	(5,035)		
Taxable income	9,965	12,351	22,316

Non-savings income	
£2,150 × 10%	215
£7,815 × 22%	1,719
Dividend income	
£12,351 × 10%	1,235
	3,169
Less tax suffered £12,351 × 10%	(1,235)
Income tax payable	1,934

Net income	£	£
Salary		15,000
Dividends		11,116
		26,116
Less: income tax	1,934	
Employee's NIC (£15,000 − £5,035) × 11%	1,096	
		(3,030)
		23,086

Trading as a sole trader would give annual net income of £(22,660 − 23,086) = £426 less than trading through a company.

Question   Small business as sole trader versus company

Let's say we have a business earning profits of £15,035.

Compare the retained profit for the business owner if he operates the business as a sole trader with a year ended 31 March 2007 to that of a company with the same year end but paying out £5,035 as a salary and the remaining post-tax profits as a dividend.

Answer

Sole Trader

Trading profits of £15,035 in 2006/07

Year ended 31 March 2007

	£
Income tax	
£(15,035 − 5,035) = £10,000	
£2,150 @ 10%	215
£7,850 @ 22%	1,727
	1,942
National Insurance	
Class 2	109
Class 4	
£(15,035 − 5,035) × 8%	800
Total Income Tax and NIC	2,851
Net income	
£(15,035 − 2,851)	£12,184

Company

Year ended 31 March 2007	
PCTCT = £(15,035 − 5,035)	10,000
Corporation tax	
£10,000 @ 19% before distribution	(1,900)
Maximum distribution is	8,100

Income tax
Salary covered by PA
Gross dividend income = £9,000

	£
£9,000 @ 10%	900
Less Tax credit	(900)
	Nil
Class 1 NIC	Nil
Net income £(5,035 + 8,100)	£13,135

As a sole-tradership the business would typically pay £2,851 in the 2006/07 tax year as income tax and national insurance contributions. The same business operating as a limited company for the same year would have a tax bill of £1,900.

5.3 Benefits and expenses

The restrictions on deducting expenses against earnings may make self-employment rather more attractive than employment as a company director. Although the same expense deduction rules apply to a company and a sole trader, the company's deductible business expenses may give rise to taxable benefits as earnings for directors.

On the other hand, the provision of fringe benefits can be an advantage of incorporation. Tax exempt benefits can be used to maximise directors' net spendable income, although care is required because not all benefits are tax-efficient.

5.4 Opening years

Companies have no equivalent of the opening year rules that apply for income tax purposes. For a sole trader or partnership, profits earned when basis periods overlap are taxed twice. Relief is available for such overlap profits but that may not take place for many years, by which time inflation may have reduced the value of the relief for overlap profits.

If a partnership is envisaged it may be worthwhile to commence trading with the prospective partner as a salaried employee for a year or so, thereby obtaining tax relief twice on his salary during the overlap period.

5.5 Losses

Losses in the first four years of an unincorporated business can be used to obtain tax repayments (using s 381 claims). In these and later years a s 380 claim permits **relief for trading losses against other income** (and capital gains) of either or both of two tax years.

With corporation tax, although there is considerable flexibility for the company itself, **a company's losses are not available to reduce shareholders' taxable income.**

5.6 Capital gains tax

One difference between companies and individuals is that **companies do not benefit from an exemption from tax on the first £8,800 of total gains** (for 2006/07).

Chargeable gains of an individual are charged to capital gains tax at 10%, 20% or 40%. By contrast, companies' gains are charged at normal corporation tax rates (30% full rate, 19% small companies' rate or 32.75% effective marginal rate.

The principal disadvantage of incorporation is the double charge to tax which arises when a company sells a chargeable asset. Firstly, the company may pay corporation tax on the chargeable gain. Secondly, the shareholders may be taxed when they attempt to realise those proceeds, either in the form of dividends or, when the shares are sold, incurring a further charge on capital gains.

If there are no tax advantages in the company owning an asset, the asset should be held outside the company, perhaps being leased to the company. The lessor may receive rent without restricting CGT and IHT business asset reliefs.

5.7 Tax cash flows

A sole trader/partner is assessable to income tax and NIC (Class 4) on a current year basis but will use a prior year basis to calculate two payments on account due on 31 January in and 31 July directly following the tax year. The balance of tax is due on 31 January following the tax year. Thus tax on profits earned in the year to 30 April 2006 (assessable 2006/07) will not be payable in full until 31 January 2008 and will be used to calculate payments on account due 31 January 2008 and 31 July 2008. **Where profits are rising this lag gives a considerable benefit**. A sole trader's/partner's drawings do not of themselves attract or accelerate a tax charge.

A company pays CT nine months after the end of its accounts period. Companies paying tax at the full rate are required to make **quarterly payments on account** based on the current year's estimated liability. As an employer it will have to account for **PAYE and NIC 14 days after the end of each tax month** in which the pay date falls.

Generally therefore a business held by a company will bear tax earlier than a business held by a sole trader or partnership.

5.8 What if things go wrong?

Sound tax planning should always take account of possible changes in circumstances. A successful business may fail or a struggling concern may eventually become profitable.

Running down an unincorporated business does not normally give rise to serious problems. The proprietor may be able to cover any balancing charges with loss relief.

Taking a business out of a company (disincorporation), or winding up a corporate trade altogether is more complex and involves both tax and legal issues. Consider the following:

- No subsequent relief is available for a company's unused losses once the trade ceases
- Liquidation costs may be considerable
- A double charge on capital gains may arise.

5.9 Personal service companies (PSCs)

The 'IR 35 provisions' (see earlier in this Text) are anti-avoidance rules which attack the provision of personal services by personal service companies (PSCs). If an individual would have been an employee if he had been working directly for a client, he will generally be subject to tax and NIC on income from the PSC as if he was in fact an employee of the client.

6 The incorporation of a business

FAST FORWARD

The incorporation of a business should be carefully planned, taking account of consequent tax liabilities. There are both advantages and disadvantages to incorporating a business. A disposal of shares can also have several tax consequences.

6.1 Why incorporate a business?

6.1.1 Advantages

(a) Retained profits subject only to corporation tax not income tax or NIC

(b) Easier to dispose of shares in a company than interest in a business – thus advantage for raising equity and selling to outside investors

(c) Pension provision can be made by employer (the company) for employees (eg directors) with no national insurance liability

(d)   Benefits for employees can be more tax efficient

(e)   Loan finance easier to arrange as lender can take out charge on company assets

(f)   Limited liability

(g)   A company arguably has a more respectable image than a sole trader or partnership

(h)   Incorporation is a means of converting the value of a business into shares which could be brought to the AIM or even achieve a full stock market quote. This provides for succession of ownership and can make the original proprietors very wealthy

6.1.2 Disadvantages

(a)   Potential double capital gains charge on assets (see above)

(b)   Trading losses restricted to set-off against corporate profits

(c)   No carry back of trading losses in opening years (ie no s 381 equivalent)

(d)   Partner's share of profit not openly challenged by HMRC provided the recipient is a genuine partner. Conversely excessive remuneration to employee/director can be challenged

(e)   NIC for employer company and employee will generally exceed the contributions required of a self-employed person

(f)   Tax payment dates for tax for a company and its employees (CT, PAYE and NIC) are generally well in advance of those for self-employed

(g)   Assets used in a business but held outside the business entity can qualify for 50% BPR for IHT. In the case of a partnership the owner merely has to be a partner but in the case of a company using an asset the owner must be a controlling shareholder

(h)   There may be statutory requirement of audit, keeping books, filing accounts etc

(i)   Disclosure requirements of published accounts may give information to employees/ competitors that business owners would not have willingly disclosed

6.2 Income tax

6.2.1 The choice of a date

When an unincorporated trade is transferred to a company the **trade is treated as discontinued for tax purposes and the cessation rules apply**. Careful consideration of the level of profit and date of transfer is required to avoid large taxable profits in one year from a basis period of more than 12 months. For example a trader with a 30 June year end will be assessed on 21 months of profit in his final year if he incorporates on 31 March (albeit subject to overlap relief) whereas only 10 months of profit will be taxed in that final year if he delays incorporation to 30 April.

6.2.2 Capital allowances

On the transfer of a trade to a company **a balancing charge will usually arise as plant and machinery are treated as being sold at market value**. However, where the company is controlled by the transferor, **the two are connected and an election may be made** so as not to treat the transfer as a permanent discontinuance for capital allowances purposes. **Fixed assets are then transferred at their tax written down values**.

6.2.3 Trading losses

Unrelieved trading losses cannot be carried forward to a company as such, but **may be set against any income derived from the company** by way of dividends, remuneration and so on, provided the business is exchanged for shares and those shares are still held at the time the loss is set off. Terminal loss relief may also be available for the loss of the last twelve months of trading.

6.3 Capital gains tax

When the transfer takes place the **chargeable assets are deemed to be disposed of to the company at their open market values**. Capital gains tax liabilities are likely to arise, particularly on land and buildings and on goodwill. The gains will be reduced by business asset taper relief.

If the whole business (or the whole business other than cash) **is transferred to the company as a going concern in exchange for shares in the company, any chargeable gains (before taper relief) are automatically rolled over through incorporation relief**, reducing the base cost of the shares on a subsequent disposal. If the shares are held until death the tax liability may never arise as no capital gains tax arises on death.

Individuals who incorporate a business can elect that incorporation relief should not apply. This election must be made within two years of 31 January following the end of the tax year in which the business was incorporated. A shorter time limit will apply when all the shares received on the transfer are disposed of in the tax year of transfer, or in the following tax year. Making the election could be advantageous for taper relief purposes where the shares are disposed of soon after incorporation.

It may not be desirable for all the assets comprised in the business to be transferred to the company. **As an alternative**, an individual can **use gift relief** to transfer chargeable business assets to a company and **defer any gains by deducting them from the base costs of the assets** for the company.

6.4 Value added tax

The transfer of assets will not be treated as a supply for VAT purposes (a transfer of a going concern (TOGC)) if all of the following conditions are satisfied.

(a) The assets are to be used by the company in the same kind of business (whether or not as part of an existing business) as that carried on by the transferor, the business being transferred as a going concern

(b) If only part of the business is transferred, that part is capable of separate operation

(c) If the transferor is a taxable person, the company is a taxable person when the transfer takes place or immediately becomes one as a result of the transfer

(d) In the case of land and buildings, the company makes an election to tax if the transferor has done so

(e) In the case of 'new' buildings the company makes an election to tax.

Note. For the last two points if the election to tax is not made by the company the supply of land or buildings is standard rated. All the other business assets can be transferred outside the scope of VAT under the TOGC rules.

An application may be made for the company to take over the existing VAT registration number. In this case the company will take over all the debts and liabilities of the business but it will be able to claim VAT bad debt relief in respect of supplies made before the transfer.

If the above conditions cannot be satisfied VAT will be charged on the transfer, but this will only represent a cash flow problem in most cases.

Customs should be notified of the incorporation within 30 days.

6.5 Stamp duty land tax

The transfer of land will be subject to Stamp Duty Land Tax as a transfer at market value. The use of the gift relief route should be considered so that land can be retained outside the company.

7 Tax efficient profit extraction

FAST FORWARD   There are several methods by which profit can be extracted from a company.

7.1 Methods of extracting profits

When trading activities are carried on through a limited company careful thought needs to be given to the level and method of extraction of the profits generated. This decision should take into account both the needs of the individual shareholders and directors as well as the needs of the company itself. For instance, the company may need to retain a certain level of profit in order to reduce its bank overdraft or fund an expansion project.

The table below compares the various methods of extracting profits in outline. They are looked at in more detail below.

Method of extraction	Company	Individual
Remuneration		
Salary	Deductible/Class 1 NICs	Taxable/Class 1 NICs
Benefits	Deductible/Class 1A NICs	Taxable
Tax free benefits	Deductible/No NICs	Tax/NI free
Dividends	Not deductible	No tax for basic or starting rate taxpayer
		Higher rate tax at 32.5%, reduced by 10% tax credit
		No NICs
Loan interest	Deductible on accruals basis as interest on a loan relationship	Taxable as savings (excl dividend) income
Rental income	Deductible	Taxable non savings income
Pension contributions		
• registered	Deductible	Tax free
• non registered	Deductible/Class 1 NICs	Taxable/Class 1 NICs

7.2 Dividends or remuneration

Director/shareholders may wish to consider either extracting profits as dividend or remuneration. Payments of dividends or remuneration will reduce a company's retained profits which means a reduction in net asset value and hence the value of the shares, ultimately reducing any chargeable gain on the disposal of those shares. However, the immediate tax cost of paying dividends or remuneration must be weighed against this advantage.

Remuneration and the cost of benefits will be allowed as deductions in computing the company's profits chargeable to corporation tax. The decision whether or not to make such payments could affect the rate of corporation tax by reducing the level of profits. However, **the national insurance cost must also be borne in mind**. A combination of dividends and remuneration may give the best result.

Question · Dividends and remuneration

A Ltd makes a profit before remuneration of £30,000 in the year to 31 March 2007. The shareholder/director is entitled to only the personal allowance. Consider the director's disposable income available by paying out the profit entirely as salary (of £27,167) or by paying it out as a mixture of salary (at £5,000, so that no national insurance contributions are payable but preserving the director's entitlement to state benefits) and a dividend of £8,100.

Answer

	Salary only £	Salary and dividend £
(a) **The company's tax position**		
Profits	30,000	30,000
Less: salary	(27,167)	(5,000)
employer's national insurance	(2,833)	
Taxable profits	0	25,000
Corporation tax at 19%	£Nil	£4,750
Cash dividend (25,000 – 4,750)		£20,250

(b) **The director's tax position**

	Non-savings £	Dividend £	Total £
Salary only			
Earnings	27,167		
Less personal allowance	(5,035)		
Taxable income	22,132		22,132
Salary and dividends			
Earnings	5,000		
Dividends (× 100/90)		22,500	
Less personal allowance	(5,000)	(35)	
	–	22,465	22,465

	Salary only £	Salary and dividend £
Non-savings income		
£2,150 × 10%	215	
£19,982 × 22%	4,396	
Dividend income £22,465 × 10%		2,247
Less tax credit on dividend (restricted)		(2,247)
Tax payable	4,611	–
Disposable income		
Salary	27,167	5,000
Less employee's national insurance		
(27,167 – 5,035) × 11%	(2,435)	
Dividend		20,250
Less tax payable	(4,611)	
	20,121	25,250

The overall saving through paying a dividend is £(25,250 – 20,121) = £5,129.

7.3 Dividend payments

If dividends are paid, timing can be important. The tax year in which a dividend is paid affects the due date for any additional tax, and if a shareholder's other income fluctuates it may determine whether or not there is any additional tax to pay. Higher rate taxpayers must pay tax at 32.5% on dividend income, subject to a 10% tax credit.

Dividends carry a 10% tax credit and are taxed only at 10% in the hands of basic rate taxpayers which means that dividends are attractive to such individuals. However, the 10% tax credit is not repayable to non-taxpayers.

The payment of dividends does allow flexibility, ie family members need not work for a company in order to receive a dividend. However, this must be weighted against the fact that the company must generate sufficient profit to pay a dividend. Furthermore, HMRC may seek to invoke anti-avoidance legislation if dividends are paid to non-working family members if those who do work for the company do not draw a commercial salary.

Most banks and building societies will recognise regular dividends from an owner managed company as income for mortgage or other loan purposes. This takes away a potential drawback of extraction of funds in the form of investment income.

Dividends are not subject to NICs.

Dividends do not give rise to an entitlement to pay pension contributions whereas remuneration and benefits do.

Dividends are not an allowable trading expense for the company.

7.4 Liquidation

An alternative to both dividends and remuneration is to retain profits in a company and then liquidate it. The company itself may have capital gains on the sale of its assets, and the shareholders will have capital gains on the liquidation, which will be treated as a disposal of their shares for the amounts paid to them. The CGT charges on the shareholders may be mitigated by spreading the capital distributions over two tax years, so as to use both years' annual exemptions. Taper relief may reduce the gains made by individual shareholders on the disposal of the shares.

This route may be worth considering when a company is set up to undertake a single project which will be completed within a few years.

7.5 Loans

A director/shareholder may choose to lend money to the company and extract profits as interest income in return.

Interest income is taxed on the director/shareholder as savings income but it is not subject to NIC. It does not count as relevant earnings for pension purposes.

From the company's point of view, tax relief for the interest will be available under the loan relationship rules (ie either as a trading expense or as a deficit on a non-trading loan relationship).

7.6 Loans by close companies

Although loans by close companies to participators are not treated as distributions, on making such a loan the company suffers a tax charge: a payment equal to the amount of the loan × 25% is made to HMRC. This tax charge cannot be recovered until the loan is repaid or written off.

7.7 Rental income

On incorporation the owner(s) may decide to retain business premises outside the company and charge rent for its use. **The advantages of this method of profit extraction are that the company will obtain a trading income deduction for rent charged up to a commercial rate. Also, no NIC is payable.**

The disadvantage is that income from a property business does not qualify as pensionable income.

For many small companies, the directors' own homes are often used for company business. It is possible to claim a deduction in the company for reasonable rent paid by the company. Care should be taken so as not to deny principal private residence relief on a proportion of the home. To do this, it must be shown that the room(s) are not used exclusively for company business, ie the occasional guest stays in the 'study'.

7.8 Pension provision

It is becoming increasingly important to save for one's own retirement. Fortunately, it is also something the government recognises as important and, as a result, pension provision has become the most efficient way of extracting funds from a family company.

Employers may set up an **occupational pension plan** for their employees. Employees who are not members of an occupational pension plan and the self employed may alternatively contribute to a **personal pension plan**. Employers may also contribute to an employee's personal pension plan.

The tax breaks for registered pension schemes are listed below.

(a) No taxable benefit for employer contributions

(b) No NIC is due on employer contributions

(c) The individual receives tax relief on his contributions

(d) The employer obtains tax relief for normal contributions actually paid during its accounting period.

(e) Pension fund grows tax free (tax credits on dividends not repayable)

(f) Tax free lump sum available up to 25% of the fund

7.9 Conclusion

The most tax efficient method of profit withdrawal hinges upon the marginal rate of corporation tax the company pays. For a small company dividends are the cheapest form of profit withdrawal. For a medium-sized or large company a bonus would seem the preferable option on the assumption that the director/shareholder is already paying maximum Class 1 primary NICs.

If the succession of the company is likely to be achieved by passing the shares down the family, profit retention will only increase the gain to be rolled over by way of a gift relief claim. As the gain rolled over is before taper relief the base cost of the shares to the next generation will be substantially reduced.

8 Tax efficient exit routes

FAST FORWARD

Capital gains and inheritance tax planning are important when disposing of a family business.

8.1 Introduction

Advice on tax efficient exit routes is probably the biggest area that a professional adviser is asked to deal with in tax planning for an owner managed business. This section will explore the key tax implications of passing on and selling the family business or company and suggest useful planning tips to help structure the business in the most efficient manner from the outset.

8.2 Capital gains tax planning

Regardless as to whether the business or company is to be sold or passed down to the next generation a capital gain is likely to arise. It is therefore essential to maximise the reliefs available.

When a company ceases trading **great care needs to be taken with the CGT taper relief** position as the following example shows.

8.3 Example: capital gains tax on exit

Mark owns all the shares in Nicholls Limited and has done so since 1995. Assume that the trade ceases on 6 April 2007. The gain Mark is likely to realise on the sale of his shares is expected to be £918,000.

If he sells the shares on 6 April 2007 the whole gain will be eligible for maximum business taper. The chargeable gain will therefore be £912,000 × 25% = £228,000.

If the company is liquidated on 6 October 2007, the disposal is treated as two separate assets, a business asset held for 9 years (post 5.4.98) and a non-business asset held for ½ year as the company was dormant. The total post 6.4.98 ownership period is therefore 9½ years (ie 114 months).

The taper relief rate applying to the non business asset would be for a 10 year ownership period as the bonus year will be given.

The gain would become:

	£
Business assets	
£912,000 × 108/114 = £864,000 × 25% =	216,000
Non business assets	
£912,000 × 6/114 = £48,000 × 60%	28,800
Chargeable gain	244,800

8.4 Inheritance tax planning

IHT is only a consideration where the family business or company is to be passed on to the next generation. An outright sale of the business to a third party does not constitute a transfer of value for IHT.

When a taxpayer wants to pass on his family business a major question exists as to whether to gift the assets now or wait until death.

If the assets are given during lifetime there may never be an IHT liability, either because the PET does not become chargeable or because the gift is covered by BPR provided the transferee still owns it (or other relevant business property) at the time of the transferor's death.

A lifetime gift will be subject to CGT at some point, either on transfer or on sale of the assets by the transferee assuming a gift relief claim is made. In addition, where gift relief is claimed the period of ownership by the transferor is effectively 'lost' as it is the untapered gain that is rolled over.

However, a transfer of assets on death receives a free uplift in the CGT base cost to current market value and any business property is passed on with the benefit of 100% BPR.

There are strong arguments in favour of the approach to hold business property until death but other points are worthy of serious consideration:

(a)   If a business is hit by recession the gain itself may be fairly low in any case

(b)   The gain may be or deferred through EIS reinvestment relief

(c)   The favoured rates of business asset taper relief may reduce a gain to an amount covered by the annual exemption

(d)   BPR at 100% may not be around forever

(e)   Free CGT uplift on assets covered by BPR may be abolished in the future.

Some other tax pitfalls exist which can be avoided provided they are identified and acted upon. The main areas as to consider include:

(a)   Holding assets, such as business premises, outside the company or partnership restricts BPR to a rate of only 50%. This reduces to nil if the shares or partnership interest are disposed of before the business premises

(b)   Where a lifetime gift is made it is important that the property remains 'business property' for the next seven years and that the transferee retains ownership of it (or owns alternative business property) to prevent a charge to IHT on a sudden death

(c)   Care should be taken not to change the nature of the company, ie a property development company becoming a property holding company

(d)   Beware of buy and sell arrangements included in the Articles of Association or partnership or shareholder agreements as BPR may be denied.

(e)   It will be important to ensure that a gift does not fall foul of the 'reservation of benefit' rules. (see earlier in this Text.)

8.5 Pre-sale dividend

It may be sensible to extract some wealth as dividends (which have a tax credit attached to them) before sale, rather than as a capital gain (with no tax credit) on sale.

8.6 Example: pre-sale dividend (1)

James has recently received an offer of £3,000,000 for his 100% holding in his investment (ie non-trading) company.

James' shares were acquired in April 2003 for £400,000. James is a higher rate taxpayer and has used his annual exemption for 2006/07. We need to determine whether James should extract £2,000,000 by way of dividend from the company prior to a sale of the shares.

Sale of shares in 2006/07

	£
Proceeds	3,000,000
Less cost	(400,000)
Gain before taper relief	2,600,000
Gain after taper relief (3 years NBA: 95%)	2,470,000
CGT at 40%	988,000
Net proceeds £(3,000,000 – 988,000)	2,012,000

Pre-sale dividend	£
Proceeds	1,000,000
Less cost	(400,000)
Gain before taper relief	600,000
Gain after taper relief (95%)	570,000
CGT @ 40%	228,000
Gross dividend £2,000,000 × 100/90	2,222,222
Higher rate tax at 32.5%	722,222
Less 10% tax credit	(222,222)
Higher rate tax liability	500,000
Net proceeds £(3,000,000 – 228,000 – 500,000) =	2,272,000

Therefore paying a pre-sale dividend has increased James' net proceeds by £260,000.

Care must be taken however if the capital gain arising qualifies for high levels of taper relief.

8.7 Example: pre-sale dividend (2)

John has recently received an offer of £3,000,000 for his 100% holding in his personal company which is a trading company.

John's shares were acquired in April 2003 for £400,000. John is a higher rate taxpayer and has used his annual CGT exemption for 2006/07. We need to determine whether John should extract £2,000,000 by way of a dividend from the company prior to a sale of the shares.

Sale of shares in 2006/07

	£
Proceeds	3,000,000
Less cost	(400,000)
Gain before taper relief	2,600,000
Gain after taper relief (25%)	650,000
CGT at 40%	260,000
Net proceeds £(3,000,000 – 260,000)	2,740,000

Pre-sale dividend	£
Proceeds	1,000,000
Less cost	(400,000)
Gain before taper relief	600,000

	£
Gain after taper relief (25%)	150,000
CGT @ 40%	60,000
Gross dividend £2,000,000 × 100/90	2,222,222
Higher rate tax at 32.5%	722,222
Less 10% tax credit	(222,222)
Higher rate tax liability	500,000
Net proceeds £(3,000,000 – 60,000 – 500,000) =	2,440,000

Therefore paying a presale dividend has decreased John's net proceeds by £300,000.

8.8 Repurchases of own shares

It may be advantageous for individuals to sell shares back to the issuing company as a repurchase of own shares (see earlier in this Text). This will be treated as a capital gain (if the conditions are satisfied) or, if not, as a distribution. If distribution treatment is preferable it may be necessary to alter the proposal to ensure the conditions are not satisfied.

9 Planning for corporate growth

FAST FORWARD

At each stage of a 'company's life' from its beginning, growth and future expansion overseas, tax planning strategies should be adopted.

Exam focus point

This section looks at a company as it begins trading, acquires additional business, and eventually expands abroad. It looks at the commercial decisions taken by the company and its shareholders at the different stages in the company's development, and summarises the tax implications of those decisions. It focuses, in particular, on those elements of corporation tax that are likely to be examined.

9.1 New company

Companies often start small. One or two individuals will set up a company using their own funds (or borrowed funds) to do so. Some shareholders may be active in running the company on a daily basis whilst others will be passive investors looking for a return on their investment.

Points to consider:

- *Is the company a close company?*

  This will impact the rate of tax paid if the company does not trade (ie full rate of CT on a CIC). Also are any benefits provided to participators (treated as dividends) or loans made to participators (trigger a charge at 25% on the company).

- *Can the shareholders receive tax relief for their investment?*

  If the company is a close company interest paid on a loan to invest in the company is qualifying annual interest (tax deduction available).

  EIS income tax relief may be available to small investors.

- *Level of tax paid on company profits*

  Small companies' rate will apply to profits below £300,000 with marginal relief for profits below £1,500,000.

  Salaries paid to employees reduce PCTCT, dividends paid to shareholders do not.

- *Losses* made can be relieved by carry back up to 12 months (if there are any profits to carry back against) or carry forward against future trading profits.

- Don't forget to consider registration for *VAT*.

9.2 Expansion in UK

A company can grow bigger by increasing its own activities or purchasing the activities of another business and either assuming those activities within itself or setting up a subsidiary company.

Points to consider:

- Single company (no associates) or group of companies. Number of associates affects CT profit bands

- If a group is formed: group relief for losses; asset transfers and tax planning regarding asset groups in respect of capital gains and losses; VAT group registration

- As PCTCT grows may need to consider payment of CT and VAT in instalments (large company)

- When a company acquires the trade of another company capital losses remain within the vendor company. Trading losses will also remain with the vendor company unless the two companies are under common ownership.

9.3 Expansion overseas

As a company grows it may consider expanding overseas.

The tax implications of the overseas business depend on the legal structure used. From a tax point of view, there are two distinct ways of establishing the business:

- It could be owned by the UK company. Under this option, it would be an overseas PE of a UK resident company

- the UK company could incorporate a new subsidiary in the overseas country to acquire the business. Under this option, it would be an overseas subsidiary of a UK resident company.

Points to consider:

- *Overseas permanent establishment (PE)*

  A PE is not a separate legal entity but is an extension of the company that owns it. The profits or losses of the PE belong directly to the company.

  Provided the PE is controlled from the UK, any trading loss made could be offset by the UK company (or group) against its income and gains of that year, reducing the company's UK corporation tax liability. Once the PE is profitable, the company owning the PE will be subject to overseas corporation tax on the PE profits, because it is trading within the boundaries of the overseas country from a PE.

  The profits will also be subject to UK corporation tax because a UK resident company is subject to tax on its worldwide income and gains. However the UK corporation tax liability, in respect of the PE profits, will be relieved by double tax relief.

- *Overseas subsidiary*

  A subsidiary is a separate legal entity. A company incorporated in an overseas country will be resident in that country for tax purposes, provided it is not managed and controlled from the UK. Its profits or losses will then be subject to the tax regime of the overseas country.

  Any trading loss of the year would be carried forward and deducted from the company's future trading profits arising out of the same trade.

  Once the company is profitable, it will be subject to tax in the overseas country. Any dividends paid to the UK parent company will be grossed up, in respect of the underlying tax suffered in the overseas country, and included in the parent company's profits chargeable to corporation tax. Double tax relief, at the lower of the overseas tax or the UK tax on the overseas income, is available.

- It is usually suggested that a PE should be used where an overseas enterprise is expected to make initial losses. This strategy enables the losses to be offset against any other profits of the company. The PE can be incorporated once it is profitable. However, the particular facts of the situation must be considered carefully.

- A subsidiary is an associate for the purpose of determining the rate of tax paid by group companies, whereas a PE is not. Accordingly, the use of a subsidiary (rather than a PE) could increase the rate of corporation tax paid by the UK companies.

10 Group tax minimisation strategies

FAST FORWARD

There are several tax planning opportunities available to groups of companies.

There are many **tax planning opportunities for groups of companies**. The following points should be considered, in addition to the points made earlier in this Text.

(a) **Minority interests should be restricted so as to ensure that the holding company has a 75% effective interest in every company. This will enable losses to be group relieved** to whichever company can make the best use of them (particularly companies in the small companies' marginal relief band).

(b) **The group can be regarded as one unit for the purposes of rollover relief** on the replacement of business assets.

(c) **The small companies rate limits will be shared equally among group members; profits may be shared to take advantage of them by fixing transfer prices for intra-group trading (transfer pricing rules generally do not apply to small and medium sized enterprises).** However, minority shareholders might then be unfairly advantaged or disadvantaged.

Careful consideration will need to be given to the number of associated companies in the group as setting up an additional subsidiary may affect the tax rate of all group companies.

(d) **VAT will arise on intra-group trading unless a VAT group is formed. It may be best to concentrate all exempt supplies in one or two companies which can be left outside the VAT group, and zero rated supplies in one or two other companies which can also be left outside the VAT group (or can form their own separate VAT group) and can make monthly repayment claims.**

(e) **Capital losses cannot be group relieved. However, an election can be made to treat any group company as though it made an asset disposal. This means that gains and losses can be netted off against each other in the same company. It will be advantageous to crystallise net gains in the company paying the lowest marginal rate of corporation tax.** However, there are restrictions on the use of pre-entry losses and gains.

11 Divisionalised v group company structure

FAST FORWARD

Careful consideration needs to be given as to whether a group structure or a divisionalised company would be better.

11.1 General principles

In certain circumstances a business can be operated through a group company structure or through a single divisionalised company.

The setting up of a **trading group has a number of implications**, namely:

(a) It is **easier to give status to a key employee** by appointing him director of a subsidiary company

(b) **Group relief of losses** is available

(c) **Assets may be transferred between the group without giving rise to a charge to tax**

(d) **Group wide rollover relief** may be claimed.

There are a number of disadvantages to a group structure that must be considered, particularly where the parent company or subsidiaries are to be sold.

Where the parent company is sold then the group would either:

(a) Sell the group and then buy back the required subsidiaries
(b) Reconstruct the group which would need tax clearances and cause delays, or
(c) Sell assets

Where a subsidiary is sold this could give rise to a capital gain although the relief for substantial shareholdings may be available.

The main advantage of a divisional structure is the fact that the **full amount of the small companies' tax bands will be available rather than being divided among all companies under common control.**

The other advantages are:

(a) **Automatic set-off losses** in respect of the various divisions
(b) **Automatic set-off of capital gains and losses**
(c) **Administration is simplified**

On the other hand, the disadvantages include:

(a)   **Lack of incentive for divisional directors**

(b)   Difficulty in giving equity interest in a venture (but may consider profit-related bonuses)

(c)   It may be difficult to find a prospective purchaser for the whole company

(d)   Group profits can decrease the possibility of making optimum use of the small companies' or the starting rate of tax.

11.2 Example: group vs divisionalised structure

Sumner Limited carries on two trades through two separate divisions. The furniture production division makes profits of £1.35m in the year to 31 March 2007. The antique furniture restoration division makes profits of £150,000 in the same year.

Sumner Limited will pay tax of £450,000 (ie £1,500,000 × 30%).

If the company were to operate the trades through two separate companies the CT limits would be divided and the tax payable would be:

	£
£1,350,000 × 30%	405,000
£150,000 × 19%	28,500
Total	433,500

This creates a tax saving of £16,500 (ie £150,000 × 11%) as part of the profit utilises the small companies' rate.

It may be worth setting up a subsidiary company and channelling £150,000 profit into it.

12 Disclosure of tax avoidance schemes

FAST FORWARD

There are disclosure requirements for promoters of direct tax avoidance schemes. Businesses may be required to disclose use of VAT avoidance schemes.

12.1 Direct tax avoidance schemes

Promoters of tax avoidance schemes have disclosure obligations. There is also an obligation on taxpayers to disclose details of schemes in certain cases.

Notification is required from a promoter of arrangements or proposed arrangements, the main benefit of which is to enable any person to obtain an advantage in relation to tax. A 'promoter' is defined as a person who, in the course of a trade, profession or business involving the provision of tax services to other persons, is to any extent responsible for the design of the arrangements, or who makes a proposal available for implementation by other persons.

The information to be given by a promoter must be provided within a prescribed period of five days after being made available. The information to be provided and the manner in which it is to be provided is set out in the regulations.

A taxpayer is required to provide details of arrangements where the arrangements have been purchased from an offshore promoter, and that promoter has made no disclosure. Disclosure must also be made by large businesses which have **entered into arrangements not involving a promoter.**

HMRC may allocate a reference number to arrangements notified under the disclosure rules. Promoters are required to notify clients of that reference number so that they can enter that number on their tax return.

Any person that fails to comply with any of the disclosure provisions is liable to a penalty not exceeding £5,000. If the failure continues after that penalty has been imposed, that person is liable to a further penalty or penalties not exceeding £600 for each day on which the failure continues.

A tax advantage is defined as relief or increased relief from tax, repayment or increased repayment of tax, avoidance or reduction of a charge to a tax. It also includes the deferral of any payment of tax or advancement of any repayment of tax or the avoidance of any obligation to deduct or account for tax. Hallmarks are laid down by regulations specifying types of notifiable schemes.

The taxes covered by these provisions are IT, CGT, CT, IHT, SDLT and stamp duty. NIC is not included.

12.2 VAT avoidance schemes

Businesses using VAT avoidance schemes must disclose their use. Certain VAT avoidance schemes ('notifiable' schemes) are put on a statutory register.

Businesses with an annual turnover of £600,000 or more that use designated schemes must inform HMRC. A designated scheme is one which has been designated by the Treasury.

Businesses with an annual turnover of £10 million or more must also inform HMRC if they use notifiable schemes, that are not designated schemes, for the purpose of securing a tax advantage.

Detailed regulations deal with the notification procedure to be used.

The penalty for failure to notify HMRC of the use of a designated scheme is 15% of the VAT saving as a result of the use of the scheme. The penalty for using other arrangements is £5,000.

Chapter roundup

- The fundamental principles of ethics should underlie all of a member's professional behaviour.

- A conflict of interest is a commonly met threat to compliance with the fundamental principles.

- If a member discovers that a client has misled him in order to obtain a tax advantage, the member has to consider his position in relation to both the client and the tax authorities.

- As a general rule, self-employment leads to lower overall tax and NIC burdens than employment.

- If someone is to be an employee, the tax effects of the remuneration package should be taken into account.

- An entrepreneur must choose between trading as a sole trader and trading through a company. That choice, and if a company is chosen, the choice between dividends and remuneration, can significantly affect the overall tax and NIC burden. Cash flow is also an important consideration.

- The incorporation of a business should be carefully planned, taking account of consequent tax liabilities. There are both advantages and disadvantages to incorporating a business. A disposal of shares can also have several tax consequences.

- There are several methods by which profit can be extracted from a company.

- Capital gains and inheritance tax planning are important when disposing of a family business.

- At each stage of a 'company's life' from its beginning, growth and future expansion overseas, tax planning strategies should be adopted.

- There are several tax planning opportunities available to groups of companies.

- Careful consideration needs to be given as to whether a group structure or a divisionalised company would be better.

- There are disclosure requirements for promoters of direct tax avoidance schemes. Businesses may be required to disclose use of VAT avoidance schemes.

Quick quiz

1   Can a member act for both a husband and wife?

2   What should you do if you suspect that a client may have taken a bribe from a customer?

3   What are the main NIC differences between the tax positions of employees and the self employed?

4   What is a major attraction of incorporation?

5   Why might a newly commencing trader employ a prospective partner at first, before forming a partnership?

6   What is the major disadvantage for an individual shareholder of an incorporated business where losses are anticipated?

7   List the methods by which profit may be extracted from a company.

8   What are the advantages of a divisionalised company structure?

9   What is the maximum initial penalty for failure to notify a tax avoidance scheme relating to income tax?

Answers to quick quiz

1   It depends on whether there are any relationships between the two that could give rise to a conflict of interest. For example they may be business partners, or one may employ the other. Even so, it may be sufficient to ensure that each is aware that you act for both, provided you keep the position under review. In other cases the conflict of interest might be such that you should not; for example if they are in the course of a divorce.

2   This is likely to be a criminal offence and you should report your suspicions to the firm's money laundering officer.

3   Employees suffer Class 1 NIC. Their employers suffer Class 1 and Class 1A NIC too.

The self employed pay Class 2 and Class 4 NIC. The rates of NIC due under these classes are smaller than Class 1 and Class 1A NIC.

4   The attraction of incorporation is limited liability. A sole trader or partner is liable for business debts to the full extent of his personal wealth. A limited company's shareholder is liable to the amount, if any, unpaid on his shares.

5   Commencing trade with a prospective partner as a salaried employee for a year or two obtains tax relief twice on his salary during any overlap period

6   A company's losses are not available to reduce shareholders' taxable incomes (unlike losses of an unincorporated business which can reduce the sole trade/partners incomes).

7   • remuneration
    • dividends
    • loan interest
    • rental income
    • pension contributions

8   • Full amount of small company tax bands available rather than being divided among all companies under common control

    • Automatic set off of trading losses in respect of various divisions

    • Automatic set off of capital gains and losses

    • Administration is simplified

9   £5,000

Now try the question below from the Exam Question Bank

Number	Level	Marks	Time
Q33	Introductory	25	45 mins
Q34	Examination	21	38 mins

Part F

Personal and corporate financial management

31

Personal and corporate financial management

Topic list	Syllabus reference
1 Personal financial management	B1,B6
2 Sources of personal finance	B2,B3,B6
3 Investment products	B3,B6
4 Business finance	B4-B6

Introduction

We have studied the various taxes which may be charged on individuals and businesses and we have considered how tax liabilities may be deferred or mitigated by careful planning. We now turn our attention to the impact of tax on personal and corporate financial planning.

Although financial planning should never be tax driven, the tax consequences must be taken into account in decision making. Tax liabilities will reduce investment returns, and must therefore be deducted in calculating net of tax income or gains. This may tip the balance between investments; a lower rate of return on a tax free investment may be greater than the actual return on a higher yielding investment for a higher rate taxpayer.

In this chapter, we look at how finance may be raised, both for personal use and for businesses, and at the tax and other considerations affecting the choice between sources of finance. The key distinction for businesses is between equity (cost: dividends – not tax-deductible) and debt (cost: interest – tax-deductible). We also look at the tax treatment of various different types of investment products.

Study guide

		Intellectual level
B	**THE IMPORTANCE OF TAXATION TO PERSONAL AND CORPORATE FINANCIAL MANAGEMENT**	
1	**The principles underlying personal financial management**	
(a)	Calculate the receipts from a transaction, net of tax and compare the results of alternative scenarios and advise on the most tax efficient course of action.	3
2	**How an individual's personal financial objectives may differ depending on their circumstances and expectations**	
(a)	Understand and apply the effect of age, family commitments, aspirations and the economy on personal financial objectives.	3
3	**The common forms of personal finance and investment products in a given set of circumstances, including ethical considerations**	
(a)	Understand and be able to compare and contrast the tax treatment of the sources of finance available to individuals.	3
(b)	Understand and be able to compare and contrast the tax treatment of investment products:	3
(i)	Deposit based investments	
(ii)	Fixed interest securities	
(iii)	Packaged investments	
(iv)	Collective investments	
(v)	Equities	
(vi)	Enterprise investment scheme	
(vii)	Venture capital trusts	
(viii)	Fixed interest securities	
4	**How a business' financial objectives may differ depending on its circumstances and the business environment.**	
(a)	Understand and be able to explain the effect of profitability, future plans, actions of competitors and the economy on a business' financial objectives.	3
5	**How taxation can affect the financial decisions made by businesses (corporate and unincorporated) and by individuals.**	
(a)	Understand and explain the tax implications of the effect of the raising of equity and loan finance.	3
(b)	Explain the tax differences between decisions to lease, use hire purchase or purchase outright.	3
(c)	Understand and explain the impact of taxation on the cash flows of a business.	3
6	**Other considerations, personal and commercial, which might affect a financial decision.**	3

1 Personal financial management

1.1 Basic principles

Although high net worth individuals may seem to be more concerned with personal financial management than the man in the street is, it would be wrong to suggest that there are no opportunities for the ordinary man. In each case the principle is the same:

(a) determine the options available
(b) calculate the after tax receipts
(c) advise on the most tax efficient course of action.

This is best illustrated by a simple example.

1.2 Example: personal financial management

Tony, aged 22, is employed on a remuneration package of £20,000 pa. He is saving towards buying a house and can save approximately £2,500 each year. He wants to have the money in a bank or building society so that he can withdraw it to pay the deposit when he finds a house, although this may not be for a year or two.

What would you advise?

The options are:

(a) to select a suitable instant access or short notice account, possibly an internet account, paying a competitive rate of interest

(b) to select a mini cash ISA.

The annual after tax receipts, assuming that Tony could achieve a rate of interest of 5% on either sort of account, are calculated as follows (Tony is a basic rate taxpayer):

(a) £2,500 × 5% = £125 less tax of £125 x 20% = £25, net receipt £100.
(b) £2,500 × 5% = £125, no tax, net receipt £125.

The most tax efficient option is to invest in a mini cash ISA. This achieves the same objectives and increases the after tax receipt by £25.

1.3 Circumstances and expectations

An individual's objectives will vary according to his current circumstances.

Tony, in the above example, is saving towards a house. Once he has acquired one, his spare income may be spent on paying a mortgage, or saving towards the cost of getting married. He may then have a few years where there are two incomes which may be spent on holidays or, if Tony is prudent, invested in pension provision.

Next on the list may be children. Not only must the cost of feeding and clothing.the children be taken into account, but Tony may also want to provide for school fees. In addition there may be a fall in income, if Tony or his wife give up work or do reduced hours, or there will be childcare costs.

When finally the children become financially independent, Tony and his wife may feel well off. At this stage they may find they need to invest a considerable amount in pension provision if they have been unable to afford regular contributions. There may be inheritances from elderly parent or other relatives to be invested. However the spectre of care home fees may be looming.

You need to ascertain the individual's current circumstances and commitments and how these are likely to change in the future before you can give proper advice. Your client may need income, or may prefer capital growth.

He may like some element of risk in his investments, but this must be balanced against what he can afford to lose. The type of investment chosen will depend not only on individual circumstances but also on the economy as a whole. Stock markets and property can slump, but can also provides returns far greater than can be obtained on money deposits.

At times where an individual has a high input into the family, whether in money or time, it may be advisable to insure against death or illness in case of need.

2 Sources of personal finance

FAST FORWARD

There are many sources of finance available, long or short term, secured or unsecured.

2.1 Introduction

Investments can only be made if funds are available. The private investor will generally have his own funds to invest, accumulated from salary or from business profits, but he may even decide to borrow money in order to make an investment which is expected to be particularly profitable. And of course, many private individuals borrow money to invest in land and buildings, buying their homes with mortgage loans.

Some individuals borrow to fund expensive lifestyles, making them even more expensive.

2.2 Sources of finance for private purposes

The following sources of finance are available to individuals for private purposes.

- Bank overdrafts
- Unsecured bank and building society loans
- Mortgage loans from banks and building societies, secured on the borrower's home
- Credit cards
- Hire purchase facilities
- Credit facilities provided by retailers

If the individual wishes to buy or improve a house, a mortgage loan is likely to be the most suitable source of finance. The fact that it is secured reduces the risk to the lender, and therefore the interest charged. For other large purchases, hire purchase facilities or the credit facilities provided by retailers may be the most suitable: the cost may be reduced as an incentive to make the purchase concerned, and using a specific facility avoids tying up a large proportion of a more general facility such as an overdraft or a credit card. An alternative to such specific facilities is an unsecured bank or building society loan, which must be repaid by agreed instalments over a fixed period.

Small and varied purchases may be made using a credit card, although if credit is taken the interest rate is very high, to reflect the risk of non-payment accepted by the credit card company. A bank overdraft facility can be useful to allow the individual to cope with times when expenditure temporarily exceeds income, perhaps because of fluctuating business profits or because of occasional worthwhile new investment opportunities such as new share issues.

2.3 Mortgage products

> A mortgage may be a repayment or interest only mortgage. Endowment policies, ISAs or pension products may be used to accumulate the capital required to repay an interest only mortgage.

2.3.1 Introduction

Most people who buy a house need to **borrow** to finance the purchase. Mortgage loans are normally repayable not later than the end of a fixed term agreed at the start of the loan.

Key term

> A **mortgage** is a loan given on the **security** of a property. The purchaser pays a proportion of the purchase price of a property – a **mortgage deposit** – and the balance is lent by the mortgage lender.

The borrower gives the lender **legal rights over the property** for the duration of the loan. While the loan is outstanding the property is the lender's security that the loan will be repaid.

If the borrower does not keep up repayments on the loan – defaults – **the lender has the right to take possession of the property**, sell it, recover the amount of the loan (assuming the sale price is higher than the loan) and pay the balance to the borrower.

If the loan is repaid according to the terms of the mortgage, the legal rights of the lender over the property cease **at the end of the term**.

2.3.2 Interest rates

The **interest rate** charged by a lender may be variable (**variable rate mortgage**). Some variable rates of interest are limited to a specified maximum but may rise or fall subject to that maximum. These are **'capped' mortgages**. Others are variable between both a maximum and a minimum rate – **'cap and collar mortgages'**.   These are not very common.

Fixed rate mortgages are available at a rate of interest which is fixed for a specific period of time.

Discounted mortgages allow a discount on the rate of interest for a specific period of time, typically six months to two years, before the borrower moves to a variable rate mortgage.

Low start mortgages are mortgages where interest only is paid to the lender for an initial period. After this period a full repayment mortgage (see below) starts on the total loan.

Deferred interest mortgages are mortgages where reduced interest is paid for a period. At the end of the period the full mortgage starts and the loan is increased by the deferred and unpaid interest.

2.3.3 Methods of repaying capital

During the term of the mortgage the borrower must pay **interest**. There are two methods of **repaying the capital**: during the term or at the end of it. It is possible to **combine the two types of mortgage**. For example, a borrower might borrow £70,000 on a repayment basis and £30,000 on an interest only basis.

With a repayment mortgage each time interest is paid to a lender, part of the capital is repaid at the same time. Payments are often of a fixed regular amount. However, flexible mortgages may allow underpayments (ie less than the regular monthly amount), overpayments or payment holidays. There may also be additional borrowing facilities.

With an interest only mortgage **the entire capital sum is repaid on the last day of the mortgage**. Most lenders will want the borrower to take some action over the term of the mortgage to accumulate sufficient money to repay the loan.

There are a number of different methods of **accumulating funds** to repay a mortgage:

(a)   via a **life insurance endowment policy**. These were very common when investment returns were high, but are less so now. The life cover in the policy, however, guarantees the receipt of a lump sum under the policy should the holder die. There are currently no tax reliefs for investing in an endowment policy, but the proceeds are normally tax free.

(b)   via a **pension,** where the borrower uses a lump sum from a pension fund to repay his mortgage. Level term assurance for a sum assured equal to the amount of the loan and for the same term should preferably run alongside the pension policy to provide a benefit in the event of the borrower's death. If this is taken out as a pension term assurance, tax relief is available for the premiums paid. The advantage of a pension mortgage is that tax relief is given on contributions into the pension fund, and the fact that the funds rolls up tax free. However only one quarter of the pension fund built up can be taken as a lump sum. For example, to pay off a £100,000 mortgage, a fund of £400,000 is required. The balance (£300,000) has to be used to buy a pension.

(c)   via an **individual savings account**, where the individual invests surplus funds in an ISA to grow tax free. The risk is that the accumulation of capital to repay the mortgage is totally dependent on the performance of the shares or funds chosen. There is a need to consider level term assurance with a sum assured equivalent to the outstanding loan.

2.4 Tax treatment of borrowings

Tax relief is only available for interest paid in limited circumstances.

Apart from business borrowings or in connection with a property letting business, where the interest paid is a deduction from profits, interest relief is only available if the interest is charged on a qualifying **loan** such as for loans to invest in close companies or partnerships. This precludes relief for interest on overdrafts or credit card borrowings.

Note that **interest relief is not available** on a loan to buy shares in a close company **if EIS relief is claimed** for the investment.

Unless tax relief is available for interest it may be advisable to repay loans if surplus funds are available. In evaluating the situation, however, as well as comparing the interest charge on the borrowing with the income generated by the surplus funds you need to take into account any capital return which may be generated if the surplus funds are invested.

3 Investment products

3.1 Introduction

There is a very wide range of investment products available to individuals, ranging from an almost risk free bank deposit to a high risk investment in shares in a small unquoted trading company under the enterprise investment scheme.

3.2 Deposit based investments

Most deposit based investments are fairly low risk investments in which an investor receives a low rate of interest in return for depositing his capital with the institution.

The products available and their tax treatment are:

Provider	Type of account	Tax treatment
Banks and building societies	Instant access accounts, notice accounts, fixed term deposits, money market accounts	Interest taxable as savings income (excl. divs). Normally paid net of 20% tax, except on money market deposits over £50,000 or if investor certifies that he is a non-taxpayer.
	Mini cash ISA	Tax free
	Child trust fund accounts	Tax free, even if deriving from parental contributions
National Savings and Investments (NS&I)	Easy access accounts Investment accounts Income bonds Pensioners bonds	Interest taxable as savings income (excl. divs). Paid gross.
	Fixed rate savings bonds	Interest taxable as savings income (excl. divs). Paid net of 20% tax.
	Capital bonds	Interest added to the bond is taxable as savings income (excl. divs) each year although not paid until encashment. Interest added gross.
	Guaranteed equity bond	Return (linked to FTSE) at end of 5 year term is taxable as savings income (excl. divs) on maturity. Added gross.
	Savings certificate, fixed interest or index linked	Bonus paid at end of term is tax free
	Children's bonus bonds	Bonus paid at end of term is tax free, even if bond bought by parent.
	Child trust fund accounts	Tax free, even if deriving from parental contributions

3.3 Fixed interest securities

A fixed interest security pays a fixed rate of interest and has a known maturity value so long as it is held until its redemption date.

A **fixed interest security** is a loan to a government, a local authority, a corporation or a building society. **The security pays a fixed rate of interest and has a known maturity value so long as the stock is held until its redemption date**.

Government securities and corporate bonds are negotiable and can therefore be traded in the market.

The securities available and their tax treatment are:

Investment	Income tax	Capital gains tax
Government securities Local authority bonds	Interest is taxed as savings income (excl. divs). Paid gross. Accrued income scheme applies.	Exempt
Company debentures and loan stock which are qualifying corporate bonds	Interest is taxed as savings income (excl. divs). Paid gross unless company is not quoted, when paid net of 20% tax. Accrued income scheme applies.	Exempt
Company debentures and loan stock which are not qualifying corporate bonds	Interest is taxed as savings income (excl. divs). Paid gross unless company is not quoted, when paid net of 20% tax. Accrued income scheme applies.	Taxable

3.4 Packaged investments

 FAST FORWARD

Collective and packaged investments may be attractive to the smaller and less sophisticated investor.

The small or unsophisticated investor may invest through a fund managed by professionals.

Some of the more commonly met investments available and their tax treatment are:

Product	Income tax	Capital gains tax
Endowment life assurance policy	None for qualifying policies (10 year term)	None for qualifying policies (10 year term)
Traded endowment policy sold on the open market	None for qualifying policies (10 year term) on first sale. Chargeable event subject to income tax if non-qualifying.	None on first sale. CGT on subsequent sales, maturity or death of policy holder.
Single premium bond	Up to 5% pa (cumulative) may be withdrawn tax free each year. Excess withdrawals chargeable. Chargeable event on maturity or sale = excess of proceeds + earlier withdrawals – original investment – earlier charges. Taxed as savings income (excl. divs) with an imputed 20% tax credit. 'Top slicing' relief available whereby rate of tax on chargeable amount calculated as if 1/n of the chargeable amount was the top slice of income, where n is the number of complete years since the last chargeable event.	No capital gains tax on chargeable event.
Purchased life annuity – annuity paid by life company which is part income and part return of capital	Income part is taxed as savings income (excl. divs) and is generally paid net of 20% tax. May be paid gross if investor certifies that he is a non-taxpayer. Capital part is tax free.	No capital gains tax.
Back to back packages, such as purchased life annuity where annuity pays premiums on endowment policy.	On each element of the package as normal.	

The **gift and loan scheme** is a particular type of scheme aimed at **reducing IHT**. It works in the following way:

(a) The settlor creates a trust to which he gives £3,000 covered by the annual exemption.

(b) The settlor subsequently lends the trustees a much larger amount of money, say £100,000. This is an interest-free loan repayable on demand.

(c) The original gift and the loan are invested in an investment bond. The trustees take advantage of the 5% withdrawal facility to repay the loan to the donor over a 20 year period.

(d) The inheritance tax implications are:

(i) The original gift is not chargeable to IHT as it makes use of the annual IHT exemption.

(ii) On the settlor's death any outstanding loan is repaid to his estate from the proceeds of the bond and may be subject to IHT. The estate is also responsible for any charge to higher rate tax which may have occurred on the encashment of the bond. Whether this is payable will depend on the settlor's income in the year of death.

(iii) The balance of the bond is paid to the beneficiaries free of IHT.

Such a scheme could fall within the pre-owned assets income tax rules (see earlier in this Text).

3.5 Collective investments

3.5.1 Introduction

A collective or pooled investment is a scheme in which a large number of small investors pool their money to purchase shares or other securities. By doing this they are able to participate in a much larger spread of investments than they could individually own and in this way they reduce their exposure to risk.

There are three main types of direct collective investments.

(a) **Unit trusts**. These are open ended funds. This means that the size of the unit trust varies with the number of units in issue. If investors wish to invest in the fund, new units are created to meet demand and the manager invests the money raised in shares or securities. Investors sell back their units to the manager who must buy them back.

(b) **Open-ended investment companies (OEICs).** These are is similar to unit trusts but issues shares rather than units. These are usually participating redeemable preference shares rather than ordinary voting shares. An OEIC can issue many types of share under one management and this is referred to as an 'umbrella fund'.

(c) **Investment trusts.** These are companies quoted on the London Stock Exchange whose business is investing in other companies' shares. The investor purchases shares in the investment trust through the market, and may subsequently sell them in the same way.

Unit trusts and OEICs may invest across the market generally, may be invested for income, or for growth, or may be invested in a particular industry sector or region of the world. If an OIEC is an umbrella fund, it is the underlying funds which are invested under these criteria. They are run by **fund managers** who are responsible for the selection and management of the shares within the portfolio.

In some funds it is possible to buy **income or accumulation units**. If accumulation units are purchased, the income is rolled up either in the price or by the issue of additional units.

3.5.2 Taxation of the individual investor

Income from units in a unit trust, shares in an OEIC or shares in an investment trust is, with one exception (see below), taxed as **dividend income carrying a non-repayable 10% tax credit**.

Some unit trust and OEICs invest mainly in interest bearing securities and so pay **interest distributions** not dividend distributions. These are **paid net of 20% tax and are taxed as savings income (excl divs)**.

Capital gains made by an investor on the sale of units in a unit trust or shares in an OEIC or investment trust will be **subject to CGT**, and losses are allowable capital losses.

3.6 Tax free investment wrappers

3.6.1 Introduction

Successive governments have encouraged stock market saving by enabling investors to hold shares and securities under a tax free wrapper. The funds may be invested directly in shares and securities, or in unit and investment trusts or OEICs where a spread of investments is needed to minimise risk.

Exam focus point

> In an exam you may advise investing in stocks and shares or collective investments. In that case the only disadvantage of investing in an ISA is the management charge that may be imposed.

3.6.2 Personal equity plans (PEPs)

PEPs were introduced to encourage share ownership. It has been impossible to make any further contributions to PEPs since 6 April 1999 but those schemes already in operation then may continue.

No tax is paid on income or capital growth for any taxpayers. There is no minimum investment period to achieve the tax free status.

3.6.3 Individual savings accounts (ISAs)

Key term

> **ISAs** are tax efficient savings accounts. They can be made up of two components.
>
> - Cash
> - Stocks and shares

There can be a single account manager or one manager for each component of the account. The investor must be resident and ordinarily resident in the UK in the year the investment is made. The investor must normally be 18 years or over. However, a cash only ISA can be held by individuals aged 16 or 17.

There are two distinct types of ISA:

(a)   **Maxi-accounts** which must normally contain a stocks and shares component and may contain the cash components (either one or both)

(b)   **Mini-accounts** which comprise a single component only.

Once an account has been designated by the manager as being of a particular type it retains that designation and cannot be altered.

Subscribing to a maxi-account in one year precludes an investor from also subscribing to a mini-account of any type in that year. **There is a general annual subscription limit for maxi-accounts of £7,000 of which a maximum of £3,000 can be in cash.**

A **mini-account** comprises a single component only. Once a mini-account, for any component, has been subscribed to for a particular tax year the only other ISA that may be subscribed to for that year is another mini-account comprising the other component.

The annual subscription limits for mini-accounts are:

(a) **Cash component accounts: £3,000**
(b) **Stocks and shares component accounts: £4,000**

Investors under 18 years of age can only invest in a cash mini-ISA.

The stock and shares element may contain medium term stakeholder products (Unit trust, OEIC and unit linked insurance). **All non-stakeholder life insurance may also be held in the stocks and shares component. Investments producing a 'cash like' return** (capital not at risk or at minimum risk) **are restricted to the cash component**.

Investments within an ISA are exempt from both income and capital gains tax. If, however, cash is held in a stocks and shares ISA a 20% deduction is made from interest received. This is not recoverable. There is no deduction from interest in a cash ISA. Also if a minor child opens a cash ISA with finds provided by a parent, the interest is taxed as the parent's income unless the £100 de minimis limit applies.

3.6.4 Child Trust Fund (CTF)

CTF accounts are available from 6 April 2005 for children born after 31 August 2002. **The CTF is initially funded by a Government voucher** (£250 or £500 for lower income families). **It is also possible for friends and family (including parents) to contribute up to a total of £1,200 a year to the account.**

The CTF is held for the child until he reaches 18. There are different types of accounts including **cash accounts, unit trusts and life products**.

There is no income tax or capital gains tax payable on the CTF. This applies even if parental contributions have been made.

3.7 Equities

Equities are high risk investments as neither the income nor the capital is secure.

When an investor buys a share in Marks and Spencer plc that is exactly what he has done; he has bought a share in the ownership of the company.

The main types of share available to investors are:

Type of share	Features
Ordinary shares	The shareholder is entitled: (a) to a share of profit distributed as a dividend (b) the right to vote on matters affecting the company (c) in the event of a winding up, to a share of assets, but note that shareholders do not take precedence over the creditors
Preference shares	(a) These shareholders are placed ahead of the ordinary shareholders for dividend payments and in the event of a liquidation (b) The dividend is usually a guaranteed amount but if the distribution to the ordinary shareholders is higher, the preference shareholders do not receive the increase
Convertible preference shares	The dividend paid on these is usually less than the non-convertible preference share but there is the option to convert to ordinary shares in the future at pre-set dates and at pre-set prices

Dividends are received with a non-refundable tax credit of 10%. The gross amount of dividends received are subject to income tax as described earlier in this Text.

A capital gain arising on shares, calculated using the matching rules, is subject to CGT. Losses are allowable losses.

3.8 The enterprise investment scheme (EIS)

The enterprise investment scheme is a scheme designed to promote enterprise and investment by helping high-risk, unlisted trading companies raise finance by the issue of ordinary shares to individual investors who are unconnected with that company.

3.8.1 Income tax relief

Individuals who subscribe for EIS shares are entitled to income tax relief. This has already been discussed earlier in this Text, but as a summary the rules are:

Individuals can claim a **tax reducer of the lower of 20% of the amount subscribed for qualifying investments** (maximum qualifying investment is £400,000 and the individual's tax liability for the year after deducting VCT relief.

If shares are issued in the first six months of the tax year (ie before 6 October), the investor may claim to have up to half of the shares treated as issued in the previous tax year. This is subject to a maximum carry back of £50,000.

The relief may be withdrawn if certain events, such as the sale of the shares, occur within three years.

3.8.2 Capital gains tax reliefs

Where EIS income tax relief is available there are also capital gains tax reliefs:

    (a)   Where EIS shares are disposed of after the three year period any gain is **exempt** from CGT. If the shares are disposed of within three years any gain is computed in the normal way.

    (b)   If EIS shares are disposed of at a loss at any time, the loss is **allowable** but the acquisition cost of the shares is reduced by the amount of EIS relief attributable to the shares. The loss is eligible for S574 ICTA 1988 relief (see earlier in this Text).

Question   Allowable losses

During 2004/05 Martin invested £35,000 in EIS shares and received relief against income tax of £35,000 × 20% = £7,000.

The shares are sold in February 2007 for £15,000. This will lead to a withdrawal of EIS relief of £15,000 × 20% = £3,000. What is the allowable loss for CGT purposes?

Answer

	£	£
Disposal proceeds		15,000
Less: cost	35,000	
EIS relief (7,000 – 3,000)	(4,000)	(31,000)
Allowable loss		(16,000)

If the shares had instead been sold outside the three year relevant period (ie so that there was no withdrawal of income tax relief), the allowable loss would instead be:

	£	£
Disposal proceeds		15,000
Less: cost	35,000	
EIS relief	(7,000)	(28,000)
Allowable loss		(13,000)

EIS reinvestment, or deferral, relief may be available to defer chargeable gains if an individual invests in EIS shares in the period commencing one year before and ending three years after the disposal of the asset (see earlier in this Text). Note that this relief is not conditional on income tax relief being available.

Exam focus point

> In the exam you may advise investing in an EIS company. Remember to point out the risks as well as the tax breaks.

3.9 Venture capital trusts (VCTs)

Key term

> **Venture capital trusts (VCTs)** are listed companies which invest in unquoted trading companies and meet certain conditions.

The VCT scheme differs from EIS in that the individual investor may spread his risk over a number of higher-risk, unquoted companies.

An individual investing in a VCT obtains the following tax benefits on a maximum qualifying investment of £200,000 in 2006/07.

- **A tax reduction of 30% of the amount invested** (40% for investments made in 2005/06). There is a withdrawal of relief if the shares are disposed of within five years or if the VCT ceases to qualify

- **Dividends received are tax-free income**

- **Capital gains on the sale of shares in the VCT are exempt** from CGT (and losses are not allowable)

In addition, capital gains which the VCT itself makes on its investments are not chargeable gains, and so are not subject to corporation tax.

Note that there is no minimum holding period requirement for the benefits of tax-free dividends and CGT exemption.

4 Business finance

FAST FORWARD

> For a business, the basic choice of finance is between debt and equity (although some equity will always be needed) and then the appropriate mix of short term and long term debt must be arranged.

4.1 Introduction

Businesses need funds in order to start up and expand, and their requirements are often far beyond the means of the entrepreneurs concerned. Outside capital may be sought from banks, from other lenders or from new shareholders or partners.

Various factors will affect the need for finance at different times in the business' life time. The types of finance are considered below, but it is useful to consider the needs that may arise.

When a business starts it will require funds to acquire premises, stock etc. Profits may be low as the business establishes itself, and the business will not wish to be burdened with large interest payments. As the company grows it will still need funds with which to expand and invest in new equipment. If the company is sufficiently profitable it may choose to retain profits within the company to finance such future expansion. This must be weighed against the expectations of external shareholders to receive dividends as a return on their capital. Once a regular pattern of dividend payments has been established, investors will expect it to continue.

Where a company has established a profitable business other entrepreneurs may set up in competition. This will force the company to adapt to preserve its share of the market, for example by cutting prices or offering special deals. This will result in reduced profitability unless the company can reduce its costs accordingly, and in the long term may affect the company's ability to acquire new equipment etc.

A slump in the economy, or in the particular sector of the economy, will also reduce a company's profitability. If the company has not maintained a sound basis this may result in a need to refinance. This usually involves persuading the banks or other investors to convert loans into equity, so reducing the annual interest payments at the expense of giving away a share in the future capital growth of the company. The worst case scenario would be to fail to refinance, resulting in the company being placed into administration or even liquidation.

4.2 Sources of finance for businesses

4.2.1 Introduction

The following sources of finance are available for businesses.

- The entrepreneur's own capital
- Bank overdrafts
- Bank loans (which may be short term, medium term or long term)
- Loans secured by mortgages of land
- Leasing and hire purchase arrangements
- Sale and leaseback arrangements
- Loans from private individuals
- Capital invested by partners
- Share issues (for incorporated businesses)
- Debenture issues (for incorporated businesses)
- Venture capital institutions

4.2.2 Private financing

An entrepreneur's own capital is readily available to his business with no conditions attached and no interest payments required (although the entrepreneur should recognise that he is giving up the opportunity to invest his capital elsewhere and earn interest on it). However, it is likely to prove to be inadequate for all but the smallest and least ambitious of business ventures, so outside sources of finance will usually have to be considered. Similarly, loans from private individuals, perhaps friends or relatives of the entrepreneur, are likely to be too small to finance a substantial business. However, interest rates and repayment terms may be favourable, so such loans should be considered.

4.2.3 Bank financing

Working capital is needed simply to carry on daily operations. Stock must be bought and creditors and employees must be paid, often before sales revenue is received. **A bank overdraft facility is often the most suitable source of finance,** because funds are available on demand and interest is only paid on the amount actually borrowed from day to day.

An overdraft is not, however, suitable for all of the financing needs of a business. Interest rates tend to be fairly high, and the lending bank could demand repayment at any time. **There is a general principle of term matching in business finance, which is that assets should be financed by funds which will be available for at least as long as the assets are expected to last.** Thus a machine which is expected to be kept for five years should be financed by a loan for five years or more, or by equity. Bank loans and debentures can be a useful source of such longer term finance, and if the loan can be secured on the assets bought with it then the interest rate may be reduced. It may also be possible to obtain loans, from banks and other lenders, at reduced rates of interest by offering a mortgage of land as security.

4.2.4 Leasing and hire purchase arrangements

Some fixed assets may conveniently be obtained under leasing or hire purchase arrangements. Under a lease, the lessee never obtains ownership of the asset, but if the lease is for the useful life of the asset and the risks and rewards of ownership are effectively transferred to the lessee (a **finance lease**), this point is unlikely to be of any practical significance. **A hire purchase agreement is effectively a finance lease, at the end of which the lessee has the option to buy the asset for a small sum.**

If a business already owns a valuable fixed asset, **finance might be obtained through a sale and leaseback arrangement.** The asset is sold, and is then leased back from the buyer so that the business can continue to use it. Such arrangements are usually made in respect of premises. They are attractive to the buyer/lessor, because the risk is low (he obtains ownership of a valuable asset at the outset). However, they should really only be considered as a last resort when other sources of finance are unavailable. In due course, the business will have to find and pay for new premises, or accept the burden of increasing lease payments.

4.2.5 Equity capital

An essential component in the overall financing package for any business is **equity capital**, which **is the form of capital most at risk in the event of business failure** but which also represents a stake in the ownership of the business, and therefore gives the investors the opportunity to profit most from the success of the business. Equity capital reflects the faith of investors in the business, and providers of loan capital will expect to see substantial equity investment before they will agree to lend money. Apart from anything else, if the business loses money lenders will be able to get their loans repaid out of the funds provided by equity investors.

In an unincorporated business, capital invested by the proprietor is equity capital. If more such capital is needed, the proprietor may take in partners. In a partnership, profits will be shared among the partners in a way which may take account of the amounts of capital invested, for example by including 'interest on capital' in the profit sharing arrangement.

Equity capital in a company is in the form of shares. Any company may issue shares to a limited range of investors, but only a public company may offer shares to the general public. A well known public company can raise very large amounts of capital through share issues, and even a private company may be able to attract a fair number of investors because of the limited liability of shareholders. Directors of a small company may, however, find that although their liability as shareholders is limited, they still have to give personal guarantees to repay bank loans to the company.

Unquoted trading companies may consider raising share capital under the enterprise investment scheme, which offers income tax reductions for qualifying investors and a capital gains tax exemption (see earlier in this Text). However, investors must be prepared to keep their shares for at least three years in order not to lose these tax benefits.

Venture capital institutions specialise in investing in growing businesses where both the potential rewards and the risk of failure are relatively high. They may offer a mixture of loans and equity finance, but they do not expect to be equity investors in a business indefinitely. They may, for example, plan to sell their shares in about five years time, perhaps following a stock market flotation.

Finally, **venture capital trusts provide finance for unquoted companies.**

For all types of external equity finance, the main advantage to the entrepreneur is that cash returns need not be paid at times when cash is short. Dividends need not be paid at any particular level, whereas if loan finance is obtained the interest must be paid and the capital must be repaid on time. The main disadvantage of external equity finance is that the entrepreneur must give up a stake in his business and in its potential for growth. Beyond a certain point, he may even lose the right to direct its affairs.

4.3 The tax implications of equity finance and of loan finance

4.3.1 Loan finance

You saw earlier in this Text that if a company is a party to a loan relationship for the purposes of its trade, any debits are deductible in computing its trading profits. If, however a loan relationship is not one for the purposes of a trade any debits or credits are pooled. A net credit on the pool is chargeable as interest income. A net deficit may be relieved in the various ways described earlier in this Text.

It is not only the interest costs of borrowing that are allowable or taxable. The **capital costs are treated similarly**. Thus if a company issues a loan at a discount and repays it eventually at par, the capital cost is allowed.

A sole trader or partnership will not obtain a deduction in respect of capital repayments of loan finance. A trading deduction will only be available in respect of interest incurred wholly and exclusively for trade purposes.

4.3.2 Equity finance

Companies can raise finance by issuing shares to shareholders. Capital can be raised in this way for trading and non-trading purposes.

Companies can distribute profits to shareholders in a variety of ways, of which the payment of dividends is the most common. **The cost of making distributions to shareholders is not allowable in computing taxable profits.**

A sole trader may make a deduction for 'interest' on his own capital in computing his profits, and partners may include amounts for interest on capital in their profit sharing arrangements, but no deduction for such interest is available for tax purposes.

4.3.3 Legal and professional expenses

Legal and professional expenses relating to capital or non-trading items are disallowable. This includes fees incurred, for example, in issuing share capital. However, a deduction is allowed to companies under the loan relationship rules for the incidental costs of obtaining medium or long term business loans and for issuing loan stock.

4.3.4 Investors

Interest income received from a company on loan stock etc is taxable income for the recipient (and will have suffered 20% tax at source if paid by an unlisted company).

Dividend income received from a shareholding in a company is taxable on an individual investor only to the extent he is a higher rate tax payer. The tax credit on dividend income can never be repaid to non-taxpayers but the tax suffered on interest income is repayable.

UK dividend income is not taxable in the hands of a company shareholder.

No gain or loss can arise to the original creditor when he disposes of his debt. A purchaser of a debt may have a chargeable gain and (unless he is connected with the original creditor) **an allowable loss.**

A debt on a security can give rise to a gain or loss to the original creditor.

4.4 The lease or buy decision

If assets are leased and the term of the lease is less than 5 years, then the lease payments are in general deductible in computing taxable profits. If they are bought on hire purchase or leased under a long term lease, then the cash price of the assets may qualify for capital allowances and the finance charges are deductible in computing taxable profits, making the tax effects very similar to those of taking out a loan and then buying the asset.

If assets are bought outright then capital allowances may be available on the purchase cost. These will be given on a reducing balance basis each year. The ultimate lease or buy decision is likely to depend on the availability of funds and whether leasing the asset allows the company to keep funds free to finance other activities.

4.5 Other considerations when raising finance

There are several non-tax considerations which are important when finance is being raised for a business. The following points should be considered.

(a) Long term assets should be financed by long term sources of finance. In addition, it is sensible not to rely totally on short term finance for working capital.

(b) The costs of different sources of finance may vary widely. Loans secured on land tend to be the cheapest form of finance, but they are relatively inflexible. Overdrafts are quite expensive, but they may be cheaper than loans in the long term because interest is only paid on the actual amount of funds needed.

(c) The effect of different sources of finance on gearing (the ratio of debt to equity) should be considered. Very high gearing can be very profitable for equity investors if things go well, but it also brings a high risk of insolvency if revenue falls. High gearing can also make potential lenders reluctant to provide any further funds.

(d) A company's shareholders will be interested in the earnings per share (EPS). High gearing tends to make EPS volatile. On the other hand, a large share issue to finance a project which will not produce profits for several years will reduce earnings per share until the new project generates adequate profits.

(e) There may be legal restrictions on borrowing. Some companies have Articles of Association which limit their borrowing, and lenders may impose restrictions on the extent to which borrowers can take out further loans. In addition, when an asset is used as security for a loan, the lender will generally want to have a first charge over the asset. Only one first charge can be given over each asset at once, and although a second charge may be given, the lender with that second charge will only be able to obtain repayment out of the proceeds of sale of the asset after the holder of the first charge has been repaid.

Chapter roundup

- There are many sources of finance available, long or short term, secured or unsecured.

- A mortgage may be a repayment or interest only mortgage. Endowment policies, ISAs or pension products may be used to accumulate the capital required to repay an interest only mortgage.

- Most deposit based investments are fairly low risk investments in which an investor receives a low rate of interest in return for depositing his capital with the institution.

- A fixed interest security pays a fixed rate of interest and has a known maturity value so long as it is held until its redemption date.

- Collective and packaged investments may be attractive to the smaller and less sophisticated investor.

- Equities are high risk investments as neither the income nor the capital is secure.

- The enterprise investment scheme is a scheme designed to promote enterprise and investment by helping high-risk, unlisted trading companies raise finance by the issue of ordinary shares to individual investors who are unconnected with that company.

- For a business, the basic choice of finance is between debt and equity (although some equity will always be needed) and then the appropriate mix of short term and long term debt must be arranged.

Quick quiz

1   What are the main sources of finance for private purposes?

2   What are the two main methods of repaying the capital of a mortgage?

3   How are the returns on NS&I savings certificates taxed?

4   What are the two distinct types of individual savings account?

5   What are the features of a preference share?

6   What income tax relief is available in respect of investments under the enterprise investment scheme?

7   What non-tax considerations are relevant to the choice of sources of finance to businesses?

Answers to quick quiz

1 (a) bank overdrafts
   (b) unsecured bank and building society loans
   (c) mortgage loans
   (d) credit cards and credit facilities provided by retailers
   (e) hire purchase facilities

2 Capital of a mortgage may be paid back during the term or at the end of the term.

3 They are tax free

4 (a) Maxi-ISAs
   (b) Mini-ISAs

5 Preference shares:

   (a) ahead of ordinary shares for dividends/liquidation
   (b) guaranteed dividend amount (but no increase if surplus)

6 EIS income tax relief is tax reducer up to 20% of amount subscribed up to £400,000.

7 (a) financing long term assets with long term finance
   (b) costs
   (c) gearing (ratio of debt to equity)
   (d) effect on earnings per share
   (e) legal restrictions

Now try the question below from the Exam Question Bank

Number	Level	Marks	Time
Q35	Introductory	15	27 mins
Q36	Introductory	10	18 mins

Exam question bank

1 The Wrights
36 mins

Eric Wright (born 31 January 1934) is a partner in a firm of architects. His taxable trade profits for 2006/07 are £21,060. In 2005, he took out a loan to buy some plant and machinery used in the partnership business. The amount of loan interest in 2006/07 was £1,000.

Eric has a bank account with the Halifax Bank. His account was credited with interest of £1,600 on 31 March 2007. In October 2006 Eric invested £10,000 in a venture capital trust.

Eric married Melanie on 10 May 2005. Melanie (born 1 April 1955) is employed as a head teacher in a local primary school. In 2006/07 she had earnings of £40,000. PAYE of £8,429 was deducted from these earnings.

Melanie received dividends of £4,500 during 2006/07. She also cashed in National Savings & Investments Certificates and received £250 interest in addition to the repayment of the capital invested.

Eric and Melanie are considering buying a cottage together in May 2007 and renting it out. The cottage will cost £100,000. The net rental income will be about £10,000 per year. Eric and Melanie have not decided exactly in what proportions they will contribute to the cost of the cottage.

Required

(a)   Compute the net income tax payable by Eric and Melanie for 2006/07.   **(10 marks)**

(b)   Explain how the rental income from the cottage will be taxed on Eric and Melanie. What advice would you give them to reduce their total tax liability? Assume Eric and Melanie have the same other income and expenditure in 2007/08 as in 2006/07 and that the rates of tax and allowances also remain the same in both tax years.   **(5 marks)**

(c)   A friend of Melanie has offered her the opportunity to subscribe £20,000 for shares in an EIS company. If Melanie does so she will borrow the money from the bank at an interest rate of 8%. Melanie's friend assures her that the company will start to pay dividends in five year's time. Alternatively Melanie could invest £20,000 to buy a 10% stake in another friend's company, and in this case dividends are likely to be paid at the rate of £1,000 in the first year, increasing by £100 pa. Melanie would like to know how much her cash outlay will be over five years for each investment.   **(5 marks)**

(Total = 20 marks)

2 Mr Lee
20 mins

You have received the following e-mail from a client, Mr Lee:

'I have just started a new job and thought that I ought to start making some pension provision now that I am in my mid-30s. My initial salary is £100,000 a year, but I am hoping that, with bonuses, it may increase in the next few years to around £500,000.

My employer operates a pension scheme and I have been given a booklet about it. The booklet says that the scheme is a 'money purchase' scheme. If I join the scheme, my employer will make contributions to the scheme in addition to the amount that I pay into it.

Could you answer the following questions:

(a)   Do I have to join my employer's pension scheme or can I make other pension arrangements? What is a 'money purchase' scheme?

(b)   If I join my employer's pension scheme, how much can I contribute to the scheme and how much can my employer contribute?

(c)   I have heard that there is tax relief on my contributions to a pension scheme. How does that work if I join my employer's pension scheme?

(d)   What benefits will I be able to receive from the pension scheme and when will I be able to receive them?'

You are required to draft an e-mail in response.   **(11 marks)**

3 Hamburg   45 mins

(a)   Hamburg retired in January 2006 at the age of 63 and used the income from investments to live on.

On 31 December 2006, he received the following interest payments on his National Savings & Investments accounts:

Easy Access Savings account	£90
Investment account	£460

Hamburg received an income payment of £6,600 from a discretionary trust set up by his aunt on 1 February 2007. The whole of the trust fund was invested in quoted shares.

Hamburg also received dividends of £15,750 during 2006/07 from his own investments.

Hamburg owned £20,000 6% Treasury loan stock which he bought in 1995. Interest is payable gross on 1 June and 1 December each year. On 21 May 2006, Hamburg sold £10,000 of the loan stock ex interest. The accrued interest due to the purchaser was £35. Hamburg sold a further £7,500 of loan stock including interest of £150 on 1 October 2006.

On 1 May 2006, Hamburg started to invest in rented properties. He bought three houses in the first three months, as follows.

House 1

Hamburg bought house 1 for £62,000 on 1 May 2006. It needed a new roof, and Hamburg paid £5,000 for the work to be done in May. He also spent £1,200 on loft insulation. He then let it unfurnished for £600 a month from 1 June to 30 November 2006. The first tenant then left, and the house was empty throughout December 2006. On 1 January 2007, a new tenant moved in. The house was again let unfurnished. The rent was £6,000 a year, payable annually in advance.

Hamburg paid water rates of £320 for the period from 1 May 2006 to 5 April 2007 and a buildings insurance premium of £480 for the period from 1 June 2006 to 31 May 2007.

House 2

Hamburg bought house 2 for £84,000 on 1 June 2006. He immediately bought furniture for £4,300, and let the house fully furnished for £8,000 a year from 1 August 2006. The rent was payable quarterly in arrears. Hamburg paid water rates of £240 for the period from 1 June 2006 to 5 April 2007. He claimed the 10% wear and tear allowance for furniture.

House 3

Hamburg bought house 3 for £45,000 on 1 July 2006. He spent £1,000 on routine redecoration and £2,300 on furniture in July, and let the house fully furnished from 1 August 2006 for £7,800 a year, payable annually in advance. Hamburg paid water rates of £360 for the period from 1 July 2006 to 5 April 2007, a buildings insurance premium of £440 for the period from 1 July 2006 to 30 June 2007 and a contents insurance premium of £180 for the period from 1 August 2006 to 31 July 2007. He claimed the 10% wear and tear allowance for furniture.

During 2006/07 Hamburg also rented out one furnished room of his main residence. He received £4,600 and incurred allowable expenses of £875.

Required

Compute Hamburg's income tax payable for 2006/07.   **(14 marks)**

(b)   Hamburg is thinking about investing in two holiday cottages in Cornwall.

Required

Outline the requirements for the cottages to be furnished holiday lettings and the income tax treatment of such lettings.   **(6 marks)**

(c)   Hamburg is thinking about selling a one half share in his main residence to his son to raise the funds to buy the holiday cottages instead of raising a bank loan. He will continue to live in the property.

Required

Advise Hamburg of any income tax consequences of this plan.   **(5 marks)**

(Total = 25 marks)

4 Taker   27 mins

(a)   Taker is employed at an annual salary of £35,000. He is not in a pension scheme, but receives the following benefits in 2006/07.

    (i)   He has the use of an 1,800 cc petrol engined motor car, which cost £20,000. Its CO_2 emissions are 177g/km. Fuel is provided for both business and private motoring, and Taker contributes £500 a year (half the cost of fuel for private motoring) for fuel.

    (ii)   He makes occasional private calls on the mobile phone provided by his employer.

    (iii)   He usually borrows his employer's video camera (which cost £600) at weekends, when he uses it to record weddings and parties for friends. He receives no payment for this, and he supplies blank tapes himself.

    (iv)   He has an interest free loan of £3,000 from his employer. Take the official rate of interest to be 5%.

    (v)   His employer pays £4,000 a year to a registered childminder with whom the employer has a contract. The childminder looks after Taker's three year old son for 48 weeks during the year.

In 2006/07, Taker pays expenses out of his earnings as follows.

    (i)   He pays subscriptions to professional bodies (relevant to his employment) of £180.

    (ii)   He makes business telephone calls from home. The cost of business calls is £45. The cost of renting the line for the year is £100, and 40% of all Taker's calls are business calls.

    (iii)   He pays a golf club subscription of £150. He does not play golf at all, but goes to the club to discuss business with potential clients. These discussions frequently lead to valuable contracts.

Required

Compute Taker's taxable earnings for 2006/07.   **(8 marks)**

(b)   Taker is considering changing his employment and has received two offers. One is from a near by company which is offering a salary of £40,000 pa and a choice of the provision of a company car with a taxable benefit of £4,000 (no private use fuel would be provided) or an increase in salary of £3,000 and a mileage allowance of 35p per business mile. If he does not accept the company car Taker would need to buy a new car costing £15,000 with annual running expenses of £2,200, including private use fuel of £500. Taker would sell the car after 3 years for 5,000, and estimates that extra interest charges over the period would amount to £1,800. Taker would drive 6,000 business miles pa.

The other offer is from a company 100 miles away, and it offers a salary of £45,000. Taker would be required to relocate, and the company would pay allowable relocation expenses of £12,000. Taker does not wish to sell his old house and would let it out unfurnished for £8,000 pa. renting a property at the new location for £6,000 pa. Alternatively the company would pay only £3,000 of relocation expenses but would provide Taker with a company flat which cost the company £120,000 four years ago and which has an annual value of £2,500. Taker could obtain an additional £2,000 rent for letting out his old house furnished. Taker estimates that he would spend three years in this job before moving back to his old house. He thinks his actual relocation costs will be £2,000 lower if he chooses the company flat.

Required

For each offer compute the effect on Taker's net income of the available options. (You may ignore NICs). **(7 marks)**

(Total = 15 marks)

5 National insurance contributions   27 mins

(a)   The following people work for Poster plc:

Albert   Managing director – works full time for the company – receives director's fees of £2,500 per month and a bonus of £5,000 in January 2007. Entitled to company car (benefit £4,500). No private fuel is provided. Provided with private medical insurance at a cost to the company of £750.

Barney   Manager, salary of £2,000 per month, and a bonus of £3,000 in January 2007.

Chloe   Cleaner, paid £120 per week.

None of the above is contracted out of the second state pension scheme.

Required

Show all NICs payable for 2006/07 in respect of these employees.   **(8 marks)**

(b)   Poster plc has had a good year and wants to reward its employees. Instead of paying bonuses it has decided that the employees should all have an additional holiday and it is offering the following options:

(i)   A week on a health farm. The place will be booked by Poster plc, and will cost £2,000.

(ii)   A week's sailing on a yacht chartered directly by the employees. The charter costs £5,000 per week, and a professional skipper a further £1,000 per week. Three members of staff must charter together, and each will take a partner.

(iii)   A voucher which may be exchanged for a holiday at a high street travel agent. The face value is £2,200, but the voucher cost the company £2,000.

(iv)   For employees with commitments that mean they cannot leave home, a payment of £1,500 cash.

Required

Explain the NICs payable under each of these options.   **(7 marks)**

(Total = 15 marks)

6 Colin Jessop

36 mins

ENVIROTECH plc
Conservation House
Valley Park
Guildford

1 April 2007

Brian Andrews
Andrews, Simmons & Finch
25 High Street
Dorking

Dear Brian,

Share Option Schemes

I wonder if you could help me with a couple of issues we are having with our share option schemes.

Bonus schemes

For the last 10 years we have been paying relatively modest cash bonuses to our workforce. It has been suggested that if we pay the bonuses in the form of shares, our employees would be committed to our company, and could see their hard work reflected in the value of their shares. Is there a tax efficient way of dealing with this?

Derek Forrest

You will be aware that Derek (assistant Chief Executive) is due to retire on 30 June 2007 after 20 years with the company.

Executive options

In 1999 Envirotech granted him the right to buy 100,000 shares for 50p each. The value of the shares at that point was about £1.50. These options were in addition to the 20,000 'approved' options you told us about at the time. Derek could exercise at any time until 2011 but actually did so last week as he is keen to get the shares before he leaves the company. The share price is currently up around £3.60. Derek wants to know what the position is for income tax and CGT.

Retirement bonus

We are considering awarding Derek a 'thank you' bonus of £30,000 in cash as a retirement gift. Derek doesn't know yet. The company has no obligation to do this, but Derek is 58 and has been with us since the beginning. He has been talking about retreating to the Algarve to play a bit of golf and the rest of the Board thought that this would be a nice gesture.

I hope you are well.

Colin Jessop

Managing Director.

You are required to write a letter to Colin dealing with his queries.   **(20 marks)**

7 Helen Strube

31 mins

(a) Helen started trading as a physiotherapist on 1 July 2001. Her accounts were initially made up to 30 June each year but in 2004 she changed her accounting date to 30 September by preparing accounts for the fifteen months to 30 September 2004. She ceased trading on 31 December 2006 and accounts were prepared for the three months to 31 December 2006.

Helen's trade profits were as follows.

	£
Year to 30 June 2002	36,000
Year to 30 June 2003	48,000
Fifteen months to 30 September 2004	60,000
Year to 30 September 2005	30,000
Year to 30 September 2006	24,000
Three months to 31 December 2006	10,000

Required

Show the taxable trade profits for each tax year. Show clearly when overlap profits arise and how these are relieved. **(10 marks)**

(b) Gemma has traded for some years preparing accounts to 30 April each year. Her business has been making profits at the rate of £2,000 per month for the last three years, but when she commenced trading on 1 May 1999 profits were only earned at the rate of £100 per month. She has decided to sell her business and is unsure whether to sell on 31 March 2007 or 30 April 2007. Gemma has no other income in 2006/07 and expects to have other income of £25,000 in 2007/08 onwards.

Required

Advise Gemma of the income tax and national insurance advantages or disadvantages of selling on 31 March as opposed to 30 April. **(5 marks)**

(c) Daniel is a self-employed designer. In 2006/07, he has taxable profits of (i) £30,000 or (ii) £35,000.

Required

Show the NICs payable by Daniel for 2006/07. **(2 marks)**

(Total = 17 marks)

8 Vivace

45 mins

(a) Vivace makes up his accounts to 31 December each year. On 30 September 2006 Vivace decided to retire and he gave his business to his son.

After claiming allowances based on the period ended 31 December 2003, the balance of his general pool stood at £8,000.

During the period from 1 January 2004 to 30 September 2006 Vivace recorded the following capital transactions.

14 September 2004	He sold machinery which originally cost £1,800 for £700.
16 September 2004	He bought a new car for a salesman for £4,000. The employee uses it privately for 25% of all its mileage.
1 December 2004	He bought secondhand machinery for £9,232.
21 March 2005	He sold plant which cost £2,000 in 2000 for £2,500.
22 March 2005	He sold the salesman's car for £3,200.

5 July 2005	He bought a Mercedes car for his own use costing £22,000. Vivace uses the car 60% for business purposes.
4 February 2006	He bought a new machine on hire purchase. A deposit of £1,800 was paid immediately. Four further instalments of £1,000 are payable annually in future years. The cash price would have been £4,000.
5 February 2006	He bought a car for the accountant for £3,000. There is no private use.
15 June 2006	He replaced his car. The Mercedes was sold for £4,000; a Volvo was bought for £18,000. 60% business use continued.
30 June 2006	Plant and equipment which originally cost £10,000 was sold for £2,602.
30 June 2006	He bought plant for £3,000.

On 30 September 2006 the plant and machinery was worth £10,000 and the Volvo was worth 16,000.

Vivace has always been a basic rate taxpayer, but his son is a higher rate taxpayer.

Required

Set out Vivace's capital allowance computations for the periods of account concerned, assuming that maximum claims are made, and advise Vivace and his son of any options open to them. Assume Vivace's business qualifies as a small enterprise for capital allowances purposes where appropriate. **(13 marks)**

(b) Simon acquired a new factory for use in his trade on 1 August 2000. The cost of the factory was as follows:

	£
Land	50,000
Cost of preparing land	10,000
Architect's fees	5,000
Offices	45,000
Factory	140,000
Total cost	250,000

Simon used the factory in his trade until 1 December 2003. The factory was then let for 2 years. Simon then used the factory again in his business until he sold it to Alicia on 1 December 2006 for £300,000 (including £80,000 for the land).

Simon makes up his accounts to 31 July and Alicia to 31 December.

Required

(i) Show the IBAs available to Simon and Alicia.

(ii) Explain how your answer would differ if the factory had been sold for £200,000 (including £80,000 for the land). (Computations are not required.) **(12 marks)**

(Total = 25 marks)

593

9 Arrol

45 mins

Arrol, a dentist, has been employed for several years as a representative by Bean Ltd, dental equipment manufacturers. His salary was £13,000 in the year ended 5 April 2006 and £12,771 in the year ended 5 April 2007. His employer provides him with a petrol engined motor car (cost £20,271) with CO_2 emissions of 237g/km. All petrol is purchased on Bean Ltd's account at a garage. Arrol makes a nominal £25 a month reimbursement to Bean Ltd for part of the petrol used by him in private usage of the motor car.

On 1 May 2006 Arrol and his wife received substantial gifts in cash and shares from a relative. On that day Arrol exchanged contracts and completed purchase of a private dental practice. Since then he has continued his employment and has worked part time in his practice. The result of the practice for the first year of trading to 30 April 2007 as adjusted for income tax but before capital allowances was a loss of £13,384. Indications are that the practice will be profitable in the year ending 30 April 2008, and after that will become very profitable.

Dental furniture (chairs, lamps etc) was purchased with the practice for £12,800. Additions to this equipment in the year ended 30 April 2007 cost £46,720 on 26 January 2007. Arrol wishes to claim the maximum capital allowances as soon as possible. None of the new equipment qualified for 100% FYAs.

In 2006/07 Arrol and his wife, who are both in their early fifties, had other income as follows.

	Arrol	Wife
	£	£
Bank interest received	235	
Building society interest received	3,005	5,012
Interest on National Savings & Investments account		1,742
Salary as receptionist in husband's practice		2,800

Required

(a) Calculate Arrol's income tax liability in 2006/07 on the assumption that he claims to have the loss incurred in 2006/07 set against his income of that year.

(b) Calculate Arrol's wife's income tax liability in 2006/07.

(c) Calculate the loss remaining unrelieved in the year 2006/07, state the alternative ways in which this loss may be used and give Arrol any advice you consider beneficial to maximise the tax relief.

(25 marks)

10 Adam, Bert and Charlie — 45 mins

(a)   Adam, Bert and Charlie started in partnership as secondhand car dealers on 6 April 2003, sharing profits in the ratio 2:2:1, after charging annual salaries of £1,500, £1,200 and £1,000 respectively.

On 5 July 2004 Adam retires and Bert and Charlie continue, taking the same salaries as before, but dividing the balance of the profits in the ratio 3:2.

On 5 May 2006 Dick is admitted as a partner on the terms that he received a salary of £1,800 a year, that the salaries of Bert and Charlie should be increased to £1,800 a year each and that of the balance of the profits, Dick should take one tenth and Bert and Charlie should divide the remainder in the ratio 3:2.

The trade profits of the partnership as adjusted for tax purposes are as follows.

Year ending 31 March	Profits £
2004	10,200
2005	20,800
2006	12,600
2007	18,000

Required

Show the taxable trade profits for each partner for 2003/04 to 2006/07 inclusive.   **(15 marks)**

(b)   Eric has been running a hardware store for several years. His shop assistant is retiring and Eric would like to take his wife Freda into the business. He is unsure whether to take her on as a part time salaried assistant, or to take her into partnership. Eric's profits are in the order of £60,000 pa before deducting his assistant's wages. If Eric took on a new assistant on the same terms as he would employ Freda he would expect to pay wages of £12,000 pa. Freda has no other income.

Required

Advise Eric of the advantages or disadvantages of employing Freda as an employee or of taking her into partnership with him

(i)   assuming Freda would receive £12,000 of income in both scenarios.
(ii)   assuming a profit share for Freda that would maximise the couples tax saving   **(10 marks)**

(Total = 25 marks)

11 Overseas — 36 mins

Susan (age 42) received the following income in 2006/07.

UK dividends	£9,000
Overseas property business income	£10,000
UK earnings income (gross)	£17,820

The overseas property business income suffered £4,705 of overseas tax before being paid to Susan.

Required

(a)   Calculate the tax payable by Susan if she has suffered £2,000 of tax under PAYE for the year.

(b)   To correct an error made on the behalf of the overseas country in 2006/07 on 1 November 2008 Susan receives from the overseas authorities a refund of £2,600 of the overseas tax suffered. What should Susan do in respect of this receipt?

(c)   Susan is likely to be sent overseas to work in Utopia for 15 months. The posting will run from 1 June 2007, although it could be altered to commence on 1 April 2007. Advise Susan on what effect this will have on her UK tax liabilities.

(d)   James, who is domiciled in Utopia and has always lived there is to be seconded to the UK for 1 year from 1 April 2007, although he will be required to carry out some duties in Utopia. Explain how he will be taxed on his earnings, and whether he will have any UK tax liability on his interest from a Utopian bank account.

(20 marks)

12 John

45 mins

John (aged 35) is employed by DEF plc, a quoted trading company. He earns a salary of £30,000 per year and in December 2006 received a one-off bonus of £6,000. He makes a monthly contribution of £195 (net) to a personal pension scheme. He has no other income since the part-time business which he also runs made no profit in this year; most years profits amount to about £5,000.

During 2006/07, John makes the following disposals:

(a)   1,000 shares in DEF plc which he bought on 10 September 2005 and sold on 28 February 2007. His gain on sale was £10,000.

(b)   His car. He bought the car on 12 July 2004 and sold it on 10 December 2006. He made a loss of £(3,000) on the sale.

(c)   A piece of land bought as an investment on 14 June 1997. John sold the land on 15 November 2006. The gain on sale was £25,000.

(d)   5,000 shares in XYZ plc held in an individual savings account. The shares were bought by John on 17 August 2002 and sold at a gain of £7,500 on 31 January 2007.

(e)   A factory. John bought the factory on 1 August 2003 and immediately used it for trading purposes until 1 November 2006. The factory was then empty until John sold it on 1 February 2007. He made a gain of £27,000 on the sale.

John had losses of £6,000 brought forward at 5 April 2006.

Required

(a)   Compute the CGT payable by John for 2006/07. Explain your treatment of each of the gains and losses.

(b)   Assuming that it is now March 2007 advise John whether there are any steps he can take to reduce his expected capital gains tax liability. He has no other chargeable assets that he intends to realise in the near future.

(25 marks)

13 Sophie Shaw

45 mins

Sophie Shaw made the following disposals in 2006/07:

(a)   A painting for proceeds of £50,000 at auction on 12 October 2006. The auctioneer's costs of sale were 1% of the gross proceeds. Sophie had bought the painting on 31 March 1982 for £2,500 (RPI March 1982 79.4).

(b)   A freehold shop on 1 February 2007 for £85,000. The shop was acquired by Sophie's husband on 1 September 2002 for £45,000. He had transferred the shop to Sophie on 30 November 2005 when it was worth £60,000. The shop was let out to a quoted company throughout the period it was owned by Sophie or her husband.

(c)   4 acres of land on 10 July 2006 for £40,000. This was part of a 10 acre plot of land acquired by Sophie in September 1995 (RPI 150.6) for £20,000 as an investment. At the date of the sale, the remaining 6 acres was valued at £24,000.

(d)   4,000 shares in JKL plc to her son Jason for £10,000 (their market value) on 23 December 2006. Sophie bought the shares on 1 February 2004 for £12,000. Jason sold the shares in January 2007 for £9,000.

On 6.4.06 Sophie had an unused capital loss brought forward of £5,000.

Sophie is a higher rate taxpayer, her husband Terry is also a higher rate taxpayer but has made no capital disposals during the year, and Jason is a student with only holiday earnings

Required

(a)   Calculate the capital gains chargeable on Sophie for 2006/07 after taper relief and the annual exemption, giving details of your treatment of the disposals. RPI April 1998 = 162.6.

(b)   Advise Sophie of any steps that could have been taken to reduce the capital gains tax liability for 2006/07.

(25 marks)

14 The Green family

45 mins

(a)   John Green acquired 20,000 shares in Miller plc on 1 May 2003 for £40,000. On 10 June 2006, Miller plc was taken over by Wall plc. Clearance was obtained from HMRC that this was a bona fide commercial arrangement. John received 1 ordinary share (worth £4.90) in Wall plc and cash of £1.60 for each Miller plc share.

(b)   John's wife made the following purchases of ordinary shares in Read plc, a quoted company.

Date	Number	Cost
		£
15 May 2005	1,800	1,900
1 March 2006	1,000	1,260

On 12 July 2006, there was a 1 for 1 bonus issue.

On 30 September 2006 she sold 3,200 of the shares for £14,000.

(c)   On 26 May 2006 Robert Green, Mr and Mrs Green's son, sold 1,450 quoted ordinary shares in Greengage Supermarkets plc for £10,150. His previous dealings in these shares had been as follows.

6 April 1998   Balance of FA 1985 pool 900 shares, cost £3,408, indexed cost £5,845
11 November 2005   Purchased 1,000 shares for £6,000

None of the shares are business assets for taper relief purposes.

Required

(a)   Compute the capital gain on the takeover of Miller plc for John Green. Show the base cost of his shares in Wall plc.   **(5 marks)**

(b)   Compute the capital gain or allowable loss on the sale of Mrs Green's shares.   **(6 marks)**

(c)   Compute the capital gain on Robert's disposal of his shares.   **(6 marks)**

(d)   State how much capital gains tax John and his wife will have to pay for 2006/07 if they have no other chargeable gains or allowable losses, but Mr Green had £17,560 of allowable losses brought forward at 6 April 2006, Mr Green's taxable income for the year is £17,000, and Mrs Green has no income. Show any amounts carried forward.   **(4 marks)**

(e)   Explain whether there would have been any advantages for John Green if instead of receiving cash on the take over of Wall plc shares he had received corporate bonds.   **(4 marks)**

(Total = 25 marks)

15 Roland Rat

45 mins

In April 1999, Roland Rat ceased in business as a sole trader and transferred the assets of his business to Mouse Trap Ltd, wholly in exchange for shares. His final accounts as a sole trader and the opening position of the company in April 1999 were as follows.

	£	Roland Rat £	£	Mouse Trap Ltd £
Fixed assets				
Goodwill		0		150,000
Freehold property		77,000		200,000
Plant and machinery (small movable items)		30,000		30,000
		107,000		380,000
Current assets				
Stock	73,200		73,200	
Debtors	63,900		63,900	
Cash at bank	41,000		0	
	178,100		137,100	
Less trade and expense creditors	(70,800)		(70,800)	
		107,300		66,300
		214,300		446,300
Capital employed				
Roland Rat capital account		214,300		
Share capital: 10,000 issued shares				10,000
Share premium account				436,300
		214,300		446,300

The freehold property is shown in Roland Rat's balance sheet at net book value being the cost in April 1983, less depreciation of £8,000. This was the date Roland commenced trading. He did not acquire an existing business. The values at which the company took over the assets have been accepted by HMRC.

Roland Rat informs you in August 2006 that the following transactions are proposed.

(i) He intends to transfer 2,500 shares in Mouse Trap Ltd to his wife for £50,000. They are a happily married couple.

(ii) At the same time he proposes to sell 2,000 shares to an incoming director at a price of £165,000, the market value.

(iii) The freehold property owned by Mouse Trap Ltd is now too small for the company's expanding trade. It is proposed to sell the property for £500,000 and use the proceeds, together with bank borrowings, to acquire larger freehold premises for £550,000.

Required

(a) Compute the chargeable gains which will arise if the above transactions proceed in August 2006, assuming that all gains are deferred where possible. State the base costs of the chargeable assets referred to above for any future disposals.

(b) Suggest whether there are any steps that Roland could have taken, either in 1999 or at the current time, to mitigate any capital gains tax liabilities. Roland's wife has only a small part time salary whilst Roland draws a substantial income from the company. Neither of them have made any other chargeable gains. (Computations are not required.)

Assume indexation	April 1983 – April 1998	0.929
	April 1999 – August 2006	0.119

(25 marks)

16 Miss Wolf, Mr Hen and Mr Fox   45 mins

(a)   On 30 June 2006 Miss Wolf assigned the lease of a building originally acquired as an investment for £30,750; the lease expires on 30 June 2022. She had acquired the lease for £8,000 on 1 January 1998 (RPI = 159.5) and the building had never been her principal private residence. RPI April 1998 = 162.6.

You may assume that the relevant percentages from the lease percentage table are as follows:

16 years   64.116
24 years   79.622
25 years   81.100

Required

Calculate the gain or loss on the assignment after taper relief.   **(5 marks)**

(b)   Mr Hen is a sole trader. He bought a factory for use in his trade on 10 July 2004 for £150,000.

On 9 November 2005, the factory was damaged in a flood. Mr Hen received compensation from the water company of £20,000 on 1 September 2006. He had incurred costs of £15,000 in July 2006 on renovations. The value of the factory after the renovations is £250,000.

On 1 December 2007, Mr Hen sold the factory for £260,000.

Required

Show the chargeable gains (if any) for Mr Hen for 2005/06, 2006/07 and 2007/08 assuming that any claims to defer gains are made and taking account of taper relief. Mr Hen made no other disposals except to utilise his annual exemption each year.   **(8 marks)**

(c)   Mr Fox bought a house on 1 August 1986 (RPI = 97.8) for £50,000. He lived in the house until 31 July 1989. He then went abroad to work as a self-employed engineer until 31 July 1994.

Mr Fox went back to live in the house until 31 January 1995. He then moved in with his sister.

Mr Fox sold the house on 31 July 2006 for £180,000.

Required

(i)   Calculate the gain on sale after all reliefs. RPI April 1998 is 162.6

(ii)   Advise Mr Fox whether he could have taken any action to reduce the gain on sale.

(iii)   Assuming Mr Fox's sister had died in July 2005 leaving her house to Mr Fox and that Mr Fox intends to sell this house also, reinvesting the proceeds of both sales in a larger house, advise Mr Fox of any steps he should take to reduce any capital gains. Mr Fox is likely to make a gain on the sale of his sister's house.   **(12 marks)**

(Total = 25 marks)

17 Mr & Mrs Brown

31 mins

Mr Brown's income tax liability for 2005/06 was £16,000. He had suffered tax by deduction at source of £4,000 and paid two payments on account of £6,000 each on the due dates.

He submitted his 2005/06 return on 31 January 2007 and made a claim to reduce his payments on account for 2006/07 on the basis that his total liability for 2006/07 would be £14,000 with tax suffered of £5,000.

He made the payments on account of £4,500 on 28 February and 14 August 2007.

Finally, on 13 March 2008 he submitted his return for 2006/07 which showed total tax due of £17,000 and tax deducted at source of £4,000. He therefore paid a further £4,000 on the same date.

Mrs Brown's tax return for 2006/07 included a transaction which it was commonly understood gave rise to a tax liability of £10,000. The return was filed in December 2007. In February 2008 another taxpayer who had undertaken a similar transaction challenged HMRC's interpretation of the legislation, succeeding before the Appeals Commissioners and the case is expected to proceed to the Courts during early 2009. If the alternative interpretation was correct it would have saved Mrs Brown tax of £8,000.

Required

(a) Outline the time limits for submission of returns and payments of tax under self assessment and detail the provisions for failure to comply. **(9 marks)**

(b) Calculate the interest on overdue tax chargeable in respect of Mr Brown's tax payments for 2006/07. You are not required to compute any surcharges payable. **(3 marks)**

(c) Advise Mrs Brown of any action she should take to enable her to take advantage of the alternative interpretation should the other taxpayer be successful before the Courts. **(5 marks)**

Note. Assume interest is charged at 6.5% per annum.

(Total = 17 marks)

18 Rodin

29 mins

Rodin dies unexpectedly on 20 December 2006. His record of lifetime transfers is as follows.

Date	£	Recipient
15.12.99	60,000	Son
21.1.02	337,000	Discretionary trust (Rodin paid the IHT)
20.8.03	46,000	Daughter
19.6.05	106,000	Discretionary trust (Rodin paid the IHT)
1.8.06	73,000	Cousin
1.9.06	300,000	Wife

Required

(a) Compute all amounts of inheritance tax due on these lifetime transfers. Assume that the nil band has always been £285,000. **(10 marks)**

(b) Comment on whether your answer would have been the same had Rodin's wife not been domiciled in the UK. **(2 marks)**

(c) Rodin's cousin wishes to give £50,000 to each of his son and daughter, and to transfer £300,000 to a discretionary trust for his grandchildren. His daughter is widowed, and he thinks it likely that in the next few months she will remarry. Rodin's cousin has not made any gifts recently. What advice would you give Rodin's cousin? **(4 marks)**

(Total = 16 marks)

19 Mr Bright

45 mins

Hubert Bright, for whom you act as tax adviser, had over the years acquired 3,000 £1 ordinary shares in Bod Ltd, an unquoted trading company with an issued share capital of 5,000 ordinary shares. All the assets of Bod Ltd are in use for the purpose of its trade. Mr Bright has been a full time working director of the company since 1980. His wife, Rose, also owns 1,000 ordinary shares in the company.

Hubert had acquired his shares as follows.

	Shares	Cost	
		£	
1.11.83	2,200	3,300	indexed cost £6,187
15.6.01	200	1,366	
18.8.06	600	3,000	

The current market values attributable to various percentage shareholdings in Bod Ltd are estimated as follows.

% Shareholding	Value of £1 ordinary share
100	40.50
80	36.67
60	25.00
40 or below	18.00

On 1 April 2007 Mr Bright sold 2,000 of his shares in Bod Ltd for £10,000 to his daughter Maxine, who sold them to an unconnected buyer ten days later.

He has made no previous transfer of assets other than a gift of £309,000 cash to a discretionary trust (which did not include Mr Bright as a beneficiary) on 1 May 2006. Mr Bright had agreed to bear any costs or taxes in respect of the gift. Apart from his shares in Bod Ltd Mr Bright currently has no other assets apart from cash of £40,000. He has left everything in his will to his son Roger. You should assume that today's date is 14 April 2007.

Required

(a)   Advise Mr Bright of his potential inheritance tax and capital gains tax liabilities assuming that he pays income tax at the marginal rate of 40%.

(b)   Advise Mr Bright on the inheritance tax implications which would arise if he were to die on 20 April 2007. (Assume that any CGT on lifetime gifts is unpaid at the date of death but that any IHT has been paid.)

(c)   Roger has suggested to Mr Bright that he should gift his shares in Bod Ltd now rather than retaining them until his death. Prepare brief notes of matters which will have a bearing on a decision in preparation for a meeting with Mr Bright.

Assume that the IHT nil rate band is £285,000 and the CGT annual exemption is £8,800 throughout and that the rules and rates of CGT and IHT are the same in 2007/08 as in 2006/07. RPIs November 1983 86.7; April 1985 94.8; April 1998 162.6.

(25 marks)

20 Trusts

20 mins

On 17 July 1999 Rhys Jones settled his portfolio of quoted shares on the RJ discretionary trust. Rhys died on 3 September 2006.

Under his will Rhys left his estate on discretionary will trusts for his sister Blodwen and her children, with the trust to be wound up and the capital to be distributed to Blodwen's children on her death.

Blodwen died on 28 February 2011.

Half of the assets of the RJ discretionary trust were distributed to beneficiaries on 5 March 2008, and the remainder was finally distributed on 18 April 2012.

Rhys made no other gifts other than to use his annual exemptions each year.

Required

(a)   Explain the occasions of charge to IHT in respect of the above transactions. Calculations are not required. **(9 marks)**

(b)   Comment on how your answer would have been affected had Rhys died on 3 July 2006. **(2 marks)**

(Total = 11 marks)

21 Fraser Ltd

27 mins

Fraser Ltd is a medium sized trading company. It has no associated companies and it makes up accounts to 31 March in each year.

The profit and loss account for the year ended 31 March 2007 showed a profit before taxation of £379,198.

The following items were included in the accounts.

Income	£
Dividend from a UK company (including tax credit)	1,655
Interest on bank deposits	6,834
Interest from gilts (gross)	2,208
Surplus on the disposal of a factory and a lease	59,106
Expenditure	
Directors' remuneration	62,075
Miscellaneous	3,837
Depreciation	13,876

The company has not paid a dividend since its incorporation. Its bank deposits and gilts are held for non-trading purposes.

The company's main factory was acquired on 1 February 1995 for £200,000, including £30,000 for the land, from Swift Ltd which had used it for manufacturing purposes since its completion on 1 February 1990. The cost to Swift Ltd was £110,000 which included £20,000 for the land, £8,000 for general offices and £6,500 for a canteen.

The company's second factory (acquired for £79,000, including £12,000 for the land, on its completion on 31 May 1997) was sold for £112,750 (including £20,000 for the land) on 15 August 2006.

Both of the company's factories have been used solely for manufacturing purposes. Maximum writing down allowances have been claimed throughout their ownership although an initial allowance was not claimed in respect of the expenditure in either building.

A lease of one of the company's retail outlets was sold on 30 April 2006 for £40,000. The term of the lease was 30 years from 1 November 1993 and the company acquired it on 1 November 1998 at a cost of £17,500. The lease percentage for 17 years is 66.470, for 18 years is 68.697 and for 25 years is 81.100.

There are no other unused losses or reliefs brought forward at 31 March 2006.

Miscellaneous expenses comprise the following.

	£
Hire purchase interest on two new fork lift trucks	783
Christmas gifts to customers: 40 executive desk diaries bearing the company's name	2,085
Entertaining customers	969
	3,837

The pool value of plant at 1 April 2006 was £nil. With the exception of the acquisition of the two new fork lift trucks under the hire purchase agreements at a cash price of £9,800 each on 1 December 2006 there were no purchases or sales of plant in the year ended 31 March 2007.

Fraser Ltd has build up a cash surplus and is considering several schemes.

The company has identified an area of the market into which it could expand. This would necessitate the acquisition of new premises, and two possibilities are under consideration.

(i)   a second hand factory could be acquired at a cost of £150,000. This factory was built in 1980 at a cost of £50,000.

(ii)   a new factory could be acquired at a cost of £400,000. Fraser Ltd would need to raise additional finance of £250,000, partly through a bank loan and partly through the issue of debentures. Initially the factory would be too large, and Fraser Ltd would let out approximately half of the building to another manufacturing company. It may be necessary to pay a tenant a premium to take a lease as there is an oversupply of premises.

Alternatively, Fraser Ltd would purchase all of the issued share capital of Simmonds Ltd, a company which already trades in this new area. The cost of the investment would be £250,000, and Fraser Ltd would need to raise £100,000 through bank loans.

To do well in the new area Fraser Ltd is likely to have to buy patents and similar rights, which it expects would cost £50,000. These will be written off over their useful lives in the accounts.

Instead of raising loan finance, Fraser Ltd is contemplating issuing new shares.

Required

(a)   Compute Fraser Ltd's profits chargeable to corporation tax for the year ended 31 March 2007.

(10 marks)

(b)   Advise Fraser Ltd of the corporation tax consequences of its proposals.   **(5 marks)**

Assume indexation	May 1997 – August 2006	0.253
	November 1998 – April 2006	0.186

(Total = 15 marks)

22 Major Ltd

36 mins

Major Ltd is a trading company resident in the United Kingdom. It has one associated company. Until 2006 Major Ltd made up accounts each year to 31 July, but decided to change its accounting date to 31 March. The information below relates to the eight month period to 31 March 2007:

	£
INCOME	
Adjusted trading profit (before deduction of any patent royalties or loan interest)	180,000
Rents received *less* expenses	30,000
Loan interest received – (see Note 1)	24,000
Capital gains	40,000
Franked investment income (FII) (received September 2006)	20,000

	£
PAYMENTS	
Patent royalties (gross figure, paid to a sole trader)	15,000
Gift Aid payment (paid September 2006)	3,000
Loan interest paid (see Note 2)	30,000

Notes

1 The loan interest was received in respect of a loan of £100,000 made by the company to Z Ltd, a main supplier of materials to Major Ltd. The directors of Major Ltd are concerned about the financial position of Z Ltd, but have decided to take no action at present.

2 The loan interest paid was to a UK bank in respect of funds raised to acquire the company's 80% interest in its associated company.

3 The patent royalties were paid for the purpose of Major Ltd's trade. All amounts accrued in the year were paid in the year.

Major Ltd is considering investing in another supplier and has identified two possibilities. 20% of the shares of S Ltd are being offered for sale by one of the retiring directors at a cost of £40,000. Alternatively Major Ltd could subscribe for new shares in T Ltd, taking either an 8% holding at a cost of £15,000 or a 40% shareholding at a cost of £80,000. Whichever acquisition is made Major Ltd would hope to sell the shares after a few years at twice its original cost, although it is possible that either of the two target companies could collapse. Major Ltd would have to borrow to fund the purchase.

Required

(a) Compute the corporation tax payable by Major Ltd in respect of the above accounting period.

(b) Advise the directors of Major Ltd in a brief memo of the taxation implications of the loan to Z Ltd proving irrecoverable.

(c) Advise Major Ltd of the tax consequences of its alternative share acquisitions.

(20 marks)

23 Hogg Ltd

23 mins

(a) Hogg Ltd prepares accounts for the year to 31 December 2006. In June 2006 it estimates that its corporation tax liability for the year will be £500,000. In January 2007 it revises its estimate to £520,000. In October 2007 it submits its return and self-assessment, showing a total liability of £525,000. The company has always paid corporation tax at the full rate.

Required

State the amounts and due dates for the payment of corporation tax by Hogg Ltd in respect of the year to 31 December 2006. **(7 marks)**

(b) State what penalties arise if a company submits its CT600 return late. **(6 marks)**

(Total = 13 marks)

24 Norma Ltd

18 mins

Norma is intending to start a new business on 1 April 2007, and anticipates a profit of £50,000 in the first year of trading. She is undecided whether to:

(a) Operate as a sole trader,

(b) Operate as a limited company and draw out all the profits as a dividend, or

(c) Operate as a limited company, draw a salary of £10,000 pa and draw out all the remaining profits as a dividend.

Required

Compare the tax and national insurance resulting from each alternative. **(10 marks)**

25 Clarke Ltd

18 mins

Alex, one of the directors of Clarke Ltd, has had a serious disagreement with the other directors over the direction in which the business should be moving, and as a consequence wishes to resign as a director and dispose of his shares. It has been agreed that Clarke Ltd will repurchase Alex's shares for £5 per share, either in March 2007 or in June 2007.

In January 1992 Alex subscribed for 5,000 shares at par. In May 2002 he purchased a further 2,000 from another director, Benny, at a cost of £3 per share. Benny had also subscribed for these share at par in January 1992. Clarke Ltd is an unquoted trading company and Alex is a higher rate taxpayer and has utilised his capital gains tax exemption on the disposal of other business assets held for over 2 years.

Required

Explain how the repurchase will be dealt with for tax purposes for Alex and indicate whether it would be preferable for the repurchase to take place in March or June 2007. **(10 marks)**

Assume indexation   January 1992 – April 1998   0.199

26 Daley plc

27 mins

Daley plc has recently become a client, having previously prepared its own accounts and corporation tax computations on the basis that reliefs should always be claimed as soon as possible. The return for the year to 30 June 2006 has been prepared but not yet filed.

The company has had the following results since it started to trade.

	Year ended 31.12.03	Year ended 31.12.04	Six months ended 30.6.05	Year ended 30.6.06
	£	£	£	£
Trading profit/(loss)	(29,000)	110,000	85,000	(200,000)
Interest income	10,000	11,000	12,000	14,000
Chargeable gains/ (allowable losses)	18,000	(5,000)	2,000	(1,000)
Gift aid donation	Nil	1,000	3,000	1,000

There are no associated companies, although Daley Ltd intends to acquire Terry Ltd in April 2007. Terry Ltd has one subsidiary company. It is expected that Daley Ltd's profits in the year to 30 June 2007 will be in the region of £150,000, and that this level will be maintained in the future.

Required

(a) Compute the corporation tax liability for all four periods on the basis that relief is claimed as soon as possible, and show all amounts to be carried forward at 30 June 2006. Assume that tax rates and allowances for FY 2006 apply to all years.

(b) Write a letter to the directors of Daley Ltd explaining how losses can be relieved and advise whether best use has been obtained for the losses.

(15 marks)

27 Huis Ltd

27 mins

(a) Huis Ltd is a close company which pays corporation tax at the small companies' rate. On 31 May 2006, six months before the company's year end, it lent £45,000 to Sartre, a shareholder. Sartre is not an employee of the company. The loan carried a market rate of interest.

The company advised Sartre on 31 March 2008 that he would not be required to repay the loan. It has also agreed to include Sartre in its medical insurance scheme at an annual cost of £1,000, and to allow him to use the company yacht (annual value £24,000) for a month each summer.

Required

Set out the tax consequences of the transactions with Sartre, giving the dates on which any amounts are payable to HMRC.

(b) Beauvoir Ltd is a close investment-holding company. It has had the following results for the last two years.

	Year ended 31.3.06	Year ended 31.3.07
	£	£
Property income	14,000	25,000
Interest income	20,000	100,000
Management expenses	36,000	45,000
Dividends received in August from non-group companies	16,000	27,000

Required

Compute the company's corporation tax liability for both years. **(15 marks)**

28 H, S and N

45 mins

H Ltd has owned 60% of the issued ordinary share capital of S Ltd since its incorporation, the remaining 40% being held by individuals. Both UK companies have always prepared accounts to 30 June, their most recent accounts showing the following.

	H Ltd		S Ltd	
	Year ended 30.6.05	Year ended 30.6.06	Year ended 30.6.05	Year ended 30.6.06
	£	£	£	£
Adjusted trading profit	2,000		30,000	100,000
Adjusted trading loss		(48,000)		
Gift aid donation paid			12,000	12,000

On 1 January 2005, H Ltd acquired 100% of the issued ordinary share capital of N Ltd, a company which had always prepared accounts to 31 December.

N Ltd's accounts for the period of 1 January 2005 to 30 June 2006 show the following.

	£
Adjusted trading profit, before capital allowances	65,250
Chargeable gain, after indexation allowance on land bought in 1992 and sold in February 2006	20,000

N Ltd had a written down value of plant at 1 January 2005 of £5,000 and had incurred expenditure as follows.

		£
3 February 2005:	new car to be used by the managing director of N Ltd 80% for business, 20% for private use	16,000
4 January 2006:	new plant	31,000
20 March 2006:	secondhand plant bought on hire purchase, the cash price being £8,000, a deposit of £2,000 being paid on the above date followed by 24 monthly instalments of £300, commencing 20 May 2006.	

The group are planning several property transactions for 1 January 2007:

(i) N Ltd will sell a factory for £200,000 realising a loss of £40,000. The factory was acquired on 1 January 2001 and was valued at £190,000 on 1 January 2005.

(ii) H Ltd will sell an office block for £250,000 realising a capital gain of £50,000.

(iii) S Ltd will sell a warehouse for £300,000 realising a gain of £70,000.

(iv) S Ltd will acquire a new warehouse at a cost of £240,000.

It is anticipated that for the year to 30 June 2007 H Ltd will have trading profits of £10,000, S Ltd of £150,000 and N Ltd of £75,000.

Required

(a) Compute the corporation tax payable by H Ltd, S Ltd and N Ltd for the above periods of account, assuming all available claims and surrenders are made to minimise the corporation tax payable by the group and that all three companies meet the definition of 'medium sized'.

(b) Draft a memorandum to the directors of H Ltd suggesting how the group can minimise the corporation tax on chargeable gains for the year to 30 June 2007.

(25 marks)

29 Exotica Inc and W Ltd

27 mins

(a) Exotica Inc (for which you act as United Kingdom tax adviser) is a company resident and incorporated in Ruritania, a country which is outside the European Community and does not have a double tax agreement with the UK. The company manufactures items of advanced industrial equipment and now wishes to increase its sales within the UK. The company has no subsidiaries and currently makes worldwide profits equivalent to £300,000 sterling a year.

It intends to acquire an office in London and to staff it with full-time salesmen assigned from its head office in Ruritania. These individuals will stay in the UK for periods ranging between six months and four years. Those staying for less than a year will reside on their own in hotels. Those staying for a year or longer will live in rented accommodation with their families. Most, but not all of them, will be non-UK domiciled, and in all cases their only source of income (apart from their employment with Exotica Inc) will be long-standing bank deposit accounts in Ruritania.

Exotica Inc is still considering whether the salesmen will be given the authority to conclude contracts with UK customers or whether such authority will be reserved for the head office only. It is also considering whether customers' orders should be met from stocks held in Ruritania or whether stocks should be maintained in the UK. While tax considerations will be taken into account, other commercial factors are likely to influence these decisions strongly. Projected additional profits from the UK operation are £75,000 a year.

Required

Advise Exotica Inc on the corporation tax implications of the various alternative courses of action still under consideration.

(b) The directors of W Ltd have decided to set up an operation in a country where the rate of corporation tax is 25%.

They are considering two alternative approaches:

(i)   to run the overseas operation as a permanent establishment of the UK company; or

(ii) to run it as a foreign-registered subsidiary of the UK company.

Required

Draft a report to the board on the taxation implications of each of the alternative proposals.

(15 marks)

30 Paul and Joe

18 mins

Paul Sand is in business as a general builder but he is also in partnership with John Rowe as 'A1 Repairs', Peter Dene as 'Kwik Repairs' and in partnership with his wife as 'Speedy Builders'.

Required

Discuss how many VAT 'persons' exist here.

(10 marks)

31 VAT groups

18 mins

It is February 2007. Barry Franklin, the Finance Director of Banner plc, has written to you, asking for your advice on certain VAT matters. Banner plc has two wholly owned subsidiaries, Flag Ltd and Ensign Ltd. All three companies are fully taxable and are included in a group registration for VAT. Two months ago, in December 2006, Banner plc acquired 75% of the ordinary share capital of Union Ltd, a partly exempt company. Union Ltd generally recovers around 60% of its input tax. To date, no action has been taken to include Union Ltd in the group registration.

As Union Ltd is not wholly owned, other group companies will be required to pay for any losses surrendered to them as group relief.

Mr Franklin has specifically asked whether Union Ltd should be included in the group registration and, if so, what action he should take in this regard.

All four companies are UK resident with an established place of business in the UK.

Required

Write a letter in reply to Mr Franklin.

(10 marks)

32 Stewart Ltd

18 mins

Stewart Ltd, a partially exempt trader, has the following information for the year ended 31 March 2007:

Supplies

Quarter ended	Taxable (excl VAT) £	Exempt £	Total (excl VAT) £
30.6.06	403,920	52,072	455,992
30.9.06	*384,177	23,194	*407,371
31.12.06	467,159	18,791	485,950
31.3.07	520,321	37,439	557,760
	*1,775,577	131,496	*1,907,073

* This includes £25,000 in respect of a computer used in the business and subsequently sold. The computer was originally purchased for £45,000 in 2005.

Input tax

Quarter ended	Re taxable supplies £	Re exempt supplies £	Non-attributable £	Total £
30.6.06	44,404	3,120	14,719	62,243
30.9.06	39,098	2,775	12,613	54,486
31.12.06	24,926	1,374	10,412	36,712
31.3.07	36,020	1,876	11,919	49,815
	144,448	9,145	49,663	203,256

Required

Calculate the amount of recoverable input tax for each quarter and the annual adjustment, if any.

(10 marks)

33 Tax planning

45 mins

You are a partner in a firm of certified accountants with particular responsibility for tax planning.

Required

Draft an answer to each of the following queries which have been passed on to you by your fellow partners. You should assume that today's date is 1 April 2006.

(a)   Client A, who is single, is about to commence business as a management consultant on 1 May 2006. She was previously employed as a school headmistress for several years at a salary in excess of £40,000 pa. The business involves virtually no expenditure on capital assets. She expects to make operating losses in her first two years of trading, after which she expects the business slowly to become profitable. She will have no other taxable sources of income. For reasons of prestige she is proposing to trade through a specially formed company, A Ltd. However, she could delay forming the company for a short while and she asks what the best course of action would be from a tax viewpoint.

(b)   Client B currently manufactures fitted bedroom furniture for the general public from a small workshop. The market is highly competitive. He has a turnover of £55,000 pa which yields a current gross profit percentage of 40% and he incurs minimal overheads. He has been offered a contract to manufacture bookcases for a VAT registered trader at a price of £10,000 a year (exclusive of any VAT). B estimates that this project would involve a similar cost structure to his existing operations. B is concerned that, since he will become liable to register for VAT if he takes on the new contract, it may not be worthwhile to accept it.

He has asked for calculations showing the net annual gain to him from taking on the contract. He has also enquired whether it would be possible to avoid the requirement to register by setting up a new company, B Ltd, to carry out the new contract. (*Note.* You are required to consider VAT issues *only*.)

(c)   Client C is about to acquire shares in a publicly quoted company for £350,000 out of his own funds. The shares currently yield a dividend of £28,000 a year paid in September and March each year. The prospects for significant capital appreciation in the future are excellent. At the end of ten years C may decide to sell some or all of the shares. It has been suggested to C by a friend, D, that instead of buying the shares himself he should form a new investment company, C Ltd. C would subscribe for 350,000 £1 shares in C Ltd, which would then use the cash to buy the shares. D has told C that he could draw out director's remuneration of up to £10,000 a year and that C Ltd could deduct this against the dividend income and that the balance of £18,000 would only be liable to the lower corporation tax rate of 19%. D has also said that C could obtain tax relief by paying premiums into a personal pension scheme. C has asked whether the advice which he has received from D is correct.

(d)   Client D is setting up in business as an aromatherapist. She is considering structuring her business either as a sole trader or through a limited company. If she operates as a sole trader she will be starting in business on 6 April 2006, making up her first accounts to 5 April 2007 with an expected trading profit of £23,000. If she uses a limited company, it will start in business on 1 April 2006, make up accounts to 31 March 2007, with expected PCTCT of £23,000. Client D would extract all available profits by way of dividends on 31 March 2007.

Client D has investment income which exactly covers her personal allowance and starting band for 2006/07. Client D wants to know how much net spendable income she would have from the business in each of these cases.

(25 marks)

34 Hulse Finds Ltd

38 mins

Paul Hulse and his friend Nick Royle set up the company Hulse Finds Ltd with Paul and Nick holding 40% of the shares each. The remaining 20% of the company is held by five of their friends. Hulse Finds Ltd runs a shop in Didsbury selling unusual objects which are sourced from around the world. Paul and Nick work full time in the management of the company but their five friends are passive investors in the business.

Paul took out a bank loan of £150,000 secured on his apartment in central Manchester to purchase his shares whereas Nick used his redundancy payout from his old employer (a large bank).

Hulse Finds Ltd incurred significant start-up costs in its first 18 months of trade. Profits chargeable to corporation tax were £60,000 and £160,000 in the years to 31 March 2006 and 2007 respectively.

During June in the second year the company made a loan to Chris Newn (one of the investor friends) of £10,000.

Nick has identified a company Sweet Nothings Ltd (SNL) as a possible acquisition. The company sells French furniture and fixtures which it imports into the UK. After negotiations with the board of directors of SNL it has been agreed that Hulse Finds Ltd can purchase the trade and assets of SNL on 1 April 2008.

SNL has trading losses which are being carried forward of £50,000 and capital losses being carried forward of £25,000. Hulse Finds Ltd will set up a wholly owned subsidiary SN2 Ltd to acquire the trade and assets of SNL.

Predicted PCTCT for the two companies for year ended 31 March 2009 are:

Hulse Finds Ltd		£250,000
SN2 Ltd	Trading profits	40,000
	Capital gains	10,000

By 2010 Paul and Nick expect the business to have grown considerably and they expect to have taxable profits of £1 million in the year ended 31 March 2010. SN2 Ltd is expected to have taxable profits of £100,000 in the same period.

Paul and Nick have been looking to expand overseas in order to take advantage of new emerging markets. They intend to start a new business in Newland on 1 April 2010.

It is anticipated that the overseas business will make a trading loss of £60,000 in the year ended 31 March 2010, a profit of £80,000 in the year ended 31 March 2011 and a profit of £100,000 per year in future years.

The system of corporation tax in Newland is broadly the same as that in the UK, although loss relief is only available to companies resident in Newland. In addition, the rate of corporation tax is 45% regardless of the level of profits and there is no withholding tax when dividends are paid to overseas shareholders. There is no double tax treaty between the UK and Newland.

You are meeting with Paul and Chris next week.

Required

Make brief notes on the following for discussion at that meeting:

(a) Any relief for Pauls' investment in the company? **(2 marks)**

(b) What is the impact, if any, of the loan to Chris and would this be different if Chris was an employee of the company? **(4 marks)**

(c) What are the tax implications of the acquisition of SNL? In particular can you suggest any way to maximise the tax advantages for Hulse Finds Ltd. **(7 marks)**

(d) Discuss the tax implications of the proposed expansion overseas. **(8 marks)**

(Total = 21 marks)

35 Financial planning

27mins

The directors of M Ltd, a medium-sized unquoted company engaged in manufacturing, have decided to embark on a major expansion of the business.

The company has a significant amount of unissued share capital and, to finance the expansion, the directors have been considering issuing further shares. They have also considered raising loan capital, using as security identified pieces of valuable property owned by the company.

Required

Draft a report to the board, dated 19 May 2006, setting out the taxation implications for the company under each of the alternative methods of raising finance.

Your report should also identify any taxation implications for the providers of this finance.

(15 marks)

36 Mr and Mrs Faulds

18 mins

Mr and Mrs Faulds are considering investment in ISAs (individual savings accounts).

Required

Draft short notes in preparation for a meeting with them scheduled for October 2006 describing the main features of this type of investment. **(10 marks)**

37 Landscape Ltd

45 mins

Landscape Ltd is an unquoted trading company that operates a nationwide chain of retail shops.

(a) Landscape Ltd employed Peter Plain as a computer programmer until 31 December 2006. On that date he resigned from the company, and set up as a self-employed computer programmer. Peter has continued to work for Landscape Ltd, and during the period 1 January to 5 April 2007 has invoiced them for work done based on an hourly rate of pay. Peter works five days each week at the offices of Landscape Ltd, uses their computer equipment, and does not have any other clients. The computer function is an integral part of Landscape Ltd's business operations. Peter considers himself to be self-employed but Landscape Ltd's accountant is not sure if this is correct.

(b) On 15 March 2007 Landscape Ltd dismissed Simon Savannah, the manager of their shop in Manchester, and gave him a lump sum redundancy payment of £55,000. This amount include statutory redundancy pay of £2,400, holiday pay of £1,500, and £5,000 for agreeing not to work for a rival company. The balance of the payment was compensation for loss of office, and £10,000 of this was not paid until 31 May 2007.

(c) Trevor Tundra is one of the Landscape Ltd's shareholders, and is not a director or employee of the company. On 6 April 2006 Landscape Ltd provided Trevor with a new motor car that had a CO_2 emissions figure of 240g/km and that had an original list price of £14,000. No private petrol was provided. On 1 July 2006 Landscape Ltd made an interest free loan of £40,000 to Trevor. He repaid £25,000 of the loan on 31 August 2006, and the balance of the loan was written off on 31 March 2007.

(d) On 1 October 2006 Landscape Ltd opened a new shop in Cambridge, and assigned three employees from the London shop to work there on a temporary basis.

    (1) Ursula Upland is to work in Cambridge for a period of 18 months. Her ordinary commuting is a daily total of 90 miles, and her daily total from home to Cambridge to home again is 40 miles. She uses her private motor car for business mileage.

(2)   Violet Veld was initially due to work in Cambridge for a period of 30 months, but this was reduced to a period of 20 months on 1 January 2007. Violet walks to work whereas the cost of her train fare from home to Cambridge is £30 per day. This is paid by Landscape Ltd.

(3)   Wilma Wood is to work in Cambridge for a period of six months. Her ordinary commuting is a daily total of 30 miles, and her daily total from home to Cambridge is 150 miles. Wilma passes the London shop on her daily journey to Cambridge. She uses her private motor car for business mileage.

All three employees worked at Cambridge for 120 days during 2006/07. Landscape Ltd pays a mileage allowance of 36p per mile for business use.

(e)   Landscape Ltd is considering setting up a share incentive plan to reward its key employees. The company would like to know how many tax and NIC free shares it can give to each employee and how long the employees concerned must hold the shares for in order to obtain this advantage.

Required

Explain the income tax implications arising from the payments and benefits that have been made or provided by Landscape Ltd to Peter, Richard, Simon, Trevor, Ursula, Violet and Wilma. Your answer should be confined to the implications for 2006/07 and should assume that Landscape Ltd meets the definition of a close company.   **(25 marks)**

Marks for this question will be allocated on the basis of:

6 marks to (a)
4 marks to (b)
4 marks to (c)
7 marks to (d)
4 marks to (e)

Assume that the official rate of interest is 5%.

Approaching the answer

You should read through the requirement before working through and annotating the question as we have done so that you are aware of what things you are looking for.

Landscape Ltd is an unquoted trading company that operates a nationwide chain of retail shops.

Employment v self employment

(a)   Landscape Ltd employed Peter Plain as a computer programmer until 31 December 2006. On that

date he resigned from the company, and set up as a self-employed computer programmer. Peter

Suggest self-employed

Suggest employee

has continued to work for Landscape Ltd, and during the period 1 January to 5 April 2007 has

invoiced them for work done based on an hourly rate of pay. Peter works five days each week at

the offices of Landscape Ltd, uses their computer equipment, and does not have any other clients.

Suggest employee

Suggest employee

The computer function is an integral part of Landscape Ltd's business operations. Peter now

Suggest employee

considers himself to be self-employed but Landscape Ltd's accountant is not sure if this is the

correct interpretation.

(b) On 15 March 2007 Landscape Ltd dismissed Simon Savannah, the manager of their shop in

Manchester, and gave him a lump sum redundancy payment of £55,000. This amount includes

| £30,000 exempt if ex gratia |

statutory redundancy pay of £2,400, holiday pay of £1,500, and

| Exempt |

£5,000 for agreeing not to work for a rival company. The balance of the payment

| Taxable |

| Taxable |

was compensation for loss of office, and £10,000 of this was not paid until

31 May 2007.

| Taxed 07/08 |

(c) Trevor Tundra is one of the Landscape Ltd's shareholders, and is not a director or an employee of

| Participator taxed on distribution |

the company. On 6 April 2006 Landscape Ltd provided Trevor with

| Calculate benefit |

a new motor car that had a CO_2 emissions figure of 240g/km and that had an original list price of

£14,000. No private petrol was provided. On 1 July 2006 Landscape Ltd made an interest free loan

| Calculate benefit |

of £40,000 to Trevor. He repaid £25,000 of the loan on 31 August 2006, and the balance of the

loan was written off on 31 March 2007.

| Taxable |

(d) On 1 October 2006 Landscape Ltd opened a new shop in Cambridge, and assigned three

| Travel deductible |

employees from the London shop to work there on a temporary basis.

(1) Ursula Upland is to work in Cambridge for a period of 18 months. Her ordinary commuting

| Temporary |

is a daily total of 90 miles, and her daily total from home to Cambridge to home again is 40

| Authorised mileage rates |

miles. She uses her private motor car for business mileage.

(2) Violet Veld was initially due to work in Cambridge for a period of 30 months,

| Not temporary |

| Temporary |

but this was reduced to a period of 20 months on 1 January 2007. Violet walks to work

whereas the cost of her train fare from home to Cambridge is £30 per day. This is paid by

Landscape Ltd.

| Temporary |

(3) Wilma Wood is to work in Cambridge for a period of six months. Her ordinary commuting is

a daily total of 30 miles, and her daily total from home to Cambridge is 150 miles. Wilma

passes the London shop on her daily journey to Cambridge. She uses her private motor car

for business mileage.

| Authorised mileage rates |

All three employees worked at Cambridge for 120 days using 2006/07. Landscape Ltd pays a mileage allowance of 36 pence per mile for business use.

'Free' shares plus matching & partnership

(e)   Landscape Ltd is considering setting up a share incentive plan in order to reward its key employees. The company would like to know how many tax and NIC free shares it can give to each employee and how long the employees concerned must hold the shares for in order to obtain this advantage.

Required

Explain the income tax implications arising from the payments and benefits that have been made or provided by Landscape Ltd to Peter, Richard, Simon, Trevor, Ursula, Violet and Wilma. Your answer should be confined to the implications for 2006/07 and should assume that Landscape Ltd meets the definition of a close company.

Marks for this question will be allocated on the basis of:

6 marks to (a)
4 marks to (b)
4 marks to (c)
7 marks to (d)
4 marks to (e)

Assume that the official rate of interest is 5%.

Answer plan

This question is helpfully broken down into parts so you should start by working out how much time to spend on each individual part:

Part (a)   11 mins
Part (b)   7 mins
Part (c)   7 mins
Part (d)   13 mins
Part (e)   7 mins

You can then work through the question methodically. The answer is written so take care not to ramble. Lots of concise points will obtain more marks than one point written about at length.

38 Marilyn Corniche

45 mins

Marilyn Corniche was widowed on 20 May 2005. Under the terms of the will of her late husband Max she benefited absolutely from his share of the family home which they had held jointly as tenants in common and the bank balances. The mortgage on the family home was repaid out of the proceeds of a joint life first death life assurance policy. In addition Marilyn benefited from a life interest in a trust owning a holiday home in Cornwall and a portfolio of quoted investments, all of which had previously been owned by Max personally. The trust property passes equally to their twin sons, Douglas and Archie, aged 24, absolutely on Marilyn's death. The chattels passed to Max's brother Mark. Max, who had died suddenly, had made no lifetime gifts. The base cost, probate value and current market value of the items contained in Max's estate are as follows:

	Base cost plus indexation to 5/4/98	Probate value May 2005	Market value February 2007
	£	£	£
Family home (½ share)	61,500	90,000	110,000
Holiday home	42,000	63,000	73,000
Quoted investments			
Spiro plc 10,000 ordinary shares	50,000		
quoted at		685-677	635-647
with bargains marked at		690, 670, 675	630, 642, 641
Unit trusts	50,000	60,300	81,000
Unit trusts contained in PEPs and ISAs	40,000	48,800	67,600
Bank deposits contained in ISAs	9,000	11,000	11,300
Bank deposit account	20,000	20,000	20,000
Chattels			
Chirico painting – Creation	4,000	5,000	7,000
Rene writing desk	8,000	7,000	4,000
Beckman's Diary – first edition	3,500	3,000	4,500

Marilyn also has £33,400 on deposit at Berkley's Bank, unit trust units invested in PEPs and stocks and shares ISAs valued at £72,000 and a cash ISA of £10,600.

Marilyn has sufficient income to live on from her own resources.

Marilyn has just been diagnosed as having terminal cancer. The prognosis is that she has less than two years to live. She is anxious to minimise the impact of inheritance tax on her estate.

Mark is a higher rate taxpayer and has already made capital gains in the 2006/07 year of £10,000. No taper relief is due in respect of these gains.

Required

(a) Calculate the inheritance tax liability that arose on Max's estate as a result of his death on 20 May 2005 and that which would arise on Marilyn's estate if she were to die today (ie February 2007). Use the nil rate band for 2006/07 for both calculations. **(8 marks)**

(b) (i) Advise on action(s) that Marilyn (and her sons) can now take to reduce the liability in (a), identifying any conditions that need to be satisfied for the plan to be effective. **(9 marks)**

    (ii) Calculate the tax saving which would result if the advice in part (b)(i) were followed.

(8 marks)

(Total = 25 marks)

Approaching the answer

You should read through the requirement before working through and annotating the question as we have done so that you are aware of what things you are looking for.

Marilyn Corniche was widowed on 20 May 2005. Under the terms of the will of her

Spouse exemption → late husband Max she benefited absolutely from his share of the family home which they had held jointly as

tenants in common and the bank balances. The mortgage on the family home was repaid out of the proceeds of

a joint life first death life assurance policy. In addition Marilyn benefited from a life interest in a trust owning a ← **Initial interest in will trust**

holiday home in Cornwall and a portfolio of quoted investments, all of which had previously been owned by Max

personally. The trust property passes equally to their twin sons, Douglas and Archie, aged 24, absolutely on

Taxable? → Marilyn's death. The chattels passed to Max's brother Mark. Max, who had died suddenly, had made

NLY death estate → no lifetime gifts. The base cost, probate value and current market value of the items contained in Max's estate

are as follows:

	Base cost plus indexation to 5/4/98	Probate value May 2005	Market value February 2007
	£	£	£
Family home (½ share)	61,500	90,000	110,000
Holiday home	42,000	63,000	73,000
Quoted investments			
Spiro plc 10,000 ordinary shares	50,000		
quoted at		685-677	635-647
with bargains marked at		690, 670, 675	630, 642, 641
Unit trusts	50,000	60,300	81,000
Unit trusts contained in PEPs and ISAs	40,000	48,800	67,600
Bank deposits contained in ISAs	9,000	11,000	11,300
Bank deposit account	20,000	20,000	20,000
Chirico painting – Creation	4,000	5,000	7,000
Rene writing desk	8,000	7,000	4,000
Beckman's Diary – first edition	3,500	3,000	4,500

Lowest of
(i) ¼ up
(ii) Average highest and lowest marked bargain

Marilyn also has £33,400 on deposit at Berkley's Bank, unit trust with units invested in PEPs and stocks and

shares ISAs valued at £72,000 and a cash ISA of £10,600. → **All subject to IHT**

Marilyn has sufficient income to live on from her own resources. — **Deed of variation**

Marilyn has just been diagnosed as having terminal cancer. The prognosis is that she has less than two

years to live. She is anxious to minimise the impact of inheritance tax on her estate.

Mark is a higher rate taxpayer and has already made capital gains in the 2006/07 year of £10,000. No taper

relief is due in respect of these gains.

Required

(a) Calculate the inheritance tax liability that arose on Max's estate as a result of his death on 20 May 2005 and that which would arise on Marilyn's estate if she were to die today (ie February 2007). Use the nil rate band for 2006/07 for both calculations. **(8 marks)**

(b) (i) Advise on action(s) that Marilyn (and her sons) can now take to reduce the liability in (a), identifying any conditions that need to be satisfied for the plan to be effective. **(9 marks)**

   (ii) Calculate the tax saving which would result if the advice in part (b)(i) were followed. **(8 marks)**

Answer plan

(a) Death of Max: Spouse exemption, residue covered by nil band

   Death of Marilyn: Calculate death estate
                       Value Spiro plc shares

(b) Deed of variation: Conditions, saving

Exam answer bank

1 The Wrights

Tutorial note. By this stage you should be proficient at setting up an income tax computation in three columns, grossing up income etc. This question also tests some new areas at Paper P6 such as age allowance, joint income and tax reducers.

(a) (i) *Eric*

	Non-savings £	Savings (excl. dividends) £	Dividends £	Total £
Taxable trade profits	21,060			
BI £1,600 × 100/80		2,000		
Less eligible interest (charge)	(1,000)			
STI	20,060	2,000	Nil	22,060
Less: PA (W1)	(6,300)			(6,300)
Taxable income	13,760	2,000	Nil	15,760

Tax

	£
£2,150 × 10%	215
£11,610 × 22%	2,554
£2,000 × 20%	400
	3,169
Less: tax reducer	
VCT £10,000 × 30%	(3,000)
	169
Less tax deducted at source	(400)
Tax repayable	(231)

(ii) *Melanie*

	Non-savings £	Savings (excl. dividends) £	Dividends £	Total £
Earnings	40,000			
Dividends £4,500 × 100/90			5,000	
STI	40,000	Nil	5,000	45,000
Less PA	(5,035)			(5,035)
Taxable income	34,965	Nil	5,000	39,965

Tax

	£
£2,150 × 10%	215
£31,150 × 22%	6,853
£1,665 × 40%	666
£5,000 × 32½ %	1,625
	9,359
Less: PAYE	(8,429)
dividend tax credit	(500)
Tax due	430

Note. Interest on the National Savings & Investments Certificate is exempt from income tax.

(b) The total income will be split 50:50 between Eric and Melanie if no declaration of underlying interests is made.

The tax liability would be:

	£
Eric £5,000 × 22%	1,100
Add tax on reduction in age allowance (W2)	278
Melanie £5,000 × 40%	2,000
Total extra tax	3,378

It would be better for the cottage to be bought by Eric as the additional income would fall within his basic rate band. If Melanie wished to have some interest in the cottage she could be given a notional 5% (say) as this would only have a marginal tax cost. A declaration for this treatment would need to be made.

Workings

1 Age allowance (aged 73 in January 2007)

	£
STI as above	22,060
Reduction £(22,060 – 20,100) × 0.5	980
PA £(7,280 – 980)	6,300

2

	£	
STI including rent	27,060	
Reduction £(27,060 – 20,100) × 0.5	3,480	
PA £(7,280 – 2,245)	5,035	(minimum)

So there is a loss of personal allowance of £6,300 - £5,035 = £1,265 × 22% = £278.

(c) *EIS investment*

Assuming the shares are subscribed for the initial investment will qualify for EIS relief at the rate of 20%. In this case the interest paid on the bank loan will not qualify for tax relief. Her outlay over five years will be £20,000 – £(20,000 × 20%) + £(20,000 × 8% × 5) = £24,000.

Purchase of 10% stake

In this case the bank interest paid will be allowed as a charge on income, but the dividends received will be liable to higher rate tax. Her outlay will be £20,000 + £(20,000 × 8% × 5) × (100 – 40)% – £(1,000 + 1,100 + 1,200 + 1,300 + 1,400) × (100 - 32.5)/90 = £20,300.

2 Mr Lee

> **Tutorial note.** Although you are asked to reply by e-mail, you must remember that you are writing to a client and present a structured reply.

To: Mr Lee@red.co.uk
From: An Advisor@taxadvice.co.uk
Date: [   ]
Re: Pension advice

Thank you for your e-mail about pension advice. My answers to your questions are as follows:

(a)   You do not have to join your new employer's pension scheme. Instead you could start a pension with a financial institution such as a bank or insurance company. However, your employer may not want to contribute to private pension arrangements so you need to bear this in mind when considering whether or not to join your employer's scheme.

A money purchase scheme is one where the value of your pension benefits depends on the value of the investments in the pension scheme at the date that you set aside ('vest') funds to produce those benefits. This is distinct from a defined benefits scheme where the benefits are defined from the outset. If you decide to use private pension arrangements, these are also likely to be money purchase arrangements.

(b)   You can contribute an amount up to 100% of your UK earnings into the pension scheme and obtain tax-relief on those contributions. You can also make any amount of further contributions, for example out of capital, but these will not obtain initial tax relief. However, since there is no income tax or capital gains tax payable by a pension fund, it may still be beneficial for such extra contributions to be made into this tax-exempt fund.

In addition, your employer can make any amount of contributions provided that the tax authorities are happy that such contributions are not excessive and so not for the purposes of the employer's trade.

However, there are two limits that you need to be aware of. First, there is an annual allowance which limits the inputs that can be paid into the pension fund. For 2006/07, this limit is £215,000. It will rise in later years, so that, for example, in 2010/11 it will be £255,000. The amounts that you contribute *and* obtain tax relief on, plus any contributions made by your employer, will count towards the annual allowance. If those contributions exceed the annual allowance, there will be a tax charge at 40% on the excess which is payable by you. This might be relevant in later years when your earnings may be above the annual allowance limit.

The second limit is the lifetime allowance limit. This is the maximum value of the pension fund that you are allowed to build up to provide pension benefits without incurring adverse tax consequences. The lifetime allowance is £1,500,000 in 2006/07, rising to £1,800,000 in 2010/11. This limit is tested against the value of your pension fund when you vest pension benefits. If your fund exceeds the lifetime allowance at that time, there will be a tax charge of 55% on funds vested to provide a lump sum and 25% on funds vested to provide a pension income. Although there are no adverse tax consequences at other times if your pension fund exceeds the lifetime allowance, it would be wise to keep an eye on how your fund is growing so that you can adjust your contributions accordingly so as to keep within the lifetime allowance.

(c)   There are two methods of tax relief for your pension contributions that might be used if you join your employer's pension scheme.

The more usual method for occupational pension schemes is called net pay arrangements. Here your employer deducts your pension contributions gross from your pay before applying income tax. This means that tax relief is given automatically at your highest rate of tax and no adjustment is needed in your tax return. As an example, if you contribute £1,000 to your pension and that amount of income would have been taxed at 40%, your pay will be reduced by £1,000 but the amount of tax that would be deducted from your pay would be reduced by £400, so that the net amount of the contribution payable by you would be £600.

The second method can only be used if your employer applies it to all of the members of the pension scheme and is called relief at source. Here an amount will be deducted from your pay which is treated as being net of basic rate tax at 22%. As you are a higher rate tax payer, you will then need to claim higher rate tax relief of 18% through your tax return. Again using a gross contribution of £1,000, your employer would withhold £780 from your pay and then you would claim an additional £180 through your tax return, again leaving a net contribution of £600.

(d)   There are two types of benefit that you can receive from your pension fund. The earliest age that you will be able to receive pension benefits is the age of 55 and you must vest your pension benefits at the latest by the age of 75. You should be able to vest pension benefits at different times between the ages of 55 and 75 depending on your financial circumstances. For example, you might decide to vest half of your pension benefits at the age of 55 and leave the remainder of the fund until a later age which can be any age up to 75.

When you vest your pension fund, you will be able to take a tax-free lump sum of up to 25% of the value of the vested funds. The remainder must be used to provide a pension income. This will be taxable in the same way as earnings. Between the ages of 55 and 75 you may decide to take an unsecured pension income where you draw down income produced by the fund, but once you reach the age of 75 you must have a secured income, usually produced by the purchase of an annuity which will give you a guaranteed income.

If you die before the age of 75, death benefits in the form of a lump sum and/or pension income may be payable to your dependants. If you die aged 75 or over, only pension income will be payable to your dependants. 'Dependants' includes a spouse/civil partner, children up to the age of 23 and certain other individuals who may be financially dependant on you or mutually financially dependant with you.

Obviously I can only outline the basics of pension provision in this e-mail as this is very complex area, so I suggest that we meet once you have decided how to proceed.

3 Hamburg

> **Tutorial note.** It is important to realise that for individuals income from a property business is computed for tax years on an accruals basis. Don't forget to look out for rent a room relief in questions. You should have spotted the possibility of a pre-owned assets charge in part (c)

(a)

	Non-savings £	Savings (excl. dividends) £	Dividends £	Total £
Income from UK property business (W1)	11,020			
Trust income £6,600 × 100/60	11,000			
Interest – EASA		90		
– investment a/c		460		
– gilt interest (W2)		640		
Accrued income on sale		150		
Dividends £15,750 × 100/90			17,500	
STI	22,020	1,340	17,500	40,860
Less: PA	(5,035)			(5,035)
Taxable income	16,985	1,340	17,500	35,825

Tax

	£
£2,150 × 10%	215
£14,835 × 22%	3,264
£1,340 × 20%	268
£14,975 × 10%	1,497
£2,525 × 32½ %	821
	6,065
Less: tax deducted on trust income	(4,400)
tax deducted on dividends	(1,750)
Tax repayable	(85)

Workings

1

	£	£
Rent		
House 1: first letting £600 × 6		3,600
House 1: second letting £6,000 × 3/12		1,500
House 2 £8,000 × 8/12		5,333
House 3 £7,800 × 8/12		5,200
		15,633
Expenses		
House 1: new roof, disallowable because capital	0	
House 1: loft insulation	1,200	
House 1: water rates	320	
House 1: buildings insurance £480 × 10/12	400	
House 2: water rates	240	
House 2: furniture £(5,333 – 240) × 10%	509	
House 3: redecoration	1,000	
House 3: water rates	360	
House 3: buildings insurance £440 × 9/12	330	
House 3: contents insurance £180 × 8/12	120	
House 3: furniture £(5,200 – 360) × 10%	484	
		(4,963)
UK property business income from 3 houses		10,670

Note. The loft insulation is a capital expense but it is specifically allowable up to £1,500.

Hamburg should claim rent a room relief in respect of the letting of the furnished room in his main residence, since this is more beneficial than the normal basis of assessment (£4,600 – £875 = £3,725). This means that Hamburg will be taxed on additional income of £350 (£4,600 – £4,250) from the UK property business.

Total property income is £11,020 (10,670 + 350)

2

	£
Interest June 2006 £20,000 × 6% × 6/12	600
Less: due to purchaser	(35)
	565
Interest December 2006 £2,500 × 6% × 6/12	75
	640

(b) If the cottages are to be treated as furnished holiday lettings, the first condition is that the lettings must be made on a **commercial basis with a view to the realisation of profit**.

Each property must be **available for letting** to the public for not less than 140 days in a tax year. Between them, the properties **must be let for at least 70 days each** in the 140 day period. For example, if the first cottage is let for 90 days in the year, the second cottage must be let for at least 50 days in the year to give an average of 70 days. If one of the cottages satisfies the 70 day test but the aggregation of the other cottage would pull the average down to below 70 days, the landlord can choose to treat the cottage which satisfies the 70 days test as furnished holiday accommodation.

In addition, **each property must not normally be in longer term occupation (ie for more than 31 days)** for more than 155 days in the year.

If the cottages satisfies these conditions, **the income from the lettings is taxed as income from a UK property business but as if the landlord was carrying on a trade** (except for the basis period rules). **This means that any losses are treated as trading losses instead of losses from the property business, capital allowance are available on furniture (instead of either the renewals basis or the 10% wear and tear allowance) and the income qualifies as relevant earnings for pension contribution purposes.**

(c) There are two income tax consequences resulting from Hamburg's proposal.

If Hamburg raises a bank loan the interest payable will be an allowable expense of the property letting, and will therefore save tax at Hamburg's marginal tax rate. Assuming Hamburg's income continues at a comparable level the rate of tax saving will be 44.5% since tax is saved at the basic rate (22%) on the property income covered by the interest and at 22.5% (32.5% - 10%) on gross dividends no longer falling in the higher rate band.

If Hamburg raises funds by selling a one half share in his house to his son but continues to live there, he will fall within the pre-owned assets rules. Unless he pays a full rental for his occupation out of after tax income he will be liable to an income tax charge on the value of the interest $\times$ 5% unless this is below the de minimis limit of £5,000. The charge will be at his marginal rate, ie effectively at 44.5% as shown above.

4 Taker

> **Tutorial note.** The CO_2 emissions of the car are rounded down to 175g/km. The baseline figure for CO_2 emissions given in the tax rates and allowances tables is 140g/km at which the % if 15%. The % increases by 1% for each 5g/km that this figure is exceeded, ie here to 22%.
>
> The telephone line rental and the golf club subscription do not qualify for a deduction because they are not paid wholly, exclusively and necessarily for employment purposes.
>
> The exemption for the first £55 per week for childcare is only available for the weeks in which the childminder looks after Taker's son.
>
> Part (b) requires you to compare the after tax effects of different options based on your knowledge of the benefits rules.

(a)

	£	£
Salary		35,000
Car £20,000 × 22%		4,400
Fuel £14,400 × 22% (partial contribution gives no reduction)		3,168
Mobile telephone – exempt		0
Use of video camera £600 × 20%		120
Loan: does not exceed £5,000		0
Childminder (4,000 – [48 × £55])		1,360
		44,048
Less: professional subscriptions	180	
cost of business telephone calls	45	
		(225)
Earnings		43,823

(b) *Company car*

If Taker chooses the company car he will be charged 40% income tax on a car benefit of £4,000, ie a cost of £1,600.

If Taker accepts the higher salary the position will be:

	£
Extra salary	3,000
Less tax @ 40%	(1,200)
	1,800
Add mileage allowance 6,000 × 35p	2,100
Add tax relief on expenses claim 6,000 × (40p – 35p) × 40%	120
Net additional income from company	4,020
Less running costs (excluding private use fuel) (2,200 – 500)	(1,700)
Less depreciation (15,000 – 5,000) × 1/3	(3,333)
Less extra interest paid £1,800 × 1/3	(600)
Net cost	(1,613)

Taking the additional salary would only cost Taker an extra £13, so the decision should be made on non-cash flow grounds.

Note. The cost of private use fuel is excluded from running costs as it would also be a cost of accepting the company car.

Company flat

If Taker moves to rented accommodation for three years the position is as follows:

	£
Relocation cost paid	12,000
Less tax on excess (12,000 – 8,000) @ 40%	(1,600)
	10,400
Net rent on old house £8,000 × 3 × (100 – 40)%	14,400
Less rent paid	(18,000)
Net inflow (before actual relocation costs)	6,800

If Taker moves to the company flat for three years the position is as follows:

	£
Relocation cost paid (not taxable)	3,000
Less tax on benefit of company flat £(2,500 + (120,000 – 75,000) × 5%) × 3 × 40%	(5,700)
	(2,700)
Net rent on old house £(8,000 + 2,000) × 3 × (100 – 40)%	18,000
Net inflow (before actual relocation costs)	15,300

If Taker chooses to rent accommodation he will be £(15,300 – 6,800) = £8,500 worse off over three years and will also have to pay an extra £2,000 in relocation costs. The relative merits of the different accommodation must also be taken into account.

627

5 National insurance contributions

> **Tutorial note**. Directors have an annual earnings period whereas the earnings period for other employees is normally equal to the period for which earnings are paid.
>
> Part (b) illustrates how different payments and benefits can have different NIC implications.

(a)   *Albert*

Total earnings are £35,000 £(30,000 + 5,000)

	£
Primary contributions	
Total earnings exceed UEL	
£(33,540 – 5,035) = £28,505 × 11% (main)	3,136
£(35,000 – 33,540) = £1,460 × 1% (additional)	15
Total primary contributions	3,151
Secondary contributions	
£(35,000 – 5,035) = £29,965 × 12.8%	3,836
Class 1A contributions	
£(4,500 + 750) = £5,250 × 12.8%	672

Barney

	£
Earnings threshold £5,035 ÷ 12 = £420	
Upper earnings limit £33,540 ÷ 12 = £2,795	
Primary contributions	
11 months	
£(2,000 – 420) = £1,580 × 11% × 11 (main only)	1,912
1 month (January)	
£(2,795 – 420) = £2,375 × 11% (main)	261
£(5,000 – 2,795) = £2,205 × 1% (additional)	22
Total primary contributions	2,195
Secondary contributions	
11 months	
£(2,000 – 420) = £1,580 × 12.8% × 11	2,225
1 month (January)	
£(5,000 – 420) = £4,580 × 12.8%	586
Total secondary contributions	2,811

Chloe

	£
Primary contributions	
£(120 – 97) = £23 × 11% × 52	£132
Secondary contributions	
£(120 – 97) = £23 × 12.8% × 52	£153

(b)   (i)   A week on a health farm. This is a payment in kind and Poster plc will be liable to Class 1A NICs on each place, at a cost of £2,000 × 12.8% = £256. There will be no NICs for the employee.

(ii)   A week's sailing on a yacht chartered by the employee. This is the payment of the employee's personal liability and so is liable to Class 1 NICs. Each employee's share of the bill is £(5,000 + 1,000)/3 = £2,000 and Class 1 NICs for each employee will be £2,000 × 11% = £220, or £2,000 × 1% = £20 if the upper earnings limit is exceeded. Poster plc will be liable to secondary Class 1 NICs, at a cost of £2,000 × 12.8% = £256 per employee.

(iii) A voucher which may be exchanged for a holiday at a high street travel agent. Vouchers are liable to Class 1 NICs even if they cannot be exchanged for cash. The cost to the employee will be £2,000 × 11% = £220, or £2,000 × 1% = £20 if the upper earnings limit is exceeded. Poster plc will be liable to secondary Class 1 NICs, at a cost of £2,000 × 12.8% = £256 per employee.

(iv) Payment of £1,500 cash. This is liable to primary Class 1 NICs of £1,500 × 11% = £165 per employee, or £1,500 × 1% = £15 if the upper earnings limit is exceeded   Poster plc will be liable to secondary Class 1 NICs, at a cost of £1,500 × 12.8% = £192 per employee.

6 Colin Jessop

Tutorial note. As Derek's option was granted under an unapproved scheme before September 2003, a charge would have arisen at the date of the grant as the option could be exercised more than ten years after the grant.

Our address

Your address

Date

Dear Colin,

Share option schemes

Thank you for your letter, I shall reply to your queries in turn.

Bonus scheme

There is indeed an approved scheme, the Share Incentive Plan (SIP) which can be used to reward employees with shares in a tax-efficient way. I set out the main features of the scheme below.

The company establishes a UK trust which acquires shares and appropriates them to employees in accordance with the plan. These shares are free of charge ('free shares'). The value of these free shares cannot exceed £3,000 to any employee in any tax year (although the award can be less). These free shares must stay in the trust for a period of five years if the award is to be completely free of income tax in the hands of the employee. If the employee removes the shares between three and five years after appropriation, there is an income tax charge on the value of the shares at award (or at withdrawal if lower). If the employee removes the shares from the trust before three years have elapsed, there will be an income tax charge on the value of the shares at the date of withdrawal.

The 'free shares' could replace your existing cash bonus scheme. The SIP provisions provide further incentives to your employees to invest in the company as outlined below.

'Partnership shares'

Employees who are awarded free shares can purchase up to £1,500 worth of 'partnership shares' from their pre-tax salary. Thus, for example, an employee can authorise Envirotech plc to deduct up to £125 per month from gross salary. This money is passed to the trustees who then acquire shares on behalf of the employee.

The income tax rules on the withdrawal of partnership shares from the trust are the same as the rules for the free shares.

'Matching shares'

Where an employee buys partnership shares, the company can award free 'matching shares'. The ratio of matching shares to partnership shares must be specified and cannot exceed 1:2 (ie the maximum value of 'matching shares' award to an employee in any tax year will not exceed £3,000).

The income tax rules on withdrawal of these shares from the trust are the same as for free and partnership shares.

'Dividend shares'

Employees can opt to reinvest the dividends on their SIP shares to acquire further shares, up to a maximum of £1,500 per annum. Any such dividends reinvested are not treated as taxable income for the participant.

Dividend shares must be held within the plan for three years to be exempt from tax. Dividend shares withdrawn within this period are treated as giving rise to a taxable dividend at the withdrawal date. The taxable dividend is equal to the cash dividend originally applied by the trustees to acquire shares on the participants behalf.

General Conditions

All employees (full or part-time) must be invited to participate in the scheme. Employees with less than 18 months service can be excluded. Employees with a 'material interest' in the company (25% or more of the ordinary share capital) must be excluded.

The shares must be ordinary shares of a class listed or a recognised stock exchange, fully paid up and not redeemable.

An employee can only participate in one SIP in any given tax year.

Derek Forrest

Executive share options

As these options were granted under an 'unapproved' scheme, Derek will have an income tax charge at the date he exercised his options. You will see from the Appendix attached that his income tax liability will be £84,000. You will note that Derek is given relief for the charge made on him when the option was granted. I have assumed that Derek is a 40% taxpayer. Please let me know if this is incorrect.

Assuming Derek sells his shares in the very near future, he will have no CGT to pay as his allowable cost is effectively equal to the market value of the shares at the date of exercise. If he retains the shares, any growth will be subject to CGT.

Retirement bonus

It is likely that the £30,000 'thank you' bonus will be taxable in full and will not be eligible for the exemption given to ex-gratia payments.

HMRC are likely to argue that the payment is made in return for services thereby making the bonus taxable under normal principles. It is therefore important that any documentation stresses that the payment is ex-gratia.

Failing this, HMRC could contend that as a payment is made to an employee 'at or near the age of retirement' the payment should be taxable in full in the same way as a benefit under a non-registered pension scheme.

I hope this deals with your queries but do please let me know if I can be of further help.

Yours sincerely

Brian Andrews.

Appendix

Derek Forrest

Calculation of tax on exercise of share options:

	£
Charge on grant in 1999	
$100{,}000 \times £(1.50 - 0.50)$	100,000
Tax on exercise	
$100{,}000 \times £(3.60 - 0.50)$	310,000
Less charged on grant	(100,000)
Amount liable	210,000
Income tax @ 40%	84,000

7 Helen Strube

> **Tutorial note.** This question is a very basic revision of material although the change of accounting date rules will have been new if you completed level 2.3. You **must** be fully competent with these basic computations at Paper P6.

(a)

	£
2001/02 (1.7.01 to 5.4.02)	
9/12 × £36,000	27,000
2002/03 (1.7.01 to 30.6.02)	36,000
2003/04 (1.7.02 to 30.6.03)	48,000

Overlap profits of £27,000 arise as a result of the trade profits accruing in the nine months to 5.4.02 being taxed in both 2001/02 and in 2002/03.

There is a change of accounting date which results in one long period of account ending during 2004/05. As a result the basis period is the fifteen months to 30 September 2004 and three months' worth of the overlap profits can be relieved:

2004/05	£
Basis period (1.7.03 – 30.9.04)	60,000
Less overlap profits 27,000 × 3/9	(9,000)
	51,000

2005/06 (year to 30.9.05)	£30,000
2006/07 (1.10.05 to 31.12.06)	
Year to 30.9.06	24,000
Three months to 31.12.06	10,000
Less overlap profits (27,000 – 9,000)	(18,000)
	16,000

The trade ceases during 2006/07 so the basis period for this year runs from the end of the last basis period to the date of cessation. Overlap profits which were not relieved on the change of accounting date are relieved against this final year's taxable profits.

(b)   Gemma will have overlap profits from the period 1 May 1999 – 5 April 2000 of 11 × £100 = £1,100. These will be relieved on cessation.

If Gemma sells her business on 31 March 2007 the basis period for 2006/07 will be 1 May 2005 – 31 March 2007, and her taxable profits will be 23 × £2,000 – £1,100 = £44,900. This will all be taxed in 2006/07, so Gemma will pay higher rate tax on £(44,900 – 33,300 – 5,035) = £6,565. The top £(44,900 – 33,540) = £11,360 of profits will only be liable to Class 4 NICs at the additional 1% rate.

If Gemma sells her business on 30 April 2007 the basis period for 2006/07 will be 1 May 2005 – 30 April 2006, and her taxable profits will be 12 × £2,000 = £24,000. Her basis period for 2007/08 will be 1 May 2006 – 30 April 2007, and her taxable profits will be 12 × £2,000 – £1,100 = £22,900. Gemma will not be liable to higher rate tax in 2006/07 but will be liable to higher rate tax in 2007/08 on £(25,000 + 22,900 – 33,300 – 5,035) = £9,565. The first £5,035 of profits in 2007/08 will not be liable to Class 4 NICs.

Thus if a 31 March 2007 date is selected, £(9,565 – 6,565) × (40 – 22)% = £540 tax will be saved, and £(11,360 × (8 – 1)% – 5,035 × 8%) = £392 of Class 4 NICs will be saved, but one month's less profits (£2,000) will be earned.

There may be other considerations to take into account, such as sale proceeds and capital gains tax.

(c) *Class 2 contributions (for both)*

		£
52 × £2.10		109

Class 4 contributions

(i)	£(30,000 – 5,035) = £24,965 × 8% (main only)	1,997
(ii)	£(33,540 – 5,035) = £28,505 × 8% (main)	2,280
	£(35,000 – 33,540) = £1,460 × 1% (additional)	15
	Total Class 4 contributions	2,295

8 Vivace

> **Tutorial note.** It is important that you become fully competent at spotting when and at what rate FYAs are available.

(a)

		FYA £	Pool £	Expensive car (60%) £		Allowances £
WDV b/f			8,000			
Y/e 31.12.04						
14.9.04	Machinery sold		(700)			
			7,300			
16.9.04	Addition – car		4,000			
			11,300			
	WDA 25%		(2,825)			2,825
1.12.04	Machinery	9,232				
	FYA @ 50%	(4,616)				4,616
			4,616			
	WDV c/f		13,091			
	Total allowances					7,441
Y/e 31.12.05						
5.7.05	Mercedes			22,000		
21.3.05	Plant sold					
	(restricted to cost)		(2,000)			
22.3.05	Car sold		(3,200)			
			7,891			
	WDA 25%/restricted		(1,973)	(3,000)	× 60%	3,773
	WDV c/f		5,918	19,000		
	Total allowances					
P/e 30.9.06						
5.2.06	Car (no FYA)		3,000			
30.6.06	Plant sold		(2,602)			
15.6.06	Mercedes sold			(4,000)		
	Balancing allowance			15,000	× 60%	9,000
15.6.06	Volvo			18,000		
4.2.06	Machine on HP		4,000			
30.6.06	Plant		3,000			
			13,316			
30.9.06	Market value		(10,000)	(16,000)		
	Balancing allowance		3,316	2,000	× 60%	4,516
	Total allowances					13,516

Notes

(1) FYA of 50% is available for small enterprises from 6.4.04 until 5.4.05 for unincorporated businesses and from 6.4.06 until 5.4.07.

(2) No WDA or FYA are available in the period of cessation.

Vivace's capital allowances for the period of cessation total £13,516, of which £4,516 arise on cessation as the plant and machinery and the Volvo are deemed to have been sold for their then market value.

As Vivace and his son are connected persons they could make a joint election for the plant and machinery and car to be treated as transferred at tax written down value, so that there was no balancing allowance/charge on cessation. The result of this election would be that Vivace's capital allowances for the period of cessation were £9,000 (on the sale of the Mercedes), and that the expenditure for Vivaces son on plant and machinery and the Volvo was £13,316 and £18,000 respectively, compared to £10,000 and £16,000 if no election is made.

Vivace's son is a higher rate taxpayer, so he will obtain 40% tax relief on this expenditure compared to Vivace's 22%. Against this must be weighed the fact that tax relief will be delayed, as WDA are given on the reducing balance basis. Also, the amount of private use of the Volvo by Vivace's son will affect the amount of allowances which will be relieved.

(b) (i) Eligible expenditure (excluding land but includes offices of 22.5% ie less than 25%) £200,000

Simon	£
Cost 1.8.00	200,000
Y/e 31.7.01 WDA 4%	(8,000)
Y/e 31.7.02 WDA 4%	(8,000)
Y/e 31.7.03 WDA 4%	(8,000)
	176,000
Y/e 31.7.04 WDA 4% (notional)	(8,000)
Y/e 31.7.05 WDA 4% (notional)	(8,000)
	160,000
Y/e 31.7.06 WDA 4%	(8,000)
Residue before sale	152,000
Y/e 31.7.07 year of sale – balancing charge (real not notional allowances)	
4 × £8,000	32,000
Alicia	
Residue before sale	152,000
Add: balancing charge	32,000
Residue after sale	184,000
Tax life ends on 1.8.00 + 25 years = 31.7.2025	
Unexpired life 18 years 8 months = 18.6667	
Y/e 31.12.06 £184,000/18.667	9,857
Next 17 years	167,569
Y/e 31.12.24	6,574
	184,000

(ii) In the computation above the factory was sold for more than cost, so the allowances actually given (but not the notional allowances) were clawed back. The residue after sale then comprises the residue before sale plus the balancing charge, which equates to the original cost less the notional allowances given.

If the factory is sold for £120,000 (excluding land) it is sold for less than cost. In this case the allowances actually given are compared to the adjusted net cost, and any excess or shortfall is taxed as a balancing charge, or relieved as a balancing allowance. The adjusted net cost is (capital expenditure – sale proceeds) × period of industrial use/period of total use, and thus reflects the fall in value attributable to the period of industrial use. The residue after sale is, as normal, the residue before sale +/– the balancing charge/allowance, but it cannot exceed the purchase price.

9 Arrol

> **Tutorial note.** The disadvantage of a s 380 claim can be that it wastes the personal allowance. Note how restricting the capital allowances claimed can avoid the wastage of personal allowances.

(a) INCOME TAX COMPUTATION

	Non-savings £	Savings £	Total £
Earnings: salary	12,771		
car benefit £20,271 × 34% (W1)	6,892		
fuel benefit £14,400 × 34%	4,896		
Bank interest £235 × 100/80		294	
Building society interest £3,005 × 100/80		3,756	
	24,559	4,050	28,609
Less s 380 loss relief (W2)	(24,559)	(4,050)	(28,609)
STI	0	0	0
Income tax liability: nil			

Workings

1 **Car and fuel benefit**

237 g/km is rounded down to 235 g/km. Excess over base figure 235 – 140 = 95 g/km.

95 ÷ 5 = 19. Taxable % = 15 + 19 = 34%.

Partial contributions towards the cost of petrol do not reduce the fuel benefit.

2 **The loss available for relief**

			£
Loss			13,384
Capital allowances:	FYA	£12,800 × 50%	6,400
	FYA	£46,720 × 50%	23,360
			43,144
Loss in 2006/07: £43,144 × 11/12 (1.5.06 – 5.4.07)			£39,549

(b) INCOME TAX COMPUTATION FOR WIFE

	Non-savings £	Savings £	Total £
Earnings	2,800		
Building society interest £5,012 × 100/80		6,265	
NS&I interest		1,742	
STI	2,800	8,007	10,807
Less personal allowance	(2,800)	(2,235)	(5,035)
Taxable income	0	5,772	5,772

		£	£
Income tax			
Starting rate band		2,150 × 10%	215
Basic rate band: savings income		3,622 × 20%	724
		5,772	939

(c) *The loss remaining unrelieved*

	£
Loss available for relief	39,549
Less used	(28,609)
Unrelieved balance	10,940

Relief for the remaining loss may be obtained:

(i)   under s 380 in 2005/06 against Arrol's total income

(ii)   under s 381 ICTA 1988 against Arrol's total income for 2003/04, 2004/05 and 2005/06 in that order, or

(iii)   by carry forward under s 385 ICTA 1988 against future profits of the practice.

A claim under s380 for 2005/06 or carry back under s.381 will obtain tax relief at a maximum of 22% and will lead to a wastage of personal allowances.

Carry forward under s.385 will obtain tax relief in 2008/09 against the profits of the year to 30 April 2008 at a maximum of 22%, and may lead to a wastage of personal allowances, unless these are covered by investment income. If any loss remains to carried forward to 2009/10 it is likely to obtain tax relief at 40% as the business is expected to become very profitable.

£29,760 of the loss derives from Arrol making the maximum claim to capital allowances. A significant proportion of this loss is wasted by being set against income covered by personal allowances. Arrol should consider restricting his claim for capital allowances to avoid wastage of personal allowance, Capital allowances not claimed are effectively carried forward in the pool of expenditure, and although they can then only be relieved on a reducing balance basis, relief will be obtained at a higher rate.

10 Adam, Bert and Charlie

Tutorial note. Always divide the profits of a period of account between the partners before you begin allocating them to tax years.

In part (b) do not forget to consider national insurance as well as tax, and also non-tax advantages/disadvantages.

(a)

	Total £	A £	B £	C £	D £
Year ending 31 March 2004					
Salaries	3,700	1,500	1,200	1,000	
Balance	6,500	2,600	2,600	1,300	
Total	10,200	4,100	3,800	2,300	
Year ending 31 March 2005					
April to June					
Salaries	925	375	300	250	
Balance	4,275	1,710	1,710	855	
Total	5,200	2,085	2,010	1,105	
July to March					
Salaries	1,650		900	750	
Balance	13,950		8,370	5,580	
Total	15,600		9,270	6,330	
Totals for the year	20,800	2,085	11,280	7,435	
Year ending 31 March 2006					
Salaries	2,200		1,200	1,000	
Balance	10,400		6,240	4,160	
Total	12,600		7,440	5,160	

	Total £	A £	B £	C £	D £
Year ending 31 March 2007					
April					
Salaries	183		100	83	
Balance	1,317		790	527	
Total	1,500		890	610	
May to March					
Salaries	4,950		1,650	1,650	1,650
Balance	11,550		6,237	4,158	1,155
Total	16,500		7,887	5,808	2,805
Totals for the year	18,000		8,777	6,418	2,805

Taxable trade profits are as follows.

	A £	B £	C £	D £
Year				
2003/04	4,100	3,800	2,300	
2004/05	2,085	11,280	7,435	
2005/06		7,440	5,160	
2006/07		8,777	6,418	2,805

(b)   (i)   If Freda is employed on a salary of £12,000 pa the tax and NI costs and savings will be:

	£
Employer's NI £(12,000 − 5,035) × 12.8%	892
Employee's NI £(12,000 − 5,035) × 11%	766
Income tax payable by Freda (12,000 − 5,035 − 2,150) × 22% + 2,150 × 10%	1,274
Income tax saved by Eric £(12,000 + 892) × 40%	(5,156)
Class 4 NI saved by Eric £(12,000 + 892) × 1%	(129)
Total saving	(2,353)

If Freda is taken on as a partner with a 20% profit share, ie £12,000, the tax and NI costs and savings will be:

	£
Class 4 NI payable by Freda £(12,000 − 5,035) × 8%	557
Class 2 NI payable by Freda £2.10 × 52	109
Income tax payable by Freda (12,000 − 5,035 − 2,150) × 22% + 2,150 × 10%	1,274
Income tax saved by Eric £12,000 × 40%	(4,800)
Class 4 NI saved by Eric £12,000 × 1%	(120)
Total saving	(2,980)

In this case the savings are £627 (£2,980 − £2,353) greater because of the reduction in NI contributions due.

(ii)   If Eric increased Freda's share of partnership profits so that Eric did not pay higher rate tax, the savings would be maximised. Freda's share of profits would be £(60,000 − 33,300 − 5,035) = 21,665. The savings would be:

	£
Class 4 NI payable by Freda £(21,665 − 5,035) × 8%	1,330
Class 2 NI payable by Freda £2.10 × 52	109
Income tax payable by Freda (21,665 − 5,035 − 2,150) × 22% + 2,150 × 10%	3,401
Income tax saved by Eric £21,665 × 40%	(8,666)
Class 4 NI saved by Eric £21,665 × 1%	(217)
Total saving	(4,043)

Note that unless Eric's share of profits is reduced below £33,540 there is no advantage in increasing Freda's share of profits because she would pay Class 4 NI at 8% whilst Eric would only save Class 4 NI at 1%.

In addition to the tax and NI advantages/disadvantages of taking Freda into partnership as opposed to employing her there are other considerations. These include the unlimited liability of partners, employment law, PAYE obligations and entitlement to state benefits.

11 Overseas

Tutorial note. Double tax relief is an important topic which could be examined in the Section A compulsory questions. Take great care when calculating the amount of UK tax on overseas income, as here, it is not always that straightforward.

(a)   2006/07 SUSAN'S TAX COMPUTATION

	Non-savings	Dividends	Total
	£	£	£
Earnings	17,820		
UK dividends (× 100/90)		10,000	
Overseas property business income (10,000 + 4,705)	14,705		
STI	32,525	10,000	42,525
Less personal allowance	(5,035)		
	27,490	10,000	37,490

	£
Income tax on non-savings income:	
£2,150 × 10%	215
£25,340 × 22%	5,575
Income tax on dividend income:	
£5,810 × 10%	581
£4,190 × 32.5%	1,362
	7,733
Less DTR (W)	(4,178)
	3,555
Less tax credit and PAYE £(2,000 + 1,000)	(3,000)
Tax payable	555

Working

DTR

UK tax on overseas income:	Non-savings	Dividends
	£	£
Total taxable income	27,490	10,000
Less overseas property business income	(14,705)	
	12,785	10,000

Income tax	£
2,150 × 10%	215
10,635 × 22%	2,340
10,000 × 10%	1,000
22,785	
Tax on UK income	3,555
Tax on total income (above)	(7,733)
UK tax on overseas income	4,178

DTR is lower of:

(i)   UK tax on overseas income £4,178

(ii)   overseas tax £4,705

(b)   A UK taxpayer can claim relief from UK tax in respect of foreign tax paid by that person. There is a clear requirement in the legislation that the taxpayer should advise HMRC if subsequently the foreign tax is adjusted by the foreign tax authority so that if a DTR claim is rendered excessive an alteration can be made.

The taxpayer must notify HMRC within one year of any adjustment to the amount of foreign tax. So Susan must notify HMRC before 1 November 2009.

Her DTR claim for 2006/07 becomes the lower of:

(i)	UK tax suffered on overseas income	£4,178
(ii)	overseas tax suffered (£4,705 – 2,600)	£2,105

ie £2,105 not £4,178 as before.

(c)   If Susan's overseas posting runs for 15 months from 1 June 2007 it will not span a complete tax year. She will continue to be resident and ordinarily resident in the UK, and will be liable to UK tax on all of her worldwide income.

If Susan's overseas posting runs from 1 April 2007 she will be abroad for a whole tax year, and as long as her visits to the UK during this period do not exceed 183 days pa or 91 days pa on average, she will be treated as neither resident nor ordinarily resident in the UK for the whole period. In this case there is no UK tax on the foreign earnings or overseas rental income.

(d)   James will be present in the UK for 183 days or more during 2007/08 and will be treated as resident in the UK, although not ordinarily resident. He will be taxed in the UK on his earnings for working in the UK, but will only be taxed in the UK on his earnings for duties carried out in Utopia and on his Utopian bank interest to the extent that the income is remitted to the UK. James should therefore try to avoid remitting such income to the UK.

12 John

> **Tutorial note.** The knowledge required in this question should be familiar to you from Paper 2.3. or F6. You should be aware that a thorough knowledge of the Paper F6 syllabus is required for candidates sitting Paper P6.
>
> Note that although chargeable gains are never included in the income tax computation, the level of income affects the rate of CGT.

(a)   John: CGT liability

DEF plc shares

Gain chargeable

Business asset for taper relief because John is an employee of this trading company

Taper relief period is 10.9.05 to 9.9.06 = 1 year

Car

Exempt asset so loss is not allowable.

Land

Gain chargeable

Non business asset taper relief

Taper relief period is 6.4.98 to 5.4.06 = 8 years plus additional year = 9 years as asset held at 17 March 1998.

XYZ plc shares

Gain exempt as shares held in ISA.

Factory

Gain chargeable

Factory is business asset between 1.8.03 to 1.11.06 (39 months) as the factory was used in John's trade.

Factory is non-business asset from 1.11.06 to 1.2.07 (3 months).

The business gain is 39/42 × £27,000 = £25,071 and the non-business gain is 3/42 × £27,000 = £1,929.

Taper relief period (whole years) is 1.8.03 to 31.7.06 = 3 years for both business and non-business parts.

Losses b/f

Set against gains in the most advantageous manner, that is, gain with least taper relief first and so on.

Summary

	Business		Non-business	
	3 yrs	*1 yr*	*9 yrs*	*3 yrs*
	£	£	£	£
Gains	25,071	10,000	25,000	1,929
Less loss b/f (best use)	n/a	n/a	(4,071)	(1,929)
Gains before taper relief	25,071	10,000	20,929	nil
Percentage of gain remaining chargeable	25%	50%	65%	n/a
Gains after taper relief	6,268	5,000	13,604	nil

	£
Total gains £(6,268 + 5,000 + 13,604)	24,872
Less: annual exemption	(8,800)
Taxable gains	16,072

Taxable income £(36,000 − 5,035)	£30,965

Basic rate band £(33,300 + [195 × 12 × 100/78])	36,300
Basic rate band left £(36,300 − 30,965)	5,335

	£
CGT payable	1,067
£5,335 @ 20%	4,295
£10,737 @ 40%	5,362
£16,072	

(b) John is paying CGT at 40% on £10,737 of his gain although he is normally a basic rate taxpayer.

He has no other capital assets he wishes to realise, so he cannot minimise his CGT liability by realising capital losses to set against the gains that have already been realised. He could reduce his CGT liability if he could shift some of the gains from the 40% band into the 20% band. As his taxable income for 2006/07 derives from his employment, he cannot reduce his income, but he could instead seek to increase the basic rate band limit.

This can be done in two ways; by making charitable gifts under the gift aid scheme, or by paying pension contributions. If John has been a basic rate taxpayer for some while he may have neglected to claim gift aid relief as it would not have reduced his own tax liability. He should review the position for 2006/07, as it is possible to make gift aid declarations after the gift has been made. However making a donation simply to save tax requires an outlay greater than the tax saved.

John is already making regular contributions to a personal pension of £195 net (£250 gross) per month. If he made a further contribution this would extend his basic rate tax band. Maximum relief would be obtained by making a payment of £10,737 gross, equivalent to £8,375 net. This would reduce his CGT liability by £10,737 × 20% = £2,147, so that the net cost of the contributions would be £8,375 − £2,147 = £6,228.

If John did not wish to make such large contributions in the long term he could temporarily suspend his normal monthly contributions from 6 April 2007. Although the contributions are being paid earlier he is thereby obtaining higher rate tax relief on them, whilst they would only be relievable at the basic rate in 2007/08.

13 Sophie Shaw

> **Tutorial note.** Again, this question covers the basics of CGT with which you must be completely familiar by the time you sit Paper P6. You are also required to consider how the CGT liability could have been reduced; there are several basic strategies.

(a) *Summary – all non business assets*

	9 yrs £	4 yrs £
Gains (W1, W2, W3)	70,880	40,000
Less loss b/f (note)	0	(5,000)
	70,880	35,000
Percentage of gain remaining chargeable	65%	90%
Gains after taper relief	46,072	31,500

	£
Total gains	77,572
Less annual exemption	(8,800)
Chargeable gains	68,772

Note. The brought forward loss is set against the gain with the lowest amount of taper relief, ie where the highest percentage of the gain is chargeable. The current year loss (W4) arises on a disposal to a connected person and cannot be set off against the other gains.

Workings

(1)   *Painting*

The costs of sale (auctioneer's costs) can be deducted from the sale proceeds.

	£
Proceeds	50,000
Less costs of sale	(500)
Net proceeds of sale	49,500
Less cost	(2,500)
Unindexed gain	47,000
Less indexation allowance $\frac{162.6-79.4}{79.4}$ (= 1.048) × £2,500	(2,620)
Indexed gain	44,380

Gain is £44,380

Taper relief period is 6.4.98 – 5.4.06 = 8 years plus 1 year as non business asset held at 17 March 1998 = 9 years.

(2)   *Freehold shop*

The transfer of the shop between the spouses is on a no gain/no loss basis. The base cost for Sophie is therefore £45,000. The value of the shop at the transfer is not relevant.

The gain is:

	£
Proceeds	85,000
Less cost	(45,000)
Gain	40,000

The taper relief period runs from 1.9.02 (the acquisition by the spouse) to 31.8.06 which is 4 years. The asset is a non-business asset.

(3)   *4 acres of land*

This is a part disposal of the land. The fraction of cost used is:

$$\frac{\text{Proceeds of sale}}{\text{Proceeds of sale} + \text{value of part remaining}} \times \text{cost}$$

that is: $\frac{40,000}{40,000 + 24,000} \times £20,000 = £12,500$

The gain is:

	£
Proceeds	40,000
Less cost	(12,500)
Unindexed gain	27,500
Less indexation allowance $\frac{162.6-150.6}{150.6}$ (= 0.080) × £12,500	(1,000)
Indexed gain	26,500

Taper relief period is 6.4.98 – 5.4.06 = 8 years plus 1 year as non business asset held at 17 March 1998 = 9 years.

    (4)   *JKL plc shares*

	£
Proceeds	10,000
Less cost	(12,000)
Loss	(2,000)

This is a loss on a disposal to a connected person. The loss is only allowable on a gain on a disposal to the same connected person.

(b)   There are several ways in which Sophie's CGT liability could have been reduced.

    (i)   Sophie should have sold the JKL plc shares and gifted the proceeds to her son. She would then have generated an allowable loss of £12,000 – £9,000 = £3,000 (assuming she had achieved the same proceeds as did Jason), instead of realising a restricted loss of £2,000 and Jason generating the loss of £1,000 which can only be used if Jason makes capital gains, which is likely to be some time in the future. Sophie would set the loss against gains tapered at 90%, so would save CGT of £3,000 × 90% × 40% = £1,080.

    (ii)   Terry has made no capital gains in 2006/07 so his annual exemption of £8,800 is unused. Sophie should have transferred one of the assets to Terry so that the gain would be realised in his hands thereby saving CGT of £8,800 × 40% = £3,520.

    (iii)   Sophie has made a part disposal of 4 acres land out of a total holding valued at £(40,000 + 24,000) = £64,000. This does not qualify for the small part disposal relief in Sophie's hands as the proceeds exceed both £20,000 and 20% of the market value of the land.

        It might, however, have been possible to have transferred part of the land to Terry so that he could make a disposal which would fall within the limits. If the land retained is valued at £24,000 the part transferred to him would have to be valued at less than £30,000 so that the disposal was of less than 20% of his holding. Terry may then deduct the proceeds of the land sold from the base cost of the land retained, thereby reducing the chargeable gain on the sale of the land. The exact amount saved would depend on the values of the various tranches of land, but as the proceeds cannot exceed £6,000 the maximum saving is £6,000 × 65% × 40% = £1,560.

14 The Green family

> **Tutorial note.** The key to a long question like this is to ensure that you allocate your time so that you are able to make an attempt at each individual requirement.

(a)   *Total value due to John Green on takeover*

	£
Shares 20,000 × £4.90	98,000
Cash 20,000 × £1.60	32,000
	130,000

Cash element exceeds both £3,000 and 5% of £130,000, so there is a part disposal

	£
Disposal proceeds (cash)	32,000
Less cost $\dfrac{32,000}{32,000+98,000} \times £40,000$	(9,846)
Gain	22,154
Base cost of Wall plc shares £(40,000 – 9,846)	£30,154

(b)   *Match post April 1998 acquisitions on a LIFO basis*

      1 March 2006

      Shares held after bonus issue 1,000 + 1,000 = 2,000

      No change to base cost

	£
Disposal proceeds (£14,000 $\times \frac{2,000}{3,200}$)	8,750
Less cost	(1,260)
Gain	7,490

      No taper relief – owned less than one year

      15 May 2005

      Shares held after bonus issue 1,800 + 1,800 = 3,600

      No change to base cost

	£
Disposal proceeds (£14,000 $\times \frac{1,200}{3,200}$)	5,250
Less cost (£1,900 $\times \frac{1,200}{3,600}$)	(633)
Gain	4,617

      No taper relief – non business asset held less than 3 years.

      The total chargeable gain on the sale of Mrs Green's shares in Read plc is £12,107 (£7,490 + £4,617).

(c)   *The disposal of Greengage Supermarkets plc shares*

    (i)   *Post 5 April 1998 acquisition*

	£
Proceeds $\frac{1,000}{1,450} \times$ £10,150	7,000
Less cost	(6,000)
Gain	1,000

        No taper relief – owned less than one year

    (ii)   *The FA 1985 pool*

	£
Proceeds $\frac{450}{1,450} \times$ £10,150	3,150
Less cost (W)	(1,704)
	1,446
Less indexation allowance £(2,923 − 1,704) (W)	(1,219)
Indexed gain	227

        Gain after taper relief (9 complete years ownership after 6.4.98 including additional year) 65% × £227   148

    Working

    The FA 1985 pool

	No of shares	Cost	Indexed cost
	£	£	£
Balance at 5 April 1998	900	3,408	5,845
Disposal (May 2006)	(450)	(1,704)	(2,923)
FA 1985 pool value remaining	450	1,704	2,922

(d)   *Summary: Mr Green*

	£
Gains	22,154
Less loss brought forward	(13,354)
	8,800
Less annual exemption	(8,800)
Taxable gains	0
CGT payable	£nil

The losses brought forward are only set against gains to bring the gains down to the annual exemption.

Loss carried forward £(17,560 – 13,354)   £4,206

Summary: Mrs Green

	£
Gains	12,107
Less annual exemption	(8,800)
Chargeable gains	3,307
CGT payable	
£2,150 @ 10%	215
£1,157 @ 20%	231
	446

(e)   If John Green had received loan stock instead of cash there would not be an immediately chargeable gain. If the corporate bonds were qualifying corporate bonds the gain of £22,154 would be deferred until the QCBs were sold, and would then be eligible for three years taper relief as the shares were held for three years (1.5.03 – 1.5.06) before the takeover. This would enable John to sell the QCBs in tranches realising sufficient gains to utilise the annual exemption over several years, and preserve brought forward losses.

If the bonds are not QCBs the base cost of the original shares would simply be apportioned between the new shares and bonds, and no gain would arise until the bonds were disposed of. Again, this allows for phased disposals.

15 Roland Rat

Tutorial note. This question requires a methodical approach. First establish the base cost of the shares and then deal with the transactions in 2006/07. You must then consider how the chargeable gains could have been reduced.

(a)   *The transfer of the business to the company wholly in exchange for shares*

(i)   The transfer of shares to Roland Rat's wife

Where a husband and wife are living together, transfers between them give rise to neither gains nor losses. There is therefore no chargeable gain on the transfer of 2,500 shares to Mrs Rat.

Mrs Rat's base cost for future disposal purposes will be as follows.

	£
	65,066

$$\frac{2,500}{10,000} \times £260,265(W)$$

(ii)   *The sale of shares to the incoming director*

	£
Proceeds	165,000
Less cost $\frac{2,000}{10,000} \times £260,265$ (W)	(52,053)
Chargeable gain before taper	112,947
Chargeable gain after taper relief (25%)	28,237

Note. Mr Rat owned shares in a qualifying company for seven complete years post April 1999 prior to the sale in August 2006. 25% of the gain is chargeable.

The base cost for the incoming director will be £165,000.

(iii)   *The sale of the freehold property by Mouse Trap Ltd*

The gain on sale of the freehold property can be rolled over against the base cost of the new property if that new property is acquired within the period from 12 months before to three years after the disposal of the old property.

The gain to be rolled over is calculated as follows.

	£
Proceeds	500,000
Less cost	(200,000)
	300,000
Less indexation allowance to August 2006	
$0.119 \times £200,000$	(23,800)
Gain	276,200

The base cost of the new property is found as follows.

	£
Cost	550,000
Less rolled over gain	(276,200)
Base cost	273,800

(iv)   *The base costs of other chargeable assets*

   (1)   Mr. Rat's shares

   $$\frac{5,500}{10,000} \times £260,265 \text{ (W)} = £143,146$$

   (2)   Goodwill owned by company

   Cost in April 1999   £150,000

Working

The gains arising on the transfer of chargeable assets to Mouse Trap Ltd are rolled over against the acquisition value of the shares in the company.

The gains arising in April 1999 are as follows.

	£
Goodwill £(150,000 − 0)	150,000
Freehold property £(200,000 − 85,000* − (85,000 × 0.929))	36,035
Gain rolled over	186,035

*£77,000 + £8,000 = £85,000.

The base cost of the shares acquired is as follows.

	£
Consideration	446,300
Less rolled over gain	(186,035)
Base cost (10,000 shares)	260,265

(b)   There are several steps that could have mitigated the CGT liabilities:

(i)   *The transfer of the business to the company partly in exchange for shares*

On the incorporation of a business, only gains attributable to a transfer in exchange for shares can be rolled over. Roland Rat could have left part of the proceeds on loan account so as to realise sufficient gains to utilise his CGT annual exemption. 50% taper relief would be available on the transfer to the company (business assets held for one year since 5.4.98) so gains of £17,600 (8,800 × 100/50) should be crystallised to utilise the capital gains exemption. The amount to be left on loan account would have been £17,600/186,035 × 446,350 = 42,227. The base cost of the shares would have been £446,300 − 42,227 − (186,035 − 17,600) = £235,638.

This stratagem reduces the base cost of the shares, but the value of the company at the time of the current share transactions would be reduced to take into account the loan account, or would have been lower had the loan account been withdrawn

(ii)   *Gift Relief*

An alternative stratagem at the time of incorporation would be to have gifted the goodwill and the freehold to the company and claim gift relief. The company's base cost would then be the market value, less the gain rolled over. The chargeable gains would then be deferred until the freehold and the goodwill were sold. The base cost of the shares would then be their market value at the time of incorporation, and this would reduce the gain on the sale to the incoming director.

When the factory is sold the gain arising will be greater as it will include the gain held over under gift relief, but it can all be rolled over against the cost of the new factory

(iii)   *Retention of freehold*

Roland could have retained the freehold outside the company, and used gift relief on the transfer of goodwill. Rollover relief would still be able on the replacement of the factory, since both the old and new factories would be owned by Roland and used by his company. Retention of the factory has advantages on the ultimate disposal of the business as it avoids the potential double charge to tax on capital gains. Provided the new factory is retained for at least two years it will qualify for the maximum business assets taper relief.

Retention of the factory will, however, reduce the price payable by the incoming director for his shares, and may reduce the marketability of the shares as investors may perceive that Roland can manipulate the company's performance due to his retention of the premises.

(iv)   *Sale by wife*

The shares sold to the incoming director have all been sold by Roland. Had part or all of the holding been transferred to Roland's wife and sold by her to the incoming director this would have utilised her annual CGT exemption, and her basic rate tax band.

16 Miss Wolf, Mr Hen and Mr Fox

Tutorial note. In part (c), no further absence can be counted as deemed occupation because Mr Fox did not go back to live in the house (compare absences followed by occupation between 1.8.89 and 31.1.95). Note also how the election as to which house is used as the PPR can be advantageous.

(a)   Miss Wolf

The lease

	£
Proceeds	30,750
Less $\dfrac{64.116\,(16\ \text{years})}{80.361\,(24\tfrac{1}{2}\ \text{years})} \times £8,000$	(6,383)
Unindexed gain	24,367
Less indexation allowance (January 1998 to April 1998)	
$\dfrac{162.6 - 159.5}{159.5} = (0.019) \times £6,383$	(121)
Gain before taper relief	24,246
Gain after taper relief (9 years)	
65% × £24,246	15,760

The percentage for 24½ years is 79.622 + (81.100 − 79.622) × 6/12 = 80.361.

Taper relief period is nine years (6.4.98 − 5.4.06 = 8 years plus additional year).

(b)   Mr Hen

2005/06

No CGT event on the damage to the factory.

2006/07

Receipt of compensation is treated as part disposal. The amount not used in restoration is not 'small'. The restoration must also be taken into account.

	£
Amount not used in restoration £(20,000 − 15,000)	5,000
Less cost plus restoration	
$\dfrac{5,000}{5,000 + 250,000} \times £(150,000 + 15,000)$	(3,235)
Gain	1,765
Taper relief (10.7.04 − 9.7.06) = 2 years, business asset	
£1,765 × 25%	£441

2007/08

Sale of factory

	£
Sale proceeds	260,000
Less cost £(150,000 + 15,000 − 3,235 − 15,000)	(146,765)
Gain	113,235
Taper relief (10.7.04 − 9.7.07) = 3 years, business asset	
£113,235 × 25%	£28,309

(c) Mr Fox

(i) *Gain on sale*

	£
Proceeds	180,000
Less cost	(50,000)
Unindexed gain	130,000
Less indexation allowance	

$$\frac{162.6 - 97.8}{97.8}\ (= 0.663) \times £50,000$$

	£
	(33,150)
Indexed gain	96,850
Exempt gain (W): $\dfrac{11\frac{1}{2}}{20} \times £96,850$	(55,689)
Chargeable gain	41,161
Gain after taper relief (9 years)	
65% × £41,161	£26,755

Working

Principal private residence relief	Exempt years	Chargeable years
1.8.86 – 31.7.89 (actual occupation)	3	
1.8.89 – 31.7.93 (up to 4 yrs due to place of work – *not* employed abroad)	4	
1.8.93 – 31.7.94 (up to 3 years any other reason)	1	
1.8.94 – 31.1.95 (actual occupation)	½	
1.2.95 – 31.7.03 (not followed by actual occupation)		8½
1.8.03 – 31.7.06 (last 3 years)	3	
Totals	11½	8½

(ii) If Mr Fox had moved back into his house before it was sold, then the two years from 1.2.95 to 31.1.97 would have been treated as a period of occupation, since Mr Fox had re-occupied the property after the period of absence. The exempt portion of the gain would have increased to 13½/20 × £96,850 = 65,374, leaving a chargeable gain of £31,476, or £20,459 after taper relief.

(iii) When Mr Fox inherited the house from his sister he had two residences available. He should have moved back to his own house for a few months. He should then have returned to his sister's house, electing for that to be treated as his PPR. Any remaining months before his old house was sold would be covered by the exemption for the last 36 months.

Provided the sister's house was sold within three years of her death any gain would also be covered by the exemption for the last 36 months.

17 Mr & Mrs Brown

> **Tutorial note**. Administration should be a very familiar topic from Paper 2.3 or F6. It can be examined in the compulsory Section A questions so you should ensure that you have a thorough knowledge of it.

(a) *Returns*

Income tax returns must be submitted by 31 January following the tax year concerned. Thus an individual's return for 2006/07 must be delivered by 31 January 2008. However, if the notice requiring the return is served after 31 October following the tax year, the filing date becomes three months after the notice. Thus, if notice to deliver the return for 2006/07 were given, say, on 1 December 2007, it must be delivered by 28 February 2008.

Where a tax return is filed late a penalty of up to a maximum of £100 can be charged. The Commissioners may impose a further penalty of up to £60 for each day for which the return remains outstanding after the taxpayer is notified of the penalty, although it cannot be imposed after the failure had been remedied.

If no application is made by the Inspector to the Commissioners and the return is not filed within six months of the filing date, the taxpayer is liable to a further maximum penalty of £100 subject to a right of appeal on the grounds of reasonable excuse. If the failure continues after the first anniversary of the filing date and the return shows that there is an outstanding liability to tax, the taxpayer is liable to a penalty equal to that outstanding tax liability.

Any penalty will be limited to the amount of tax outstanding for the year and this will be mitigable.

As an alternative to completing their own calculation, the taxpayer can request HMRC assistance and submit a return by 30 September following the tax year (or, if later, two months from the date of the notice requiring delivery of a return). The Officer of Revenue and Customs must then raise an assessment in accordance with the information contained in the return and provide the taxpayer with a copy of the assessment.

Payments of tax

Although an individual is not normally required to file a return until 31 January following the tax year, payments on account are required on 31 January in the tax year and on 31 July following it. These payments are required where an individual has either made a self-assessment or been assessed to tax following submission of his tax return for the previous tax year and the amount of the assessment exceeded the tax which was deducted at source: this excess is known as the relevant amount. Tax deducted at source includes PAYE, tax credits on dividends and income tax deducted or treated as paid. The taxpayer is required to pay 50% of the previous year's relevant amount on each of 31 January in the tax year and 31 July following it.

If the taxpayer believes that the current year's income tax and Class 4 NIC liability will be less than the previous year's amount, he may claim to reduce each payment on account may then be reduced to 50% of the amount which the taxpayer believes will be due. If the taxpayer fraudulently or negligently makes a false statement in connection with such a claim, he will be liable to a penalty equal to the amount of tax lost. Interest is charged on the amount by which payments on account are reduced if the reduced amount finally becomes payable. The interest runs from the due date of payment for the payments on account.

Income tax and Class 4 NICs due, in excess of the payments on account, together with the whole of any CGT, must be paid on 31 January in the following year.

Interest on overdue tax is charged on all unpaid tax from the due date. Where the balance of tax (due on 31 January following the year) is unpaid more than 28 days after the due date, a surcharge of 5% of the unpaid amount is also applied. If it remains unpaid more than six months after the due date, there is a further 5% surcharge. The surcharge carries interest from the date imposed to the date paid.

(b) *Mr Brown*

Due dates of tax – 2006/07

Payments made	Paid	No claim to reduce payments on account	Due date
£		£	
4,500	28 February 2007	6,000	31 January 2007
4,500	14 August 2007	6,000	31 July 2007
4,000	13 March 2008	1,000	31 January 2008
13,000		13,000	

Interest due

Payments on account:

	£
£4,500 × 28/365 × 6.5%	22.44
£4,500 × 14/365 × 6.5%	11.22
£1,500 × 406/365 × 6.5%	108.45
£1,500 × 225/365 × 6.5%	60.10
Final payment:	
£1,000 × 41/365 × 6.5%	7.30
	209.51

(c) Mrs Brown's tax return was prepared in accordance with the practice prevailing at that time. She will therefore be precluded from making an error or mistake claim for the revised treatment if the court case should go in the taxpayer's favour.

Mrs Brown is, however, able to amend her tax return at any time up until 31 January 2009. She should therefore file an amendment to her return, using the more favourable treatment.

It is likely that HMRC will open an enquiry into her tax return, thereby enabling them to amend the return should the taxpayer fail in the Courts. Even at that stage Mrs Brown could appeal against any amendment HMRC made on closing an enquiry if it was likely that the matter would progress to higher courts.

18 Rodin

> **Tutorial note.** This answer follows the 'steps' set out within the text but in a streamlined format which is equally acceptable in the exam.

(a) **IHT paid during Rodin's lifetime was as follows.**

15.12.99

	£
Gift	60,000
Less: A/E (1999/00)	(3,000)
A/E (1998/99) b/f	(3,000)
PET	54,000

This gift was a PET so no lifetime tax was due.

21.1.02

No gross chargeable transfers were made in the seven years prior to 21.1.02 so all of the nil band remained available for use. This means the IHT paid by Rodin was:

		£
Gift		337,000
Less: A/E (2001/02)		(3,000)
A/E (2000/01) b/f		(3,000)
		331,000

			£
IHT	£285,000	× 0% =	Nil
	£ 46,000	× 20/80 =	11,500
	£331,000		11,500

The gross chargeable transfer after annual exemptions was: £331,000 + £11,500 = £342,500.

Check: tax £(342,500 − 285,000) = £57,500 × 20% = £11,500.

> **Tutorial note**. The nil band of £285,000 was used in calculating this lifetime IHT because you were told in the question to assume that the nil band has always been £285,000. In practice you would use the nil band applicable on 21.1.02 when calculating the lifetime tax on a gift made on 21.1.02.

20.8.03

	£
Gift	46,000
Less: A/E (2003/04)	(3,000)
A/E (2002/03) b/f	(3,000)
PET	40,000

This was a PET so no lifetime tax was due.

19.6.05

Gross chargeable transfers of £342,500 had been made in the seven years prior to 19.6.05 so none of the nil band remains and the lifetime IHT due was:

	£
Gift	106,000
Less: A/E (2005/06)	(3,000)
A/E (2004/05) b/f	(3,000)
	100,000

	£
IHT: £100,000 × 20/80 =	£25,000

The gross chargeable transfer after annual exemptions was £100,000 + £25,000 = £125,000

Check tax £125,000 × 20% = £25,000.

1.8.06

	£
Gift	73,000
Less: A/E (2006/07)	(3,000)
PET	70,000

This was a PET so no lifetime tax was due.

1.9.06

This was an exempt transfer to Rodin's spouse so no lifetime tax was due.

IHT due as a result of death.

As a result of death, IHT will be due on transfers made in the seven years before the death.

Lifetime transfers

15.12.99

This PET was made more than seven years before death, so no IHT arises as a result of death.

21.1.02

Gross transfer after annual exemptions	£342,500

None of the nil band had been used in calculating death tax in the seven years before 21.1.02 so the IHT due on death is:

			£
£285,000	× 0%		Nil
£57,500	× 40%		23,000
£342,500			23,000

Less taper relief at 40% (4-5 years)	(9,200)
Death tax after taper relief	13,800
Less lifetime tax paid	(11,500)
IHT due on death	2,300

20.8.03

All of the nil band has been used in calculating death tax on gifts made in the seven years prior to 20.8.03, so the death tax due on this now chargeable PET is:

	£
PET (valued at 20.8.03)	40,000

IHT @ 40%	16,000
Less taper relief @ 20% (3-4 years)	(3,200)
IHT payable by daughter (80%)	12,800

19.6.05

All of the nil band has been used in calculating death tax on the gifts made in the seven years prior to 19.6.05, so the death tax due on this gift is:

Gross chargeable transfer	£125,000

	£
£125,000 × 40% =	50,000
Less lifetime tax	(25,000)
Tax due on death	25,000

1.8.06

No nil band remains so IHT due on this now chargeable PET is:

PET (valued at 1.8.06)	£70,000

£70,000 × 40%	£28,000

No taper relief as death occurs within 3 years of the gift.

1.9.06

No IHT arises on an exempt transfer to a spouse.

(b) If Rodin's wife had not been domiciled in the UK only the first £55,000 of the transfer would have been exempt. The balance of the transfer would still be a PET, so there would be no IHT to pay unless Rodin died within seven years. The additional IHT that would be due following Rodin's death would be £(300,000 − 55,000) × 40% = £98,000.

(c)   The gift by Rodin's cousin into the discretionary trust is a CLT which is in excess of the nil rate threshold of £285,000. He should therefore make this gift first to ensure that the annual exemption for the current year and the previous year are set against this transfer, so reducing the amount of lifetime IHT payable. If Rodin's cousin pays the tax the gift would need to be grossed up, so the immediate IHT saving would be £3,000 × 2 × 20/80 = £1,500, whereas if the trustees paid the tax the saving would be £3,000 × 2 × 20% = £1,200.

The gifts to the two children are PETs and no tax will be payable unless Rodin's cousin dies within seven years of the gifts. If he does the total IHT payable will in fact be unaffected by the timing of the gifts.

Rodin's cousin could delay his gift to his daughter until her marriage so that he can utilise the marriage exemption. For a parent the exemption is £5,000. Should Rodin's cousin die within seven years of the gift this will save IHT of £5,000 × 40% = £2,000. There is a small element of risk should Rodin's cousin die more than seven years after the gift to the son, but within seven years of the gift to the daughter.

19 Mr Bright

> **Tutorial note**. Note the different valuation rules for CGT and IHT. The shares are valued at market value for CGT purposes. For IHT purposes the diminution in value principle is used to value the shares.

(a)   *Capital gains tax liability*

	£
Gain on shares (W)	12,914
Less annual exemption	(8,800)
Taxable gain	4,114

As Mr Bright's marginal rate of income tax is 40%, the marginal rate of CGT is 40%. The CGT is £4,114 × 40% = £1,646.

Inheritance tax liability

The gift to the discretionary trust is a chargeable lifetime transfer. As he pays the tax, grossing up is necessary. Two annual exemptions of £3,000 each (for 2006/07 and 2005/06) are available to reduce the net transfer.

	£
Transfer	309,000
Less: A/E (2006/07)	(3,000)
A/E (2005/06) b/f	(3,000)
Net transfer	303,000

There have been no previous transfers so all of the nil band remains available for use in calculating the IHT on this transfer.

		£
£285,000	× 0%	Nil
£18,000	× 20/80	4,500
£303,000		4,500

Gross transfer is thus £307,500 (£303,000 + 4,500). The IHT payable by Mr Bright is £4,500.

Check: tax £(307,500 – 285,000) = £22,500 × 20% = £4,500.

The gift to Maxine on 1 April 2007 is a potentially exempt transfer so no tax is due during Mr Bright's lifetime.

Working

Post 5.4.98 acquisitions

18.8.06

	£
Proceeds (600 × £18)	10,800
Less cost	(3,000)
Chargeable gain	7,800

There is no indexation allowance after April 1998. No taper relief due since owned for less than one year.

15.6.01

	£
Proceeds (200 × £18)	3,600
Less cost	(1,366)
	2,234

The shares are a business asset for taper relief purposes. As they have been owned for five complete years after 6.4.98 only 25% of the gain is taxable.

£2,234 × 25% = £558

FA 1985 Pool

	No of shares	Cost	Indexed cost
Pool at 5.4.98	2,200	3,300	6,187
Disposal	(1,200)	(1,800)	(3,375)
	1,000	1,500	2,182

	£
Disposal proceeds (1,200 × £18) (market value)	21,600
Less cost	(1,800)
	19,800
Less indexation allowance £(3,375 – 1,800)	(1,575)
	18,225
Chargeable gain after taper relief (6.4.98 – 5.4.06; business asset 25%)	4,556

	£
August 2006 acquisition	7,800
June 2001 acquisition	558
FA 1985 pool	4,556
Total gain on shares	12,914

(b) If Mr Bright were to die on 20 April 2007, the potentially exempt transfer to Maxine on 1 April 2007 would become chargeable. The amount of this transfer, applying both the diminution in value principle and the related property rules (since Mrs Bright owns 1,000 shares) is as follows.

	£
Before the transfer, Mr Bright had 3,000 shares in a holding of 3,000 + 1,000 = 4,000 shares (80%), worth £36.67 a share	110,010
After the transfer, Mr Bright had 1,000 shares in a holding of 1,000 + 1,000 = 2,000 shares (40%), worth £18 a share	(18,000)
	92,010
Less actual proceeds	(10,000)
	82,010
Less business property relief: unavailable because shares sold by date of Mr Bright's death	(0)
Transfer of value (no annual exemptions available)	82,010

On Mr Bright's death, his remaining shares would also be valued using the related property rules, as follows.

	£
1,000 shares in a holding of 2,000 shares, worth £18 a share	18,000
Less business property relief at 100% (unquoted shares)	(18,000)
	0

The inheritance tax liabilities which would arise on Mr Bright's death on 20 April 2007 are as follows.

1 May 2006 transfer

Gross transfer (valued on 1 May 2006)	£307,500

IHT at death (no taper relief – death within 3 years)

		£
£285,000	× 0%	Nil
£ 22,500	× 40%	9,000
£307,500		9,000
Less: Lifetime tax paid		(4,500)
Tax payable at death		4,500

1 April 2007 transfer

	£
Transfer of value 2007	82,010
Less: A/E (2006/07 – already used)	–
A/E (2005/06 – already used)	–
	82,010

All nil band used in previous seven years so IHT due on death is:

£82,010 × 40% = £32,804

Death estate

	£
Shares	Nil
Cash	40,000
Less CGT liability	(1,646)
	38,354

IHT at 40% = £15,342

The trustees of the settlement must pay IHT of £4,500.

Maxine must pay IHT of £32,804.

Mr Bright's personal representatives must pay IHT of £15,342.

(c) Notes for meeting

Immediate gift of shares in Bod Ltd:

(i) PET for IHT purposes, only chargeable if Mr Bright dies within seven years.

(ii) BPR only available on Mr Bright's death within seven years if Roger retains the shares and they are still eligible for BPR.

(iii) Disposal for CGT purposes. Gain can be held over; reduction in rate of taper relief if Roger disposes of the shares within two years.

(iv) Loss of influence over running of Bod Ltd; Mrs Bod has a 20% holding.

Retention of shares in Bod Ltd until death:

(i)   BPR likely to be available on Mr Bright's death, so no IHT.

(ii)   Tax free uplift to market value at date of death for CGT purposes.

(iii)   Retention of influence over running of Bod Ltd; Mr & Mrs Bod each have a 20% holding.

(iv)   If Roger is involved in the business he may be unhappy not to have received shares whilst his sister purchased shares at an undervalue.

20 Trusts

> **Tutorial note**. Work through the transactions methodically to identify when an IHT charge will arise.

(a)   Death 3 September 2006

RJ discretionary trust

The occasions of charge are:

17 July 1999: CLT by Rhys. If Rhys pays the tax this will be grossed up. The full £285,000 nil rate band is available.

5 March 2008: exit charge on the assets distributed. This is calculated using 30% of an assumed rate of tax scaled down by 34/40 to reflect the number of complete quarters that have elapsed since the settlement was created. The assumed rate is calculated using a transfer equal to the initial value of the settlement with prior transfers equal to the chargeable transfers made by Rhys in the seven years prior to the settlement (£nil).

17 July 2009: principal charge calculated using 30% of an assumed rate. The assumed rate is calculated using a transfer equal to the value of the settlement at the date of the anniversary with prior transfers equal to the chargeable transfers made by Rhys in the seven years prior to the settlement (£nil) plus the transfers made on 5 March 2008.

18 April 2012: exit charge on the assets distributed. This is calculated using 30% of the assumed rate of tax calculated at the last principal charge scaled down by 11/40 to reflect the number of complete quarters that have elapsed since the anniversary.

Rhys Jones discretionary will trust

3 September 2006: charge on death estate. The full £285,000 nil rate band is available as the Rhys Jones discretionary trust was set up more than seven years earlier.

28 February 2011: exit charge on the assets distributed. This is calculated using 30% of an assumed rate of tax scaled down by 17/40 to reflect the number of complete quarters that have elapsed since Rhys Jones' death. The assumed rate is calculated using a transfer equal to the initial value of the settlement with prior transfers equal to the chargeable transfers made by Rhys in the seven years prior to the death (£nil).

(b)   Death 3 July 2006

RJ discretionary trust

 If Rhys dies on 3 July 2006 this will be within seven years of the settlement and there will be additional IHT to pay by the trustees. This will be taken into account in computing the IHT payable on the advance on 5 March 2008 as it will reduce the initial value of the settlement.

Rhys Jones discretionary will trust

As death occurred within seven years of the transfer to the RJ discretionary trust there will be no nil rate band remaining, and this will increase the IHT due on death.

When computing the exit charge due on the distribution of the capital on 28 February 2011 the chargeable lifetime transfer by Rhys to the RJ discretionary trust will be an assumed prior transfer, so increasing the rate of IHT payable on the exit charge.

21 Fraser Ltd

> **Tutorial note**. The first part of this question is revision of material that you should know well from Paper 2.3. The second part requires you to apply your knowledge to several diffrenet proposals.

(a) CORPORATION TAX COMPUTATION

	£
Trading income (W1)	338,105
Interest income £(6,834 + 2,208)	9,042
Chargeable gains (W3)	36,468
PCTCT	383,615

Workings

(1) *Adjusted profit computation*

	£	£
Net profit per accounts		379,198
Add: depreciation	13,876	
gifts (over £50 each)	2,085	
entertaining	969	
		16,930
		396,128
Less: dividend including tax credit	1,655	
bank interest	6,834	
interest from gilts	2,208	
surplus on disposal of factory and lease	59,106	
net balancing charge (W2)	(11,780)	
		(58,023)
Taxable trading profit		338,105

(2) *Capital allowances*

(a) The plant

	£
FYA £9,800 × 2 × 40%	7,840

Note. The question stated that Fraser Ltd meets the criteria of medium-sized enterprise, so it is eligible for the 40% FYA on the purchase of plant and machinery.

(b) *The first factory*

	£
Original cost (excluding land)	90,000
Assuming the canteen is used by both manufacturing and office staff, only the general offices are in theory disallowable. However, being not more than 25% of the cost, the offices qualify for relief.	
Since the factory was sold above cost and there had been no non-industrial use the residue of expenditure for Fraser Ltd is	90,000
WDA is £90,000/20	4,500

(c) *The second factory*

The cost (excluding land) was £67,000.
The factory was sold for more than cost, so there is a balancing charge equal to the allowances given.

	£
9 years × 4% × £67,000	(24,120)
Net balancing charge	(11,780)

(3)　Chargeable gains

(a)　The lease

	£
Proceeds	40,000
Less cost	

$$£17,500 \times \frac{66.470 + \frac{1}{2}(68.697 - 66.470)}{81.100} = \frac{17.5 \text{ years}}{25 \text{ years}} \qquad (14,583)$$

	£
Unindexed gain	25,417
Less indexation allowance to April 2006	
$0.186 \times £14,583$	(2,712)
Chargeable gain	22,705

(b)　The factory

	£
Proceeds	112,750
Less cost	(79,000)
Unindexed gain	33,750
Less indexation allowance to August 2006	
$0.253 \times £79,000$	(19,987)
Indexed gain	13,763

Total gains are £(22,705 + 13,763) = £36,468.

(b)　Purchase of second hand property

The factory was originally built in 1980 and so its 25 year tax life has expired, no industrial buildings allowances will be available for the expenditure.

The factory will cost £150,000. The two disposals by Fraser Ltd during the year to 31 March 2007 realised proceeds of £152,750, so Fraser Ltd can make a claim to roll over all but £2,750 of the gains realised in the year ended 31 March 2007.

Purchase of new property

Assuming the new property is being sold by a speculative builder, Fraser Ltd will be able to claim industrial buildings allowances on the full cost of the building, but excluding land. If the purchase was not from a speculative developer the amount eligible for allowances would be limited to the construction cost.

If half of the factory is let out, the IBAs on that part will be set against the rental income received, and not allowed as a trading expense.

Rent received, less IBAs and property expenses, will be taxed as property income. if a reverse premium is paid to induce a tenant to take a lease, this would be an allowable property expense. The premium would normally be spread over the life of the lease for accounting purposes, and this would also apply for tax.

Any interest paid on bank borrowings or debentures would be allowable, either as a trading deduction or as a deduction from interest income, but not as a deduction from property income. It would be necessary to identify how the borrowings had been applied, and to apportion the interest payable between trading and non-trading.

If Fraser is to use half of the factory itself, the cost of that half will be £200,000, so that full rollover relief will be available. Rollover relief is not available against let property.

Purchase of subsidiary

If a subsidiary is purchased Fraser Ltd will not be able to roll over any of the gains from the disposals in the year ended 31 March 2007 as shares are not qualifying assets. No tax relief will be available for the cost of the shares until Fraser Ltd disposes of them, and the disposal may then be exempt as the disposal of a substantial shareholding.

Any interest paid on borrowings for the share purchase will be allowed as a deduction from non-trading interest.

As there will now be an additional company in the group, this will affect the small companies limits, and since Fraser Ltd is a marginal company this may increase the corporation tax payable.

Purchase of patents etc

The tax treatment of patents etc follows the accounting treatment. Fraser Ltd will therefore obtain a deduction for the cost of these intangible fixed assets over their useful lives. Any royalties payable will be allowed as an expense. As the patents are to be used in the trade the costs will be trading expenses; if Fraser Ltd acquires the subsidiary the patents should therefore also be acquired by the subsidiary.

Equity capital

If Fraser Ltd realises funds through the issue of shares rather than by raising loans, then there will be no interest payments to deduct in the accounts. Investors may require the payment of dividends; these are not tax deductible.

22 Major Ltd

> **Tutorial note.** It is important to distinguish between trading and non-trading loan relationships. Interest on the former is dealt with as trading income whilst interest on the latter is dealt with as interest income.

(a)   *Mainstream corporation tax*

	£	£
Trading profit per question	180,000	
Less patent royalties	(15,000)	
Taxable trading income		165,000
Property income		30,000
Capital gains		40,000
		235,000
Less charges: Gift Aid		(3,000)
Less non-trade deficit (£24,000 – £30,000)		(6,000)
PCTCT		226,000
Add Franked investment income		20,000
'Profits'		246,000

The eight month accounting period all falls within financial year 2006.

Small companies' lower limit	£300,000 × 8/12 × ½	£100,000
Small companies' upper limit	£1,500,000 × 8/12 × ½	£500,000

Small companies' marginal relief applies

Corporation tax

	£
£226,000 × 30%	67,800
Less small companies' marginal relief	
(11/400 × (£500,000 – £246,000) × 226,000/246,000)	(6,417)
Corporation tax	61,383

Working

Income tax

The loan interest was received from another UK company so it would have been received gross.

Interest on the bank loan is paid gross.

Charitable donations are paid gross under the gift aid scheme.

(b)
To:	The Directors of Major Ltd
From:	Certified Accountant
Date:	31 March 2007
Re:	Tax implications of the loan to Z Ltd becoming irrecoverable

It will not be possible for any amount of the loan written off to be deducted in computing Major Ltd's trading profits. This means that if the loan is written off in the company's profit and loss account, the amount written off must be added back to compute trading profits. Instead **any amount written off will be treated as a deficit on a non-trading loan relationship**. This means that **it will initially be deducted from income arising on non-trading loan relationships in the same accounting period. Any overall net deficit can be**:

(i) **Set against the company's total profits in the same accounting period,** or

(ii) **Set against income from non trading loan relationships arising in the previous twelve months**, or

(iii) **Set off against non-trading profits in the following period**, or

(iv) **Surrendered as group relief**.

Signed: Certified Accountant

(c) *General considerations*

Any dividends received on the shares acquired are not subject to corporation tax, but will be taken into account in determining the rate of corporation tax applicable to Major Ltd's profits chargeable to corporation tax. Any interest paid on borrowings to fund the purchase would be allowed as a deduction from non-trading interest, and if there is a deficit it can be relieved as described above.

Purchase of 20% holding from a retiring director

If Major Ltd purchases a 20% holding from a retiring director no tax relief will be obtained for the cost of the shares until they are sold. Provided the shares are held for at least twelve months and the target company is a trading company, the conditions for the substantial shareholding exemption to apply are likely to be satisfied so that any gain on disposal would be exempt. Conversely, if the target company collapses the loss would not be allowable. If it appears that the target company is declining it may be worthwhile attempting to sell the shares within twelve months of acquisition to ensure the loss is allowable.

Subscription for 5% holding

If the target company is a trading company and has gross assets of not more than £7million before the subscription and not more than £8million afterwards, it is likely that the investment will qualify for relief under the corporate venturing scheme. Major Ltd would obtain immediate tax relief of 20% of the £15,000 subscribed for the shares, ie £3,000. If the shares are disposed of within three years the relief is withdrawn.

As the shareholding will be less than 10%, it will not qualify for the substantial shareholding exemption. If a gain is made on the disposal it will be fully taxable. If there is a loss it will be allowable, and if the investment did qualify for CVS relief it will be possible to claim for the loss to be set against other income rather than capital gains.

Subscription for 40% holding

Even if the issuing company satisfies the conditions for CVS relief it will not be available since the holding is in excess of 40%.

The substantial shareholding exemption will however apply in the same way as for the purchase of a 20% holding as described above.

23 Hogg Ltd

> **Tutorial note**. Again, the information required in this question should be very familiar knowledge to you from Paper 2.3.

(a)   The due dates for the payment of corporation tax by Hogg Ltd in respect of the year to 31.12.06 are:

	£	£
14 July 2006 (1/4 × £500,000)		125,000
14 October 2006 (1/4 × £500,000)		125,000
14 January 2007 (1/4 × £520,000)	130,000	
plus underpaid 2 × £(130,000 − 125,000)	10,000	
		140,000
14 April 2007 (1/4 × £520,000)		130,000
1 October 2007 100% × £525,000		
− £125,000 − £125,000 − £140,000 − £130,000		5,000
Total		525,000

(b)   There is a £100 penalty for a failure to submit a return on time, rising to £200 if the delay exceeds three months. These penalties become £500 and £1,000 respectively when a return was late (or never submitted) for each of the preceding two accounting periods.

An additional tax geared penalty is applied if a return is more than six months late. The penalty is 10% of the tax unpaid six months after the return was due if the total delay is up to 12 months, and 20% of that tax if the return is over 12 months late.

24 Norma Ltd

> **Tutorial note**. This question takes a situation of an individual commencing a new trade and contrasts the tax treatment of trading as a company or as an unincorporated business. It is simply a question of applying your knowledge of the tax rules to the given scenario.

	(a) Sole trader £	(b) Dividend £	(c) Dividend + salary £
Company			
Profits	N/A	50,000	50,000
Less salary			(10,000)
Less employers NI (10,000 – 5,035) × 12.8%			(636)
			39,364
Less corporation tax @ 19%		(9,500)	(7,479)
Profits available for dividend		40,500	31,885
Individual			
Profits/salary	50,000		10,000
Dividend 40,500/31,885 × 100/90		45,000	35,428
Less PA	(5,035)	(5,035)	(5,035)
Taxable income	44,965	39,965	40,393
Income tax payable			
2,150 @ 10%	215	215	215
31,150/-/2,815 @ 22%	6,853		619
-/31,150/28,335 @ 10%		3,115	2,834
11,665/-/- @ 40%	4,666		
-/6,665/7,093 @ 32.5%		2,166	2,305
	11,734	5,496	5,973
Less tax credits -/45,000/35,428 @ 10%		(4,500)	(3,543)
	11,734	996	2,430
National insurance			
Class 2 52 × £2.10	109		
Class 4 (50000 – 33,540) × 1% + (33,540 – 5,035) × 8%	2,445		
	2,554		
Class 1 employees (10,000 – 5,035) × 11%			546
Net cash received			
Profit/Salary	50,000		10,000
Net dividend		40,500	31,885
Less income tax	(11,734)	(996)	(2,430)
Less national insurance	(2,554)		(546)
	35,712	39,504	38,909

From this it can be seen that Norma's net receipt is greatest if she operates as a company and withdraws all the profits as dividend. The net inflow is, however, only marginally lower if she draws a £10,000 salary. She may choose to draw a salary to ensure that her national insurance record is up to date, or if she wants to pay pension contributions in excess of the £3,600 limit available to all individuals.

It should also be noted that corporation tax is payable 9 months after the year end, PAYE and class 1 NI are payable monthly during the tax year, and any income tax not collected through PAYE and class 4 NI is payable by instalments on 31 January in and 31 July following the tax year, and any balance on the following 31 January.

25 Clarke Ltd

Since Clarke Ltd is an unquoted trading company the capital treatment will automatically apply if the conditions are satisfied. Alex is selling all of his shares, so the reduction to 75% or less of his interest is clearly satisfied. The buying out of a dissident shareholder/director is generally accepted by HMRC as being for the benefit of the company's trade. The shares subscribed for in 1992 have been held for more than the requisite five years, whereas the shares purchased in May 2002 will only qualify if the repurchase is delayed until June 2007.

Disposal March 2007

May 2002 acquisition – distribution treatment.

	£
Distribution – excess of proceeds over subscription 2,000 × £(5 − 1)	8,000
Higher rate tax thereon £8,000 × 100/90 × (32.5 − 10)%	2,000

	£
Capital gain	
Proceeds not treated as distribution 2,000 × £5 − £8,000	2,000
Less cost 2,000 × £3	(6,000)
Capital loss	(4,000)

January 1992 acquisition – capital treatment.

	£
Capital gain	
Proceeds 5,000 × £5	25,000
Less cost 5,000 × £1	(5,000)
Less indexation £5,000 × 0.199	(995)
	19,005
Less capital loss	(4,000)
Gain	15,005
Gain after taper relief (>2yrs business asset) £15,005 × 25%	3,751
CGT payable @ 40%	1,500

Total tax liability £2,000 + £1,500 = £3,500.

Disposal June 2007

May 2002 acquisition – capital treatment.

	£
Capital gain	
Proceeds 2,000 × £5	10,000
Less cost 2,000 × £3	(6,000)
Gain	4,000
Gain after taper relief (> 2 yrs business asset) £4,000 × 25%	1,000

January 1992 acquisition – capital treatment.

	£
Capital gain	
Proceeds 5,000 × £5	25,000
Less cost 5,000 × £1	(5,000)
Less indexation £5,000 × 0.199	(995)
Gain	19,005
Gain after taper relief (> 2 yrs business asset) £19,005 × 25%	4,751

Total gains £(1,000 + 4,751) = £5,751.

CGT liability £5,751 × 40% = £2,300.

Delaying the disposal until June 2007 enables the capital treatment to apply to the total shareholding, and saves tax of £3,500 − £2,300 = £1,200. It also delays the due date for payment of the tax by one year.

26 Daley plc

> **Tutorial note**. The computation should have been very straightforward revision of core Paper 2.3 material. Your discussion of loss relief is required to take the form of a letter to the directors, and you should ensure that you give a full and clear explanation.

(a)   *Profits chargeable to corporation tax*

	Year ended 31.12.03 £	Year ended 31.12.04 £	6 months ended 30.6.05 £	Year ended 30.6.06 £
Trading profits	–	110,000	85,000	–
Less s 393(1) relief	–	(1,000)	–	–
	–	109,000	85,000	–
Interest income	10,000	11,000	12,000	14,000
Chargeable gains	18,000	–	–	–
(losses are carried forward)	–			
	28,000	120,000	97,000	14,000
Less s 393A(1) current period relief	(28,000)	–	–	(14,000)
	–	120,000	97,000	–
Less s 393A carryback	–	(60,000)	(97,000)	–
	–	60,000	–	–
Less gift aid donation	–	(1,000)	–	–
PCTCT	–	59,000	–	–
CT @ 19%	–	11,210	–	–
Unrelieved gift aid donation	–	–	3,000	1,000

Loss memorandum		
Loss	29,000	200,000
Less s 393A(1) relief	(28,000)	(14,000)
Less s 393A(1) relief (6 months)		(97,000)
Less 6/12 × £120,000 (restricted)		(60,000)
Loss carried forward	1,000	29,000

A trading loss of £29,000 is available at 30 June 2006 to carry forward against future profits of the same trade, and there is also a capital loss of £4,000 to carry forward against future chargeable gains at 30.6.06.

(b)   My address

The directors of Daley Ltd

Their address

Date

Dear Directors

Relief for losses

I am writing to set out for you how Daley Ltd can obtain relief for losses that it has incurred during its first few years of trading. The company has incurred two different types of losses, capital losses and trading losses.

Capital losses

Capital losses incurred must first be set against any capital gains made in the same accounting period. Any capital losses which cannot be so offset are carried forward and set against capital gains in future accounting periods, as soon as they arise. The offset is automatic, and cannot be disapplied. Capital losses cannot be carried back.

Daley Ltd incurred a net capital loss of £5,000 in the year ended 31 December 2004. this cannot be carried back against the capital gains of £18,000 arising in the year to 31 December 2003 but is carried forward. £2,000 must be offset against the capital gains arising in the 6 months to 30 June 2005, leaving £3,000 of unrelieved capital losses to carry forward. Further capital losses of £1,000 arise in the year to 30 June 2006, and these are added to the £3,000 brought forward, so that capital losses of £4,000 are carried forward at 30 June 2006.

Trading losses

Trading losses can be relieved in several different ways, and there are strict rules about how the reliefs interact.

(i)   A claim can be made for trading losses to be relieved by set off against other income of the same accounting period. Other income includes interest income, property income, miscellaneous income and capital gains. The trading loss is, however, set off before gift aid donations are deducted, so that if the trading loss exceeds the other income, the gift aid donation is unrelieved.

        If the claim is made, the amount of trading loss that is set off is the lower of the company's other income or the trading loss. It is not possible to restrict the claim, for example to prevent gift aid donations from being unrelieved.

(ii)   If a claim has been made under (i) but not all of the trading loss has been relieved, then a claim may be made for the unrelieved amount to be carried back against the company's other income of the previous twelve months. Other income is as above, before the deduction of gift aid donations.

        Again, the amount of trading loss that is set off is the lower of the company's other income or the trading loss, and the claim cannot be restricted.

        If the previous accounting period is not twelve months long, then the loss will be carried back against the other income of the previous accounting period, then against the relevant proportion of the other income of the accounting period before that. For example, if the previous accounting period is six months long, then any loss carried back is set against the profits of the six month accounting period, then against 6/12ths of the profits of the accounting period before that (assuming it is 12 months long). When apportioning the profits it is acceptable to apportion the profits before deducting gift aid donations, and then to deduct the gift aid donations from the profits which fell outside the twelve month carry back period.

(iii) Any trading loss which has not been relived by a claim under (i) or (ii) is carried forward and set off against future profits from the same trade. The set off is automatic, is made against the first available profits, and is equal to the lower of the available loss and the available profits. It is not possible to restrict the amount of loss offset.

Best use of loss

Whilst making a claim under (i) or (ii) for offset against other income achieves relief at the earliest possible time, it may not achieve the best use of the loss. The rate at which a company pays corporation tax for an accounting period depends upon the level of its profits for that accounting period, so that a company may pay corporation tax at a higher rate in some accounting periods than in others. It may, therefore, be preferable to carry a loss forward if it will obtain a higher rate of relief, although this must be weighed against the disadvantage of receiving relief later.

The rates of corporation tax over recent year have been as follows:

- Before 31 March 2006 the starting rate of nil% applied to profits under £10,000

- Before 31 March 2006 an effective rate of 23.75% applied to the next £40,000 of profits

- The small companies rate of 19% applies to profits of up to £300,000 (before 31 March 2006 it applied if profits exceeded £50,000)

- the small companies marginal rate of 32.75% applies to the next £1,200,000 of profits

- the full rate of 30% applies to profits in excess of £1,500,000.

These limits are reduced where companies are associated, so that if Daley Ltd acquires Terry Ltd in April 2007 the small companies limits will be reduced from £300,000 to £100,000 and from £1,500,000 to £500,000 for the year to 30 June 2007.

Loss of year ended 31 December 2003

A claim was made for this loss to be set against other income of the same accounting period, and the balance was carried forward against the loss of the year to 31 December 2004. This meant that £10,000 was relieved at the starting rate of 0%, £18,000 at the marginal rate of 23.75% and £1,000 at the small companies rate of 19%. Had the loss been carried forward only, it would all have been relieved at the small companies rate of 19%. This claim cannot be amended.

Loss of the year to 30 June 2006

It is proposed that a claim should be made for the loss of the year to 30 June 2006 to be relieved against current and prior year profits. This will result in relief of £40,705 being obtained as follows:

Y/e 30.6.06   9/12 × £10,000 × 0% + 9/12 × £4,000 × 23.75% + 3/12 × 14,000 × 19% = £1,377, and gift aid of £1,000 is wasted

6m/e 30.6.05   £97,000 × 19% = £18,430, and gift aid of £3,000 is wasted

y/e 31.12.04   £60,000 × 19% = £11,400

y/e 30.6.07   £29,000 × 32.75% = £9,498

If the whole loss of £200,000 is carried forward the relief obtained will be £51,750:

y/e 30.6.07   £50,000 × 32.75% + 100,000 × 19% = £35,375

y/e 30.6.08   £50,000 × 32.75% = £16,375

In addition relief will be obtained of gift aid donations of £4,000 that would otherwise have been wasted, ie a further £760 (4,000 @ 19%).

It must be borne in mind that the relief will be delayed compared to a current year and carry back claim.

If I can provide any further information please do not hesitate to contact me.

Yours sincerely

Certified Accountant

27 Huis Ltd

> **Tutorial note**. The tax consequences of close company status are designed to ensure that people do not use this type of company as a means of avoiding tax.

(a) The loan to Sartre will lead to Huis Ltd being required to make a payment of £45,000 × 25% £11,250 to HMRC. This amount is payable at the same time as the mainstream corporation tax for the accounting period, so it is payable by 1 September 2007. (Note that if Huis Ltd were a 'large' company the tax on the loan is subject to the quarterly instalment regime.)

When the loan is written off on 31 March 2008 the company will be entitled to a refund of 25% of the amount waived (ie £45,000 × 25% = £11,250 refund). This refund will be due nine months after the end of the accounting period of the write off, ie it will be due on 1 September 2009.

Sartre will be deemed to receive income of £45,000 × 100/90 = £50,000 in the year in which the loan is written off, 2007/08. There will be no further basic rate liability, but if the income falls within the higher rate threshold, tax of 32.5% will be payable by 31 January 2009. That is, Sartre will be taxed just as if he had received a net dividend of £45,000.

The provision of private medical cover and the use of the yacht are provisions of benefits to a shareholder who is not an employee. Each year they will be treated as net distributions of £(1,000 + 24,000 × 1/12) = £3,000 pa. This is equivalent to gross income of £3,000 × 100/90 = £3,333. No further tax will be payable if Sartre is a basic rate tax payer, but if he is a higher rate taxpayer he will have a higher rate tax liability of £3,333 × (32.5 – 10)% = £750, payable by 31 January following the end of the tax year through self-assessment.

Huis Ltd will not be able to deduct the medical insurance premium nor the running costs of the yacht for that month in its corporation tax computation.

(b) Because Beauvoir Ltd is a close investment-holding company, the full rate of corporation tax applies. Excess management expenses are carried forward.

	Year ended 31.3.06 £	Year ended 31.3.07 £
Property income	14,000	25,000
Interest income	20,000	100,000
	34,000	125,000
Less management expenses – current	(34,000)	(45,000)
– brought forward (note)		(2,000)
PCTCT	–	78,000

Note. £2,000 carried forward from ye 31.3.06

Corporation tax at 30%	£23,400

28 H, S and N

> **Tutorial note**. It is important to realise that N Ltd counts as associated for the whole period to 30.6.05 despite the fact that it was only acquired on 1.1.05.

(a)   *H Ltd: corporation tax computations for the accounting periods of 12 months to*

	30.6.05	30.6.06
	£	£
Trading profit	2,000	–
Chargeable profits	2,000	–
MCT payable	£–	£–

Note. Starting rate applies for y/e 30.06.05 (W3)

S Ltd: corporation tax computations for the accounting periods of 12 months to

	30.6.05	30.6.06
	£	£
Trading profits	30,000	100,000
Less charges	(12,000)	(12,000)
Chargeable profits	18,000	88,000

S Ltd: corporation tax computations for the accounting periods of 12 months to

	30.6.05	30.6.06
	£	£
Corporation tax		
£18,000 × 19%	3,420	
£88,000 × 19%		16,720
MCT payable	3,420	16,720

Note. small companies' rate (SCR) applies in both periods (W3).

N Ltd: corporation tax computations for the accounting periods of 12 months and 6 months to

	31.12.05	30.6.06
	£	£
Adjusted profit split 12:6	43,500	21,750
Less capital allowances (W2)	(4,250)	(17,569)
Trading profits	39,250	4,181
Chargeable gain	–	20,000
	39,250	24,181
Less group relief surrendered by H Ltd (W1)	(19,625)	(24,000)
Chargeable profits	19,625	181
Corporation tax		
	£	£
£19,625 × 19% and W4	3,729	17
MCT	3,729	17

Note. SCR applies for Y/e 31.12.05.

Workings

(1) *Group relief*

	£
Loss of H Ltd y/e 30.6.06 available for group relief	48,000
Surrendered to N Ltd	
6 months to 31.12.05 lower of ($^{6}/_{12}$ × £48,000) or ($^{6}/_{12}$ × £39,250)	(19,625)
6 months to 30.6.06 lower of ($^{6}/_{12}$ × £48,000) or £24,181	(24,000)
Loss of H Ltd carried forward	4,375

Group relief is not available for S Ltd because it is only a 60% subsidiary.

Note. The group relief to N Ltd in the 6 months to 30.6.06 wastes most the starting rate band of £3,333 × ¼ = £833 falling into FY 05. This could be avoided by restricting group relief claimed for the 6 months to 30.6.06 by £1,486. This would incur additional CT of £1,486 × $^{3}/_{6}$ × 19% = £141 for FY 06, but if relief could be obtained by H Ltd in the year to 30.6.07 this may be preferable.·

H Ltd should not make a S.393A(1) carry back claim as this would waste starting rate relief in y/e 30.6.05.

(2) *Capital allowances*

		Pool	Expensive car	Allowances
	£	£	£	£
12 months to 31.12.05				
WDV brought forward		5,000		
Addition: car			16,000	
WDA 25%/£3,000		(1,250)	(3,000)	4,250
		3,750	13,000	
6 months to 30.6.06				
WDA 25% × 6/12		(469)	(1,500)	1,969
Additions: plant	31,000			
plant on HP	8,000			
	39,000			
FYA 40%	(15,600)			15,600
		23,400		17,569
WDV carried forward		26,681	11,500	

Private use of an asset does not restrict the capital allowances available to a company.

In a short period of account writing down allowances are pro-rated but first year allowances are not.

(3) *Upper and lower limits*

Y/e 30.6.05 and 30.6.06 there are three companies associated. Even though N Ltd only became associated with H and S on 1 January 2005 it is counted as associated for the whole period to 30.6.05. Thus small companies' limits for FY 2005 and FY 2006 are:

UL   £1,500,000 ÷ 3 = £500,000
LL   £300,000 ÷ 3 = £100,000

For N Ltd's six months to 30.6.06 these limits must be halved.

Starting rate limits for FY 2005 are: £50,000 ÷ 3 = £16,667
                                            £10,000 ÷ 3 = £3,333

Of N Ltd's AP to 30.6.06 only 3 months fall in FY 2005, so the starting rate limits for those three months are multiplied by $^{3}/_{12}$.

£16,667 × 3/12 = £4,167

£3,333 × 3/12 = £833

(4)   *6m to 30.6.06*

     3m FY 05 and 3m FY 06

     PCTCT is £181

     FY05

     PCTCT of £91 falls below starting rate lower limit

	£
0% × £91 =	nil

     FY 06
     PCTCT of £90 taxed at 19%

	£
19% × £90	17
MCT	£17

(b)   To: The Directors of H Ltd
     From: Certified Accountant
     Date: 31 December 2006
     Re: Minimisation of corporation tax on property transactions

There are several factors which will affect the corporation tax liability on the proposed disposals.

(i)   Of the £40,000 loss on the disposal of the factory by N Ltd, 4/6 x £40,000 = £26,667 accrued before N Ltd joined the H Ltd group and cannot be offset against gains on the disposals by H Ltd and S Ltd.

(ii)   Rollover relief is available against the purchase of the new warehouse. As the cost is only £240,000, which is less than the proceeds from either of the sales by H Ltd and S Ltd, the claim should be made to roll over £40,000 of the gain on the sale of the office block by H Ltd. The balance of £10,000 cannot be rolled over, as there are surplus proceeds of £10,000.

(iii)   H Ltd pays corporation tax at the small companies rate, N Ltd will pay corporation tax at the small companies rate on the first £25,000 of any capital gains and at the small companies marginal rate on any excess, and S Ltd pays tax at the small companies marginal rate. It is therefore preferable for the gains to be realised by H Ltd so as to bear corporation tax at the lowest rate. An election should be made for S Ltd to be treated as disposing of the warehouse to H Ltd before its sale, and for N Ltd to have transferred the factory to H Ltd immediately before sale.

The net position is then:

	£
Sale of factory	(13,333)
Sale of office block – surplus proceeds	10,000
Sale of warehouse	70,000
Total gains	66,667
Corporation tax £66,667 × 19%	12,667

N Ltd will have a pre-entry loss of £26,667 carried forward.

Signed: Certified Accountant

29 Exotica Inc and W ltd

(a)   If the salesmen have authority to conclude contracts, there will almost certainly be a permanent establishment in the United Kingdom, and its profits would therefore be liable to UK corporation tax. The holding of stocks would not, however, by itself show that there was a permanent establishment.

Taxable profits would be determined as if the permanent establishment had an arm's length relationship with the company, so that tax liabilities could not be manipulated by transfer pricing. Profits would be liable to tax at 30%, because the small companies' rate and marginal relief are not available to non-resident companies.

(b)   REPORT

To: The Board of Directors
From: Certified Accountant   Date: 1 November 2006
Subject: Taxation implications of the overseas operation

(i)   UK taxation arises on the profits of an overseas permanent establishment (PE), and any losses of such a PE will, provided that the PE is controlled in the UK, be aggregated with the profits or losses of the UK division. UK taxation will, subject to paragraph (ii) below, only arise on the profits of an overseas subsidiary controlled abroad to the extent that those profits are remitted to the UK (for example as dividends, or as interest on loans). Losses of an overseas subsidiary cannot be relieved against the UK company's profits, as group relief is only available between UK resident companies and between UK and EU resident companies in certain restricted circumstances.

(ii)   Foreign tax will arise on the profits of both PEs and subsidiaries. There may also be foreign withholding taxes on profits of a subsidiary remitted to the UK. To the extent that the same profits suffer both foreign and UK taxation, double taxation relief will be available, either under a treaty or under the UK's unilateral relief provisions. The usual effect is that the overall tax rate is the higher of the average UK rate on the UK company's profits and the foreign rate subject to an overall 30% ceiling.

(iii)   Assets cannot be transferred outside the scope of UK taxation to a foreign subsidiary on a no gain/no loss basis, so capital gains may arise. However, any such gains may be deferred until shares in the subsidiary are sold. If assets are transferred to a PE, there is no change of ownership so CGT is not triggered.

(iv)   A subsidiary will only be treated as not UK resident if it is not incorporated in the UK and its central management and control are abroad.

Signed: Certified Accountant

30 Paul and Joe

> **Tutorial note**. These rules are really designed to stop people avoiding VAT by establishing several different businesses with a turnover below the registration threshold.

VAT law recognises a 'taxable person' rather than a business. All business activities of the same person are regarded as a single VATable activity, and are brought within the same registration if the person is, or is required to be, registered. The same individual is a single 'person' for all activities carried on in his own capacity; and two partnership activities are also a single person, if exactly the same people are partners in both firms.

Conversely, related business activities may be regarded separately under VAT law if they are carried out by different 'persons'. Examples of different persons would be:

- individuals
- partnerships with different partners
- different limited companies.

HMRC may question whether there really is a separation of activities between different persons. If the activities are in reality carried on by someone else, they will form part of that person's taxable turnover, even if that person argues that the supplies are made by another.

In this situation, there are four possible taxable persons:

- Paul Sand trading alone (as a sole trader)
- Paul Sand and John Rowe
- Paul Sand and Peter Dene
- Paul Sand and Mrs Sand.

HMRC may question the reality of any of the partnerships. They will consider whether the parties involved are closely bound by financial, economic and organisational links.

For example HMRC may consider whether there is:

- a proper written partnership agreement
- evidence of the parties' intentions
- actual sharing of profits (not just income or expenses)
- notification of customers, suppliers and other authorities (eg on stationery)
- authority of partners to bind the firm
- ownership of common assets.

They may also consider how the business is treated for direct tax purposes.

If they consider any of the partnerships to be artificial, the activities of that partnership will be treated as carried on in conjunction with the sole trade.

Conversely HMRC may also issue a business splitting direction.

31 VAT groups

> **Tutorial note**. Marks may be specifically allocated for letter writing skills. Would you have gained them here?

Our address

Your address

Date

Dear Mr Franklin

GROUP REGISTRATION

I am writing in reply to your recent enquiry regarding Union Ltd, specifically the question of whether that company should be included in the group VAT registration and the procedure for so doing.

First, I would confirm that group registration is possible, since all the companies are either established or have a fixed establishment in the UK and they are all under common control.

It would be advisable for Union Ltd to be included in the group registration, for two reasons:

(1)   To avoid the need to account for VAT on intra group transactions and hence minimise the risk of VAT being underdeclared in error. For example, the group relief payments to which you refer in your letter would not normally constitute consideration for taxable supplies and so would not give rise to the need to account for VAT, even between companies which are not in a group registration. However, in certain circumstances HMRC might argue that the 'group relief payments' in fact amount to consideration for a taxable supply, giving rise to an output tax liability; for example, if the payments were linked to services provided by Union Ltd to other group companies.

By including Union Ltd in the group registration, such potential problems are avoided.

(2)   As Union Ltd is partly exempt, around 40% of any input tax it incurs is irrecoverable.   If Union Ltd is not included in the group registration, any standard-rated supplies which it receives from other group companies would generate additional irrecoverable VAT.

It is also necessary to consider, however, the effect of including a partly exempt company in the group registration. This will depend in part on the partial exemption method used by Union Ltd at present and the method to be used by the group if Union Ltd is included. Under the standard method, more of Union Ltd's overhead input tax would become recoverable but some of the group's would be lost.

It should however be borne in mind that the partial exemption de minimis limit will apply to the group as a whole and is not multiplied by the number of companies in the group registration.

So far as the procedure is concerned, an application needs to be made to HMRC for Union Ltd to be added to the group registration. All applications to join an existing VAT group will automatically be approved by HMRC and will take effect from the date they are received by HMRC (or such earlier or later time as HMRC may allow). HMRC will not normally permit retrospective grouping, so Union Ltd will have to be accounted for separately until you make the application.

HMRC do have the power to refuse an application within 90 days of its receipt if the application does not meet all of the eligibility criteria (which should not be a problem in your case) or presents a risk to the revenue. It is not thought that a slight improvement in the partial exemption position would be sufficient to warrant a refusal on the grounds of risk to the revenue; the improvement would have to go beyond the simple effects of grouping, so something 'artificial' would have to be involved.

Please do not hesitate to contact me if I can be of further assistance.

Yours sincerely

Certified Accountant

32 Stewart Ltd

> **Tutorial note**. Remember to round up the percentage recovery to the nearest whole number.

(a)   Residual input tax

	6/06 £	9/06 £	12/06 £	3/07 £	Total £
'T' (note 1)	403,920	359,177	467,159	520,321	1,750,577
'T + E'	455,992	382,371	485,950	557,760	1,882,073
T/T + E (note 2)	89%	94%	97%	94%	94%
Residual tax	14,719	12,613	10,412	11,919	49,663

Notes

(1)   Excludes sale of capital asset used in the business.

(2)   Rounded up to nearest whole percentage point.

(b)   Exempt input tax

	6/06 £	9/06 £	12/06 £	3/07 £	Total £
Direct	3,120	2,775	1,374	1,876	9,145
Share of residual	1,619	757	312	715	2,980
	4,739	3,532	1,686	2,591	12,125
De minimis? (note)	N	N	Y	N	N

Note. Less than £625 pm and less than 50% of the total

(c)   Recoverable input tax

	6/06 £	9/06 £	12/06 £	3/07 £	Total £
Direct	44,404	39,098	24,926	36,020	144,448
Exempt de min			1,686		
Share of residual	13,100	11,856	10,100	11,204	46,683
	57,504	50,954	36,712	47,224	191,131

Total recovered in the four quarterly returns: 192,394

Annual adjustment – due to HMRC   (1,263)

The annual adjustment will be made by reducing the input tax for the return period to June 2007.

33 Tax planning

> **Tutorial note**. In this question it was important to allocate your time carefully between each of the queries raised.

(a)   Incorporation should take place when the business starts to make profits, on 1 May 2008. Advantage can then be taken of s 381 ICTA 1988 loss relief, which is only available to unincorporated businesses. This relief is against income of the three tax years preceding the year of loss, taking earlier years first. Relief will be obtained against the salary of the last few years before Client A became self-employed, leading to repayments of tax.

(b)   B's current annual profit is £55,000 × 40% = £22,000.

With the contract, B's turnover will be over the registration limit so he will have to register for VAT. He will be able to charge VAT on top of the contract price, as the customer is registered and will be able to reclaim the VAT. However, as the business is highly competitive he will have to absorb the

VAT which he will have to charge to other customers, and not increase his prices. This will be offset to some extent by the fact that he will be able to reclaim VAT suffered on his purchases. Thus his overall profit margin on normal sales will be reduced to 40% × 100/117.5. The new annual profit will be as follows.

	£	£
Normal sales		55,000
Less VAT on normal sales × $^7/_{47}$		(8,191)
		46,809
Less normal purchases £55,000 × 60%	33,000	
Less VAT on normal purchases × $^7/_{47}$	(4,915)	
		(28,085)
Profit on normal sales		18,724
Contract sales	10,000	
Less cost of contract sales £10,000 × 60%	(6,000)	
		4,000
Revised annual profit		22,724

The increase in annual profit will therefore be £22,724 – £22,000 = £724. It is for B to decide whether this makes it worthwhile to accept the contract.

If B attempted to avoid VAT registration by having a separate company handle the contract, HMRC could aggregate the turnovers of B's own business and the company's business, making both B and the company liable to register. The consequence would be that no saving would be achieved.

(c) It is in general bad planning to hold an asset likely to rise in value in a company. When the asset is sold, the company will have to pay corporation tax on the gain (at 30% in this case, since close investment-holding companies are not entitled to the small companies' rate or to marginal relief). If the proceeds are paid out as a dividend, further tax will be suffered by higher rate taxpayers. If they are paid out in the course of winding up the company, the shareholders will have chargeable gains on their shares.

The scheme has several other flaws. UK dividend income is not taxable in the hands of a UK company so there is no question of a deduction for the director's fees from the company's taxable income, as it will not have any taxable income. Also, the payment of the fees will have adverse consequences as both primary (employee's) and secondary (employer's) Class 1 NICs will arise. Finally, the income of a controlling director of an investment company is not treated as relevant earnings for the purposes of personal pension schemes, so no tax relief for premiums above the contribution threshold (£3,600 per year) would be available.

(d) *Sole trader*

	£
Profits	23,000
IT £23,000 × 22%	(5,060)
NIC Class 2 £2.10 × 52	(109)
Class 4 £(23,000 – 5,035) × 8%	(1,437)
Net spendable income	16,394

Company

	£
CT £23,000 × 19%	4,370
Net profits before distribution (£23,000 – £4,370)	18,630
Dividend × 100/90	20,700
Less tax credit	(2,070)
Net spendable income	18,630

34 Hulse Finds Ltd

> **Tutorial note**. Although the question may appear long on first reading note how it breaks down into a series of points.

(a)   The interest paid by Paul on the loan to acquire the shares in the company is qualifying annual interest. This is because Hulse Finds Ltd is a close company (it is controlled by Paul and Nick) and Paul works full-time for the company. Qualifying annual interest is an allowable charge on income that is deducted in arriving at Paul's statutory total income, and consequently reduces his taxable income.

(b)   Hulse Finds Ltd is a close company and has made a loan to a participator, Chris. Accordingly, the company should have paid HM Revenue & Customs (HMRC) £2,500 (25% of the loan) by 1 January 2008 (ie nine months after the end of the accounting period). HMRC will repay the £2,500 when the loan is repaid by Chris or waived by Hulse Finds Ltd. The company would not have had to make any payment if Chris had worked full-time for the company, as the loan is for less than £15,000 and Chris does not own more than 5% of Hulse Finds Ltd.

(c)   The tax implications arising out of the acquisition are:

(i)   The capital losses of SNL will remain with SNL. SNL has sold its trade and assets to Hulse Finds Ltd and capital losses remain with a company when it sells its trade. SNL can use its capital losses to relieve any gains arising on the assets sold to SN2 Ltd.

(ii)   The trading losses of SNL will also remain with SNL and will not to be transferred with the trade. Where a company sells its trade to an unconnected company, any trading losses remain with the vendor company. SNL may be able to offset the losses against any capital allowance balancing charges arising on the sale.

It is possible for trading losses to be transferred to the purchaser when a company sells its trade to another company, but only when certain conditions are satisfied. Broadly, the same persons must beneficially own at least 75% of the business both before and after the sale. These conditions would have been satisfied if SNL had formed a subsidiary, Newco, sold its trade to Newco, and then sold Newco to SN2 Ltd.

SNL is the legal and beneficial owner of its trade prior to the sale. If the trade had been sold to Newco, SNL would no longer be the legal owner of the trade but would still be the beneficial owner as it owns Newco.

In such circumstances, Newco could have used the trading losses against future trading profits arising from the same trade, provided there was no major change in the nature or conduct of its trade within three years of the purchase by Hulse Finds Ltd.

(iii)   There are now two companies in the Hulse Finds Ltd group. Accordingly, the limits used to determine the rate of corporation tax payable must be divided by two. The corporation tax liability of the group is continued as follows:

	£
Hulse Finds Ltd	
£250,000 × 30%	75,000
Less marginal relief (£750,000 − £250,000) × 11/400	(13,750)
	61,250
SN2 Ltd	£
£50,000 (£40,000 + £10,000) × 19%	9,500
Group tax liability	70,750

(iv) Consideration should have been given to Hulse Finds Ltd acquiring the trade of SNL without the use of a separate subsidiary. This would have resulted in a single company with profits chargeable to corporation tax of £300,000 (£250,000 + £50,000) and a lower tax liability as asset out below:

Hulse Finds Ltd (owning the trade of SN2 Ltd)

	£
£300,000 × 19%	57,000
Reduction in tax liability (£70,750 – £57,000)	13,750

(d) The tax implications of the Newland business depend on the legal structure used. From a tax point of view, there are two distinct ways of establishing the business:

(i)   It could be owned directly by Hulse Finds Ltd (or SN2 Ltd). Under this option, it would be an overseas permanent establishment of a UK resident company.

(ii) Hulse Finds Ltd (or SN2 Ltd) could incorporate a new subsidiary in Newland to acquire the business. Under this option, it would be an overseas subsidiary of a UK resident company.

Overseas permanent establishment

A permanent establishment is not a separate legal entity but is an extension of the company that owns it. The profits or losses of the permanent establishment belong directly to the company.

Provided the permanent establishment is controlled from the UK, the trading loss made in the year ended 31 March 2010 could be offset by Hulse Finds Ltd (or SN2 Ltd) against its income and gains of that year, reducing the company's UK corporation tax liability. Once the permanent establishment is profitable, the company owning the permanent establishment will be subject to 45% Newland corporation tax on the permanent establishment profits, because it is trading within the boundaries of Newland from permanent establishment.

The profits will also be subject to UK corporation tax because a UK resident company is subject to tax on its worldwide income and gains. However, the UK corporation tax liability, in respect of the permanent establishment profits, will be fully relieved by double tax relief as the rate of corporation tax in Newland is higher than that in the UK. Accordingly, there will be no UK corporation tax to pay on the permanent establishment's profits.

Overseas subsidiary

A subsidiary is a separate legal entity. A company incorporation in Newland will be resident in Newland for tax purposes, provided it is not managed and controlled from the UK. Its profits or losses will then be subject to the tax regime of Newland.

The trading loss of the year ended 31 March 2010 would be carried forward and deducted from the company's future trading profits arising out of the same trade.

Once the company is profitable, it will be subject to tax in Newland at the rate of 45%. Any dividends paid to the UK parent company will be grossed up, in respect of the underlying tax suffered in Newland, and included in the parent company's profits chargeable to corporation tax. Double tax relief, at the lower of either the overseas tax suffered or the UK tax on the overseas income, is available. Accordingly, no UK tax will be due on the overseas dividends as the rate of tax in Newland exceeds that in the UK.

It is usually suggested that a permanent establishment should be used where an overseas enterprise is expected to make initial losses. This strategy enables the losses to be offset against any other profits of the company. However, the particular facts of the situation must be considered carefully.

The use of a permanent establishment in Newland will enable Hulse Finds Ltd (or SN2 Ltd) to offset the losses against its profits for the year ended 31 March 2010. This will save UK corporation tax at a maximum rate of 30%.

The use of a subsidiary would mean that the losses could not be offset in the year ended 31 March 2010, as the subsidiary will not have any other income. However, in the following year the losses will reduce that year's profits and save tax in Newland at 45%.

Accordingly, provided the group is willing to wait for a year (from a cash flow point of view) a greater tax saving can be achieved by using a subsidiary in Newland rather than a permanent establishment. This assumes, of course, that the anticipated profits materialise in the year ended 31 March 2011.

It must also be recognised that a subsidiary is an associate for the purpose of determining the rate of tax paid by group companies, whereas a permanent establishment is not. Accordingly, the use of a subsidiary (rather than a permanent establishment) could increase the rate of corporation tax paid in the UK companies. However, on the facts given, whether a permanent establishment or a subsidiary is used makes no difference to the liabilities of the UK companies in the year ended 31 March 2010.

35 Financial planning

Tutorial note. The choice between equity and debt finance is a very important consideration when raising additional funds.

Report

To: The Board of M Ltd

From: Certified Accountant

Date: 19 May 2006

Re: Taxation consequences of alternative methods of raising finance

The choice of raising additional funds to finance a major expansion of the business can be summarised as being between loan capital or equity. A major distinction between the two forms of financing is that interest payable on borrowings is deductible for corporation tax purposes whereas dividends payable to shareholders are not.

Loan capital

Interest is tax deductible on an accruals basis under either from trading profit (if put to a trading use) or from interest income.

If the loan interest being paid represents an annual payment other than to a UK bank or a UK resident company, income tax should be deducted at source and accounted for to the Collector of Taxes.

Costs of obtaining loan finance will be treated as tax-deductible in the same manner as interest payable on the loan. In contrast, costs in respect of issuing share capital are not deductible for CT purposes.

Interest income received by the providers of loan finance is taxable. It will be interest income of a company and subject to tax at normal corporation tax rates. Individuals in receipt of interest income will be subject to tax on the gross amount at either 20% or 40%.

Equity finance

Dividends represent appropriations of profit after tax. They are not tax deductible and any costs associated with the raising of share capital are not tax deductible.

With regard to providers of equity finance, there are tax benefits available to investors who invest in Enterprise Investment Scheme (EIS) shares:

(1)   An individual subscribing for new ordinary shares in an unquoted trading company can claim income tax relief at 20% for an investment of up to £400,000 per tax year. If the EIS shares are held for three years, there is exemption from capital gains tax on a disposal of the shares. A capital loss may arise on a disposal before or after expiry of the three year period but it is restricted by reducing the issue price by the amount of relief obtained.

(2)   Chargeable gains realised by individuals may be deferred provided that those gains are reinvested in the ordinary shares of a qualifying EIS unquoted trading company. The reinvestment of gains must be made in the period twelve months before to three years after the relevant disposal. The gain is deferred and does not therefore crystallise before a subsequent disposal of the new EIS shares.

If you wish to discuss further any of the above points do not hesitate to contact me.

Signed: Certified Accountant

36 Mr and Mrs Faulds

> **Tutorial note**. This question required you to draft notes for a meeting so an answer in bullet point format would have been perfectly acceptable.

Notes for meeting regarding individual savings accounts (ISAs)

- Investments within an ISA are exempt from both income and capital gains tax.

- There is no statutory minimum period for which an ISA must be held. A full or partial withdrawal may be made at any time without loss of the tax exemption.

- To open an ISA an investor must, in general, be aged 18 or over. However, a cash ISA can be held by individuals aged 16 or 17

- A husband and wife each have their own limits.

- ISAs can be made up of two components.

  - Cash
  - Stocks and shares (which may include life insurance policies)

- There are two distinct types of ISA:

  - **Maxi-accounts** which must contain a stocks and shares component and may contain a cash component

  - **Mini-accounts** which comprise a single component only.

- A '**maxi-account**', must contain a stocks and shares component with or without a cash component. Subscribing to a maxi-account in one year precludes an investor from also subscribing to a mini-account of any type in that year. **There is an annual subscription limit for maxi-accounts of £7,000 of which a maximum of £3,000 can be in cash.**

- A **mini-account** comprises a single component only. Once a mini-account, for either component, has been subscribed to for a particular tax year the only other ISA that may be subscribed to for that year is a mini-account comprising the other component. **The annual subscription limits for mini-accounts are:**

  - Cash component accounts: £3,000
  - Stocks and shares component accounts: £4,000

37 Landscape Ltd

> **Tutorial note.** Make sure you make an attempt at each part of the question and do not spend too long on any one part.

(a) *Peter Plain*

The distinction between employment and self employment is a fine one. Employment involves a contract of service, whereas self employment involves a contract for services. Taxpayers tend to prefer self employment because the rules for the deductibility of expenses are more generous but the following factors suggest that HMRC will regard Peter as an employee rather than self employed:

(i) Peter works five days each week: If Peter cannot work when he chooses it suggests the **company has control** over him and he is an employee

(ii) Peter **uses the company's equipment**

(iii) Peter **does not have any other clients**

(iv) The **computer function (and hence Peter) is an integral part of the company's business.**

Other factors HMRC may consider are:

- **whether Peter must accept further work**
- **whether the company must provide further work**
- **whether Peter hires his own helpers**
- **what degree of financial risk Peter takes**
- **what degree of responsibility for investment and management Peter has**
- **whether Peter can profit from sound management**
- **the wording used in any agreement between Peter and the company.**

(b) *Simon Savannah*

The **statutory redundancy pay of £2,400 is exempt from income tax.** However, **both the holiday pay of £1,500 and the £5,000** in respect of the agreement not to work for a rival company are taxable in 2006/07.

The balance of the lump sum redundancy payment is £46,100 (£55,000 – £2,400 – £1,500 – £5,000). If the payment is a genuine *ex gratia* redundancy payment, £27,600 (£30,000 – £2,400) is exempt. £8,500 is taxable in 2006/07. The balance of £10,000 is taxable when received in 2007/08.

(c) *Trevor Tundra*

Landscape Ltd is a close company and Trevor Tundra is a participator. This means that Trevor will be treated as though he has received dividends equal to the earnings that would have arisen in 2006/07 if he had been a director or an employee of Landscape Ltd:

	£
Car (£14,000 × 35%) (W)	4,900
Loan (£40,000 × 2/12 × 5%) + (£15,000 × 7/12 × 5%)	771
Loan written off	15,000
Taxable benefits	20,671

Working

CO_2 emissions = 240 g/km
Above baseline figure 240 – 140 = 100g/km
Divide by 5 = 20
% = 15 + 20 = 35%

(d)   *Ursula, Violet and Wilma*

Ursula, Violet and Wilma are all working in Cambridge in the performance of their duties. **Tax relief is available for the cost of travel between home and Cambridge, if Cambridge is a 'temporary' place of work. A place of work is classed as a temporary workplace if the employee does not work there continuously for a period which lasts (or is expected to last) more than 24 months.**

Therefore, the cost of all of Ursula's travel to Cambridge qualifies for tax relief. The mileage allowance that Ursula receives from the company falls within the authorised mileage rates and so is tax free and she can make an expense claim as follows:

	£
Authorised mileage rates	
(120 × 40 =) 4,800 × 40p	1,920
Less mileage allowance received (4,800 × 36p)	(1,728)
Expense claim	192

As Violet was initially expected to work in Cambridge for more than 24 months the train fare initially paid by Landscape Ltd is a taxable benefit. However, from 1 January 2007 no taxable benefit arises in respect of the train fare because Violet's period of secondment to Cambridge is no longer expected to exceed 24 months.

Wilma should be entitled to full tax relief for the cost of her journey's to Cambridge. Wilma will be assessed on a benefit as follows:

	£
Mileage allowance received (120 x 150 =) 18,000 × 36p	6,480
Less authorised mileage rates 10,000 × 40p	
8,000 × 25p	(4,000)
	(2,000)
Taxable benefit	480

(e)   Landscape Ltd can give an employee up to **£3,000 worth of 'free' shares a year**. Employees can buy **'partnership'** shares with their pre-tax salary up to a maximum of 10% of gross earnings, subject to an upper limit of £1,500 per year.

In addition, employers can give employees up to two free matching shares for each partnership share purchased. Provided the shares are held for **five years before disposal**, employees will not be subject to income tax or NIC on them. If the shares are held for more than three years but less than five years, tax and NIC is due on the lower of the market value of the shares on the date they were given to the employee and the market value at the date of withdrawal.

38 Marilyn Corniche

Tutorial note. The shares in Spiro plc fell in value between May 2005 and February 2007 as the valuation of Spiro plc shares at May 2005 is lower of:

¼ up

$$\frac{(685 - 677)}{4} + 677 = 679$$

Mid-bargain

$$\frac{690 + 670}{2} = 680$$

ie 679 × 10,000 = £67,900

whereas the value of shares at February 2007 is £63,600.

This means that the optimal solution would be for the deed of variation to be made in respect of all the assets passing to Marilyn except the Spiro plc shares. The shares would then be included in Marilyn's death estate at their lower value and consequently less IHT would be due on them.

However, the examiner did not require this level of complexity in your answer and we have produced below the answer that the examiner expected.

(a) *Inheritance tax liability on the death of Max Corniche 20 May 2005*

All of Max's estate (except the chattels) passes to Marilyn for IHT purposes, either outright or under trust of which Marilyn is entitled to the interest in possession. Therefore the **spouse exemption** applies to these assets.

The chattels passing to Max's brother total £15,000 (£5,000 + £7,000 + £3,000) and are covered by the nil rate band.

Therefore, there is no IHT payable on the death of Max.

Inheritance tax liability on death of Marilyn Corniche February 2007

Marilyn has the initial interest in Max's will trust, so the assets of that trust are liable to IHT as if they were part of Marilyn's estate.

	£	£
Free estate		
Personalty		
Berkley's Bank a/c	33,400	
Unit trust units in PEPs and ISAs	72,000	
Cash ISA	10,600	
Ex-cash ISA from Max	11,300	
Bank deposit a/c from Max	20,000	
	147,300	
Realty		
Family home (whole)	220,000	367,300
Settled property		
Personalty		
Spiro plc (W)	63,600	
Unit trusts	81,000	
Unit trusts – PEPs and ISAs	67,600	
	212,200	
Realty		
Holiday home	73,000	285,200
Gross estate		652,500

	£
Tax is:	
£285,000 × 0%	Nil
£367,500 × 40%	147,000
	147,000

Working

Valuation of Spiro plc shares at February 2007 is lower of:

¼ up

$$\frac{(647-635)}{4} + 635 = 638$$

Mid-bargain

$$\frac{642+630}{2} = 636$$

ie 636 × 10,000 = £63,600

(b)   (i)   **A deed of variation could be executed, passing assets now owned by Marilyn but deriving from Max's estate, directly to Douglas and Archie.** The deed of variation can apply both to assets passing directly to Marilyn and to those passing to the interest in possession trust. It includes the share of the house owned as tenants in common which passes to Marilyn under the will.

The following conditions must be satisfied:

(1)   the variation must be made before 20 May 2007 (**within 2 years of Max's death**)

(2)   it must be made **in writing** by Marilyn

(3)   the variation must not be made for consideration

(4)   the variation must include a statement that the assets subject to the variation will to be treated as devolving for IHT under its terms rather than under the terms of the will. The statements must be made by Marilyn and **by the personal representatives of Max's estate as more IHT will become payable in respect of his estate as a result of the variation.**

A similar statement can be made for CGT so that the variation is not a disposal for CGT and Douglas and Archie will take the assets at their value at Max's death.

(ii)   The assets subject to the variation are:

	May 2005 £	*Feb 2007* £
Passing outright		
Family home (1/2 shares)	90,000	110,000
Ex-cash ISA from Max	11,000	11,300
Bank deposit a/c from Max	20,000	20,000
Spiro plc shares	67,900	63,600
Passing into life interest trust		
Unit trusts	60,300	81,000
Unit trusts – PEPs and ISAs	48,800	67,600
Holiday home	63,000	73,000
	361,000	426,500

Max's chargeable estate at death is therefore £(361,000 + 15,000 (note)) = £376,000.

The IHT on Max's estate is therefore:

	£
£285,000 × 0%	Nil
£91,000 × 40%	36,400
	36,400

Marilyn's chargeable estate at death is £(652,500 − 426,500) = £226,000.

Marilyn's estate now falls within the nil band. The IHT saved on Marilyn's estate is therefore £147,000 (see above).

The overall IHT saving is therefore £(147,000 − 36,400) = £110,600

Note. £15,000 of chattels left to Max's brother (5,000 + 7,000 + 3,000).

Pilot Paper

BPP
LEARNING MEDIA

Section A: BOTH questions are compulsory and MUST be attempted

1   Hutt plc has owned the whole of the ordinary share capital of Rainbow Ltd and Coronet Ltd since 1998. All three companies are resident in the UK. Their results for the year ended 31 March 2007 are as follows:

	Hutt plc £	Rainbow Ltd £	Coronet Ltd £
Taxable trading profit/(loss)	(105,000)	800,000	63,000
Capital gain	144,000	–	–
Rental income	65,000	–	–
UK bank interest receivable	2,000	57,000	18,000

Hutt plc's rental income of £65,000 per annum arises in respect of Hutt Tower, an office building acquired on 1 April 2006.

In the year ended 31 March 2006 Hutt plc had a trading profit of £735,000, UK bank interest receivable of £2,000 and a capital loss of £98,000, which was carried forward as at 31 March 2006.

Hutt plc and Coronet Ltd both carry on trades in the UK. Rainbow Ltd conducts both its manufacturing and trading activities wholly in the country of Prismovia. The system of corporation tax in Prismovia is mainly the same as that in the UK although the rate of corporation tax is 28%. There is no double taxation agreement between the UK and Prismovia.

Hutt plc has agreed that it will purchase the whole of the share capital of Lucia Ltd, a UK resident engineering component manufacturing company, on 1 July 2007 for £130,000.

Hutt plc will need to take out a loan to finance the purchase of Lucia Ltd. The company intends to borrow £190,000 from BHC Bank Ltd on 1 July 2007. BHC Bank Ltd will charge Hutt plc a £1,400 loan arrangement fee and interest at 7.25% per annum. Hutt plc only needs £130,000 of the loan to buy the share capital of Lucia Ltd and intends to use the balance of the loan as follows: £45,000 to carry out repairs to Hutt Tower; and the remainder to help fund the company's ongoing working capital requirements.

Lucia Ltd is a UK resident company. The scale of its activities in the last few years has been very small and it has made tax adjusted trading losses. As at 31 March 2007 Lucia Ltd has trading losses carried forward of £186,000. The company's activities from 1 April 2007 to 30 June 2007 are expected to be negligible and any profit or loss in that period can be ignored. Because of the small scale of its activities Lucia Ltd has not been registered for value added tax (VAT) since March 2006. In arriving at the purchase price for the company, the owners of Lucia Ltd have valued the company's trading losses at £35,340 (£186,000 at 19%), as Lucia Ltd has always been a small company.

On the purchase of Lucia Ltd, Hutt plc has plans to return the company to profitability and the budgeted turnover of Lucia Ltd for the nine months ended 31 March 2008 is as set out below. All amounts relate to the sales of engineering components and are stated exclusive of VAT. It can be assumed that all categories of turnover will accrue evenly over the period.

			£
UK customers:	–	VAT registered	85,000
	–	non-VAT registered	25,000
European Union customers:	–	VAT registered	315,000
	–	non-VAT registered	70,000
Other non-UK customers			180,000
			675,000

Lucia Ltd will incur input VAT of £7,800 per month from 1 July 2007 in respect of purchases from UK businesses. It will also purchase raw materials from Dabet Gmbh for £17,000 in November 2007. Dabet Gmbh is resident and registered for VAT in Germany.

Lucia Ltd owns a factory that was built in May 1971 at a cost of £210,000. The factory was acquired by Lucia Ltd on 30 June 2003, for £270,000. It can be assumed that the factory's current value of £80,000 will not change in the foreseeable future. On 1 January 2008, Lucia Ltd will sell this factory and take out a short lease on a new, larger one. The indexation allowance applicable to the period June 2003 to January 2008 can be assumed to be £27,000.

It is proposed that an office building owned by Coronet Ltd be sold to Lucia Ltd in May 2008 at its market value. This building will then be sold on by Lucia Ltd, to Vac Ltd, an unconnected third party in June 2008, giving rise to a capital gain of £92,000. The intention is that this gain will be reduced by the capital loss arising on the sale of the factory.

Required:

(a) Describe and evaluate the options available in respect of the trading losses of Hutt plc for the year ended 31 March 2007. Your answer should include a recommendation on the most tax efficient use of these losses, together with details of and time limits for any elections or claims that would need to be submitted, assuming that the losses are to be used as soon as possible and are not to be carried forward. (13 marks)

(b) Prepare a report for the management of Hutt plc concerning the acquisition of Lucia Ltd. The report should be in three sections, addressing the three sets of issues set out below, and should, where appropriate, include supporting calculations.

    (i) **The purchase price**
    Comment on the valuation placed on Lucia Ltd's trading losses, by the owners of Lucia Ltd.

    Provide an explanation of the tax treatment of the loan arrangement fee and the interest payable on the loan of £190,000, assuming that Hutt plc continues to have bank interest receivable, in the year ended 31 March 2008, of £2,000. (9 marks)

    (ii) **VAT issues**
    Provide an explanation of the date by which Lucia Ltd will be required to register for VAT in the UK and any other relevant points in respect of registration.

    Provide a calculation of the VAT payable by, or repayable to, Lucia Ltd in respect of the period from registration to 31 March 2008.

    With reference only to the facts in the question, suggest ONE disadvantage of Lucia Ltd entering into a group VAT registration with Hutt plc. (6 marks)

    (iii) **The office building**
    Advise on the tax implications of the proposed sale of the office building by Coronet Ltd to Lucia Ltd in May 2008. Your answer should consider all relevant taxes.

    Evaluate the proposed strategy to reduce the capital gain arising on the sale of the office building by offsetting the capital loss on the sale of the factory, on the assumption that both Lucia Ltd and Coronet Ltd will pay corporation tax at the rate of 30%, for the year ended 31 March 2009. (9 marks)

Appropriateness of the format and presentation of the report and the effectiveness with which its advice is communicated. (2 marks)

You may assume that the tax rates and allowances for the financial year to 31 March 2007 and for the tax year 2006/07 will continue to apply for the foreseeable future.

(39 marks)

2 Your manager has had a meeting with Pilar Mareno, a self-employed consultant, and has sent you a copy of the following memorandum.

To   The files
From   Tax manager
Date   31 May 2007
Subject Pilar Mareno – Business expansion

Pilar Mareno (PM) has been offered a contract with DWM plc, initially for two years, which will result in fees of £80,000 plus VAT per annum.

In order to service this contract, PM would have to take on additional help in the form of either a part-time employee for two days a week, or the services of a self-employed contractor for 100 days per year. She would also have to acquire a van, which would be used wholly for business purposes. PM has decided that she will only enter into the contract if it generates at least an additional £15,000 per annum, on average, for the family after all costs and taxes.

PM's annual profitability and the profit generated by the contract (before taking into account the costs of the part-time employee/contractor and the van) are summarised below.

	Existing business £	New contract £
Sales	210,000	80,000
Less: Materials, wages and overheads	(120,000)	(35,000)
Profit per accounts and taxable profit	90,000	45,000

Supplies made under the contract will be 65% standard rated and 35% exempt for value added tax (VAT) purposes; this is the same as for PM's existing business. £31,500 of the costs incurred in relation to the contract will be subject to VAT at the standard rate. The equivalent figure for PM's existing business is £100,000.

PM has identified Max Wallen (MW) as a possible self-employed contractor. MW would charge £75 per day plus VAT for a contract of 100 days per year, with a rate of £25 per day plus VAT in respect of any days when he is ill (up to a maximum of 8 days per year). PM has a spare copy of the specialist software that MW would need but MW would use his own laptop computer.

Alternatively, PM could employ her husband, Alec (AM), paying him a gross annual salary of £7,600. AM would have to give up his current full time job, but would expect to do other part-time employed work earning a further £10,000 (gross) per annum.

PM estimates that a second hand van will cost £7,800 plus VAT or alternatively, a van could be leased for £300 plus VAT per month. We can assume that if the van is purchased, it will be sold at the end of the two year contract for £2,500 plus VAT.

Tax manager

An extract from an email from your manager is set out below.

Please prepare a memorandum for me, incorporating the following:
1 Calculations to demonstrate whether or not Pilar's desired annual after tax income from the new contract will be achievable depending on:
   – whether she leases or buys the van; and
   – whether she employs Alec or uses Max Wallen.

You may find it easier to:
(i) work out the after tax cost of buying or leasing the van. (When calculating the annual cost of the van, assume that the total cost can be averaged over the two years of the contract.)

    and then to consider:

(ii) the after tax income depending on whether Alec is employed or the self-employed contractor, Max, is used.

> 2   A rationale for the approach you have taken and a summary of your findings.
>
> 3   Any other issues we should be considering in respect of Pilar employing Alec, including any alternative to employment.
>
> 4   It seems to me that HM Revenue and Customs may be able to successfully contend that Max Wallen would be an employee, rather than a self-employed contractor. Prepare your figures on the basis that he is self-employed but include a list of factors in your memorandum, based on the information we have, that would indicate either employed or self-employed status.
>
> Take some time to think about your approach to this before you start. Also, as always when working on Pilar's affairs, watch out for the VAT as it can get quite tricky. I suspect the VAT will affect the costs incurred so you'll need to address VAT first. Pilar's estimate of the profit on the contract will have ignored these complications.
>
> Tax manager

You have extracted the following further information from Pilar Mareno's client file.
–   None of Pilar's VAT inputs is directly attributable to either standard rated or exempt supplies.
–   Alec has worked for a UK bank for many years and is currently paid an annual salary of £17,000.
–   The couple have no sources of income other than those set out above.

Required:

Prepare the memorandum requested by your manager.

Marks are available for the four components of the memorandum as follows:

1. **Relevant calculations.**   (16 marks)

2. **Rationale for the approach taken and summary of findings.**   (2 marks)

3. **Other issues in respect of Pilar employing Alec, together with any suggestions as to an alternative to employment.**   (2 marks)

4. **The employment status of Max Wallen.**   (3 marks)

Appropriateness of the format and presentation of the memorandum and the effectiveness with which the information is communicated.   (2 marks)

You may assume that the rates and allowances for the tax year 2006/07 will continue to apply for the foreseeable future.

(25 marks)

Section B: TWO questions ONLY to be attempted

3 Stanley Beech, a self-employed landscape gardener, intends to transfer his business to Landscape Ltd, a company formed for this purpose.

The following information has been extracted from client files and from meetings with Stanley.

Stanley:
- Acquired a storage building for £46,000 on 1 July 1998 and began trading.
- Has no other sources of income.
- Has capital losses brought forward from 2002/03 of £11,400.

The whole of the business is to be transferred to Landscape Ltd on 1 September 2007:
- The market value of the assets to be transferred is £118,000.
- The assets include the storage building and goodwill, valued at £87,000 and £24,000 respectively, and various small pieces of equipment and consumable stores.
- Landscape Ltd will issue 5,000 £1 ordinary shares as consideration for the transfer.

Advice given to Stanley in respect of the sale of the business:
- "No capital gains tax will arise on the transfer of your business to the company."
- "You should take approximately 30% of the payment from Landscape Ltd in shares with the balance left on a loan account payable to you by the company, such that you can receive a cash payment in the future."

Advice given to Stanley in respect of his annual remuneration from Landscape Ltd:
- "The payment of a dividend of £21,000 is more tax efficient than paying a salary bonus of £21,000 as you will pay income tax at only 25% on the dividend received, whereas you would pay income tax at 40% on a salary bonus. The dividend also avoids the need to pay national insurance contributions."
- "There is no tax in respect of an interest free loan from an employer of less than £5,000."
- "The provision of a company car is tax neutral as the cost of providing it is deductible in the corporation tax computation."

Stanley's proposed remuneration package from Landscape Ltd:
- An annual salary of £40,000 and an annual dividend of approximately £21,000.
- On 1 December 2007 an interest free loan of £3,600, which he intends to repay in two years time.
- A company car with a cost when new of £11,400. The only costs incurred by the company in respect of this car will be lease rentals of £300 per month and business fuel of £100 per month.
- The annual employment income benefit in respect of the car is to be taken as £3,420.

Landscape Ltd:
- Will prepare accounts to 31 March each year.
- Will pay corporation tax at the rate of 19%.

Required:

(a) (i) Explain why there would be no capital gains tax liability on the transfer of Stanley's business to Landscape Ltd in exchange for shares. Calculate the maximum loan account balance that Stanley could receive without giving rise to a capital gains tax liability and state the resulting capital gains tax base cost of the shares. (8 marks)

(ii) Explain the benefit to Stanley of taking part of the payment for the sale of his business in the form of a loan account, which is to be paid out in cash at some time in the future. (1 mark)

(b) Comment on the accuracy and completeness of the advice received by Stanley in respect of his remuneration package. Supporting calculations are only required in respect of the company car. (9 marks)

Ignore value added tax (VAT) in answering this question.

You may assume that the rates and allowances for the financial year to 31 March 2007 and the tax year 2006/07 will continue to apply for the foreseeable future.

(18 marks)

4   Mahia Ltd is an unquoted, UK resident trading company formed in May 2000. One of its shareholders, Claus Rowen, intends to sell his shares back to Mahia Ltd on 31 July 2007. Another shareholder, Maude Brooke, intends to give some of her shares to her daughter, Tessa.

The following information has been extracted from client files and from meetings with the shareholders.

Mahia Ltd:
–   In May 2000 the company issued 40,000 shares at £3.40 per share as follows:

Claus Rowen	16,000
Charlotte Forde	12,000
Olaf Berne	12,000

–   Olaf sold his 12,000 shares to Maude Brooke on 1 October 2005 when they were worth £154,000.

Claus and Charlotte:
–   Have always lived in the UK.
–   Are higher rate taxpayers who use their capital gains tax annual exemption every year.

Maude:
–   Was born in the UK, but moved to Canada on 1 April 2003 with her daughter, Tessa.
–   Has not visited the UK since leaving for Canada, but will return to the UK permanently in December 2012.
–   Is employed in Canada with an annual salary equivalent to £70,000.

Sale of shares by Claus:
–   Charlotte and Maude want to expand the company's activities in the UK but Claus does not. The shareholders have been arguing over this matter for almost a year.
–   In order to enable the company to prosper, Claus has agreed to sell his shares to the company on 31 July 2007.

Gift of shares by Maude:
–   Maude will gift 4,000 shares in Mahia Ltd to her daughter, Tessa, on either 1 August 2007 or 1 June 2008.
–   She will delay the gift until 1 June 2008 (Tessa's wedding day) if this reduces the total tax due.
–   The tax due in Canada will be the same regardless of the date of the gift.
–   She has made no previous transfers of value for UK inheritance tax purposes.
–   For the purposes of this gift, you should assume that Maude will die on 31 December 2011.

Market values of shares in Mahia Ltd on all relevant dates are to be taken as:

Size of shareholding %	Market value per share £
< 25	10.20
25 – 35	14.40
> 35	38.60

Market values of the assets of Mahia Ltd on all relevant dates are to be taken as:

	£
Land and buildings used within the trade	1,400,000
Three machines of equal value used within the trade	15,000
Motor cars used by employees	45,000
Quoted shares	42,000
Inventory, trade receivables and cash	145,000

Required:

(a)   Advise Claus on the tax treatment of the proceeds he will receive in respect of the sale of his shares to Mahia Ltd. Prepare a calculation of the net (after tax) proceeds from the sale based on your conclusions. (8 marks)

(b)   Advise Maude on the UK tax consequences of gifting the shares to Tessa and prepare computations to determine on which of the two dates the gift should be made, if the total UK tax due on the gift is to be minimised. Your answer should consider all relevant taxes. (10 marks)

You may assume that the rates and allowances for the tax year 2006/07 will continue to apply for the foreseeable future.

(18 marks)

5 Vikram Bridge has been made redundant by Bart Industries Ltd, a company based in Birmingham. He intends to move to Scotland to start a new job with Dreamz Technology Ltd.

The following information has been extracted from client files and from meetings with Vikram.

Vikram Bridge:
- Is unmarried, but has been living with Alice Tate since 1996. The couple have four young children.
- Receives dividends of approximately £7,800 each year and makes annual capital gains of approximately £1,200 in respect of shares inherited from his mother.
- The couple have no sources of income other than Vikram's employment income and the £7,800 of dividends.

Made redundant by Bart Industries Ltd on 28 February 2007:
- Vikram's employment contract entitled him to two months' notice or two months salary in lieu of notice. On 28 February 2007 the company paid him his salary for the two-month period of £4,700, and asked him to leave immediately.
- On 30 April 2007 the company paid him a further £1,300 in respect of statutory redundancy, together with a non-contractual lump sum of £14,500, as a gesture of goodwill.

Job with Dreamz Technology Ltd:
- Starts on 1 October 2007 with an annual salary of £38,500.
- The company will contribute £9,400 in October 2007 towards Vikram's costs of moving to Scotland.
- In November 2008, the company will issue free shares to all of its employees. Vikram will be issued with 200 shares, expected to be worth approximately £2,750.

Moving house:
- Vikram's house in Birmingham is fairly small; he intends to buy a much larger one in Glasgow.
- The cost of moving to Glasgow, including the stamp duty land tax in respect of the purchase of his new house, will be approximately £12,500.
- To finance the purchase of the house in Glasgow Vikram will sell a house he owns in Wales, in August 2007.

House in Wales:
- Was given to Vikram by his mother on 1 September 1999, when it was worth £145,000.
- Vikram's mother continued to live in the house until her death on 1 May 2007, when she left the whole of her estate to Vikram.
- At the time of her death the house had severe structural problems and was valued at £140,000.
- Vikram has subsequently spent £18,000 improving the property and expects to be able to sell it for £195,000.
- Vikram is keen to reduce the tax payable on the sale of the house and is willing to transfer the house, or part of it, to Alice prior to the sale if that would help.

Required:

Prepare explanations, including supporting calculations where appropriate, of the following issues suitable for inclusion in a letter to Vikram.

(a) **The capital gains tax payable on the sale of the house in Wales in August 2007, together with the potential effect of transferring the house, or part of it, to Alice prior to the sale, and any other advice you consider helpful.** (7 marks)

(b) **The inheritance tax implications in respect of the house in Wales on the death of Vikram's mother.** (2 marks)

(c) **The income tax treatment of the receipt by Vikram of the shares in Dreamz Technology Ltd.** (3 marks)

(d) **How Vikram's job with Dreamz Technology Ltd will affect the amount and date of payment of the income tax due on his dividend income for 2009/10 and future years.** (6 marks)

Ignore national insurance contributions in answering this question.

You may assume that the rates and allowances for the tax year 2006/07 will continue to apply for the foreseeable future.

(**18 marks**)

End of Question paper

1 (a) Options available in respect of the trading losses of Hutt plc of £105,000

(i) Within Hutt plc

The loss can be offset against the profits chargeable to corporation tax of Hutt plc for the year ended 31 March 2007.

	£
Capital gain	144,000
Less: capital loss brought forward	(98,000)
	46,000
Rental income	65,000
Interest income	2,000
Profits chargeable to corporation tax	113,000

Hutt plc, Rainbow Ltd and Coronet Ltd are associated as Hutt plc controls the other two companies. As a result, the small companies rate lower limit for the purposes of determining the rate of corporation tax is reduced from £300,000 to £100,000. Accordingly, Hutt plc will pay corporation tax at 30% less marginal relief. This means that the first £100,000 of the company's profits will be taxed at 19% and the final £13,000 at the marginal rate of 32¾%.

A current period offset has to be made before losses can be carried back to the previous twelve months. The trading loss for the year ended 31 March 2007 is less than the profits chargeable to corporation tax and therefore a claim to carry back the losses cannot be made.

(ii) Group relief

Hutt plc, Rainbow Ltd and Coronet Ltd are in a group for group relief purposes as Hutt plc controls at least 75% of the other two companies. Any amount of the loss can be surrendered to each of the two subsidiary companies in order to reduce their profits chargeable to corporation tax. The maximum surrender is the profits chargeable to corporation tax of the recipient company.

Coronet Ltd has profits chargeable to corporation tax of £81,000 (£63,000 + £18,000). As stated above, due to the number of associates, the small companies rate lower limit is reduced to £100,000 (£300,000 x ⅓). Accordingly, Coronet Ltd will pay tax at 19%.

The profits chargeable to corporation tax of Rainbow Ltd exceed £500,000 (£1,500,000 x ⅓) and therefore, the company will pay UK corporation tax at the rate of 30%.

However, Rainbow Ltd has a permanent establishment in Prismovia as it manufactures and trades in that country. The profits arising in Prismovia will be taxed in that country at 28%. Double tax relief will be available in the UK in respect of the Prismovian tax suffered, up to a maximum of the UK tax on the Prismovian profits; any surrender to Rainbow Ltd must ensure that relief for the foreign tax suffered is not lost.

The maximum surrender that can be made to Rainbow Ltd whilst preserving relief for the foreign tax is calculated as follows.

	£
Trading profit ((£800,000 x 2%) / 30%)	53,333
Interest income	57,000
	110,333

(iii) Recommendations

In order to maximise the tax saved the losses should be offset against the profits taxed at 32¾% in Hutt plc and the profits taxed at 30% in Rainbow Ltd whilst preserving the relief for the foreign tax suffered.

Accordingly, £13,000 of the losses should be offset against the profits chargeable to corporation tax in Hutt plc with the balance of £92,000 (£105,000 – £13,000) surrendered to Rainbow Ltd. This is less than £110,333, and therefore, preserves relief for all of the foreign tax.

When making a claim to offset a company's trading loss against its total profits, it is not possible to specify the amount to be offset; all of the losses available will be offset subject to the level of taxable profits. Accordingly, in order to achieve the desired result, the two claims must be made in the following order.

1. An election to surrender losses of £92,000 to Rainbow Ltd. This must be made by 31 March 2009, i.e. within one year of the filing date of the claimant company's tax return. Both Rainbow Ltd and Hutt plc must elect.
2. An election to offset the remaining losses (£13,000) against the total profits of Hutt plc should be submitted by the same date, i.e. within two years of the end of the period in which the loss was made.

Tutorial note

The tax computation of Rainbow Ltd for the year ended 31 March 2007 following the group relief claim is set out below. Group relief of £57,000 is offset against the interest income with the balance of £35,000 being offset against the trading profit in order to maximise the double tax relief.

	£
Trading profit (£800,000 – £35,000)	*765,000*
Interest income (£57,000 – £57,000)	*–*
Profits chargeable to corporation tax	*765,000*
Corporation tax @ 30%	*229,500*
Less Double tax relief (£800,000 x 28%)	*(224,000)*
Corporation tax payable	*5,500*

(b)   Report to the management of Hutt plc

To	The management of Hutt plc
From	Tax advisers
Date	1 June 2007
Subject	The acquisition of Lucia Ltd

(i)   The purchase price

Valuation of the trading losses in Lucia Ltd

Lucia Ltd has no profits in the year ended 31 March 2007 or the previous year against which to offset the losses.

The trading losses arose before Lucia Ltd joined the Hutt plc group, and therefore, they cannot be surrendered to any of the group members.

The losses cannot be carried forward as there will be a change of ownership of Lucia Ltd after its activities have become negligible. Losses arising prior to the change of ownership cannot be offset against profits arising once the trade has been revived.

The losses cannot be used, and therefore, they have no value.

Loan from BHC Bank

Hutt plc is to enter into a loan relationship with BHC Bank. Any amounts charged to the company's profit and loss account in respect of the relationship are allowable deductions for tax purposes. Accordingly, a tax deduction is available for the interest and the loan arrangement fee on the accruals basis.

On the assumption that the loan arrangement fee is charged to the profit and loss account in full in the year ended 31 March 2008, the total amount charged in the accounts will be £11,731 (£1,400 + (£190,000 x 7.25% x 9/12)). The income from which this amount can be deducted in the corporation tax computation depends on the use made of the finance obtained.

	Finance £		Allowable cost £
For the purpose of investments:			
Acquisition of Lucia Ltd	130,000		
Repairs to Hutt Tower	45,000		
	175,000	175/190 x £11,731	10,805
For the purpose of the trade:			
Working capital requirements	15,000	15/190 x £11,731	926
Total finance obtained	190,000		11,731

Where the finance has been used for trading purposes, the cost of £926 is deductible in arriving at Hutt plc's taxable trading income.

Where the finance has been used for non-trading purposes, the cost of £10,805 is deductible from Hutt plc's interest income in respect of loan relationships. This results in a deficit, or loss, of £8,805 (£10,805 – £2,000) in the year ended 31 March 2008.

The deficit can be:
- Offset against other income and gains of Hutt plc of the same accounting period.
- Offset against the interest income of Hutt plc of the previous 12 months.
- Surrendered as group relief to companies within the group relief group.
- Carried forward and offset against future non-trading income and gains.

The most tax efficient use of the deficit will depend on the level of profits in Hutt plc and the other group companies in the year ended 31 March 2008.

(ii) VAT issues

Registration

All the supplies made by Lucia Ltd are taxable supplies for the purposes of VAT. The company must register for VAT:
* If its taxable supplies in the previous 12 months exceed £61,000; or
* If its taxable supplies in the next 30 days are expected to exceed £61,000.

It is anticipated that the company's supplies in the nine months ended 31 March 2008 will be £675,000 and that these supplies will accrue evenly over the period. This amounts to supplies of £75,000 per month. Accordingly, Lucia Ltd must register with effect from 1 July 2007 and must notify HMRC by 30 July 2007.

Lucia Ltd intends to make supplies to non-VAT registered customers in the European Union (EU). If Lucia Ltd is responsible for the delivery of the goods it should be aware that once its supplies in any one particular member state exceed that state's 'distance selling' threshold, it may be required to register for VAT in that state.

VAT in respect of the nine months ended 31 March 2008

	£
Output tax	
UK customers – VAT registered (£85,000 x 17½%)	14,875
UK customers – non-VAT registered (£25,000 x 17½%)	4,375
EU customers – VAT registered – zero-rated	–
EU customers – non-VAT registered (£70,000 x 17½%)	12,250
Other non-UK customers – zero-rated	–
Acquisition from Dabet Gmbh (£17,000 x 17½%)	2,975
	34,475
Input tax	
In respect of purchases from UK businesses (9 x £7,800)	70,200
Acquisition from Dabet Gmbh	2,975
	73,175
Repayment of VAT due (£73,175 – £34,475)	38,700

Disadvantage of entering into a group VAT registration

Lucia Ltd makes mainly zero-rated supplies and is in a VAT repayment position. It can improve its cash flow position by accounting for VAT monthly and receiving monthly repayments of VAT. It would not be in a position to do this if it were to register in a VAT group.

Under a group registration, the group's representative member will account for VAT payable to HMRC on behalf of all group companies. It may be some time before Lucia Ltd's accounting system is aligned with that of Hutt plc. The existence of two different systems may create administrative difficulties in preparing a group VAT return.

Note – Only one of the above disadvantages was required

(iii) The office building

Tax implications of the sale of the office building from Coronet Ltd to Lucia Ltd

Corporation tax
At the time of the transfer, Coronet Ltd and Lucia Ltd will be in a capital gains group as they will both be 75% subsidiaries of Hutt plc. Therefore the transfer of the office building will be deemed to occur at no gain, no loss. Lucia Ltd will have a capital gains tax base cost in the building equal to the cost to Coronet Ltd plus indexation allowance up to the date of the transfer.

Value added tax (VAT)
The transfer will be outside the scope of VAT if the two companies are in a VAT group.

If the two companies are registered separately, the treatment depends on whether or not Coronet Ltd has opted to tax the building. If it has, then the transfer to Lucia Ltd will be standard rated and VAT must be charged. If it has not, the transfer will be an exempt supply.

Stamp duty land tax
There will be no stamp duty land tax on the transfer as both companies are 75% subsidiaries of Hutt plc.

Relief of the gain on the sale of the office building to Vac Ltd
The loss arising on the sale of the factory will be £190,000 (£270,000 - £80,000). Indexation allowance is not available to increase a loss.

Lucia Ltd acquired the factory before it joined the Hutt plc group. Accordingly, the factory is a pre-entry asset and that part of the loss that arose prior to 1 July 2007 is restricted in use. In particular, it cannot be offset against gains arising in other companies in the Hutt plc group or gains on assets transferred from other group members on a no gain no loss basis.

As at 1 January 2008, Lucia Ltd will have owned the factory for four and a half years, of which four years are outside of the Hutt plc group. The pre-entry element of the loss is £168,889 (£190,000 x 4/4.5).

The pre-entry element of the loss could be computed by reference to the market value of the building at the time Hutt plc acquires Lucia Ltd. However this would not be advantageous in this case as the whole of the loss would then be a pre-entry loss.

The balance of the loss of £21,111 can be offset against the gain on the office building. Based on a corporation tax rate of 30%, this will save tax of £6,333.

There is no need to actually transfer the office building to Lucia Ltd in order to relieve the gain in this way. Coronet Ltd and Lucia Ltd can simply elect to treat the gain as if it has been made by Lucia Ltd. The election must be submitted by 31 March 2011, ie within two years of the end of the accounting period in which the disposal of the office building occurs.

2

To	The files
From	Tax assistant
Date	1 June 2007
Subject	Pilar Mareno - Business expansion

This memorandum considers the implications of Pilar Mareno (PM) accepting the DWM plc contract.

Rationale and approach
PM has decided to accept the contract if it generates at least £15,000 per annum on average for the family after all costs and taxes.

PM will either employ her husband, Alec, or use the services of Max Wallen, and will either buy or lease a van. However, it can be seen from workings 3 and 4 that it is cheaper to buy rather than lease the van, and therefore, there are only two options to consider.
- Employ Alec and buy a van – Appendix 1
- Use Max Wallen and buy a van – Appendix 2

Summary of findings
The contract generates sufficient after tax income whether PM buys a van and employs Alec or uses Max Wallen. However, the issues raised below in relation to PM employing Alec should be considered before a decision is made.

Issues in respect of Pilar employing Alec

1. Alec has worked for a UK bank for many years. It is risky to give up an apparently secure job in exchange for a two year contract requiring two days work a week and other, as yet unidentified, part-time work.

    Accordingly, Alec should obtain advice as regards his personal situation. If we are asked to provide this advice we must recognise that Pilar and Alec would be two separate clients. The work would have to be managed in such a way as to ensure that we do not allow the interests of Pilar to adversely affect those of Alec or vice versa.

2. PM and Alec should consider forming a partnership. This would reduce national insurance contributions as Alec would only pay 8% on his share of the profit plus class 2 at £2.10 per week whereas the cost of employer and employee class 1 contributions where Alec is an employee is 12.8% and 11% respectively.

    Alec's profit share could be more than £7,600. This would enable income currently taxed at 40% in PM's hands to be taxed at 22% in Alec's hands. However, this saving in income tax would be offset by increased national insurance costs as the national insurance on PM's marginal income is only 1% whereas Alec would pay 8%.

Employment status of Max Wallen
Max's employment status will be determined by reference to all of the facts surrounding his agreement with PM.

Factors indicating employee status
1. It appears that Max has to do the work himself and cannot use a substitute.
2. Max is to be paid by the day rather than by reference to the performance of particular tasks.
3. Max is to be paid for the days when he is sick.
4. Max is to be provided with the specialist software he needs to do the work.

Factors indicating self-employed status
1. Max provides his own laptop computer.

Tax assistant

Tutorial Note

There is insufficient information provided regarding other factors, such as the level of control over Max's work, to justify their inclusion within the terms of the brief provided.

Appendix 1 – Employ Alec and buy a van

	£
Profit on contract	45,000
Irrecoverable VAT due to partial exemption (W1)	(8,054)
Salary paid to Alec	(7,600)
Class 1 secondary NIC re Alec ((£7,600 – £5,035) x 12.8%)	(328)
	29,018
Income tax and class 4 NIC due (£29,018 x (40% + 1%))	(11,897)
	17,121
Increase in Alec's income (W2)	402
Purchase of van (less than cost of leasing van) (W3 and W4)	(1,704)
Income of family after all taxes	15,819

Tutorial Note:
The salary paid to Alec is a cost as far as Pilar is concerned. The effect of the salary on Alec's income is calculated in working 2, below.

Appendix 2 – Use Max Wallen and buy a van

	£
Profit on contract	45,000
Irrecoverable VAT due to partial exemption (W1)	(8,054)
Fees paid to Max Wallen (100 x £75)	(7,500)
Irrecoverable VAT on fees (£7,500 x 17½% x 35%))	(459)
	28,987
Income tax and class 4 NIC due (£28,987 x (40% + 1%))	(11,885)
	17,102
Purchase of van (less than cost of leasing van) (W3 and W4)	(1,704)
Income of family after all taxes	15,398

Workings

(1) **Irrecoverable VAT due to partial exemption**

	£
Without the new contract:	
In respect of the existing business (£100,000 x 17½% x 35%)	6,125

This is below the annual de minimis limit of £7,500 (£625 x 12) and is fully recoverable.

	£
With the new contract:	
In respect of the existing business (as above)	6,125
In respect of the costs of the DWM contract (£31,500 x 17½% x 35%)	1,929
	8,054

This exceeds the annual de minimis limit and is irrecoverable.

Tutorial Note
Pilar's taxable turnover is not affected by the sale of the van as it is a capital asset.

(2) **Increase in Alec's income**

	£
Increase in gross salary ((£7,600 + £10,000) – £17,000)	600
Less income tax and NIC (£600 x (22% + 11%))	(198)
Increase in after tax income	402

Tutorial Note
At the margin, Alec pays income tax at the basic rate of 22% and NIC at 11%.

(3) **Cost of purchasing van**

	£
Net cost (£7,800 – £2,500) for two year period	5,300
Income tax and class 4 NIC saved (£5,300 x (40% + 1%))	(2,173)
Irrecoverable VAT (£7,800 x 17½% x 35%)	478
Income tax and class 4 NIC saved (£478 x (40% + 1%))	(196)
	3,409
Average cost per year (£3,409 x ½)	1,704

(4) Cost of leasing van (per year)

	£
Lease rentals (£300 x 12)	3,600
Income tax and class 4 NIC saved (£3,600 x (40% + 1%))	(1,476)
Irrecoverable VAT (£3,600 x 17½% x 35%)	220
Income tax and class 4 NIC saved (£220 x (40% + 1%))	(90)
	2,254

3 (a) Use of a loan account

(i) The split of consideration between the shares and loan account

Where all of the assets of Stanley's business are transferred to Landscape Ltd as a going concern wholly in exchange for shares, any capital gains arising are relieved via incorporation relief such that no capital gains tax liability arises.

However, where part of the payment received from the company is in the form of a loan account, Stanley will have chargeable gains as set out below. For Stanley to have no liability to capital gains tax in 2007/08, his chargeable gains must equal the annual exemption of £8,800.

	£
Gain on building (£87,000 – £46,000)	41,000
Gain on goodwill	24,000
	65,000

Gains after incorporation relief:

$$£65,000 \times \frac{\text{Value of the loan account}}{£118,000} \qquad y$$

Less: Capital losses brought forward	(11,400)
	z
Taper relief – business assets owned for at least two years	x 25%
Chargeable gains	8,800

Gains after incorporation relief, y, must equal £46,600 ((£8,800 x 4) + £11,400).

The value of the loan account needs to be £84,597 (£46,600 x £118,000/£65,000) such that the gains after incorporation relief are £46,600 (£65,000 x £84,597/£118,000).

The shares will have a capital gains tax base cost of £15,003 computed as follows.

	£
Market value of assets transferred to Landscape Ltd	118,000
Less Consideration left on loan account	(84,597)
	33,403

Incorporation relief:

$$£65,000 \times \frac{£33,403}{£118,000} \qquad (18,400)$$

	15,003

(ii) The benefit of using a loan account

The loan account crystallises capital gains at the time of incorporation without giving rise to a tax liability due to the availability of capital losses, taper relief and the annual exemption. This reduces the gains deferred against the base cost of the shares in Landscape Ltd from £65,000 to £18,400 such that any future gains on the disposal of the shares will be smaller. Stanley can extract £84,597 from Landscape Ltd in the future with no 'tax cost', by having the loan repaid.

(b) Advice on Stanley's remuneration package

(i) Dividend

The advice in respect of the dividend is accurate but not complete as it ignores the cost to Landscape Ltd. Because Stanley owns Landscape Ltd, he must consider the effect on the company's position as well as his own.

Dividends are not tax deductible. The profits paid out as a dividend to Stanley will have been subject to corporation tax at 19%. On the other hand, Landscape Ltd will obtain a tax deduction at 19% for a salary bonus together with the related national insurance contributions.

There will be an overall tax saving from paying a dividend as opposed to a salary bonus. However the benefit will not be as great as suggested by the advice that Stanley has received due to the different treatment of the two payments in the company.

(ii) **Interest free loan**

The advice in respect of the loan is again accurate but not complete. The loan will not give rise to an employment income benefit as it is for not more than £5,000, but the advice again ignores the position of the company.

As it is controlled by Stanley, Landscape Ltd will be a close company. Accordingly, the loan to Stanley is a loan to a participator in a close company, and as Stanley owns more than 5% of the company's share capital there is no de minimis in this case.

Thus, Landscape Ltd must pay an amount equal to 25% of the loan (£900) to HMRC. The payment will be due on 1 January 2009, i.e. nine months and one day after the end of the accounting period in which the loan is made.

When the loan is repaid by Stanley, Landscape Ltd may reclaim the £900. The repayment by HMRC will be made nine months and one day after the end of the accounting period in which the loan is repaid.

(iii) **Company car**

The advice in respect of the company car is not correct because of the difference in the tax rates applying to the company and to Stanley, and the liability to Class 1A national insurance contributions.

	£
Tax cost of providing car:	
Class 1A national insurance contributions	
£3,420 x 12.8%	438
Income tax on benefit (£3,420 x 40%)	1,368
	1,806
Tax saved:	
Cost of providing car (£400 x 12)	4,800
Class 1A national insurance contributions	438
	5,238
Corporation tax @ 19%	995
Net tax cost (£1,806 – £995)	811

4 (a) Sale of shares in Mahia Ltd

The proceeds received on a purchase by a company of its own shares are subject to either income tax or capital gains tax depending on the circumstances.

The normal assumption on a purchase of own shares by a company is that any payment you receive for the shares, over and above the amount originally subscribed for them, would be an income distribution, and treated in the same way as a payment of a dividend. The net amount received, less the amount originally subscribed, would be grossed up by 100/90 and included in your taxable income.

Alternatively, where the transaction satisfies the conditions set out below, the proceeds are treated as capital proceeds giving rise to a capital gain. Your proposed sale of shares to Mahia Ltd satisfies these conditions and will therefore give rise to a capital gain.
- Mahia Ltd is an unquoted trading company.
- The purchase of shares is for the benefit of the company's trade as the disagreement between you and your sisters is having an adverse effect on the company's trade.
- You are resident and ordinarily resident in the UK.
- You have owned the shares for more than five years.
- You are selling all of your shares such that your holding is reduced by at least 25% and you will own less than 30% of Mahia Ltd following the sale.
- The purchase is not part of a scheme designed to avoid tax.

Advance clearance can be obtained from HM Revenue and Customs, to confirm that the capital treatment applies to a purchase of own shares.

The capital gains tax arising on the sale and the net cash proceeds after tax will be:

	£
Shares sold (40% x 40,000)	16,000
Proceeds (16,000 x £38.60)	617,600
Less: Cost (16,000 x £3.40)	(54,400)
	563,200
Taper relief	
Business asset owned for more than two years – 75% relief	(422,400)
	140,800
Capital gains tax at 40%	56,320
Proceeds after tax (£617,600 – £56,320)	561,280

Tutorial note
Mahia Ltd is a trading company such that its shares are business assets for the purposes of taper relief despite the fact that it owns investments in quoted companies. This is because its non-trading activities are no more than 20% of its overall activities.

(b) Gift to Tessa

Capital gains tax (CGT)

Maude lives in Canada and is non-UK resident and not-ordinarily resident. In addition, she is not a temporary non-resident for the purposes of capital gains tax as her stay in Canada will be for more than five years.

Accordingly, there will be no UK CGT on the gift of the shares to Tessa.

Even if Maude were a temporary non-resident, there would be no capital gains tax on the gift of the shares as she acquired them after she left the UK.

Inheritance tax (IHT)

As the shares are situated in the UK, UK IHT will be due on any transfers of value concerning them, regardless of the domicile of the transferor. Therefore, we do not need to consider Maude's domicile.

The gift by Maude to Tessa will be a potentially exempt transfer (PET) and no IHT will be payable. In addition, if Maude were to survive seven years from the date of the gift, there would be no IHT to pay on death. However, the question asks us to assume that Maude will die on 31 December 2011. As this date is within seven years of the proposed dates of the gift, there would be a potential liability to IHT on death for each proposed date as follows:

Gift on 1 August 2007

	£
Value of shares before gift (12,000 x £38.60 (50% holding))	463,200
Value of shares after gift (8,000 x £14.40 (33.3% holding))	(115,200)
Fall in value	348,000
No BPR as Maude has not owned the shares for two years	
Annual exemptions for 2007/08 and 2006/07	(6,000)
	342,000
IHT (40% x (£342,000 – £285,000))	22,800
IHT after taper relief (4 to 5 years) (£22,800 x 60%)	13,680

Tutorial Note
On 1 August 2007 Mahia Ltd will have 24,000 issued shares as the shares sold by Claus to the company will have been cancelled.

Double tax relief may be available to reduce this UK liability, in respect of any inheritance taxes payable in Canada.

Gift on 1 June 2008

	£
Fall in value (as above)	348,000
Business property relief (BPR)	
$£348,000 \times \dfrac{£1,605,000 \ (£1,400,000 + £15,000 + £45,000 + £145,000)}{£1,647,000 \ (£1,605,000 + £42,000)}$	(339,126)
	8,874
Marriage exemption	(5,000)
Annual exemptions for 2008/09 and 2007/08 (part only)	(3,874)
	0

Maude should make the gift on 1 June 2008 as this produces a nil IHT liability due to the availability of BPR. This presupposes that Tessa will continue to own the shares or replacement business property up to the date of Maude's death on 31 December 2011, and so preserve the entitlement to BPR.

Stamp duty

As the transfer of shares is made by way of gift, i.e. for no consideration, no stamp duty is payable.

5   (a)   Capital gains tax payable on the sale of the house in Wales

Your taxable capital gain on the sale of the Welsh property will be computed as follows.

	£
Proceeds in August 2007	195,000
Less: Cost (market value as at 1 September 1999)	(145,000)
Enhancement expenditure	(18,000)
	32,000
Taper relief (£32,000 x 75%)	24,000
(non-business asset held for seven years)	
Less: Annual exemption (£8,800 – £1,200)	(7,600)
Taxable capital gain	16,400

Giving the house or part of it to Alice prior to the sale will not reduce the gain as you and Alice are not married. If you make a gift to Alice a capital gain will arise by reference to the market value of the property in exactly the same way as if you had sold the property to an unconnected third party. The gain on such a gift cannot be deferred as the house is not a business asset.

The basic rate band remaining after taxing your income in 2007/08 is as set out below.

When reviewing the computation please note that you do not have any taxable income from Bart Industries Ltd in 2007/08; the payments you received on being made redundant are taxed as follows.
- The payment in lieu of notice of £4,700 is taxed in 2006/07, the year of receipt.
- Statutory redundancy pay is not taxable.
- A non-contractual lump sum up to a maximum of £30,000 is not subject to income tax.

The relocation costs paid by Dreamz Technology Ltd are exempt from income tax up to a maximum of £8,000.

	£
Employment income – Dreamz Technology Ltd	
Salary (£38,500 x 6/12)	19,250
Removal costs (£9,400 – £8,000)	1,400
Dividend income (£7,800 x 10/9)	8,667
	29,317
Less: Personal allowance	(5,035)
Taxable income	24,282
Basic rate band	33,300
Basic rate band remaining	9,018

The computation of your capital gains tax liability is thus:

Capital gains tax: £		£
9,018	@ 20%	1,804
7,382	@ 40%	2,953
		4,757

An additional year of taper relief would be available if you were to delay the sale until after 1 September 2007. This would reduce the tax due by £640 (£32,000 x 5% x 40%).

(b)   Inheritance tax due in respect of the house in Wales

Usually, where a gift is made to an individual more than seven years prior to the donor's death, as in the case of your mother's gift of the house to you, there are no inheritance tax (IHT) implications on the death of the donor. However, because your mother continued to live in the house after she gave it to you, the gift will be taxed under the rules applying to 'gifts with reservation of benefit'.

In these circumstances, HM Revenue and Customs will ignore the original gift as, although the asset was gifted, your mother continued to use it as if it were her own. Therefore, the house will be included in your mother's death estate for IHT purposes at its market value at the date of her death, ie £140,000.

(c) Shares in Dreamz Technology Ltd

The income tax treatment of the issue to you of shares in Dreamz Technology Ltd depends on whether the shares are issued via an approved share incentive plan or not.

Where there is no share incentive plan, the market value of the shares received (£2,750) will be taxable as employment income in 2008/09, i.e. the year in which you receive them.

If there is a share incentive plan approved by HM Revenue and Customs then an employer can give shares to its employees, up to a maximum value of £3,000 per employee per year, with no income tax consequences. However, the shares must be kept within the plan for a stipulated period and income tax will be charged if they are withdrawn within five years.

If you withdraw the shares from the plan within three years, income tax will be charged on their value at the time of withdrawal. If you withdraw them more than three years but within five years, income tax will be charged on the lower of their value when you acquired them and their value at the time of withdrawal.

(d) Amount of income tax on dividend income

When you worked for Bart Industries Ltd you were not a higher rate taxpayer as your taxable income was less than £33,300, as set out below. Accordingly, your dividend income was taxed at 10% with a 10% tax credit such that there was no income tax payable.

	£
Employment income (£4,700 x ½ x 12)	28,200
Dividend income (£7,800 x 10/9)	8,667
	36,867
Less Personal allowance	(5,035)
Taxable income	31,832

In 2009/10 your annual salary from Dreamz Technology Ltd less the income tax personal allowance is £33,465 (£38,500 – £5,035). As this exceeds £33,300, all of your dividend income will fall into the higher rate tax band such that it is taxed at 32½% less a 10% tax credit. This gives rise to income tax payable on the dividend income of £1,950 (£8,667 x 22½%).

Date of payment of income tax on dividend income

The tax due in respect of your dividend income must be paid on 31 January after the end of the tax year (i.e. on 31 January 2011 for 2009/10) under self-assessment. You do not have to pay the tax earlier than this by instalments as the amount due is less than 20% of your total annual income tax liability as set out below. The income tax on your employment income from Dreamz Technology Ltd will continue to be collected under the PAYE system.

	£
Taxable employment income (£38,500 – £5,035)	33,465

Income tax:

£		£
2,150	@ 10%	215
31,150	@ 22%	6,853
165	@ 40%	66
Income tax liability on employment income		7,134
Income tax liability on dividend income (£8,667 x 32½%)		2,817
Total annual income tax liability		9,951
Less: PAYE (equal to liability on employment income)		(7,134)
Tax credit on dividend income (£8,667 x 10%)		(867)
Income tax payable via self-assessment		1,950
Threshold for payments by instalments (£9,951 x 20%)		1,990

Pilot Paper P6
Advanced Taxation

Marking Scheme

		Available	Max
1 The Hutt plc group			
(a) Hutt plc trading losses			
Within Hutt plc			
Current year offset		0.5	
Available profits		1	
Application of the small companies rate limits		1	
Effective rate of tax/relief		1	
No carry back opportunity		0.5	
Group relief			
Relevant companies		0.5	
Available relief		0.5	
Coronet Ltd:			
Available profits		0.5	
Effective rate of tax		1	
Rainbow Ltd:			
Effective rate of UK tax		0.5	
Tax position in Prismovia		1	
Effect of DTR		2	
Recommendation			
Identify correct objective		1	
Hutt plc – profits at 32¾%		0.5	
Rainbow Ltd – the balance		0.5	
Order of elections		1	
Group relief election – both companies/time limit		1	
Current year offset election/time limit		1	
Total for (a)		**15**	**13**
(b) (i) The purchase price			
Trading losses:			
No current relief in Lucia Ltd		0.5	
No group relief with reason		1	
No carry forward with reasons		1.5	
Conclusion		0.5	
Loan from BHC Bank			
Tax deduction per accounts treatment		1	
Total amount allowable in the period		0.5	
Amount relating to trading purpose		1	
Amount relating to non-trading purpose		2	
Uses of deficit		2	
Recommendation		0.5	
Total for (b) (i)		**10½**	**9**
(ii) VAT issues			
Registration			
Historic and future limits		1	
Registration and notification dates		1	
Distance selling thresholds		0.5	
Calculation			
Output tax		2.5	
Input tax		1	
Disadvantage of group VAT registration – either of			
Lucia Ltd in repayment position; or administrative difficulties		1	
Total for (b) (ii)		**7**	**6**

	Available	Max
(iii) The office building		
Sale from Coronet Ltd to Lucia Ltd		
Capital gain		
CGT group	0.5	
Consequences	1	
VAT		
If group registration	0.5	
If no group registration	1.5	
Stamp duty land tax	1	
Sale of building to Vac Ltd		
Loss on sale – no IA	0.5	
Pre-entry asset		
Identify	0.5	
Consequences	1	
Calculation of post-entry loss/tax saving	1	
Use of market value	0.5	
Election re notional transfer – availability	1	
Both companies and time limit	1	
Total for (b) (iii)	**10**	**9**
Format and style		
Appropriate style and presentation	1	
Effectiveness of communication	1	
Total for format and style	**2**	**2**
Total for Q1	**44½**	**39**

2 Pilar Moreno

(1) Calculations

	Available	Max
Employ Alec:		
Net profit of contract	0.5	
Alec's salary and class 1 secondary NIC	1.5	
Irrecoverable VAT/purchase of van	0.5	
Tax and NIC saved	0.5	
Increase in Alec's income:		
Identification of issue	1	
Calculation	1.5	
Use Max:		
Fees paid	0.5	
Irrecoverable VAT on fees	0.5	
Tax and NIC saved	0.5	
Supporting calculations		
Irrecoverable VAT:		
Identification of issue	1	
Current partial exemption position	1	
Application of de minimis	1	
Irrecoverable amount with new contract	1	
Purchase of van:		
Net cost	0.5	
Irrecoverable VAT	1	
Tax and NIC saved	1	
Cost per year	0.5	
Leasing van		
Rentals	0.5	
Irrecoverable VAT	1	
Tax and NIC saved	1	
Total for (1)	**16½**	**16**

(2) Rationale and summary

	Available	Max
Reference to Pilar's income criterion	1	
Conclusion re van and implications	1	
Summary of findings	1	
Total for (2)	**3**	**2**

		Available	Max
(3)	**Employment of Alec**		
	Secure job, short-term contract	1.5	
	Use of partnership	2	
	Alec would be a separate client from Pilar	1	
	Total for (3)	4½	2
(4)	**Employment status of Max**		
	Depends on all of the facts	0.5	
	Each valid factor – ½ mark (max 5 factors)	2.5	
	Total for (4)	3	3
	Format and style		
	Appropriate style and presentation	1	
	Effectiveness of communication	1	
	Total for format and style	2	2
	Total for Q2	28	25

3 Stanley

			Available	Max
(a)	**(i)**	**Split of consideration**		
		Incorporation relief – 3 conditions	1.5	
		Amount of future cash payment:		
		Rationale – gains to equal annual exemption	1	
		Gains on transfer of business	1	
		Gains after incorporation relief:		
		Incorporation relief	1	
		Capital loss and taper relief	1.5	
		Calculation of gains after incorporation relief	0.5	
		Solving to find value of the loan account	1	
		CGT base cost of shares:		
		Value of assets transferred for shares	0.5	
		Incorporation relief	1	
	(ii)	**Benefit of using a loan account**		
		Capital gains	1	
		Extract funds with no tax cost	0.5	
		Total for (a)	10½	9
(b)		**Advice on remuneration package**		
		Dividend		
		Advice is correct but incomplete with reason	1	
		CT position re dividend	0.5	
		CT position re bonus	0.5	
		Conclusion with reason	1	
		Interest free loan		
		Advice is correct but incomplete with reason	1	
		Close company	0.5	
		Loan to a participator and reason	1	
		Tax due /when	1	
		Repayment position	0.5	
		Company car		
		The advice is not correct with reason	1	
		Calculation		
		Tax cost	1	
		Tax saving	1	
		Total for (b)	10	9
		Total for Q3	20½	18

		Available	Max
4	**Mahia Ltd**		
(a)	**Sale of shares by Claus**		
	Purchase of own shares		
	Identify and distinguish between the two possible treatments	1	
	CGT treatment applies	1	
	Reasons why:		
	Unquoted trading company	0.5	
	Resident and ordinarily resident	0.5	
	Owned for more than 5 years	0.5	
	Not part of a scheme to avoid tax	0.5	
	For benefit of company's trade with reason	1	
	Reduction in holding criteria	1	
	Availability of advance clearance	1	
	Calculation		
	Gain before taper relief	1	
	Taper relief	1	
	Net of tax proceeds	0.5	
	Total for (a)	**9½**	**8**
(b)	**Gift to Tessa**		
	CGT		
	No CGT due	0.5	
	Reasons why:		
	Not resident or ordinarily resident	0.5	
	Asset acquired after becoming resident abroad	0.5	
	Not temporarily non-resident	0.5	
	IHT		
	IHT applies, shares are UK property	0.5	
	Gift on 1 August 2007		
	Fall in value	1	
	No BPR with reason	1	
	Chargeable transfer (2 x annual exemption)	0.5	
	Taper relief available	0.5	
	Calculation of tax due	0.5	
	Reference to DTR	0.5	
	Gift on 1 June 2008		
	Assumption re Tessa's continued ownership	1	
	BPR	1	
	Marriage and annual exemptions	1	
	Advice	1	
	Stamp duty		
	Not applicable, gift	0.5	
	Total for (b)	**11**	**10**
	Total for Q4	**20½**	**18**

BPP
LEARNING MEDIA

			Available	Max
5	**(a)**	**Taxable capital gain on the sale of the house**		
		Computation of capital gain		
		Untapered gain	0.5	
		Taper relief	1	
		Annual exemption	0.5	
		Effect of gift to Alice	1	
		Computation of basic rate band remaining	2	
		Treatment of payments on redundancy	1	
		Capital gains tax payable	1	
		Advice to delay sale	1	
		Total for (a)	**8**	**7**
	(b)	**Inheritance tax due in respect of the house**		
		Gift more than seven years prior to death	0.5	
		Gift with reservation rules apply	0.5	
		Consequences	1	
		Total for (b)	**2**	**2**
	(c)	**Shares in Dreamz Technology Ltd**		
		Identify two possible treatments	0.5	
		Treatment if no share incentive plan	1	
		Exemption under share incentive plan	1	
		Withdrawal from plan within five year	1	
		Total for (c)	**3½**	**3**
	(d)	**Amount of income tax on dividend income**		
		Tax position whilst working for Bart Industries Ltd		
		No tax payable on dividends	1	
		Computation	1	
		Tax position whilst working for Dreamz Technology Ltd	1.5	
		Date of payment of income tax on dividend income		
		Due date with reason	1.5	
		Computation	2.5	
		Total for (d)	**7.5**	**6**
		Total for Q5	**21**	**18**

Tax tables

The following tax rates and allowances are to be used in answering the questions

Income tax

Starting rate	£1 – £2,150	10%
Basic rate	£2,151 – £33,300	22%
Higher rate	£33,301 and above	40%

Personal allowances

	£
Personal allowance	5,035
Personal allowance aged 65 to 74	7,280
Personal allowance aged 75 and over	7,420
Income limit for age-related allowances	20,100

Car benefit percentage

The base level of CO_2 emissions is 140 grams per kilometre.

Car fuel benefit

The base figure for calculating the car fuel benefit is £14,400.

Pension scheme limits

Annual allowance	£215,000
Lifetime allowance	£1,500,000

The maximum contribution that can qualify for tax relief without any earnings is £3,600.

Authorised mileage allowances

All cars:	
Up to 10,000 miles	40p
Over 10,000 miles	25p

Capital allowances

		%
Plant and machinery		
Writing down allowance		25
First year allowance –	plant and machinery	40
–	low emission motor cars (CO_2 emissions of not more than than 120 g/km) (17 April 2002 to 31 March 2008)	100

For small businesses only: the rate of plant and machinery first-year allowance is 50% for the periods from 1 April 2004 to 31 March (6 April 2004 and 5 April 2005 for unincorporated businesses) and 1 April 2006 to 31 March 2007 (6 April 2006 and 5 April 2007 for unincorporated businesses).

Long-life assets

Writing-down allowance	6

Industrial buildings

Industrial buildings Writing-down allowance	4

Corporation tax

Financial year	2004	2005	2006
Starting rate	Nil	Nil	-
Small companies (SC) rate	19%	19%	19%
Full rate	30%	30%	30%
Starting rate lower limit	10,000	10,000	-
Starting rate upper limit	50,000	50,000	-
Lower limit	30,000	300,000	300,000
Upper limit	1,500,000	1,500,000	1,500,000
Marginal relief fraction:			
Starting rate	19/400	19/400	-
Small companies' rate	11/400	11/400	11/400

Marginal relief

$(M - P) \times I/P \times$ marginal relief fraction

Value Added Tax

Registration limit	£61,000
Deregistration limit	£59,000

Inheritance tax

First £285,000	Nil
Excess	40%

Capital gains tax: annual exemption

Individuals	£8,800

Capital gains tax: taper relief

The percentage of the gain chargeable is as follows:

Complete years after 5 April 1998 for which asset held	Gains on business assets (%)	Gains on non-business assets (%)
0	100	100
1	50	100
2	25	100
3	25	95
4	25	90
5	25	85
6	25	80
7	25	75
8	25	70
9	25	65
10	25	60

National insurance (not contracted-out rates)

		%
Class 1 employee	£1 – £5,035 per year	Nil
	£5,036 – £33,540 per year	11.0
	£33,541 and above per year	1.0
Class 1 employer	£1 – £5,035 per year	Nil
	£5,036 and above per year	12.8
Class 1A		12.8
Class 2	£2.10 per week	
Class 4	£1 – £5,035 per year	Nil
	£5,036 – £33,540 per year	8.0
	£33,541 and above per year	1.0

Rates of Interest

Official rate of interest	5.0%
Rate of interest on underpaid tax	6.5% (assumed)
Rate of interest on overpaid tax	2.25% (assumed)

Stamp Duty and Stamp Duty Land Tax

	Rate
Ad valorem duty	
Residential property:	
£125,000 or less [1]	Nil
£125,001 to £250,000	1%
£250,001 to £500,000	3%
£500,001 or above	4%

[1] for non residential property, the nil rate is extended to £150,000

Shares	0.5%
Fixed duty	£5

Calculations and workings need only be made to the nearest £.

All apportionments may be made to the nearest month.

All workings should be shown.

Index

Note. **Key Terms** and their page references are given in **bold**.

Review Form & Free Prize Draw – Paper P6 Advanced Taxation (UK) FA 2006 (03/07)

All original review forms from the entire BPP range, completed with genuine comments, will be entered into one of two draws on 31 January 2008 and 31 July 2008. The names on the first four forms picked out on each occasion will be sent a cheque for £50.

Name: _____ Address: _____

_____

_____

How have you used this Text?
(Tick one box only)

☐ Home study (book only)

☐ On a course: college _____

☐ With 'correspondence' package

☐ Other _____

Why did you decide to purchase this Text? *(Tick one box only)*

☐ Have used BPP Texts in the past

☐ Recommendation by friend/colleague

☐ Recommendation by a lecturer at college

☐ Saw advertising

☐ Saw information on BPP website

☐ Other _____

During the past six months do you recall seeing/receiving any of the following?
(Tick as many boxes as are relevant)

☐ Our advertisement in *ACCA Student Accountant*

☐ Our advertisement in *Pass*

☐ Our advertisement in *PQ*

☐ Our brochure with a letter through the post

☐ Our website www.bpp.com

Which (if any) aspects of our advertising do you find useful?
(Tick as many boxes as are relevant)

☐ Prices and publication dates of new editions

☐ Information on Text content

☐ Facility to order books off-the-page

☐ None of the above

Which BPP products have you used?

Text	☑	Success CD	☐	Learn Online	☐
Kit	☐	i-Learn	☐	Home Study Package	☐
Passcard	☐	i-Pass	☐	Home Study PLUS	☐

Your ratings, comments and suggestions would be appreciated on the following areas.

	Very useful	Useful	Not useful
Introductory section (Key study steps, personal study)	☐	☐	☐
Chapter introductions	☐	☐	☐
Key terms	☐	☐	☐
Quality of explanations	☐	☐	☐
Exam focus points	☐	☐	☐
Questions and answers in each chapter	☐	☐	☐
Fast forwards and chapter roundups	☐	☐	☐
Quick quizzes	☐	☐	☐
Question Bank	☐	☐	☐
Answer Bank	☐	☐	☐
Index	☐	☐	☐

Overall opinion of this Study Text   Excellent ☐   Good ☐   Adequate ☐   Poor ☐

Do you intend to continue using BPP products?   Yes ☐   No ☐

On the reverse of this page are noted particular areas of the text about which we would welcome your feedback. The BPP author of this edition can be e-mailed at: suedexter@bpp.com

Please return this form to: Nick Weller, ACCA Publishing Manager, BPP Learning Media Ltd, FREEPOST, London, W12 8BR

Review Form & Free Prize Draw (continued)

TELL US WHAT YOU THINK

Please note any further comments and suggestions/errors below

Free Prize Draw Rules

1   Closing date for 31 January 2008 draw is 31 December 2007. Closing date for 31 July 2008 draw is 30 June 2008.

2   Restricted to entries with UK and Eire addresses only. BPP employees, their families and business associates are excluded.

3   No purchase necessary. Entry forms are available upon request from BPP Learning Media Ltd. No more than one entry per title, per person. Draw restricted to persons aged 16 and over.

4   Winners will be notified by post and receive their cheques not later than 6 weeks after the relevant draw date.

5   The decision of the promoter in all matters is final and binding. No correspondence will be entered into.